REMARKABLE PRAISE FOR CROSSROADS: THE LIFE AND MUSIC OF ERIC CLAPTON

"Schumacher covers a tale of unhappy . . . relationships, . . . addiction and the tragic death of the performer's infant son, while giving full account of Clapton's significant accomplishments as guitarist and vocalist."

—*Publishers' Weekly*

"Evenhanded . . . humanizes the guitar hero . . . meatier than the average fan bio."

—*Kirkus Reviews*

"An informed and eminently fair biography."

—*New York Daily News*

"A necessary addition to the pop-music library."

—*Booklist*

"Schumacher portrays Clapton as a gifted but human musician . . . effectively binds together the . . . aspects of Clapton's complicated personality and wraps them around the rocker's impressive musical achievements."

—*Boston Herald*

"Truly something for everyone in this exceptionally well written biography."

—*Blues Revue*

"Comprehensive . . . a far more professional book than the average quickie rock bio."

—*Milwaukee Journal Sentinel*

"An in-depth, entertaining examination."

—*Flint Journal*

"A rare animal in the music bio section . . . straightforward and surprisingly even handed."

—*Buffalo News*

"A full scale, serious look."

—*Ingram*

"An excellent biographical treatment."

—*Midwest Book Review*

"The perfect biography."

—*Record Collector*

"Faithful, factually accurate."

—*Mojo*

Crossroads

Crossroads

The Life and Music of
ERIC CLAPTON

Michael Schumacher

CITADEL PRESS
Kensington Publishing Corp.
www.kensingtonbooks.com

CITADEL PRESS BOOKS are published by

Kensington Publishing Corp.
850 Third Avenue
New York, NY 10022

All Kensington titles, imprints, and distributed lines are available at special quantity discounts for bulk purchases for sales promotions, premiums, fund-raising, educational, or institutional use. Special book excerpts or customized printings can also be created to fit specific needs. For detail, write or phone the office of the Kensington special sales manager: Kensington Publishing Corp., 850 Third Avenue, New York, NY 10022, attn: Special Sales Department, phone 1-800-221-2647.

First printing: March 2003

10 9 8 7 6 5 4 3 2

Printed in the United States of America

Library of Congress Control Number: 2002113404

ISBN 0-8065-2466-9

For Emily Joy, who looks wonderful tonight

. . . and always.

Contents

Acknowledgments

My gratitude, first and foremost, to the many people who spoke to me for this book: your observations were invaluable. My appreciation, also, to those who checked portions of this biography for accuracy, and to those who granted me permission to quote from their interviews with Eric Clapton. Each contribution, no matter how large or small, strengthened the book.

Special thanks to Virginia Lohle, who very well may be Eric Clapton's biggest fan, and who has made a special point of connecting Clapton fans around the world.

Mary Ann Naples, Laurie Chittenden, Lauren Marino, Liz Welch, and Shila Patel played significant roles in seeing this book into publication. Thank you all for your patience and help.

Thanks to Dona Chernoff, who set this book in motion, and to Kim Witherspoon and Maria Massie for keeping it from becoming derailed.

A tip of the cap to those who assisted in ways that may not be apparent, or who helped keep me somewhat steady during the writing of this book: Ken and Karen Ade, Jim Sieger, Glen Puterbaugh, Amelie Littel, Carol Edwards, Peter Spielmann, Judy Hansen, Frank Falduto, and Mark Gumbinger.

Finally, love and gratitude to my wife, Susan, and children, Adam, Emily, and Jack Henry. Your contributions become more evident with every book.

—MICHAEL SCHUMACHER

Crossroads

Prologue

The house lights go down, and countless lighters are struck and held aloft, winking in the darkness like thousands of votive candles flickering in a cathedral. People are on their feet, shouting and applauding, sending a huge surge of energy through the arena.

Backstage, Eric Clapton battles his customary preconcert jitters. He loves to perform, but he's always nervous before stepping out onstage. He's putting himself on the line at each concert, and he won't relax until he's torn off at least one good solo.

This time around, he's taking the stage in his true identity. This is his Nothing but the Blues tour, and for the first time in his many jaunts through the States, he will be playing literally nothing but the blues.

Somehow this manages to be both a luxury and a necessity for the world-renowned guitarist.

He has always considered himself a bluesman. He grew up listening to Muddy Waters and Big Bill Broonzy, Little Walter and Robert Johnson; the first numbers he was proud of playing on his guitar were songs he'd heard on imported American blues records. The music has never been second nature to him—it is his only nature.

Still, his enormous success as a pop star has obscured some of his identity. People want to hear "Wonderful Tonight," "Let It Rain," or any number of his hit singles, and what people want to hear is what record company executives would like him to produce. It's a tough, cynical business, where artistry is expected but only occasionally rewarded, where identity can be established by a bullet on the *Billboard* charts or by a four-minute video played (or ignored) by MTV or VH1.

Clapton knows this. He's been victimized by the mind-set in the past, and he's even gone along with it willingly at times. In trying to please people, he's wandered off his own musical path, but he's never strayed too far from it.

Now he's back where he belongs, playing the music he loves.

• • •

In all likelihood, the tour would never have occurred had it not been for a string of events that took him from one of the lowest points in his life to one of the highest. Just three years earlier, he had suffered one of life's greatest losses, when his son, Conor, died in a terrible accident. As a way of coping with the loss, Clapton wrote a series of beautiful ballads dedicated to Conor, including "Tears in Heaven," a profound and moving song that, by speaking the universal language of grief, touched millions of people worldwide. Not long after the song's release, Clapton appeared on the MTV program "Unplugged," where he gave his most personal performance to date, playing "Tears in Heaven" for the first time in public and framing the all-acoustic television concert with a selection of blues songs that had influenced him as a musician.

The response was overwhelmingly favorable. Warner Brothers, Clapton's record company, pushed to issue the "Unplugged" concert as an album, but Clapton balked at the notion, claiming that the show wasn't up to his highest standard, and that only a limited number of people would be interested in buying the album. The record company prevailed, and to Clapton's amazement, *Unplugged* not only received the best reviews of a Clapton album in more than a decade, but it also became his all-time best-selling work.

It got better. When the Grammy Award nominations were announced the following year, *Unplugged* was cited in nine categories, winning in six, including honors for best song, album, and record—not a bad haul for an artist who had managed only one Grammy for his work over the previous three decades. Clapton was clearly stunned by the long-overdue recognition, which arrived at a time when he was at his most vulnerable, when he was reassessing his past and trying to determine a direction to take in the future.

The Grammy awards afforded Clapton no less than the opportunity to reclaim his identity, and with *From the Cradle*, his album of blues standards, he has done just that. In an interview conducted shortly before the album's release, Clapton called *From the Cradle* his most personal statement to date, and while the remark may seem a bit curious, given the fact that he wrote none of the songs on the record, it makes perfect sense on another level. Clapton has never been one to offer a lot of detail about his private life. For someone of his stature and longevity in the business, he has been all but reclusive, consenting only sparingly to interviews—usually when he has a new album to promote. When he does speak for the record, he measures his responses as if he might have to pay for them someday. He is by nature a private, modest man, never quite convinced that the public cares about what he has to say—or, if they do, that it is any of their business. What people need to know about him can be found in his music.

And now, as he steps to the stage and into the spotlight, he is ready to define himself once again, playing the kind of music that belongs only to bluesmen.

one

Motherless Child: Early Blues Roots
1945 – 68

I'm driven by things that happened to me early in my life, and I recognize it. I was raised by my grandparents, *thinking* that they were my parents, up until I was nine years old. That's when the shock came up, when I found out—from outside sources—that they weren't my parents, they were my grandparents. I went into a kind of . . . shock, which lasted through my teens, really, and started to turn me into the kind of person I am now.

Which is . . . I think it's impossible for me to say, but I'm fairly secretive, and insecure, and madly driven by the ability to impress people or be the best in certain areas. I mean, all of this I've come to terms with in the last five years or so. But up until then, I wasn't really aware of *what* was driving me.

*e*ric Patrick Clapton has never been an easy person to define. To those who know him, he can be in turns friendly and open, moody and withdrawn, self-assured, self-doubting, down to earth, elitist, sensitive, self-absorbed; at one moment he can seem terribly impulsive, and the next he can be coolly calculating. His obsessions have been well documented throughout his years of public life, whether they be his pursuit of fine Italian clothing, priceless art, beautiful women, and expensive sports cars or his hellish struggles with drug and alcohol dependency. As a musician, he is a fierce perfectionist, yet he disdains any kind of polish that threatens to remove the raw, natural beauty of a simple blues line. He is a genuinely shy human being who has chosen to place himself center stage, a bandleader who also sees himself as a journeyman guitarist.

Such contradictions, in the case of a well-known performer, raise very few eyebrows. Fans accept—perhaps even expect—their heroes to be a little offbeat or contradictory, if not downright weird. Publicists and agents revel in the notion that their clients are moving targets, subjects of continuing public interest and press coverage. Performers devote lifetimes to designing their images and myths, redefining themselves in ways that raise the stakes at the marketplace. It's all part of the game.

For Clapton, however, the contradictions signify a lifelong search for his own identity as a person and an artist. His interviews, granted sparingly over the years, indicate as much. At any given moment, he can appear to be at home with who he is and what he is doing, yet a few years down the road, he might reject his previous stance and move on to something else.

Both uncertainty *and* self-confidence act as catalysts in his career. They direct him as a musician, just as they drive all true artists to reach for perfection. As Clapton himself admits, he is not just a performer out to pick up a paycheck. He is constantly seeking that magic level, where the music is a spiritual medium connecting his mind to the thousands of minds in his audience.

After all, Clapton's forte—improvisation in public performance— invokes the risky business of spontaneous self-definition, even if it's framed within the flash of a few moments. The performer's soul lies naked, awaiting acceptance. If, as in Clapton's case, the artist has spent a lifetime trying to determine his own identity, such spontaneity cries out for approval, and Clapton is stung by a lack of response to his work.

· · ·

Clapton's journey toward self-discovery and public acceptance began modestly enough, in a rural English village about thirty miles south of London. It was only appropriate, for one who liked to describe himself as a journeyman, that he be born and raised in a village of laborers.

Patricia Molly Clapton was only sixteen years old when she gave birth to her first child, Eric, on March 30, 1945, in the front room of her parents' large house in Ripley, Surrey. Under the usual circumstances, the arrival of one's firstborn would be an event celebrated by family, friends, and neighbors, but in a village such as Ripley, a traditional community with small-town values, a single mother's pregnancy was more an occasion for gossip than congratulations.

Eric's father, a married man named Edward Fryer, was a Canadian airman stationed in England during the waning days of World War II. In his free time, he played piano in dance hall combos, and he and Pat Clapton had met at one of his gigs in Surrey. Their relationship, such as it was, was doomed from the beginning, for Fryer had every intention of returning to his wife and native country as soon as his tour of duty in England had come to a close.

Fryer's departure was very difficult for Pat Clapton; there would be no easy resolution to her pregnancy, no natural father around to help raise her child. Eric would never get the whole story about his father's background, and he knew better than to ask many questions about him. "It's difficult for me to approach the subject without sensing a great feeling of hurt," he stated when asked about his background, noting that he had seen a photograph of his father, and understood that he had died relatively young. Outside of that information, though, he was not inclined to pursue details about him. "For me to dig it all up again, even for my own sake, I don't think it's worth it."

Raising a child on her own posed serious challenges to Eric's mother. Barely more than a child herself, Pat was anything but prepared to meet her maternal obligations and take on the local gossip mill. It would be better, she ultimately concluded, if her mother and stepfather raised her son. This difficult decision would haunt her with feelings of guilt and regret for years to come, but at the time she viewed it as best for her son's welfare. She left when Eric was two.

Jack and Rose Clapp turned out to be ideal, loving surrogate parents, eager to cater to Eric's every need. A journeyman plasterer and bricklayer,

Jack Clapp was a custom fit in Ripley's hardworking, close-knit community. His wife, Rose, had been a widow when they met. Rose's daughter, Pat, was the product of her marriage to her first husband, Reginald Clapton, whose surname was passed down to Eric.

As an adult, Eric Clapton would scoff at the notion that his childhood had been unhappy. The composition of his family, he'd admit, had been out of the ordinary, but his grandparents had done their best to assure him a proper upbringing. Mum and Dad, as he called them, were "very fun-loving people," and while they were by no means wealthy, they made certain that Eric never lacked the clothing and toys that other children had. If anything, they overindulged him.

Exactly when Eric learned the truth about his biological mother is not known for certain. Clapton has said that he was about nine years old when he learned of his illegitimacy. Rose Clapp, however, dated the revelation to a much earlier time. "We told him when he was five, just before he went to school," she told biographer Ray Coleman, explaining that she felt Eric needed to understand why she and her husband identified themselves as guardians, not parents, on his school forms and legal papers.

It is possible that both memories are accurate. All accounts concur that Clapton was nine when he saw his mother for the first time since she had left him. At the time of that meeting, Pat had married and borne two more children, including a son three years younger than Eric. Clapton might have known that the Clapps were not his biological parents, but he had no memory of his natural mother.

In any event, Clapton's early childhood appears to have been reasonably normal, given the circumstances. His early school years, begun at the Ripley Church of England Primary School when he was five, found Eric impressing his teachers with his facility in English and art, even as he muddled his way through more challenging math courses. Since he was shy and rather small in stature, he was not one to distinguish himself in the schoolyard.

His artistic aptitude was apparent when he was very young. Eric loved to draw, and he always seemed to be at work on some new picture, filling sheets of paper, or even the pages of his grandmother's recipe book, with drawings of animals or cars or other objects that caught his fancy; for a while, he enjoyed sketching pictures of men eating meat pies—a preoccupation that he could never explain, but which amused him when he remembered it as an adult. When he was six, he took first place in an art contest for his drawing of a Western scene, complete with cowboys, horses, and cactuses. Some of this talent, his mother surmised, might have been inherited from his natural father, who enjoyed painting as a pastime.

Eric's early interests in music also came naturally, and at a young age. "It was a very musical family background," he'd say, pointing out that both of his natural parents, as well as his grandmother, played piano. Rose Clapp was fond of sitting at the family's upright piano and singing the songs of the day, and she encouraged Eric to entertain guests at family gatherings. "As a tiny tot," Clapton remembered, "I was inevitably put up in the big bay window, they would pull the curtains, and I would sing, 'I Belong to Glasgow.' That was before I was aware of show biz."

Rose and Jack Clapp supported Eric's enthusiasm for music, though they were not the type of people who saw a career in music as a realistic means of self-support. They supplied Eric with toy instruments, but as the years passed and they further witnessed Eric's skill in sketching, they became convinced that if he was going to use his creative impulses as an adult, it would probably be as a commercial artist.

. . .

The reappearance of Eric's mother proved to be traumatic.

Upon leaving Ripley, Pat Clapton had moved to Germany and married a Canadian soldier named Frank McDonald. She eventually moved to Canada with her husband and had two children with him. In 1954, she decided to return to England for an extended stay with Eric and her parents.

His mother's arrival—and the inevitable revelation of her identity—troubled Eric deeply. He had learned to accept the notion that his family was different from others in the village, but as far as he was concerned, living with the Clapps was no different from living with one's own parents. Now, all of a sudden, he had to contend with the presence of his biological mother, as well as her six-year-old son from her marriage to Frank McDonald. To a nine-year-old lacking the maturity to sort out and analyze his feelings about such complex circumstances, the situation was almost unbearable. It was only natural that he would harbor some resentment toward the woman who he felt had abandoned him as a toddler.

His confused emotional state was compounded by his mother's reluctance to treat him like her son, even in private—a decision that Pat did not arrive at easily. She believed that Rick, as she called him, needed a sense of continuity in his upbringing, and her acting like his mother, even if only temporarily, would disrupt that continuity. Rose and Jack Clapp had been his parents to that point, and they would also be his parents after she returned to Canada; better to let them act as parents now. In addition, she had overcome the troubles of her own youth and rebuilt her life in Canada; she had a husband and children who knew very little about her past. As difficult as it was, she decided to maintain a distance from Eric while she was in England.

Then there was the issue of having to explain who she was when they appeared together in public. To avoid embarrassment and keep the gossip hounds at bay, the family, at Eric's urging, decided to have Pat pose as Eric's sister, rather than as his mother.

It would take years—until Eric's adulthood—for the two to be able to live comfortably with the truth. Up to the point of his mother's arrival, Eric had been very little trouble to his grandparents. Although he was very independent and solitary, and could be moody at times, he had generally been agreeable and polite, both at home and away. He could be strong-willed, almost fanatical on occasion, about doing things his own way, but this had never been a serious problem.

This changed as Eric tried to deal with the trauma of finally encountering his mother and having her around. He grew moody and aloof, which only served to isolate him further from schoolmates. Not surprisingly, his classwork began to slide, much to the alarm of teachers accustomed to having a model student on their hands. Eric's grades fell and he showed no sign of regaining the focus needed to bring them back up.

During these difficult times, a significant change was taking place. For Eric, the confusion resulting from his actually meeting his mother underscored a long-standing belief that, as a loner, he was different from his classmates; but rather than work at trying to find a way to fit in, Eric decided to take another approach. He would use his shyness as a way of distinguishing himself.

"I wanted to be different from everyone else," he recalled. "I sensed that I was, so I developed the philosophy of flaunting it, but [not] in an outgoing way. Instead, it was very introverted. I wanted to be a beatnik before beatniks were even heard of in Ripley. I was the village beatnik."

In hindsight, Clapton's decision, made at such an early age, proved to be enormously important. First, in acknowledging his differences from the average kids in Ripley, he was setting in motion his pursuit of his own identity. Second, in recognizing that his background left him with an unstable if not rootless sense of personal history, he was unwittingly placing himself in a category shared by many of the people he would grow up to admire and emulate—the blues musicians and singers of America.

· · ·

Eric was vaguely aware of a different kind of music being produced in the United States. Like others his age, he had listened to a lot of radio while he was growing up in postwar England. Most of what he heard was standard fare—the pop songs of the day—but as he grew a little older, he began to hear a new kind of music steeped in rhythm and blues, known in America as rock 'n' roll.

His first exposure to this kind of music came when he was ten or eleven years old. "There was a funny Saturday-morning radio program for children, with this strange person, Uncle Mac," he said. "He was a very old man with one leg and a strange little penchant for children. He'd play things like 'Mule Train,' and then every week he'd slip in something like a Buddy Holly record or a Chuck Berry record. And the first blues I ever heard was on that program; it was a song by Sonny Terry and Brownie McGhee, with Sonny Terry howling and playing the harmonica. It blew me away."

It was also during this period that Eric heard Big Bill Broonzy for the first time. An authentic country bluesman from America's Deep South, Broonzy had played an instrumental role in bringing blues to Chicago. He wrote hundreds of blues and interpreted hundreds more, and in the later years of his life, he proved to be an articulate spokesman, capable of closing the gap between black and white audiences. Two of his songs, "Hey Hey" and "Key to the Highway," became favorites of the young Eric Clapton.

These sounds contrasted with the music Eric was accustomed to hearing around the house. From radio to parlor piano to the phonograph records around the Clapp house, there never seemed to be a shortage of music to be heard and appreciated. Eric's mother was a big-band fan, and Eric was fond of the Glenn Miller, Harry James, and Benny Goodman records that she played. Pat's older brother, Adrian, who had moved back into the Clapp household after a stint in the service, had a large collection of jazz records that Eric enjoyed.

However, as much as he liked the sounds produced by a bandleader like Stan Kenton, Eric discovered he enjoyed this "new" music more. Blues seemed to come from a place that was both universal and almost ancient; its eloquence rested in its purity, stated with a simplicity that only accentuated its emotional power. It could make the hair on your neck stand up; it could make you cry.

Rock 'n' roll gave this music an added dimension. With its heavy rhythms and amplified instruments, it had the ability to plug into youthful energy. A Chuck Berry song told a complete story in just a handful of verses, its impact riding on guitar licks that, in time, would be studied and imitated by every kid who picked up an electric guitar. Somehow, rock 'n' roll had raised a musical ante. It was the voice of rebellion, and nowhere was this as clear as in the voice of Elvis Presley, the Mississippi upstart who grounded his music in the blues he'd heard in his youth.

When Eric Clapton first heard this music, he knew he had to learn to play it. He pestered his grandparents until they bought him, first, a plastic guitar that he could neither play nor keep in tune, and then, for his thirteenth birthday, a gut-string Spanish guitar, which they purchased at an instrument shop in Kingston for 14 pounds—a princely sum in 1958.

Oddly enough, learning to play the Hoya guitar was anything but agreeable to the novice musician. Without instructions or lessons at his disposal, Eric had to learn the chords on his own. He would sit up in his room for hours on end, listening to records or the radio, trying to copy the music that he heard, inventing his own chords as he went along. Over the months, the neck of the guitar started to warp, and a frustrated Clapton began to lose interest in his latest obsession.

"I couldn't really get the hang of it," he admitted in an interview thirty-five years later. "I tried and tried, but got nowhere with it. I finally gave up after a year and a half."

• • •

School continued to be a problem. After failing his eleven-plus grammar school exams in 1959, Eric transferred to St. Bede's Secondary Modern School, where he was expected to get his studies back on track. His grades did improve, but his time at the school was rather difficult. Eric was the kind of oddball that schoolmates found difficult to warm up to. At a time when the social pecking order among adolescent boys was established by their prowess in competitive games, Eric was a miserable failure, with neither the physical coordination nor the desire to prove himself in sports. "I was the one," he said, "that used to get stones thrown at me because I was so thin and couldn't do physical training very well. One of those types. I was always the seven-stone weakling. I used to hang out with three or four other kids who were all in the same kind of predicament. The outcasts. They used to call us 'the loonies.'"

Even if Clapton could laugh at the memory as a successful adult, the experience was nevertheless painful to endure in his youth.

Nor did it help that Eric preferred to spend most of his time by himself, wrapped in his own sullen thoughts. Rather than make any attempt to socialize, he would be off on his own, riding his bicycle along the country-side or drawing in a sketchbook. While distancing himself from others, he developed a sizable chip on his shoulder, a defense mechanism that suggested, OK, if you won't have anything to do with me, I don't need you either. The resentment helped stave off loneliness.

Eric spent two years at St. Bede's, improving enough academically for admission to Hollyfield Road School in Surbiton, where he was able to focus on his art interests at a more intense level. Rose and Jack Clapp were pushing him to think about a career as a commercial artist, perhaps in the field of stained-glass design, and Eric worked hard to qualify for studies at the Kingston College of Art. Unfortunately, as far as these plans were concerned, he had picked up the guitar again and was training himself with a passion that would ultimately redirect his future.

This time around, Clapton did not let the difficulties of learning to play the instrument on his own deter him. He was no longer content just to wrestle with the mechanics of playing the guitar; he was obsessed with determining and copying the *feeling* of the masters. There were many styles of blues guitar to be heard in the records he was picking up or listening to in the record stores, and Eric pushed himself to learn as much about each as he could. His endless practicing drove his grandparents half crazy, but by now they were all too familiar with Eric's obsessive tendencies. They had given him a portable Grundig Cub reel-to-reel tape recorder as a gift, upon which he recorded hours upon hours of his practicing, hoping that he could duplicate the sounds he heard from the likes of Big Bill Broonzy, Muddy Waters, and other favorites.

The slow learning process offered its own small rewards, such as the time when Eric was practicing in the stairwell of his grandparents' home and heard an encouraging echo from his guitar resounding off the walls.

"It sounded like a record," he remembered. "Normally, if you sat and played the guitar in here, it wouldn't be very inspiring, but when it suddenly had that echo, it sounded like Elvis or Buddy Holly. And I thought, 'Yeah, this could be . . . the world had better watch out.' You know. 'I'll put this on tape.' And that's the way it started."

His motives, he noted, weren't entirely artistic. He was painfully aware that he did not fit in with his peers at school. He didn't run with the popular crowd, and he was terribly shy around girls. He had nowhere to fit in. Learning to excel on a musical instrument offered him the opportunity to be noticed.

"Guitar playing—it's like a bluff," he said. "Covers up all your wimp things. If you can get that down . . . I mean, the first recognition I ever got amongst the crowd I used to hang out with was for my guitar playing."

That would certainly prove to be the case when, at age sixteen, Eric moved on to the Kingston College of Art. While studying at Hollyfield, Eric had put together an impressive enough art portfolio to gain admission to the school on a probationary basis. According to the conditions of his admittance, Eric would attend classes for a year, after which his performance would be evaluated. If he did well enough in his studies and assembled an acceptable portfolio of work, he would be allowed to continue on to his second term at the school.

While enrolling, Eric was asked to choose between Kingston's fine arts and graphics schools. Since he hoped to become a commercial artist, Eric selected the graphics school—a decision he regretted from his first day of classes. The students in the graphics school took a businesslike approach to their artwork, whereas the fine arts division seemed to house the interesting, creative types—the kind of people who liked the bohemian lifestyle that Eric found appealing at the time.

Before long, music had replaced art studies and become Eric's number one priority. He attended classes and haunted London's art galleries, but he did very little to build up the portfolio he was required to present to school officials at the end of the year. Instead, he devoted most of his free hours to practicing guitar or listening to records, his guitar being as much a companion on campus as his books. When his occasional absences from

•

classes became more frequent, the school's headmaster sent a warning letter to the Clapps, warning them that Eric was in danger of dismissal if he did not improve in his studies.

The letter, along with Rose Clapp's scolding, had little effect on Eric, who was totally submerged in his own course of study.

In Eric's private study, the discipline was Blues, the master Robert Johnson.

•   •   •

Over the course of his career, Eric Clapton would be influenced by a number of American blues artists, but with the possible exception of Muddy Waters, no one would ever come close to approaching the profound effect that Robert Johnson had on Clapton and his music.

Ironically, Clapton had never heard of Johnson when he initiated his study of American blues, but when he did, the country bluesman represented no less than a validation of Clapton's sense of musical vocation. "It was almost like I'd been prepared each step to receive him," Clapton explained, saying that his study was "like a religious experience that started out by hearing Chuck Berry, and then at each stage I was going further and further back, and deeper and deeper into the source of the music, until I was ready for Robert Johnson."

Such a statement was no exaggeration. One did not simply listen to Johnson's music and tear off a quick cover version of one of his songs. To blues players, Johnson's name elicited unequaled reverence. Although the entire body of his work could be found on two records, Johnson's music had incredible range, which Clapton was quick to acknowledge: "Both of the Robert Johnson albums actually cover all of my desires musically. Every angle of emotion is expressed on both those albums."

Then there were the sketchy details of Johnson's life, which, by the time Clapton heard them, had reached mythical proportions. You heard talk about his wife and child dying in childbirth, about wanderlust that led him to roaming all parts of North America. His musical and extracurricular activity—the drinking and womanizing—in the Deep South "jook" houses were legendary. There was the account of Johnson's poisoning by the jealous lover of one of his barroom flings. However, all these stories shriveled in the presence of the ultimate Robert Johnson myth—the tale of how he sold his soul to the devil in exchange for his uncanny guitar-playing ability.

The larger-than-life facts of Johnson's twenty-seven years on earth only served to underscore the heavy emotional content of such classic Johnson compositions as "Love in Vain," "Terraplane Blues," "Hellhound on My Trail," and "Cross Road Blues."* When he first heard Johnson's *King of the Delta Blues Singers* recording, Eric Clapton found the singer's anguish almost too much to take.

"It came as something of a shock to me that there could be anything that powerful," he admitted, noting that Johnson seemed to break all the standard maxims regarding tempo and harmonics. "It was almost as if he felt things so acutely he found it almost unbearable. . . . It called to me in my confusion, it seemed to echo something that I had always felt."

Johnson's music set a standard that was both challenging and terrifying. Clapton realized that it would have been pointless to imitate Johnson's voice and style. Instead, he searched for a way to integrate the raw emotion of Johnson's music into the modern sounds of amplified blues and rock 'n' roll.

• • •

Clapton's personal study of the blues indicated how obsessive he could be. By Clapton's thinking, it wasn't enough to know some of the big names, or be aware of the important, influential songs; he had to know *everything* about the music. He was driven to learn all about the different styles of blues, when and where they had been played, and how the different styles had cross-pollinated and influenced each other. Learning this involved delving into the geography of the United States and the country's cultural history. It also meant learning about the kind of music that had been largely ignored even by its native land.

*Clapton retitled the song "Crossroads" when he recorded it with Cream.

These new interests all but spelled an end to his schooling. His formal studies at Kingston College of Art continued their downward spiral. He was, as he put it, "a general nuisance," the kind of underachiever that school administrators were all too happy to weed out. He would bring his guitar to school and give regular lunchtime performances in Kingston's cafeteria, and on those occasions when he wasn't giving impromptu concerts, he could often be found in a nearby pub, getting too drunk to attend his afternoon classes. He was far too busy playing records to work on his art portfolio.

Eric had just turned seventeen when he was called in and asked to present his first year's work. Of the fifty students in his class, he had done the least. The work he had actually completed was acceptable and showed plenty of promise, but the portfolio was far too slender for Eric to pass his probationary period at the school. Any remaining intentions of a future in commercial art disappeared when Eric was dismissed from Kingston in the spring of 1962.

Oddly enough, Eric was shocked by this rejection. Now that he had been bounced from school, he had to find a job, and the prospects were grim. He was not accomplished enough to secure employment as a regular musician in any of London's pubs. He had worked sparingly in the past, so he had few skills and little experience to bring to the job market.

If Clapton's dismissal from school had been unfortunate, its timing could not have been better. London's blues scene was on the rise. The Ealing Club had opened on March 17, 1962, joining such establishments as the Barrelhouse Club, the Flamingo, and the Marquee in presenting some of the best local talent in jazz, blues, and rhythm and blues. Veteran musicians Alexis Korner and Cyril Davies, along with the younger, yet highly regarded Georgie Fame, were kings of the scene, founding such bands as Blues Incorporated, the Cyril Davies All Stars, and the Blue Flames. London had become a veritable musical stewpot, offering a spicy entree of newcomers that included such soon-to-be-well-known names as Brian Jones, John Baldry, Paul Jones, Charlie Watts, Ginger Baker, Keith Richards, Jack Bruce, and Mick Jagger.

Eric Clapton wandered into this scene fresh from his art school expulsion. He haunted London's coffeehouses and pubs, taking in the shows, watching other musicians ply their trade, polishing his own performance skills with an occasional onstage appearance of his own. He would also turn up in the clubs around Richmond and Kingston, playing for drinks, a bite to eat, or a place to sleep overnight. He lacked confidence in his singing ability, but he found that, if he could not find someone to sing while he played, he could do passable versions of country blues like Big Bill Broonzy's "Hey Hey," Jesse Fuller's "San Francisco Bay Blues," and Bessie Smith's "Nobody Knows You When You're Down and Out."

Clapton found it easy to distinguish himself in the clubs. The scene was still developing, and newcomers with talent were greeted as welcome new additions. Clapton was easily as good as or better than most of the competition around, and he quickly discovered that he could find work almost anywhere. "If you were pretty good you could work all the time and you'd get fairly well paid and you were successful," he remarked in an interview three decades later, dispelling any notions that he had ever been a starving young artist paying heavy dues. "It was easy to be successful if you had what was necessary, which was the right musical taste."

Although he would characterize himself during that period as "just a blues aficionado with a guitar, attempting to sing," Clapton was pleased to have found a personal outlet for the music he loved. "You could play that kind of music in a pub, be the hero of all your friends, and get free drinks," he noted. "And finally I'd something I could do that no one else could do."

His enthusiasm was not entirely shared by his grandparents, who believed that music, for all the pleasure it offered as a hobby, promised little in the way of a decent living. They had been patient when Eric was dismissed from art school, but they found their tolerance tested as the months passed along and Eric spent most of his waking hours at home practicing his guitar, showing no sign of actively looking for a job.

Jack Clapp eventually suggested that Eric might be able to earn some money by working as his assistant. For the next several months, Eric accompanied his grandfather to building sites, where he would mix cement and mortar for Jack's bricklaying jobs. It was tough, physical work, and Eric marveled at the dexterity required to do a proper job in short order. The lesson was not wasted on him.

"It was magic to watch him work," said Clapton, obviously still proud of his grandfather's ability, even after the passing of many years. "To attempt to do it, to get a trowel and lay some plaster in a straight line up a wall was something that very few people could do. He could plaster a room in maybe two hours, and it was phenomenal. It was a work of art."

Though he was not the preachy type, Jack Clapp would talk to Eric about values from time to time. Eric, however, didn't need lengthy lectures about developing a work ethic. He had learned all he needed to know by observing his grandfather at work, and those youthful lessons were maintained throughout his adult life, where hard work and the attention to detail would help set him apart from his peers.

"It was mainly by watching him," said Clapton of his grandfather, "that I realized that little things are all-important. He was a true craftsman. In fact, he was a journeyman."

. . .

Manual labor, whatever it had to offer, was not for a talented young musician with growing ambitions. Clapton knew as much, even if he had no clear direction of how—or if—he would be making a living with his guitar. He and another guitarist named Dave Brock had played occasional gigs in some of Surrey's folk clubs, but Eric was restless, anxious to move on to something better. He wanted to redeem himself in the wake of his art school fiasco—to prove that his interest in music was not a passing fancy—but he was confused about the next step to take.

"I didn't know what to do, so I asked my family to get me an electric guitar," he said. "It became clear that I would have to make a go of it."

For his first electric guitar, Eric selected a red twin cutaway Kay, an American model that had received its British endorsement from Alexis Korner. The instrument's hefty 100-pound price tag, picked up by the

Clapps on the installment plan, acted as a motivating factor for Eric: if his grandparents were going to make that kind of investment in his musical future, he had better find some way to reward their faith.

The guitar purchase coincided with Eric's early-1963 entry into his first formal band, an outfit originally called Rhode Island Red and the Roosters, which was quickly shortened to the Roosters.

Clapton's involvement with the band was a happy accident. Guitarist Tom McGuinness, one of the Rooster's cofounders, was dating a young woman who had attended Kingston College of Art the same year that Clapton was there. She was aware of Eric's growing reputation, and she introduced McGuinness to him at a prearranged meeting at a Kingston hotel. Eric was hired on the spot.

The Roosters' other founder, pianist Ben Palmer, shared Clapton's fanaticism for the blues, and the two hit it off immediately. In earlier days, Palmer had spent plenty of time discussing, playing, and listening to blues music with future Rolling Stones guitarist Brian Jones and future Manfred Mann vocalist Paul Jones. When he and McGuinness had been planning the formation of the Roosters, Palmer had hoped to play Chicago-style blues exclusively.

From a musical standpoint, the Roosters might have been a cut above a garage band, but not by much. Palmer was more an aficionado than a musician dedicated to a future in the business, and two of the group's other members, singer Terry Brennan and drummer Robin Mason, would not have long-term careers in music. McGuinness and Clapton were in it for the long haul, but they were still learning their craft and would not blossom for a couple of years.

"I knew just about enough to be able to play and keep up that end of it," was Clapton's evaluation of his talent at the time, and McGuinness would not dispute the assessment. "I'd love to be able to say that the minute Eric picked up a guitar I knew he was a genius, but that wasn't the case at that time," said McGuinness. "I never felt that I was in the presence of someone who would turn out to be as good as Eric Clapton."

Their musical inexperience aside, the Roosters devoted themselves to a sound that refused to compromise the purity of raw blues to some of the slicker sounds being produced by pop-oriented British groups of the day. The band would gather at the Prince of Wales pub in New Malden, or at the Wooden Bridge Hotel in Guildford, where they would rehearse arrangements of songs by such American blues artists as Howlin' Wolf, Freddie King, and Muddy Waters, as well as offerings by rock 'n' rollers like Fats Domino, Little Richard, Larry Williams, and Chuck Berry. Working now with amplification, Clapton experimented with feedback and note bending, though most of these early efforts fell short of their intended effects.

Like the seemingly endless number of bands springing up in England at the time, the Roosters struggled for gigs—paying or otherwise. They played any venue available, from private parties to the pub circuit around London, Windsor, Kingston, and West Wickham. As a general rule, the money was terrible but the experience was good. The people frequenting the blues clubs were as fanatical about their music as the musicians themselves, and what the typical audience lacked in sheer numbers was made up for in enthusiasm. For a serious young guitarist like Eric Clapton, the appreciative response and camaraderie overshadowed the poor remuneration for services.

For some of the others, this was not the case. Only Clapton and Brennan had steady income from other sources, and the few gigs the band was getting were hardly enough reward for the hours of rehearsing and the problems the Roosters had to endure getting from job to job. Robin Mason was the only band member with a car, which would be overburdened with five musicians and all their equipment when the group had to travel to a gig. "It was a nightmare, but it was great fun," said Clapton of the experience.

The Roosters lasted about six months before disbanding, victims of heavy competition and lack of transportation. It was probably just as well, for there were already disputes among members over the direction the Roosters were taking; Ben Palmer wanting to stay with Chicago blues, while Clapton and McGuinness hoped to expand into other forms of blues-based music, including rock 'n' roll. As time would show, Clapton was a man of complex musical ambitions, never content to stay put for any noteworthy period of time. It was time to move on.

. . .

In retrospect, 1963 was one of the most important years in rock music history. In the United States, the sound of street-corner doo-wop, along with the refined harmonies of the Everly Brothers and such pop quartets as the Four Freshmen and the Four Lads, had been incorporated into Chuck Berry–influenced rock and mixed with dashes of teenage innocence, resulting in music that made the Beach Boys one of America's most success-ful new bands. For those looking for more adult content in their music, the East Coast folk scene, spearheaded by Bob Dylan, a young Minnesota singer-songwriter found ways to combine traditional folk and country blues with lyrics reflecting a growing concern with social inequity and global warfare.

The influence of American music, particularly rhythm and blues, could be felt all over England in a glut of new groups that, within a year, would break through on an international level. Four musicians from Liverpool, calling themselves the Beatles and playing anything from self-written pop tunes to American Motown music, were taking the country by storm. The Rolling Stones, a blues-based quintet deriving their name from a Muddy Waters song, had taken up residence at the Crawdaddy Club and were playing before shoulder-to-shoulder crowds. In Newcastle, a young singer named Eric Burdon assembled his American-blues-based group, the Ani-mals, while in Birmingham, Stevie Winwood, all of sixteen years old, propelled the Spencer Davis Group with some of the most soulful vocals ever produced in rock music.

It was a good time to hang out—which was precisely what Eric Clapton did in the period immediately following the disbanding of the Roosters. He and Ben Palmer would jump from club to club, listening to the different bands, Eric occasionally sitting in with a group for a song or two. Even then, Clapton drew a distinction between what a band did on record and what it did onstage, and he preferred the performance aspect of the music business, where musicians could improvise on songs that were otherwise limited by the time restrictions on records.

Almost exactly a month after parting ways with the Roosters, Clapton was offered the opportunity to join another outfit, a Liverpool band called Casey Jones and the Engineers. As it turned out, the band was little more than a marketing setup for a young singer named Brian Casser, who had recorded a single for Columbia and needed a group of backing musicians to promote it in live performances.

A master of self-promotion, Casser had taken his marginal talents a long way, first in leading a band called Cass and the Casanovas, and then in fronting an outfit known as Casey Jones and the Governors. Casser, whose repertoire included everything from Mersey-beat pop to blues standards, managed to build a following in Hamburg as well as in England, and this success, coupled with the music industry's obsession with any band coming out of Liverpool, led to a recording contract with Columbia. When Casser recorded his single, "One Way Ticket," his "Engineers" were sessions musicians, not his own touring band. With the release of the record came the sudden need to find musicians to help promote it.

When Clapton heard that Casser was looking for two guitarists for his band, he talked to Tom McGuinness and the two signed on. Clapton later admitted that he was enticed by the prospects of touring England and making a little money—and maybe, eventually, cutting an album—but he soon grew bored with backing a singer who specialized in stage acrobatics and music he had no interest in. "It was a very heavy pop show and I couldn't stand it for long," he remarked years later. "I was such a purist, and the band was Top Twenty, which at the time was disastrous."

Clapton stayed with the band for a month, performing a total of seven gigs in London, Manchester, Macclesfield, and Reading. He had decided, early in his brief tenure with Casey and the Engineers, that he would be leaving the group as soon as he found an opening somewhere else.

That opening presented itself in October 1963, when Eric ran into Keith

Relf, a singer-harmonica player he knew from his days of playing at the folk clubs around Kingston and Richmond. Relf and a friend, Paul Samwell-Smith, had formed the Metropolis Blues Quartet, which, in mid-1963, had expanded to a quintet and changed its name.

The group now called itself the Yardbirds.

Smokestack
Lightning
1963–65

I couldn't see what was so wonderful about competing with the Liverpool sound and all of that, trying to jump on the bandwagon; there was still a great part of me that was very much the blues purist, thinking, "Music is this, it's not that."

eric Clapton's brief membership in the Roosters and Casey Jones and the Engineers had been fruitful in his development as a performing musician. In less than a year's time, he had gained the reputation, at least among area musicians, of being one of the best young blues guitarists around. He was confident as a soloist, and he brought to the stage a sense of personal style that set him apart from the lead guitarists in other bands. He knew what he wanted to play, how he wanted to play it, and what he wanted to look like while he was playing it.

Clapton's familiarity with the Yardbirds went back to the group's earlier permutation as the Metropolis Blues Quartet, and his acquaintance with a couple of the band's members dated back further yet, to his art school days. He admired the band's devotion to electric Chicago blues, even if, in his expanding self-confidence, he was somewhat disdainful of the way the group's guitarists played.

On one occasion, while attending a Metropolis Blues Quartet performance at a Kingston pub, he had watched in disgust as Paul Samwell-Smith, eventually the Yardbird's bassist but then playing guitar, took a solo during one of the songs. After the show, Clapton approached Samwell-Smith with a rather audacious request.

"Would you do me a favor?" he asked his future bandmate.

"Yeah, Eric, what is it?" replied Samwell-Smith.

"Don't play any more lead guitar."

The point was not lost on Samwell-Smith, who was not fond of playing solos in the first place.

Later, after the band had changed its name to the Yardbirds and hired Tony Topham as its guitarist, Clapton was equally harsh and outspoken in his criticism. He could do better than Topham, he informed some of the band members, and they had to agree. Not that it took much persuasion for the Yardbirds to dismiss Topham and appoint Clapton as his replacement: at the time, Tony Topham was all of sixteen years old, and his parents were worked up about the prospects of his traveling all over England and staying out until all hours when he might be better off attending art school and eventually finding gainful employment in a more stable occupation. Topham's release from the band came as a relief to all parties involved—except, of course, the young guitarist himself, who, oddly enough, wound up playing and writing about the blues later in his life. After Topham's departure, the Yardbirds consisted of Eric Clapton on lead guitar, Chris Dreja on rhythm guitar, Samwell-Smith on bass, and Jim McCarty on drums, with Keith Relf playing harmonica and handling the band's vocals.

Clapton had an immediate and important impact on the band. The Yardbirds' repertoire included songs by Howlin' Wolf, Snooky Pryor, John Lee Hooker, Bo Diddley, and Chuck Berry, among others, and Clapton was already familiar with the material when he took over the guitar duties. His skills, however, added a new dimension to the Yardbirds' performances. Rather than play standard cover versions of the songs, which the band had been doing prior to Clapton's appearance on the scene, the Yardbirds began to put their own signature on the music. Clapton could play extended guitar solos, which, along with Keith Relf's ability to do the same on harmonica, afforded the band the opportunity to stretch out and improvise. The "rave-up," as the Yardbirds called it, had been born.

In the era of the two-minute pop song, the rave-up was as unlikely as one could have imagined, its origins stemming more from jazz improvisation than anything pop music was producing. In a song such as "Smokestack Lightning," a favorite among their fans, the Yardbirds would begin with a straight reading of the Howlin' Wolf standard, the band playing basic accompaniment while Keith Relf sang the song's verses. During the instrumental breaks, however, the musicians would break tempo, starting slowly and working steadily toward a loud, relentless climax, only to fall away and repeat the process. This series of peaks and valleys, controlled by the Yardbirds' rhythm section, encouraged the open-ended solos that became the trademark of the rave-up. Depending on inspiration and crowd reaction, a song could go on indefinitely—and often did.

In addition to the recognition he received for his guitar work, Clapton was getting a lot of attention for his appearance, which was unlike what people were accustomed to seeing in rock musicians. Instead of following the long hairstyles that were becoming the rage among musicians, Clapton kept his hair short and neatly groomed in a mod fashion, and he eventually turned up in a military-style crewcut that really set him apart from his peers. His choice of clothing was equally individualistic, eschewing both the bohemian and uniform styles typical of his contemporaries. He loved the Ivy League styles available in some of London's West End clothing shops, and it was not uncommon to find his onstage outfit consisting of a dress shirt with a button-down collar, a tie, a vest or Ivy League jacket, either dress slacks or blue jeans, and white socks. He also liked to accent his wardrobe with long, flowing scarves. To Clapton, the choice of what to wear was an important decision that helped further define the performer.

"I always used to buy jazz albums on Blue Note," he would recall, "and even when I was just buying blues albums I'd go into the record shops and flip through the bins and pick out something by Miles Davis, and see this guy impeccably dressed. The way these guys presented themselves attracted me to the jazz world much more than the music. They were *sharp*. And people like Ray Charles would go to a session wearing a shirt and tie and suit."

His interest in style would never change. Two decades up the road, when he was one of rock's highest-ranking stars, he would be spending a small fortune on Italian designer clothing and changing the way he looked from album to album.

. . .

The Yardbirds were already enjoying regular Sunday night engagements in Richmond's Crawdaddy Club when Clapton joined the band. Located in the Station Hotel, the Crawdaddy was one of the most successful clubs in the area. The Rolling Stones had cut their teeth in the club, acting as the Crawdaddy's resident band until September 1963, when their first single, "Come On," fared just well enough on the British charts to warrant the band a low-rung position in a touring package that included the Everly Brothers, Bo Diddley, and Little Richard. The Yardbirds had been hired to fill the void.

The early appearances of the Yardbirds at the Crawdaddy were far from ideal. The Rolling Stones had built quite a following during their stint at the club, and their replacements were not enthusiastically greeted by their die-hard fans. To Crawdaddy regulars, the Rolling Stones offered a hard-edged alternative to the country's Mersey beat scene, and the Yardbirds, while playing the right kind of music, were just imitations.

Giorgio Gomelsky, the twenty-nine-year-old proprietor and talent promoter at the Crawdaddy, felt otherwise. He had watched the Stones' rise in popularity and had even, for a brief period of time, acted as the group's informal manager. Gomelsky strongly believed in the Yardbirds' ability and potential, and he was determined to guide them along in their career. Not about to repeat the scene he'd had with the Stones, which saw Mick Jagger and company signing on with another agent just as they were about to break through to commercial success, Gomelsky insisted that a proper management contract be drawn up between him and the Yardbirds. A meeting was held at the home of Keith Relf's parents, and the contract was signed by Gomelsky, the individual members of the Yardbirds, and, since the musicians were under twenty-one, their parents. Rose Clapp signed with Eric.

The arrangement paid immediate dividends. An avid fan of the blues, Gomelsky was helping put together the American Blues Festival, which included a touring group of such American blues artists as Muddy Waters, Willie Dixon, Memphis Slim, and Sonny Boy Williamson. The festival, held at the Fairfield Hall in Croydon, was an enormous hit, receiving such overwhelming response that Williamson was persuaded to remain in England at the end of the tour. The legendary blues harpist needed a backing unit for his own string of dates in the country, and Giorgio Gomelsky convinced him to use the Yardbirds in this capacity.

For Clapton, the notion of playing with a blues artist of Williamson's reputation was a dream come true. Aleck "Rice" Miller—aka "Little Boy Blue," aka Sonny Boy Williamson II—had known or recorded with some of the most revered blues singers of the twentieth century. He had played harmonica on Elmore James's historic recording of "Dust My Broom," and he had been a friend and traveling companion of Robert Johnson; his appearance on radio's "King Biscuit Time" in the 1940s had established him a reputation that, in time, would earn him a recording contract with Chess Records, one of the most influential American blues labels. Although he was sixty-six years old when he met Eric Clapton and the Yardbirds, and had less than two years to live, Williamson was still capable of high-energy performances worthy of players half his age.

Clapton's work with Williamson was both humbling and educational. Eric was proud of his knowledge of the blues—to the point that he took a lofty stance in relation to his bandmates. He could be elitist in his attitudes, and he would shrug off or criticize any music that failed to meet his standards, particularly anything he deemed to be too pop oriented. He fancied himself—and correctly so—to be the most gifted musician in the Yardbirds, and this, coupled with his highbrow attitude about the blues, could make him a difficult companion.

Sonny Boy Williamson provided him with his comeuppance. Even in his advancing age, Williamson was a firebrand. He drank heavily and would turn up drunk for many of his shows, but even in this state he proved a top-notch performer. The Yardbirds often found themselves hanging on for dear life, hoping to keep up with him during the gigs. It didn't help, either, that Williamson could be openly disdainful of these five white British kids trying to play black American music.

Williamson, like many established blues artists, harbored resentment about the way rock 'n' roll was capitalizing on its blues influences. Black singers and musicians had toiled in obscurity, living impoverished lives on the road and performing under every conceivable condition—all to keep the blues alive and to peck out whatever existence they could muster. Their music was part of a native oral tradition, a validation of lives that might otherwise have disappeared from history's notice, or even from the memory of their own families. The music was meant to be passed along, from generation to generation.

In time, some of the best of the bluesmen had migrated from the Deep South to Chicago, where they plugged in their instruments and invented a blues with a strong kick, the amplified "Chicago blues" that directly influenced rock 'n' roll. Even then, the black musicians enjoyed regional popularity but were never adequately compensated, in money or renown, for their work. Whites felt no qualms about paying to see them play and then insisting that they eat and sleep in segregated restaurants and hotels.

When the young, white British musicians and blues aficionados began purchasing the blues records being imported to the United Kingdom from America, the older bluesmen found new career opportunities. They were not only selling their music overseas; they were also in demand for personal appearances. Sonny Boy Williamson was not alone in feeling ambivalent about this newfound popularity. During one of his many visits to the Marquee Club, Clapton saw Little Walter playing with a pickup band of English musicians. The famous blues harpist was drunk and obnoxious, impatiently barking out orders to his support group. People were outraged by his behavior, but to Clapton, those in attendance should have felt *fortunate* to be seeing Little Walter in the first place. "You take the rough with the smooth," he said. "You're lucky he's alive and that he condescends to play for you."

Condescending was an apt description for Sonny Boy Williamson's attitude toward the Yardbirds. The musicians, he felt, were pathetic in their attempts to play the music he'd been performing his entire life. They were little more than snotty white kids attempting to cash in on the hardscrabble existences of the American bluesman. "Those Englishmen want to play the blues so bad," he sneered, "and they play it so bad!"

Aware of his own shortcomings, Clapton had little choice but to agree.

"When Sonny Boy came over we didn't know how to back him up," he admitted. "It was frightening, really, because this man was real and we weren't. He wasn't very tolerant, either. He did take a shine to us after a while, but before that he put us through some bloody hard paces."

The problem, Clapton pointed out, went beyond the fact that the Yardbirds had been together for a relatively short period of time and were still learning how to play as a cohesive unit. Williamson expected his backing band to be familiar with his music, and he became abusive during rehearsals when he called out a song title and certain members had no idea what song he was talking about. In Clapton's case, the lesson to be learned focused on the idea that there was a major difference between being familiar with a song and actually *knowing* it.

"I knew his songs," he said. "I had *heard* them, but at that point in time it hadn't occurred to me that to know a song was different to being familiar with it. I thought it would be in a key, and it would have a tempo. I didn't realize that the detail was important. It didn't occur to me that there would be a strict adherence to a guitar line, to an intro, to a solo. And that's what I learned very quickly with him. Because he didn't just want to count it off. That's what really shook me up—I thought we could get away with just busking it, and he wasn't at all happy with that. I mean, we would rehearse, but still, even then, we were nowhere near getting it right to his satisfaction."

Williamson, the Yardbirds quickly learned, wasn't interested in their rave-up style of playing. He demanded certain structure and discipline in his show, which the band was damn well advised to follow, even if that structure wasn't readily apparent to the individual members.

As the weeks passed, however, the relationship between Williamson and the Yardbirds improved. Because he knew more than the others about the blues in general and Williamson in specific, Clapton assumed the role of liaison between the Yardbirds and the aging bluesman, and while Williamson never did warm up to the band to such an extent that everybody could relax, there was a better line of communication between all parties involved.

"I thought we'd done pretty well," said Clapton of the period that the Yardbirds worked with Williamson, taking exception to some of Williamson's remarks about the Yardbirds. The problem was in the direction the band was taking, not in its ability. "By that time, the momentum of the band was toward becoming a pop group, and this man arrived and took it all back down to the basic blues. And I had to almost relearn how to play. It taught me a lot; it taught me the value of that music, which I still feel."

Giorgio Gomelsky thought it might be a good idea to record some of the music, and Horst Lippman, a German record producer and one of the blues tour organizers, was brought in to cut a live album of one of the shows.

Recorded on the evening of December 8, 1963, at the Crawdaddy, the album, *Sonny Boy Williamson and the Yardbirds*, features nine Williamson songs that, in retrospect, didn't do justice to the band's talents. The Yardbirds were always a better unit onstage than in the recording studio, recognized for enthusiastic performances that minimized the band's musical weaknesses, but that confidence is missing on *Sonny Boy Williamson and the Yardbirds*. The group sounds tentative, as if intimidated by Williamson and the fact that their performance was being taped. While their interpretations of such Williamson songs as "Mister Downchild," "Pontiac Blues," and "Baby Don't Worry" are certainly nothing to be embarrassed about, they lack the innovative playing necessary to elevate the album to a plateau beyond standard fare. With only a few scattered, exceptional moments, Clapton's guitar work is limited to fills, buried beneath the rhythm section and Williamson's harmonica. With the Yardbirds, Clapton's guitar exchanges alongside Keith Relf's harmonica had been one of the group's musical strengths, but it is not much in evidence on *Sonny Boy Williamson and the Yardbirds*. The backing band, in this instance, was not about to upstage the headliner.

On the other hand, the album is a noteworthy historical document. British musicians would record notable works with influential black American blues artists—the Chess "London Sessions" recordings, featuring Howlin' Wolf, Bo Diddley, Muddy Waters, and Chuck Berry, spring immediately to mind—but *Sonny Boy Williamson and the Yardbirds* was one of the first attempts to release a record featuring a master and his pupils.

• • •

The Yardbirds closed out 1963 with the Williamson concerts, their weekly Sunday night dates at the Crawdaddy, regular appearances at London's Studio 51, and various one-nighters elsewhere. Clapton moved into an apartment with Keith Relf and Chris Dreja. With steady money coming in, he lived a carefree life, spending almost all of his extra money on his wardrobe and guitars. He had purchased a red Fender Telecaster shortly after joining the Yardbirds, and he would favor this particular instrument throughout his time in the band, though he was now trying out other models, including a Fender Jazzmaster, a Gretsch, and Dreja's Gibson ES335.

As demand for the Yardbirds increased, Giorgio Gomelsky stepped up his efforts to get the group into venues with greater visibility than just the average pubs. By early 1964, the Yardbirds were attracting standing-room-only crowds at the Crawdaddy, drawing larger audiences than even the Rolling Stones during their heyday at the club, and Gomelsky used this success to secure a Friday night residency in London's Marquee club. These engagements, along with a series of new gigs at the Star Club in Croyden, afforded the band its best exposure yet, and the British press was beginning to take notice.

It was time, Gomelsky decided, to think about recording an album, or at least a single. The first order of business was to cut some demos to show prospective record companies, and with this in mind Gomelsky booked studio time in the tiny R. G. Jones studio in Morden, Surrey.

The seven tracks recorded in the studio were drawn from the Yardbirds' regular stage repertoire, and varied in their measure of success. A cover of John Lee Hooker's "Boom Boom," though adequate, was nothing special; the same could be said of the band's version of Chuck Berry's "I'm Talking About You." "Honey in Your Hips," a Keith Relf original, and "I Wish You Would," a cover of a Billy Boy Arnold song, fared much better, finding the Yardbirds in representative form, especially given the limitations of the two-to-three-minute singles format.

Clapton was jarred by his first experience in the studio. He felt anxious and self-conscious about playing in this setting, and he discovered that hearing the tapes of his performances could be unnerving. "You realize how clumsy you sound," he said. "What feels so sophisticated and smooth as you're doing it sounds so rough on playback."

Whatever their flaws, the demos were polished enough to earn the Yardbirds their first recording contract. Executives at Decca listened to the songs but judged them to be too similar to the music being released by their other young blues band, the Rolling Stones. EMI liked the music and, after seeing the Yardbirds onstage, decided to sign the group. EMI's recording strategy involved using both studio and live work: the lp would be a live album, capturing as much of the band's onstage, rave-up style as could be put on two twenty-minute album sides, whereas the studio would be used to record the Yardbirds' first single. Ideally, the people who supported the band by attending their performances would also be buying the single.

In the long run, this was an interesting decision, given Clapton's lifelong habit of drawing a weighty distinction between his studio and live recordings. Clapton has issued more live recordings than most rock artists, but unlike those who use the live album as a way to recycle hits, Clapton has used the live recording as a way of breaking from what he considers to be the limitations of the studio. "When you're in the studio, you can't really stretch out much," he explained. "You have more license to experiment onstage."

In Clapton's opinion, his best studio music has been accomplished when the machines were shut off and he was working on a particular song arrangement or guitar lick. The spontaneity is lost when the musician can erase a portion of a studio tape and rerecord. Conversely, playing live is like working without a net. The musician faces more risk of failure, but the rewards—especially the instant connection with an audience—are greater.*

The album, *Five Live Yardbirds*, recorded at the Marquee less than a month after the contract signing, was marred by sonic imperfection, but it still managed to represent the Yardbirds at their onstage best. The band stuck with its tried and tested staples—songs by Howlin' Wolf ("Smokestack Lightning"), John Lee Hooker ("Louise"), Sonny Boy Williamson ("Good Morning Little Schoolgirl"), the Isley Brothers ("Respectable"), Bo Diddley ("Pretty Girl," "Here 'Tis," and "I'm a Man"), and Chuck Berry ("Too Much Monkey Business"). The Marquee's acoustics were anything but ideal for the recording of an album, and this, combined with the limitations of recording on an antiquated two-track tape machine, made for sound quality no better than one finds on a good bootleg recording. But even this had an element of charm: the raw sound gives the music immediacy rather than the sense that a product is being filtered through high-tech studio contraptions. You feel the bodies being pressed together in the packed house, the frenzied movement with the music, and the occasional pause of excited anticipation.

Clapton makes his presence felt on *Five Live Yardbirds* much more than on the Sonny Boy Williamson venture. Harmonica is still the dominant instrument on some of the tracks, but the backing instruments play a greater role in the overall mix. Clapton's playing is still largely imitative of the original blues versions he'd heard on records, but he performs with more authority than he did on *Sonny Boy Williamson and the Yardbirds*. This

---

*Clapton eventually found a compromise in 1994's *From the Cradle*, an album recorded "live" in the studio, without overdubs or fixes.

is especially evident in songs such as "Too Much Monkey Business" and "Respectable," which go a long way in explaining why Clapton was being introduced to audiences as "Slowhand."

The nickname, bestowed on Clapton by Giorgio Gomelsky in humorous reference to Clapton's blistering speed on lead guitar, was also a play on words. When Clapton would break a string—which was becoming more and more frequent as he worked at bending notes—the audience would engage in a slow handclapping while he changed strings. Hence: Slow-Hand-Clap-Ton. The nickname stuck, and Clapton would use it as the title for his highly successful 1977 recording.

. . .

By mid-1964, the phenomenon known as the British Invasion was changing from a one-group charge to a full-scale assault on the American music scene. The Beatles' appearances on "The Ed Sullivan Show," watched by millions of screaming teenagers and their incredulous parents, had opened the doors, creating a furious interest in any band originating from England. Three Beatles songs ("I Want to Hold Your Hand," "She Loves You," and "Can't Buy Me Love") held the number one position on the *Billboard* charts from February 1 to May 8, supplanting such middle-of-the-road adult fare as Bobby Vinton's "There! I've Said It Again" and the Singing Nun's "Dominique" at the top of the charts. *A Hard Day's Night*, the Beatles' first movie, was the rage of the season. As the months wore on, more groups were added to the roster, and their music ran the gamut from the Rolling Stones' version of the Buddy Holly classic "Not Fade Away" to the Dave Clark Five's remake of the Contours' "Do You Love Me." Eric Burdon and the Animals scored a major hit with their interpretation of the classic "The House of the Rising Sun," and by the end of the year, Manfred Mann would check in with "Do Wah Diddy Diddy," which became a staple of every teenage dance band in America. The word was out: there was plenty of money to be made in the United States.

Giorgio Gomelsky was ready to cash in, and he worked overtime to see that his clients achieved the fame and wealth that he envisioned for them.

As the Yardbirds learned, there was never a shortage of work. They were always in demand on the club scene, and their manager was pushing to get a single recorded. At times, it seemed as if they had no lives outside of their work.

For Eric Clapton, the workload was both a blessing and a curse. He was honing his skills on guitar and doing what he loved to do, yet at the same time, he was growing increasingly concerned about the band's artistic integrity. He was not interested in adapting his standards to reach the lowest common denominator, which, all too often, was what popularity and chart success was all about, and he had nothing but contempt for what he considered to be crass commercialism in the recording business.

This concern was not an issue when the Yardbirds visited London's Olympic Sound Studios in April and recorded their first single, "I Wish You Would." That song, backed by "A Certain Girl," fit well within the Yardbirds' blues framework, and the recording could in no way be misconstrued as commercial compromise—which is to say, the critics liked it and the public ignored it. Gomelsky, however, was able to use the single as a sales tool in arranging for the Yardbirds' first television appearance, on the BBC's "Go Tell It on the Mountain" program.

Clapton had good reason to stand firm in his commitment to playing the blues. The Yardbirds had been well received when they backed Sonny Boy Williamson at the British Rhythm and Blues Festival at Birmingham Town Hall on February 28, and his reputation as a guitarist had grown to such an extent that he was asked to work as a sessions musician for blues pianist Otis Spann. The May 4 session, held at Decca Studios and supervised by Mike Vernon, the Decca house producer who had worked with the Yardbirds on their early demos, was one of the highlights of Eric Clapton's early days as a musician. Spann's half brother was none other than Muddy Waters, one of Clapton's idols. Clapton not only played alongside him in the studio but was asked to play lead guitar for the two songs on which he performed. It was heady stuff for a kid who had just reached his nineteenth birthday, and it only served to strengthen his conviction that the blues were the musical path he was meant to follow. Clapton would always feel close to Muddy Waters, never forgetting how warm he had been toward him that day in the studio, and he would credit him as being "very instrumental in forming my correct identity as a blues musician."

The summer months saw a continuation of Clapton's busy schedule. After a brief vacation with Giorgio Gomelsky in Switzerland, the Yardbirds appeared at the fourth annual National Jazz and Blues Festival held in Richmond. What might have been one of the year's high points for the band was tarnished when Keith Relf, a lifelong asthmatic, suffered a collapsed lung and was hospitalized. Mick O'Neill, a singer for the Authentics, filled in for Relf, and the band went on as scheduled. After their performance, the Yardbirds took part in a jam session that included such luminaries as Mike Vernon, Graham Bond, Georgie Fame, and Ginger Baker.

That same month the band returned to Olympia Sound Studios to record their second single, "Good Morning Little Schoolgirl." With Relf still out of commission, the Yardbirds could only lay down the single's backing track, which pushed back the record company's intended September release date for the record. A few weeks later, Relf rejoined his bandmates in the studio, where he finished the vocals for "Good Morning Little Schoolgirl," and the Yardbirds cut "I Ain't Got You," the B side of their single, which featured one of Clapton's best early guitar solos.

By this point, Clapton was growing more and more disenchanted with the direction the band was taking. Some of the group—Paul Samwell-Smith and Giorgio Gomelsky in particular—were eager to find the commercial success that would free them from the grueling one-nighters on the pub circuit and maybe even earn them a trip to the United States, where the Beatles and Rolling Stones were already enjoying success. At the very least, they felt, they should be getting better exposure in their home country.

Clapton couldn't have cared less about any of this. His musical ambitions, for the time being at least, were limited. With the exception of seeing Chicago, the blues capital of America, he had very little interest in touring the United States or appearing on television. He was quite happy being a hero on the local club scene, where there always seemed to be enough wine, women, and song to go around. The package tours, such as the ones the Yardbirds did with Billy J. Kramer and the Dakotas in September and October, and with Jerry Lee Lewis in November, were disappointing in an artistic sense: indeed, the bands would be seen by a lot of people, but the performances were little more than trotting out the latest single, playing several other songs, and leaving the stage for the next act. Clapton despised such concessions to the hit makers.

In addition, he and Samwell-Smith had clashed throughout their time together in the Yardbirds. To Clapton, Samwell-Smith was the epitome of the polite, middle-class boy who lived with his parents and took the middle-of-the-road approach, the kind of guy Clapton had looked down on during his bohemian art school days. Clapton was especially put off by the fact that Samwell-Smith favored folk and pop-oriented music and felt that the Yardbirds ought to move toward the mainstream music scene.

Two November recording sessions revealed the division with stunning clarity. The first, held in the Yardbirds' customary Olympia Studio, produced two completed songs, a cover of the Shirelles' "Putty in Your Hands," a throwaway number that found the band taking no new strides in their music, and "Got to Hurry," an outstanding blues instrumental that showcased some very confident guitar work from Clapton. The latter also represented Clapton's first attempt at songwriting, even though its authorship was credited to one "O. Rasputin," which, in reality, was Giorgio Gomelsky's pseudonym.

The second session, at London's IBC studios, was produced by Manfred Mann, who was currently riding high on the charts with "Do Wah Diddy Diddy." The only song produced in the session, "Sweet Music," was a pop tune as far removed from the Yardbirds' style of music as a band such as Gerry and the Pacemakers was removed from the Rolling Stones. The vocal duet of Keith Relf and Paul Jones, lead vocalist in Manfred Mann's band, was syrupy and uninspired, while the Yardbirds' instrumentation was laconic at best.

Little hope remained for Eric Clapton's continuing participation in the

Yardbirds. The personality clash between Clapton and Samwell-Smith intensified over the ensuing months, as Samwell-Smith, with the encouragement of Giorgio Gomelsky, began to assume a stronger voice in the band's affairs. Clapton made no effort to hide his dissatisfaction, and it was clear to all that he was not the team player he had once been. He was now just biding his time, waiting for something to happen.

· · ·

The Yardbirds' first lp, *Five Live Yardbirds*, was issued by Columbia Records in England in December 1964. The timing of the album's release was ironic, given what the Yardbirds had been when the album was recorded and what they were when it was actually presented to the public. The band now shunned almost all pub appearances in favor of package tours, and its music was moving away from the kind of music it had played in the old Marquee days. A comparison of the live version of "Good Morning Little Schoolgirl" on *Five Live Yardbirds* and the studio version, recorded a few months later and released as a single, gave listeners a strong indication of where the Yardbirds were going. The live version, performed at the Marquee for an older audience, was faster paced, with the slightest hint of lechery bubbling just beneath the surface of its otherwise innocent lyrics; the studio version was obviously aimed at a much younger group of record buyers, many of whom were teenagers already plugged into the far less menacing sounds of the Beatles and BBC television programs like "Ready Steady Go."

As it turned out, the Fab Four knew of the Yardbirds. Brian Epstein, the Beatles' manager, was also working with Billy J. Kramer, and he was aware of the response the Yardbirds had received when the band had toured on the Kramer package tour. When the Beatles assembled the roster of performers for their Christmas concerts at the Hammersmith Odeon Theatre in London, the Yardbirds were added to a lineup that included Freddie and the Dreamers, Jimmy Saville, and Sounds Incorporated. Under normal circumstances, the opportunity for an up-and-coming band to share a billing with the most popular band of its time would have been nothing less than golden, especially if the newcomers had product to promote. For the Yardbirds, however, this was not the case, for its lead guitarist, at the time of the shows, had already announced in private his intentions to leave the group.

Clapton's plans had been hastened by two major events: the group's recording of the hit single "For Your Love" and the formal appointment of Paul Samwell-Smith as the leader of the Yardbirds. To Clapton, both events represented an irreversible trend of which he wanted no part.

Recording "For Your Love" left Clapton bitterly disappointed. Still searching for the elusive commercial hit, the Yardbirds had considered a number of songs that they ultimately deemed to be unsuitable. Through the process of discussion and elimination, the band finally settled on two possibilities, an Otis Redding song called "Your One and Only Man," which Clapton favored, and "For Your Love," a new number written by Graham Gouldman, which Paul Samwell-Smith wanted to record. According to the plan, the Yardbirds would record both songs and then decide which to release as their next single.

By pop standards, "For Your Love" was not a bad song, but it was not a Yardbirds type of song, either. To Clapton's amazement, the predominant instruments on the recording—harpsichord and bongos—were played by hired studio musicians, and the only time the Yardbirds could be heard together was on the song's bridge, which lasted all of a few seconds, and even that was given to the band as a concession to Clapton after he became openly upset by the arrangement.

With the exception of Clapton, the band was ecstatic when it heard the playback. Keith Relf's mournful voice was in excellent form, and there was no denying that "For Your Love" posed the greatest commercial appeal of any of the Yardbirds' recorded songs to that point. Any plans to record the Otis Redding song were scrapped. The decision rattled Clapton to the breaking point.

"Sam did his first and everyone just said, 'Oh, that's it. No need to try yours,'" Clapton said of the experience. "So I thought, 'Fucking hell!' and I got really upset and bore a grudge, and I think that when they said it I actually made up my mind that I wasn't going to play with them anymore. It was like kids, you know."

The other turning point—the Samwell-Smith appointment—had been a long time coming. As one of the band's cofounders, Samwell-Smith had always exerted a certain authority over the others, and since he and Giorgio Gomelsky were philosophically close in terms of what both felt was in the best interests of the Yardbirds, it was only natural that Gomelsky would turn to Samwell-Smith when he decided to create a more rigid framework for the band. Based on the band's popularity in recent months, Gomelsky was convinced that the Yardbirds were headed for a new level of success, and such success would demand a stronger sense of discipline—something more businesslike.

With this in mind, Gomelsky dispatched a formal memo to all members of the Yardbirds. From this point on, he said, Paul Samwell-Smith was in charge of the band, and if members had suggestions, complaints, or other comments that they wished to make about the band, they should direct them either to himself or Samwell-Smith.

Clapton seethed when he read the memo. He was not certain which was worse, the appointment of Samwell-Smith as the musical director of the Yardbirds or the idea that Samwell-Smith was now in the position to set day-to-day policy and actually punish those who refused to follow it. Either way, the situation was intolerable to Clapton, and he decided that there was no way he would work under those conditions. Shortly after receiving his memo, Clapton visited Gomelsky's office and informed him that he was leaving the band. To Clapton's surprise, Gomelsky let him go without raising a fuss.

"He could have slapped something on me," Clapton recalled, mentioning the contract he had signed when Gomelsky had been brought on board as the group's manager. "He could have really made it tough for me, but he didn't. He just said, 'OK.'"

Keith Relf shrugged off Clapton's departure in a brief, rather sarcastic statement that hit the target dead center: "He loves the blues so much I suppose he didn't like it being played badly by a white shower like us."

What Clapton's young ego might have found difficult to embrace was the notion that the Yardbirds had grown weary of his attitude and, in all likelihood, were as eager for him to go as he was to leave. No one needed the tension. As gifted as he was, Eric Clapton was expendable, a fact brought to light when the band hired a young guitarist named Jeff Beck to replace him. Like Clapton, Beck would register his own huge impact on the Yardbirds, playing on some of their most memorable songs and earning his own reputation as one of rock's most influential guitarists. The Yardbirds would miss Eric Clapton, but probably not as much as he would have estimated.

. . .

Clapton stayed on with the Yardbirds for a couple of months after submitting his resignation, helping them honor prior commitments and performing a number of one-night gigs. It was not a pleasant time. The Yardbirds had been founded out of friendship and mutual devotion to the blues, yet, in Clapton's eyes, both had disintegrated to varying degrees during his year and a half with the band. Although he would be harsh in his assessment of the events leading up to his leaving the Yardbirds—and particularly critical of Samwell-Smith—in the immediate years after his departure, he would eventually appraise it with a more objective view. He concluded that he had initially been seduced by the elements of rock 'n' roll that attract a lot of young musicians—the money, the women, and the chance to see the world—only to grow disillusioned when he realized that he would not be able to have these things *and* maintain all of his musical standards.

"For Your Love," issued in England in March 1965 and in the United States a month later, hovered near the top of the music charts, which had become extremely competitive in the midst of the British Invasion. It found its way to the number two position in England while reaching the number six spot in America. An album of the same title, containing the Yardbirds' singles from the Clapton era, their B sides, and a few loose ends such as

"Putty in Your Hands" and "Sweet Music," was released in the United States in June.

By that point, Clapton was long gone, well on his way in his singular pursuit of playing the blues music that he loved, even as his former mates reached and surpassed the wildest dreams of their own foggy youth.

three

Deification
1965–66

I was so deadly serious about what I was doing. . . . I was in it to save the fucking world! I wanted to tell the world about the blues and to get it right. Even then, I thought I was on some kind of mission, so in a way I thought, Yes, I *am* God, quite right.

ric Clapton was just about to turn twenty when he and the Yardbirds parted company in March 1965. He had no clear sense of what to do. He was in virtually the same uncomfortable position he'd been in when he was dismissed from art school and had to make some kind of decision about how he intended to spend his life.

The Yardbirds experience had reduced him to a state of confusion. For all his dogmatic talk about playing the blues and remaining true to his sources of inspiration, Clapton was beginning to doubt himself. His last days with the Yardbirds had left him feeling "very lost and alone"—ever the outsider.

"I started wondering if I *was* a freak," he conceded. "They all wanted the simple things of success and the charts, and what was wrong with that? 'What's the matter with you? Why don't you want this?' And I began to think that I was really crazy."

For help in sorting through his thoughts, Clapton looked up Ben Palmer, his old friend and former bandmate in the Roosters. Palmer, too, had grown disillusioned with the music business, and he had set aside his musical ambitions after the Roosters broke up. He was now living in Oxford, earning his living as a wood-carver. Palmer invited Clapton to move in with him and stay as long as he wanted, an invitation Eric wasted no time in accepting.

Clapton had hoped to talk Palmer into forming a new blues band with him, but Palmer would hear nothing of it. He was happy doing what he was doing, he said, and he wanted no part of a business that, as far as he could tell, was almost as concerned with how one looked and dressed as it was with the music one created.

Despite such feelings, Palmer was an excellent sounding board. He and Clapton sat for hours and exchanged ideas about blues, the music business, Clapton's future, or life in general. Palmer sympathized with his friend's desire to play the music of his choice, and he encouraged him to remain faithful to that goal. The two sat and played music together at Palmer's place, unencumbered by any pressure to perform, delighted to be playing for the pure joy of making music. Eric talked about his fantasy of going to the United States and seeing the blues clubs and musicians in Chicago, and he tried to sell Palmer the idea of joining him on such a journey.

As the weeks passed, Clapton could feel himself healing emotionally; his self-confidence returned. He would always be grateful for Palmer's contribution to his improved state of mind, declaring that Palmer, by just sitting and listening, "made me feel human again."

In the aftermath of his Yardbirds experiences, Clapton had considered leaving the music business and pursuing a career in art or maybe even working as a laborer again. He now understood that it was really only a matter of time before he would be back to performing again. It was inevitable: his talent and reputation would not allow him to remain inactive for long. The opportunity arose just a few weeks after he had moved up to Oxford. Palmer's phone rang, and on the line was bandleader John Mayall, with a compelling proposal: Would Clapton be interested in taking over the guitar spot in his band, the Bluesbreakers?

. . .

One of the most influential bandleaders on the British blues scene, John Mayall would spend his entire career employing and developing young musicians, many of whom would go on to reach their own impressive levels of success. Eric Clapton was just one such name. Others Bluesbreakers alumni would include John McVie, Peter Green, and Mick Fleetwood, founding members of Fleetwood Mac; Jack Bruce, who, in a year would be joining forces with Clapton in Cream; Mick Taylor, guitarist with the Rolling Stones after the death of Brian Jones; and Hughie Flint, drummer with McGuinness-Flint. In time, Mayall would be labeled "the father of British blues"—a title he was less than enthusiastic about embracing, not so much because he refused to accept his role in popularizing the blues in England as because he hated to make any concession to age. At the time of his call to Clapton, Mayall was a seasoned thirty-two-year-old veteran of the music scene, highly regarded for his abilities as both a bandleader and musician.

Mayall's initial curiosity about the blues sprang from his early exposure to jazz.

"My first main obsession," he explained, "was to buy every single 78 that came out that had the word boogie in it! And that was really the whole thrust of my interest at that point. I had so many of these and became so bitterly disappointed with most of them, because they were big band stuff and they called it boogie. Out of all that, Albert Ammons and Pete Johnson were the two who I really was most impressed with." Through auctions and mail-order catalogs, Mayall was able to obtain a voluminous collection of imported American records, ranging from country blues to jazz. The more music he heard, the more he realized that American blues were his favorite.

Mayall taught himself to play piano, guitar, and harmonica, and after serving a stint in the army and then attending art school, he became serious about pursuing a career in music. He assembled a band called the Powerhouse Four, which was actually just Mayall and drummer Pete Ward, along with anyone they could draft to play bass and guitar, the personnel changing from gig to gig. Mayall's next stop was to form and lead the

Blues Syndicate, a popular Manchester-area band that provided him with his first exposure to club audiences. At the end of 1962, the Blues Syndicate was opening for Alexis Korner's Blues Incorporated at a jazz club called the Bodega. Korner, then the elder statesman of the British blues scene, took a liking to Mayall and encouraged him to test his band's skills in the London clubs. Mayall, who was already thirty and working a day job as a graphic designer, agreed that it was time to find out if he had what it took to succeed in the business.

The Blues Syndicate played a weekend in London in early 1963, and while the band was well received, its members were not prepared to pull up stakes and switch their base of operations from Manchester to London. Mayall, all but overwhelmed by what he had seen of the blues scene in the city, decided to establish a band of his own.

He called his backing band the Bluesbreakers, a title he would maintain over the years, even though the lineup would change frequently. The first unit consisted of Mayall, guitarist Bernie Watson (a veteran of Cyril Davies's All Stars), bassist John McVie, and drummer Pete Ward. Mayall, who was married and had three children, continued to work his day job and drive to the band's weekend gigs until he felt confident that he could earn a living on his music.

It made for a demanding schedule, not only for Mayall but for others in the band as well. John McVie worked a day job in a tax office, and he found alternating a regular job and performing in a band a grueling experience. "During the week," he said, "I kept working in the tax office, while Mayall was a commercial artist. On weekends, we'd leave our jobs and play a Friday all-nighter in London, then drive way up north and do Saturday and Sunday shows, arriving home by five on Monday mornings. I'd have to be at the tax office at nine to talk to enraged Irishmen about their screwed-up tax returns. At the end of nine months I said, 'This is enough,' and turned professional."

The early Bluesbreakers performances, Mayall allowed, were a far cry from what he hoped to do, but with a lot of work and some shuffling of personnel, the band began to sound much better. Mayall and his group enjoyed regular engagements at the Marquee and Flamingo clubs, as well as one-nighters in clubs throughout the area, and the exposure paid off. Decca producer Mike Vernon attended some of the Bluesbreakers performances, and after some dickering with the powers that be, he was able to persuade his record company to commit itself to recording a Bluesbreakers single and album.

The deal was similar to the Yardbirds' first contract: the initial single "Crawling up a Hill"/"Mr. James") would be put together in the studio, while the album (*John Mayall Plays John Mayall*) would be recorded at one of the Bluesbreakers' concerts. Neither sold well, but Mayall, like so many of his blues contemporaries, had already learned that the real living was to be made onstage, in clubs with sweaty walls, filled with fans entranced by the power of a night's performance.

The Bluesbreakers continued to change personnel at a remarkable rate. Drummer Hughie Flint replaced Pete Ward, and guitarist Bernie Watson was replaced by Roger Dean, a skilled musician but not rooted enough in Chicago-style blues. Mayall patiently tried to teach him, but Dean never seemed to get the hang of it. Faced with the need for a different guitarist in his band, Mayall immediately thought of Eric Clapton. He had seen Clapton at work in the Yardbirds on a number of occasions, and he had jammed with the Yardbirds at the Twisted Wheel in Manchester. He had been impressed with the young guitarist's potential.

"Eric was the only one I'd heard in England who had any of what the blues was all about," Mayall recalled. "The others [in the Yardbirds] didn't have what Eric had—but, then, nobody has what Eric had."

Like so many others who tried to pinpoint the precise nature of Clapton's talent, Mayall was hard pressed to define what separated Clapton from other guitarists on the scene. "He was totally amazing, he was the first guitar player I'd heard who had it. *It*, you know, the elusive *it*, and nobody I'd talked to ever seemed to know what *it* was. Having listened to records all my life, I could spot it instantly. He was obviously the one to go for, it was magic."

Mayall knew of Clapton's availability from all the hoopla raised by the media when he left the Yardbirds, and if he needed any further reassurance about Clapton's commitment to the blues, he was convinced after reading a Clapton interview published in *Rave*, in which Clapton went on at some length about why he could not compromise his standards in exchange for a place on the pop music charts. As far as Mayall was concerned, Clapton's playing on "Got to Hurry," the flip side of the "For Your Love" single, underscored the point.

To introduce Clapton to his bandmates, Mayall played the song for John McVie and Hughie Flint—the Bluesbreakers' rhythm section—on a jukebox in Nottingham. They, too, were taken by Clapton's ability, and they voted to bring him into the group. All that remained was the nasty task of telling Roger Dean that his services were no longer needed.

• • •

Once a decision had been reached to admit Eric Clapton into the Bluesbreakers, no auditions were necessary: from Clapton's recordings with the Yardbirds, his reputation among British musicians, and his considerable following, it was clear to the Bluesbreakers that this was the guitarist they were seeking.

Clapton, however, was prepared to raise his own musical stakes. In the Yardbirds, he had been busy cutting his chops and establishing his name. As gifted as he was, he had ultimately been just another band member—a lesson he'd learned during his last session when he tried to convince the Yardbirds to record the Otis Redding song. Now, with a new band and another chance to play authentic blues, he was prepared to push himself and his fellow band members to a new level—from being good but derivative to being nothing less than cutting edge.

Several factors inspired such confidence. Clapton realized, even when he was being overly modest or self-critical, that he possessed greater technical and creative ability than his competition in other bands. Furthermore, from his conversations with Ben Palmer, he was utterly convinced that he had made the appropriate decision when he left the Yardbirds on the cusp of stardom. Finally, he not only believed that the Bluesbreakers were the best vehicle for pursuing his own musical vision; from those times when he had seen the group in concert, he was also confident that he could add something special to a band that already played well but had room for improvement.

In John Mayall, Clapton had found someone who could actually compete with his own love of the blues. Mayall had the most comprehensive blues collection Clapton had ever seen, and Eric spent countless hours at Mayall's house in London's Lee Green, listening to records and discussing them with Mayall, constantly learning new songs to add to his ever-expanding repertoire. Mayall generously offered Clapton a room in his house, and this became Clapton's garret. In a monastic room barely wide enough to hold a narrow bed, but as private as any woodshedding musician could ever hope for, Clapton practiced and practiced, learning new guitar licks from the likes of Freddie King, Muddy Waters, Otis Rush, B. B. King, and Buddy Guy.

These studies were immediately noticeable onstage. In his early Bluesbreakers solos, Clapton imitated the guitar solos he was hearing on Mayall's records, but as time passed and he grew more confident in his ability to create his own variations of the classic performances, Clapton added his own personal touch to his solos, with results that caught both the band and its fans off guard.

"When Eric joined the Bluesbreakers, the sound of the band changed dramatically," recalled Hughie Flint. "To be fair, he worked his way into the group at first—he was a little bit tentative. Then he gained in confidence and started to amaze me."

Clapton had little choice but to adapt quickly. He made his first public appearance with the Bluesbreakers without so much as a rehearsal with them, and within several days of joining the band, he found himself in London's BBC studios, playing a three-song set for live radio.

On May 12, the Bluesbreakers were summoned to a CBS studio in London for a recording session with Bob Dylan. The American singer-songwriter was making his first full-scale tour of England, and he was in town for appearances at the Royal Albert Hall. While in London, Dylan was asked by Columbia Records officials to tape a brief promotional message for a record convention being held in the United States, and Dylan figured that as long as he was in the studio he might as well look up John Mayall, whose single "Crawling up a Hill" had caught his attention.

In time, Clapton and Dylan would become good friends, but their first meeting was mostly forgettable. Dylan and his producer, Tom Wilson, had been drinking, and the studio environment was disorganized. Dylan, who often preferred to write and work out arrangements for new songs in the studio, improvised with the Bluesbreakers for about two hours, with very little emerging from the session except a still-unreleased version of his song "If You Gotta Go, Go Now." "We did a lot of his blues songs, which he was making up," Clapton remarked. "He was sitting at the piano and we just joined in."

As far as the Bluesbreakers were concerned, the studio time was little more than a sloppy jam session. The band was accustomed to a much more structured approach to making music. John Mayall was authoritarian in his methods of running his unit, commanding a discipline that was virtually unheard of in the rather hedonistic bands of the time. Drugs and alcohol were strictly forbidden—to such an extent that, on one occasion, a drunken John McVie was tossed out of Mayall's van and left by himself on a country road, forced to find his own way home.

Life on the road could be a test. When traveling, Mayall slept in a bunk that he'd built in the back of his van, while the others had to find a way to catch some sleep while sitting up in the front seat. Or, if the Bluesbreakers happened to be playing in Manchester, Mayall would stay overnight at his parents' house, leaving the bandmembers outside in the van.

"He didn't get you a hotel or anything," complained Clapton of the situation. "So there were these disadvantages being in that band! It wasn't all roses."

• • •

In June, John Mayall led the Bluesbreakers into the studio to lay down their first Clapton-era tracks: the single "I'm Your Witchdoctor"/"Telephone

Blues," and a third song, "On Top of the World," which would surface on blues anthology albums long after Clapton had left the band. Producing the session was the future Yardbirds and Led Zeppelin guitarist Jimmy Page, one of England's premier studio musicians at the time.

Mayall wrote both sides of the single. "I'm Your Witchdoctor" was a short, uptempo blues placing Clapton mostly in the background, supporting Mayall's vocals with tasteful fills. Conversely, Clapton stood very much at the forefront of "Telephone Blues," a slow blues that found Clapton using his guitar to answer Mayall's vocal phrasing. As he had been in the Yardbirds, Clapton was adept at fashioning compelling guitar interplay with the band's harmonica, creating a textured sound that added a sense of urgency to the instrumentation. Clapton's solo—one of his longest on a studio cut to that point—was a slicing, aggressive bit of work that accentuated the "fat note" sound of his Les Paul guitar. More than any previously recorded Clapton song, "Telephone Blues" offered the promise of the kind of guitarist Clapton would be, first, when he recorded *John Mayall's Bluesbreakers with Eric Clapton* in 1966, and then, a short time later, when his solos took flight in Cream.

The three Bluesbreakers cuts were only the beginning of the recording Clapton would do in what turned out to be a very busy month. Clapton enjoyed working with Jimmy Page, and the two met later that same month to put down some basic guitar tracks at Page's house. At first the seven cuts, recorded on a two-track reel-to-reel tape recorder, offered very little to get excited about, but when Page later overdubbed harmonica, bass, and piano, provided by Mick Jagger, Bill Wyman, and Ian Stewart of the Rolling Stones, the music took on a sense of historical importance.

Clapton concluded his month of recording sessions by putting together another single, this time as a duet with John Mayall, for release as a limited edition on Mike Vernon's independent Purdah label. Vernon wanted to present an authentic Chicago blues sound, and the Mayall-Clapton tandem came through for him with two splendid sides, "Lonely Years," a Mayall-written song featuring Mayall on vocals and harmonica and Clapton on guitar, and "Bernard Jenkins," a Big Maceo–influenced instrumental that featured a piano-guitar duet that showed just how musically compatible Mayall and Clapton had become in a span of less than three months.

Vernon was pleased with the results, which had been achieved by employing a tried-and-tested studio setup. "We did it straight mono, one microphone stuck up in the middle of the studio, just piano, voice, and guitar," Vernon remembered. "To this day it's the only record I've ever made that sounds as if it was made in Chicago."

All the recording work, sandwiched between a touring schedule that had the Bluesbreakers playing all over England in a nonstop string of one-nighters, became more than Clapton wanted to deal with—so much so that he began to take advantage of his stature in the band. Knowing full well that, as the Bluesbreakers' main attraction, he was not about to be fired for his infractions, Clapton missed an occasional performance, leaving his mates in the unenviable position of having to cover for him. Such behavior flew in the face of Mayall's disciplinarian approach to running a band, not to mention professionalism in general, but there was little that Mayall could do. With the Yardbirds, Clapton had already displayed his willingness to pack up and leave a successful band, and Mayall had no reason to doubt that he would quit the Bluesbreakers if he was so inclined.

Mayall had good reason for such feelings. He and Clapton weren't nearly as tight as they had been in the early days, and Clapton was now subjecting the band to the same moodiness and temperamental outbursts that had characterized much of his tenure in the Yardbirds. Clapton would grumble about Mayall behind his back, criticizing his singing and methods of running a band; he could be critical of Flint and McVie as well. Over the passing months, Clapton grew tired of the whole scene, and on a number of occasions he found himself just going through the motions onstage.

In August, Clapton decided that he needed a vacation from the grind. He approached Mayall and told him that he was taking an indefinite leave of absence from the band. He wanted to see the world, he explained, but he planned to do it as a kind of working holiday, as a musician working his way around the globe. He would be heading up a group of friends who were essentially amateur musicians with just enough talent to pose as a working unit.

Mayall, anything but pleased by Clapton's announcement, had no choice but to watch his star performer pursue his youthful folly.

. . .

As half-baked as the plan might have seemed, Clapton embraced the notion of reliving the sense of freedom he had enjoyed in earlier days. Rather than toil night after night in small, crowded clubs, playing essentially the same music every night, this new outfit could play whatever it felt like playing. The environment would be loose and easy.

The idea had risen from Clapton's drinking bouts with a group of his friends. After his brief stay at John Mayall's house, Clapton had moved into an apartment occupied by poet-puppeteer Ted Milton and his brother Jake. The Covent Garden flat was frequented by a number of mutual friends, including Ben Palmer, who, at Clapton's urging, had put aside wood-carving and moved to London for another attempt at making music. Most days, the group would hang around the apartment, listening to a lot of jazz and blues, drinking and talking and, in general, carrying on like a group of college kids. "They were wino days," Clapton recalled years later. "Everyone was drinking wine by the gallon and getting wiped out at three o'clock in the afternoon."

From these sessions came the scheme for a strange, world-traveling ensemble called the Glands. Besides having the British Isles' leading guitarist, the Glands were made up of Ben Palmer on piano; Bernie Greenwood, a doctor, on saxophone; John Baily, a psychology student, as the band's vocalist; Bob Ray, a trumpeter, handling chores on bass; and drummer Jake Milton. According to the plan, the group members would pool their money, purchase a double-decker bus, and work their way east, stopping in Greece for some performances before heading to Australia. They would save hotel expenses by living on the bus.

These preliminary plans proved to be a bit ambitious, but by August the

Glands somehow managed to find a way to get their show on the road. The double-decker bus idea was scratched in favor of a large American station wagon, which was packed to the hilt with musicians, equipment, and anything else the band could squeeze in. Once in Greece, the Glands found work at an Athens nightclub, backing a band called the Juniors, a local favorite specializing in British Invasion pop songs.

The job was a fiasco from the start. Not surprisingly, the Glands were incapable of playing the kind of blues that Clapton and Palmer originally wanted to perform, so the set list was adjusted to include basic rock 'n' roll numbers. The pay was horrible, but the Glands were in no position to protest their wages or negotiate for more money. The club owner, either by design or oversight, had neglected to secure the necessary work permits for the Glands, and he threatened to turn Clapton and his friends over to the authorities if they complained too loudly or quit. Then, just when it seemed as if things could get no worse, the Juniors were involved in a terrible car accident that killed one member and left another critically injured. Without his headliners, the club owner couldn't afford to keep his place open. The Glands suddenly found themselves in a tough spot, stuck in a foreign country without any means of supporting themselves.

In an effort to salvage a rapidly sinking situation, Clapton volunteered to play in both the Juniors and the Glands, an offer the club owner gratefully accepted. Unfortunately for Clapton, this new arrangement meant that he was now working for hours on end, with very little down time. This was of no concern to the club owner, who was busy trying to find a way to keep Clapton in Greece as his house band's guitarist while ridding himself of the Glands. The solution, he determined, was as simple as seeing that the authorities were made aware of the work permit situation: he could use his influence with the local police to protect Clapton, while the rest of the Glands were told they could no longer work in Greece. As a bargaining chip in his ongoing negotiations with Clapton, the owner kept the Glands' equipment, which meant nobody was going anywhere until he and Clapton consummated some kind of deal.

The trip that had begun as a lark had now turned into a nightmare, and in a scene worthy of a good dime-store novel, Clapton and his friends began to plot their escape. Clapton set the plan in motion by telling the owner that he would stay on as a member of the house band on the condition that the Glands' equipment be released. The owner agreed, and he returned all of the equipment except for Clapton's, which was kept locked in the club. While Clapton continued to play with the Juniors, the Glands sold their equipment for escape funds. Finally, on the planned escape date, Clapton approached the club owner and calmly informed him that he would have to have his guitar restrung before he could play another gig. The owner, knowing that Clapton still had clothing and a valuable Marshall amplifier in the club, allowed Eric to leave with his guitar. Outside the club, Clapton was picked up by his friends and whisked to the train station, where he and Ben Palmer caught the Orient Express back to England, while John Baily and Bernie Greenwood proceeded on to Australia. The adventure had cost Clapton an amp, but in light of his hostage scenario in Greece, it seemed like a small price to pay for freedom.

To Clapton, the drudgery of club dates with John Mayall and the Bluesbreakers was looking better all the time.

. . .

Before Clapton left for Greece, John Mayall had assured him that he harbored no hard feelings about his leaving the Bluesbreakers, and that Eric would be welcome to rejoin the band at any time in the future. Whatever his feelings about being left in a lurch, Mayall kept his promise when Clapton returned to England in November and asked for his old job back.

The Bluesbreakers had changed personnel while Clapton was away. John McVie had been banished in August after another drinking episode, replaced by Graham Bond Organisation alumnus Jack Bruce. Mayall had tried out other guitarists to take Clapton's place, and he had finally settled on Peter Green just a few gigs prior to Clapton's return. Green, a wonderful guitarist in his own right, had performed well for the Bluesbreakers, and was understandably angry when Mayall cut him from the band.

Jack Bruce and Eric Clapton shared the stage for only a month before Bruce left for a job playing bass for Manfred Mann, but during their brief period together, Clapton and Bruce brought the Bluesbreakers performances to a wild new level. Having come from a jazz background, Bruce preferred to improvise onstage, which encouraged Clapton to take off into some uncharted territory of his own.

Clapton appreciated the fresh new approach. "There was something creative there," he said of his work with Bruce. "Most of what we were doing with Mayall was imitating the records we got, but Jack had something else. He had no reverence for what we were doing, and so he was composing new parts as he went along playing."

Clapton enjoyed this kind of improvisation, which was a test not only of one's prowess on guitar but also of one's ability to sustain a creative flow over an extended period of time. He had not been skilled enough with the Yardbirds to take this to the limit, and while he had improvised to a certain extent during his first stint with the Bluesbreakers, Clapton found that Mayall preferred to structure his song arrangements a little more tightly than the free-form approach that Bruce liked to take during solos.

Onstage, Clapton was *cool* personified. To the uninitiated, he might have seemed aloof, perhaps arrogant, as he stood stock still, his back quite often to the audience, his fingers working across his guitar's strings and fretboard with an ease that seemed vaguely sensual yet somehow not in conjunction with the slicing sounds coming from his amplifier. Such were the beginnings of Clapton's image as guitar hero. To his dismay, the legend "Clapton is God" started to appear all over London's subway walls, while a growing legion of fans pressed ever tighter in the clubs where the Bluesbreakers played.

Others in the band took notice. "The audiences in Britain really grew, and they were all youngsters," observed Hughie Flint. "The clubs were full of young dudes at the front, sort of playing [air guitar] like Joe Cocker—looking at their lord and master."

John Mayall was also aware of the fact that many of the people coming to Bluesbreakers shows were actually coming to see Clapton. Such enthusiasm for his guitarist, he felt, was merited. He had seen a few guitar players in his time, but Clapton was an original. "He was a very moody player," said Mayall. "By that I mean he'd conjure up these incredible moods and intensity. The things he did with a slow blues—when he *felt* like playing a slow blues—could send shivers down your spine. I just cannot recall anybody else ever doing that." The fanatical following, Mayall explained, was evidence of Clapton's growing influence: "With my band, Eric became *the* way to play."

The adulation had a mixed effect on Clapton. Although he was uncomfortable with the "Clapton is God" graffiti in the subway stations, he also realized that he was the best thing going on the local blues scene. He had always aspired to be a star. The boy in him craved the attention, the blues purist appreciated the recognition. Still, he remained skeptical of his deification in the eyes of his fans. Words that easily offered could just as easily be retracted.

There were additional reasons to stay humble. For all the praise he received, Clapton realized that he was essentially a one-dimensional band member. Unlike John Mayall, who wrote some of the Bluesbreakers' songs, handled most of the vocals, and played piano, organ, guitar, and harmonica, Clapton limited himself to playing one instrument. He didn't possess enough confidence in his singing ability to do much more than some background singing. He wrote very little music.

This did not bother him. For the time being, he was content in his role as featured player in one of England's most highly regarded blues bands.

• • •

Clapton began 1966 by appearing as a guest guitarist on three songs recorded by American blues pianist Champion Jack Dupree. The Mike Vernon–produced session featured an all-star band that included Clapton, Dupree, John Mayall, and future Bluesbreakers drummer Keef Hartley. Clapton's contributions, though solid enough, were marginal.

His work was much more noticeable a month later, in March, when he fronted his own one-off band for a blues anthology being put together for the Elektra label. The band, presented as Eric Clapton and the Powerhouse, was actually the brainchild of producer Joe Boyd and Manfred Mann vocalist Paul Jones. For some time, Boyd had been trying to assemble a unit of England's best blues players for his anthology, but most of the musicians he tried to get were bound by contracts to other companies and could not play for Elektra. This was the case with John Mayall (though not his band), and with certain members of the Spencer Davis Group, another successful blues-oriented band that Boyd wanted to record.

With Paul Jones acting as his intermediary, Boyd was able to assemble the Powerhouse by using members from three different bands. Paul Jones brought along fellow Manfred Mann member Jack Bruce to play bass, while Bluesbreaker Eric Clapton invited Ben Palmer to sit in on piano. The Spencer Davis Group's involvement was perhaps most creative. Drummer Pete York was enlisted without a hitch, but singer-organist Stevie Winwood had contractual obligations, which Boyd was able to circumvent by having Winwood appear under the nom de plume of Steve Anglo. With three soon-to-be-superstars (Clapton, Winwood, and Bruce) in the fold, the Powerhouse was an aptly named unit, yet, from a historical perspective, it might have been even more noteworthy: Paul Jones's first choice for drummer was Ginger Baker, who was soon to join Clapton and Bruce in Cream.

Clapton and Boyd selected the music the band recorded. "I Want to Know," a barrelhouse blues, highlighted the harmonica work of Paul Jones, while "Steppin' Out," a Bluesbreakers staple, offered the world a taste of things to come, with Clapton and Bruce providing some excellent solo work. Oddly enough, a slow blues version of Robert Johnson's "Crossroads," with Winwood taking the chores on lead vocals, bore little resemblance to the blistering uptempo arrangement that became Clapton's signature song in the future.

The band members worked well together and would have made a formidable working unit, but it was understood from the outset that this was to be a one-shot deal. Nevertheless, Jack Bruce, who had left Manfred Mann and was again filling in with the Bluesbreakers during a John McVie absence, felt that his renewed camaraderie with Eric Clapton, along with the concept of forming a supergroup with the best players from several groups, was significant. "There were no thoughts of making a band at that time," he commented of the Powerhouse experience, "but it probably helped to make the Cream thing happen later."

. . .

That day was rapidly approaching—it was less than a hundred days from the time of the Powerhouse recordings—but first there was the matter of documenting Clapton's tenure in the Bluesbreakers.

John Mayall's first plan was to record another live album along the line of *John Mayall Plays John Mayall*. During his year with the Bluesbreakers, Eric Clapton had developed his creative and technical abilities on guitar at an astonishing rate, and Mayall hoped to preserve on a live album some of the soaring solos that left people speechless. "He hit those peaks quite regularly in clubs," Mayall pointed out, "but that's very hard to capture on a studio recording."

With this in mind, Mayall set up to record a Bluesbreakers show at the Flamingo Club. The performances, featuring Jack Bruce standing in for John McVie, were on the mark, particularly the band's hard-edged interpretations of "Have You Ever Loved a Woman" and "Hoochie Coochie Man." Unfortunately, the recording conditions at the Flamingo were awful. To make matters worse, the primitive two-track reel-to-reel tape machine used to record the show was malfunctioning, leaving Mayall's proposed record with muddy sound made worse by dragging tape speed. Mayall scrapped his plans for a live album—though some of the performances were later released as part of the *Primal Solos* lp—and booked studio time.

This, in retrospect, was a fortuitous turn of events, for the product of those sessions, *John Mayall's Bluesbreakers with Eric Clapton*, will always stand as one of the great British blues albums of the period. The record's twelve songs, culled from the band's regular set list, run the gamut from Mayall originals to covers of such American blues icons as Robert Johnson,

Freddie King, Ray Charles, Otis Rush, and Willie Dixon. In addition, the album remains one of the most significant *guitar* records of its time.

The recording session quickly turned into an engineer's nightmare. The tiny size of the studio became a major issue when Clapton announced that he intended to turn his amplifier on full volume in an attempt to approximate the sustain and distortion characteristic of his onstage solos. Engineer Gus Dudgeon wanted Clapton's microphone in the standard placement near the amp, but Clapton insisted that his amp be moved across the room to a position where he would be able to employ a maximum range of effects from his guitar. To the engineer, this meant that there would be a certain amount of sound bleeding as Clapton's guitar was picked up by other microphones in the room, but Clapton was in no frame of mind to negotiate the issue.

"I had a definite rebel stance about the whole thing," he recalled. "I was on top of my craft, and I was completely confident, and I didn't give a shit about what anyone thought. I mean, we made the record in two days, and I told the engineer where to put the microphone, and that's the way it went. If you didn't like what I was doing, then you weren't on the same planet as me."

Given the level of Clapton's performance on *Bluesbreakers with Eric Clapton*, it is possible that he was the sole inhabitant of his own planet at the time of the album's recording. Jimi Hendrix had yet to visit England and turn the country on its ear with his outrageously innovative techniques, and Jeff Beck, Clapton's closest artistic contemporary (then working with the Yardbirds), had yet to record some of his more innovative experiments with guitar feedback, distortion, and sustain. Although the recording of the album bore no special significance for Clapton and the rest of the Bluesbreakers other than its being an honest attempt to preserve the best of their onstage repertoire at the time, the result was nothing less than a defining moment in Clapton's musical development.

There was nothing tentative about Clapton's playing on the album. His self-confidence was evident in every solo, whether he was reworking a chestnut such as Otis Rush's "All Your Love" or providing bold colors to original Mayall compositions such as "Double Crossing Time" (which Clapton cowrote) and "Have You Heard," the latter offering a solo that, over the course of Clapton's career, would rank among his best. Although he was obviously breaking new ground, Clapton never shied away from paying tribute to others, from his stinging salute to Freddie King in "Hideaway" to his humorous homage to John Lennon's "Daytripper" riff in the Bluesbreakers' rendition of the Ray Charles masterpiece "What'd I say."

Two songs, positioned back to back on the album, place Clapton's growth in perspective. The first, "Ramblin' on My Mind," is Clapton's reverential nod to his spiritual mentor, Robert Johnson. In time, Clapton would perform or record a fair percentage of the Johnson song catalog, but it would never be a particularly easy task. As Clapton would admit, his high esteem for Johnson's original versions, most notably "Hellhound on My Trail," kept him from so much as attempting to record his own arrangements of the songs, while in those instances in which he did use his own arrangements, he felt obliged to honor the original somehow within the context of the new. "Ramblin' on My Mind," a slow blues with plenty of room for tasteful solo work, would appear to be a natural selection, but Clapton pushed his own musical ambitions even further by designating this song for his first lead vocal performance on record. The prospect filled him with self-doubts.

"The leap came in accepting that this thing was going to go on plastic and would be recorded," he explained. "Accepting that took a lot of convincing from John, who really kept having to tell me that it was worth it."

To accommodate Clapton's misgivings, Mayall recorded the vocal track after the others had left the studio. "He was a bit shy about singing for the first time on record, but it worked out after a couple of takes," said Mayall of the session. "He just didn't want anybody listening in case it didn't work out."

If Clapton reveals his protégé identity on "Ramblin' on My Mind," he establishes his own arrival on "Steppin' Out." By 1966, Clapton had become proficient enough on guitar to feel confident in trying to imitate single-note passages played on other instruments in his favorite songs. He was intrigued by the harmonica notes of Little Walter, and he even attempted to match some of Ray Charles's piano licks on the Bluesbreakers version of "What'd I Say." In "Steppin' Out," he is again working on a basic piano piece—this time by bluesman Memphis Slim. The fat tone of his Gibson Les Paul, combined with John Mayall and producer Mike Vernon's decision to flesh out the song with a horn section that sounds as if it had been shipped over from America's Atlantic Studios, gives the song a flavor that goes beyond the Chicago-style blues that the Bluesbreakers specialized in. On "Steppin' Out," Clapton is truly announcing the direction he would be taking in the future, beginning with Cream and extending, off and on, over the next three decades.

Released in August 1966, *John Mayall's Bluesbreakers with Eric Clapton* shot up the British charts, spending ten weeks in the Top 10. Such success, unprecedented in British blues history, might have been partly the result of John Mayall and the Bluesbreakers' growing and very loyal following. More likely, however, the album's popularity could be traced to Mayall's decision to include Clapton's name on the album cover: when the album was finally hitting the record racks in England, Eric Clapton had already left the Bluesbreakers and was sharing a very bright spotlight in rock's first power trio—an unlikely group of mercurial musicians with the nerve to refer to themselves as the cream of the crop.

four

Power Trio
1966–68

I think we aimed to start a revolution in musical thought. We set out
to change the world, to upset people and to shock them.

*e*ric Clapton's defection from the Bluesbreakers surprised no one,
nor was it as acrimonious as when he had left the Yardbirds. To John
Mayall and his cohorts, it was quite apparent that Clapton had gone as far
as he could go with the Bluesbreakers, that he was ready to explore other
avenues in his music. "By the time he was finished with me, he wasn't
playing very well at all, because he didn't feel like it," Mayall commented.
"He wanted to do something else. After a year with me he had developed
his style to a point where he wanted to go still further but in another
direction."

Clapton agreed with the assessment. "It was always just wanting to do
something better or basically just move on," he said, maintaining that he
had been pleased with the album he'd made with the Bluesbreakers and
was not really unhappy with the band. The problem, he continued, was
that "the ambition wasn't really going. John was quite happy to stay on
the club circuit and play the same kind of music, changing a few numbers
here and there. But there was something inside me that said there was
more to do or different places to go."

Clapton's mood swings were more pronounced as his time with the
Bluesbreakers drew to a close. Part of the problem, he would later confess,

stemmed from his tendency to find fault in any group he was in; it wasn't easy to be virtually living with three bandmates and not have things get on one's nerves. In addition, he was growing tired of England altogether. He still yearned to get to the United States and witness the blues scene in Chicago, and he believed that he was reaching a dead end in his own country.

Most important, perhaps, was another battle going on inside his head. He continued to feel ambivalent about the "Clapton is God" business and the adulation of his fans. He felt the pressure that comes from being the object of hero worship, yet at the same time, he was extremely confident of his standing as a musician—his self-assurance boosted, no doubt, when a readers' poll, conducted by *Melody Maker* in March 1966, elected him lead guitarist in a fantasy supergroup of British musicians.

Also cited in the poll was drummer Ginger Baker, who was presently between bands and looking for a way out. The best way, Baker figured, was to start a band of his own. He knew Clapton from the several occasions when Eric had sat in on Graham Bond gigs, and he had been very impressed with Clapton's ability. Clapton, he decided, would be the ideal guitarist for the kind of band he wanted to form.

Baker and Clapton met again in June 1966, at a Bluesbreakers gig in Oxford. By this point, Clapton was all but finished with John Mayall's group. Baker sat in with the band for a while, and after the show he approached Clapton backstage. The Graham Bond Organisation, he informed Clapton, was thinking about breaking up.

"I like the way you play," he said. "Would you like to start a band?"

"Yeah," Clapton replied, "but I'd like to have Jack Bruce as well."

Clapton's response was innocent enough. He remembered the special onstage chemistry he'd felt with Bruce when the bassist had played with the Bluesbreakers, and he was eager to work with him in the new band that Baker was proposing. When he recommended Bruce, Clapton did not realize that, in effect, he was asking Ginger Baker to work in close quarters with his sworn enemy.

· · ·

The Jack Bruce–Ginger Baker feud was legendary to anyone who had closely followed the Graham Bond Organisation for any length of time. Their intense dislike for one another had occasionally erupted into onstage pyrotechnics, such as the time Baker threw his drumsticks at Bruce, only to have to duck to avoid the double bass that Bruce heaved back at him, the two then duking it out onstage like a couple of schoolboys bloodying knuckles on the playground. Baker had tried to fire Bruce near the end of his time with the band, but Bruce had refused to leave. As far as Baker was concerned, it was a case of good riddance when Bruce switched over to Manfred Mann in late 1965.

To the delight of Graham Bond fans, Bruce and Baker's volatile personalities were matched by the intensity of their musicianship. The Graham Bond Organisation specialized in a blend of jazz and blues that encouraged extended, free-form solos, and as the group's rhythm section, Baker and Bruce fanned improvisational fires that were not easily matched by other bands on the scene. Both were incredibly active on their respective instruments, each playing as if his was the featured instrument in the band.

Not surprisingly, both came from solid musical backgrounds. Born on May 14, 1943, in Glasgow, Scotland, Jack Bruce came from a family with little money—a situation that bore some influence on his musical training. According to Bruce, he learned to play cello simply because "it was the only instrument that the school had to give away free." This proved to be fortunate, for Bruce's classical training not only endowed him with an appreciation of all forms of music but also meant that he learned to read and write music, which he would find very useful later in life.

One of Bruce's teachers played bass, and Jack learned to love the instrument from listening to him play it. As a teenager, Bruce learned to play bass himself—a considerable achievement, given the fact that he was small and had to all but wrestle with the bulky instrument. Bruce was gifted enough to be offered a scholarship to the Scottish Academy of Music, but his time there was to be an unhappy association. "I was thrown out because they didn't like the direction I was taking," said Bruce, explaining that he was then more interested in playing blues and jazz bass than classical cello.

After his expulsion, Bruce kicked around for a while, living the bohemian life, playing in small jazz combos and traveling around Europe. He landed a position in a band called the Scotsville Jazzmen, which gave him occasion to meet Ginger Baker. The Scotsville Jazzmen were performing on the same bill as Baker's group, the Burt Corvey Sextet, at the Cambridge Maid Ball.

Almost four years older than Bruce, Baker had taken a long, difficult path to a position where he could place judgment on Jack Bruce's performance. Born in London on August 19, 1939, Peter "Ginger" Baker was raised by his mother and her sister in an impoverished household. Both women lost their husbands during World War II, and they discovered that the only way to survive was to pool their resources. "We were very poor," Baker recalled. "My mother worked in a tobacco shop to support my sister and me."

Despite the financial hardship, Baker's childhood was not an unhappy one. He excelled in school and was athletic enough that he considered a career as a professional bicycle racer. His interest in music developed relatively late. At fourteen, he played trumpet for a short period of time but quit when he was told that his teeth weren't shaped right for the instrument. A year later, without any prior training or experience, he sat down at a drum set and started playing. To his surprise, it all came naturally to him.

At sixteen, Baker quit school and was playing professionally, sitting in with jazz bands that needed a drummer. Over the next few years, he held down regular jobs with a variety of bands, playing music ranging from Dixieland to Big Band, including a three-month Scandinavian tour with Sister Rosetta Tharpe. Renowned British drummer Phil Seamen attended one of Baker's performances and, appreciating the young drummer's talent, took Baker under his wing, initiating a strong friendship that greatly influenced Baker's playing.

Baker's growing reputation on the jazz scene helped connect him to many established and upcoming players. One of his most important early meetings was with Dick Heckstall-Smith, one of the country's best young tenor sax players. Baker was happy to learn that he and Heckstall-Smith shared many of the same musical interests and ambitions, and they were playing together in the Burt Corvey Sextet the night Jack Bruce turned up and asked if he could sit in with the group.

"Jack wanted to sit in and we didn't want him to," remembered Baker, "so we played a really difficult ballad and he played all the notes right. Then we sort of played a jam with him, and we were very impressed with him."

For the next four years, Baker, Bruce, and Heckstall-Smith became a sort of roving unit in England's music circles. All three spent time together in Alexis Korner's Blues Incorporated before hooking up with Graham Bond—a pianist first with the Corvey Sextet and then briefly with Blues Incorporated—to form the Graham Bond Organisation during the heyday of the country's interest in American blues.

Baker essentially ran the Graham Bond Organisation, and under his leadership the group blossomed into one of England's most popular bands, competing with Alexis Korner's Blues Incorporated, Cyril Davies's All-Stars, and John Mayall's Bluesbreakers for gigs in the country's best venues. With success came the inevitable internal squabbling, especially between Jack Bruce and Ginger Baker, both of whom had strong wills, fiery tempers, and outspoken opinions about the creative direction the band should be taking. The tension led to some marvelous onstage playing. Baker disliked Bruce's "busy" style of bass playing and insisted that he tone it down, which only led to more furious playing from Bruce, who was using a six-string bass and incorporating regular guitar runs in his work. The musical (and occasionally physical) duels onstage drove the Graham Bond Organisation to new heights.

By 1966, both Bruce and Baker were ready for changes in their respective careers. Baker had grown tired of working in the Graham Bond Organisation, and Bruce had already served in the John Mayall and Manfred Mann units. Neither Bruce nor Baker expected to work with the other again—that is, until an interested third party named Eric Clapton decided that the two would be a perfect combination for the kind of band in which he wanted to work.

. . .

Clapton was adamant about having Jack Bruce in the band: if Bruce refused to play, he told Baker, he wouldn't play either. He was interested in creating the best music that England had to offer, personality conflicts be damned.

Baker agreed that the band's potential was far too important to be undermined by problems from the past, so he drove to Bruce's home to offer a truce. Bruce was intrigued by the idea of forming a supergroup, but he hesitated to work with Baker again. Finally, after some discussion, Bruce relented.

Predictably, all three had different ideas about what the new band would be. All agreed that a trio would be the best format for the group, although they talked for a while about asking Stevie Winwood to join. With his vocal gifts and great ability on keyboards, Winwood would have brought quite a bit to the group, but Winwood's own band, the Spencer Davis Group, was enjoying such commercial success that Winwood was not inclined to leave for an untested unit. Besides, both Jack Bruce and Ginger Baker favored the idea of remaining a threesome.

"I always liked trios in the jazz situation," Bruce explained. "I always liked people like Ornette Coleman, who played these piano-less quartets, which are trios. There's a bareness, a spare quality that I like." Baker felt similarly, noting that "the trio [gave] us a chance to spread out."

Bruce and Baker envisioned the band in more of an improvisational jazz vein—Cream, Bruce once joked, was "the only jazz band to go platinum so far"—while Clapton hoped it would be more of a blues-based unit. He liked the guitar-bass-drums format he'd heard on a Buddy Guy and Junior Wells album, and he figured he would be fronting a Chicago blues trio, his guitar backed by a powerful rhythm section.

Such fantasies were quickly put to rest when he and the others held their first rehearsal in the front room of Ginger Baker's Neasden house. The three jammed for hours, playing familiar songs or improvising new songs on the spot. All three marveled at how natural they sounded together. They played well as a unit, yet there was plenty of room for each instrumentalist to shine. Clapton, who had privately fancied himself to be a leader in the Bluesbreakers, immediately understood that he would not be dictating the path this new band would be taking; he probably had the least forceful personality in the trio. If anything, the band's musical direction would be directed by the incredible individual talents of its members. "The minute we started playing," said Clapton of that first rehearsal, "I realized it was a fully solo-oriented kind of thing, with three of us going at it strong."

Jack Bruce became the group's lead singer almost by default. Not only did he have more experience as a vocalist than Clapton but when he arrived at Baker's house, he brought along a number of new songs that he'd written for the band—songs that he wound up singing at the rehearsal. Although he was not one to shy away from the microphone and had enjoyed singing with Graham Bond, Bruce did not fancy himself to be the lead singer for a band, but Clapton demurred when Bruce suggested that he handle the task. Bruce had a strong yet malleable voice, well suited to a variety of song types, and Clapton and Baker agreed that he was the right man for the job.

Clapton, Bruce, and Baker decided to keep the band's existence a secret until certain logistics had been worked out. For openers, neither Clapton nor Baker had left their respective bands, and they needed time to give proper notice to the Bluesbreakers and the Graham Bond Organisation. Then there was the issue of what the new band was going to call itself. Clapton proposed "Sweet and Sour Rock 'n' Roll," but this suggestion was rejected in favor of another Clapton idea. "We're the Cream," he said at one point during the group's first get-together, an elated reference to the talent in the group. "That's the name of the band." The others agreed.

Next on the band's agenda was finding someone to look after their business affairs. While in the Graham Bond Organisation, Baker and Bruce had been managed by Robert Stigwood, an Australian trying to make a name for himself in the British entertainment industry. Stigwood's business background was far from pristine—he'd lost almost as much money on some ventures as he had gained on others—but Ginger Baker, a savvy businessman in his own right, believed that Stigwood had done a good job handling the Graham Bond Organisation, and he recommended him highly to Clapton and Bruce. The three met with Stigwood, discussed their goals for Cream, and signed individual management contracts with him.

By early June, rumors of the band's existence were starting to circulate. A brief article published on June 11, 1966, in *Melody Maker* announced the formation of "a sensational new 'groups' group' starring Eric Clapton, Jack Bruce, and Ginger Baker" that would be making public appearances within a month. This was news to the band members, who hadn't practiced enough to perform together onstage. For Clapton, the news item proved to be embarrassing because he was still officially a member of John Mayall's Bluesbreakers and had continued to play club dates with the band, even as he was busy rehearsing with a new one. Jack Bruce was livid, especially when he learned that the news item had come as a result of a conversation between Ginger Baker and Chris Welch, a reporter friend.

Equally unhappy with the announcement—and justifiably so—was John Mayall, who might have suspected Clapton's pending defection, but who nevertheless was incensed when he had to read about it in the newspaper rather than hear it from the man himself. Clapton had fancied himself to be a professional when he joined the Bluesbreakers, but there had been times when he'd shown very little evidence of it. He came and went as he pleased, operated under a separate set of rules from the other band members, and had the gall to lay a lot of attitude on the group to boot. As the band's main attraction, Clapton had challenged, intentionally or otherwise, Mayall's leadership of the Bluesbreakers. Clapton may have believed that he was a working pro, but all too often he acted like a petulant musical prodigy. The least he could have done was approach Mayall with his plans before the press got its hands on the item.

Once the word was out, there was no denying the group's existence, and on the heels of the *Melody Maker* article, Robert Stigwood issued a formal announcement. "They will be called Cream and will be represented by me for agency and management," he wrote. "They will record for my Reaction label and go into the studios next week to cut tracks for their first single. Their debut will be at the National Jazz and Blues Festival at Windsor in July, where their single will be released."

Ready or not, Cream had been born, and it was time to face the world.

. . .

From the beginning, Eric Clapton had certain misgivings about the band—and for good reason. For one thing, he was unclear about his role in the group; Cream's musical direction had yet to be defined. In addition, public expectations, at least among blues devotees, were high. Finally, the Baker-Bruce truce was, at best, tenuous.

Clapton worried about how the band would come off onstage. He was not nearly as experienced in the jazz-influenced style of improvisation as the other two, and neither Bruce nor Baker knew a whole lot about the blues. The date of the Windsor festival was rapidly approaching, and Cream didn't have enough songs in its repertoire to fill out a full set list.

In retrospect, the lack of material worked to Cream's advantage, for it led to the lengthy instrumental jams that became the group's calling card. "We had maybe three-quarters of an hour's material," noted Clapton. "When it became clear that we needed more than that, we just stretched the numbers out and then that became VOGUE! It was purely accidental."

Before appearing at the blues festival, Cream performed a preliminary show at one of the Bluesbreakers' old Manchester haunts, the Twisted Wheel. The low-key affair resembled an average pub date, with very little to either encourage or discourage the band—which was precisely what the band wanted. Neither Clapton nor his mates believed that the Cream experience would be anything but what they had gone through in the past. They expected to play in small to medium-sized clubs, record an album or two, and, if their playing was as good as they thought it could be, make some kind of impact on the English music scene. "We didn't want to be big in any way," Clapton admitted long after the fact, still surprised by how things had turned out.

However modest their ambitions, Cream got a dose of reality the very next day at the National Jazz and Blues Festival, where thousands of fans braved a driving rainstorm for the band's official, open-air debut. As Clapton had predicted, Cream did not have enough material for the scheduled hour-long set, but those in attendance wouldn't have noticed. The extended solos—Baker on drums in "Toad," Bruce on harmonica in "Traintime," and Clapton on virtually every other song—whipped the crowd into a frenzy. Clapton's anxiety about audience response to Cream dissipated, to be replaced by a nagging feeling that it was all too much, that the crowd would have roared its approval to anything he played. Any remaining notions of a modest blues trio disappeared during that single bittersweet performance.

Robert Stigwood did a good job booking the kind of gigs the band originally wanted, and in the weeks following the Windsor festival, Cream traveled all over England, playing the club and university circuit in London, Edmonton, Kensington, and Stockport. Between shows, they went to the studio and recorded their first single, as well as tracks for their debut album.

Clapton would always insist that Cream was really two distinct units— a performing band and a studio band—and this was very much in evidence on their first recordings. The single "Wrapping Paper"/"Cat's Squirrel" stood as a strong example of the musical differences within the band, the latter being a traditional blues arranged by Eric Clapton, the former an original pop composition that, at first glance, had little to do with what Cream was all about except for its faint, bluesy backdrop. When asked about the single, Clapton would claim that "Wrapping Paper" was an intentional departure: it was Cream's way of keeping their fans a little off balance, of assembling something in the studio that ran against the grain of what the public expected as a result of seeing the band's live performances.

The song introduced the world to the Jack Bruce–Pete Brown writing team, a tandem that produced some of Cream's most memorable songs. A poet, Brown had been a part of London's jazz and poetry readings backed, on different occasions, by Jack Bruce on bass or Ginger Baker on drums. Brown had a nodding acquaintance with Bruce at that time, as well as with

Eric Clapton, who was rooming with Ted Milton, another poet on the scene.

Ironically, it was Ginger Baker who brought Pete Brown and Jack Bruce together. Baker was a friend of Brown's, and when Cream started working in earnest, he called the poet for help on the lyrics to a song he was writing, a piece called "Sweet Wine." The two went over to Jack Bruce's Hempstead flat, where Bruce was working on several new songs, including the music for "Wrapping Paper." Brown wound up writing the lyrics for that song, as well as for Cream's second single, "I Feel Free," while Baker found an altogether different lyricist for "Sweet Wine"—Jack Bruce's wife, Janet Godfrey.

The issue of songwriting credits became the first wedge driven between group members. Because Cream worked on song arrangements together, Ginger Baker believed that the songwriting credits (and the all-important publishing revenue) should be divided equally among band members. Clapton and Bruce disagreed. The credits, they argued, should go to the principle songwriters and lyricists. Baker would always resent the Bruce-Brown credit on "Wrapping Paper," since he felt that he and Clapton both contributed significantly to the writing and arrangement of the song.

Pete Brown, recipient of a large percentage of Cream's publishing royalties, was also a target of Baker's resentment: "I had worked on some things with Ginger and then he would say, 'Oh, I'm afraid I lost your lyric and I had to do something else.' Later on, when he was not being very pleasant, he virtually accused me of stealing his birthright by writing all those songs and copping a living from them. He perhaps felt he should have been doing it. On the other hand, with all due respect, I did help the main hits along quite a bit, which did quite a lot for them, and besides he didn't come up with as much stuff as I did."

Not all of the tension proved to be harmful. The division of musical styles turned out to be an asset for the band. *Fresh Cream*, the group's grossly underrated first album, recorded in several sessions over the summer of 1966, presented a healthy mixture of traditional blues and original compositions. Clapton had been teaching the band some of his favorite blues, and his influence is evident in Cream's recordings of Robert John-son's country blues, "From Four until Late," Muddy Waters's "Rollin' and Tumblin'," Willie Dixon's "Spoonful," and Skip James's "I'm So Glad." Bruce, who seemed to have written several new numbers every time the band got together, pitched in "I Feel Free," "Sleepy Time Time," "N.S.U.,"* and "Dreaming"—all songs with a pop bent. Besides "Sweet Wine," Baker contributed "Toad," his popular drum solo number written as an homage to Mike Felana's drumwork in the Johnny Birch Octet's "Toes."

On *Fresh Cream*, Clapton continues his evolution as a guitarist, further developing his technique even as the music itself moved more toward rock. The use of distortion and sustained notes, employed to great effect on the earlier Bluesbreakers album, is nothing short of revolutionary when placed in the context of such rock-oriented songs as "I Feel Free" and "N.S.U." Clapton, however, uses these effects with restraint: on one of the early takes of "Sweet Wine," the guitarist fired off a solo composed almost entirely of wild guitar feedback, but this version, recorded before the release of Jimi Hendrix's *Are You Experienced*, was deemed too radical for the rock-blues fusion that Cream was working on and was replaced by a more conservative version of the song.

In fact, compared to where Cream was going, all of *Fresh Cream* appears to be musically conservative. Seven of the album's songs ("N.S.U.," "Sleepy Time Time," "Sweet Wine," "Spoonful," "I'm So Glad," "Toad," and "Rollin' and Tumblin'") would turn up on other albums in greatly expanded live arrangements, full of the over-the-top improvisation for which Cream would become known, but in retrospect, some of the shorter versions hold up better. The band is more focused, working together as a unit rather than as three individuals furiously competing with each other. (Clapton's guitar duet with Jack Bruce's harmonica in "Cat's Squirrel" is

---

*"N.S.U.," one of two Cream titles released with just initials, stood for Non-Specific Urethritis, a sexual dysfunction among males. The inside joke was typical of the band's "Goon Show" humor.

so tight that it sounds as if the two musicians have created a sort of synthesized sound.) For a first effort, *Fresh Cream* can compete in quality with the first albums by the Beatles, Rolling Stones, Bob Dylan, or any number of other groups or individuals who would go on to establish themselves at the pinnacle of rock music stardom.

• • •

Ever the perfectionist, Eric Clapton expressed dissatisfaction with *Fresh Cream* when it was issued in December 1966. "It could have been better," he proposed, noting that he was not pleased with the production techniques used on the album, and that the band had evolved considerably between the time of the album's recording and the time of its release.

That much was true enough. Although Jack Bruce acted informally as Cream's musical director in the studio, none of the three had enough exposure to record production to work on some of the finer details that would distinguish their later efforts. The album was billed as a Robert Stigwood Production, but the label had more to do with Stigwood's independent marketing technique than his ability to do much of anything in the studio.

Nor was there any denying that Cream was moving ahead at a dizzying pace—a progression that, for Clapton, could be marked by the arrival of Jimi Hendrix in London. Prior to Hendrix's arrival, Clapton's reputation as a guitarist went virtually uncontested. After all, he was "God"; no one was as masterful or innovative on his instrument.

All that changed—at least in Clapton's eyes—when Chas Chandler, bassist for the Animals and a friend of the band's, turned up at a Cream concert at Central London Polytechnic with a young black American guitarist in tow. Chandler dropped by Cream's dressing room, introduced Hendrix to the group, and asked if Hendrix could sit in for a song or two.

Ginger Baker was especially leery of the proposal. Cream was still in the process of establishing itself, and Baker was not at all keen on the prospects of some young kid upstaging the band's guitarist. Hendrix could sit in, Baker said, but only if Clapton stayed onstage as well.

Clapton had no serious reservations about playing with Hendrix, although, as he said later, he "had a funny feeling about him." Clapton was intrigued by Hendrix, who wore flashy clothes and stood at the dressing room mirror, primping with his hair. For all the pizzazz, he seemed shy—that is, until he hit the stage.

Hendrix played two songs that evening, including a version of Howlin' Wolf's "Killing Floor" that caused Clapton's jaw to drop. Somehow Hendrix managed to play both rhythm and lead at the same time, with an intensity that Clapton could not believe. A couple years earlier, Clapton had been floored by the stage theatrics of Buddy Guy, who played his guitar as if he were attacking it, and who loved to jump around onstage, or even leave the stage and wander through the audience while he played. Hendrix took this kind of performance to another level. He could play his guitar behind his back or with his teeth; at one point he pretended to be making love to it. To Clapton, it was incredible that Hendrix could play *and* perform at such a high level.

Jack Bruce and Ginger Baker were less receptive. Bruce praised Hendrix's act, but he worried about the effect it had on Clapton. "He blew everybody's mind because he played all over the guitar, with his teeth and everything," Bruce said. "It must have been difficult for Eric to handle because he was 'God,' and this unknown person comes along and burns."

Ginger Baker took offense to some of the theatrics. "He bugs me a little bit with all his showmanship," he said in an interview not long after the show. "Maybe I'm an old man but to me Jimi gets carried away. . . . He's a great guitar player but he pushes his act too far."

True to form, Clapton based his assessment on the success of Hendrix's performances, rather than on feelings of competition. "He did everything that he did for the rest of his career in those two songs," Clapton reflected. "It just blew the audience away; they'd never seen anything like it before."

Although naturally wary of someone with that kind of power, Clapton was not intimidated by Hendrix. From a musician's standpoint, he loved hearing and watching a true craftsman at work. For a change, *he* could be the fan.

Hendrix's influence on Clapton was immediate, with a favorable effect on Clapton's outlook in Cream. "I was still at that time pretty uptight by the fact that we weren't playing one hundred percent blues numbers," he noted, "and to see Jimi play that way I just thought, 'Wow!'—that's alright with me! It just sort of opened my mind up to listening to a lot of other things and playing a lot of other things."

Clapton played his own important role in helping to shape Hendrix's career. The American guitarist had known of Clapton prior to his visit to London—one of the selling points in getting Hendrix to England in the first place was Chas Chandler's promise to introduce him to Clapton—and Hendrix wanted to see how Clapton fared in the trio format. He had yet to put together a band of his own, but within weeks of his sitting in with Cream, Hendrix had assembled the Jimi Hendrix Experience, a trio that, in a way, turned out to be an American counterpart to Cream.

The Polytechnic meeting was only the beginning of the Clapton-Hendrix story. Aside from a few words backstage, the two musicians barely spoke to each other at the gig. The true introduction took place unexpectedly a short time later, when Clapton walked into a London restaurant and found Hendrix in the middle of an interview with *Beat International*. Hendrix invited Clapton to sit at the table with him, and in the ensuing conversation, his and Clapton's relationship grew from one of mutual admiration to one of genuine friendship. The two huddled at the table, drinking and talking long after the interview had ended, both waxing philosophical about playing guitar, the music business, the idea of working a regular nine-to-five job, women, and where they hoped to be in the future. Clapton allowed that he wouldn't have minded having a lot of money and expensive cars but added that he hated the idea of having to consider where he was going to be twenty years up the road. Hendrix, in turn, was both moved and delighted by the conversation. At one point he grasped Clapton's hand and kissed him, declaring, "I just kissed the fairest soul brother in England."

Clapton and Hendrix saw a lot of each other over the ensuing weeks, talking for hours on end and exchanging ideas about guitar technique and equipment. Their friendship—and gentle rivalry—would continue until

Hendrix's death in 1970, providing an ironic footnote to the countless debates over who was the better and more influential guitarist, the Hendrix school arguing in favor of Hendrix's open-ended innovation, the Clapton school standing by Clapton's purist approach, both sides refusing to accept the powerful influence the two guitar giants had on each other.

• • •

Unlike "Wrapping Paper," which had gone nowhere on the charts, "I Feel Free" moved up to the eleventh spot on the British charts, while *Fresh Cream* soared to the sixth slot in album sales. Cream toured extensively in support of the album, balancing a hectic schedule of club and university appearances with a handful of radio spots on BBC Radio's "Saturday Club."

As Cream's popularity grew, it became clear that the band was outgrowing some of the smaller clubs they'd been playing. It was also apparent that the group was ready to travel outside of England to reach an even greater audience. The big goal, of course, was to line up a visit to the United States, but until that time arrived, there were other countries in Europe to explore. From mid-February to mid-March, Cream played a string of critically acclaimed shows in France, Holland, Germany, and Scandinavia.

Upon their return to England, Clapton, Bruce, and Baker learned that Robert Stigwood had succeeded in getting Cream booked for a ten-day run on "The Fifth Dimensional," an American radio show hosted by disc jockey "Murray the K" Kaufman. The popular New York radio personality had earned a national reputation stemming from his friendship with and promotion of the Beatles and, as a result, he had become one of the most important "discoverers" of new talent in the rock industry. Held in Manhattan's RKO Theater, "The Fifth Dimensional" was as much an endurance test as a promotional venue for artists: the show ran five times a day and featured as many acts as could be squeezed into a one-hour slot—sometimes as many as twenty groups per segment. After the show, audiences changed and the show was repeated. Some shows were played for an empty hall and some for standing-room-only crowds. For every three-minute number performed, a band could be assured of waiting around for a couple hours for the chance to play again. It was, quite simply, one version of rock 'n' roll hell.

Cream shared the bill with a number of notable groups, including The Who, Simon and Garfunkel, Wilson Pickett, the Lovin' Spoonful, the Blues Project, and Mitch Ryder and the Detroit Wheels, and from shared misery arose a camaraderie between musicians. Eric Clapton was united with an old friend, Who guitarist Pete Townshend, while Ginger Baker palled around with Keith Moon, The Who's talented but decisively strange drummer. Onstage, Cream would play one song, using equipment already set up by another band—usually The Who—playing for an audience that wanted the kind of showmanship they saw in other bands; they were invariably disappointed.

When he was away from the mayhem, Clapton enjoyed his first look at New York City, where something interesting always seemed to be going on. He haunted the music shops and clothing boutiques; he even attended a huge "be-in" in Central Park. It was the era of the hippie, complete with wild clothing and psychedelic music and almost limitless sex and drugs, and Clapton was all too happy to take in as much as he could. The New York music scene, he discovered, was jumping with talent, and from hanging out in Greenwich Village clubs, Clapton met a number of influential artists, including Al Kooper and Frank Zappa. To his delight, there was always somewhere to jam. He sat in with bands on any number of occasions, but one particular session would always stand out in his mind: a three-hour jam with one of his idols, B. B. King. Clapton found the great bluesman playing at the Café Au Go Go. Formal introductions were made, and before long Clapton was onstage with King, joined by Al Kooper and Elvin Bishop in a marathon blues improvisation that was recorded but never released.

To Clapton's delight, the American groupie scene was no different from what he had encountered earlier in the Yardbirds. As a celebrity, he could cash in on his star status for all the one-nighters he wanted, and for someone who was naturally shy to begin with, but who nevertheless admitted to having youthful fantasies about sleeping with a thousand women, this was a bonanza. In the era before AIDS, when the United States was charging through its sexual revolution, Clapton was able to have all the sex he could handle with only marginal risk and no need for personal attachment.

In New York, huge groups of young women hung around the RKO Theater, hoping to connect with the musicians appearing on the Murray the K show. Clapton characterized the scene as "red hot," and while he was more than happy to take part in it, the romantic in him hated the notion of looking on the lines of expectant young women as just a meat market.

"As a rule they're the most incredibly warm people," he said, when asked about the groupie scene, perhaps showing a hint of guilt from his overindulgence. "I mean, there are a few exceptions—chicks who are just out to be superstar groupies because it's become the in thing to do, but in the early days they were just chicks who wanted to look after you when you were in town. If making love to you was going to make you happy, they'd make love. If you were tired and didn't want to make it, they'd cook you a meal and make you feel at home. They really were 'ports of call.'"

Clapton's statement was revealing about the way he regarded women, then and in the future. He would always have a difficult time maintaining long-term relationships, partly because his libido would drive him to women other than his partner at the moment, partly because he found it almost impossible to remain satisfied with anything—or anyone—over an extended period of time, and partly because his attitudes toward women in general were lagging behind the times. At his best, Eric Clapton was a chauvinist; at his worst, a sexist. Even in his more enduring relationships, Clapton expected his women to be at his beck and call, to be the kind of domestics who cooked his meals, ironed his clothes, and kept the house tidy. In his mind, he was clearly the authority figure.

His casual relationships, affairs, and one-night stands followed suit. Over the course of Clapton's life, countless women were indeed "ports of call," as he so indelicately put it, although, in all fairness, it should be noted that Clapton was far too sensitive to treat them as nothing but sex objects. For all his chauvinism, he could also be very warm, tender, romantic, and thoughtful. If anything, his attitudes were shaped by his unusual background, his upbringing in the traditional Surrey community, his natural shyness toward (yet strong attraction to) women, and his status as a rock star.

Clapton celebrated his twenty-second birthday a few days before the end of Cream's "Fifth Dimensional" engagement. By then, he and his bandmates were so fed up with the program that they were just going through the motions onstage, hoping to survive the experience and get on with their next important piece of business, the recording of their second album. April 3—the last day of the engagement—finally arrived. To mark the end of the ordeal, Clapton had planned to stage a food fight, for which he had purchased dozens of eggs and huge sacks of flour. Word of the prank leaked out, and Murray the K put an end to the frivolity by threatening to withhold the band's paychecks if the fight took place. Clapton responded by using the foodstuffs in the different dressing rooms, causing a major flood in Pete Townshend's room when his shower stall overflowed. As far as Clapton was concerned, it was an appropriate finale to a forgettable experience.

· · ·

If ever there was a year with a rock 'n' roll sound track, 1967 would have to lay claim to the honor. Flower Power was in full bloom, and every band on both sides of the ocean seemed to be vying to create a sound track for a strange epoch compressed into just a few calendar months, blossoming in the sweet scents of what would be known as "The Summer of Love." The Beatles issued *Sgt. Pepper's Lonely Hearts Club Band*, the Doors and Grateful Dead released their self-entitled first albums, the Rolling Stones checked in with their song about "Ruby Tuesday," and Procol Harum put out their dreamy "A Whiter Shade of Pale." West Coast bands with such strange names as the Jefferson Airplane, Quicksilver Messenger Service, Moby Grape, Sopwith Camel, Country Joe and the Fish, and Electric Flag enjoyed great local success and varying national recognition. The mood in the music industry was decisively psychedelic.

Cream's contribution was *Disraeli Gears*. From its orange Day-Glo cover to some of its songs' psychedelic lyrics, the album addressed a precise moment in time, yet its music managed to survive without sounding too dated. As unbelievable as it may seem today, given the amount of time and effort and money devoted to any given recording, *Disraeli Gears* was put together over the course of only a few days, in the time immediately following Cream's appearance on Murray the K's show.

The band had arrived in America with a sheaf of new songs. Jack Bruce and Pete Brown had come up with memorable material, including "SWLABR,"* a song destined to become an FM-radio classic; the uptempo blues "Take It Back," which Cream had already performed during one of their "Saturday Club" appearances on the BBC; and two powerful new works called "White Room" and "Sunshine of Your Love." Clapton's songwriting contributions were less substantial, at least in terms of sheer numbers. Beside helping with the writing of "Sunshine," he had only one other new composition to offer—"Tales of Brave Ulysses," a tour de force that Cream would often use to open their concerts.

Ahmet Ertegun, head of Atlantic Records, was far from enthusiastic about the demos of the songs he'd heard. In Ertegun's opinion, the songs were too experimental to be commercial. Other Atlantic executives dismissed "White Room" and "Sunshine of Your Love" as being so much "psychedelic hogwash." Oblivious to the notion of hurting Jack Bruce's feelings, officials wondered why Clapton, their designated band leader, had not written more new music, and why Bruce was singing virtually all of Cream's material.

Ertegun assigned the album's technical direction to Atlantic's house

---

*The initials stand for "She Walks Like a Bearded Rainbow," but Jack Bruce, the song's author, was a little embarrassed by the psychedelic title and decided to call it by initials.

engineer, Tom Dowd, a recording sessions veteran with top-shelf credentials. Dowd had worked with such artists as John Coltrane, Ray Charles, and Otis Redding, and had been the engineer on such classics as Bobby Darin's "Mack the Knife" and Aretha Franklin's "Respect." In addition, he had helped design Atlantic's innovative, state-of-the-art studio, which was fully equipped to accommodate the large-band sound of the label's jazz and R & B acts.

For all his experience in the studio, Dowd had spent very little time working with rock bands, so Atlantic hired Felix Pappalardi, a gifted musician and producer, to act as an intermediary between Cream and Tom Dowd. Pappalardi took a light-handed approach in producing a record, preferring to bounce ideas off musicians to giving them strict direction. That was definitely the approach to take with a band like Cream, whose members tended to be stubborn about maintaining creative control of their material.

Like the engineer on the Bluesbreakers recording, Tom Dowd quickly learned that Clapton had his own ideas about how to set up the studio. Artists recording at the Atlantic studios traditionally used the house amplifiers, with which Dowd was totally familiar. Clapton and Bruce, however, marched in with huge stacks of Marshall amps, prepared to record at the volume they set for their concerts.

"They recorded at ear-shattering level," Dowd recalled. "I'd never worked with a band with the order of power in the studio that these chaps had. Everyone I'd worked with before was using Fender Deluxes or Twins—six- and seven-piece bands that didn't play as loud as this three-piece did."

Cream started off by recording "Lawdy Mama," a traditional blues arranged by Clapton in homage to Albert King. Liking the song but wanting something different, Felix Pappalardi erased Clapton's vocals, took the recording home, and, along with his wife, Gail Collins, wrote new lyrics for it. The result, "Strange Brew," eventually released as the album's first single, was an odd mixture of influences, from the song's traditional melody to Clapton's direct transcription of an Albert King guitar solo to the new lyrics. It was a good start.

Like an artist beginning a new painting with a fresh palette, Clapton went to the Atlantic studios with the intention of creating his album with entirely new colors coming from his guitar. He had become even more adept in his feedback and sustain techniques, and from the time he'd spent with Jimi Hendrix he had added a fuzz box and wah-wah pedal for new effects. At the time, the wah-wah pedal was still relatively new, and Clapton's use of it on "Tales of Brave Ulysses" was one of the high points of *Disraeli Gears*. Using the wah-wah in four descending notes throughout the song, Clapton carved out the song's sense of drama, which was then given depth by Ginger Baker's drumming and a powerful vocal performance by Jack Bruce. The song was designated B side status on the "Strange Brew" single, though it was easily the stronger of the two sides.

The centerpiece to *Disraeli Gears*—and eventually a best-selling single— was "Sunshine of Your Love," a song that began as a tribute to Jimi Hendrix. Earlier in the year, Clapton and Bruce had attended a Hendrix show at London's Saville Theatre. After the show, Jack Bruce, thunder- struck by Hendrix's performance, had gone home and written the memora- ble guitar lick that runs throughout "Sunshine." He and Pete Brown struggled to find lyrics to match the riff, and after one particular all-night session, during which very little was accomplished, a tired, frustrated Jack Bruce grabbed his upright bass and, staring out the window and playing the song's main riff, sang, "It's getting near dawn, when lights close a tired eye ..." The song had its first line. It was a simple as that.

When Bruce ran through the number for Clapton and Baker, all enthusi- astically agreed that he was onto something, but the song was nowhere near finished. The pacing was wrong, and it lacked a chorus or bridge. Baker solved the first problem by counting off a slower, African beat, which ultimately became the song's tempo. Clapton came up with the bridge ("I've been waiting so long ..."), which gave the song its title. All three felt that they had a hit on their hands.

The people at Atlantic were not so certain, and the song was initially rejected. Fortunately for Cream (and Atlantic), Booker T. Jones, leader of Booker T. and the MG's and one of Atlantic's most respected studio musicians, was in the studio when Cream was running through the song one day. He listened to it and told the record company's bosses that he thought it was excellent. On the basis of Booker T.'s recommendation, Cream was given the go-ahead to record "Sunshine of Your Love," which in time became one of Atlantic's all-time best-selling singles.

The band was hitting a creative peak, and *Disraeli Gears* fell together nicely, from the music itself to the titling and packaging of the album. Clapton's roommate, Australian painter Martin Sharp, who had written the lyrics for "Tales of Brave Ulysses," did the album's cover art, which perfectly matched 1967's psychedelic mood. For some of the album jacket's memorable photos, cameraman Robert Whittaker took the band to Ben Nevis, the highest point in the United Kingdom. The band, tripping on acid, romped around the rugged terrain throughout the photo shoot. Afterward, Clapton raced Baker down the mountain, both stumbling and falling, oblivious to the sheer drops around them.

The album's title was the result of the kind of humorous wordplay typical of the times. Looking for something offbeat, the band members tossed around puns such as "Elephant Gerald" and "Duke Elephant," but nothing came of it. A few weeks later, after Cream had returned to England, the band members and some of their roadies were talking about Scotland's recent winner of the Tour de France. The topic switched to a discussion about a racing bicycle that Clapton had purchased, with Clapton asking Baker, the band's resident bicycling expert, about the bike's gears. One of Cream's roadies said that Clapton's bike came equipped with "disraeli gears"—instead of "dérailleur gears"—and the group, laughing hysterically, realized that they had the pun they were looking for. The title stuck.

· · ·

Back in England, Cream resumed a busy schedule whereas, in hindsight, the band might have been better off taking a short break from their activities.

The group's unity, eroded by the pace they had maintained in New York, was again in question. Recording *Disraeli Gears* had taken a lot out of the three men. There had been the usual friction that is common to collaboration on creative ventures, and egos had been bruised. Ginger Baker felt that Jack Bruce was a bit too assertive in the studio, and he stewed over what he believed was a lack of proper respect and credit for his contributions to the band's songwriting. Bruce, on the other hand, was still smarting from the emphasis that Atlantic placed on Clapton's role in Cream when, in fact, he had written the great bulk of the album's songs, played several instruments to Clapton's one, sang most of the lead vocals, and generally acted as the band's creative director in the studio. He still admired Clapton's musical ability and valued his friendship, but he couldn't help but envy the attention he was receiving. Nor did it help that, for some time, the band had been billed as The Cream starring Eric Clapton.

There was no question that Clapton was the band's onstage leader, but not like Jimi Hendrix was the leader of his trio. Jack Bruce and Ginger Baker brought their own circle of fans to the band, but Clapton followers were more obvious, to the extent of even dressing like him. At one time in the early going, when Clapton favored wearing military-style jackets onstage, it wasn't at all uncommon for Cream to walk out to a sea of similar jackets in the audience.

Imitators notwithstanding, Clapton tended to follow, rather than set, fashion. After seeing Jimi Hendrix and Bob Dylan in frizzy, Afro-style hairdos, Clapton had his hair frizzed in a similar fashion. His choice of clothing, although colorful and interesting, was really a reflection of the outlandish hippie garb of the day. In response to the popularity of psychedelic art, he hired the Fool (the pseudonym for two Dutch artists-designers best known for the mural they painted for the Beatles' Apple boutique) to paint his favorite Gibson guitar in a rainbow of colors and pastel designs.

Robert Stigwood continued to manage Cream's affairs in a way that was part business savvy, part blind luck. He had the band appearing on radio and television shows in support of the June release of "Strange Brew," and he arranged for them to play again at the annual Jazz and Blues Festival in Windsor. In one of his stranger arrangements for the band, he landed Cream a job playing and singing for a Falstaff beer commercial, a promotion that sounded utterly preposterous with Bruce wailing an advertising pitch over Cream's heavy-handed playing; mercifully, the commercial never saw the light of day. Stigwood declined, however, to accept a slot in the Monterey Pop Festival, the now historic outdoor concert spectacle that kicked open the doors to commercial success for a number of new acts, including Jimi Hendrix, Janis Joplin, and The Who. For all his hits and misses, Stigwood will be forever remembered for bringing Cream to San Francisco. Stigwood, a hard-line negotiator, had been dealing with West Coast promotor Bill Graham, an equally feisty businessman, and after some hard-nosed bargaining, an agreement was reached.

On the West Coast during the Summer of Love, Graham's Fillmore Auditorium (soon to be renamed Fillmore West) was *the* place for a band to appear. Graham ran a tight ship, overseeing all aspects of concert promotion and production. He could never claim to be as musically knowledgeable as his peers, but he possessed uncanny instincts for packaging the right acts for his concert hall's stage.

When he booked Cream, Graham knew very little about the band. *Fresh Cream* had served up dismal sales figures, *Disraeli Gears* had yet to be released, and with the exception of Murray the K's show in New York, Cream had never appeared on an American stage. Still, Graham had heard through the grapevine that Cream was a band to be reckoned with, and he signed the group for what others might have judged to be an ill-advised two weeks at the Fillmore, paying them a sum total of $5,000 for their work. During the first week, Cream performed as the support group for the Paul Butterfield Blues Band; the second week, they topped a bill that included the Electric Flag and Gary Burton. The packaging proved to be excellent: the Butterfield Blues Band and Electric Flag, featuring such artists as Paul Butterfield, Mike Bloomfield, and Elvin Bishop, played the kind of amplified blues that attracted just the sort of crowds that would be receptive to Cream's music.

Clapton and Graham hit it off from the start—or, that is, as soon as

Clapton understood that Graham's regulations applied to *all* performers, stars and unknowns alike, and that you either did things his way or you didn't play. Graham, for instance, had a rule prohibiting performers from leaving the Fillmore once they had checked in. One day Clapton decided to go for a walk between shows. He was promptly confronted by Graham, who informed him, in no uncertain terms, that he was going nowhere. Clapton, who was accustomed to a much looser situation in the British clubs, was surprised by Graham's rather dictatorial approach, but he soon came to realize that, in an era of sex and drugs and rock 'n' roll, when authorities could—and would—make life miserable for everyone from concert hall promoters to music fans, some rules of order were necessary. Graham, Clapton concluded, ruled the Fillmore like the head of a traditional household. "It was like a little family," he remarked. "Once I got to know that, once I got to know where the limitations were, then it was great. I was very, very at home there." Graham, in return, took a liking to Clapton, deeming him to be "the ultimate of all gentlemen." At the end of Cream's two-week engagement at the Fillmore, he showed his appreciation for their work by giving each band member a gold watch.

Cream could not have found a better place to play. Set up to hold 900 people (though it ran up several times that number on numerous occasions), the Fillmore provided a more intimate concert backdrop than the gigantic halls Clapton would be playing in the future. The atmosphere was laid-back, with stoned or tripping patrons getting lost in the music and the Fillmore's renowned light show. Anything went, as long as a semblance of order was maintained. The musicians, too, were given plenty of leeway. Cream was told that they were free to play anything they wanted. They could work off a set list or they could jam all night.

Clapton was amazed by this open, almost otherworldly environment, and he and the band responded with some of Cream's most innovative work to date. On a typical night, Clapton, Bruce, and Baker would walk out in front of a packed house and play about a half dozen songs, all featuring lengthy improvisations that excited band and concertgoers alike. American audiences had never heard anything quite like it before, and they responded enthusiastically. Cream's performances sold out, night after night.

The response caught Clapton by surprise. When leaving for the United States, he had anticipated that some people might be familiar with Cream through word of mouth or underground radio stations, but the overwhelming reaction to the band's music was more than he could have imagined. He had envisioned America, with its blues roots, to be a sort of musical Mecca, but he'd heard enough complaints to the contrary from bluesmen traveling through England to wonder whether Cream would be accepted in the country. The communal San Francisco scene banished any of his doubts.

"Every little move you make and every little note you play is being noticed, being devoured, accepted or rejected," Clapton told an interviewer shortly after the Fillmore concerts. "You know that whatever you do is going to be noticed and you do it right. You got to do your best 'cause they know if you're not doing your best."

Between the music business in England and that in the United States, he favored the American scene, noting that "there is less competition and more encouragement here from musician to musician. Music thrives wildly in England because they are jealous of someone else's success. They're jealous so they have to do better. Here you're encouraged. Everybody digs everybody else and they don't hide it."

Throughout his career, Clapton would be asked to compare his British and American experiences, and he would always be forthright in saying that he felt more appreciated in the United States than in his own country. Cream's reception during their Fillmore dates initiated this attitude but, as Clapton was to learn, the good feelings of the Summer of Love represented a temporary and artificial setting. The real test would come later.

· · ·

The word on Cream spread like wildfire, and other cities were quickly added to the band's itinerary. There were shows from coast to coast, including the Whiskey Au Go Go in Los Angeles, the Psychedelic Supermarket in Boston, and the Village Theater and Café Au Go Go in New York, the tour running all the way through September and halfway into October. No matter where they appeared, they were greeted by enthusiastic fans eager to hear half-hour jams of songs like "Spoonful" or "I'm So Glad." When looking back on Cream's success, the band members would view this period as the height of their performances.

"The beginning of the peak was on our first U.S. tour at the first gig at the Fillmore," said Jack Bruce. "The crowd started shouting things like 'Just play anything,' which we did. We just started playing what came into our heads, instead of going out to play set tunes. And that's when we realized that this is where it's at. But we didn't go beyond that; we just got better at it."

Eric Clapton had mixed feelings about the long solos. He was pleased with much of what Cream was doing onstage, but as time went on and he saw other bands imitating what Cream was doing, he was less enthralled with it. In some of his darker moments, he criticized the lengthy improvisations as "taking a liberty" with the band's fans. "We leaped in and took advantage of it," he said of Cream's popularity. "When we saw that in America they actually wanted us to play a number for a whole hour—one number—we just stretched it."

Ginger Baker allowed that Cream was catering to the wishes of their fans, and that audience response was such that people wouldn't have known if Cream played badly, but he felt that the onstage jamming was worthwhile if the group continued to grow. Keeping a creative edge was the key. "Sometimes when we have a bad night," he said at the time, "we get forced into clichés. We've all got original clichés that we fall back on during bad moments."

Despite the differing outlooks, all agreed that Cream should be recorded onstage. A live album—or maybe even a more ambitious project involving a two-record set, one album recorded live, one done in the studio—was projected for the near future.

One of the highlights of Clapton's stay in America occurred in September, when he received an invitation from Tom Dowd to play a guitar solo on a song being recorded by Aretha Franklin. The assignment was a plum, finding Clapton in the studio with the likes of guitarists Jimmy Johnson, Bobby Womack, and Joe South, as well as legendary sax player King Curtis. Clapton responded with outstanding guitar work that harkened back to some of the short but very effective work he had done during his John Mayall period. The song "Good to Me as I Am to You," appeared on Franklin's *Lady Soul* album, released in March 1968. For Clapton, the session marked a strong finale to a trying period in the United States.

Ironically, the tour that truly established the band also proved to be its undoing. The months of traveling and performing placed a great strain on the individual band members, and by the time Cream returned to England at the end of the year, Bruce and Baker were again at each other's throats. The band needed a rest, but with its popularity hitting a peak—*Disraeli Gears*, released in November, reached number four in America, number five in England—Cream could not afford the luxury of a vacation. Stigwood had already set up a full slate of club dates in England, along with radio and television appearances. Then, as a tune-up for another tour of the United States, Cream played a week's worth of gigs in Scandinavia. Nerves were badly frayed by the time Clapton, Baker, and Bruce returned to America in February 1968 for what would become the longest tour undertaken by a British band to that point.

First at hand, however, was the task of recording another album, and for this Cream checked back into New York's Atlantic Studio. This time around, with a successful album and tour behind them, Cream was in more of a position to control the content of their record. Felix Pappalardi and Tom Dowd were back at the soundboard, but there was no longer any discussion, from them or Atlantic officials, about the band's punching out a commercial hit. In a recent interview with *Melody Maker*, Clapton had announced that Cream was finished recording singles. The band had progressed beyond the three-minute singles formula, and he was no more inclined to sell out to commercialism now than when he had been with the Yardbirds.

From the outset, the album was conceived as a two-record set, which, in 1968, was still a very ambitious, costly, and relatively unusual venture for a rock band. Felix Pappalardi shared Cream's belief that the band differed substantially between what it did in the studio and what it did onstage, and as a producer, Pappalardi was fascinated by the concept of having one record present the band in a controlled studio environment, and having another feature long, onstage solos focusing on the individual work of each member. To get the project started, he had visited England the previous December and worked with the band on the writing and arranging of a number of new songs. Somehow, in the midst of their grueling concert schedule, Cream had found time to enter the studio and record the backing tracks for two of the new album's songs—"White Room," a Jack Bruce–Pete Brown number originally intended for *Disraeli Gears*, and "Born Under a Bad Sign," a cover of an Albert King song.

Cream had a wealth of material for the studio album. Clapton himself had no new original material to offer, though he wanted to cover both the Albert King song and Howlin' Wolf's "Sitting on Top of the World." Ginger Baker had been writing songs with Mike Taylor, a classically trained, avant-garde jazz pianist, and three of their songs ("Those Were the Days," "Passing the Time," and "Pressed Rat and Warthog") were pegged for the current album. As usual, the Bruce-Brown team came in with the most material, including "Politician," a scathing attack on political hypocrisy; "As You Said," a string piece that was a total change from what Cream had been doing; "Deserted Cities of the Heart," a work of psychedelic poetry; and "White Room."

Due to Cream's touring schedule, the recording was divided into two series of sessions, one to lay down the basic tracks and a later session to complete the tracks and insert overdubs. This was not especially good news to the already overworked band members. Bruce and Baker were still at loggerheads, Clapton was disgusted with the whole mess, and all three were exhausted from nonstop touring and recording that had begun a year earlier. Such conditions were bound to have a distracting effect on the recording sessions. "The album got bogged down in a lot of places," Felix Pappalardi wrote in a memoir of the recording sessions, "because Cream was working very hard on tour. They were tired and they just wanted to get away."

Nevertheless, the band labored to get each song precisely as they wanted it. With an eight-track tape machine at their disposal—as opposed to the standard four-track machines used in all other studios at the time—Cream had plenty of room for experimentation and overdubbing. Clapton, for example, appeared on three separate guitar tracks on "Politician," once playing rhythm and twice on overdubbed leads that crisscross from the right to left speakers when played on a stereo. Bruce played both a four-string and a six-string bass on separate tracks on "Pressed Rat and Warthog." Strings and horns were added throughout. To those accustomed to Cream's three-piece, live sound, the final product was quite a departure, disappointing to some, but there was little question that the studio sides of *Wheels of Fire* represented the first time Cream used the recording studio to maximum advantage.

This portion of the album has worn well over the years—perhaps better than the live portion, which reviewers tended to prefer when the album was released in August 1968. Clapton's guitar work sounds as vital as ever, from the straight blues readings in "Born Under a Bad Sign" and "Sitting on Top of the World" to the absolutely incendiary solos in "White Room" and "Deserted Cities of the Heart." There is the usual playful humor ("Pressed Rat and Warthog," recited by Ginger Baker, who originally wanted his young daughter to read the poem for the record) and the psychedelic lyricism that was almost standard at the time. By using strings, horns, even tubular bells and a calliope, Cream succeeds in blending classical influences with the hard-edged contemporary sound that they helped create.

To record the second album of the set, Pappalardi shipped rented recording equipment from Los Angeles to Cream's shows at San Francisco's Fillmore West and Winterland.* A mobile recording studio, consisting

---

*The live sides of *Wheels of Fire* were subtitled "Live at the Fillmore West," but in reality only "Toad" was recorded in this venue; "Spoonful," "Traintime," and "Crossroads" were taken from the Winterland concerts.

of two eight-track machines, four speakers, and a console, manned by Pappalardi, Tom Dowd, and Bill Halverson, a young West Coast engineer, was stationed outside the auditoriums. "Tom and Bill carefully set up all the mikes onstage and made preparations," Pappalardi remembered. "I don't think the audience ever knew what was going on. The shows went on as scheduled and we didn't miss a note."

Altogether, six shows were taped, from which came the four songs included on *Wheels of Fire*, as well as numbers eventually placed on *Goodbye*, Cream's final album, and two other live albums released after Cream had disbanded. The group was in top form, playing different sets each night in order to give Pappalardi a maximum number of selections from which to choose. Pappalardi hoped to include a song focusing on the talents of each member of Cream, and in the cases of Jack Bruce and Ginger Baker, the choices were easy. Bruce was featured on "Traintime," Baker on "Toad." Clapton, however, was problematic, mainly because the guitarist and his producer could never agree on which solo constituted Clapton's best. Eventually, they decided to include "Spoonful," a nearly seventeen-minute magnum opus that caught the band giving maximum treatment to the Willie Dixon song they had originally recorded for *Fresh Cream*.

The best song—by far—on the live album was Cream's muscular work-out on Robert Johnson's "Crossroads." Singing lead for the only time on *Wheels of Fire*, Eric Clapton gave his best, most confident vocal performance of all his recordings with Cream. In the past, on "Ramblin' on My Mind" with John Mayall's Bluesbreakers, and "Four Until Late" with Cream, Clapton had preferred not to stray too far from the country-blues arrangements of the originals. On "Crossroads," he and his mates turned the song into a forceful blues rave-up, proving Robert Johnson's influence on rock 'n' roll.

The individual members of Cream always insisted that each member was a soloist within the group structure. It was this friction, caused by three instrumentalists soloing at the same time, that made the band work as a whole. Nowhere in the volume of their recorded work, onstage or in the studio, is this as apparent as on "Crossroads." Clapton plays furious solos layered over Jack Bruce's equally fiery bass runs, while Ginger Baker directs the band from a world of his own, creating a spontaneous and wholly original sound. Given the passion of the solo performances on "Crossroads," it seems almost miraculous that Cream is able to return to the song itself. On "Spoonful," as well as other live recordings, Cream had typically used the song as a framework for extensive solo work, but on "Crossroads," the spirited solos give the song even greater definition.

The four live cuts on *Wheels of Fire*, although extremely popular at the time of their release, are better seen as historical documentation of the band than as durable music. All four numbers—especially "Crossroads" and "Spoonful"—have high points capable of astonishing listeners today, but in retrospect, Baker's drum solo on "Toad" and Bruce's harmonica solo on "Traintime" seem excessive and repetitive. As a result, both solos diminish the songs' impact and detract from the tremendous talent of the two performers.

Indeed, by the time *Wheels of Fire* was released and reviewed by critics and record buyers, Eric Clapton had heard The Band's *Music from Big Pink* and was ready to move on to a simpler format with shorter songs and fewer notes, and with a new accent on the melody of the song itself.

• • •

Newsweek ran a feature on Cream in its March 18, 1968, issue, giving the band its best publicity yet in the United States. In a favorable review of one of the group's Winterland shows, the *Newsweek* writer lauded each member's virtuosity and ability to improvise, saving his highest praise for Clapton. "Both Baker and Bruce are superbly skilled musicians," wrote the reviewer, "but Clapton is the creme de la creme. . . . At best he is a melodist, scampering along a wandering line that never stops or falters in inventiveness." Interviewed for the piece, Clapton talked about the band's lengthy solos, complimenting Baker and Bruce for their abilities to jam onstage. From the tone of Clapton's comments, Cream seemed to be moving happily along, but in fact, the band was dangerously close to hitting the breaking point. When they weren't openly fighting, Baker and Bruce weren't speaking to each other. They were now in the habit of checking into separate hotels and taking separate cars to their shows.

"The bone of contention with me was the incredible volume," said Baker, noting how both Bruce and Clapton were playing into huge stacks of Marshall amps that blasted out music at such overwhelming volume as to cause a substantial buildup of wax inside his ears. In addition, since his drums were not miked, Baker was shredding his hands by pounding his drums in an effort to be heard over the din. "Friends of mine would come to the gigs and say, 'Yeah, man it was great, but the only time I heard you was during the drum solo.' The rest of the night I was completely inaudible."

Sparks flew when Baker asked Bruce to turn down the volume. Bruce wasn't about to listen to anyone tell him how to play his instrument—especially Baker, of all people, who was asserting his authority in much the same manner as he did when they played together in the Graham Bond Organisation.

For his part, Clapton had grown weary of acting as a mediator in the disputes between the two. At one time, he had tried to keep peace between them for the welfare of the band, but he was beginning to wonder about the way they worked as a unit. "I just experimented one night," he recalled. "I stopped playing halfway through a number and the other two didn't notice. . . . I just stood there and watched and they carried on playing 'til the end of the number. I thought, well fuck that."

The warfare depressed him, literally leaving him in tears on one occasion a couple of months earlier, when they were playing in Denmark. The hostilities never erupted into fisticuffs, as had happened in the Graham Bond Organisation, but the vicious verbal lashings, as far as Clapton was concerned, were incomprehensible.

If all this weren't enough, Clapton found himself in hot water on the evening of March 19, 1968, when he was arrested—along with Neil Young, Jim Messina, and Richie Furay of Buffalo Springfield—and charged with being present at a place where marijuana was being used. Clapton and the others had been at a Topanga Canyon party when sheriff's deputies from

Los Angeles County responded to a complaint about the noise at the party, and all had been taken to the station and booked. Had the penalties if found guilty been less steep, Clapton might have laughed at the irony of the bust: he could not go onstage without getting a strong whiff of marijuana smoke coming from his audience. As it was, however, if convicted he stood to receive a maximum $500 fine and/or six months in jail, not to mention the future problems he'd encounter whenever he tried to enter the United States for a concert tour. Such penalties worried him, but his attorney was able to get the charges reduced to disturbing the peace. (Even these charges failed to stick, and a few months later, Clapton was acquitted due to a lack of evidence in the case against him.)

The tour continued, taking Cream in a zigzagging pattern across the United States, the band playing in every kind of available venue, from university halls to huge convention centers. To the band members, the earnings were more than anyone could have imagined, yet the tour exacted its own price in exchange. Ginger Baker had started using heroin and on occasion became violently ill onstage. Jack Bruce kept threatening to leave the band and, at one point, when Cream was in Canada, had actually tried to catch a flight back to England; he was retrieved at the airport by roadies, who brought him back to his hotel. Fed up with all the craziness, Clapton placed a number of calls to Robert Stigwood and told him that he was quitting the band. As Baker's and Bruce's discontentment became noticeable to the public, rumors circulated that the band was breaking up—rumors that were emphatically denied.

For all the turmoil, the music kept the band united, at least as far as the public could tell. Cream's concerts sold out everywhere they went, and their performances received rave reviews. The overdubbing work on *Wheels of Fire*, accomplished during a ten-day break from the tour in April, went well, and Atlantic executives pushed to get the album out as soon as possible. As an entity, Cream seemed to be almost invincible, even as its members grew farther apart.

Oddly enough, Cream's fate was largely determined when *Rolling Stone* magazine ran a cover story on Clapton in its May 11, 1968, issue. Under normal circumstances, musicians, publicists, and record company executives would jump through hoops for such exposure, but Clapton's "Rolling Stone Interview"—his longest meeting with the American press to date—was a mixed bag. Always a reluctant interview subject, Clapton came across as cranky at times and elusive at others, revealing only sparse details about his own background and current band, preferring instead to talk about the American music scene, its fans, and its British counterparts. Significantly, he said nothing about the recording of Cream's new album.

In a companion piece, interviewer Jon Landau wrote a long review of a recent Cream concert, and his analysis was to sting Clapton for some time to come. While he found great merit in Cream's musical talent, Landau was anything but an adoring fan, and he admitted being put off by all the onstage improvisation. Labeling Clapton "a master of the blues clichés of all the post–World War II blues guitarists," the reviewer then assailed what he felt was a lack of creativity in Clapton's solos: "Clapton's problem is that while he has vast creative potential, at this time he hasn't begun to fulfill it. He is a virtuoso at performing other people's ideas." Baker and Bruce were given similar treatment.

Not surprisingly, Clapton felt betrayed by the review. Up to that point, the media had been hanging on Cream's every note, elevating the band and its members to what seemed a newly created pantheon in rock music. Clapton prided himself on his ability to play creative solos, yet here was a reviewer—and an American no less—accusing him of being derivative and unimaginative.

"All during Cream I was riding high on the 'Clapton is God' myth that had been started up," he admitted. "I was flying high on an ego trip. I was pretty sure I was the best thing happening that was popular. Then we got our first kind of bad review which, funnily enough, was in *Rolling Stone*. The magazine ran an interview with us in which we were really praising ourselves, and it was followed by a review that said how boring and repetitious our performance had been. And it was true! The ring of truth just knocked me backward; I was in a restaurant and I fainted. And after I woke up, I immediately decided that that was the end of the band."

Clapton had suspected the truth for some time, but seeing it stated in print forced him to abandon all the ego gratification and look at the music for what it was.

"Once we'd got our wings we couldn't play a note wrong," he said, remembering the incredible audience response. "I thought, this isn't right because the music we're playing is useless. OK, it had its moments, but it's not what they deserve. They're paying too much, they're applauding too much and it made me feel like a con man. I don't want to feel like a con man. I want to feel that I've earned what I've got."

Cream would continue to perform for another six months after Clapton reached his decision, but for Clapton, the period was anticlimactic. It simply took that long to leave.

five

Do What You Like
1968-69

We started out with very big ideas . . . and gradually it started to lose the original concept of what we were going to do. Finally we were just living up to our commitments—just doing the tour and playing the album. It didn't come off as well as we had intended. Our names got in the way—you know, all that super-group hype.

eric Clapton's decision to leave Cream was not made solely on the basis of a bad review. He could—and would—survive all kinds of negative commentary. Seeing the review only prodded him into reassessing the strengths and weaknesses of what he was doing at that moment. Equally influential in his decision to move on was his introduction to the work of five musicians who, rather than stroking their egos by calling themselves the Cream, simply referred to themselves as The Band.

Clapton explained: "I got hold of an acetate of The Band, listened to it and thought, 'What's going on?' I'm in a group that's a raging success, it's a *con*, it makes a lot of money, I'm trying to appreciate it, and here's a band that's been working for ten years and *that's* where I'd like to be."

The "acetate" in question was a bootleg copy of *The Basement Tapes*, the legendary recordings made by The Band with Bob Dylan in Woodstock, New York, where Dylan was staying while recovering from a serious motor-cycle accident. *The Basement Tapes*, along with The Band's first formal release, *Music from Big Pink*, heralded nothing less than a new direction for American popular music. In an era catering to consciousness frozen in a single, often drug-induced moment, The Band was harking back to a timeless spirit, their music steeped in rhythm and blues, their lyrics invoking biblical images passed down through the ages. The group's unique song arrangements, featuring two keyboards, were deceptive: what appeared to be simple, back-to-basics music was, in fact, a complex, thoughtful layering of sound, devoid of flash but as rewarding as a gulp of clear well water to a parched throat. Robbie Robertson, the group's guitarist, was a tremendously gifted instrumentalist capable of the kind of solos popular at the time, but instead of blistering eardrums with a volley of rapid-fire notes, Robertson used his guitar for effect, his fills adding subtle color and definition to any given song.

"When I heard that," said Clapton, "I felt we were dinosaurs and what we were doing was rapidly becoming outdated and boring. *Music from Big Pink* bowled me over 'cause I thought that's where everything should be going and we were nowhere near it."

Although he had no way of knowing it at the time, Clapton had a connection to this group of four Canadians and one American: both he and The Band had worked with Sonny Boy Williamson. In their early days, when they were an R & B band calling themselves the Hawks, The Band had been Williamson's backing unit during one of the bluesman's tours of the Deep South. Williamson had taken a liking to the Hawks and was considering the notion of signing them on as his permanent backing band at the time of his death in 1964. In Williamson's opinion, there was an authenticity to the Hawks' playing that had been absent in the more imitative work he had witnessed a short time earlier in England, when he had played with Eric Burdon and the Animals and the Yardbirds. The Hawks, he felt, were naturals.

A few years later, Eric Clapton drew the same conclusion, and it would influence his music more than he ever could have predicted at the time.

• • •

For the time being, however, he was still connected to the juggernaut that was taking the world by storm. Money rolled in from Cream's American tour, and the group's first two albums caught a second wind in sales. By the end of the year, *Disraeli Gears* would rank as *Cashbox*'s top-selling album.

In May, just a few weeks before returning to England, Cream appeared on "The Smothers Brothers Show," where they performed "Sunshine of Your Love" along with a lip-synched version of their new single "Anyone for Tennis?" Written for use in the motion picture soundtrack of *The Savage Seven*, "Anyone for Tennis?" was another collaboration between Clapton and Martin Sharp, though it proved to be far less successful than their initial effort, "Tales of Brave Ulysses." Clapton struggled for some time to find a melody to match Sharp's lyrics but never came up with anything that fully satisfied him. The song was recorded during the *Wheels of Fire* sessions, but rather than include it on the new album, Cream issued it as a single, backed by Ginger Baker's "Pressed Rat and Warthog." The single flopped miserably, tarnishing an otherwise outstanding year of record releases.

Upon their return to England, Cream decided that it was no longer possible to ignore or deny the persistent, circulating rumors about the band's impending separation. The group had kept up a fairly good front throughout the weeks on end of one-nighters in the United States, dismissing rumors that all was not well, despite what was now open evidence to the contrary. "All rumors of a breakup are denied," Clapton emphatically informed *Rolling Stone* near the end of Cream's American tour, though he knew otherwise.

It was time to face the truth, but it wasn't easy. *Wheels of Fire* was about to be issued, and it seemed wrong to announce the breakup of the band on the eve of the release of its magnum opus; there had to be some sense of closure. With this in mind, Robert Stigwood announced that Cream would indeed be splitting up as rumored, but not before a farewell tour of the United States and a final appearance at London's Royal Albert Hall.

The news was greeted with mixed feelings, especially in England, where fans were disappointed, bitter and angry that the band had chosen to spend the bulk of its existence in the United States instead of its own homeland.

Questioned about this perceived incongruity, Jack Bruce offered a very candid response. Cream, he said, had always aspired to make good music and good money—in that order—and the United States was where the money was. They could tour nonstop in England and never enjoy the kind of payrolls they picked up in America. "It is simply a question of pure economics," Bruce concluded.

The economic angle was impossible to dispute. In the United States, the demand for *Wheels of Fire* was so great that the record had achieved gold record status before it was shipped, and it would eventually become the first two-record set to go platinum. With the exception of the Royal Albert Hall, no English concert venues could compete with the enormous halls found in every major American city. It only made good business sense that these musicians, all with bright but still very uncertain futures, would cash in while the money was there for the taking.

For all their popularity in the American press, and the string of good reviews they had received in the past, Cream could not escape a brutal *Rolling Stone* review of *Wheels of Fire*, written by Jann Wenner, the publication's publisher-editor. "Cream," began Wenner, "is good at a number of things; unfortunately song-writing and recording are not among them." The review only got worse. Wenner had very little use for the studio album. "White Room," he wrote, was a pointless repeat of "Tales of Brave Ulysses," suffering from what Wenner called "the Sonny Bono-ish production job"; "Passing the Time," in the reviewer's opinion, was "a stone bore." Jack Bruce was savaged throughout the piece, criticized for bass playing that was "much too busy," for a harmonica style that was "loudly amateurish," and for a voice that was not suited to blues singing. Wenner was amused by "Pressed Rat and Warthog" and wrote kindly of "As You Said," but beside these songs and "Politician," which he damned with faint praise, he found very little to get excited about on the studio record.

The live album fared much better in the review. It was, wrote Wenner, "the kind of thing that people who have seen Cream walk away raving about and it's good to at last have it on record." After trashing "Traintime" as an unworthy effort, Wenner went on to cite "Toad," "Crossroads," and "Spoonful" as the highlights of the album, before concluding his lengthy review with its only indisputable truth: "The album will be a monster."

Wheels of Fire moved up the charts quickly. Significantly, rather than release a single from the album to help goose its sales, the record company issued "Sunshine of Your Love," backed by "SWLABR"—both from *Disraeli Gears*—as Cream's fifth single. The marketing strategy worked: the huge success of the single helped maintain interest in *Disraeli Gears*, giving Cream two albums on the charts to go along with its most recent single. There seemed to be no stopping the band.

· · ·

Clapton did very little resting during Cream's brief hiatus from touring. He deepened his friendship with George Harrison, and from the association sprang a number of sessions projects, the most notable being the work he did for the Beatles' *White Album*.

Harrison and Clapton had met almost four years earlier, when the Yardbirds played as part of the Beatles' 1964 Christmas program. While talking about music, the two determined that they differed in their musical preferences, Harrison favoring American rockabilly to Clapton's American blues. There had been the usual uneasiness that occurs when members of competing bands get together, but these feelings were overshadowed by their genuine high regard for each other. Clapton believed that Harrison's talents were being stifled in the Beatles, where John Lennon and Paul McCartney were always at the forefront, and he tried to encourage Harrison to take more of a step forward in the band.

The two saw each other occasionally over the next several years, though commitments to their respective bands kept their friendship from developing further. Then, in late 1967, Harrison contacted Clapton about working with him on a non-Beatles project—the soundtrack for Joe Massot's film *Wonderwall*. The music featured an Eastern sound influenced by the Beatles' visit to India, and Harrison was looking for a Western sound to run counterpoint to the dominant sounds of sitar, sarod, tabla, and tambura.

Clapton—listed on the album's credits as Eddie Clayton—visited the Abbey Road studios and recorded blues guitar lines for some of Harrison's music, thus beginning a sideline foray into sound track recording that he would engage in, off and on, for the next twenty-five years.

With the establishment of Apple, their record company, the Beatles were branching off into producing other artists' albums, and with their reputations and connections, it took very little effort on their part to assemble an impressive roster of studio musicians for any given project. For the George Harrison–produced Jackie Lomax album, Clapton found himself working in the studio with the makeshift band of himself and Harrison on guitar, Klaus Voorman on bass, Nicky Hopkins on piano, and Ringo Starr on drums. After months of free-form onstage performance, the loose, congenial studio setting for these recordings represented a welcome change from the onstage competing and offstage fighting. That same month, Clapton recorded four songs as a sessions guitarist for his old friend Mike Vernon, who was producing an album for blues singer Martha Velez, using a studio lineup that included Jack Bruce, Christine McVie, Mitch Mitchell, Jim Capaldi, and Brian Auger.

Of all Clapton's sessions work, none would equal the recognition he received for the time he spent in Abbey Road Studio Number Two on September 6, when he joined the Beatles to play the memorable guitar solo on George Harrison's song "While My Guitar Gently Weeps." At first, Clapton was hesitant to accept Harrison's invitation to play on the cut. No one, he pointed out to Harrison, ever sat in as a guest musician on a Beatles album.

"He wanted me to play the guitar on the cut because he couldn't do it the way he wanted to hear it," Clapton recalled, making a point to mention that he did not agree with Harrison's misgivings about his own ability to play the solo himself. "I thought he should have played guitar on it," continued Clapton, "but it was great for me to do it. We agreed that I wouldn't get paid for it or have my name mentioned."

Harrison had his own vivid recollection of the historic session. According to Harrison, the other three Beatles didn't care for the song, but Clapton's playing swayed their opinions. The solo, one of the best to grace any Beatles album, was wonderfully expressive—an exact match with Harrison's moody lyrics and melody. Even so, Clapton was apprehensive about the way it worked for the band.

"We listened to it back," remembered Harrison, "and he said, 'Ah, there's a problem though; it's not Beatley enough.' So we put it through the ADT [automatic double-tracker], to wobble it a bit."

Despite the idea of not listing him in the album's credits, Clapton's participation in the session became one of the music industry's worst-kept secrets. Beatles fans were obsessive about knowing the most minute detail behind the recording of every Beatles song, and it took them no time at all to determine that Cream's famous axman had applied his skills to one of the *White Album*'s most notable songs, or to uncover the news that his sweet tooth had been the inspiration for "Savoy Truffle," another Harrison entry on the album.

The Clapton-Harrison friendship would help stimulate valuable work on the part of both musicians in future years. It would also lead Clapton to some of the high and low points of his life, beginning when Harrison introduced him to his wife, setting in motion a chain of events that both men were essentially incapable of altering.

• • •

Cream's farewell tour opened in Oakland on October 4, 1968, and from there the band moved on to perform in fourteen cities, including Los Angeles, Chicago, Dallas, Miami, and New York. Gone were the days of the band's playing small to medium-sized concert venues; for this tour, Cream was booked into the largest halls available, with gross earnings of $25,000 per show—a whopping figure for a concert at the time. Many of the shows were recorded for a projected final album.

Cream was given a hero's welcome throughout the tour. Packed houses greeted them everywhere, and fans, perhaps sensing that they were witnesses to important music history, roared their approval from the moment Cream walked onstage and tuned their instruments to the final note of their encore. During their performance in New York's Madison Square Garden, Clapton, Bruce, and Baker were presented their platinum records for *Wheels of Fire*. Nineteen sixty-eight had been a very rough year, with Americans having to deal with the assassinations of Martin Luther King, Jr., and Robert Kennedy, as well as tremendous urban violence capped by a police riot at the Democratic National Convention in Chicago. Cream was in no position to heal wounds caused by such brutality, but their music, like all welcome music, provided at least a temporary diversion from the woes of what seemed like a world living on spiritual and political faultlines.

Even in such turbulent times, Clapton continued to define his role as that of an entertainer. Though it was fashionable for rock bands to issue songs with a sense of social conscience—the Beatles released "Revolution" and the Rolling Stones "Street Fighting Man" in 1968—Clapton preferred to take a different approach. "Politician"—a staple at all Cream concerts— expressed a cynical view of politics, and "Anyone for Tennis?" had been a stab at social commentary, but for the most part, Clapton remained uncomfortable with the idea of being anyone's spokesperson or role model.

Before leaving the United States, Clapton took a side trip to upstate New York, where he met with Bob Dylan and members of The Band. He had been introduced to Robbie Robertson when Cream was in Los Angeles, and Robertson had invited him to meet the rest of the group in upstate New York. "I had to go and see what they looked like," Clapton said, "so I went up to Woodstock and visited, and they turned out to be *great* people, *incredibly* great people, very intelligent, very tight."

To Clapton, these down-to-earth people "looked like characters from the Hole in the Wall Gang," as opposed to Cream, who, he felt, had become "psychedelic loonies." He couldn't help but be impressed by The Band's low-key approach to making music, and by the way the group's members got along, which seemed to be the opposite of what Cream had become.

Still, for all of Cream's problems, there was a kind of nostalgic sadness at seeing the band come to an end. No group of musicians could have gone through the trials of heavy-duty touring and recording without members' developing some deep feelings toward each other, and the intensity of the love-hate relationship between the members of Cream would never again be matched in Clapton's professional life. In the midst of all the warfare, some incredible music had been produced.

At no time was this as apparent as when Cream took the stage on November 26 for two final performances at the Royal Albert Hall. Backing the band was a relatively unknown group calling itself Yes, and Rory Gallagher's band, Taste. Both shows were sold out, and thousands of turned-away fans milled around in the street outside the hall, battling the odds of finding an occasional stray ticket, keeping a vigil that both honored and mourned the end of the band. Onstage, Cream ran through a set list of their biggest hits, performing selections from all three of their albums. The first show, Clapton would later lament, was cut shorter than Cream would have liked because the hall needed to be cleared and prepared for the second performance. In both shows, Cream played as a unit, all differences set aside for one last, memorable evening. Fans rushed the stage and showered Clapton with confetti, the band played three encores, and no one wanted the party to end. For a few fleeting moments, all three members of Cream, elated by the great music made that evening and the crowd's overwhelming response to it, considered calling off the breakup of the group.

"I was really depressed for two or three days afterwards," Jack Bruce said. "It was quite moving. I just didn't expect it."

Clapton was also surprised by the fans' reaction—"It was a great reception, as good as any we have had anywhere," he said—but he realized, as did the others, that one good evening was not enough to hold the group together. The band's problems had never been resolved.

As a parting gesture, Cream released its fourth album, *Goodbye*, which, like their previous recording, combined live and studio work. Cream had originally intended to release another two-record set, similar in format to *Wheels of Fire*, but they did not have enough suitable material to pull it off. Rather than settle on substandard material which, in all likelihood, their fans would have purchased anyway, Clapton, Bruce, and Baker selected three standout concert performances ("I'm So Glad," "Politician," and

"Sitting on Top of the World") and three studio-produced songs—one written by each member of the band. The contrast between the onstage and studio bands was once again evident: the live material sizzled with energy unleashed, the accent squarely on the virtuosity of the three individual musicians, whereas the studio material focused on melody and song arrangement.

The new Jack Bruce–Pete Brown number, "Doing That Scrapyard Thing," was a nostalgic look at better days, complete with the kind of striking images characteristic of all of Brown's lyrics; to achieve the unusual organlike sound running throughout the song, Clapton used a Leslie speaker that had been specially set up for guitar. Ginger Baker's contribution to *Goodbye*, "What a Bringdown," was a commentary on the group's breakup, cleverly concealed in disjointed lyrics.

The Clapton piece, "Badge," cowritten by George Harrison, was far and away the highlight of the album. As Harrison recalled, the song was written when he, Clapton, and Ringo Starr were at his place, relaxing and working on nonsensical lyrics. "That whole song was quite silly," Harrison told interviewer Timothy White. "Ringo was sitting around drinking, out of his brain, saying anything. The part about 'Our kid, now he's married to Mabel,' well, 'our kid' is a common Liverpool expression that usually means your younger brother. We were amusing ourselves."

The song's title stemmed from a funny misunderstanding that occurred that same evening, when Clapton misread Harrison's handwriting. "We were writing down the lyrics at George's house," Clapton remembered, "and as Ringo and I were shouting them out George was writing them down. It said Badge [on the lyric sheet] but what it meant was actually the bridge. I said that's a good name for a song and it stuck."

Neither Harrison nor Starr received a writing credit on the album jacket (though Harrison would be cited in subsequent songwriting credits); nor was Harrison cited for his work as a guest guitarist on the song. On the finished product, Harrison played rhythm guitar until the song's bridge, at which point Clapton joined in, his guitar plugged into a Leslie to achieve the distinctive arpeggio that accents the bridge. Harrison's contribution to the recording was noted only through the use of the humorous pseudonym L'Angelo Misterioso.

Oddly enough, "Badge," an immensely popular song throughout Clapton's career, went nowhere when it was initially issued as a single, backed by "What a Bringdown," in April 1969. Perhaps this was due to the success of *Goodbye*, which topped the charts in both the United States and England, or because the public was being fed an excess of product ("White Room"/"Those Were the Days" had been released in January 1969); whatever the reason, the song's chart failure was an unfortunate close to the recording career of a band that, in just three years' time, had created a body of work that greatly influenced the direction that rock music would be taking for some time to come.

• • •

The Cream experience left Clapton burned out and feeling as if he were betraying the path he wanted to follow as a musician.

"I've been on the road seven years and I'm going to take a holiday," he said at the time. "I went off on a lot of different things since Cream formed. But I found I have floated back to straight blues playing. I got really hung up, trying to write pop songs, and create a pop image. It was a shame because I was not being true to myself. I am and always will be a blues guitarist."

Cream had never been a blues band per se; if anything, it derived its musical structure from jazz combos. In this framework, Clapton was strictly hit or miss. On the good nights—and there were many—he could play forever, taking his audiences into creative regions of his mind that seemed to explode with musical imagery and color. On the bad nights—and there were more than he wanted to face or admit—he would be filling time, running over familiar turf. Either way, he was rarely reciting the blues, at least not the way he wanted to play them, and he was bothered that his fans seemed willing to accept anything he had to offer.

Years after the breakup of Cream, Clapton was able to analyze the band's successes and failures with an objective eye. On a personal level, he had paid a devil's price for all the fame and fortune, exchanging his sense of identity for the security of being in a successful band: "All through Cream, I was lost, really, *trying* to find an identity but not really knowing whether I had one or not." He was, he concluded, a kind of musical chameleon, adapting to the musical standard the band had set.

It was, he'd say, one hell of a ride while it lasted. "With Cream," he explained, "there was a camaraderie that not many people could have experienced in their lifetimes. I mean the three of us, chemically, were so suited to one another that there were times when we would all get stoned— we did a lot of drugs in those days, nothing heavy, but acid and grass— and we started to develop a complete language that no one else could understand. And I think that only a really tight family type of group can really experience or understand what that type of relationship is like. We had a rapport where we could be in a room, the three of us, surrounded by people and no one else could get *in* at all. It was a tight, closed shop and we could direct that malevolently, or humorously, at anyone we liked. In any situation, we were totally secure."

In the period immediately following the Albert Hall concerts, Clapton hung around with friends, avoiding the public light and enjoying a break from the action. With earnings from Cream, he purchased Hurtwood Edge, a sprawling, twenty-room mansion in Ewhurst, Surrey. The fortress, complete with pools and gardens and set on spacious grounds in the Surrey countryside, was just the kind of retreat that Clapton wanted. He was far too famous to walk around London unnoticed, and he faced a constant stream of visitors whenever he was in his apartment in the city. Sergeant Norman Pilcher was busy earning his reputation for busting rock stars during drug raids, and Clapton wanted no part of him. At Hurtwood Edge, he could keep the world at arm's length.

There was one person Clapton wanted to see at his estate, an attractive young woman named Alice Ormsby-Gore. The daughter of Lord David Harlech, Alice caught Eric's eye when she visited Hurtwood Edge with some interior designer friends hired to work on the estate. Clapton, who could be shy around women to begin with, took a cautious approach with

Alice: not only was she the daughter of Britain's former ambassador to the United States but she was only sixteen years old at the time of their meeting.

Clapton moved slowly with her, taking her through a formal courtship lasting nearly a year, before asking her to move in with him. During that period, he got to know Lord Harlech and his family well. Lord Harlech liked Clapton and didn't discourage him from seeing his daughter. For Clapton, this was important. He'd had a number of girlfriends in the past, including a model he'd dated and even lived with during his time in Cream, but none had quite struck his fancy like Alice. With the exception of his future wife, Clapton would spend more time with Alice than with any other woman in his life.

• • •

Clapton's holiday from the music scene, for all his good intentions, was short-lived. The Rolling Stones were putting together a Christmas television special that they were calling "Rock 'n' Roll Circus," and they invited Clapton to join a stellar lineup that included the Stones, The Who, John Lennon and Yoko Ono, Taj Mahal, Jethro Tull, and a host of others. Clapton spent most of his time jamming with a makeshift group made up of himself on lead guitar, John Lennon on rhythm guitar, Mitch Mitchell on drums, and Keith Richards on bass. The band ran through several takes of the Beatles' "Yer Blues," as well as Buddy Holly's "Peggy Sue," on which Mick Jagger appeared as a guest vocalist. Sadly, the Rolling Stones judged their own performances to be substandard and the show never reached the air, though bootlegs of the show circulated for years to come.

Clapton enjoyed the sessions, and while he did not miss the craziness characteristic of Cream's final months on the road, he was not ready to quit touring or performing either. In mulling over what direction he wanted to take, he kept coming back to the idea of forming a band with a keyboard player. The keyboards on the studio cuts on *Goodbye*, largely influenced by the music of The Band, had given Cream's music a new sound, and Clapton wanted to continue in this direction.

Fortunately for Clapton, Stevie Winwood, one of rock's premier keyboardists and vocalists, was currently unemployed. Winwood's band, Traffic, had recently broken up for many of the same reasons that had led to the disbanding of Cream. Clapton had known Winwood from Stevie's days with the Spencer Davis Group, and over the years both had agreed that it would be ideal if they were to work together someday.

Winwood owned a secluded cottage in Berkshire, and Clapton stopped by one day in late December to pay an informal visit. Not surprisingly, the two wound up jamming together for hours, improvising from twelve-bar blues or playing songs they both knew. The chemistry was right, and the two renewed their hopes of working with each other on a project.

Clapton and Winwood met frequently over the ensuing weeks, playing at Winwood's cottage or at Hurtwood Edge. Winwood wrote a handful of new songs that he and Clapton rehearsed. Both had discussed the possibility of forming a band—perhaps using Otis Redding's rhythm section of Donald "Duck" Dunn and Al Jackson—but neither was in any particular rush to do so. That changed in a hurry when Ginger Baker joined them at one of their jam sessions. Baker made no secret of his wanting to join any band they might be putting together, and Winwood was in favor of it.

Clapton, however, was ambivalent. He and Baker had grown very close while they were in Cream, and Clapton had promised Baker that they would work together on his next project, but hooking up with him so soon after breaking away from Cream was not an ideal scenario. Clapton hated the prospects of acting again as referee in any personality clashes that might pop up, and he feared that any band with Clapton and Baker as members would be seen as a new permutation of Cream, which would only bring back some of the undue expectations and adulation he was trying to escape. Baker rehearsed with Clapton and Winwood on subsequent occasions, building his own case through his music and his open campaigning for the job, and that, along with Winwood's persistent belief that Baker could only make the projected band's music better, wore down Clapton's resistance. Baker was officially in. Lacking a name for the band, the trio simply called itself Clapton, Baker, Winwood.

The press was on the case almost from the beginning, and by the time the group entered London's Morgan Recording Studios in February to lay down the initial tracks for its first recording, rumors of a new supergroup were running rampant in music papers and magazines on both sides of the Atlantic. In the United States, *Rolling Stone* took a low-key approach, noting that Clapton was working on a new album for Atlantic Atco, "the implication—but implication only—being that Winwood will be on the album with him." For his part, Clapton similarly tried to downplay the formation of a band. For all he knew, he told the British press, Winwood might be added to a new version of Cream.

In many respects, the new band bore a strong resemblance to Winwood's early edition of Traffic, with Winwood writing virtually all of the new material, taking all of the lead vocals, and playing keyboards, guitar, and bass. Clapton had one new song, "Presence of the Lord," a piece inspired partly by his religious convictions and partly by his feelings of contentment after moving into his new home. Baker chipped in "Do What You Like," a song designed to allow each band member a substantial solo. Much of the early studio work was devoted to the band's jamming and getting used to playing together, the group working on covers of Billy Roberts's "Hey Joe," Buddy Holly's "Well All Right," and Sam Myers's "Sleeping in the Ground."

If Clapton thought the new band was going to have all the time it needed to develop into a finely tuned unit, he was sadly mistaken: as reports of the group's recording endeavors made the rounds in the music papers, the clamor for an album and tour increased. Concert promoters offered the band huge sums for appearances, and the press portrayed the band, which had yet to offer any music to the public, as rock's answer to the second coming. Such unfounded faith amused Clapton, who suggested that the new group be called Blind Faith. From such cynicism rose a band that was as ill-fated as it was talented.

. . .

To work effectively onstage, Blind Faith needed a steady bass player, and after considering a number of possibilities, the group settled on Rick Grech, a member of Family. An adequate bassist well suited to blending into a band already known for three superstar musicians, Grech will always be remembered for bringing electric violin to rock 'n' roll. His violin solo on "Sea of Joy" would become one of the high points of Blind Faith concerts.

Grech was touring with Family when he received an invitation to join Blind Faith, and he immediately joined the new band in the studio for work on their album and rehearsals for the group's inaugural tour. Even after all the practice and time together in the studio, the band was still in no condition to take its show on the road: it had yet to establish its own sound or identity, and its members needed more time to develop into a cohesive unit.

That much was apparent when Blind Faith was officially unveiled at a free concert on June 7, 1969, in London's Hyde Park. An ocean of over 100,000 fans, pumped up from weeks of media hype, greeted the band in one of the largest festival gatherings to that point. The band opened with their cover of "Well All Right," followed by Stevie Winwood's "Sea of Joy." Clapton kept a very low profile, looking every bit the sideman as he huddled next to his Marshall amps and played along. His bluesy solo on the next song, "Sleeping in the Ground," established his presence as a major player in the band, but he was again in the background when Blind Faith offered a reading of "Under My Thumb" that paled next to the Rolling Stones' original. Three covers in the first four numbers: hardly an auspicious beginning for a supergroup.

The band's performance improved measurably when it moved into the original material, including an electric arrangement of Stevie Winwood's beautiful ballad "Can't Find My Way Home" and Ginger Baker's drum solo number "Do What You Like." Baker could still ignite a crowd with his trademark double-bass-drum roll, and there was plenty of fire in the Clapton-Winwood guitar exchange on "Had to Cry Today." Still, the overall quality of the show left much to be desired. Those expecting an unparalleled performance from some of rock's most respected musicians were instead served a competent, yet far from definitive, workout.

Clapton himself expressed disappointment in Blind Faith's debut performance. "I came offstage at that Hyde Park concert shaking like a leaf because I felt once again that I'd let people down," he said.

The band members agreed that they needed more time to smooth out their repertoire, but the tour dates had already been set. After a brief, eight-date excursion to Scandinavian countries, Blind Faith departed for the United States for a string of dates in amphitheaters and stadiums that, in retrospect, proved the ruling power of the dollar in the music industry. The money was on the table, and everyone—band, management, record company, and concert promoters—reached out for a share of the take. As a general rule, the concerts were brief and the sound was lousy. Fans welcomed Blind Faith with long, thunderous standing ovations before each show, only to grow restless when they could not hear the band, or when they realized that they had been charged exorbitant ticket prices to see a group that, by all indications, could still use more rehearsal.

Most alarming of all was a pattern of violence that followed the band as it made its way across the country. The huge venues demanded large security forces, and a number of Blind Faith gigs were marred by clashes between police and concertgoers. After the concert in New York's Madison Square Garden, fans rushed to the stage in search of souvenirs, only to be beaten back by a phalanx of police. The ensuing riot, which lasted over half an hour, was as ugly as anything the band members had ever witnessed in a concert setting: fans were beaten senseless, Winwood's electric piano was destroyed in the mayhem, and Ginger Baker, who had tried to help restore order from the stage, was clubbed by a police officer mistaking him for a hippie troublemaker.

Such tension was bound to have a profound effect on the band, and Winwood and Grech suffered the most. From their experiences on Cream's farewell tour, Clapton and Baker had faced enormous, demanding audiences, and they had also dealt with the despair that accompanies a bad night onstage. Neither Winwood or Grech had faced such an overwhelming tour experience in their former bands. Winwood, for one, admitted that the blame for the fiasco ultimately belonged to the band.

"The show *was* vulgar, crude, disgusting," he said. "It lacked integrity.

There were huge crowds everywhere, full of mindless adulation, mostly due to Eric and Ginger's success with Cream and, to a more modest extent, my own impact. The combination led to a situation where we could have gone on and farted and gotten a massive reaction. *That* was one of the times I got so uninspired.

"The attitude backstage was, 'These people think we're great, and we better damned well *give* them something great,' but it didn't help. And it wasn't the audiences' fault. The blame all rightfully belonged in our laps. We did not sound good live, due to the simple lack of experience being a band. We'd had no natural growth, and it was very evident onstage."

Nor, in such circumstances, was there any chance of growth within the band. As Blind Faith worked its way westward across the United States, playing July dates in Philadelphia, Baltimore, Kansas City, and Chicago, as well as in Toronto and Montreal in Canada, the band members grew farther apart. Winwood and Baker were at odds, as were Clapton and Baker, but rather than try to work things out, as he had done in Cream, Clapton started to spend more time with Blind Faith's support group, Delaney and Bonnie and Friends.

Clapton and Delaney Bramlett met after Blind Faith's Madison Square Garden debacle. Clapton had watched the Delaney and Bonnie show that night, and he had been impressed that the group appeared to be enjoying itself while making good music, seemingly oblivious to all the hoopla surrounding the Blind Faith circus. Clapton was additionally pleased to discover that Bramlett, a Mississippi native, shared his taste in music, particularly his devotion to Robert Johnson.

Over the course of the next several days, Clapton and Bramlett cemented their friendship. With three days off between the Madison Square Garden show and their next scheduled appearance in Philadelphia, Winwood, Grech, and Baker had all flown back to England, hoping to regroup their thoughts in the wake of the violence in New York. Clapton stayed behind and hung out with Delaney Bramlett. The two talked in great detail about the music business and their favorite performers. At one point, Bramlett mentioned that Clapton had a good singing voice and asked him why he didn't sing more onstage. Clapton replied that it wasn't necessary for him to sing much in Blind Faith—not when the band had one of the finest vocalists in rock music. Besides, Clapton added, he didn't have a lot of confidence in his voice. Bramlett was hearing none of it. If Clapton didn't use his gift, Bramlett argued, God would take it away.

Clapton held his ground. "No, man," he said. "I can't sing."

"Yes you can," insisted Bramlett. "Hit this note: Ahhhh . . ."

It took some effort, but Clapton finally matched the note. Once that barrier had been broken, Clapton gave Bramlett's encouragement more serious consideration. "I started to feel that if I was to gain his respect, I ought to really pursue this," he recalled. "That night we started talking about making a solo album with his band."

· · ·

Just as Clapton's exposure to The Band's music had spelled the beginning of the end for Cream, so did his developing friendship with Delaney Bramlett initiate his withdrawal from Blind Faith. In Clapton's mind, the contrast between his and Bramlett's bands was so evident that it took very little thinking to determine which direction he wanted to take. Blind Faith was a big, awkward machine, a music-industry product lumbering on artificial appendages, making plenty of money but edging nevertheless toward the scrapyard. Delaney and Bonnie and Friends, though not as musically accomplished as the individual members of Blind Faith, were having *fun*, rocking out nightly with their blend of blues, gospel, and rock 'n' roll.

What fans and critics alike could not understand was that Clapton *wanted* to disappear into the framework of a band. He might have been naive in thinking that he could ever again be anything but the meal ticket for whatever band he was in—the onstage focus of attention, certainly—but he was neither willing nor prepared to assume leadership in any group. In Cream, he had willfully deferred to the more forceful personalities of Jack Bruce and Ginger Baker; in Blind Faith, it was Baker and Stevie Winwood. Throughout Blind Faith's tour of the United States, reporters annoyed Clapton with questions about why he didn't step forward more often, why he allowed Winwood to dominate the band. Such queries, to Clapton, were pointless: as he continued to develop his identity as a musician, he had no desire to lead or to follow; he only wanted to belong.

The tour matured Clapton as an artist and as a person. He had always distrusted the seductive factors of big bucks and fan adulation, but he had also felt that he could exert some kind of personal control over them. His experiences in Cream, especially toward the end, had eroded some of these beliefs, but to nowhere near the extent of the Blind Faith tour, which forced him to face the possibility of living in a wasteland of his own making. Clapton reacted by pulling away from the band and retreating to the safety of another. At the same time, he began to examine his spiritual side.

To a great extent, Clapton's self-examination had its roots in a strange incident that occurred after Blind Faith's concert in Minneapolis on August 1. Clapton's song "Presence of the Lord," played at every Blind Faith gig, attracted the attention of the Christians in his audience, and after the Minneapolis show, he answered a knock on his dressing room door, to be greeted by two young Christians who had somehow managed to elude the arena's security system. The two men presented Clapton with what had to have been the most unusual request he'd heard in his time in the music business.

"Can we pray with you?" they asked.

Not knowing how to respond, Clapton went along with them. The three knelt down and prayed and, as Clapton recalled, he felt very peaceful when they were finished. While they were talking afterward, Clapton offered to show the two men a Jimi Hendrix poster that he'd picked up at a head shop earlier in the day. When he pulled the poster from the package and unrolled it, he was stunned to find another poster—a portrait of Jesus that he'd never seen before—instead.

In all likelihood, a swap of posters had taken place somewhere along the line. Or it's even possible that the wrong poster had been packaged at the head shop. Clapton, however, viewed the poster of Jesus as nothing short of a miracle, and his visitors were inclined to agree. The young Christians, Clapton reasoned, had been sent to his dressing room door for a purpose, and he would do well not to ignore what might have been a true religious experience. Over the following weeks, he regaled anyone who would listen with accounts of the miracle, driving the Cream entourage half crazy with his zeal. "I ran around, telling everyone I was a born-again Christian and God-knows-what," he said, rather sheepishly, years later.

At the time, though, the experience represented an important anchor in Clapton's life. The name, Blind Faith, might have been coined in a rock star's cynicism, but as Clapton toured with the group, he found himself groping to find something to believe in within the context of his music— or his own life. These feelings, of course, were not far removed from the backbone of the old Negro spirituals, or from contemporary blues for that matter, in which singers depended upon their spiritual strength for survival. Clapton's quasi-religious experience, coming when it did, afforded him at least temporary faith and strength.

Clapton always considered himself a spiritual person, but not in the openly religious, churchgoing sense. He would pray from time to time, either in thanksgiving or in supplication, but he never allowed himself the luxury of using his faith as a crutch.

"I suppose I'm kind of a casual Christian," he answered, when asked about his spirituality. "I believe that if I pray for something, then it may come along; if I don't then I don't get it. You know, it's just good to be good, if you can be good."

Although he had great tolerance for others' beliefs—tolerance that would be sorely tested on a number of occasions by George Harrison's religious fervor—Clapton had little patience for people who waited around to be saved. In times of trouble, it was up to the individual, not some act of God, to provide the path to survival.

• • •

Blind Faith's self-titled album was released on August 19, 1969, just as the band was playing out the second half of its American tour. Preorders for the recording approached the half million mark, but distribution in the United States hit a snag when a controversy broke out over the album's cover photo of a pubescent eleven-year-old girl, shown naked from the waist up, standing in a field and holding what appeared to be a silver model airplane. The sight of a nude child, holding what could have been interpreted as a phallic symbol, outraged many dealers, who refused to sell the records. Atlantic Records responded by printing an alternate cover showing the four band members in rehearsal at Clapton's estate. The album quickly rose to number one on both the American and British charts, but the controversy over the Bob Ciderman photograph continued.*

Unfortunately, the backlash to the cover art deflected attention from what turned out to be a surprisingly good effort, given the short period of time the band had been together when it was recorded. Producer Jimmy Miller, who had worked in the studio with Traffic, succeeded in combining some of the best elements of Traffic and Cream in a way that showcased the wide-ranging talents of each musician without the heavy-handedness found on some of the earlier Cream and Traffic albums. Cream fans might have been surprised by Clapton's acoustic guitar and Baker's brushes and splash cymbals on "Can't Find My Way Home," whereas Traffic fans might have raised an eyebrow hearing Winwood play the kind of rock guitar licks the world expected from Clapton. With the exception of "Do What You Like," on which all four members were given a chance to solo, Miller maintained a subtle approach to the production. Solos were kept short, the songs held to a reasonable length. Clapton's wah-wah solo on "Presence of the Lord" topped the list of the album's highlights, which also included Baker's drum solo on "Do What You Like," Grech's violin work on "Sea of Joy," and Winwood's keyboard work on "Well All Right."

Looking back on the album, long after they were able to separate the band that made the record from the one that toured the United States, both Steve Winwood and Eric Clapton expressed pleasure with the way *Blind Faith* turned out.

---

*For years after the album's release, people speculated that the young red-haired girl in the picture was Ginger Baker's daughter, Neatty. In fact, the subject of the photo was the daughter of a friend of Ciderman's.

"The album stands up very well on its own merits," said Winwood. "It's better to have a good record and a bad tour than vice versa. Memories always mellow, but the record lingers on intact. At least the album indicates that we could get on a bit musically."

Clapton agreed with the assessment. "I think it's a lovely album. I like its looseness. It's like a supersession record, except it's got a little something more than that. You can feel there's a lot of longing in the band."

The only longing the band had as it wound down its U.S. tour was to honor its commitments and get out of the country in one piece. No matter where they played, there seemed to be tension between concert attendees and security forces. At times it seemed as if the kids were more interested in heckling the police than in the music being played onstage. To refocus attention and keep peace, Blind Faith resorted to playing popular Cream or Traffic songs.

The lunacy hit bottom at the band's concerts in Los Angeles and Phoenix. At the Los Angeles Forum, the four Blind Faith members looked out at a line of police standing in front of the stage; skirmishes broke out everywhere, and the house lights were turned on three times during the concert so police could chase down and arrest unruly fans. Phoenix was even worse. The show at the Memorial Coliseum, the band's last gig in the continental United States before leaving for a finale in Hawaii, had an ominous prelude when the police barred Clapton from walking out into the crowd to watch the Delaney and Bonnie set. The real trouble occurred after a relatively uneventful show, when Blind Faith was joined onstage by both of their support bands for the customary encore jam of "Sunshine of Your Love." Bonnie Bramlett was dancing at the edge of the stage when a plank broke, sending her into a ten-foot free fall. In the confusion that followed, Delaney Bramlett was clubbed with a nightstick as he rushed to his wife's aid, Ginger Baker confronted a policeman about the incident and was nearly arrested, and a full-scale riot broke out in the audience. The band barely escaped the stage.

Clapton had seen enough, and though there had been no formal discussion about breaking up the band, he had no doubt that it had played its last gig in Hawaii. In the months ahead, there would be rumors galore about a Blind Faith tour of England and Europe, or of another album from the band. None of it would occur. Winwood would look into assembling a new edition of Traffic, as well as recording with Baker and Grech in Air Force.

Having faced the demise of two high-profile groups in less than a year's time, Clapton was prepared to try something entirely different.

Why Does Love Got to Be So Sad?
1969–70

It was a make-believe band. It wasn't me, it was another band. We were all hiding inside it. Derek & the Dominos—the whole thing was . . . assumed. So it couldn't last. I mean, I had to come out and admit that I was being me. I mean, being Derek was a cover for the fact that I was trying to steal someone else's wife.

After Blind Faith's final concert in Honolulu, Eric Clapton flew to Los Angeles to spend a few days with Delaney and Bonnie Bramlett. Delaney still hoped to produce a Clapton solo album, and he continued to work on Eric about developing his singing. He also believed that Clapton should pursue his talents as a songwriter. "Presence of the Lord" had demonstrated Clapton's ability to write a wonderful song, and Bramlett urged him to try it again. At first Clapton was reticent. He was a guitar player, he argued. In Blind Faith and Cream, he had been quite content to let Stevie Winwood and Jack Bruce handle the singing and songwriting chores; they were more adept at them than he was. Why not stick to what you do best, he wondered, and leave the rest to those who managed it better?

Bramlett was an interesting example to the contrary. He was by no estimation the world's greatest singer or songwriter, and his guitar skills were, at best, passable. Nevertheless, he fronted a band that included such notable musicians as Bobby Whitlock, Jim Gordon, Carl Radle, Bobby Keys, and Jim Price, and he was respected for his skill in staging a top-flight concert. Singing, Bramlett tried to explain to Clapton, didn't have to be a chore; it could be fun. Clapton simply had to change his way of looking at it.

The two spent their time together talking and jamming, unwinding from the Blind Faith tour. Clapton wanted to bring Delaney and Bonnie and their band to England for some concerts in the country and, if possible, a tour of Europe, and from their discussions an informal deal was struck: Delaney would do the tour if Eric joined his band as its lead guitarist; in return, Delaney would produce Clapton's solo album. Clapton left the United States in early October, encouraged by the prospects.

He had barely touched down in England and unpacked his bags when he received a telegram from John Lennon, inviting him to play as part of his makeshift Plastic Ono Band at a rock 'n' roll revival show in Toronto. Clapton found the idea appealing. Lennon had not played onstage since the final Beatles tour in 1966, and other names slated for the festival included Bo Diddley, Chuck Berry, and Little Richard—all people who had influenced Clapton when he was first listening to rock 'n' roll and learning to play guitar. Problem was, the concert was to take place that very evening. The telegram arrived at Hurtwood Edge literally a few hours before Lennon and company were scheduled to fly to Toronto, so there was no time to make plans or rehearse. Nevertheless, Clapton grabbed his equipment and met the group at Heathrow.

Rehearsals were held on the plane. Lennon ran through a short set list with Clapton, bassist Klaus Voorman, and drummer Alan White. Clapton and Lennon worked out their parts on acoustic guitars so they would not disturb the other passengers on the plane. Lennon kept the repertoire simple: three rock 'n' roll standards ("Blue Suede Shoes," "Money," and "Dizzy Miss Lizzy"), one Beatles song ("Yer Blues"), and two Lennon solo works ("Cold Turkey" and "Give Peace a Chance"), to go along with two avant-garde feedback-drenched Yoko Ono numbers ("Don't Worry

Kyoko" and "John John"). All were songs that any good pickup band could waltz through with minimal practice. One can only imagine the scene in the first-class section of the plane, as two of the world's most recognizable faces, joined by one of rock's top guitarists and two other musicians, went over a bunch of songs that, only hours later, would be performed for thousands of screaming fans and eventually released on an album. One particular passenger stood out for Clapton. "There was a guy there who was a Gillette salesman—I'll never forget that—and he was trying to give us free razors, 'cause we all had beards," he remembered with some amusement.

When they landed in Toronto, John and Yoko were immediately picked up by a limousine and driven to Varsity Stadium, a scene that did not sit well with Clapton, who was left with the others to find a way to the stadium. Backstage, both Clapton and Lennon came down with a bad case of jitters, Lennon becoming physically ill from anxiety, Clapton trying to battle his way through his own nervousness by snorting cocaine, which he had begun to do on occasion to ease his nerves. Instead Clapton became so sick that he vomited and passed out. He was shaking when he walked out in front of the packed stadium crowd for the band's midnight show.

Whatever fears the band may have had were not evident in the music played that evening. After explaining to the crowd that the band had never worked together before, Lennon led the group through fairly safe readings of "Blue Suede Shoes" and "Money," followed by a high-voltage rendition of "Dizzy Miss Lizzy" that came close to matching the Beatles' own version. With each song, the band seemed to grow more confident. Clapton entered a superb blues solo to close out "Yer Blues," and from there he moved into some slashing and grinding guitar work that brilliantly complemented Lennon's tortured vocals on "Cold Turkey." The Yoko Ono songs contrasted sharply with the festival's "oldies" motif, eliciting a mixed response from the crowd. As a whole, the concert was an enjoyable experience for Clapton and a complete reversal of the problems he'd witnessed while touring with Blind Faith just two months earlier.

Back in London, Clapton resumed his retreat from the spotlight. He spent a lot of time in the city's recording studios, working in sessions for album projects by Rick Grech, Doris Troy, Leon Russell, and Shawn Phillips. It was a time of great camaraderie between American and British musicians, and any given studio session could turn into a meeting of some of the most respected names from both sides of the ocean. When, for example, Doris Troy decided to record a new arrangement of the Beatles' "Get Back," she found herself singing over a backing track performed by Clapton, George Harrison (who also produced the session), Ringo Starr, Klaus Voorman, Billy Preston, Bobby Keys, and Jim Price—quite a backing band for someone who was only marginally known. The easygoing sessions not only afforded Clapton a badly needed respite from the high-visibility work he'd been doing in recent months but also put him in contact with some of the musicians who would be working with him on his own solo album.

Delaney and Bonnie Bramlett arrived in England on November 10, 1969, two weeks before their tour with Clapton was scheduled to open in Germany. In keeping with the loose, informal atmosphere that everyone wanted for the tour, Delaney, Bonnie, and their entire band moved into Hurtwood Edge, where rehearsals took place on an impromptu basis, the band sitting around and enjoying each others' company as much as it prepared for the tour. On some days, the entire group would relocate to the Olympic or Trident Studios in London for some preliminary work on Clapton's solo album, though only one usable song ("Lovin' You Lovin' Me") came out of the sessions.

The German segment of the tour, which included concerts in Frankfurt, Hamburg, and Cologne, was a nightmare. Although the tour was being formally billed as "Delaney and Bonnie and Friends with Guest Star Eric Clapton," fans were more interested in the guest star than in the rest of the band. This was understandable enough, given Clapton's international star status, but concert promoters made matters worse by hyping the shows as Eric Clapton appearances.

"It was the promoters who were wrong," reflected Delaney Bramlett. "The kids in Germany had been led to believe Eric Clapton was going to do a single set and not just play with somebody else's band, which of course was incorrect, but the promoters saw it as a quick way to sell tickets."

Plenty of tickets were sold, but to the frustration of those attending the concerts in Germany, Clapton was just another band member onstage. Indeed, he played all the guitar solos and sang background vocals, as he had done in Cream and Blind Faith, but these were Delaney and Bonnie shows, with an entirely different brand of music, and Clapton was hesitant to upstage them. Angry fans jeered the band with boos and catcalls, the worst taking place in Cologne, where the crowd was so disruptive that the band left the stage after only four numbers.

The reaction was quite the opposite of what Clapton intended when he brought the band overseas and lent his name and musicianship to the Delaney and Bonnie cause. "I joined Delaney's band," he explained, "because I was in total awe of him, and I thought everyone *else* should see this. I knew that I had the drawing power, even then. I could make the public aware of them just by putting my name on the bill."

The grumbles, then and later, were that Clapton was far too talented to be wasting his time on a band like Delaney and Bonnie and Friends. To the cynics, the band was just another white soul group working hard to sound black. The critics knew nothing of Clapton's debt to Delaney Bramlett, nor were they interested, in the wake of Clapton's previous bands, of hearing Clapton play Delaney and Bonnie's brand of music. As far as they were concerned, there was far too much Bramlett and Company, and far too little Clapton.

The group fared much better when they returned to England and opened their British tour at the Royal Albert Hall on December 1. The highly anticipated concert had been surrounded by rumors of guest appearances ("There is some talk about the band being joined at the Hall by such notables as George Harrison, John Lennon, and a couple of Rolling Stones," reported *Rolling Stone*) and though Harrison was backstage during the show, the Albert Hall appearance featured only the advertised band. The concert was a hit, starting off a seven-city, thirteen-show itinerary that included stops in Bristol, Birmingham, Sheffield, Newcastle, and Liverpool.

Clapton was not the only special guest star to grace the stage during this segment of the Delaney and Bonnie tour: to the delight of fans and the press alike, George Harrison decided to end his long absence from performance and joined the group onstage. Clapton had been trying to persuade Harrison to do this since the Bramletts had arrived in England, but the notoriously shy Beatle had put him off. After the Albert Hall show, Harrison had spoken of how much he enjoyed the performance, and Clapton responded by offering to pick Harrison up the next morning and bring him on the tour. If Harrison doubted the sincerity of Clapton's offer, he learned otherwise when the Delaney and Bonnie tour bus pulled up outside his mansion. Put on the spot in such a way, he had little choice but to join them. "I just grabbed a guitar and an amp and went on the road with them," he remarked. He stayed with the band for the remainder of its British tour.

In the strictest sense, touring with Delaney and Bonnie did not represent a step forward in Eric Clapton's career, though it did signify a suitable coda to his standing as a musician at the decade's end. In a half dozen years, he had played with four notable bands; he had toured the world, recorded a lot of music, and seen all sides of the music business—and all before his twenty-fifth birthday. The past two or three years had been so intense that some form of burnout was probably inevitable, and with Delaney and Bonnie, Clapton was putting his career in a holding pattern. The workaholic was having a good time.

• • •

Clapton closed out an eventful year with yet another appearance with John Lennon and Yoko Ono. This one, held on December 15 at London's Lyceum Ballroom and billed as "Peace for Christmas," turned out to be a splendid affair combining the talents of the Toronto version of the Plastic Ono Band with Delaney and Bonnie and Friends, George Harrison, Billy Preston, Keith Moon, and several friends of the band members. Unlike the show in Toronto, Clapton and Lennon were relaxed onstage, playing before their countrymen, and they led the huge ensemble in a version of

"Cold Turkey" that wound up on Lennon's 1972 solo album, *Some Time in New York City*.

With four months gone since the final Blind Faith concerts, Clapton realized that it was time to work in earnest on a new project. Shortly after the first of the year, he flew to Los Angeles and joined Delaney Bramlett in the studio to lay down tracks for the solo album. He and Bramlett had written a handful of new songs during their tour of Europe—not enough for an entire album but a good start. Clapton still harbored misgivings about doing the album, which Delaney was calling *Eric Sings*, but Bramlett was not about to let him find any rationale for backing out of the project. "He was prepared to be my coach," said Clapton, "and no one had ever offered that to me before. He was the first person to instill in me a sense of purpose."

Clapton allowed that, in working with him, Bramlett might have been working out some of his own musical aspirations. He and his band had built up quite a following just by having Clapton on their tour, and now, in the Los Angeles studio, Delaney had a good vehicle to promote his own songwriting skills. Not that Bramlett was simply using the more famous musician for his own gain: as Eric was quick to point out, he and Delaney had grown very close over the past year, and much of Delaney's prodding on the project was the result of genuine friendship.

"He's such an enthusiastic, generous character, and incredibly affectionate—if he becomes your buddy he's your bosom buddy," Clapton remarked of Bramlett. "He's also ambitious too. A very strange combination. So, I mean, he'd sit down and write a song and tell you you'd written part of it! He'd write most of it and then say, 'Don't you remember that's the part you put in the other day.' If you thought about it you'd realize you hadn't actually done any of it, so it was kind of like he was giving you this song and also selling himself through it at the same time. I mean, I actually put some of it together—a few words here, a few riffs there and a chord, but the mainstay was him."

There is little disputing Delaney Bramlett's profound influence on Clapton's first solo album, *Eric Clapton*, released in August 1970. Bramlett produced the recording, provided his band as the nucleus of Clapton's studio musicians, and wrote or cowrote eight of the album's eleven songs. He also introduced Clapton to his friend J. J. Cale's song "After Midnight," which Clapton covered on the album and released as a single. Bramlett's influence, though, was not entirely for the best, at least as far as record buyers were concerned. People expecting another Cream or Blind Faith album were sorely disappointed with the album, and compared to the sales figures for recordings by Clapton's previous bands, *Eric Clapton* fared poorly in the marketplace. Reviews of the album generally ran from lukewarm to negative, with very few critics sympathetic to the new musical direction Clapton was taking.

Despite such negative reaction, *Eric Clapton* plays better today than a number of his other solo projects. Three of the album's songs—"After Midnight," "Blues Power," and "Let It Rain"—are Clapton standards, and time has been kind to a couple others as well. Both "Easy Now," a love ballad that owes much of its musical direction to Clapton's friendship with George Harrison, and "Bottle of Red Wine," a shuffle that was a concert favorite of Clapton's for several years, bear up well over repeated listenings.

The album's lasting importance, however, may not have as much to do with the artistic merits of its individual songs as with the path it provided for Clapton. By writing and singing his own songs, Clapton was now more complete as an artist. He would write better songs in the future, and his voice would improve with age, but it is unlikely that he would have pursued his singing and songwriting skills had it not been for his hit-or-miss experiences on *Eric Clapton*.

• • •

Immediately following the recording sessions, Clapton joined Delaney and Bonnie for a monthlong tour of the States that coincided with the release of *On Tour With Eric Clapton*, an album recorded at the two Delaney and Bonnie concerts in Craydon on December 7. The tour, which included an appearance on "The Dick Cavett Show," went smoothly enough, though Clapton was beginning to grow weary of the codependence he shared with Delaney and Bonnie. He was happy to be back in England in early March.

Once home, his first priority was to finish his solo album. He still wanted to work on the lyrics and overdubs of "Let It Rain," and he had brought the master tape of the song back to England. Under the usual circumstances, this would have posed no problem, but an odd misunderstanding over the tape led to the album's being released in less than optimum shape.

"I left the tapes in L.A. for Delaney to mix them, and he was waiting on me to finish one of the tracks," Clapton explained. "He didn't realize that I was waiting on him to mix the tracks and send them over. Finally, my manager got kind of impatient and told Atlantic to send the tapes to me, and I mixed them very badly. Atlantic heard them, didn't like 'em. Then they sent them to Tom Dowd, who mixed them again. So they were mixed three times in all. I never heard Delaney's mixes until it was too late—the record was already out."

Clapton spent the better part of March and April mixing the tapes and working in the studio on projects for Stephen Stills; Ashton, Gardner and Dyke; and Jonathan Kelly. In addition, he sat in on sessions for Ringo Starr's first post-Beatles single, "It Don't Come Easy," though he was not on the final, released version of the song.

His finest hour as a sessions musician occurred during this busy work period. Chess Records had come up with the idea of linking some of rock's top musicians with the blues masters who had influenced them, and Clapton was invited to play on the Howlin' Wolf recording.

Clapton jumped at the opportunity. The Chicago blues legend had been part of his musical consciousness since he first began playing guitar. "Smokestack Lightning" had been an integral part of Clapton's stage repertoire with the Yardbirds, and Cream had covered "Sitting on Top of the World" on its *Wheels of Fire* album. Clapton relished the opportunity not only to meet and work with the man but also record with a core band made up of Stevie Winwood, Bill Wyman, and Charlie Watts—a unit that would be anyone's dream band.

This, however, was only part of his motive for wanting to make the record. "The other reason I did that session," he said, "was that for a long time I'd really wanted to meet his guitarist, Hubert Sumlin, because he did some things that freaked me out when I was picking up the guitar—that stuff on 'Goin' Down Slow,' just the weirdest playing." To Clapton, Sumlin's playing was "just amazing."

He was shocked, then, when he learned that Sumlin had not been invited to participate in the session, that the Chess executives wanted to stick to their concept of having the teacher surrounded by a supergroup of his pupils. Clapton responded by threatening to pull out of the project unless Sumlin was brought to England for the sessions. After some tension, a compromise was reached: Sumlin could play on the record, but only as a rhythm guitarist; Clapton would be playing lead guitar. Clapton was still dissatisfied. "Hubert ended up supplementing, playing rhythm, which I thought was all wrong," he grumbled, "because he knew all the parts that were necessary and I didn't."

Clapton had reasons for his apprehension. He had been out of his element when he worked as a backing guitarist for Sonny Boy Williamson in 1964, but he had been young and brash going into that project, unaware of the idea that Williamson had a preferred way of doing his material; now he was a much better musician and an internationally known figure, and he was also much wiser about the intricacies of playing the blues properly. He wanted no part of repeating his youthful problems with Howlin' Wolf.

His fears turned out to be justified. At six-foot-three and nearly 300 pounds, Chester "Howlin' Wolf" Burnett was an imposing physical presence—with a gruff manner to match his size. When he arrived at London's Olympic Sound Studios in April, Howlin' Wolf fully expected these young British musicians to know his songs and be able to play them correctly, and he flew into a rage when he discovered that his backing musicians wanted to take an improvisational approach. Unlike Howlin' Wolf's previous sessions with the likes of Willie Dixon, Muddy Waters, Buddy Guy, and Hubert Sumlin in a disciplined studio setting, the British musicians were accustomed to working in an easygoing environment and playing ideas off each other. Howlin' Wolf made it clear from the outset that he intended to have things his way.

"His attitude was the same as Sonny Boy's," Clapton recalled. "You know, 'We're going to do "Little Red Rooster," and it goes like this. And it doesn't go like anything *you* think it goes like.' He was tough and aggressive, and a certain amount of the guys in the studio were just too shook up to come back the next day. And I was pretty shook up, too. It scared me. You see, I was already going along a different path. I was a rock musician. And it's not that I'd left my blues roots behind, it's just that I'd forgotten a lot of the ways things went. And to get it all back in the space of an evening is no easy job. But I spoke to the producer from Chicago [Norman Dayron], who said, 'Well, come back again tomorrow, it'll be all right.' And I did, and it was better."

Hubert Sumlin had seen his share of Howlin' Wolf's dark moods. He had fought with him—even had his dental work rearranged during one especially nasty altercation—but their relationship had ultimately rested on the common denominators of professional trust and respect. Howlin' Wolf knew he was not long for the world, and while a part of him resented the fact that he was dying at a time when blues was enjoying its greatest success ever, another part accepted the reality that one of the ways his music would live on was through young talents like those with him in the London studio. The realization drove him to work the musicians even harder.

"The hardest confrontation I ever had was when Howlin' Wolf tried to teach me to play 'Little Red Rooster,'" said Clapton. "He was saying to me, 'Listen, son, you've got to learn this because after I'm gone, someone's got to keep this alive.' Part of me fought this, and I thought, 'No, I'm not taking that!'"

But take it he did, not only in the studio, where Howlin' Wolf literally took his hand and guided him through the playing of "Little Red Rooster," but also in the continuing development of his own identity as a musician. He *was*, he decided, part of the lineage of blues musicians, and if he was going to maintain a place in that heritage, he had to accept the responsibilities that went along with it.

"It introduced me to the reality of playing," he said of the Howlin' Wolf sessions. "Up until then it had always been a bit of a fantasy: listening to records and harboring a sense of belonging to it. Which no one could really shake until I met the real guys, and then I felt a bit of a stranger. But it fortified my urge to get it right. Because once you get the reward, it made you realize that there was something there."

The sessions proceeded slowly. Howlin' Wolf needed dialysis on a daily basis, and a machine was installed in the studio to allow him the chance to work with only minimal interruption. Still, there were days when he was unable to work, and on one of those days, Clapton took Hubert Sumlin to Hurtwood Edge to show him his home, have dinner with him, and present him with a gift.

"He took me down to the basement, where he had all these guitars," said Sumlin. "It looked like a factory, with every style you can imagine. Three and a half walls of this room just lined with guitars. He said, 'Pick out a couple of these guitars, Hubert, I'm giving you two of them.' I walked all the way around the room, looking at every one of them. Then I saw this case sitting in the middle of the room. I sat down on the floor and said, 'What's in there?' He said, 'It ain't nothing, man.' I asked if I could take a look. He said, 'You don't want that.' I opened the case and took this beautiful Fender Stratocaster out and started playing it right there, sitting on the floor."

The guitar in question turned out to be Clapton's regular guitar. While working with Delaney Bramlett on the *Eric Clapton* album, Clapton had set aside his customary Gibson Les Paul in favor of a Stratocaster, which gave him a leaner sound, and though he hated the idea of giving away a favored new instrument, Clapton offered it to Sumlin.*

*Clapton could be very touchy about his guitars. Over the years, he would give any number of them away, including a favored instrument such as the psychedelic guitar that he used in Cream. On the other hand, he attached a weighty significance to the almost spiritual relationship between the musician and his guitar. On one occasion, when someone tried to hand him Muddy Waters's guitar, he refused to so much as touch it; on another occasion, he threw a fit in the recording studio when Stephen Bishop picked up Clapton's guitar and began to play it.

"Take it, man," he said to Sumlin. "At least I know it's got a good home. Just promise me that if I ever want it back you'll give it to me."

Sumlin held on to the guitar for two years, but he would never play it onstage. He eventually returned it to Clapton, when the two ran into each other at a Montreaux Jazz Festival. A torch was being passed.

. . .

Clapton's time with Howlin' Wolf produced one of the better blues records of its time. Released in August 1971, *The London Howlin' Wolf Sessions* featured spare but lively blues arrangements of such Howlin' Wolf classics as "Sitting on Top of the World," "Wang Dang Doodle," "I Ain't Superstitious," and "Little Red Rooster." Two outstanding tracks from the sessions, "Goin' Down Slow" and "Killing Floor," did not make the album but subsequently turned up on the 1974 Muddy Waters–Howlin' Wolf combination album, *London Revisited*.

Not long after the conclusion of the Howlin' Wolf sessions, Clapton heard from Bobby Whitlock, who was interested in working with him and maybe even forming a band. Clapton was definitely interested. Whitlock was an exceptional keyboard player and vocalist, and Clapton valued the time they spent together during the Delaney and Bonnie tours. Clapton suggested that Whitlock fly to England and move in with him at Hurtwood Edge. Before long, Clapton was engaged in the kind of jamming and songwriting sessions he had enjoyed with Stevie Winwood prior to the official formation of Blind Faith. The two discussed bringing in Jim Keltner, a much-sought-after studio drummer, as part of the new unit, but they ultimately selected Jim Gordon and Carl Radle, Delaney and Bonnie's rhythm section, to play drums and bass, respectively.

All three musicians had been busy since Clapton had seen them last. After their Delaney and Bonnie tour with Clapton, they had asked Delaney Bramlett for raises in pay, and they had been fired on the spot. They were not unemployed for long. Leon Russell, who had worked with the group on the *Eric Clapton* album, was assembling a large band to back Joe Cocker on his *Mad Dogs and Englishmen* tour, and he invited the three to work in the troupe. Whitlock, Gordon, and Radle jumped aboard for what turned out to be a memorable yet maddening tour.

For Clapton, the new band was ideal. Everyone was familiar with the music from his solo album, so whenever they decided they might want to tour, all they would really need to do was work up a few new songs and they would be ready to go before the public. Since Alice was away on an extended holiday in Israel, Clapton invited Gordon and Radle to move in with him, and they reprised the informal jam sessions and rehearsals that typified Delaney and Bonnie's stay half a year earlier. As before, there was little structure to the creative process. The group might improvise for hours on a song like "Johnnie B. Goode," or they might just sit around, get stoned, and hash out fragments of new songs. The band had no name, and no one was in any hurry to set up club dates or concerts.

They had been together only a few weeks when Clapton received a call from George Harrison. The former Beatle was ready to record his first solo album, and he was hunting around for backing musicians. Clapton told Harrison that he and the others would be happy to work on the album, on the condition that Harrison talk his producer, the immensely gifted but equally eccentric Phil Spector, into working with the new band on its first single.

Over the next three months, while working on Harrison's *All Things Must Pass*, Clapton's band became a polished unit. Dave Mason, a former member of Traffic, was also contributing to the Harrison album, and he was informally drafted into Clapton's band as a second guitarist. His tenure, however, was brief: with his own solo album to promote, Mason had little time to work with a new band.

He did appear with Clapton and the rest when they made their first official public appearance at the Lyceum Ballroom in London on June 14, 1970. The show had been booked as an Eric Clapton appearance, but just before going onstage, Clapton decided his band needed a name. Tony Ashton, a longtime Clapton associate, suggested that they call the group Del and the Dominos, Del being his nickname for Clapton. Del and Eric were combined, and the band had a name—Derek and the Dominos.

The band's name, a humorous bit of whimsy on the part of its leader, who still fantasized a scenario in which he could play onstage without the baggage of his reputation, fooled no one. The Dominos' set list drew heavily from Clapton's solo album, so there would be no pretense, then or ever, that the group would be anything but an Eric Clapton band. As Clapton would realize, it was too late to become just another player in a band. It had not worked when he had attempted it in Delaney and Bonnie and Friends; it would not work now. Not that the anonymity really mattered: the band's name, he'd say in interviews over the years, was intended in good fun, as if the identity of the Dominos' Derek was rock's worst-kept secret.

Four days after appearing at the Lyceum, Derek and the Dominos entered Apple Studios to cut their first single, "Tell the Truth"/"Roll It Over." As promised, Phil Spector was in the control room, and the Dominos, still with Dave Mason on guitar, were joined by George Harrison. With three guitars in the band, Derek and the Dominos promised to deliver an entirely different sound from what was usually associated with Eric Clapton.

"The basic concept of Derek and the Dominos," recalled Bobby Whitlock, "was that we didn't want any horns, we didn't want no chicks, we wanted a rock 'n' roll band. But my vocal concept was that we approached singing like Sam and Dave did: he sings a line, I sing a line, we sing together."

"Tell the Truth" was ideal for that format. Written by Bobby Whitlock after one of the late-night rehearsals at Hurtwood Edge, with a final verse added later by Clapton, "Tell the Truth" was originally recorded as an uptempo rocker, the vocal exchange between Clapton and Whitlock serving notice that the Dominos might be Clapton's most soulful group yet. However, the pace of the single was entirely too fast—especially when compared to the better, slower version that eventually appeared on *Layla and Other Assorted Love Songs*—and the song's ending was entirely too abrupt. The band may have been able to describe the sound it was seeking, but it was not present on "Tell the Truth." The single would be withdrawn almost as soon as it was released in September.

Judging from the large volume of Clapton-related music being recorded and issued during the summer and fall of 1970, one would not have been surprised to find some confusion in Clapton's perception about his current musical identity. His solo album hit the music shops in August, giving the public a look at Eric Clapton the vocalist. In the studio, he was preoccupied with a new band of his own, as well as album projects for George Harrison and Dr. John. He also played on Jonathan Kelly's single "Don't You Believe It," issued in June, and on King Curtis's "Teasin'," which was released a month later. If all that wasn't enough, Clapton's past was well represented with "new" albums by Cream (*Live Cream, Volume 1*) and Delaney and Bonnie (*On Tour with Eric Clapton*).

Clapton, it appeared, was everywhere, but which role best defined the real Eric Clapton?

The question hung in the air like a puzzling riddle waiting to be solved.

．　．　．

For all his activity and success in the music business, Clapton was entering a prolonged period of personal crisis that would take him years to resolve. On an artistic level, the turmoil would provide him with the grist needed for his finest work; on the psychological level, it would torment him to the darkest regions of despair, nearly costing him his life.

His problems began during the making of George Harrison's *All Things Must Pass* album. Over the past two years, Clapton and Harrison had grown extremely close. Each was a frequent guest at the other's mansion— Harrison had written "Here Comes the Sun" while sitting in the garden at Hurtwood Edge—and the two were mutually sympathetic after the disintegration of their respective bands. The breakup of the Beatles had been traumatic for all four members of the group, and Harrison had taken refuge from the attendant bedlam by breaking away from the public light and immersing himself in both his work and in his deep devotion to Eastern religion.

Clapton had spent a lot of time with Harrison during this difficult time, and as a result, he had many occasions to cross paths with Harrison's wife, Pattie, an ex-model who was one of the most stunningly beautiful women Clapton had ever seen. The former Pattie Boyd had been on his mind, off and on, since his days with Blind Faith. The Harrisons lived a short drive away, in Esher, and with each visit to their estate, Clapton found himself more attracted to the woman married to the man he called his best friend.

"I went to Esher several times," he told Ray Coleman, his British biographer, "and every time I went, after a nice time with George and Pattie, I remember feeling a dreadful emptiness—because I was certain I was never going to meet a woman quite that beautiful for myself. I knew that. I knew I was in love. I fell in love with her at first sight—and it got heavier and heavier for me."

Clapton tried every subtle ploy he could think of to get Pattie's attention—including briefly courting her younger sister—but it became clear that he was getting nowhere. She considered him a friend and nothing more. The two flirted from time to time, but nothing came of it. As the wife of a Beatle and a successful career woman in her own right, Pattie Boyd Harrison was such a public figure that Clapton considered her unapproachable. He brooded about the situation, even fantasized about having a fling with her as a form of retribution for a time when Harrison stole one of his own girlfriends, but he refrained from making open advances.

All this changed during the period that Clapton was working on *All Things Must Pass*. Feeling neglected by a husband who seemed to be more devoted to his work and religion than to her, Pattie Harrison began to flirt more seriously with Clapton. Her actions, she'd later admit, had been intended to make her husband jealous, but the ploy backfired: Harrison didn't seem to notice, while Clapton fell even more deeply in love with her. She was surprised—both pleased and unnerved—when Clapton finally revealed the depth of his feelings for her.

Over the following weeks, Clapton desperately pursued Pattie, but to no avail. She, too, felt that an affair was out of the question, given her position in the public eye, along with her belief that, as a married woman, she should remain loyal to her husband, even if she was unhappy with him. Clapton's declarations of love, though flattering, made her extremely uncomfortable.

Pattie's unavailability only fueled Clapton's obsession with her. With no one to confide in, and no means of resolving his dilemma, Clapton was hounded by depression, loneliness, despair, confusion, sadness, and frustration. He even rejected his Christianity, blaming religion—and Harrison's religious convictions specifically—for Pattie's unhappiness. (Somehow, almost miraculously, he managed to put in day after day in the studio with George Harrison, hiding his feelings and recording solid music for his friend's album.) Fortunately for Clapton, Alice was still out of town, so he was not in the position of having to disguise his feelings around an inquisitive lover.

There was only one outlet for expressing his deepest emotions, and with a new band and a fellow songwriter nearby, and unrequited love acting as a touchstone to his creativity, Clapton began to construct the foundation of an album that would put his feelings on the line. The blues, of course, had always been grounded in the expression of such powerful feelings, and for the first time in his life, Clapton had ample emotional resources, combined with the creative flint, to truly live on blues power.

Each composition for the projected album seemed to be rooted in deep, almost unbearable melancholia. "Have You Ever Loved a Woman," a blues he had known since his days with John Mayall, now took on special significance, with its open reference to a man's falling in love with his best friend's woman and being helpless to pursue his feelings. Bobby Whitlock, though unaware of the actual roots of Clapton's emotional turmoil, picked up on it and proved to be an ideal writing partner. A new song, "Why Does Love Got to Be So Sad," was a number that virtually wrote itself.

One new song was so painfully specific, yet so totally universal in what it expressed, that it was destined from the beginning to be a classic. Clapton had recently received, as a gift from a friend, a volume entitled *The Story of Layla and Majnun*. In this Persian tale, a young man is driven insane when he falls in love with a beautiful, unavailable woman. Clapton loved the sound of Layla's name, and that, along with the general theme of the story, became the basis of a song about his feelings for Pattie Harrison. While writing the song, Clapton addressed Pattie as directly as possible, confessing his anguish and begging her to remain open to his love. In three tightly written verses, Clapton stated his case and entered his plea, his song drawing its life source from a history of heart-wrenching, musically expressed drama that could be traced back to a Mississippi delta blues singer named Robert Johnson, and to such songs as "Hellhound on My Trail," "Love in Vain," and "Crossroads."

"Layla" was the kind of song that one could use as an album's cornerstone. Clapton recognized this immediately, and even though the song was still unfinished, he had Robert Stigwood contact Tom Dowd, his old engineer from Cream, who was now producing records out of his own studio in Miami. It was time to record.

seven

Crossroads
1970–78

It was something I *had* to go through. . . . Perhaps it took that to get
me on my feet again. You can't go up without coming down.

*d*erek and the Dominos flew to Miami in late August. The
band had played a string of club dates in England earlier in the month,
occasionally mixing a new song into a set list drawn mostly from Clapton's
solo album, but the smaller-hall gigs were generally devoted to the band's
learning to play better together. Clapton wanted no repeats of the problems
he had experienced with Blind Faith, where the band was recording and
touring before it was ready, and in this area he was successful: the band
that set up in Miami's Criteria Studios was extremely tight as a working
unit.

No one expected the double album that ultimately came out of the
sessions. If anything, the Dominos were short on material. Clapton and
Whitlock had a handful of original songs, along with several standard blues,
that they wanted to record, but very little was firmly committed for the
project. Clapton had written one especially strong song, "Bell Bottom
Blues," that he and the band would record early on, but he had yet to
introduce the Dominos to "Layla," which he still figured to record as a
ballad or blues shuffle.

Although they were scheduled to open another tour of England in less
than a month, the Dominos were in no hurry to lay down the tracks for

As a teenager, Eric Clapton played with a band called The Roosters, with (from left to right) Clapton, Robin Mason, Terry Brennan, Tom McGuiness, and Ben Palmer. The band, pictured here in 1962, was very short lived. *(Tom McGuiness/Star File)*

Positioned near their stacks of Marshall amps and playing at ear-shattering volume, Jack Bruce, Ginger Baker, and Eric Clapton perform Cream's farewell concert in London's Royal Albert Hall. *(Barrie Wentzell/Star File)*

With the money earned from the phenomenal success of Cream, Clapton purchased Hurtwood Edge, a sprawling mansion in the Surrey countryside.

(Barrie Wentzell/Star File)

Clapton in 1968, at the height of the psychedelic era. *(Jeffrey Mayer/Star File)*

Eric Clapton and Alice Ormsby-Gore around the time of announcing their engagement in 1969. *(Hulton Archive/Getty Images)*

At the height of his popularity, Clapton left the super-group scene and toured with Delaney and Bonnie and Friends, a relatively unknown American band. Delaney Bramlett encouraged a reluctant Clapton to sing, which led to Clapton's highly successful solo career. *(Joe Sia/Star File)*

Clapton (back facing camera) contributed the famous guitar solo in the Beatles' "While My Guitar Gently Weeps," solidifying his friendship with George Harrison. The two, shown here in the studio during the recording of Harrison's *All Things Must Pass*, worked frequently together.

(Barrie Wentzell/Star File)

Derek and the Dominos, with (from left to right) Bobby Whitlock, Eric Clapton, Jim Gordon, and Carl Radle, created *Layla and Other Assorted Love Songs*— arguably Clapton's finest moment as a musician—but excessive drug use undermined the band's effectiveness as a touring unit, and eventually led to its early demise. *(Elliot Landy/Star File)*

In August 1971, Clapton joined an all-star lineup for George Harrison's Concert for Bangla Desh. It was one of only a few public appearances during Clapton's battles with heroin addiction. *(Chuck Pulin/Star File)*

Pete Townshend (right) coaxed Clapton out of seclusion for two historic shows at the Rainbow Theatre on January 13, 1973.
(Barrie Wentzell/Star File)

the new album. The band members moved into a hotel on the Atlantic and spent their days lounging in the sun, swimming in the ocean, taking saunas, or resting. Recording sessions took place in the evenings. During their first week in Miami, most of the group's time at Criteria was spent jamming and piecing together scraps of new song material. It was almost as if the band were in a holding pattern, waiting for something to happen.

The "happening," as it turned out, was named Duane Allman, and his introduction to the band was a happy accident. Just prior to working with Clapton and his band, Tom Dowd had been producing *Idlewild South*, the new album by the Allman Brothers Band. Duane Allman, the group's brilliant slide guitarist, was a longtime Clapton fan, and when he learned that Eric was coming to Miami to record, he asked Dowd if he could stop by the studio to meet him. When Dowd told Clapton of his conversation with Allman, Clapton was equally enthusiastic about setting up a meeting. He had admired Allman from as far back as his studio days with Atlantic Records—especially for his guitar solo on Wilson Pickett's version of "Hey Jude"—and he urged Dowd to introduce him to Allman. "I'm *dying* to see him play," Clapton told his producer.

It so happened the Allman Brothers Band was scheduled to play a benefit in Miami the following Saturday night. Clapton canceled his studio session for that evening, and he and Dowd drove together to see the show.

"I just remember driving down to this park," said Clapton of that evening, "and while we were parking the car about half a mile from this open-air gig I just heard this wailing guitar coming through the air, louder than anything else. You could just hear the band and then this really high in the air sound like a siren. It was just amazing. We walked down to the gig, sat down in front of the bandstand, and there were The Allman Brothers."

Since they didn't have tickets for the concert, Clapton and Dowd had to sneak into the show. Not only did they find a way in, but they wound up with a unique vantage point. Remembered Dowd: "They had a barricade between where the public was and the riser for the band, sandbags and gobos up there to keep the people back. They got us in by the side of the stage and we crawled in on our hands and knees, so we wouldn't obscure the stage, and propped ourselves against these sandbags, sitting on our butts, looking up with our hands holding our knees together."

Duane Allman, Dowd recalled, was in the middle of a solo when he and Clapton took their places just a few yards away from the band. When Allman saw Clapton, he froze on the spot, bringing his solo to an abrupt ending. While the band tried to cover for him, Allman stood dumbfounded onstage, staring down at Clapton, utterly amazed to see him sitting on the grass in front of him. "It scared Duane to death!" Gregg Allman said of his brother's peculiar reaction to Clapton's presence at the concert.

Formal introductions were made after the show, and Clapton invited the entire band to Criteria Studios for a jam session that wound up lasting all night. Clapton and Allman were naturals together, neither feeling competitive about the other's reputation or ability, both sharing the same musical interests. Clapton had not felt such instant affinity toward a fellow musician since he had connected with John Mayall five years earlier, and he had never worked with a guitarist who made him feel as completely at ease. "When you get two people like that in the studio," he explained, "you're really listening to one musician some of the time and the other one is standing off. Then he steps in and it's just like very kindred."

Allman still hoped to be able to sit in the studio while the Dominos worked on their album. He mentioned as much to Clapton, who wasn't at all interested in having him hang out as an observer.

"Get out your guitar," he told Allman. "We got to play."

• • •

Allman was not immediately available to join the Dominos full-time in the studio. The Allman Brothers Band had a few remaining concerts on their tour, so Duane left Miami to complete his obligations with the band. In his absence, Derek and the Dominos recorded several new songs, including "I Looked Away" and "Bell Bottom Blues," the two numbers that eventually opened the *Layla* album.

The recording sessions were elevated to a higher, more intense level when Allman returned. Future years would indicate that Clapton played at his best whenever he was in a two-guitar band, working with another guitarist who kept him from getting sloppy or lazy, and this was undeniably the case when he had Duane Allman in the studio. Allman's slide playing on "Anyday" added the perfect splash of color to Clapton and Whitlock's soulful vocals, while his slashing duet with Clapton on "Why Does Love Got to Be So Sad?" pushed Clapton to some of his best work yet.

His greatest influence was on "Layla," and though his name would never appear in the songwriting credits, Allman was absolutely fundamental to the song's development.

"He wrote the riff," Clapton said of Allman's contribution—the blazing, twelve-note riff that runs throughout the song. "I just had the main body of the song, and it wasn't enough. It needed an intro, a motif."

Allman, Clapton would learn later, had "borrowed" the riff from Albert King's "As the Years Go Passing By," but in its greatly sped-up tempo, it sounded original. It entirely changed the emotional center of the song. With Allman's hard-driving blues lick powering the song forward, Clapton sounded as if he was at wit's end—which, in fact, he was when he wrote the piece.

As good as it sounded, the song's new tempo created a problem: as it now stood, it had no acceptable ending. An abrupt conclusion would have diminished the intensity of the music, and a fade-out would have detracted from the urgency of Clapton's lyrics. The song needed a sense of resolution or closure.

The solution—the beautiful piano piece that closes out the song—came from an unexpected source. Jim Gordon, Clapton accidentally discovered, had been working in the studio while the others were away, writing and recording songs for his own solo album, composing his music on the piano. Clapton came by the studio unexpectedly and heard Gordon playing a striking melody. When he learned what his drummer was doing, Clapton asked if he could use the piano fragment as the ending for "Layla." Gordon agreed, and the song was finally completed.

Once the band got down to recording seriously, the album took very little time to complete; the bulk of the recording and overdubbing was accomplished in a ten-day stretch. Songs seemed to materialize out of nowhere. Between the blues covers and original compositions, the group soon had more than enough material for one album, and talk quickly turned to converting the project into a two-record set. To fill out the album, Carl Radle came up with "It's Too Late," a Chuck Willis number that added a strong country dimension, while Bobby Whitlock contributed "Thorn Tree in the Garden," a sad love ballad made even more striking by Whitlock's emotional vocal. To round out the collection, the band recorded Jimi Hendrix's "Little Wing" as Clapton and Allman's tribute to one of rock's most influential guitarists.

"Layla" has been called one of rock's greatest songs, and *Layla and Other Assorted Love Songs* one of its finest albums, and those working on the album were certain that they had been involved in something very special. "When I finished doing the *Layla* album," commented Tom Dowd, "I walked out of the studio and said, 'That's the best goddamn record I've made in ten years.' I was high as a kite." "I'm as proud of that as any album I've ever been on," proclaimed Duane Allman, who had worked on a few classics in his time.

Inexplicably, Clapton's greatest achievement was a miserable sales failure when it was released at the end of the year. In interviews, Clapton attributed the problem to the band's anonymity (the album cover was just a painting, with nothing to identify the record's title or artists), but in retrospect this seems far-fetched. Clapton's name was listed prominently on the album's back cover, and just in case people might have missed the bandleader's true identity, Polidor distributed thousands of "Derek is Eric" buttons to the record-buying public. More likely, the album's initial poor showing might indicate that the public was wary of new Eric Clapton product. The guitar hero had been all but absent on the Delaney and Bonnie tour and on his first solo album, and a new Clapton offering, featuring players from that album and the Bramlett tour, might have scared off potential buyers. In addition, with the glut of Clapton-related product on the market, it is possible that record buyers were hitting a kind of saturation level, at least for the time being. Whatever the reasons, a couple of years would pass before the public caught up with the direction and pace set on this magnificent record, at which point Clapton had all but disappeared from view and was living in an extended period of semiretirement.

. . .

The recording of *Layla and Other Assorted Love Songs* proved to be the high point for Derek and the Dominos. The band began to disintegrate almost as soon as Duane Allman left the studio to rejoin his own band and the Dominos returned to England. In the past, Clapton had seen creative differences, ego problems, and personal ambition contribute to the downfall of his bands; this time around, excessive drug use led to his group's demise.

It had started earlier, in England, when Clapton and the Dominos were working on George Harrison's solo album. Cocaine was the main drug of choice, but its usage had not become intrusive to the studio work. As Clapton would recall, his dealer required him to purchase some heroin whenever he bought cocaine, but this, too, was not a problem, since Clapton and the band feared the drug and didn't want to get too heavily involved with it. Clapton would snort a small amount of the heroin from time to time, but the rest piled up by the bagful in a drawer in his home.

Things changed measurably when the Dominos hit Miami, where cocaine was so readily available that Clapton and his friends could order it from a newsstand near the beachfront hotel. At first, the drug use was rather casual, but it picked up dramatically as the band's workload increased and the group members were spending more and more time in the studio. All of a sudden, the studio became a veritable warehouse of mind-altering substances, legal and illegal, from beer and wine and whiskey to marijuana, cocaine, heroin, hashish, and assorted uppers and downers.

"We were dabbling and fucking around with everything," Clapton remembered. "It was like a snort of coke in one nostril, a snort of smack in the other, a pint of cheap wine in one ear, a bottle of Scotch in the other—it was just full out."

Oddly enough, Clapton explained, the drugs seemed to enhance the group's creativity—or at least leave them with the impression that they were at peak performance. Life in the studio was a hermetic existence with an otherworldly quality to it. Musicians zonked out of their minds could move about freely and without reprisal from the real world; they could jam endlessly, record music, piece together new songs, or overdub parts on already recorded songs, their altered states only encouraging them to stretch the limits further, telling them that anything they did was adventuresome and acceptable.

Both Tom Dowd and Atlantic chairman Ahmet Ertegun were alarmed by the extent of the drug and alcohol abuse in the studio, and both attempted to exert a gentle influence to get the band members to slow down. Ertegun broke down in tears as he told Clapton that he knew where all the substance abuse was going to take the band; he'd been down this horrible road with Ray Charles years earlier. Like so many drug abusers in denial, Clapton tried to assure Ertegun that he had everything under control.

The addiction, Clapton would later claim, was a slow, almost undetectable process, and he and the others found no reason to quit—not as long as good music was being recorded. The camaraderie between band members was reaching its zenith, the group's creativity as solid as it would ever be. Nevertheless, the band's stability was being eroded by chemical dependency. As they would later learn, there was no reclaiming the innocence of their early days, when everything was friendly and all that mattered was the creation of good music.

. . .

In September, Clapton and his mates flew back to London to begin a monthlong tour of England. The shows, held in smaller halls and without a lot of advance publicity about the Dominos' being Clapton's band, went off well enough, but for Clapton, returning to England meant the resumption of his unresolved situation with Pattie Harrison.

This time around, Pattie was more responsive to Clapton's advances. She and her husband had not patched up their marital difficulties, and she was feeling as neglected as ever, in need of the kind of attention and affection that Clapton desperately wanted to give her. She and Eric met in secret on a number of occasions, first after a chance meeting at the theater, when she stayed overnight with Clapton in the city, and then on several subsequent occasions when she joined Eric at Hurtwood Edge.

Clapton pursued her relentlessly. He had her listen to *Layla and Other Assorted Love Songs*, and then offered her the book that had inspired the title cut. For Pattie, the internal conflict was stronger than ever. She cared for Eric but she was frightened by the extent of his passion for her. She was not the kind of person easily given to carrying on extramarital affairs, and the international fame of both her husband and her suitor, plus the fact that she still had strong feelings for George, only added to the tremendous stress of what seemed like an unresolvable dilemma.

Still, she had to make a choice, and no matter which way she went, she was bound to deeply hurt someone she loved. After agonizing over the matter for what seemed like a lifetime, she met with Eric and told him that she had decided to stay with her husband and try to work through the difficulties in their marriage.

Clapton was not about to walk away from Pattie without a fight. Stunned by her decision, he countered with a frightening ultimatum. Pulling out a packet of heroin, he told Pattie that if she refused to stay with him, he would take the drug as a way of dealing with her rejection. He couldn't bear to be without her. Eric's threats horrified Pattie, but she stood by her decision. They would not see each other for nearly three years.

Clapton was still trying to cope with this turn of events when he was dealt another stunning blow. Shortly after returning to England, he had been delighted to learn that Jimi Hendrix had recently concluded a series concerts in Sweden, Denmark, and West Germany, and was presently in London, taking a break from touring. Clapton contacted Hendrix and the two agreed to get together at a Sly and the Family Stone concert at the Lyceum Ballroom on September 18, 1970. On the afternoon of their scheduled meeting, Clapton visited a West End guitar shop, where he saw and purchased a left-handed Stratocaster as a gift for Hendrix. He took the guitar with him to the Lyceum that evening, but Hendrix, who had agreed to appear onstage with Eric Burdon's group, War, later that evening, had disappeared before Clapton could reach him after the concert. "He was in a box over there," Clapton explained, "and I was in a box over here, and I could see him, but I couldn't . . . we never got together."

Nor would they ever see each other again, for Jimi Hendrix died within hours of Clapton's seeing him in his box at the Lyceum.

Clapton was devastated by the loss. After hearing of Hendrix's death, Eric wandered around his estate, unable to cope with the news, feeling abandoned and lonely. "When Jimi died," he noted fifteen years later, "I cried all day because he'd left me behind."

Suddenly, the Dominos' recording of "Little Wing" took on an added, highly charged dimension. Clapton had intended it as a tribute to a living legend, but now that Hendrix was gone, the song hit on a different emotional level. Performing it onstage became a kind of catharsis, night after night, in which Clapton bore witness, as well as he could, to his own wonderings about why he, and not his friend, was still alive.

. . .

Somehow, in the face of such defeating emotional setbacks, Clapton managed to endure. His tour of North America had its high points, but far too often the shows were rough around the edges and poorly represented the band's capabilities. Before leaving Miami for their concerts in England, Derek and the Dominos had scored an enormous amount of cocaine to take on the road during their forthcoming American tour, and while the band members would have been loath to admit as much, the drug use was probably as responsible as anything for the Dominos' uneven level of performance.

Clapton may have hit a creative peak during the recording of *Layla*, but his popular appeal continued to diminish in America. Robert Stigwood had lined up a variety of outlets for the band's concerts, ranging from small university halls to huge auditoriums, but he was finding it difficult to fill the larger venues. Not helping matters was a *Rolling Stone* review panning one of Derek and the Dominos' early shows, the reviewer criticizing Clapton in particular for being off in his performance. In the eyes of fans and critics alike, Clapton had gone from being God to being mortal—and mortal was not enough.

The typical Dominos set, as in their appearances in England, offered a sampling of blues covers, numbers from Clapton's solo album, and new material from the yet-to-be-released *Layla* album. On the good nights, the band would use songs such as "Tell the Truth" or "Let It Rain" as the framework for extended jams, but, as had been Clapton's experience with Cream, on bad nights the improvisations sounded uninspired and aimless. "After Midnight" and "Layla" were two notable omissions from the set list. As good as "Layla" was, and as beneficial as it might have been for Clapton to perform it on the eve of the new album's release, Clapton found that he could not simultaneously play "Layla" 's distinctive riff and sing the song's chorus; he needed a second guitarist.

In early November, while the Dominos were well into their North American tour, Clapton received a call from Robert Stigwood, who told him that Jack Clapp was critically ill and had been taken to a Guildford clinic. Clapton rushed back to England. He had seen his grandparents only on occasion in recent years, but their relationship remained warm, even as Clapton's star continued to rise and he had less and less time for them. Clapton still felt a debt of gratitude to his grandparents for the way they had raised him, and he found it very difficult to watch Rose suffer through her husband's final days.

With so much turmoil in his life, it was only natural that Clapton would turn to any available source of inspiration, comfort, or even temporary relief. His use of drugs, including heroin, grew heavier as the Dominos' tour progressed, and probably served to numb some of the pain caused by his love for Pattie Harrison and the recent deaths of Jimi Hendrix and his grandfather, but this did little to lift his spirits. For that, he needed something else.

During the Derek and the Dominos tour, Clapton hooked up with a Pentacostal disc jockey who accompanied him through a portion of the tour. The dj initially approached Clapton as a friend concerned about his spiritual welfare, and Clapton, bothered by self-doubts and the recent events in his life, was grateful to find someone who seemed to care more about him as an individual than as a celebrity. The dj, however, strongly disapproved of Clapton's drug use, and he was soon railing about how the devil was taking over his soul, the sermons only making Eric feel even worse about himself than he already did. Clapton finally lost his patience when, in the midst of a group of people, the dj announced that he wanted to conduct a prayer meeting.

"Well, maybe not *right* now," Clapton advised, noticing that the dj's proposal had made the others in the room uncomfortable.

"Look," the dj angrily replied, "I've come to every gig of yours and I've watched you doing your gig. What about you watching me do mine?"

The man stormed out when Clapton refused to pray, ending Clapton's brief interest in born-again Christianity. As far as Clapton could tell, the whole thing had been a show, with the disc jockey more interested in the level of his performance than in the quality of his message. The man might have been genuinely concerned about the state of Clapton's soul, but he was lacking so much as a clue as to what measures to take to heal it.

The extent of Clapton's problems was manifest when he tried to use a short break in the Dominos' touring schedule to produce an album by Buddy Guy and Junior Wells. Clapton had jammed with Guy and Wells in Paris, when the two blues greats were acting as the support group for the Rolling Stones, and after the show he had suggested to Ahmet Ertegun that Atlantic cut an album by the two. Ertegun said that his label would put out the record, but only on the condition that Clapton produce the album.

Unfortunately for all concerned, Clapton was in terrible shape when he arrived at Criteria Studios for the sessions. He had not used heroin in several days, and he was feeling the torturous effects of withdrawal. Since no one knew about his habit, he pretended to be ill. "I was completely underequipped mentally and emotionally in every way to deal with this situation," he recalled. "I shouldn't have been there. I was sweating and dying inside."

Clapton had talented people with him in the studio. Dr. John was there to lend his talent on piano, and the Dominos were hanging around, ready to work if the occasion arose. In addition, Tom Dowd was on hand to assist with the production. Clapton, however, was in no condition to make the necessary production decisions, and after a while, Dowd suggested to Clapton that he go home. The album, *Buddy Guy and Junior Wells Play the Blues*, was eventually released in 1972, but its sound was as lackluster as its title, and Clapton would be haunted for years by a sense of guilt that he'd let two of his heroes down.

Derek and the Dominos slogged through the remainder of their U.S. tour, honoring obligations more than making good music, occasionally outplayed by their support act, a then relatively unknown singer-songwriter named Elton John. An appearance on "The Johnny Cash Show" caught them in good form, playing "It's Too Late," as well as a raucous version of "Matchbox" with Cash and Carl Perkins, but such tight playing was now more an exception than the rule. The drug use, as Clapton later commented, had taken its toll.

"I don't know how we got through it with the amount we were taking," he confessed. "I couldn't do it; I would die now. Even the idea of it frightens me. But it definitely wore the band down and introduced a lot of hostility that wasn't naturally there. It drove a wedge between each one of us."

The band returned to England in December. By all rights, with a new album on the market and a big money-making tour behind them, Derek and the Dominos should have been a happy, if exhausted, unit. Instead, they were barely alive, victims of rock's well-documented excesses. They were finished as a touring band.

. . .

As 1970 came to an end, Clapton was entering his own dark night of the soul. His personal and professional lives were a shambles, and he had no clear direction that he intended to take. He could no longer claim to be just a casual drug user, but his increasing intake had not rendered him helpless or apathetic, either. All that would come later, with a vengeance that Clapton would regret for the rest of his life.

For the time being, he tried to maintain. He was still a major figure in the rock establishment, and that alone provided him entrance to inner sanctums denied people of lesser rank.

One such instance occurred in mid-December, not long after Clapton's return to England, when he was invited to a birthday party for Keith Richards in London's Olympia Sound Studios. The Rolling Stones were at work on their *Sticky Fingers* album, and had taken a break from the sessions to throw a party for Richards. Over two years had passed since the death of Brian Jones, and during that time Clapton's name had been bandied about as a possible replacement for the Stones' brilliant guitarist. Clapton, though, had been preoccupied with a band of his own, and the Rolling Stones decided to give the position to Mick Taylor, a John Mayall alumnus. After Richards's party, Clapton gave the Stones a taste of what might have been when the band set up in the studio and Clapton played on the recording of a new song entitled "Brown Sugar." (Unfortunately, that particular take of the song, also featuring Al Kooper on keyboards, would not be included on the album, and would be available to the public only through bootlegs.)

Other studio sessions followed. The Dominos reunited briefly in January, not to record a project under their own name but to serve as a backup band on Bobby Whitlock's solo album. The album, released as *Bobby Whitlock*, provided a hint of where the Dominos might have progressed had "Derek" not been so much at the band's center: the gospel- and blues-tinged music was an ideal avenue for Whitlock's singing and songwriting, and it would have been a worthy addition to the Dominos' own work, had Whitlock been allowed a stronger position in the band.

The division between the members of the group was evident to all when Derek and the Dominos gathered in Olympic Sound Studios in April and May, and tried to record their second studio album. The good-time feelings present during the recording of the band's initial album were long gone, replaced by rancor and competition between the members. In addition, two important people were missing from the recording sessions. Duane Allman had been killed in a motorcycle accident the previous year, and since the album was being recorded in England, Tom Dowd was not present to add the stabilizing influence he had contributed to *Layla*. The Dominos were still capable of making good music, as the five tracks eventually released on Clapton's *Crossroads* compilation would indicate, but such high points seemed almost coincidental when placed in the context of the quarreling between band members in the studio. Egos had reached such an inflated state that they were easily bruised by the kind of creative disagreement common during recording, and that, along with the level of paranoia brought on by months of heavy drug abuse, led to tension that no one could overcome.

The anger and frustration boiled over when Clapton suggested to Jim Gordon that his drumming was wrong for one particular song they were working on.

"Well," Gordon shot back, "the Dixie Flyers are in town. You can get their drummer." Evidently, Clapton had made a previous remark about another band's drummer—a favorable statement that Clapton didn't remember making—and Gordon's reaction was based on resentment about those earlier remarks.

Clapton lost whatever patience he had left for the band. He put down his guitar and walked out of the studio. Derek and the Dominos, he decided, were finished.

"There was no going back," he recalled. "It was time to move on. Or time to just go and hide and rest."

And hide he did—literally. "I remember to this day being in my house, feeling totally lost and hearing Bobby Whitlock pull up in the driveway outside and scream for me to come out. He sat in his car outside all day, and I hid. And that's when I went on my journey into the smack."

. . .

The "journey," as Clapton so delicately put it, lasted for nearly three years, from May 1971 to April 1974, marking a period of professional seclusion that found Clapton working in public only on rare occasions, and private isolation that found him ignoring or insulting friends and relatives alike, leaving them fearing for his life. Throughout the period, his management and record company tried to downplay his mysterious disappearance from the public. Clapton, they claimed, was tired and burned out and in need of a rest—which, in fact, was true enough. The word *semiretirement* crept around music circles, but those in the know realized, after a point, that Clapton's absence from the scene involved something dark and menacing. In the wake of the drug-related deaths of Brian Jones, Jimi Hendrix, Janis Joplin, Jim Morrison, and others, there were plenty of whispers about Clapton's being rock's next casualty.

It's easy, in hindsight, to attribute Clapton's drug addiction and behavior to the kind of self-destructive tendencies for which so many artists are known. He certainly had his reasons for falling apart, ranging from his unrequited love for Pattie Harrison to the recent deaths of his grandfather and Jimi Hendrix, from his disillusionment with superstardom to the failure of his latest band. Clapton recognized his self-destructiveness, even if, in a textbook case of denial, he found a way to romanticize it all.

"When I first started using [heroin]," he said, "George [Harrison] and Leon [Russell] asked me, 'What are you doing? What is your intention?' And I said, 'I want to make a journey through the dark, on my own, to find out what it's like in there. And then come out the other end.'"

Such sentiment, Clapton acknowledged, was relatively easy to state. He had his music to fall back on, as well as a girlfriend and a large support group of friends and family to bail him out—even if he recognized the latter only subconsciously. He could afford to test his limits.

This, however, is only part of the explanation. As difficult as it may be to believe, given the horrible, destructive properties of a drug such as heroin, Clapton's withdrawal from public was also a rather convoluted measure of self-preservation. He had just passed his twenty-sixth birthday, and during his brief professional career, he had reached heights achieved only by an elite few at such an early age. He had felt the proverbial walls closing in on him—from the demands of fans and record company officials to his own musical standards—all exacting their individual tolls, all driving him like a pinball off polarized hazards of egotism and self-doubt. The rock 'n' roll establishment could do terrible damage to someone as sensitive as Clapton, and with his personal life in disarray, a withdrawal or retreat was not only unsurprising—it might have been necessary.

Drugs, as Clapton would later lament, were not the answer. On a typical day, he would sleep late and then spend most of his waking hours in a heroin-induced haze, passively strumming his guitar, building model cars and airplanes, lying around, listening to music or watching television . . . vegetating. Visitors were discouraged, the mail went unopened and the phone unanswered. According to his own estimation, the cost of his habit rose slowly but dramatically, going from approximately £150 a half-ounce when he started to £250–300; at the depth of his addiction, he was spending nearly £1,000 a week on heroin. Ironically, the enormous expense was an offshoot of Clapton's need for self-preservation: snorting heroin, though much safer than injecting it, required more powder to achieve comparable highs, and was therefore much more expensive.

At first, Clapton's absence from the public was barely noticed. Entertainers of all types were famous for taking breaks after especially active work periods. However, as the months passed, with little or no word from Clapton, the unanswered or unreturned telephone calls, along with his rarely going out in public, began to alarm family members and friends long accustomed to hearing from him on a regular basis. When people dropped by to visit, more often than not Clapton would leave them knocking on an unanswered door, or he would refuse to meet them if Alice let them in. When he did manage to pull himself together enough to meet people, he could be lethargic at best or irritable at worst. Either way, visitors were regarded as intruders to be dispatched as quickly as possible.

Throughout this period, Alice Ormsby-Gore was a godsend—the enabler who looked after Clapton's needs, took care of household chores, ran his flak with visitors, and even purchased the drugs that he required. She, too, had been using heroin and was addicted to it, but she placed Clapton's needs before her own, to the extent of suffering through withdrawal when the drug supply was running short and she gave Clapton the heroin she would have been using herself.

Like many substance abusers, Clapton deluded himself into thinking that no one could tell that he had a problem. He believed that he could hide his addiction, and he would become angry if someone saw through the ruse and addressed the issue with him. In looking back, he was ashamed of his behavior. "All I learned in those days," he allowed, "was a lot of bad things. I learned how to be unreliable. I learned how to be negative, how to hide and how to insult people, all the worst things in life."

If nothing else, Clapton played no favorites when it came down to finding victims for his deplorable behavior. When his mother learned of his condition and came to see him, he stayed in his room and refused to meet with her, leaving her with Alice for hours on end. Ben Palmer received no better treatment when he twice drove down from Wales to check in on his friend. On his first trip to Hurtwood Edge, Palmer was left knocking on the door; neither Eric nor Alice answered. The second time around, he was greeted by a zonked-out and irritable Eric Clapton, who let him know, in no uncertain terms, that he wasn't welcome.

George Harrison remained a confidant during those dark days. Clapton permitted Harrison entry into Hurtwood Edge where he might otherwise turn others away, and despite his feelings for Harrison's wife, he considered George his closest friend. He was therefore in a very tough spot when, in July 1971, Harrison asked him to play at a benefit he was organizing to help relieve the victims of the war, floods, and famine in Bangladesh. Performing onstage was about the last thing he wanted to do, but the cause was a worthy one, and he was never one to turn down a favor for Harrison. He and Alice were on their way to New York the last week of July.

. . .

Clapton barely made it to the concert.

Before leaving England, he had arranged to have a supply of heroin waiting for him in New York, but when he arrived he was horrified to learn that the deal hadn't gone through. Alice ran frantically around the city, trying to find the supply he needed, while Clapton holed up in his hotel, racked by withdrawal sickness that left him virtually helpless. The heroin on the street, Clapton discovered, had been cut many times over, and while it might have been fine for those injecting it, it was far too weak to hold up to the strength of his habit. Although Harrison was conducting daily rehearsals for the shows, Clapton was far too weak to think about picking up a guitar and practicing with the band.

All efforts to obtain the heroin failed, and for a while it looked as if Clapton might not appear at the show. At the last minute, one of the cameramen filming the concert offered Clapton some of the methadone he was taking for an ulcer. The morphine-based drug was, at best, a poor substitute, but it was sufficient to get Clapton on his feet.

The two shows at Madison Square Garden on August 1, 1971—one in the afternoon and one in the evening—featured such names as Clapton, Harrison, Leon Russell, Ringo Starr, and, as the ultimate surprise, an appearance by the reclusive Bob Dylan. Harrison had hoped to reunite the Beatles for the occasion, but those hopes fell through when Paul McCartney failed to make a firm commitment and John Lennon backed out at the last minute. Even so, the performances, filmed for theatrical release, were a monstrous success, finding Harrison playing such Beatles hits as "Something," "Here Comes the Sun," and "While My Guitar Gently Weeps," and Dylan singing "Mr. Tambourine Man," "Just Like a Woman," and "A Hard Rain's A-Gonna Fall."

Although no one in attendance would have noticed, Clapton struggled through the shows, trying to hold his own in the all-star band, acting as a sideman on most of the concerts' numbers. His solo on "While My Guitar Gently Weeps" drew roars of approval from the packed house, but by his own account, he was carried by the others onstage. "It wasn't me at all," he said, characteristically harsh in his judgment of his performance. "I just wasn't there. I wasn't there at all." If his bandmates had a problem with his performance, they didn't let on in public. To a grateful George Harrison, bringing together all the musicians on short notice with very little rehearsal was almost too much to ask. "That whole show was a stroke of luck," he admitted.

The concert would be Clapton's last stage appearance—with the exception of his turning up for an unexpected ten-minute jam with Leon Russell in December—for nearly a year and a half. As soon as he was back in England, he resumed his self-imposed isolation, venturing away from his home for occasional trips into town or visits with his grandmother.

Clapton's name, however, did not sink from sight, and for that he could thank the clever and creative efforts of his manager and record company. Robert Stigwood worked effectively at deflecting speculation about the nature of Clapton's problems, standing by his statements about Clapton's needing a break from his feverish activities in recent years. Stigwood manipulated the rumor mill like the skilled veteran he was, denying rumors that might prove damaging to his client, neither confirming nor denying reports—such as those saying that a new Dominos album was forthcoming, or that Clapton had completed a second solo album—if it meant keeping Clapton's name in print. If, for example, people wanted to believe that Clapton had coproduced an album by George Harrison, as was reported in *Rolling Stone* on January 4, 1973, Clapton could only benefit from the speculation.

One of the tastier rumors involved Clapton's working with John Lennon on a project known as "The John and Yoko Mobile Political Plastic Ono Band Fun Show." On September 29, 1971, Lennon and Yoko Ono had written Clapton a long letter detailing plans for a touring band that, in Lennon's words, would be "a kind of 'Easy Rider' at sea": a cruise ship would be rented and fully staffed, carrying a core group of musicians (Lennon, Ono, Clapton, Klaus Voorman, Jim Keltner, and Nicky Hopkins) who would travel the world, giving concerts in such countries as Russia, China, Hungary, Poland, Australia, and Japan. A film crew would come along to capture the festivities for one of Lennon and Ono's avant-garde movies. The main priority, Lennon insisted to Clapton, would be for the tour to be fun and laid-back.

At another time, Clapton might have leaped at such an opportunity. Lennon's plans were certainly compatible with Clapton's love of being a sideman in a band, and the former Beatle was much better equipped to pull off another magical mystery tour than Delaney and Bonnie had been with theirs. Still, after all his problems with securing drugs in the biggest city in the United States, Clapton couldn't begin to entertain the notion of spending lengthy periods at sea and trying to obtain heroin in foreign countries. In the end, Lennon's proposal, like so many of his improbable but compelling ideas, fell through—but not before rumors of it, including Clapton's name as part of the deal, made the rounds in music publications.

With Clapton refusing all interview requests and recording no new material, Atlantic Records had to work overtime to keep "new" Clapton product in the record bins. Luckily for the record company, Clapton's workaholism prior to his retirement left a number of new albums on which he appeared as a guest guitarist, including Dr. John's *Sun, Moon and Herbs*, *Jesse Ed Davis*, *Stephen Stills 2*, James Luther Dickenson's *Dixie Fried*, and Duane Allman's *An Anthology*. In addition, the company released *Live Cream Volume II*, two major Clapton compilations (*The History of Eric Clapton* and *The Best of Eric Clapton*), a live album by Derek and the Dominos (*In Concert*), and the single "Layla"/"Bell Bottom Blues." Clapton's name received a further boost when George Harrison's *Concert for Bangla Desh*, a three-record set capturing the benefit concert in Madison Square Garden, was released. To those not paying attention, or those willing to buy anything with Clapton's name attached, it was as if Eric had never left the business.

Clapton may not have been in the studio recording new music, but he was never far from a guitar. Most days, he played for at least a short while, improvising songs off blues licks, recording his singing and playing on a cassette recorder. Not much came from all the playing, but he always knew, even when his addiction was at its worst, that he would be playing again someday. He just needed more time and a good reason.

• • •

To finance the high cost of his heroin supply, Clapton considered selling some of his valuable guitars—or even one of his cars. He was still quite wealthy, but his allowance from Robert Stigwood could not accommodate both his day-to-day living expenses and his drug habit, and he hated the notion of Stigwood's knowing how bad his addiction really was. Stigwood may have suspected the worst, but he stayed away from Hurtwood Edge and avoided discussing any of his suspicions with Clapton. Eric would always be grateful for Stigwood's discretion in advancing him money without asking a lot of questions.

Two other people close to Clapton—Lord Harlech and Pete Townshend—were especially supportive during his long journey through addiction to eventual recovery. Lord Harlech had his daughter's health and welfare to consider, but he felt a great fondness for Clapton as well. It was not only painfully difficult to watch Eric and Alice slip deeper and deeper into heroin addiction, but as one of Great Britain's most highly regarded citizens, Lord Harlech stood to face significant public embarrassment if the British press ever decided to pursue the rumors floating around about his daughter and Clapton. Harlech tried everything he could think of— from pleas to at least one threat to turn Clapton in if he didn't seek help— but he remained patient and supportive when his efforts went unheeded.

Townshend's friendship was an interesting study. He and Clapton had grown close when both were in New York for the Murray the K shows in 1967, and both had hung out together with Jimi Hendrix when Hendrix had first arrived in London. Their relationship, though, was an improbable one, given the tendency of both to be stubbornly outspoken, if not highfalutin, about their musical preferences, and the two were quite different in their tastes. Their friendship endured despite these differences, and Townshend was there for Clapton during his most trying days. Alice would call Townshend at all hours and ask him to come to Hurtwood Edge, presumably to help with the latest crisis, and Townshend would invariably make the hour and a half drive, usually to discover Alice was strung out from giving Clapton her heroin and needing comfort herself. Townshend, who had been clean from drug use for some time, tried to be sympathetic, though he couldn't help but be deeply troubled and somewhat put off by the condition Eric and Alice were in.

Clapton turned to Townshend in August 1972, when he decided to go back over the unfinished tapes of the second Derek and the Dominos album and see if there was anything salvageable from the sessions. Clapton had built an eight-track recording studio in his home, and he wanted Towns-hend to help him mix the tapes. The work went poorly, mainly because the music was incomplete as recorded, but also because Clapton had a change of heart about the project almost as soon as Townshend arrived at Hurtwood Edge. The indecision, Clapton confessed to Townshend, was due mostly to his addiction. He wanted to work, but he wasn't certain that he was up to it.

Townshend refused to give up so easily. Clapton, he decided, needed to get away from his home, even if only for a short while, and with this in mind, he managed to persuade Eric into flying to Paris to see The Who perform at the Olympia Stadium. As soon as they returned, Townshend huddled with Lord Harlech, who was involved with organizing Fanfare for Europe, a series of events intended to commemorate England's entry into the Common Market. Both Townshend and Lord Harlech believed that a Clapton concert might be both proper for the series and good therapy for Clapton personally. It took some persuading, but Clapton finally agreed to do the show.

• • •

By the end of 1972, Clapton was testing the waters for a possible return. He was still hidden away most of the time, but there were indications that, given the right project, he might consider coming out of retirement.

In August, about the same time he was working with Pete Townshend on the Dominos tapes, Clapton agreed to appear with Stevie Wonder at the Great Western Festival in London, with performances at the Rainbow Theater to follow. The concerts were canceled when the Rolling Stones, also scheduled to appear at the festival, dropped out because of contractual problems. Wonder, however, invited Clapton to record with him, and the two met at London's Air Studios in October to work on the title cut for an (unreleased-to-date) album called *I'm Free*. Finally, in what turned out to be an unlikely series of aborted projects, Clapton was contacted about working on George Harrison's follow-up to *All Things Must Pass*—an album with a working title of *The Magic Is Back*. (Apparently it wasn't, for that album, like Wonder's, never saw the light of day.) Although the projects didn't pan out, it was encouraging to see Clapton doing even a limited amount of work.

The main event was the concert scheduled for the Rainbow Theater on Saturday, January 13, 1973. Pete Townshend had assembled a band of top-notch musicians to back Clapton, including Eric's old Blind Faith mates Stevie Winwood and Rick Grech, Faces guitarist Ronnie Wood, and Traffic drummer Jim Capaldi, along with percussionist Rebop and drummer Jimmy Karstein. Ronnie Wood volunteered his home for rehearsals, and for ten days prior to the concert, the group ran through a selection of songs that dated as far back as Clapton's days with Cream. Townshend, by his own admission, was worried about pulling off the show, and there was some tension when the makeshift band ran through the songs, but Clapton was loose and confident during the rehearsals, showing few effects from his two years away from working with a band. For all his initial reservations about doing the show, Clapton was ready to face an audience again.

Demand for tickets was tremendous—so much so that a second show was quickly added to the evening. Fans lined up outside the box office the night before tickets went on sale, and the two shows sold out in a couple of hours. George Harrison, Elton John, Jimmy Page, Ringo Starr, and Joe Cocker were among the many luminaries present in the 3,000-seat theater, joining die-hard fans primed to witness nothing less than the resurrection of a rock icon.

The Average White Band opened the show with an hour-long set that received warm response from a crowd that was interested in seeing only one person. Unfortunately, that person had yet to appear when his support group was leaving the stage. The concern backstage mounted as the minutes passed. Townshend whispered a short prayer in private, while Robert Stigwood and Ahmet Ertegun nervously sipped at their drinks. The scheduled starting time of the show came and went, still with no word from Clapton. The tension was suddenly broken when, fifteen minutes after the show was to start, a side door to the stage swung open and Eric and Alice walked in.

The delay had been the result of Clapton's choice of clothing for the evening—a white suit he had worn in his Derek and the Dominos days. During his two-year absence, Clapton had added considerable weight to what had once been a very slender frame, and he no longer fit into the suit's trousers. Alice let out the pants by sewing in a six-inch patch of material, but the alterations had taken time.

The crowd at the Rainbow Theater was on its feet, applauding wildly, when the band introduced as Eric and the Palpitations took the stage, Clapton flanked by Ronnie Wood and Pete Townshend. The searing riff from "Layla" acted as an informal announcement of what people could already see: Eric Clapton was back, even if for only a night. His playing, initially tentative, picked up as he gained confidence in himself. The set list read like a greatest hits compilation of Clapton's career to that point: "Layla," "Badge," "Bell Bottom Blues," "After Midnight," and "Crossroads." There were even a few surprises, such as "Bottle of Red Wine," a chestnut from his solo album, and "Pearly Queen," an old Traffic number. The concert was flawed, with the band showing signs of its brief time together, but as far as the audience was concerned, the show could have gone on all night.

A number of people tried to stay for the second show, adding to an already hectic scene and delaying the start of the second performance by an hour. While ushers and security people frantically tried to clear the hall for a new audience, Clapton relaxed with his bandmates, ridding himself of several weeks of preconcert anxiety.

The second show was a great improvement over the first. The band, warmed up from the earlier concert and playing more as a unit, seemed to draw energy from the powerful emotional responses of the crowd. Clapton's playing was more dominant and authoritative than in the first show. A beautiful blues solo on Bessie Smith's "Nobody Knows You when You're Down and Out" was followed, a short time later, by a solo on "Presence of the Lord" that was so intense that Clapton ruined his wah-wah pedal and had to finish the evening without it. During "Let It Rain," in a scene lifted from the pages of Clapton's Yardbirds days, the band improvised a lengthy percussion jam while Eric had a broken string replaced, Townshend concluding the twelve-minute interlude by shattering a set of maracas and tossing them to the crowd. As an encore, Clapton ended where he began—with a second performance of "Layla."

Clapton was happy with the evening as a whole, though he admitted afterward that he felt a little intimidated before going on for the first set. "I was very nervous, felt sick, the whole bit," he told a reporter, conceding that he was "in a daze" for the first few numbers. "Then it suddenly clicked and I began to get some confidence. But I still thought that we didn't play enough, yet afterwards they told me that we went on too long."

Clapton was overwhelmed by the response he received at the shows, and he was pleased by the enthusiastic reviews published in the music papers. His playing may not have been perfect, but he had lost very little during his two-year layoff. Unfortunately, he needed more than an onstage tune-up to prepare himself for reentry into the music scene; he still had an addiction to overcome.

eight

Return of Slowhand
1973–75

I'm a very extreme person and I live in a very extreme way. If I spend
all that time hibernating, I have to bounce back right into the other
direction when I finish—go right out in front again. . . . I was twitching
to do something and that's the only thing I knew to do.

he Rainbow concert signified only a temporary return. Months
passed without Clapton's showing any indication that he had plans other
than to continue his habits of hiding out and taking drugs. Lord Harlech
was especially concerned, perhaps because he realized that Clapton's failure
to respond to his comeback show was proof positive of the deadly nature
of his addiction. His daughter, Alice, was only twenty and she, too, appeared
to have lost the self-respect necessary to overcome her problems with
drugs. Harlech pleaded with them to seek professional help, but neither
was ready to respond.

Still trying to bide time during Clapton's absence, RSO—a new record
company formed by the Robert Stigwood Organization—issued *The Rainbow Concert* in September. The six-song album, offering selections culled
from both concerts, passed over some of the true highlights of the evening.
Worse yet, the album suffered terribly from recording problems, offering
sound quality that was not much better than a good bootleg. Sound separation in the music was virtually nonexistent, so Clapton's solos wound up
mixed in a stew of music that sounded heavy-handed and lacking any

definition. Fans listening to the album on the heels of Clapton's two other recently released live albums (*Live Cream Volume II* and Derek and the Dominos' *In Concert*) must have wondered how much farther Clapton could fall: the album didn't match all the fanfare raised at the time of the Rainbow concerts.

In fact, Clapton was reaching the end of the line. He was ingesting two grams of heroin a day—and sometimes more. His financial situation was growing grim, and he realized that he would either have to start working again or face the prospects of selling off possessions to bankroll his current lifestyle. He remained unconcerned about his own health, but Lord Harlech was finally reaching him with his worries about Alice. Harlech had heard of a radical form of neuroelectric addiction treatment developed by a Scottish doctor named Meg Patterson, and he urged Eric and Alice to give her method a try. Clapton resisted the advice for a while, but he eventually gave in.

"It finally came to the point," he remembered, "where I could see that [Lord Harlech] was worried about [Alice], so I thought, well, OK, if it gets her off, I don't mind going along with it because I can see the concern of a father for his daughter and I'm not doing any good, so let her see if she can get cured. I wasn't actually looking for a cure myself. I was quite happy to go on. It just so happened that I got cured as well."

· · ·

Dr. Meg Patterson had come across her addiction treatment in 1972, while she was working at a hospital in Hong Kong. A physician associate at the hospital had been using electroacupuncture as a form of anesthesia, and both he and Dr. Patterson had observed that sending an electrical current through acupuncture needles not only deadened nerves during surgery but also eased withdrawal symptoms among those patients addicted to drugs. Dr. Patterson subsequently invented a clip-on device, in which electrodes were attached to the ears and given stimulation via wires connected to a small, hand-held box. She had recently moved back to England and was working on ways to perfect the treatment when Eric Clapton and Alice Ormsby-Gore visited her Harley Street home in London.

After their initial consultation, Dr. Patterson and a nurse moved into Hurtwood Edge to help administer the treatment, monitor its progress, and make certain that Eric and Alice stayed away from drugs. This proved to be difficult, for the addicts were now, in effect, returning to the scene of the crime. For all Dr. Patterson knew, small stashes of heroin could have been hidden anywhere in the spacious building or on the grounds. In addition, Alice had problems with alcohol as a result of giving Clapton her heroin when the supply was running low. Alice had taken to drinking large amounts of vodka and was now addicted to alcohol as well as to heroin. After a week at the Clapton estate, Dr. Patterson suggested that Alice be treated at a clinic elsewhere, and that Eric move in with her and her husband, George, and their three children.

This was hardly good news to Clapton, who was now being asked to remove himself from all the constants in his life over the past three years, but he packed some clothes, grabbed an acoustic guitar, and settled in with the Pattersons.

Nights were the most difficult. During the daylight hours, Clapton could use Dr. Patterson's neuroelectric treatment, which, in effect, shocked him into distraction from his withdrawal symptoms and cravings for heroin. At night, however, he could not use the machine, and he would grow so restless he couldn't sleep. During some of the tougher evenings, Meg would offer Eric a sleeping pill, which she really hated to do, and on others George would sit up with Clapton, trying to talk him through his difficulties.

A former missionary, George complemented Meg's treatment perfectly by working on a person's spiritual needs while his wife dealt with the physical ones. George and Eric would talk for hours at a time, with Clapton repeating all the old reasons for his getting involved with heroin, but George wasn't buying. Indeed, he argued, many musicians had used heroin—and far too many had died as a result—but heroin itself did not make one creative; it might help bolster existing talent and creativity, but it did so artificially. An artist could look within himself, without the use of drugs, and find the spiritual aesthetic needed to produce great work.

After a couple weeks with the Pattersons, Clapton's withdrawal symptoms were gone and he was ready for the next phase of his treatment—a period of hard labor designed to work him back into good physical shape. To accomplish this, Clapton was shipped up to Wales, where he spent a month working on a farm owned by Frank Ormsby-Gore, Alice's brother. The years of physical inactivity had left Clapton soft and out of shape, but after a few weeks of baling hay, chopping wood, and doing any sort of manual labor necessary around the farm, he was trim and well tanned, looking better than he had appeared in many years. He and Frank got along well, and on occasion, after a long day's work, the two would repair to the local pub, where they would spend hours talking and getting drunk. Meg Patterson frowned on the use of alcohol during her rehabilitation program, but Clapton insisted, then and in the future, that it was a necessary part of his split from heroin.

With each day on the farm, Clapton gained more confidence about the possibilities of resuming his career. He was playing guitar and writing new songs, and he began to think about recording a new album, which, he hoped, might be followed by a world tour. His spirits had lifted substantially from the low point he had experienced in the early stages of his treatment, and he now felt that he was able to face the pressures that, at one time, had driven him from doing what he loved.

There was, however, one critical matter that needed to be resolved, and that became apparent when Alice joined Eric in Wales.

In recent weeks, as he withdrew from chemical dependency and felt his mind clearing, Clapton caught himself thinking more and more about Pattie Harrison. His time with Alice, he reasoned, was reaching an end, even though Alice still harbored the hope that they would be able to resume their relationship after their rehabilitation.

The last couple years had been brutal to their relationship. The two had spent much of their time together arguing, and while Alice in particular · continued to have very strong feelings about Eric, the sense of codependency, strongly developed at the height of their addiction, had damaged the way Eric and Alice dealt with each other. Meg Patterson had suggested that the two stay apart during their respective rehabilitation processes, and she further advised them to sleep separately when they were together on the farm in Wales. Clapton found this significant. He candidly told Alice of his feelings for Pattie Harrison, and after much discussion, the two reached the same painful conclusion: they would be better off going their separate ways.

After a month in Wales, Clapton went home with renewed determination: he would finish putting his life in order, and to do this, he had to move quickly and decisively. He visited Robert Stigwood's office and advised him that he was ready to record again. Stigwood was to contact Tom Dowd in Miami and book the Criteria Studios for sessions—the sooner the better. Clapton then called Carl Radle, his bassist with Derek and the Dominos, and asked if he could recommend musicians for recording and touring. Radle had sent Clapton tapes of the work he was doing in the States— work that had a distinct country bent—and Clapton explained that he was looking to record something more laid-back than the guitar-oriented bands of his past. On the heels of the success of such bands as Cream and Led Zeppelin, every new group in the book seemed to be blasting out power chords on guitar, and Clapton wanted to do something else. He favored a sound more like what he'd heard from the American singer-songwriter J. J. Cale. Radle suggested drummer Jamie Oldaker and keyboardist Dick Sims, two Tulsa musicians he had been working with in recent months. Although Clapton had no way of knowing it at the time, these musicians would be his core unit for the next five years.

"I wasn't actually *looking* for a band," he remarked later. "But I was *hoping* something like that would happen. If I had been looking for a band, I'd have rounded up better-known musicians. Everything along the route was accidental. The only person I knew was Carl, and I knew I could trust him."

Next on his agenda was to resolve, one way or the other, his obsession with Pattie Harrison, and to accomplish this he took a very direct, aggressive approach. When he ran into the Harrisons at a party at Robert Stigwood's estate, he confronted George with his feelings.

"I'm in love with your wife," he told Harrison. "What are you going to do about it?"

"Whatever you like, man," Harrison replied. "It doesn't worry me. You can have her and I'll have your girlfriend."

Harrison's response was not as flippant as it might seem, nor was Clapton's challenge as brazen as it appears on the surface. The Harrisons had been growing apart for years and, as George would admit himself, they probably should have split up sooner. "In this life," he said later that year, talking to reporters questioning him about his breakup with Pattie, "there is no time to lose in an uncomfortable situation."

This, of course, was precisely how Clapton felt. He had stutter-stepped around the issue for years, feeling the weight of depression pull him down as far as he dared to go. In taking a less forceful approach, he had dragged the scene out longer than need be, and in confronting the Harrisons, he was pushing the issue to resolution, risking everything on that one single moment.

Not that everything was settled that very instant: shocked by the scene, Pattie rushed out, leaving both men behind. She was stunned by Clapton's approach, but she was equally hurt by her husband's response. The confrontation might not have been proper in the civilized British sense of manners, but it helped clarify the situation for Pattie. She eventually left the party with George, but this time Clapton had really gotten through to her.

. . .

Now that he was back in circulation, Clapton began to hit his old haunts again, often in the company of Pete Townshend, who turned out to be a formidable drinking buddy. Townshend was currently working with film director Ken Russell on a film adaptation of The Who's rock opera, *Tommy*, and he asked Clapton if he would be interested in playing the part of a preacher in the film. The one song he would be singing was Sonny Boy Williamson's "Eyesight to the Blind"—the only nonoriginal song in

Townshend's creation. Clapton agreed to do the part, and for three days he hung around an army base where the film was being shot, bored by the endless hours of waiting, a bit uncomfortable in the movie milieu, but ultimately turning out a credible performance.

On April 10, 1974, Robert Stigwood officially announced Clapton's comeback with a party at The China Garden restaurant in Soho. The attendant press was offered a one-line statement—"Robert Stigwood announced today that Eric Clapton is leaving for the U.S.A. to begin work on a new album"—and turned loose on a celebrity-laden gathering that included Clapton, Townshend, Elton John, Ronnie Wood, Long John Baldry, and Rick Grech. Tanned and fit, with short-cropped hair and the beginnings of a beard, Clapton was a far sight removed from the rather shoddy-looking figure who had appeared at the Rainbow Theatre fifteen months earlier—the last time the press had been given access to him.

Clapton chatted with reporters who, after submitting less than kind reviews of his previous albums, were suddenly in his corner. He talked about his plans for an album and tour, but other than mentioning Carl Radle, he offered no hints about the musicians that he might be working with. This led to all kinds of speculation, from rumors of a Cream reunion to another Derek and the Dominos album. Expectations ran high. "At press time," one reporter wrote, "the rest of his band members remain the reclusive genius's secret, but there's a fine betting chance some superjamming will go on."

• • •

Superjamming was precisely what Clapton hoped to avoid. He'd had his fill of playing the role of superaxman, and he was hell-bent on making his new album a total departure. Unlike his time with Derek and the Dominos, when he spent an inordinate amount of time worrying about whether he should be disguising his identity as a band leader, he was now enthusiastic about being a front man. This time around, it was definitely going to be Eric Clapton and His Band.

When he arrived in Miami, Clapton was lacking a definite plan for his new album. He had a couple of new songs he wanted to record, as well as a standard blues number or two, but other than that, he was open to anything. Carl Radle, Jamie Oldaker, and Dick Sims were still in Oklahoma, fulfilling recording obligations as sidemen, and while he waited for them to show up in Miami, Clapton tinkered with new songs and worked with Tom Dowd on the tapes of the second Derek and the Dominos album. Upon hearing Clapton's ideas for the new album, Dowd suggested a blending of a mellow sound with the harder-edged rock material that Clapton fans were used to hearing, the idea being that Clapton would be more effective and better received in his new identity if he displayed his versatility. As always, Clapton trusted Dowd's judgment.

In addition to this work, Clapton spent some time jamming in the studio with George Terry, a local sessions guitarist he had met in Miami during the making of *Layla and Other Assorted Love Songs*. Terry had his own rhythm section, and they worked with Clapton in the studio for a while, but Clapton decided to keep only Terry when Radle and the others showed up. Terry was a custom-made second guitarist who instinctively knew when to act as accompanist and when to push Clapton as a kind of foil. He also had the distinction of introducing Eric to the music of Bob Marley and the Wailers, when he played Marley's *Burnin'* for Clapton. One of the songs on the album, "I Shot the Sheriff," caught Clapton's fancy, and he decided to record it for possible inclusion on the new album.

Clapton's catch-as-catch-can attitude about making the record spilled over into the way he completed his roster of studio musicians. Al Jackson, drummer for Booker T. and the MG's, was in town and hanging around the studio, and Clapton employed his services for one song. Keyboardist Albhy Galuten, a Criteria Studios regular who worked with Clapton on *Layla*'s "Nobody Knows You When You're Down and Out," was also enlisted for the new record. Other musicians came and went. Some—most notably Stephen Stills—were excluded from the sessions because Clapton didn't want to upset the chemistry that was beginning to develop among the musicians already on hand.

The most important new member, in terms of influence on the album's sound, was Yvonne Elliman, a young singer who had gained her reputation when she appeared in the role of Mary Magdalene on the *Jesus Christ Superstar* album. Not surprisingly, her involvement on the Clapton project was a happy accident, the result of a peculiar chain of events. Elliman was married to RSO executive Bill Oakes and, as a fan of Clapton's, she had accompanied her husband to Miami with the hope of meeting Eric.

"I just wanted to go *peek* at him," she explained. "I got to the studio and started talking to him and I started to sing some background vocals. We started writing. We wrote one song ["Get Ready"] together. And somehow he asked me to be in the band."

Singing duets with a woman was a new experience for Clapton. He had sung with Bonnie Bramlett and Rita Coolidge on his first solo album, but their voices were strictly in the background. With Elliman in the band, Clapton had a bold new dimension to match the new direction his music was taking. Elliman could provide a smooth, distinct harmony on the ballads, yet she was equally adept at singing in a gritty rhythm and blues style on the uptempo numbers. The decision to include her on the album was nothing short of brilliant.

Clapton and his band stayed at 461 Ocean Boulevard, in a spacious house graced with palm trees and a view of the ocean. Having the band members around produced the same effect as when Clapton invited Delaney and Bonnie and Friends, and then the Dominos, to move into his home in England: people could not only jam until all hours if they so desired but they grew comfortable with each other along the way. In addition, Criteria Studios was kept open twenty-four hours a day for Clapton, assuring him of the opportunity to record if and when the mood struck him.

After a slow start, the album quickly began to take shape. New songs sprang from studio jams. Such Clapton favorites as Robert Johnson's "Steady Rollin' Man," Elmore James's "I Can't Hold Out," and Johnny Otis's "Willie and the Hand Jive," featuring some of Clapton's most confident vocals ever, gave the album a sense of play that contrasted with the moody, confessional tones of "Please Be with Me" and "Give Me Strength." George Terry's "Mainline Florida," developed off one of Terry's guitar riffs, added a rock 'n' roll touch to recordings that were otherwise laid-back. In taping a couple dozen songs, the band reached out to blues, rock, folk, gospel, soul, and reggae, the music arising from a directional uncertainty that only urged the band to explore every musical avenue.

"That's why things were loose at that time," reflected George Terry. "[Eric] had to find out what he was going to do. Some days he'd just completely clam up, and other days he'd be a fireball. I never knew what to expect, so I just played it by ear."

As did Clapton, who was now playing Dobro and acoustic guitar almost as much as his Stratocaster. In making the album this way, Clapton realized that he was taking as many risks as he took on his first solo album—perhaps more, given the fact that *Eric Clapton* presented a sound similar to the already familiar Delaney and Bonnie style, whereas this new album was quite a departure from his previous studio work with Derek and the Dominos. In reinventing himself, Clapton had to face his own self-doubts. For example, as much as he liked "I Shot the Sheriff," he was not entirely convinced that his arrangement of the song was appropriate for the album. "I didn't think it was fair to Bob Marley, and I thought we'd done it with too much of a white feel or something," Clapton would say years later, fully appreciating the irony of the song's becoming his first number one single in America, as well as its part in introducing Marley's music to the public.

Clapton's worries proved to be unfounded. Marley had no problem with the new arrangement of his song, and not long after it was issued, he called Clapton and the two talked at length about it. Clapton was curious about the autobiographical nature of the song. What had really happened? Had Marley shot the sheriff? Marley played it cagey. Parts of the song, he informed Clapton, were based on fact, but he wouldn't say which parts.

Clapton would hear from Marley again, when the reggae star was touring England, but he wouldn't actually meet him face-to-face until he went to see a Marley performance at the Hammersmith Odeon. On that occasion Clapton visited Marley backstage and they had a warm conversation that left Clapton very impressed with Marley. "He was just a *great* guy," recalled Clapton. "He was serious about what he was doing, but he was very gentle."

The music press buzzed with excitement as word of Clapton's recording sessions in Miami made the rounds. ERIC CLAPTON IN U.S.: SOMETHING'S HAPPENING HERE, proclaimed a *Rolling Stone* headline, the story posing questions about the album he was cutting, the musicians he was using, and whether he intended to tour in support of the record. "Eric Clapton is in the studio again, fresh from a welcome-back party in London and surrounded by enough heavyweight paraphernalia to suggest that Something Big is in the offing—but still enveloped by the protective innuendo that has turned him into one of big-time rock's mystery men."

The "mystery man" avoided the media, reserving any remarks he might have had for the inevitable onslaught of interview requests he'd be facing when the album, tentatively entitled *Feed the Cook*, was released. When the press eventually learned about his Ocean Boulevard digs, Clapton retreated with his band to an enormous yacht supplied by Robert Stigwood. He would go public only when the time was right.

• • •

When it was released in August 1974, *461 Ocean Boulevard* was greeted by wide-ranging critical response. The adjective *laid-back* popped up at one point or another in virtually every review of the album—not necessarily in a complimentary way.

"Without a doubt, this is the most tasteful, laid-back, unassuming, unadventurous and yet totally meticulous album I've ever heard in my whole life," wrote one reviewer, seeing that all bases were covered, but also making clear the opinion that this record was not *Layla*. Another reviewer was even less kind: "Between laid-back and listless, between the tastefully restrained and the downright niggardly, the line can be perilously thin. . . . What is disturbing is not that Clapton plays differently, but that he plays so little." Other notices commended Clapton's new approach, one reviewer going so far as to state that *461 Ocean Boulevard* was "probably the truest representation of who and what Eric Clapton really is."

The real superlatives, almost to the review, were reserved for Clapton's singing, which seemed to surprise critics as much as Clapton's change in musical direction. "His singing is good, improving with each successive re-emergence," offered one critic, who perceptively observed that the album, coming in the aftermath of Clapton's well-publicized personal problems, was "a painfully positive attempt to retain an equilibrium." Another wrote: "Clapton's voice is so soothing you might call it sultry. If there's much truth to the theory that Clapton lost a certain percentage of instrumental facility during the course of his heroin addiction (a rationalization for his sparse guitar showoffmanship throughout the LP), he certainly made up for it in his voice."

Generally speaking, the reviews immediately following the release of *461 Ocean Boulevard* were more a reaction to the changes in Clapton's style than analyses of the overall merits of the album. In years to come, after numerous listenings had given people the chance to grow comfortable with the record, the album would rightfully gain the reputation of being a Clapton masterwork. Whereas it initially seemed to be the antithesis of *Layla and Other Assorted Love Songs*, it eventually grew to be regarded as a superb display of another side of Clapton—as radical a departure, perhaps, as Bob Dylan's strapping on an electric guitar at the Newport Folk Festival in 1965 but every bit as legitimate.

Placed in the context of all Clapton's recorded music, the songs have withstood the test of time. "I Shot the Sheriff" continues to be a concert staple, and "Let It Grow," with its long synthesizer-enhanced fade-out and beautifully layered vocals, still ranks as one of Clapton's finest pop performances. None of the songs sound dated, and Clapton's voice is as compelling now as it was in 1974. In subsequent albums, Clapton would try to recapture the magic that graced this recording, but he would never succeed. Like *Layla*, *461 Ocean Boulevard* was a once-in-a-lifetime work that will remain one of the important defining moments in Clapton's career.

. . .

Madness followed the Criteria sessions. After three years in dull, drug-induced seclusion, Clapton was full of manic energy, ready to burst out.

He was feeling playful, and he wanted to put together a tour that reflected this spirit.

Robert Stigwood was all for launching a gigantic march across America, an idea not shared by his young assistant and right-hand man (and present Clapton manager), Roger Forrester. Clapton, argued Forrester, was still fragile from his period of inactivity and substance abuse, and he had replaced heroin with alcohol, which created uncertainties of its own. Clapton, Forrester felt, needed time to ease into his return. Stigwood might have understood Forrester's concerns, but he vetoed his ideas nevertheless, and a nationwide tour, lasting most of the summer, was booked.

The band rehearsed in Barbados. Clapton kept things loose with a variety of practical jokes that included staging a huge spaghetti fight, which, as time would show, was only a hint of craziness to come. From Barbados, the group flew to Scandinavia for warm-up concerts in Stockholm and Copenhagen. After the Denmark show, Clapton found himself netting some unsavory headlines when he got so drunk he had to be carried out of a Danish strip club. This bit of "silliness," as *Melody Maker* delicately termed it, inaugurated a tour characterized by heavy drinking, onstage antics, and in some cases, destructive behavior.

"That tour was drowned in alcohol," noted Yvonne Elliman, who often wound up as Clapton's drinking partner. "We were all a bunch of lunatics, and we were falling into the rock band ritual, where you break things in hotel rooms and you throw food at each other and you release everything."

Not all of the antics had a negative effect. Some were good, clean fun, even if they did tend to confuse audiences. Clapton employed "Legs" Larry Smith, the former drummer of England's quirky Bonzo Dog Doo-Dah Band, to act as the tour's eccentric master of ceremonies, and every night, as the house lights were dimmed for the show, Smith would come running out onstage, armed with a plastic ukelele and attired in anything from wild polka dot pants to a formal evening gown. He would then introduce Clapton, who more often than not would make his entrance wearing an equally outrageous outfit chosen from a wardrobe of strange neckties, oversized pants, beat-up jackets, or even a see-through raincoat. Somehow, the outlandish entrance seemed an appropriate introduction to the band's first song, a poignant interpretation of Charlie Chaplin's song "Smile."

To concertgoers, such antics might have seemed out of character for a man who tended to present himself in interviews as a serious, occasionally brooding musician. However, there was another side to Clapton—a side that reveled in slapstick humor, pranks, and practical jokes—that surfaced when he was away from the spotlight. Friends and family members loved to hear the stories of Eric's latest road escapades, and this tour featured more than just a few, from food fights to one outrageous occasion when he peeled off his clothes and shocked passengers by streaking down the aisles of a commercial flight. For Clapton, the moments of humor and drunken revelry were releases of long-built-up tension.

From an aesthetic standpoint, the early portion of the tour was a mixed bag. The shows were advertised as Eric Clapton and His Band, but Clapton habitually remained in the background and relied on a band that had yet to totally jell as a unit. The music press covering the tour was not enthusiastic about Clapton's reluctance to assume onstage leadership, but they were even less amused by a couple of the shows in which an obviously drunk Clapton walked onstage and put on a subpar show. One such instance occurred in Buffalo, where Clapton engaged in a long drinking session with members of The Band before slogging his way through a performance.

The quality of the shows steadily improved, especially after the band had more time to play together and Clapton adapted to playing again in front of the enormous crowds that filled the stadiums and arenas on each step of the tour. Concertgoers, informed by the media of Clapton's problems of recent years, greeted him with a hero's welcome, happy to see that he had survived his battles with the demons that had kept him away. *Time* magazine heralded his return in a story praising his growth as a musician and individual; *Rolling Stone* ran an excellent cover story interview by Steve Turner, in which Clapton candidly addressed questions about his problems with heroin. To the hundreds of thousands of people who saw the shows, there was plenty of reason to celebrate.

The concerts proved to be a nice mixture of the electric and acoustic sides of Clapton, the early portions of the shows devoted to quieter songs such as "Let It Grow," "Can't Find My Way Home," or "Easy Now," the later portions opening up into some excellent blues jams on "Have You Ever Loved a Woman?," "Tell the Truth," and "Crossroads." In keeping with the partylike atmosphere, numerous "special guests" turned up for onstage jams with Clapton. Freddie King, a longtime Clapton influence, played in two of the shows, and Todd Rundgren took the stage for the encore at the concert in Madison Square Garden. In Atlanta, Clapton was joined by Pete Townshend and Keith Moon of The Who, and John Mayall sat in on a blues jam in Long Beach, California.

No guest, however, was more welcome to Clapton than Pattie Harrison, who joined him early on in the tour. Clapton's confrontation with the Harrisons in England, along with a subsequent conversation between Eric and Pattie in private a short time later, had convinced Pattie that her marriage was truly over. George had done nothing to keep her with him; if anything he had been generous, if not cavalier, about her relationship with Clapton. ("I'm friends with Eric—really," he told a *Rolling Stone* reporter, when word of the relationship reached the press. "I'd rather she be with him than some dope.") Pattie left her husband within a few weeks of her conversation with Eric, and she had been staying with her sister Jenny in Los Angeles when she received a phone call from Clapton, who asked her to join him on the tour. She readily accepted the invitation.

The first leg of Clapton's U.S. tour ended in early August. By the usual Clapton standards, a summerlong tour would have been quite enough, and while the long string of concerts, along with the constant travel and hotel living, were indeed physically and psychologically exhausting, Eric remained energetic and ambitious, ready to take on the world. "I Shot the Sheriff" was moving up the singles chart, and the demand for *461 Ocean Boulevard* was the greatest for a Clapton album in years. Hoping to cash in on this surge in popularity, Robert Stigwood penciled in a busy schedule for the remainder of the year, including another brief swing through the States and a four-concert stint in Japan, before closing out with a series of shows in Europe.

Clapton had most of August and September free, but rather than return to England for a break from the action, or even take a vacation in the United States, he went back to work in the recording studio, first as a guest guitarist on a new album by Freddie King, then to do a new album of his own. For someone who, less than a year earlier, was uncertain about his future in the music business, Clapton had returned with a vengeance.

• • •

The original plan was to record the new album in South America. Clapton was fond of Latin rhythms, and he was prepared to continue his exploration into new musical avenues with more reggae and perhaps a song or two with a Brazilian sound. Clapton and Pattie flew to Rio to check out the prospects, but they left the country after several days and canceled any plans for making an album there when they learned of an outbreak of spinal meningitis in the area.

Clapton was then prepared to record the new album in the familiar Criteria setting, but Tom Dowd had another idea. If Clapton intended to record a lot of reggae on the album, Dowd suggested, they should all go to Jamaica—to the source of the music itself. They could record at the Dynamic Sound studio in Kingston.

The Rolling Stones had recently cut their *Black and Blue* album at the studio, and when contacted by the Clapton camp, Mick Jagger had spoken highly of the studio. Kingston could be a little rough, he said, but one could easily avoid the crime and violence by renting houses on the North Shore and flying into Kingston every day. Clapton and his entourage initially attempted to follow Jagger's suggestions, but the daily commute to and from the studio proved to be more bother than it was worth, and they soon checked into the Terra Nova, an English colonial–style hotel in the center of the city.

Clapton enjoyed recording in Jamaica. Once again, he had arrived in the studio with very few songs to record, but unlike the *Ocean Boulevard* sessions, which found him trying to break in a new band and work out new songs at once, he now knew the group well enough to piece together new material with little difficulty. He and George Terry wrote a sequel to "I Shot the Sheriff" entitled "Don't Blame Me (I Didn't Shoot No Deputy)," and the band put together a reggae version of the classic spiritual "Swing Low Sweet Chariot." Clapton also worked out a new blues arrangement for Blind Willie Johnson's "We've Been Told (That Jesus Is Coming Soon)" to complement an adaptation of "The Sky Is Crying," one of Clapton's favorite Elmore James songs.

The feeling, as before, was loose and easy. Clapton had grown comfortable with his role as bandleader, and he was more at ease in hashing out the production details of his recordings. In addition, he had Pattie around for much of the time, which made recording considerably less stressful. Ironically, the peace of mind led to a record that many critics deemed to be too artistically safe.

There was no question that the album was as far removed from the Clapton sound as anyone might have imagined. Clapton had added Marcy Levy, a former background singer for Bob Seger, to sing with him and Yvonne Elliman, but the vocal arrangements, though suitable to the gospel, spiritual, and reggae sounds on the album, removed any noticeable Clapton signature from a record that was even more acoustic and less guitar-oriented than its predecessor. As Clapton himself admitted, the album featured very little that could be played onstage. Nevertheless, he was prepared to defend the record from its detractors. "I wanted that laid-back feel," he said. "I love it. Everyone in the band loved every track on the album." Critics, however, felt otherwise. Most commented favorably on Clapton's singing, noting that it was good to see him apparently at peace with himself, but the general take on the album was one of disappointment: "no growth, no strain, no sense of challenge."

In some respects, there was plenty of challenge in just getting the album out to his satisfaction. Although he maintained artistic control over the music that went on the album, Clapton faced difficulties elsewhere. His original title—*The Best Guitarist in the World*—*There's One in Every Crowd*—was rejected outright, as was his choice of cover art. The title, record company officials said, could be misinterpreted, and after much discussion, the "Best Guitarist" half of the title was dropped, leaving only the confusing title of *There's One in Every Crowd*. The proposed artwork—a Clapton drawing of a man holding a drink—was similarly dismissed, the record company contending that it was too much like Bob Dylan's artwork on *Planet Waves*. Clapton ultimately settled on a cover photograph of one of his dogs, though his drawing did appear in the album's gatefold.

Clapton might have suspected that he would run into trouble with the public's accepting his new album. In interviews, he held out the hope that it might be a sleeper along the lines of *Layla*, which had grown on people after repeated listenings, but he also conceded that it was off the beaten path. His own band had told him as much. For this reason, he withheld several reggae numbers, including two that had been recorded with reggae legend Peter Tosh, from the finished product.

Record buyers, as always, placed the bottom-line judgment on the album, and when *There's One in Every Crowd* was released in April 1975, very few people were carrying the album to the cash register. Clapton fans, it seemed, still demanded their guitar hero.

. . .

When the touring finally came to a halt toward the end of the year, Eric and Pattie settled into Hurtwood Edge. The estate had fallen into disrepair over recent years, and Pattie took on the task of trying to restore it to some of its former luster. Living with Clapton, she determined soon enough, was much different from living with George Harrison, and she was bothered by some of Clapton's habits. She was appalled, for instance, to see how nonchalant Eric could be in his treatment of such costly possessions as his immense wardrobe and record collection.

Their relationship, initially formed in an aura of desperation and mutual reliance, developed steadily. Clapton could be old-fashioned and chauvinistic in his attitudes toward women, but he could also be very sensitive and romantic. Pattie appreciated the attention he gave her—something that had been missing in the months before her breakup with her husband. Although Harrison remained steadfast in his insistence—to Clapton and the media—that he could accept the turn of events in the strange triangle that had developed over the years, Clapton remained touchy about the issue, and his relationship with Harrison, at least for the time being, resembled an uneasy truce.

To their chagrin, Eric and Pattie had very little time to establish any kind of domestic life at Hurtwood Edge. Between the enormous success of *461 Ocean Boulevard* and his extensive touring, Clapton had earned enough money to throw him into a high tax bracket, and to get around paying oppressive taxes, Clapton was instructed that he would have to spend almost all of the year out of his own country. He would be allowed up to sixty days in England, but only on the condition that he didn't work. Clapton, quite understandably, was infuriated by this disclosure, yet he had little choice but to comply.

While the Robert Stigwood Organization busied itself in booking tours for the band in Hawaii, New Zealand, and Australia, Clapton checked out and rented a new place in the Bahamas, on the aptly named Paradise Island. In Clapton's mind, the small island just north of Nassau was not a bad base of operations, but it was a far cry from home. His beachfront house, built by an American lawyer named Sam Clapp, was a magnificent Spanish-style structure stocked with luxurious imported antique furniture and priceless artwork. The beach in Clapton's backyard turned out to be the same beach used as a setting in the Beatles movie *Help*—an irony that, in all likelihood, did not escape Pattie's notice. The home, at best, was a great place to vacation, but it lacked the character of Hurtwood Edge.

Before leaving for another long series of concerts, Clapton went into the studio and worked on an album by Arthur Louis, a Jamaican who had moved permanently to England and was currently making a name for himself as one of the country's few genuine reggae artists. One of the songs being recorded, a reggae interpretation of Bob Dylan's "Knockin' on Heaven's Door," caught Clapton's attention—so much so that he would record it as his own single a few months later, using essentially the same arrangement, much to Louis's disapproval.

Clapton celebrated his thirtieth birthday on March 30, 1975, a week before leaving for the opening of his tour in Honolulu. To commemorate the occasion, Robert Stigwood threw a huge party at his estate, with such guests as Rod Stewart, Elton John, Ronnie Wood, and Ringo Starr; Alice Ormsby-Gore, with whom Clapton had remained on friendly terms, made an appearance, as did Eric's mother, who delighted guests by teaming up with Elton John and singing pub tunes until the wee hours of the morning. The all-night party acted as an informal send-off for a man who, in the months ahead, would be seeing very little of his friends or native country.

nine

Further on Up the Road
1975-77

I got fed up with the thing about "The Legend"—I wanted to be something else and I wasn't really sure what it was. I was just latching on to people and trying to be like them to see if something else would emerge, and all that *did* emerge in the long run is what I am now.

ric Clapton's band, maligned by some members of the press as not being worthy of Clapton's prodigious talents, had developed into a tight, cohesive unit. Clapton and Carl Radle had been playing together since the Delaney and Bonnie days, signifying the longest continuous period that Eric had worked with any musician, and while the Clapton–George Terry tandem had been operating for less than a year, the two were as artistically compatible as any two-guitar lineup Clapton would ever work with.

Clapton's long year of touring began in April. He spent most of the month in New Zealand and Australia, the band playing large venues in Melbourne, Sydney, Adelaide, and Perth. To Clapton's bitter disappointment, Pattie had to remain behind: she and George Harrison had been busted for pot possession in 1969, thanks to the efforts of the ever-vigilant Norman Pilcher, who took special pride in nailing rock stars for drug infractions, and as a result of her conviction, Pattie was not allowed in the United States or, as it so happened, New Zealand. In time, Clapton would prefer to hit the road alone and would, in fact, ban spouses or lovers from accompanying their mates on his tours, but for the moment, he missed Pattie and was angry that such relatively minor events in her past kept them from being together.

After the Australian dates, Clapton returned to Great Britain, where he intended to spend a week before joining Pattie in the Bahamas. According to the plan, he and Pattie would relax for a short period prior to Clapton's lengthy U.S. tour. His stay in England, however, wound up lasting several weeks, courtesy of a serious automobile accident that, had he been less fortunate, might have taken his life.

The accident occurred a couple days after the band's return to England. Still wired from the trip, and feeling the effects of jet lag, Clapton had slept very little and was looking for something to pass the time. On a whim, Clapton offered to show George Terry one of his prized new possessions, a silver-gray Boxer Ferrari, which at that point had been driven less than a hundred miles—and most of these miles had been logged by Clapton's mechanic. Clapton then decided to take the car for a spin, and he was no more than a couple of blocks' distance from Hurtwood Edge, driving down a narrow road, when he suddenly found himself sharing the road with a semi headed straight toward him. With nowhere to go, Clapton tried to squeeze past the huge truck. He didn't make it. The semi hit the Ferrari on the door, destroying the car and pinning Eric in the wreckage.

When Clapton didn't return from his drive, George Terry grew concerned and set out to look for him. He was horrified when he saw the semi and the ruined car in the road, but he was even more surprised when he ran to what was left of the Ferrari and saw Clapton.

"Eric's sitting in the car with a smile on his face," Terry recalled. "He's got blood coming out of his ears and nose, and his nose is broken, and he's sittin' there smilin' and laughin': 'Oh boy, scratch another $40,000 car!'"

"It was too quick to know what happened to me or how close to death I'd come," Clapton explained. "When the firemen came to cut me out, I was sitting there with blood pouring down my face, smiling. So I must have been grateful to be alive, even though I didn't know."

An ambulance rushed Clapton to the hospital. In addition to the broken nose, Clapton had a number of cuts and bruises and was in shock, but his injuries were relatively insignificant in comparison to what might have happened. In the end, there was only one major source of concern: some fragments of flying glass had entered one of Clapton's ears, and doctors worried that trying to remove them might puncture his eardrum. Rather than immediately clean out the ear, the attending physicians decided to see if nature would force out the bits of glass. For several days, nothing happened and Clapton remained deaf in the one ear. When word of this injury leaked out, the music press and radio station disc jockeys speculated that Clapton might have sustained permanent, or even career-threatening, damage. Fortunately, their fretting turned out to be unwarranted. Within two weeks, all the glass had been removed, Clapton's hearing had been fully restored, and he was on his way to Paradise Island.

· · ·

The U.S. tour, like all Clapton visits to the country, offered an array of highs and lows, guest performers, and memorable moments. With Carlos Santana and his band backing Clapton, the concerts promised guitar pyrotechnics galore, and the two musicians gave the huge crowds their money's worth, whether performing separately with their respective bands, or during the encore to Clapton's set, when Santana would join Eric for an extended jam on Sonny Boy Williamson's "Eyesight to the Blind." Santana's presence undoubtedly prodded Clapton into playing his very best, if for no other reason than the fact that Clapton was never happy about the prospects of being upstaged by his support act.

"We did a show at Nassau Coliseum, where John McLaughlin jammed with us," Santana recalled. "Clapton waited for John to say his thing and for me to say my thing, and then he came out with a *switchblade*, man. You know, he doesn't play fast, but like my conga player, Armando Peraza, says, 'He gets inside the note.'"

The media took notice. In their write-ups of the tour's shows, rock writers endorsed Clapton and his band with a vigor absent from reviews of his previous tour.

"Erratic performances that featured a lazy Clapton letting the band take over have been replaced by a healthy display of stability and pride," wrote one reviewer. "Gone are the days Clapton lethargically kicked off concerts with a timid acoustic greeting. These days, he opens straight away with a full bodied version of 'Layla.'"

The band—and George Terry in particular—was singled out for its great improvement: "George Terry, very much Clapton's right-hand man throughout the show, must carry a lot of the credit for injecting vitality and a fresh approach into these well-worn classics. . . . Throughout, he matches the lead note for note, forcing Clapton, as it were, to play somewhere near his peak."

Clapton's sets, as on his tour the previous year, changed from show to show, with the individual band members getting a turn in the spotlight at different points in each performance. Yvonne Elliman handled vocal chores on "Can't Find My Way Home," and George Terry sang the lead vocals on "Mainline Florida." The highlights continued to be the blues songs, particularly "Further on up the Road," on which Clapton and Terry traded scorching blues licks that, on any given night, could bring the crowd to its feet. On occasion, the audience pressing toward the stage or dancing in the aisles would threaten to turn an otherwise spirited concert into an ugly scene, but Clapton had learned from previous experiences the basic fundamentals of crowd control from the stage. By interspersing ballads with uptempo numbers, and crowd-pleasing standards with new or relatively unknown songs, Clapton managed to keep the emotional response at a level that avoided the tension and violence characteristic of earlier tours.

The success of the tour, contrasting with the failure of *There's One in Every Crowd*, convinced RSO Records that a live album was needed to balance not only the corporate ledgers but also the general perception of Clapton's career. Clapton had always differentiated between his onstage and studio work, but the differences between the two artistic personae had become so distinct over the past two years that people were in danger of losing sight of the fact that both were essential parts of the same musician. For all his attempts to shed his guitar-hero image on vinyl, Clapton still played some of his hottest solos onstage. A live album, decided RSO, would unite the images.

Clapton resisted the idea. Such an album, he argued, wouldn't necessarily accomplish this goal, since each one of his concerts offered highly variable performances and different set lists, and two sides of a record couldn't begin to capture what his band was all about.

Clapton's argument was not without merit. As bootleg albums of concerts from this period indicate, the highlights of any given show were the blues numbers, which tended to run from six to fifteen minutes each. In the era before the compact disc, when an artist was given a limited amount of time per album side—generally twenty-five minutes at the top end—Clapton would have been able to fit only a handful of his blues numbers on the live album. In addition, there would be very little, if any, thematic unity to such a recording.

Luckily, Clapton had Tom Dowd to help him sift through these problems. Dowd understood Clapton's reluctance to engage in any project simply for commercial gain ("He doesn't *owe* anybody any hit records or hit albums," he told one interviewer at the time), yet he could also see the validity of the record RSO proposed. He had an outstanding tape of Clapton and Terry working out on "Have You Ever Loved a Woman?" and this recording alone, he told Clapton, justified a live album. Clapton finally agreed, on the condition that Dowd himself put the album together.

Given the wealth of material at his disposal and the time restrictions the album format placed on him, Dowd did a magnificent job of piecing the album together. The record, he decided, should focus on Clapton's guitar playing, mainly on the blues numbers. To place as many songs as possible on the album, Dowd had to do some judicious editing. He broke Clapton's

"Rambling on My Mind"/"Have You Ever Loved a Woman?" (almost always performed together as a lengthy medley) into two separate songs, and faded out his long solo on "Drifting Blues,"* a slow, acoustic blues that worked as an effective contrast to Clapton's wah-wah solo on "Presence of the Lord." (In addition, the best available version of the song found Clapton playing snatches of "Ramblin' on My Mind," which would have been repetitive.) The resulting album, released in August as *E.C. Was Here*, contained only six songs, but each entry displayed a particular facet of Clapton's guitar skills. It may not have been a definitive statement, but it was a worthy sampler.

Critics applauded the effort. One reviewer, confessing boredom with the perennial debates over which guitar player ranked at the top of the heap, offered high praise for Clapton's blues playing, calling *E.C. Was Here* "a triumph, even for those who don't care for guitar players as heroes." "Clapton sings and plays with the authority, looseness and self-confidence of bluesmen twice his age," wrote another, noting that Clapton's long suit would always be his blues-playing ability; "*E.C. Was Here*," he continued, "despite a few minor flaws, demonstrates just how far the art of blues guitar can be developed."

· · ·

While in America, Clapton found time to sandwich in some light studio work, first on his single "Knockin' on Heaven's Door," and then on projects with the Rolling Stones and Bob Dylan, the former for a projected Clapton single that, unfortunately, never saw release.

In retrospect, "Knockin' on Heaven's Door" probably deserved a better fate than the indifference with which it was greeted. Clapton's reggae arrangement was pleasing enough, and the playing on the single was first-rate. However, the public, for whatever reasons, seemed unprepared for

---

*The song was eventually restored to its entirety when the album was reissued on compact disc.

an uptempo Island rendition of Bob Dylan's dark song, and the record sank almost as soon as it was issued.

His work with the Rolling Stones didn't even make it that far. Earlier on the tour, while enjoying an off day in New York, Clapton had hooked up with the Stones at their concert at Madison Square Garden, where he played lead guitar on their classic "Sympathy for the Devil." A short time later, the Stones joined Clapton and his band in the Electric Lady studios, where Clapton was busy putting together a new song called "Carnival to Rio." In a festive studio environment, fueled by a fair amount of drinking, Clapton and the Stones recorded numerous takes of the song that, not surprisingly, rocked harder than most of Clapton's recent studio efforts. Clapton, George Terry, Keith Richards, and Ronnie Wood took turns as soloists. The early takes had a rough-hewn quality that Clapton appreciated, and he intended to include the song on his next album, but contract snafus kept the song from being issued.

The Dylan session occurred on July 28, 1975, during a monthlong break from the tour schedule. Clapton was vacationing on Paradise Island when Dylan contacted him and asked if he would be interested in playing slide guitar on his new album. Clapton accepted without hesitation. There was, however, one hitch: all of his guitars had been shipped ahead to the West Coast, where the second leg of his tour was scheduled to begin. A comedy of errors followed. Clapton had a Dobro shipped in by air from London, but it was broken in transit. Attempts to rent guitars in New York produced nothing that Clapton was comfortable using. He finally just turned up at the studio and borrowed an instrument from folksinger Erik Frandsen, one of a dozen guitarists hanging around the studio during the recording sessions.

Dylan, in typical fashion, was looking for a spontaneous feeling to his music, but the lack of organization in the studio, along with the presence of what appeared to be half the musicians working on the East Coast, led to confusions that made recording difficult. Clapton took a place in the corner of the room and hung on while Dylan led those assembled through a number of songs. Dylan's informal method of recording was as mind-boggling to Clapton in 1975 as it had been when he tried to record with John Mayall a decade earlier—"What's happened to Zimmie?" Clapton was quoted as muttering as he left the studio—but Eric enjoyed himself nevertheless. "There were a lot of guitarists there," he told interviewer Barbara Charone a short time after the session, "but, you see, I can get off on a song just sitting there listening. My attitude is to go in there and do whatever I can, but if there's someone who can do it better, I'll just lay out."

Most of Clapton's guitar work, including his playing on "Hurricane," the successful single from the album, was ultimately wiped from the master tape. His guitar remained intact on "Romance in Durango," which meant that, between working in the studio with the Beatles and Dylan, Eric Clapton had recorded with the most influential band and the most influential singer-songwriter in rock's brief history.

. . .

Clapton rode the crest of one of his busiest work periods with energy that bordered on the manic. He was, by nature, an obsessive personality, but if that hurt him during his extended periods of drug and alcohol abuse, it also kept him very motivated, if not entirely focused, artistically. His tour of the States, and then of Japan, earned him a lot of money and reestablished his reputation as one of rock's top performing artists. On that kind of roll, he was not about to let up.

While touring, Clapton had begun to write songs for yet another album. The new record, he decided, would have a harder edge than his previous two studio releases. Ronnie Wood joined him in the Bahamas during a break from touring, and together they tried to work out some new material, but the going was slow. The environment, Clapton reasoned, wasn't right.

Unfortunately, Criteria was now out of the question, as was his usual producer, Tom Dowd. As Clapton learned, problems had developed between RSO Records and Warner Brothers, the company contracting Atlantic Records and Dowd, and as a result of unresolved differences between the labels, Dowd was not permitted to work with Clapton or any other RSO artists. Under these circumstances, the new album promised to be more of a departure than Clapton had originally anticipated.

In a move that would produce mixed results, Clapton decided to record his new album in California. Members of The Band had constructed a twenty-four-track studio in a beachfront ranchette in Malibu, christened it Shangri-La, and, as Band drummer Levon Helm recalled, "used it as a clubhouse and studio where we and our friends could record albums and cross-pollinate one another's music." The place, Clapton discovered, had its own strange history. At one time it had been an upscale bordello; years later its stables had housed television's Mr. Ed. Shangri-La was presently a musician's paradise—an aptly named place where work could be play—and on any given day, some of the world's finest recording artists would pop in for impromptu sessions, with wildly varying results.

Clapton and his band spent nearly three months at Shangri-La, hanging out and recording with the likes of The Band, Bob Dylan, Van Morrison, Ringo Starr, Pete Townshend, Joe Cocker, Billy Preston, Ronnie Wood, and Eric's old friend from the early days, Georgie Fame. In the aftermath of a year of heavy-duty touring, Clapton was all but taking a vacation. As a result, the sound and arrangement of his songs depended on who happened to be in the studio on the day a song was recorded.

"One of the reviews," recalled Clapton, "said that I was 'cronying'—hanging out and getting everyone to play on the record—and actually it was true, but . . . it was a very, very strong time at the studio, because it had been empty and hadn't been used, and suddenly all these people showed up from nowhere, and it was very hard to get any work done, because people kept walking in and picking up instruments and just playing. So the album's got that on it, and if that's wrong, well, fuck it!"

Not surprisingly, many of the songs had a strong Band-influenced quality to them. During his stay in California, Clapton had grown especially close to Richard Manuel, The Band's troubled but highly gifted piano player, who cowrote one of Clapton's new songs and whose influence can be heard on nearly every other cut. Rick Danko, the group's bassist, contributed to the songwriting, and the entire unit played on the record. "All Our Past Times," a Clapton-Danko number written about Eric's friendship with Richard Manuel, could easily have been placed on one of The Band's albums.

Under normal studio recording conditions, Clapton would have struggled to get anything down, but he thrived at Shangri-La. He was still in the playful, partying mood that had begun with his initial *461 Ocean Boulevard* tour, and he was willing to let the Shangri-La sessions play out in their own way. His birthday happened to fall in the midst of these sessions, and a star-studded jam session occurred during a party thrown for him. Billy Preston, backed by The Band, sang several Ray Charles numbers, Bob Dylan ran through a medley of Beatles songs, and Van Morrison played "Stormy Monday" and "Who Do You Love?"—all to the accompaniment of Clapton, Jesse Ed Davis, Ronnie Wood, and Robbie Robertson on guitar. Afterward, the group sat around and were entertained by an outrageous Dylan monologue that took apart the individual members of the Beatles, one by one.

The sessions became Clapton's answer to *The Basement Tapes*. Songs were written and recorded in collaboration on the spur of the moment. And it was the comfortable, homey surroundings that encouraged a directness and simplicity that gave many of the songs their charm. Although the album from these sessions, *No Reason to Cry*, bore Clapton's name on its cover, it was Eric's ultimate group project.

All told, Clapton and Friends recorded several dozen songs, many of them instrumentals and other standards that did not make the final cut for the album. Some wound up being recorded by others. "This Be Called a Song," a Clapton original, turned up on Ringo Starr's next album, while "Seven Days," an excellent new Dylan song that Dylan hoped would be included on *No Reason to Cry*, didn't make it on either, but was eventually recorded for individual projects by Ronnie Wood and Joe Cocker.

In his own way, Dylan was as much a catalyst for the music coming out of the sessions as The Band. Dylan was still riding high from the success of his Rolling Thunder Revue tour, a gigantic ensemble event that encouraged community spirit among the many musicians taking part in the tour. Though he was clearly the star of the Revue, Dylan had enjoyed standing back and letting everyone take a turn at center stage, and his music had been restructured by the unique talents of the people on board. In addition to bringing this egalitarian spirit to Shangri-La, Dylan contributed "Sign Language," one of the album's better tracks, on which he and Clapton shared lead vocal chores.

Dylan also contributed to the sessions' growing legend with some over-the-top behavior. Recalled Clapton: "He came down and we were trying to work and he goes in there and swans around for a little while in a black leather suit he's just got, and he managed to steal my percussionist's chick, who had one leg in a cast because she'd broken it. Not only that, but he stole all the clothes off Woody's [Ronnie Wood's] bed, took the chick out through the window and shagged her in the tent in the garden outside the studio he had there ready for the occasion. With a cast on her leg! Outrageous fellow!"

Clapton was pleased with *No Reason to Cry*, and over the years he would continually list it as one of his favorites among his own albums. A good portion of these sentiments, however, can undoubtedly be attributed to the pleasurable recording experience. A more objective view finds *No Reason to Cry* an album full of high and low points, and if it is not Clapton's best effort from an artistic standpoint—and it's far from it—it may very well be his most interesting. The noteworthy moments—Clapton's slow blues solo on his cover of Otis Rush's "Double Trouble," his vocal work in general, but specifically his duets with Bob Dylan and Rick Danko—are offset by some of the more embarrassing ones, such as "Beautiful Thing," the album's awful opening cut, or Clapton's blatant imitation of the California sound in "Innocent Times." Calling the record uneven is an understatement.

The rock critics lost their patience with the album and served Clapton some of the most savage reviews of his career. "There's little here that compels you to really listen," wrote a reviewer for *Creem*, complaining of the derivative nature of the songs. Rock critic Dave Marsh, writing for

Rolling Stone, took Clapton to task for producing safe, formulaic music: "This riskless music is invariably boring—which pretty much sums up this album."

The grumblings were beginning to reach an uncomfortable level. During his first decade as a professional musician, Clapton had enjoyed the best reviews imaginable. Critics had lauded him as nothing less than a guitar revolutionary; now they were putting him down as just another burnt-out case. As far as they were concerned, the Muse had slid somewhere beyond his sight and his ventures into other kinds of music were mediocre. To his harshest critics, Clapton was using his reputation to pander subpar product to a gullible public, all at the cost of his shuffling away from the kind of music he did best.

. . .

The critical response to *No Reason to Cry* had little effect on its sales. Despite less-than-stellar showings by Clapton's two most recent albums, and the fact that no hit singles were culled from the new one, *No Reason to Cry* sold well on both sides of the Atlantic, making the album Clapton's most successful new work since *461 Ocean Boulevard*. Such was the enigma of Clapton's career: an album such as *Layla*, highly acclaimed by critics and destined to become one of rock's classic albums, struggled to get out of the gate, whereas a much lesser recording such as *August*, released a decade after *No Reason to Cry* and holding the dubious distinction of being almost universally panned by critics, became Clapton's best-selling album to that point.

After completing his recording sessions, Clapton hung around Los Angeles for another month, working in Shangri-La and other local studios on album projects by Rick Danko, Kinky Friedman, Joe Cocker, Stephen Bishop, Ringo Starr, and Corky Laing. For Clapton, the entire West Coast experience was like a working holiday, a retreat from his grueling schedule the year before. Depending on his mood or the circumstances, Clapton might take in a show at a local club, such as the time when he and Rick Danko popped in at the Roxy for a Crusaders show, only to wind up onstage jamming with Stevie Wonder and Elton John, or he might just sit around, enjoying drinks and conversation with the Shangri-La set.

His prolonged holiday came to an end in July 1976, when he began his first tour of England in a half dozen years. Clapton had originally hoped to limit his performances to small halls and vacation resorts, but the demand for tickets was such that he had little choice but to include a few of the larger venues on his itinerary. The tour started smoothly enough, with a preliminary show in Hemel Hempstead before Clapton officially kicked off the tour with a July 31 appearance at London's Crystal Palace Bowl.

The unique setting at the Crystal Palace created all kinds of problems for the band. The outdoor venue featured a bandshell stage, which, for both security and aesthetic reasons, was removed from the audience by a small, shallow lake. During Clapton's show, which included guest performers Larry Coryell, Ronnie Wood, and Freddie King, dozens of enthusiastic fans jumped into the lake and worked their way to the stage, an uncomfortable situation for band members surrounded by electric wires. The concert came off without incident, though Clapton kept it shorter than his usual show.

Whatever uneasiness Clapton might have felt during that show, however, was nothing in comparison to the embarrassment he caused himself a few nights later, on August 5, at a performance in Birmingham, when he walked onstage drunk and caused a furor by mouthing off about Enoch Powell, a much despised political figure known for his outspoken, controversial opinions on minority immigration and race relations.

"Do we have any foreigners in the audience tonight?" he called out as the applause for his first song was dying down. "If so, please put up your hands. . . . I think we should vote for Enoch Powell."

The remark was the nadir of poor taste, and it couldn't have been delivered at a more unfortunate location. Racial tension was on the rise in Birmingham's working-class community, and the last thing people there needed was a lecture from a drunken, high-handed pop star on how Great Britain, with its influx of foreigners, was becoming a colony.

"What started it," Clapton later explained, "was the upsurge in London of Arab money-spending and their total lack of respect for other people's property—'How much is Hyde Park?' and all that—and for some reason it all came pouring out of me that night." The reason for his outburst that evening, Clapton intimated in a letter of explanation published in *Sounds*, was not only that he'd been drinking too much and was loose-lipped as a result, but that "one foreigner had pinched my missus's bum."

Clapton had no idea that his offhand remarks would be taken seriously, but in weeks to come, he was severely criticized by the media and his fans alike, and he found himself backpedaling to prove that he was anything but racist. The remarks' residual effects lasted for a long time, directly leading to the formation of "Rock Against Racism" as well as queries about the incident wherever he went.

"It still lives to this day," he complained to an interviewer a year later. He had been recording in Jamaica with Ginger Baker, he said, and the local rastas and West Indians gave him funny looks when he was out in public; one even came out and asked him directly if he was racist. "It's a shame," said Clapton, "because there's nothing I can do. I keep saying, 'No, man, it was a joke. I was drunk.' And that doesn't help, because they don't like people who drink either."

Clapton's problems, apparent in his onstage remarks and in his subsequent attempts to explain them, were rooted in his political naïveté. Indeed, his remarks were insensitive and poorly timed, but they were not racist in nature, as some of his critics claimed. On his best day, Clapton couldn't approach the political acumen of John Lennon or Bob Dylan, who both managed to ruffle more than a few feathers with some of their political pronouncements; he was far too grounded in his conservative blue-collar background and his pampered life as a rock star, far too politically naive to pull off any kind of sarcastic or satirical remark.

Clapton would later concede as much, claiming that he was uncomfortable with having to feel a moral responsibility to his fans.

"I also question the artistic ego—whether or not an artist should be allowed just to vent his opinion—because we're not cut out for that job," he said. "I've been in situations where I had to take back what I said. Many times. 'Cause I've mouthed off."

Unfortunately, Clapton didn't take this approach in the Powell fiasco. Instead, he compounded his problems by trying to counterpunch his critics. Rather than simply admit that he might have spoken out of turn, Clapton defiantly held his ground, unrepentant in the face of blistering criticism. Such stubbornness, totally in character for Clapton, who had a tendency to arch his back whenever he was under fire, didn't serve him well. He was stung by the criticism—particularly from those who suggested that he was the worst kind of hypocrite of all, a racist earning a living off black people's music—but he was not astute enough to engage in any kind of effective damage control. He could only plow ahead and hope the storm would subside in time.

• • •

In hindsight, the Enoch Powell incident illustrated a much greater problem for Eric Clapton than an occasional lapse in good judgment. Clapton was drinking entirely too much, and his attempts to write off the incident as an unfortunate result of his being drunk might have served as a warning signal had Clapton given it some serious thought. That kind of contemplation, sad to say, would only occur much later, when the drinking reached a state where it was literally life threatening.

For the time being, he used all kinds of rationalizations for his drinking, all of which had a kernel of legitimacy at the core. He initially drank as a calming substitute for his problems with heroin. On tour, it was something he did to release the boredom of road life and the tension of the stage. With Pattie, it was something he used to help release the long-term anxiety connected with his trying to win her over. In England, when he was away from the road and in a comfortable setting, Clapton truly enjoyed the pub life, where he could shed his celebrity image and become one of the guys.

In general, Clapton's drinking had little adverse effect on his performances. He'd experienced some drinking-related problems in the early stages of his 1974 comeback tour of America, as well as in a rare concert or so over the ensuing two years, but these were exceptions to the rule. Clapton prided himself in his ability to conceal the effects of his drinking, claiming that only those close to him could tell. Nevertheless, his drinking could be a strain, especially for Pattie, who was appalled by some of his public drunkenness, or by his occasionally bringing friends—or even strangers he'd met at the pub—to sleep off a bender at Hurtwood Edge.

Clapton's faux pas, though troubling, did not damage the remainder of the band's British tour, and Clapton put in some fine performances in his homeland. Afterward, rather than leave the country for a period of relaxation in the Bahamas before an upcoming string of shows in the United States, Clapton stayed in England, reacquainting himself with friends he hadn't seen during his extended absence. On September 7, 1976, he and Pattie attended a luncheon commemorating what would have been Buddy Holly's fortieth birthday. The party, put together by Paul McCartney, was a splendid affair, with Norman Petty (Holly's cowriter) the guest of honor and a number of rock luminaries in attendance.

Later that same day, Clapton wrote what came to be regarded as his most romantic love song. Oddly enough, the tune was written in a fit of pique, while Clapton waited for Pattie to get ready for a party. According to Clapton, they were already about two hours late for the affair, and Pattie was making no attempt to hurry things along. At one point, Clapton had checked on her progress and, seeing her trying on still another outfit, told her rather impatiently that she looked wonderful as she was. He then proceeded to go back downstairs, pick up a guitar, and write a ballad he called "You Look Wonderful Tonight." Clapton's anger, in this case, probably served him well: the new song was deeply romantic without being terribly sappy.

Not that Clapton's sentiments in the song weren't heartfelt. One couldn't fake such tender, specific lyrics. "Every now and then," he said later, when talking about the song, "you fall in love again, albeit with the same woman, just one night for some reason—something she's said or the way she's approached a situation, and bang! you're in love again, and it's such a strong feeling you can't do anything else but write it down."

The song, in its shortened title of "Wonderful Tonight," not only became an automatic entry on set lists for Clapton concerts for years to come, but it would also become a standard played at weddings throughout the world. For Clapton, the ballad showed just how far his relationship with Pattie had progressed from the days when he wrote "Layla." He was happy, confident.

. . .

Clapton's current U.S. tour, in comparison to his tours in 1974 and 1975, was an abbreviated affair, beginning in St. Petersburg, Florida, and passing through thirteen cities in the South and Southwest. Since he wasn't covering the entire country, Clapton taped his appearance at the Convention Center in Dallas and allowed it to be broadcast on the "King Biscuit Flower Hour" syndicated radio program. The performance sparkled, with Freddie King sitting in on an incendiary version of "Further on up the Road" that was eventually released on King's *1934–1976* album.

The tour ended in Los Angeles. After the final show in Los Angeles, Clapton headed out to Shangri-La, where he spent several days rehearsing with The Band for their upcoming Last Waltz concert in San Francisco. Eric and Pattie enjoyed their time at the ranch, winding down from the tour, their leisure hours spent at Shangri-La's huge bar, where they met and relaxed with Ronnie Hawkins, Ringo Starr, Ronnie Wood, and other guests.

As originally conceived by Robbie Robertson, The Last Waltz was to be a celebration of The Band's colorful history. The show would be presented at Bill Graham's Winterland on Thanksgiving evening, with The Band playing a full concert of its own, as well as acting as the house band for a full roster of special guest musicians who had been influential to The Band throughout the group's career. The guest list included Ronnie Hawkins, Dr. John, Van Morrison, Muddy Waters, Joni Mitchell, Neil

Young, Neil Diamond, Ringo Starr, Paul Butterfield, Eric Clapton, and, if it could be arranged, Bob Dylan.

It was not a modest undertaking by any means, but at the time the initial plans were being drawn up, no one could have predicted how epic in proportion the evening would become. Bill Graham, for one, was a walking hyperbole, incapable of doing anything small-scale, and when he and Robertson began planning in earnest, Graham suggested that the concert be preceded by a holiday feast, which meant feeding turkey, stuffing, mashed potatoes, gravy, salad, pumpkin and mincemeat pies—the whole works—to more than 5,000 people. Then there was talk of documenting the historical occasion on film, and what started out as a sort of home movie idea blew up into a major theatrical production, complete with sets, a shooting script, and acclaimed director Martin Scorsese running the show.

The November 26, 1976, show lived up to its advance billing. For all the acrimony that had sprung up during the planning of the event, especially between Robbie Robertson and Levon Helm, The Band gave one of its finest performances. Dylan had agreed to do the show but threatened to back out when he learned that it was being filmed, and relented only at the last minute. Clapton and The Band played "All Our Past Times," followed by a version of "Further on up the Road" that found Clapton and Robertson trading guitar licks that proved why they had both earned their reputations as two of rock's finest instrumentalists. The three-hour concert concluded with The Band and all their guests gathering onstage for a powerful singalong of "I Shall Be Released."

No one wanted the show to end, so an onstage jam commenced after the official program ended. Clapton had no intention of participating in the jam, but he found himself "persuaded" by an ever-persistent Bill Graham.

"He was just standing there like a guest," Graham said of Clapton. "I said, 'You guys *have* to play.' But nobody had asked them to go out for the jam. So I walked Clapton out. What a *night!*" (Levon Helm saw Graham's method of persuasion as being a little more forceful. "Bill Graham dragged Clapton out and strapped him in his guitar for the jam," he wrote in his autobiography.)

Clapton was not resisting too much. If anything, he wanted to stand back and take in the show. It had been eight years ago to the day that he had stood onstage at the Royal Albert Hall, partaking in a farewell concert of his own. Ironically, The Band had played a significant role in his decision to leave Cream. Now he himself was watching the end of an era.

. . .

His next public appearance was, in every respect, much more toned down.

The show's genesis can be traced to a meeting of the Round Table, a group of British businessmen who staged events to raise money for charity. These events, for the most part, tended to be upper-crust affairs, and the Round Table was looking for a change of pace for its annual Valentine's dance in Cranleigh. To the amazement of his Round Table peers, a member named Roger Swallow suggested that they contact Eric Clapton. Swallow pointed out that Clapton lived nearby, and there was an outside chance that he'd be willing to play the dance. The Round Table gathering found the recommendation uproariously funny, but Swallow was undaunted by their cynicism. He wrote Clapton a formal invitation to play.

Clapton called Swallow as soon as he received the letter. "That show of yours . . ." he started, "I'll do it." There was, Clapton continued, one condition: there could be no publicity for the affair. Clapton would play the show for free, but if word of his appearance leaked out, or if his name was connected to the event in any way, the deal was off.

The dance was an ideal scenario for Clapton. The funds raised from the show were earmarked to purchase new equipment for a local hospital, which offered Clapton the rare opportunity to actually witness benefit funds being put to good use. The show itself could be a lot of fun, providing Clapton with another chance to mingle with the locals and play a small club.

For backing musicians, Clapton looked up Ronnie Lane. Clapton's friendship with the former Faces guitarist went back a long way. Lane's mobile sound studio had been employed for recording Clapton's Rainbow concert, and Clapton's and Lane's professional paths had crossed repeatedly over the ensuing years. Most recently, Clapton and Lane had worked together in cutting the first demo of "Wonderful Tonight."

Lane offered the services of his band, Slim Chance, for the Cranleigh event. Clapton and his mates christened themselves Eddie Earthquake and the Tremors, and it was in this spirit of having a good time that they all took the stage at the Cranleigh Village Hall and played to an audience of 350 friends, locals, and members of the Round Table. Clapton and Lane sang two-part harmony on "Goodnight, Irene," and the band played a selection of Slim Chance numbers, blues and folk standards, and an occasional Clapton song. One of the evening's highlights occurred when Pattie and Ronnie Lane's wife, Katy, did a spontaneous can-can during one of the numbers. All told, it was the kind of occasion that Clapton wished would take place more often.

He was by no means alone in the pleasure he derived from playing small, unannounced gigs. In the era of big-buck recording and touring, most high-profile artists fantasized about returning to the days of their youth, when expectations weren't as high and they could play for the pure joy of it. Gary Brooker, keyboard player for Procol Harum, was one such musician, and he addressed the issue by opening the Parrot Inn, a pub within short driving distance of Hurtwood Edge. Brooker held regular blues jams at the pub and turned the profits over to charity. When Clapton heard about these gigs, he became a regular in the group of musicians calling themselves the Parrot Band. As pleasurable as these informal performances were, they had a practical side as well, leading to professional contacts that spilled over into other projects. Saxophonist Mel Collins, a pub regular, would be invited to play on Clapton's next album, *Slowhand*, and Brooker would become Clapton's keyboardist within a couple of years.

The Clapton-Lane association provided its own significant contact. Shortly after playing the Cranleigh dance, Clapton sat in on recording sessions for a Pete Townshend–Ronnie Lane album (eventually released as *Rough Mix*). Producing the sessions was Glyn Johns, a talented engineer and producer who had worked with the Rolling Stones, the Beatles, and The Who on various projects, and who had originally been slated to work on Clapton's *Rainbow Concert* album. Clapton liked Johns personally and admired his professionalism, and by the time the *Rough Mix* sessions had been completed, he had drafted Johns to work as his producer on his forthcoming studio album.

. . .

Clapton and Johns made a decent team, but at times their relationship would be tested and strained by their differing approaches to recording. Clapton was accustomed to taking his time in the studio, allowing songs to develop from jam sessions and an exchange of ideas between musicians. This approach had been effective with Tom Dowd, who by nature possessed an artist's mentality, and who could be patient with musicians as they sorted through ideas. Glyn Johns was a bit more traditional in his approach. He, too, was sympathetic to the difficulties of the creative process, but he was more apt to try to move things along, aware of the high cost of studio time.

When Clapton entered London's Olympic Sound Studios the final week of May to lay down tracks for what would become *Slowhand*, he only knew that "Wonderful Tonight" would somehow anchor the album. He hoped to record "Alberta," a country-blues standard the band had been playing in recent concerts, but he couldn't get it down to his satisfaction and abandoned the song after recording seven takes. He also recorded Arthur "Big Boy" Crudup's "Mean Old Frisco," a personal favorite that gave him the chance to work on slide guitar.

The album, like most Clapton efforts, took time to develop. As Clapton himself would later admit, the band's playing was uninspired, and when compared to a superior effort such as *Layla*, *Slowhand* came across as "really lightweight." Part of the problem, he conceded, was the time that lapsed between when a song was written and when it was recorded; some of the new songs had been written months ago, and the band's enthusiasm for them had dimmed after repeated playings.

A greater obstacle, in all likelihood, was the album's clear lack of direction. In the wake of *No Reason to Cry*, Clapton was again reinventing his sound and image, moving closer to his J. J. Cale influences, his Tulsa band's sound and, even more specifically, his admiration for country artist Don Williams. Clapton had befriended Williams toward the end of the previous year, appearing with him onstage at the Hammersmith Odeon and introducing him to some of his friends. Williams's influence was apparent throughout *Slowhand*, not only in "We're All the Way," the Williams song covered on the record, but in some of Clapton's mellow, understated vocal phrasing.

The resulting album featured fine individual efforts that didn't seem to fit together as a cohesive unit. Three songs—J. J. Cale's "Cocaine" and two original numbers, "Wonderful Tonight" and "Lay Down Sally" (the latter a tribute to Cale), enjoyed enormous popularity on radio stations and at future Clapton concerts. "Peaches and Diesel," an original composition, was a beautifully expressive instrumental. As good as these and other songs were, one couldn't listen to the album and get a strong sense of the artist. The record sounded too much like a gathering of loose ends and influences.

From a critical standpoint, *Slowhand* received the familiar mixed reviews that had become customary for Clapton albums in the mid-seventies. Where some critics had totally dismissed Clapton as a figure from the past ("The only people I can see getting into *Slowhand* are hopeless nostalgics and hero worshippers"), others appeared to have learned to accept his way of making records ("a few good tracks interspersed between the usual filler"); unqualified endorsements were difficult to find.

The album was skillfully marketed—Clapton toured extensively in its support, and radio stations offered a lot of airtime to its two singles ("Wonderful Tonight" and the double-sided "Lay Down Sally"/"Cocaine")— and the public responded by making *Slowhand* another major success in the Eric Clapton canon. It may not have been a classic, but it was a favorite.

• • •

After appearing on five Clapton albums and working onstage as a regular part of the band since 1974, Yvonne Elliman decided it was time to leave and pursue a solo career of her own. Her role in the group had decreased over the last year or so, as Marcy Levy took a more active hand in songwriting and singing onstage, and rather than just fade into the comfortable position of lifetime backup singer, Elliman reasoned that she ought to see if she could succeed as a headliner. With a full slate of concerts scheduled for the upcoming year, Clapton had to decide whether he should replace her, which would have been difficult—and probably unnecessary, under the circumstances—or leave the band as it was. He chose to stick with Marcy Levy as his only female vocalist.

The recent tours had taken a lot out of the band, and to make his European trip more interesting, Clapton came up with the idea of traveling from city to city by rail. This was not, however, to be just a rock 'n' roll version of a whistle-stop campaign. To ensure maximum comfort and a sense of playfulness in the business at hand, Clapton rented two luxurious German coaches, complete with sleeping quarters to house the band and, as the crowning touch, secured the use of the dining car from the Orient Express. Throughout the tour, the cars were hooked up with trains along regularly scheduled routes, which took the Clapton entourage all over Europe.

Clapton thoroughly enjoyed the experience. "It is the only way to travel," he said, confessing that he had some initial reservations about how they were going to pull off the tour without any serious problems. "I really thought that we'd wake up one morning and find ourselves hundreds of miles on the wrong side of Europe."

The tour passed through Denmark, Germany, Holland, Belgium, France, and Switzerland. Slim Chance played as Clapton's support band, and throughout the tour, Clapton and Ronnie Lane spent a lot of time together, occasionally amusing themselves by posing as beggars and panhandling spare change from unsuspecting travelers. The high jinks kept them loose. Pattie and George Harrison's divorce became final during the tour, and gossipmongers hounded Eric and Pattie about their plans. True to form, Clapton remained vague about the details of his private life, revealing very few details to the press.

The shows fulfilled fans' expectations, especially in Brussels, where Clapton received his best response of the tour, and in Paris, where Ringo Starr walked onstage and played tambourine during "Badge." Most disappointing, without question, was the band's concert in an Ibizan bullring. Clapton looked forward to the concert, envisioning a rather quaint atmosphere somewhat similar to what he'd have if he were playing in an American rodeo, and to add a touch of festivity to the event, he chartered a yacht to take his entourage from Cannes to Ibiza. His experience in Spain, however, was a nightmare. The bullring offered dreadful acoustics, and for dressing rooms the band members were given cubicles used to operate on gored matadors, complete with blood gutters running off the tables.

"It was all a bit grim," Clapton reflected afterward. "I thought it was going to be a lovely old building like a rodeo place and it turned out to be a concrete monstrosity in the middle of nowhere."

He couldn't leave the place quickly enough.

ten

The Shape You're In

1978–82

Part of my character is made up of an obsession to push something to the limit. It can be of great use if my obsession is channeled into constructive thought or creativity, but it can also be mentally or physically or socially destructive.

*t*hroughout the mid- to late seventies, Eric Clapton's life and music took a slow downward turn. At first the shift was barely detectable and probably would have been hotly disputed by Clapton himself, had someone presented him with the idea. After all, he had conquered his drug addiction and won over the woman of his dreams, and he was working steadily with a long-standing band. Tickets to his concerts were in constant demand, and if his singles and albums weren't actually topping the charts, they continued to make a healthy dent in them. Most people would have been happy to settle for his life.

On the other hand, there were indications that, in an artistic sense, Clapton was suffering from tired blood. His new studio work was becoming more derivative and less innovative, especially when compared to his work of a decade earlier, when he stood at the forefront in defining the direction of blues and rock guitar. His albums were pleasant enough, but they were losing their sense of urgency.

The same could be said of Clapton's concerts. There was no disputing the man's musicianship—he had few peers when he was really cooking onstage—but as the decade wore on and Clapton grew more comfortable with his role as bandleader, far too many of his performances carried an aura of slick predictability, as if he had cashed in on the edginess that made his earlier work stand out, and was now ready to coast.

Clapton would always allow that his best work came from a sense of personal crisis—"in order to create, you've got to have pain"—but at this point in his life, he had settled into a fairly easy groove. As his manager was fond of telling him, he was in a position where he could retire at any time and never have to worry about money again. As a form of self-motivation, Clapton tried to tell himself that this wasn't the case, that he would always have to work, yet he also knew that there was little chance of his ever feeling the financial pinch of his youth, when he'd play a set in exchange for sandwiches and drinks.

His alcohol intake during the later years of the decade had increased steadily, to the point where it was becoming a concern to those around him. He had by no means turned into a common drunk, but his drinking habits had nonetheless eroded his working relationship with his band. Similarly, it had undermined the growth of his relationship with Pattie. Clapton, who had been drinking since he was fifteen, was slow to recognize the subtle yet damaging effects that his brandy consumption had on the constants in his life, but he was about to learn.

• • •

By the end of 1978, much of the proverbial writing was on the wall. Clapton spent the early portion of the year on another long tour of North America, followed by three large-stadium festival concerts with Bob Dylan. *Slowhand* was enjoying great success, and Clapton was eager to record a follow-up album while it was riding high on the charts. Dylan had offered Clapton two new songs ("If I Don't Be There by Morning" and "Walk Out in the Rain") to record for his next album. These numbers, along with "Tulsa

Time," a country shuffle written by Don Williams's guitarist, Danny Flowers, were slated as cornerstone works for the projected new album.

Unfortunately, the recording sessions, which ran off and on over a spread of several months, ranked among the worst in Clapton's professional career. Bogged down by the apathy common to groups that have been working together for too long without a break, the sessions lacked the creative give and take that had sparked previous sessions. Clapton was anything but pleased. Once again, he was working with producer Glyn Johns, as well as his usual band, but he couldn't seem to get things rolling. Clapton made it through the recording by virtue of sheer willpower, but the resulting album, *Backless*, was a hodgepodge marking the nadir of Clapton's seventies recordings.

The album had its moments. "Tulsa Time" continued the country-flavored trend established in "Lay Down Sally," though Clapton's latest cover of a J. J. Cale tune, "I'll Make Love to You"—another natural in this vein—was an insipid effort. "Watch Out for Lucy" and "Golden Ring," two Clapton originals, were passable efforts featuring fine vocal work, while "Promises" was a pop song with all the markings for chart success as a single. Overall, however, the album was just too familiar and friendly, with very few defining colors: listeners are left yearning for Clapton to rear back and snarl.

Clapton hit the road as soon as he had completed his work on the album. Documentary filmmaker Rex Pyke joined the Clapton entourage as they reprised their tour of Europe by train, but on this journey, a lot of the original charm was absent. Marcy Levy and George Terry had left the band after the *Backless* sessions, but rather than find new personnel to fill the void, Clapton toured with the group's three remaining members, which meant a shift in song arrangements that had to be worked out on the job. Clapton's performances, though acceptable, were mostly given on automatic pilot, and often under the influence of alcohol. If Pyke's film, *Eric Clapton's Rolling Hotel*, failed to capture Clapton at his artistic peak, it did depict, with stark, refreshing honesty, a look at musicians on the road.

The film's portrayal of Clapton was not always flattering, which goes a long way in explaining why it was never commercially released. In some of the performance segments, Clapton was obviously drunk onstage, and while such footage might have been interpreted as evidence of a musician's durability in the midst of the already well-documented excesses of life on the road, it was hardly an image-builder for an entertainer whose work had been under fire in recent years.

Then there was an unsettling episode involving Muddy Waters, Clapton's support act on the tour. The sixty-three-year-old bluesman was suffering from bronchitis, but rather than travel with Clapton and his band in the luxury of the train, where he could have traveled in comfort, Waters was assigned a spot on the crowded tour bus. Ben Palmer, traveling with the entourage, forcefully argued that Waters, for the sake of his health, ought to be allowed on the train, but his pleas fell on deaf ears. Waters remained on the bus.

A tour of the United Kingdom followed, taking Clapton through a nine-city, ten-concert jaunt in a two-week period. The shows, still featuring Muddy Waters as Clapton's support act, were a bonanza for blues fans, especially on those occasions when Clapton, goosed by Waters's playing, would kick his own playing up a notch. In Glasgow, he played "Kindhearted Woman Blues," a Robert Johnson song he never played in concert, and in Guildford, he was joined onstage by George Harrison and Elton John during "Further on up the Road," one of the few songs that seemed to inspire him every night, regardless of his mood or physical state. When the tour ended, Muddy Waters stayed on in England for a few performances, Clapton joining him onstage during one of his London shows.

• • •

Like most musicians, Clapton led a dramatically different life on the road from the one he was accustomed to at home. While on the road, the pace was immeasurably faster, and as the constant center of attention, Clapton was quite naturally self-absorbed. The constant ego stroking by fans and, to a lesser extent, the media, coupled with the nightly glare of the spotlight, can lull a star into a vortex of self-indulgence that could be difficult, if not impossible, to set aside at the completion of a tour. Believing, as the center of attention, that any kind of behavior is acceptable—and often it is to fans—it was easy for Clapton to engage openly in heavy drinking without fear of disapproval.

When Clapton returned to his home in December, he was not prepared to slow down. Pattie, who had endured her share of various hardships during her previous marriage to one of the most recognizable faces in the world, was not of the disposition to tolerate another cycle of hedonistic pop star behavior. It was bad enough that Eric was no longer allowing girlfriends and spouses to accompany band members on the road and Pattie had to endure long periods of his absence; she was not about to put up with sloppy behavior when he was at home. Throughout the holiday season, she and Eric fought over his habits, especially his drinking.

Clapton made little effort to change his ways. His drinking, he felt, was under control, and he sure as hell didn't need to be hearing any grief about it from Pattie or anyone else. He could sense that he and Pattie were drifting apart, but he viewed the problem as a temporary one. Somehow or another, things would work out.

The quarreling continued long after the holiday season had ended, and in February 1979, Clapton crossed over the line in such a way that he nearly lost Pattie for good. Pattie had been seeing a lot of Jenny and Susie McLean, twin models, and on one occasion, after Jenny had stayed overnight at Hurtwood Edge, Pattie had caught Eric seriously flirting with her. To make matters worse, Clapton was annoyed with Pattie for interrupting his little dalliance, and he scolded her for it. Pattie left immediately for her sister's home, saying nothing to Eric about where she was going. She called a couple days later, only to learn that Jenny McLean was still at the Clapton estate. Stunned and confused, she flew to Los Angeles to stay with friends, setting no date for her return.

Clapton, meanwhile, carried on with his affair, even as he prepared for a brief tour of Ireland, to be followed by an extensive, three-month excursion to the United States. As far as he was concerned, his relationship with Pattie was on hold, if not finished completely.

. . .

Fortunately for Clapton, Roger Forrester felt otherwise. Over time, Forrester had become a close friend and confidant, as well as the man essentially running Clapton's career, and Forrester knew Clapton well enough to be totally convinced that Eric and Pattie would eventually be reunited. Nevertheless, he worried that Clapton would create a lot of problems for himself if he was seen or photographed by the British press, and he warned Clapton to be cautious about being seen in public with Jenny McLean.

Such concerns, Clapton argued, were unfounded. He was losing interest in the affair, and was presently thinking of ways to work things out with Pattie. The press, he further insisted, wasn't all that interested in what he was doing or whom he was seeing.

Spotting an opening in the argument, Forrester played what proved to be his trump card. The press not interested? He could get Clapton's picture in the paper any time he wanted to—the very next day, in fact.

Clapton remained unconvinced. "Ten thousand quid says you can't do that," he scoffed.

The wager was placed, and as soon as Clapton had left for home, Forrester called the *Daily Mail*'s gossip columnist. Eric and Pattie, Forrester announced, would be getting married the following Tuesday in Tucson, Arizona—the day before the opening of Clapton's U.S. tour.

The item appeared in the next day's paper. Clapton was furious with Forrester for backing him into a corner. The story, he complained, would be all over the papers before he had the chance to talk to Pattie, straighten out their problems, and formally propose to her. His only option now was to place an immediate, long-distance call to California and propose over the telephone.

Clapton's call was a fiasco. Pattie wasn't in, so Eric asked Rob Fraboni, with whom Pattie was staying, to deliver the message for him. It was urgent,

Clapton explained, that Pattie get the message as soon as possible. Fraboni jotted Clapton's proposal on the back of an envelope and set out to find her.*

Not surprisingly, Pattie wasn't ready to accept Eric's proposal on the spot. She had a few questions for the man who, only a few weeks earlier, seemed to have discarded her for someone else. Where was Jenny? she asked, when she received Clapton's message and returned his call. Gone, replied Clapton. Why the big rush to get married? Clapton explained his bet with Forrester. Pattie found the circumstances totally distasteful, and she told Eric that there was no way she could marry him this way. Clapton persisted and finally, after great discussion, Pattie relented.

The wedding took place three days later, on March 27, 1979. In an effort to mislead the press and ensure at least minimal privacy during the hastily prepared affair, Roger Forrester booked six Tucson churches, and a Clapton lookalike was employed, not only to confuse the media but also to take the required blood test for a groom who was frightened of needles. The private ceremony, held at the Apostolic Assembly of Faith in Jesus Christ church, went smoothly, with Rob Fraboni standing in as best man and Myel Fraboni and Chris O'Dell, one of Pattie's friends, acting as matron and maid of honor.

The honeymoon had to be put on hold; Clapton had tour dates to honor. He brought Pattie along for a handful of shows, bringing her onstage and singing "Wonderful Tonight" to her at his tour opener in Tucson, but after these few early shows, he insisted that she head back to England. Pattie was crushed, but as far as Clapton was concerned, rules were rules, and one of his steadfast laws of the road was wives and lovers were not allowed on tour. There would be no exceptions. Pattie had no recourse but to return to England and wait.

To the outsider, Clapton's actions might have appeared terribly callous

---

*The wording of Clapton's proposal read more like an ultimatum than a romantic plea: Pattie, said Clapton, was to marry him the following Tuesday in Tucson or "get on her bike."

and unromantic, especially when they involved the woman who had been the inspiration for two of his most passionate love songs, but in all matters professional, Clapton insisted that his word was final. His work demanded total concentration and control. Pattie understood this, even if she had trouble accepting it, and while Clapton's sending her back to England might not have been the ideal way to begin a marriage, it was the kind of hard-nosed decision that had allowed Clapton to survive in a tough, grueling business.

As it turned out, he had another bombshell to drop a few months later—this one involving the members of his band.

. . .

Clapton's band now included Albert Lee, a well-respected, veteran guitarist whose résumé included a recent stint with Emmylou Harris's Hot Band. Lee had been added at the suggestion of Roger Forrester, who felt that a second guitar would bring a fuller sound to such concert staples as "Badge" and "Layla." Lee's country background made him a natural for the featured songs from *Backless*, and his capability to handle both rhythm and occasional lead guitar chores provided Clapton with more onstage options.

The early portion of the tour snaked through the Southern states, working its way eastward at a steady clip. In Atlanta, on one of his nights off, Clapton attended a B. B. King show, joining King onstage for an improvised blues encore. The duet had the crowd on its feet. Despite all his recent work in a country vein, Clapton could still trade licks with the best of the bluesmen.

Having Muddy Waters as his support act didn't hurt. As Clapton later admitted, Waters had been largely responsible for directing him back to the blues when he was in danger of losing his way. Clapton and Waters spent a lot of their spare time talking, and while Waters was not one to criticize Clapton's work, he had a way of inconspicuously prodding Clapton toward his proper path. "I love listening to your band," he'd tell Eric, "but my favorite song you do is 'Worried Life Blues.' That's really where you're at, and you should realize that. You should realize it and be proud of it."

Waters's subtle point wasn't wasted on Clapton, who took Waters's fatherly advice to heart. "I think that was as close as I ever got to having a guru," Clapton said.

In May, during a three-week break separating the first and second segments of his U.S. tour, Clapton flew back to England to relax and spend some time with Pattie. On May 11, 1979, he joined friends Charlie Watts and Georgie Fame in a makeshift band that played at producer Glyn Johns's wedding reception, but such festivities were only a prelude for things to come. While Eric had been busy in America, Pattie had put together a huge garden party to celebrate their marriage. The guest list read like a Who's Who of British recording stars, including Paul McCartney, Ringo Starr, George Harrison, Mick Jagger, Keith Richards, Denny Laine, and Jack Bruce. A temporary stage was constructed, and the party featured various combinations of musicians, including Clapton, jamming on rock 'n' roll oldies by the likes of Little Richard, Jerry Lee Lewis, and Lloyd Price. To the amazement of the attendant rock press, the three former Beatles briefly set aside their ongoing legal hassles and performed "Sgt. Pepper's Lonely Hearts Club Band," setting off another volley of rumors about a possible Fab Four reunion.*

There was a downside to the festivities, a cruel prank that revealed a nasty side to Clapton's sense of humor. As the evening stretched on and the jam sessions continued, some of the musicians began to comment that Jack Bruce was taking the music far too seriously, and with Clapton's approval, they moved away from Bruce, leaving him in his own corner of the stage and, eventually, alone on the stage. Clapton thought it was all very funny. Unfortunately, his view wasn't shared by the butt of the joke, who retreated from the stage in tears.

The second part of Clapton's tour in America spelled the end of his five-year association with Carl Radle, Dick Sims, and Jamie Oldaker as a working unit. Clapton and his band had been drifting apart over the past

*Ironically, John Lennon later said that, had he been invited, he would have flown to England and joined his former mates onstage at the party.

year or so, partly because his mates were American and Eric never felt totally at home with them, partly because the long time they'd spent together had led to less-than-inspiring work, and partly because the heavy drinking on the road created tensions that were difficult to overcome. Clapton felt that he needed a change, but he waited until he had completed his American tour. Then, and in a move that seemed uncharacteristically ruthless, if not cowardly, he sent pink-slip telegrams telling the three men that their services were no longer needed.

Carl Radle took the news especially hard. His friendship with Clapton had begun a decade earlier, when Clapton was a member of Blind Faith and he was working with Delaney and Bonnie, and he had been Clapton's bassist from Derek and the Dominos to the present. During Clapton's uncertain beginnings as a band leader, and throughout his period of alcohol-induced unpredictability onstage, Radle had acted as the band's elder, directing operations when Clapton was incapable of it. When Clapton was recovering from heroin addiction and trying to assemble a new band, Radle had rounded up his unit. Sadly, less than a year after being fired from Clapton's band, Radle died of a kidney infection induced by alcoholism and drug addiction.

He deserved a better fate, and Clapton recognized as much. "I hold myself responsible for a lot of that," he said of Radle's demise, confessing that he never saw Radle again after he had cut him loose from the band. Radle, he admitted with some regret, had saved him when his career looked bleak, but he had ultimately turned away from Carl. "I have to live with that."

Of course, Clapton had no way of foreseeing Radle's fate. All he was interested in at the time was forming a band made up of fellow British musicians, and for this he turned to a rhythm section of bassist Dave Markee and drummer Henry Spinetti—two rock-solid sessions musicians he had worked with in the past, most notably on the Pete Townshend–Ronnie Lane *Rough Mix* album—and former Joe Cocker keyboardist Chris Stainton. He kept Albert Lee as his second guitarist. In assembling an all-British band, Clapton hoped to achieve a tighter unity. Theoretically, they could get together on short notice, without having to make extravagant travel arrangements, and as fellow countrymen, they would have more in common.

The group's first tour was the typical Claptonian endurance test, with dates ranging all over Europe and the Far East. There was, however, one new wrinkle: for years, Clapton had expressed interest in touring some of the Iron Curtain countries, where young fans were hungry for appearances by rock stars, previously banned by the countries' Communist leaders. With concerts scheduled in Yugoslavia and Poland, he was finally breaking through.

Unfortunately, the shows in Poland turned out badly, leaving Clapton emotionally battered and uncertain about his power as an internationally known entertainment figure. The first performance, in Warsaw's Palace of Culture, was uneventful, though the huge audience, composed largely of Polish dignitaries and people with connections, was slow to respond to Clapton and his band. The next evening, in the Katowice Stadium, was an entirely different story. Clapton had barely started his show when wildly enthusiastic fans began to clash with police and security personnel. Over the years, Clapton had learned that he could defuse potentially explosive situations by playing ballads or slow blues, but in Poland, where fans were ecstatic about the sheer prospects of seeing Clapton play anything at all, the ploy was a failure. Police clubbed teenagers dancing in the aisles and Maced others moving toward the stage. Clapton watched in horror as young people were beaten and dragged away by their hair. In the ensuing bedlam, some of Clapton's road crew were roughed up and the band's sound system was badly damaged. After the show, Clapton sat in his hotel room and wept.

"Anywhere else in the world we could help the kids by telling them to cool it," he reflected. "But there, I'm powerless because of the language problem and because the authorities are so heavy. The whole place reminds me of the Third Man."

For Clapton, crowd response was the whole point of performing. He felt an intense need to connect with his audience on a spiritual level, and he was depressed on those occasions when this didn't happen. He hated orchestrated crowd response, in which people were not allowed to move out of their seats until a predetermined time—usually during the final songs of the evening. Such arrangements robbed both performers and audience alike of spontaneous interaction. The scene in Poland was unbelievable.

"How could I play when I saw kids right in front of the stage, underneath me, being pushed about?" he complained to biographer Ray Coleman. "The only sin of those kids was to show their enjoyment. The way they were treated was sickening."

Infuriated by the violence, Roger Forrester demanded reassurance that the police wouldn't stage a repeat performance at the next evening's concert. The unrepentant security forces insisted that it was their right to maintain order in any way they saw fit. Facing the prospects of further violence, Forrester and Clapton agreed that they might be better off by canceling the second show and moving on. The cancellation meant that the band had to relinquish its earnings from the first show, but Clapton was prepared to make the concession. He left the country as quickly as he could.

. . .

The band's tour of the Far East, begun in Bangkok, Manila, and Hong Kong before moving on to an eleven-show run in Japan, fared much better. Clapton loved playing in Japan, and his shows there found him in top form, playing a mixture of hits, blues, and selections from his last two albums. His two shows in the Budokan Theater in Tokyo were recorded in their entirety, with the December 3, 1979, performance being issued in May 1980 as *Just One Night*.

The double album, which *Rolling Stone* less than happily labeled "the definitive document of Clapton's post–*461 Ocean Boulevard* era," caught the essence of the highs and lows of Clapton's work in the latter part of the decade. As the seventies drew to a close, Clapton was still playing it safe, a certain degree of his caution undoubtedly due to the fact that he was working with a new band. On *Just One Night*, such songs as "Wonderful

Tonight" and "Lay Down Sally" were virtual note-for-note transcriptions of their studio album versions; in contrast, the extended solos in "Double Trouble," "Worried Life Blues," and "Further on up the Road" captured some of the old Clapton panache. At times, Clapton sounded a little uncertain, as if he were measuring his notes rather than playing intuitively, and at other times his fretwork sounded tired and familiar, as if he simply wanted to get through a song and move on to another. Still missing—and obvious in its exclusion from all Clapton live albums to that point—was "Layla." Despite its shortcomings, the album had its charm. If it lacked the raw, intense energy of *E.C. Was Here*, it did offer enough moments of inspiration to recommend it to record buyers who wanted to hear the guitar demonstrations that had been missing on recent studio albums.

Just One Night revealed Clapton's all-English band to be a talented, technically refined unit, adept at handling the framework of Clapton's music but not especially creative when it came to improvising or breaking new ground. This was all the more evident when Clapton, with Glyn Johns at the production helm, tried to put together his first studio album with the group. By all rights the situation should have been ideal. To beef up his sound and add another creative force to the band, Clapton had invited the prodigiously talented Procol Harum keyboardist and songwriter Gary Brooker into his group, giving him a two-keyboard configuration similar to what had been successful in The Band. Still, for reasons no one could quite understand, Clapton and his band couldn't jell in the studio. For a change, Clapton had a wealth of new material to consider, including a number of Brooker originals to complement what Clapton himself had written, but the songs, when recorded, sounded languid even by Clapton's laid-back standards.

To a large extent, Clapton had only himself to blame. He was the band's leader, but he was reluctant to push his musicians in the studio. If anything, he needed motivation to rise above his own natural tendencies toward laziness. Yet, as he would later lament, his band took its cues from him, and the more he laid back, the more they followed suit.

In all, the group recorded thirteen songs over a two-month period, including numbers with Gary Brooker and Albert Lee on lead vocals, but the album, when played to RSO executives, was rejected outright as being too eclectic. RSO wanted a hit—and something with the Clapton stamp on it. As it stood, the proposed album had far too much of Brooker's influence for the record executives' tastes.

The rejection was painful to Clapton, who was already suffering from an extended period of self-doubt. His heavy use of alcohol—now a bottle of brandy a day—often dumped him in a state of moody introspection, where he would become tearful about what he considered his failures or inadequacies. During those moments when his guard was down, he would admit to friends that he was losing his sense of direction; he wanted to play the blues rather than make commercially successful pop music. For diversion he attended soccer games or hung out with Gary Brooker and other friends, but the inner demons always managed to return. The rejection of his latest studio effort seemed to confirm his suspicions.

Touring, though ego inflating on a night-to-night basis, offered no long-term reassurance. That much was evident when Clapton toured the United Kingdom to promote the release of *Just One Night*, only to return unhappy. Like other pop icons, Clapton knew all too well that he would be revered simply for showing up at a concert; fans were in no way a reliable gauge for a performance's success. Clapton could earn roomfuls of money by playing the stadium circuit in America, but such success would not answer his own haunting questions about his creativity.

Temporary relief arrived from an unexpected source. Tom Dowd, Clapton's former producer and mentor, was presently available to work with Clapton, and he invited Eric and his band to join him for recording sessions at the Compass Point Studios in Nassau. The change of recording venues, along with Dowd's patience and guidance, helped a great deal. Dowd suggested some significant changes in the arrangements of some of the previously recorded songs, most notably on "Rita Mae," a shuffle that was sped up and given a new, hard-nosed guitar riff that transformed the song into a rocker suitable for extended onstage soloing. "I Can't Stand It," another uptempo number, was capable of meeting any record executive's demands for Top 40 material, while covers of Muddy Waters's "Blow Wind Blow" and Sleepy John Estes's "Floating Bridge" fulfilled Clapton's need to record the blues.

The resulting album, *Another Ticket*, was an honest, admirable effort, even if it wasn't another *Layla* or *461 Ocean Boulevard*. Like its predecessors released in the late seventies, *Another Ticket* represented Clapton's never-ending compromise to satisfy both his own creative urges and the demands of his fans, and as such, it was doomed to sound like another Clapton miscellany. But Clapton had worked harder on this album than on any studio record in recent memory, and the effort was apparent in the final product. The bluesy backdrop that Clapton sought for the album came through on many of the cuts, while his country influences remained intact, ringing clear in "Something Special" and his autobiographical "Hold Me Lord," a plea for help that, in its own way, was as heartfelt as the sense of contentment expressed in "Presence of the Lord."

Still, for all its admirable qualities, the album didn't stack up as a totally realized package. Clapton recognized as much, but given the difficulty he had experienced in just getting the album recorded, he was prepared to release it and move on. There would be other albums up the road.

• • •

Under the usual circumstances, Clapton would have hit the tour circuit to promote his new album, and this was indeed what his management had in store for him: a few warm-up shows in Ireland, followed by a single date in London's Rainbow Theatre, and then his most extensive tour yet of the United States. Clapton, however, was in poor physical condition, and eight stops into his fifty-seven-show American tour, after complaining of severe stomach pain, he was rushed to a hospital, only to learn that his professional career had to be put on indefinite hold.

Clapton's drinking, it appeared, had finally caught up with him. He had been suffering for some time from pain in his back, but he didn't regard the discomfort as a particularly serious matter. He was given a prescription for painkillers and that was sufficient, at least in the beginning. After a while, however, he built up a tolerance to the painkillers and required more and more of the medication for relief, to the point where he was taking dozens of pills a day. By the time he had begun his American tour, he was in such pain that he was finding it difficult to sleep at night.

Clapton, who had an aversion to hospitals in general, and to needles specifically, tried to grit his teeth and work his way through the tour without seeing a doctor, but his condition deteriorated. He was administered a painkilling shot before his March 13, 1981, show in Madison, Wisconsin, but its effects were marginal; he was barely able to make it through the show and left the stage doubled over in pain.

The next scheduled show was in Minnesota, but before allowing Clapton to take the stage, Roger Forrester insisted that he have a doctor take a look at him. A thorough check up, complete with X rays of Clapton's back, revealed a group of ulcers, including one the size of a mandarin orange, ready to burst. Clapton was immediately admitted to United Hospital in St. Paul.

The remainder of the tour was canceled and the press briefed on Clapton's condition. Pattie flew in from England to be with her husband, and Pete Townshend, in another extraordinary display of friendship, traveled to Minnesota to cheer Clapton up. Fans from around the world flooded the hospital with flowers and cards.

Clapton healed gradually during a hospital stay that lasted a month. Doctors were brutally frank with him, telling him that he had come within hours of dying from a perforated ulcer. In the future, they advised, he would have to take better care of himself, which meant regulating his diet and avoiding rich or spicy foods (Clapton favorites) and, most importantly, staying away from alcohol. Clapton balked at the ban on drinking, and by arguing that it would be too difficult to quit drinking entirely, he was able to persuade his doctors to allow him a couple drinks per day, a bargain he had no intention of keeping.

Upon his April 17 release from the hospital, he decided to take a brief vacation in Seattle. One of his passions, cultivated as a result of his friendship with Gary Brooker, was fly fishing, and Clapton reasoned that a restful fishing trip would be good therapy. This might have been true, had his luck been running better, but as it was, he had no sooner set foot in Seattle than he was on his way back to the hospital, this time to recover from injuries sustained in an automobile accident.

He had been having dinner with friends in Seattle's Park Hilton Hotel, and following a brief argument with his personal assistant over whether he could have a drink, he decided to leave dinner early. The restaurant's hostess offered him a ride, but in her excitement over actually sitting in a car and talking to a world-famous celebrity, the twenty-year-old woman ran a red light and was hit broadside by a taxi. The impact pushed the 1977 Honda Civic carrying Clapton and his driver into a telephone pole.

Clapton was taken by ambulance to a local hospital, where he was treated for minor cuts and bruised ribs. During their examination of Clapton, doctors also determined that Eric was suffering from pleurisy, and that one of his lungs was partially closed. The next day, after a night's treatment with a vaporizer, Clapton was on his way back to England, where the country's naturally damp air would boost the healing process. He would be out of circulation for the next five months.

. . .

By all indications, Clapton had learned very little from his close call in the United States: in no time at all, he was back to his usual daily dosage of alcohol, with no sign of cutting back. Both he and Pattie liked to drink, and since, by his own standards, he was essentially inactive, doing no recording or touring, he had plenty of time to sit around the house and indulge himself.

Even without a tour to promote it, *Another Ticket* rose up the American and British music charts. "I Can't Stand It," the album's first single and a bona fide hit, played a substantial role in stimulating the album's sales, and the reviews, if not glowing, were kind in their assessment of the recording's merits. "As an artist often criticized for mellowing out," wrote a reviewer for *Rolling Stone*, "Eric Clapton has succeeded in making very popular music from an authentic and deeply tragic blues sensibility. He addresses both the heart and the charts in the same way: with a bullet."

Another Ticket was the final album in Clapton's long-standing association with both his management and record company. In recent years, Clapton had been less than satisfied with the way the Robert Stigwood Organization handled his career. Stigwood had made a good buck on him, especially from Cream, and Clapton questioned some of Stigwood's business practices. According to the rumor mill, Stigwood had bankrolled the Bee Gees, his other main act, with some of Cream's earnings. Although he had no real business sense himself and wasn't inclined to take an active interest in all the financial angles of his career, Clapton didn't want to feel he was being taken advantage of either. He had greater confidence in the way he had been handled by Roger Forrester, and he was convinced that Forrester was capable of managing him on his own.

Changing record companies involved both financial and creative considerations. Forrester was interested in setting up an independent record label for Clapton, similar to the RSO deal, in which a major record company would act as the distributor for the independent, artist-controlled label. In such a scenario, the artist would have more control than in the standard record company agreements. A fierce bidding war broke out between companies wanting to sign the Clapton label, with Warner Brothers eventually winning the battle. In future years, the corporate giant would exert its own influence on Clapton's career—and not always for the best.

Polidor responded to the loss of Clapton by issuing two greatest hits packages in just over a year's time. The first, *Timepieces: The Best of Eric Clapton*, an eleven-song compilation of studio fare from the seventies, included "Knockin' on Heaven's Door," which had never appeared on an album, but overall, the selections on the album were predictable, with six of the entries culled from *461 Ocean Boulevard* and *Slowhand*, Clapton's two most popular albums of the decade.

The second compilation, *Timepieces, Volume II: "Live in the Seventies,"* issued in 1983, was an oddity that left much to be desired. The idea of releasing two greatest hits collections—one of studio songs released as singles, the other of stage performances—signaled appropriate recognition of the division Clapton placed between his sessions and concert work, and the live album could have been a masterwork, given the performance tapes in the record company's vaults. Instead, five of the album's eight selections were drawn from Clapton's Budokan concert, two from his comeback tour, and one from Derek and the Dominos. The Budokan selections were especially questionable, since four of the five cuts had appeared on *Just One Night*, which had been issued less than four years earlier, and the other, "Knockin' on Heaven's Door," had appeared in its studio permutation on the earlier hits collection. In light of what it could have been, the album was a major disappointment.

Neither album was of any special interest to Clapton. He was more concerned with what the future had in store than in dredging up the past.

. . .

During his extended period of inactivity, Clapton did a lot of fishing and attended an occasional concert in London, but it was a very sedate period. By fall 1981, he was itching to get back on the road. His management booked a tour of Scandinavia, to be followed by a year-ending series of dates in Japan.

Before embarking on these journeys, Clapton marked his first public appearance since his hospitalization with three highly publicized charity gigs for Amnesty International. These concerts, known as The Secret Policeman's Other Ball, were a huge success, featuring music by Clapton, Phil Collins, Jeff Beck, Donovan, and Sting, as well as comedy skits by such renowned British comedians as John Cleese, Billy Connolly, and Rowan Atkinson. Clapton's performances, later released on both album and video, were rather subdued by his usual standard, finding Clapton content to play second fiddle to Jeff Beck, who joined him onstage for several numbers, including "Crossroads" and "Further on up the Road."

In the past, Clapton had been willing to turn the solos over to other accomplished guitarists. His historic onstage jams, dating back to his friendship with Jimi Hendrix, included Freddie King, B. B. King, Carlos Santana, and numerous others. As far as Clapton was concerned, there was no need to worry about who was the biggest gunslinger in the business. It was the music that mattered.

On the other hand, there was some speculation, brought up from time to time in reviews of his concerts, that Clapton was losing the fire.

Some of this criticism was undoubtedly accurate. Clapton had been working as a full-time musician for nearly two decades, playing his more popular numbers countless times, and it would have been natural for him to lose a certain degree of enthusiasm for these songs. As a means of combating such apathy, he changed his set lists from night to night, but that still didn't guarantee that he would be up for every number, or even every concert. In addition, Clapton was extremely sensitive to how audiences reacted to his performances, and an unresponsive crowd could affect the way he played.

Then there was the unknown factor of how greatly Clapton's alcoholism influenced the quality of his performances. The worst instances, such as those times early in his comeback tour, when he had been so drunk that he virtually had to be carried off the stage at the end of a concert, had been well documented, but he had been in much better control of his drinking in recent years. He could play a show on finger memory alone. His collapse from ulcer complications might have served as an indication that he had to change his habits, but at that point he was too far down the road of alcoholism to heed the warning.

"My mind was pretty shut down," he recalled of the time. "I was so overtaken by booze and dope, I was like a zombie. I'd shut down safety valves, and was really pushing myself. And what I did collapse from was ulcers, in fact. I should have known I had ulcers, but I was taking so many things to kill the pain that I'd blotted it out. Even then, I still carried on drinking."

Roger Forrester was terribly concerned about Clapton's excessive drinking, but he realized that Clapton was far too stubborn to entertain anything he would have to say on the subject. Managing Clapton meant not only taking care of Eric's business affairs but overseeing aspects of his personal life as well. This could be quite a burden, but Forrester had held up admirably under it. Somehow, the machinery of Clapton's life and career continued to function.

That changed the evening of a scheduled performance in Tokyo, when Clapton shocked Forrester by announcing that he didn't want to go onstage. Clapton had groused about not wanting to perform in the past, but that had been part of the long-tour ritual, a matter of motivation. This time he was serious. Clapton had broken out in an angry rash all over his body, and while Eric tried to write it off as food poisoning, Forrester recognized it for what it was. Clapton's liver was reacting to years of alcohol abuse. Alarmed by Clapton's physical condition, Forrester risked his friendship with Eric and told him, in no uncertain terms, that he was an alcoholic and needed immediate attention.

Forrester's words stung Clapton, who had never been called an alcoholic before. Forrester knew him as well as anyone, and he had endured Clapton's excesses for much of his professional career. Still, Eric couldn't believe what he was hearing. He'd been drinking his entire adult life—often to excess—but that didn't make him an alcoholic. He was in control of himself.

To his credit, Forrester persisted, even though he realized that Clapton was far too stubborn to be pushed into anything he didn't want to do. The issue, Forrester insisted, had nothing to do with business or Clapton's ability to perform, though he would gladly cancel Clapton's remaining tours and put his career on indefinite hold. What mattered was Eric's health. Something had to be done.

Clapton put off doing anything for the time being and somehow managed to get through his tour of Japan. Nevertheless, Forrester's words got through to him, and after returning to England, he told his manager that he would spend the holiday season at home and consider some kind of treatment afterward. He offered no concrete promises, but to a worried Roger Forrester, even a slight concession was a step in the right direction.

• • •

Clapton was on a flight to Minnesota in early January.

The holiday season at home had been a disaster. Clapton drank heavily throughout the period, and on Christmas Day, when Pattie had friends and members of Eric's family and hers over for dinner, Eric had become so obliterated that he stumbled off to the basement and fell asleep. Not long after this fiasco, Clapton talked to Roger Forrester and agreed to be placed into a rehabilitation facility.

Forrester's choice of the Hazelden Foundation's clinic in the United States was an excellent one. Not only was it one of the most highly regarded rehab facilities in the world, but it would remove Clapton from all sources of temptation in his own country, which, historically, had proved to be too great for Clapton.

Forrester accompanied Clapton on the trip. Clapton drank heavily throughout his flight to the States, and he was thoroughly trashed by the time his plane touched down in Minnesota. Eric recoiled when he saw the clinic's huge concrete buildings, which reminded him of a prison compound. And to complete his sense of isolation, he was informed that he could have no visitors, including Roger Forrester, during his initial two-week detoxification process. He was on his own. Forrester saw that Clapton was formally admitted to the clinic, and then checked into a nearby hotel to wait for the results.

For the next four weeks, Clapton was literally institutionalized. He practiced a rigid daily schedule, mixing with others who had found themselves enslaved by a bottle and learning that alcoholism was a type of addiction that required rigid measures to overcome. To his fellow inmates, he was just another face; celebrity meant nothing. Clapton's physical withdrawal from alcohol was eased somewhat by initial doses of Librium, but he quickly discovered that any chance of successfully overcoming alcoholism depended on his own resolve. His daily routine required that he take care of himself in every respect. This included making his own bed, something that had always been done for him, and setting the dinner tables for the twenty-eight people in his unit. He sat in on group therapy sessions and was administered a battery of psychological tests.

Early on, he wasn't entirely convinced that he needed to be in the facility. Many of the people around him were in much worse shape, and Clapton believed that he could mark his time in the clinic, return to England, and resume his life as it had been before. His attitude changed dramatically when he was forced to face the effect his drinking had on the woman he had devoted his life to. Pattie had filled out a questionnaire and described, in very frank and brutal detail, how tough he had made life for her during his years of heavy drinking, how uncommunicative he had been. Clapton broke down when he read the questionnaire aloud to several other inmates. He had never intended to hurt Pattie with his drinking, but from what she had written, her life had been deeply affected by it. The questionnaire became a turning point. From there on out, Clapton approached his rehabilitation with the resolve of a zealot.

It wasn't easy. Once he had accepted his alcoholism and its effects on others, Clapton began to rely on the clinic for answers, which went against the grain of his rehab therapy. As part of his treatment, Clapton was to take care of himself and make his own decisions; to rely on others was only transferring dependency. In group sessions, he was expected to bare his soul, which was another hurdle to a man like Clapton, who had worked throughout his career to maintain a level of privacy despite his celebrity status. Nevertheless, once he began to open himself up to those around him, Eric found the group sessions very beneficial.

Clapton's time at Hazelden was extremely important from another perspective. For years he had been a pampered rock star with all kinds of people around him to look after his every need; he knew very little about many of the things that average people take for granted, from how to make a bed to how to use a credit card. Most important, perhaps, was the fact that he had failed to realize that, rock star or working stiff, he had no excuse for behaving in a manner that hurt himself or others.

The month finally passed and Clapton returned to England, determined not to touch another drink again. He joined Alcoholics Anonymous and began attending their meetings. His drinking, he felt, had taken him to the brink of insanity; he would never let that happen again.

. . .

In the period immediately following his recovery from heroin addiction, Eric Clapton had attacked his working life with a ferocious appetite, as if a heavy workload would keep his mind off the travails of his recent past. It was no different after his treatment for alcoholism: Clapton enjoyed a brief period of inactivity in England, and then instructed Roger Forrester to set up a tour of the United States.

The tour, Clapton would later lament, was taking on far too much, far too soon—not unlike his comeback tour in 1974. Although he was again in good health and confident in his ability to move on with his career, Clapton still required some time for psychological healing, and a road tour was not the ideal place for that to happen. Without the drinking and parties, there was very little to do to fill time. For Clapton, the tour amounted to doing the concerts, going back to the hotel for some rest, packing the next morning, traveling, and then repeating the routine. Touring had become a chore.

"It was the first time I'd really gone out there to do my job, instead of going out to have a good time," he recalled, noting that he'd really had to search to find enjoyable aspects of the road life. The concerts themselves, with the loud, amplified instruments and noisy crowds, were not as much fun as they had been when he could take the edge off with a drink or two. Things improved when Clapton realized that he had to change his approach. "Suddenly," he explained, "a lightbulb went on in my head: 'You can make the most of this. You know, this is what you've been paid to do, and you can enjoy it, or you can hate it.'"

Compared to his other visits to the States, the tour was much less exhaustive. The monthlong series of dates included only seventeen shows, and the individual performances were limited to ninety minutes. Whenever possible, Clapton attended Alcoholics Anonymous meetings in the cities he visited, which led to a funny scene at an AA meeting in Minneapolis, where half the people in attendance were wearing Eric Clapton T-shirts purchased at the previous evening's show. In this and other AA meetings, Clapton was pleased to find that his celebrity had very little bearing on the business at hand. Guitar-hero status was checked at the door.

Clapton enjoyed the tour more and more as it went on, and he had mixed feelings about seeing it come to an end. The final show in Miami featured what turned out to be Clapton's final performance with Muddy Waters, a jam on Waters's "Blow Wind Blow." Waters died less than a year later.

"That was a fantastic tribute and a great memory," Clapton remarked of his last encounter with Waters.

The Clapton-Waters relationship was truly special. Clapton had been intimidated by Sonny Boy Williamson and Howlin' Wolf, who reminded him, in no uncertain terms, that he was a white boy playing a black man's song. He could be more at ease with someone like Buddy Guy, who had cut his chops as a sessions guitarist for Willie Dixon, Howlin' Wolf, Muddy Waters, and a host of others, but who had shared experiences, onstage and in the studio, that made Clapton feel as if they were peers. Freddie King fell somewhere in between. Clapton could be friendly with him, but he was nevertheless awed by some of King's trappings—the women, booze, guns and knives . . . reminders that King was from a different place.

Clapton's relationship with Muddy Waters grew slowly and naturally. Waters, more than any living bluesman, had influenced Clapton when he was first learning to play the guitar, and Waters had been in the studio when Eric played for the first time as a sessions musician. To Clapton, Muddy Waters was a larger-than-life figure, and he knew better than to assert himself on Waters when they were getting to know each other. He addressed Waters the way a respectful pupil might address a teacher.

In time, their friendship deepened, to the point where Waters proclaimed Eric to be his adopted son and accepted him into his family, inviting him to parties and cookouts at his house, where he let his guard down and exhibited a zany sense of humor that contrasted with the powerful image that Clapton had of him. Waters would talk to Eric about his music and his influences, and Clapton hung on his every word, amazed that he would be offered the musings of his boyhood hero. To Clapton, Waters was an exemplar of the bluesman he wanted to be.

"Whenever I get depressed," he said, not long before Waters's death, "when I've lost my way and want to know exactly what I should be doing, I always turn, at this point in time, to Muddy Waters. I always find in him a great well of spiritual comfort—the man is strong, you know. And that is where I belong."

. . .

Clapton was eager to get back in the studio and record a new album, his first on the new label, so after returning to England, he holed up in a cottage in Wales and wrote several new songs he hoped to include on the record. Some of the new tunes, such as "Slow Down Linda" and "The Shape You're In," had plenty of kick to them, promising a stronger rock 'n' roll base than Clapton's more laid-back albums from the seventies. "Pretty Girl," a particularly lovely ballad, had the potential to be the 1980s' version of "Wonderful Tonight."

When he flew to the Bahamas to record in Nassau's Compass Point Studios, Clapton felt strongly that he had the basis for his best album since *Slowhand*. His band, however, failed to respond to Clapton's ideas for the new material. In concert, the band had been a good working unit, especially on the music from *Backless* and *Another Ticket*, but Clapton had a difficult time coaxing his players to step things up a notch for the new recording. They seemed sluggish. "The thrill was gone," Clapton said later, "and there was a feeling of paranoia in the studio because they sensed it, too."

Not all of the problems, however, could be attributed to the band's slow response to Clapton's new material. In the months following his release from Hazelden—and particularly the weeks prior to his arrival at Compass Point Studios—Clapton could be edgy and irritable, sharp-tongued some times and uncommunicative at others. His songwriting stint in Wales had been largely an excuse for a short-term separation from his marital problems with Pattie. In Nassau, he was moody and aloof, spending a lot of his time alone and leaving his bandmates confused about what they were expected to be doing in the studio. As a leader, he was sorely lacking.

Still, with high hopes for the new album, Clapton was caught in a predicament. He hated telling band members how to play their parts, which was insulting to musicians of their caliber. After two weeks of studio work, with not a single track completed to his satisfaction, Clapton was convinced that something radical had to be done. Tom Dowd, acting in his familiar role of production midwife, urged Clapton to fire the entire unit and start over. Roger Forrester flew in from England, prepared to act as Clapton's hatchet man if Eric preferred that he do the dirty work.

Clapton considered his options and decided to do the firing himself. He would keep Albert Lee, but the rest—Gary Brooker, Dave Markee, Chris Stainton, and Henry Spinetti—would have to go. He brought the musicians together and delivered the bad news. They had been a wonderful touring band, he told them, but they weren't getting the job done in the studio. He would be hiring studio musicians for this new album, so there was no point in their hanging around.

Clapton agonized over his decision. This group of musicians had been with him throughout his dark days of alcoholism, supporting him during a very trying time, and there he was, clean and sober, firing people who had been good friends, as well as bandmates. He and Gary Brooker in particular went back a long way; they had been fishing partners and pub buddies for ages. Like Carl Radle before him, Brooker was extremely upset by the firing, and Clapton, perhaps with the way he treated Radle in mind, worked hard to reestablish his friendship with Brooker.

Ironically, Clapton's decision to fire the members was largely the result of advice he'd received at Hazelden. He'd been told that he needed to be more assertive. If something bothered him, he ought to attack the problem rather than keep his feelings to himself. Pent-up emotions searched for the kind of release that alcohol provided.

Clapton tried to be diplomatic yet firm when he gathered the group together. He explained, as well as he could, that his decision was purely business and nothing personal, but even that was a hard slap at musicians who considered themselves consummate professionals. Although he realized that firing the band could cost him valued friendships, he stuck by his decision. Too much was at stake for him to take a lesser stand.

. . .

Over his years working as a producer, Tom Dowd had spent time with some of the best sessions musicians in the business, and he was happy to use his connections to help Clapton put together a studio unit for his new album. Not that it would have been all that difficult: musicians would have lined up around the block—and then some—for the chance to work on an Eric Clapton project.

The studio band was Clapton's best as a solo musician. Besides Albert Lee and Chris Stainton (who was invited back into the fold after he returned to England), the unit consisted of Donald "Duck" Dunn, the bassist for Booker T and the MG's, who had worked as a sessions musician with Otis Redding and countless Stax and Atlantic artists; drummer Roger Hawkins, who was part of the legendary Muscle Shoals studio musicians, and who had previously worked with Clapton in the Aretha Franklin sessions; and Ry Cooder, arguably the best young slide guitarist in the business, who had been enlisted early in his career by the Rolling Stones for work on *Let It Bleed* and *Sticky Fingers*. Clapton had seen a Cooder concert in London earlier in the year, and he couldn't believe his good fortune to have someone of his ability willing to play as a sideman on his album. Dunn, in Clapton's estimation, was as good a bassist as he'd worked with to that point.

The group meshed from the beginning. On their first day in the studio, they recorded a cover of Albert King's "Crosscut Saw" that gave Clapton a glimpse of what was to come. This was no laid-back outfit. They played with a burning intensity, and if Clapton intended to hold his own in the group, he would have to stretch himself a great deal more than in his

Eric Clapton and Patti Boyd attend the premiere of the movie version of The Who's *Tommy* in 1975. *(Hulton Archive/Getty Images)*

Jimmy Page, Eric Clapton, and Jeff Beck—all guitar alumni of the Yardbirds—joined forces in a series of benefit concerts to raise funds to research multiple sclerosis. *(Michael Brito/Star File)*

Patti Boyd and Eric Clapton arrive at the LIVE AID extravaganza in Philadelphia. Clapton's appearance at the internationally televised event boosted his career to new heights.
(Vincent Zuffante/Star File)

Stevie Ray Vaughan and Eric Clapton in 1990. Vaughan died in a helicopter crash after he and Clapton performed in East Troy, Wisconsin.
(John Bellissimo/Star File)

Eric Clapton's and Bob Dylan's paths crossed on numerous occasions, with mixed results. Flanked by Steve Cropper (left) and Dylan, Clapton performed at the 1992 Madison Square Garden concert commemorating Dylan's twenty-five years in the music business. *(Chuck Pulin/Star File)*

Clapton's album *Unplugged* earned him six Grammy awards, including Album of the Year, Song of the Year, and Record of the Year in 1993. *(Jeffrey Mayer/Star File)*

Clapton's brief affair with Italian model Lory Del Santo led to the birth of Eric's son Conor in 1986. Conor's tragic death in 1991 inspired "Tears in Heaven," one of Clapton's greatest songs. *(Rex Features)*

Clapton surprised many by marrying Melia McHenry in 2002. They are seen here with their young daughter Julie Rose. *(Rex Features)*

The Journeyman: Eric Clapton in 2001. Gone are the psychedelic clothes of the 1960s and the stylist outfits of the following decades, replaced by the garb of the workingman. *(VDL/Star File)*

previous band. Like the studio veterans they were, they played selflessly, their ears tuned to the way the band sounded as a unit on the final product.

The result was a very solid album, which, if anything, was too polished for its own good. By now Clapton had the formula down pat: cut an album with a healthy blend of cover tunes and originals, complete with several possibilities for commercial singles, balanced by blues numbers for the hard-core blues fans. *Money and Cigarettes*, as the album was called, had all of the above, plus it managed to be a deeply personal statement. In "The Shape You're In," Clapton chided Pattie about her own drinking problems, while he was unsparing of his own inner turmoil in "Ain't Going Down." Two songs ("Pretty Girl" and "Man in Love") found Clapton proclaiming his love for Pattie in lyrics that walked a fine line between sensitive and sappy.

To record buyers reading the musician credits and expecting a guitar album, *Money and Cigarettes* was a mixed bag. The album presented a number of brief but notable exchanges between Clapton and his guitar mates, but these moments were typically downplayed in favor of Clapton's long-established habit of emphasizing the songs themselves. "If one focuses only on guitar pyrotechnics," wrote one critic in a generally favorable review of *Money and Cigarettes*, "much of the record is sort of like a no-contact black-belt karate demonstration, artful if not hard-hitting."

Clapton was accustomed to such criticism—and much worse. *Money and Cigarettes* may not have turned out exactly the way he envisioned it, but it ultimately stood as a telling statement about his powers of survival and recuperation. At the beginning of the year, he had been in such awful physical condition that such an album would have been all but impossible to pull off, but here he was, only months later, singing and playing with authority, his career back on track and moving full speed ahead.

eleven

Behind the Sun
1983–86

I think I sold myself a long time ago. I made some kind of deal with myself to get along, to please people, to make life easy, I think. It disturbs me a little to hear myself say that, but I have to admit it because otherwise who am I kidding?

Clapton toured tirelessly in promotion of *Money and Cigarettes*, spending much of the six months between February and July 1983 on the road in the United States and Great Britain. "(I've Got a) Rock and Roll Heart" was released as the album's first single, and radio play of the song, coupled with Clapton's tour, boosted the album's sales to a respectable level.

Nonetheless, the album and tour didn't go over without controversy. Camel cigarettes sponsored the tour, claiming "the music of a guy like Eric Clapton fits the interest profile of a Camel smoker." The endorsement provoked a storm of protest from the American Lung Association, as outraged officials of the organization complained that a man of Clapton's stature ought to be setting a better example for the young people attending his concerts. They were disappointed to see him smoking onstage, holding a cigarette on the cover of his latest album, and accepting corporate sponsorship from a major tobacco company.

Much more positive to Clapton's image—and satisfying to the guitarist himself—was the Silver Clef Award presented to him by Princess Michael of Kent at a charity lunch on June 24. Clapton had received numerous awards throughout his career, including the annual *Playboy* and *Melody Maker* readers' poll awards for best guitarist, but the Silver Clef, awarded for outstanding achievement in British music, bore special significance for him. He had always felt uneasy about his standing in his homeland, so the award, bestowed on him after an especially trying year, pleased him immensely.

The award's timing was also noteworthy, as Clapton was approaching his twentieth anniversary in the music business. Although he had dreamed of making an impact on music way back when he'd started out playing blues covers with the Yardbirds in smoky, sweaty pubs, he would never have suspected that two decades later he would be one of the world's best-known and highest-paid musicians. A concert tour now earned him more than his grandfather had made in his lifetime, and a career in masonry or design would never have brought him the things he had become accustomed to—designer Italian clothes, Ferraris, and thoroughbred racehorses.

To celebrate his twenty-year milestone, Clapton decided to stage two huge charity events at the Royal Albert Hall, the first to benefit Ronnie Lane's Action Research into Multiple Sclerosis (ARMS) fund, the second to raise money for the Prince's Trust, a charitable organization overseen by the Prince of Wales. The ARMS benefit struck very close to home, because Clapton's old friend Ronnie Lane was himself afflicted with multiple sclerosis. Lane had tried everything to combat the disorder, but very little had been helpful. He did notice some restorative effects after taking a radical hyperbaric oxygen treatment, and with funds from the benefit, Lane hoped to purchase a hyperbaric machine that could be made available to MS patients in London.

Clapton needed to hear no more. He had been deeply moved at the sight of his friend's failing health, and if there was anything he could do to help Lane and others in his position, Clapton was all for it. "When I saw Ronnie," he said, "I knew that there was a way that I could help him, that it was possible to do this. It doesn't take much. It just takes a little bit of time and a little bit of sincere work."

Clapton, who had devoted a fair share of time and work to charitable organizations in the past, was being modest concerning his involvement in the ARMS benefit. His vision for the show—and for the Prince's Trust concert the following evening—was enormous, and the logistics of lining up the shows were trying. Besides booking London's most venerable hall for the performances, Clapton and his management were attempting to assemble the most impressive group of musical talent ever to grace a stage at one time—and all for charity.

Fortunately, he had many friends who shared his feelings for Ronnie Lane. Glyn Johns volunteered to produce the show, and a video crew was put together to film the ARMS benefit for eventual commercial release; the production was to be paid for by the musicians themselves. Clapton was gratified to see so many of his peers willing to pack away their egos and wallets for two evenings. When the lights were dimmed for the September 20, 1983, ARMS performance, Clapton had assembled a lineup that included drummer Charlie Watts and bassist Bill Wyman of the Rolling Stones; singer-guitarist Andy Fairweather-Low, formerly of Amen Corner; Kenney Jones, drummer for The Who and onetime mate of Ronnie Lane in Faces; Steve Winwood and Chris Stainton on keyboards; and a host of others. The evening's biggest coup, however, was the securing of England's three most accomplished guitarists—Clapton, Jeff Beck, and Jimmy Page, all alumni of the Yardbirds—to perform individual sets. The three had never appeared on the same stage before.

People got their money's worth and then some. Clapton went on first, playing a seven-song set that established the evening's pace with some torrid fretwork on a medley of "Ramblin' on My Mind" and "Have You Ever Loved a Woman," as well as on "Rita Mae," which also featured percussion pyrotechnics from Ray Cooper. Clapton remained onstage during Stevie Winwood's set, which included a rendition of the Spencer Davis Group's hit "Gimme Some Lovin'," a perennial crowd pleaser. After an intermission, Jeff Beck and his band performed their brand of Beck's jazz-rock fusion, as well as Beck's hit "Hi Ho Silver Lining." The evening's final and perhaps most eagerly anticipated set belonged to Jimmy Page, who had become reclusive since the disbanding of Led Zeppelin three years earlier. Following Clapton and Beck would have been a challenge to any guitarist on his best night, and Page seemed hesitant at first, as if he were reacquainting himself with the spotlight. He fulfilled all expectations, however, with an intense instrumental arrangement of the Led Zeppelin classic "Stairway to Heaven."

In an evening filled with emotional high points, the best was yet to come. As soon as Page had finished his set, the entire ensemble, including Clapton and Beck, joined him onstage for three songs—"Tulsa Time," "Wee Wee Baby," and "Layla." Despite their mutual admiration, Clapton and Beck felt a professional competitiveness, which was evident when they dueled during the solos in the evening's closing numbers. The camaraderie between the musicians, galvanized by their deep regard for Ronnie Lane, elevated the show to a level rarely achieved in the rock industry. Fans wept at the end of the evening when Lane was led onto the stage to lead the ensemble in "Bombers Moon" and "Goodnight Irene."

The show was repeated the following evening at the Prince's Trust charity concert. Clapton, who acted as a sort of ringmaster in what he later described as a circuslike atmosphere, enjoyed the carefree feeling of the shows. These shows were special to all involved. "After the Albert Hall concert," offered Bill Wyman in a statement reflecting the ensemble's shared enthusiasm, "everybody was so knocked out by the fun and the camaraderie of it that they said, 'We gotta do this again!'"

And so they did. A nine-concert ARMS benefit tour of the United States was organized, with two opening dates in Dallas, followed by three shows in San Francisco, two in Los Angeles, and two in New York. The lineup stayed the same, with the exception of Stevie Winwood, who had other obligations and was unable to attend. Winwood was replaced by Paul Rodgers and Joe Cocker, whose performances of "Seven Days" and "With a Little Help from My Friends" nearly stole the nightly shows. The press joked as rock's dinosaurs went on tour, but their cynicism was quickly put to rest when some of the sixties' best-known musicians put on a series of events that *Rolling Stone* deemed "the concert of the year." At a time when yuppies were the fashion of the day, a group of aging rockers brought back the spirit of an era believed to have been long gone.

• • •

For Clapton, there was a price to be paid for all the work, no matter how well intended. The long periods away from home—the tour to promote *Money and Cigarettes*, then the ARMS benefit tour, and, in early 1984, a trip through Europe and the Middle East—had created considerable tension with Pattie. Much of it was probably inevitable. When Eric quit drinking he used work as a form of therapy, as a means of taking his mind off some of the hardships associated with it. By his account, he was out earning a living, doing what any performer and man of the house would be doing. According to Eric, there were good reasons for all his absences.

Pattie wasn't buying it. She had hated playing the role of celebrity's wife during her previous marriage, and she wasn't going to play it now. Eric's tour ban on spouses had originally stemmed from the idea that it was difficult enough to keep band members in harmony; the last thing they needed was the added aggravation of dueling partners. This might have sounded good in theory, but it was damned hard to practice—at least without ruffling feathers or raising suspicions. Pattie was quite familiar with the long-standing tradition of musicians' dalliances on the road, but even if she could trust her husband in this respect, she couldn't accept being away from him for such long periods of time. If nothing else, she wanted a life of her own.

Unfortunately, she and Eric would never get together on these terms. For twenty years music had been Eric's life, the source of his living and identity. The domestic life was not for him. He would have liked to have had a child—which, sadly, Pattie couldn't give him—but even this wouldn't have dramatically changed the way he lived. He was simply too self-absorbed, both artistically and by nature, to make major adjustments in his behavior.

Oddly enough, Eric's abstention from drinking had caused problems in the Clapton household. During the period immediately following his return from Minnesota, Clapton was withdrawn around the house, which, to Pattie, was a little unnerving. He had never been one to socialize a lot when he was off the road, but now that he was trying to put his drinking behind him, he felt uncomfortable around those who drank too much. Rather than hang out in pubs, Clapton found other ways to occupy his free time. He spent a small fortune on Italian suits. He became obsessed with fishing. He took an active interest in the West Bromwich Albion Football Club, his favorite soccer team.

None of these activities included Pattie, and by the beginning of 1984, the Clapton marriage was seriously strained. Eric still cared very deeply about his wife—as shown in "Never Make You Cry" and "Behind the Sun," two new songs written during this period—but he was at a loss as to how to patch things up. Pattie, too, was caught without answers. She needed room to grow, and as far as she could tell, it wasn't happening with her husband. Something had to change.

· · ·

When Clapton returned to his rental cottage in Wales to write songs for another album, his problems with Pattie were very much on his mind. His new songs reflected that mental state, but they also indicated a shift in direction. Clapton felt that he had fallen into a creative rut, and he hoped the new album would spell significant change. Record buyers' tastes had shifted over the past decade, but Clapton's sound during that period had remained essentially the same.

Clapton wanted a moody, atmospheric feeling for the new record, and to achieve this effect he began to experiment with synthesizers. In the past, he had joked that synthesizers, with their ability to mimic almost any instrument's sound, would put him out of business, but by 1984, they figured prominently in the success of some of rock's most popular bands. One such group was Genesis, headed by Phil Collins, a friend and neighbor of Clapton's. Eric knew very little about Genesis's music, but he had worked previously with Collins in the studio and was comfortable with his production values.

"I heard the way he was producing John Martyn, and I heard Phil's own things, and I thought I would like to have him do my record," said Clapton, explaining his decision to hire Collins to produce his new album. "He's got a great understanding of synthesizers and how they can be used without becoming overpowering."

Collins also possessed a trait that instantly endeared him to Clapton: a deep regard for all forms of black American music, from urban blues to rhythm and blues, from Motown to soul. Clapton had been impressed by Collins's ability to combine time-honored black music with a contemporary sound of his own, and he hoped some of this would rub off on his new album.

It didn't hurt either that, as a longtime fan of Eric's music, Collins was knowledgeable of Clapton's strengths and weaknesses and had ideas about how to bring out his best in a fresh new approach. "Eric's last couple albums were a little bland, productionwise," Collins offered candidly, "so when Eric asked me to produce him, I thought it would be a great chance to shake up his music and make it stand again. He had written some great songs, was off the booze, playing and singing better than ever."

Behind the Sun, an album borrowing its title from a Muddy Waters line, was recorded and mixed over a two-month period at Air Studios in Montserrat, and it delivered on the promise to be a very different Clapton album. To record the album, Clapton used his touring band of Duck Dunn, Chris Stainton, and Jamie Oldaker (who had replaced Roger Hawkins during Clapton's previous U.S. tour), adding percussionist Ray Cooper and keyboardist Peter Robinson to fill out the sound. Beside working as the album's producer, Phil Collins played drums on the recording, giving it a heavy rhythmic feeling. The big difference by far was the use of synthesizers, especially on Clapton's guitar. Clapton had purchased a Roland guitar synth, which he used when overdubbing many of the guitar solos of the album, and the result was a very nontraditional guitar album.

Behind the Sun was as radical a departure as *461 Ocean Boulevard* had been a decade earlier. Like its predecessor, the new album displayed an astonishing range of song types, from its faithful cover of Eddie Floyd's classic rhythm and blues number "Knock on Wood" to its short, contemplative title song, featuring only Collins on synthesizer and Clapton on guitar. "Same Old Blues," an eight-minute opus anchoring the record, and "Just Like a Prisoner" presented Clapton solos so savage that they were almost frightening. This was Eric Clapton at his utter best, slicing off confrontational, rapid-fire notes that attacked the listener with relentless, feral intensity. (In fact, Clapton had recorded the "Same Old Blues" solo in anger, after he learned that his band members, sensitive to his past problems with alcohol, were excluding him from their parties. Clapton responded with this solo, and by calling the band together and admonishing them for not having faith in his ability to stay away from liquor.)

Clapton and Collins were thrilled when they listened to the playback of the album's recorded tracks. It had variety, a new sound, and a measure of artistry that had been lacking on Clapton's more recent efforts. Unfortunately for Collins and Clapton, the bigwigs at Warner Brothers did not share their enthusiasm for the record. In their opinion, it was far too eclectic, with nowhere near enough material for the singles market. Clapton would have to cut several songs and replace them with commercially oriented tunes before the company would put the product on the market.

After getting over their initial shock at hearing the news, both Clapton and Collins seethed about the decision. What the hell did Warner Brothers know about the music of Eric Clapton, Collins wondered. There they were, in their corporate offices halfway around the world, judging artistic endeavors with all the critical acumen of bean counters.

Their anger, like their shock, subsided, leaving them with the reality of the situation. Warner Brothers had recently dumped Van Morrison from their roster, and if the company was capable of dropping someone of Morrison's enormous talents, it could—and would—release Clapton just as easily. Clapton had no choice but to comply with the company's wishes.

. . .

In April 1984, the same month that Clapton was finishing the mixing on the original version of *Behind the Sun*, former Pink Floyd bassist-songwriter Roger Waters issued *The Pros and Cons of Hitchhiking*, an album so intellectual and artsy that it made Clapton's new work look positively mainstream. Recorded the previous August, *Pros and Cons* featured a splendid cast of musicians, including a guest appearance by Eric Clapton himself.

Clapton had always been intrigued by Pink Floyd's music. In 1968, when asked about his favorite performing groups on the British music scene, Clapton, then with Cream, had immediately cited Pink Floyd. The band, he said, was working in a way unlike any group he had heard in America. This was high praise indeed, coming at a time when Clapton was bowled over by the psychedelic scene in the States, and when his own band was one of the top touring attractions in rock.

Recording with Waters had been a thoroughly enjoyable experience. Clapton was again in the background, happily submerging his own artistic ego in another man's work, feeling no pressure to lead or make important creative decisions. Clapton's guitar and Dobro playing on the record lent a strange quality to Waters's spacy music, and his solo on "Sexual Revolution," by his own estimation, was one of his best as a sideman. When they had finished recording the album, an elated Clapton had told Waters that he would accompany him as his guitarist if he ever decided to perform the album on tour. Less than a year later, Waters held Clapton to his word.

The Waters tour was about the last thing that Roger Forrester wanted for his client. Eric had a tour of his own looming in the near future, and he had an album to complete. Touring with Waters, Forrester argued pointedly, made no sense at all. Clapton was far too big a name to be working as a sideman, and while his name would undoubtedly help ticket sales for the tour, he had nothing in common with Waters or his music.

As time would prove, Forrester was totally on the mark in his assessment of the situation, but Clapton's involvement in the tour paid unexpected dividends in terms of his future work. Michael Kamen, one of the group's keyboardists, was a classically trained musician with an interest in film scoring, and as a result of his association with Kamen, Clapton would find a new career sideline in the very near future. Tim Renwick, the band's rhythm guitarist, would wind up working in Clapton's touring band in less than a year, and Katie Kissoon, one of Waters's backing vocalists, would become a regular background singer in future Clapton bands.

The tour itself, as Forrester had predicted, was a less than rewarding experience for Clapton. He hadn't worked as a regular, nonleading band member in fifteen years, and he found the performances with Waters to be challenging, not only in a musical sense, when he had to find a way to fit into the unit, but in a personal, ego-deflating sense. "It really was off the beaten track for me," he stated. "That gig was like playing John Cage or Stockhausen—wearing headphones with click tracks going, being ready for cues, and things like that." Waters's high-tech approach to his live shows, complete with a complex light show and films playing on three screens projected over the stage, was different from anything Clapton had ever used.

Clapton accompanied Waters for nine shows, including appearances in Stockholm, London, Zurich, and Paris. His playing was top-notch, but he soon grew bored with what he considered to be a bloodless, pretentious show. As it was, he went out of his way to keep his own tours as loose and easy as possible; to his chagrin, the Waters tour had a star-quality atmosphere that put him off.

His tenure with Waters ended after ten shows in North America. Before leaving for these dates, he had appeared at a Bob Dylan show in London's Wembley Stadium, at a performance that featured Carlos Santana, Van Morrison, Chrissie Hynde, and Mick Taylor. The Dylan show marked a strong contrast to what Clapton had been experiencing with Roger Waters: the music was spontaneous and loose, and if it all seemed a little scruffy, it was also more fun to play. When Waters added dates to his tour the following year, Clapton was no longer part of the band's roster.

• • •

Pattie moved out of Hurtwood Edge and into a London apartment in November, while Eric was out with his own band, touring Australia. The move had been coming for a long time. When talking about their marital problems, Eric and Pattie had discussed the possibility of a trial separation, and both had agreed that it might be for the best.

Despite all the discussion, Clapton was stunned when Pattie actually left. He blamed himself for her departure, and over the next several months, he tried everything he could think of to talk her into returning. He called her repeatedly on the phone, took her to lunch, sent her roses. The conversations and meetings were cordial enough, but Pattie didn't budge. She needed time and space of her own.

The British press, which had been rumoring the separation for months, stayed on the story like bloodhounds, adding to Clapton's suffering. "It really did hurt," he said afterward, "because it hadn't occurred to me up until that point that it was really anyone else's business. And when you see it all in black and white, it tends to become almost a little too real. You start believing what you read, and it multiplies the grief of all of it."

The separation capped a trying year for Clapton. The two mainstays in his life—his work and his marriage—were a shambles. Both, in his eyes, were imminently salvageable, and he approached the task of repairing his life with the determination that had seen him through the hard times in his past.

While trying to woo Pattie back, he also put the finishing touches on the *Behind the Sun* album. Unable to come up with replacement songs, Clapton had challenged his record company to provide the kind of hit-single material they wanted him to record. The company responded by sending Clapton demos of three songs ("Forever Man," "See What Love Can Do," "Something's Happening") written by a Fort Worth songwriter named Jerry Lynn Williams. Clapton liked the tunes and agreed to do them.

Warner Brothers brought Clapton to Los Angeles to record under the supervision of Lenny Waronker and Ted Templeman, two of the company's top-ranking officials. Rather than use his own band, Clapton worked with a group of local sessions musicians known as the "A Team" that included bassist Nathan East, keyboardist Greg Phillinganes, guitarist Steve Lukather, and drummer Jeff Porcaro—the last two being alumni of Toto. The highly polished productions were just the kind of upbeat pop songs

Warner Brothers was looking for, and though each was a potential hit single, the songs as a group were a bad fit on *Behind the Sun*. They sounded awkward next to the Phil Collins–produced numbers, and they disrupted the mood Clapton was trying to establish on the album.

"Forever Man" became the album's first single, and to promote both album and single, Clapton stepped in front of the cameras to make his first video. Not surprisingly, given the fact that he had never been an animated stage performer, Clapton was not interested in putting together a gimmicky story-line video. He would defer to the changing demands of the industry's sales and marketing divisions, but not at the cost of his music's integrity. As a compromise, he was filmed—by the award-winning video directors Kevin Godley and Lol Creme—performing the song with his band. Even then, Clapton had mixed feelings about the experience.

"It was fun," he said, "but I think it goes against the grain for me. It's a concession to the star-making machinery." There had been a time, he mentioned, when he enjoyed seeing early films of Chuck Berry or Jerry Lee Lewis, but modern business had taken the charm out of it by producing so many videos. The glut of videos, in Clapton's opinion, was robbing music lovers of some of their imagination: "Music for me has always been something to close your eyes to, to have your own picture."

Clapton put such feelings aside and tried to take a philosophical approach to the entire *Behind the Sun* experience. In interviews, he was forthright in expressing the resentment he harbored over seeing his music rejected. He had never been a commercialist—not as a teenager with the Yardbirds, not now. Still, he claimed to have found something valuable in his trials.

"It was very character-building for me to have to face that," he said, "and I am grateful for that situation. It lopped a lot off my ego and gave me a little taste of humility, which I may have been in great need of."

. . .

Clapton held a similarly humble outlook when trying to patch up his marriage. He had been mistaken, he admitted, in not including Pattie more in his career, and he should have been more sensitive when he was quitting his own drinking but berating Pattie for hers. In assessing blame for their separation, Clapton was prepared to shoulder most of the responsibility.

The separation had given both Eric and Pattie the chance to stand back and look at their relationship in a different light, and neither was prepared to abandon the marriage at this point. Both had engaged in brief flings during their separation, but these had only served to show how much they missed each other. Clapton had been thoroughly miserable during the holiday season, his first without Pattie in years. He continued to campaign for a reunion, and Pattie finally agreed to take a short vacation in Israel with him in February. The two talked at length during the ten-day trip, analyzing the nature of their relationship, and by the time they returned to England, Pattie was ready to move back into Hurtwood Edge. The paparazzi had a field day when Eric and Pattie turned up together for the London opening of Terry Gilliam's film *Brazil*.

"We found out," said Clapton, addressing the issue of the trial separation, "that there was a fairly strong bond there that we hadn't considered at all. Neither of us had really understood this, but there's a real thread that holds us together. In actual fact, it was a good thing for us to have split, because we had a chance to find out how much we really did miss one another."

The reconciliation, however, was not going to be easy. Clapton's 1985 schedule was one of the busiest of his career, with tours of Scandinavia, the United Kingdom, Japan, and Italy sandwiched around another gargantuan swing through the United States. As one of his concessions to Pattie, Clapton called off his "no wives" rule, giving Pattie the option of joining him on the road for the first time since the early days of their marriage.

Buoyed by the turn of events in his life, Clapton turned in some of the finest performances of his career. His band, now featuring Tim Renwick on second guitar, handled the new songs from *Behind the Sun* as if they'd been playing them for years, and Clapton's solos regained some of their old bite. Fans and rock writers alike were appreciative of Clapton's rejuvenated playing. "Here was rock's most influential and longest-reigning guitar hero," wrote one reviewer, "playing as if his life depended on it, and the sheer authority of his phrasing and that cold-blooded guitar sound were transcending the ordinary pop event just as easily as they did in 1965."

On May 8, 1985, Clapton made a rare appearance on American television, on "Late Night with David Letterman." The audience was treated to Clapton performances during the program's commercial breaks, as Eric ran through instrumental versions of "Layla," "Lay Down Sally," "Knock on Wood," and several others with Paul Shaffer and his band. The real treat, for fans of Clapton's music, was seeing Eric play "White Room" for the first time since his final show with Cream. With the exceptions of "Badge" and "Crossroads"—and, on an extremely rare occasion, "Sunshine of Your Love"—Clapton had religiously avoided performing Cream songs at his shows. With such a huge catalog of songs to choose from, Clapton saw no need to dig that far into his past for stage material. The 1985 tours found him bringing back some old chestnuts, including "Steppin' Out," from his Cream and John Mayall days, and "Motherless Children," from his *461 Ocean Boulevard* album. Clapton enjoyed playing "White Room" on the Letterman show so much that he immediately added it to the tour set lists.

The year was clearly turning into one of Clapton's best. *Behind the Sun* was holding its own on the charts, and the concerts were as successful as ever. *Rolling Stone* ran another cover story interview and, in an unprecedented move, *Guitar Player* devoted its entire July issue to Clapton. A major biography, the first to be written with Clapton's cooperation, was being prepared. There was even an Eric Clapton signature model Stratocaster guitar being designed.

Clapton found all the attention a bit overwhelming, but after enduring some difficult years in his past, he was prepared to enjoy a stretch in which the planets seemed to be lined up in his favor.

．　．　．

If any single event in Eric Clapton's career boosted his popularity to an almost unimaginable level, it would be his three-song set at the Live Aid concert on July 13, 1985.

Organized by Bob Geldof to raise funds to relieve the starving people in Africa, Live Aid was the largest single rock event in history, featuring dozens of the world's best-known rock acts. Nothing remotely similar had been attempted before, and it took a man of Geldof's skill and stamina to plan a show that would run simultaneously in two locations (JFK Stadium in Philadelphia and Wembley Stadium in London), be televised worldwide to over a billion and a half viewers, and feature performances by Clapton, Phil Collins, U2, Sting, Mick Jagger and Tina Turner, Stevie Wonder, Neil Young, The Who, Elton John, and many more.

Clapton was understandably apprehensive when he arrived in Philadelphia for the event. It was one thing to be a headliner on a tour and quite another to be working as just one act in an incredibly talented lineup. To top things off, it was a scorching hot day, and Clapton was afraid he might pass out from the heat, anxiety, and exhaustion.

A technical glitch almost ruined the show. As Clapton started to sing his first song, he noticed that he couldn't hear himself in the monitors, and when he moved closer to the microphone, he received an electrical shock from the mike. The sudden jolt surprised him, and he spent much of the first song trying to find a way to maneuver as close as possible to the microphone without actually touching it with his mouth.

But the crowd didn't even notice. The opening chords of "White Room" had them on their feet. Clapton's power chords were accompanied by the familiar sound of thumping tom-toms, but for this show, Clapton had two drummers—Jamie Oldaker, his regular tour drummer, and surprise guest Phil Collins, who had played at Wembley Stadium earlier in the day and, after the show, flew via the Concorde to play in Philadelphia. Clapton's wah-wah solo at the end of "White Room" brought back memories of another era, when a younger, thinner Clapton could bring down the house with the solo for Cream. Happily, a forty-year-old Clapton could still do the same.

"She's Waiting," Clapton's next number, was from the new album. Clapton sang confidently and with great authority. As this taste from the new album would show, his voice had improved enormously over the years. The band had been playing the song regularly on Clapton's U.S. tour, and including it in the brief set was a nice piece of marketing strategy. A few weeks earlier, "She's Waiting" had been released as the second single from *Behind the Sun*.

The final song, "Layla," needed only its familiar introductory guitar riff to whip the already worked-up crowd into an absolute frenzy. Clapton's soaring guitar notes, played over the piece's closing piano passage, served as a spectacular finale to one of his most memorable performances.

Clapton's appearance at Live Aid offered proof, to those who needed to be reminded, that he was still a major force on the music scene. He could hold his own against the army of young musicians seeking the hero worship he had once shrugged off. Twenty years in the business hadn't diminished his talents; if anything, he was a sharper and broader musician than ever.

• • •

Sales in Clapton's albums, including those recorded with Cream and Derek and the Dominos, jumped dramatically in the weeks following Eric's appearance at Live Aid, adding luster to a U.S. tour that had become an overwhelming artistic and financial success. As usual, a number of the shows featured special guest appearances, including Carlos Santana, Stephen Bishop, and Lionel Richie. Clapton had struck up a friendship with Richie at the Live Aid benefit, and after the two performed together at the tour's final show in Seattle, Clapton joined Richie in a local studio to add guitar to his song "Tonight Will Be Alright."

Clapton's torrid work schedule in 1985—tours of Japan and Europe followed his three months in the United States—only served to underscore the extent to which the man had disappeared into the artist: Clapton's life *was* his work. He certainly wasn't alone in this regard. Great artists, almost without exception, are willing to sacrifice everything for their creative endeavors. Marriages and friendships fall apart, personal lives hang in tatters, health problems develop—all as a result of the unbelievable focus needed to endure. To the casual observer, fed only an occasional tidbit about the man behind the music, Eric Clapton appeared to have escaped his greatest pitfalls. He seemed to have more lives than a cat; he was one of rock's great survivors.

Nevertheless, he paid a price for his artistry and fame. He never had, nor was he willing to make the concessions to have, the kind of relationship or marriage that most people take for granted. Although he was surrounded by wealthy and influential friends, he was essentially a lonely man. Even the work itself drove him like a demon master. Despite all the music he had made, he was still searching for new sounds and directions.

His marriage was in its final stages. Pattie had accompanied him on much of his tour, including the Live Aid performance, but their reconciliation had been difficult. Eric was always preoccupied with the business at hand, and Pattie was learning that he could be as isolated from her when they were together on the road as she had been when she was at home alone, awaiting his return from a tour. She remained the rock star's wife, someone to be patronized or tolerated, but never truly included. It was a status that would never change, regardless of Eric's best intentions.

Clapton ended any slim chance of salvaging his tumultuous marriage when he was on a nine-concert swing through Italy. While in Milan, he met Italian model Lory Del Santo, and the two were soon inseparable. Unlike his past affairs and one-nighters, which were kept discreet and out of the eyes of the media, Clapton made very little attempt to hide his relationship with Del Santo. The two were seen together at a Buddy Guy–Junior Wells concert in London after Clapton's tour of Italy, as well as at a subsequent Sting concert in Milan, where Eric performed as a guest guitarist. Clapton was definitely smitten by the beautiful aspiring actress.

Pattie had withstood her husband's dalliances in the past. In a business of seemingly endless temptations, sexual fidelity was extremely difficult, if not impossible, for many musicians to practice, and if Eric had let her down in this regard, Pattie could at least deal with it as a matter of Clapton's admitted weakness for—and the constant availability of—beautiful women.

The affairs had always been temporary, and Eric had always found a way to make up for them.

Pattie had even found a way to deal with an affair that, for most women, would have been impossible to forgive. While recording *Behind the Sun* in Montserrat, Clapton had taken up with a twenty-eight-year-old woman named Yvonne Kelly. The affair, unlike Clapton's other flings, had long-term results: On January 11, 1985, Kelly gave birth to a daughter, Ruth, who Clapton would support and secretly acknowledge to be his child.

Clapton had always wanted to have children, which, unfortunately, Pattie was biologically unable to have. Clapton conceded to the press that their marriage had suffered as a result, but the issue had not been enough to drive them apart. Somehow, almost miraculously, the marriage had survived Clapton's affair with Yvonne Kelly.

His more recent affair with Lory Del Santo changed all that. Del Santo, too, had become pregnant with Eric's child, and while Clapton had been very quiet about the Kelly pregnancy, he was openly pleased about the prospects this time around. After telling Pattie about Del Santo's pregnancy, Eric asked his wife to stand by him, even in the face of media gossip that was certain to be uncomfortable, if not humiliating, for Pattie. Clapton still believed that the marriage could be worked out. Pattie wasn't so sure.

She stayed with Eric for the time being, but this latest turn of events had effectively closed the door on the marriage.

"It was more than she could cope with," Clapton said a year later, after the birth of his son.*

· · ·

Clapton spent the early portion of 1986 hanging around, making only an occasional public appearance, unwinding from the previous year's activities.

---

*According to biographer Christopher Sandford, Lory Del Santo considered having an abortion when she learned that she was pregnant. Clapton vehemently opposed it, going so far as to threaten to kill himself if she went through with it.

He had closed out the year with a number of guest appearances, including onstage jam sessions with Buddy Guy and Junior Wells, Sting, and Dire Straits. In February, he joined the Rolling Stones, Pete Townshend, Jeff Beck, and Jack Bruce in an all-star tribute honoring the memory of Ian Stewart, the former piano player for the Rolling Stones, who had recently died of a heart attack.

The real work was just up the road. Two years had gone by since Clapton had recorded the rejected version of *Behind the Sun,* and it was time to put new product on the market. Clapton admitted that the rejection amounted to "my mortality staring me in the face"; he was keenly aware of the pressure on him to record bankable material. This meant finding a more contemporary sound.

To achieve this, he put together an altogether new studio band, a basic four-piece unit steeped in rhythm and blues and soul music yet highly skilled at playing the funkier, dance-oriented music popular at the time. Nathan East and Greg Phillinganes, the sessions players who had worked with Clapton in Los Angeles on the three new *Behind the Sun* tracks, were hired to play bass and keyboards. Phil Collins was again enlisted to produce the record and play drums in the band.

The album, with a working title of *One More Car, One More Rider,* presented Clapton with a new set of challenges. In gathering a lineup of songs suitable to the singles market, Clapton had all but written himself out of instrumental work. The songs on hand didn't accommodate guitar solos.

"They were just straight songs, with middles and choruses," Clapton explained. "To put a solo in just for the sake of it was definitely wrong in some cases. So we had to really pare it down and make whatever was there good, you know, and relevant to the song."

Two songs—"Miss You" and "Holy Mother," positioned back to back on the album—had openings for strong solos, and Clapton turned in two high-powered solos, as if to compensate for the lack of them elsewhere on the album. Both had an underlying blues feeling to them, but when placed in the context of these new songs, the solos created the kind of artistic, old blues–contemporary sound counterpoint Clapton had been trying to achieve on his last two albums.

"Holy Mother" was especially poignant. Cowritten with Stephen Bishop as a tribute to The Band's Richard Manuel, who had recently committed suicide, "Holy Mother" had more than a nodding stylistic acquaintance with "Layla," in which Clapton wove powerful emotional threads, laying bare his secret feelings and suffering, only to find a sense of resolution by the end of the song. The new song had a similar quality. Angry, wounded, and horribly depressed, Clapton implores the Holy Mother to help him find peace of mind. He then launches into a solo that ultimately brings the same sense of closure found in the piano piece at the end of "Layla." Clapton's guitar begins slowly, repeating the emotional theme of the song, only to lift noticeably by the end of the song. In his music, Richard Manuel, "the holy madman," as Clapton called him, had given the world a priceless gift, and the only proper way to eulogize him was to give back some of that music. In this solo, Clapton does just that.

The three other members of Clapton's band brought much more than their talents as backing musicians to the studio; all could write and arrange. This, of course, was no great surprise in the case of Phil Collins, who had already earned a reputation as one of the most well-rounded craftsmen in the business. Greg Phillinganes and Nathan East, though immensely respected by their peers, turned out to be pleasant surprises to those unfamiliar with their work. Both inched Clapton closer to the funk and soul sounds that he wanted for the record, and Phillinganes cowrote "Miss You" and "Tearing Us Apart," two of the album's noteworthy works, with Clapton.

From an artistic standpoint, the sessions produced extreme results. Clapton's vocal duet with Tina Turner on "Tearing Us Apart" was an inspired piece of singing, but his work elsewhere, particularly on the Lamont Dozier–written tracks ("Run" and "Hung Up on Your Love") seemed forced, almost contrived. For all the beauty of his guitar playing on "Holy Mother," Clapton was surprisingly disappointing on his cover of Robert Cray's "Bad Influence." Phil Collins's production, generally successful on *Behind the Sun*, fell short on these new songs. A lot of Clapton was being lost in the mix.*

Clapton recognized the departure he was undertaking on his new album, and he became defensive, even testy, in his interviews about it. He had heard the criticism that *Behind the Sun* was too heavily influenced by Phil Collins, and he was prepared to hear the same about his latest work.

"People will say that *Behind the Sun* and *August* are really Phil Collins records," he told an interviewer at the time. "Fine—if that's all they can hear, they're not listening properly. I'm in there with as much as I've got, but not in a competitive way. If I did, it would be a mess. It works pretty good for me to allow people to be themselves rather than trying to lay down the law."

. . .

If anyone was affecting Clapton's work, it was Robert Cray, a young guitarist of enormous range and articulation. Like Clapton, Cray was well versed in his blues history, and he could play any style of blues. Not surprisingly, he had been heavily influenced by Clapton when he was taking up guitar.

Duck Dunn had given Clapton a cassette of Cray's music several years earlier, and while Clapton had been very impressed with Cray's ability, he had never seen one of his shows. All that changed when Clapton performed at the Montreux Jazz Festival in Switzerland. Present at the festival was Otis Rush, one of Clapton's early influences, and Clapton was delighted to finally be able to play "Double Trouble" and "Crosscut Saw" with Rush during his set. Clapton's own performance, featuring his new road band of Phil Collins, Nathan East, and Greg Phillinganes, went very well, with Robert Cray standing in with the band for a guitar jam on "Ramblin' on My Mind" and "Have You Ever Loved a Woman?"

For Clapton, the Robert Cray set was an eye-opener. To see Cray onstage

*Ironically, the best song to come out of the sessions, a sexy rocker called "Lady of Verona," was left off the album. Clapton's celebration of his affair with Lory Del Santo was judged to be too controversial for the record.

was like watching a black counterpart of himself in his youth: there was the same devotion to the blues, the same dedicated, uncompromising fretwork. "I sat and watched his set and I just freaked out," Clapton recalled, thoroughly impressed by Cray's interest in building on traditional blues.

The two became instant friends, and though their relationship didn't exactly mirror the friendship that Clapton had with Muddy Waters, it bore some interesting similarities, especially in the way that Robert Cray helped Clapton redirect his attention to playing the blues. In recording the new album, Clapton had once again veered away from his true path, and despite his protests to the contrary, he seemed to recognize as much. Less than a year after meeting Cray, with a newly released album climbing the charts faster than any of his work in nearly two decades, Clapton would begin talking about recording an entire album of blues standards. He offered no apologies for his commercial ventures, but he also made it very clear that he still considered himself a bluesman.

That part of his identity would never change, even if it did seem to be pushed aside from time to time.

twelve

Journeyman
1986–90

I keep seeing *myself* at a crossroads. Always going through that same sort of shift, where you come up to a situation and don't know which way to go. I'm never, ever in a permanent situation. I'm never really satisfied with my lot, I'm always looking for something more. I'm never really sure where I'm going. I'm directionless, you know.

August, named after the birth month of Clapton's son, Conor, was issued in November. With only an occasional exception, critics turned up their noses at the album, finding it far too removed from the Clapton realm to be taken seriously. Some of the reviewers were pleased by the album's sharper rock 'n' roll edge—"This new lp is full of the sort of hard-driving rock Clapton is famous for," wrote one critic, who viewed *August* as "Clapton's best work in years"—but most critics had long since written off Clapton's forays into musical forms that, in their opinion, didn't suit his talents. The reviews, as usual, had little effect on the album's acceptance among record buyers, who made it Clapton's best-selling work as a solo artist.

Clapton's popularity was reaching phenomenal heights. A new generation of fans—kids who might have seen a Yardbirds or Cream album tucked into their parents' record collections—was discovering Clapton on its own. They might have heard a song such as "I Shot the Sheriff" or "Cocaine" on the radio, but the Live Aid performance had gone a long way in connecting the Clapton of Cream's "White Room" and Derek and the Dominos' "Layla" with the Phil Collins–produced Clapton of recent years.

With the boost in popularity came a greater demand for appearances, and while Clapton did little touring in 1986, he did fill his time with a number of studio and onstage guest performances. One of the more interesting adventures was his involvement with a gala sixtieth birthday bash for Chuck Berry. The two-concert event, filmed for commercial release, brought together a solid roster of American and British musicians, including Clapton, Keith Richards, Robert Cray, Joey Spampinato of NRBQ, and Berry's former piano player, Johnnie Johnson. A year earlier, Clapton had been a part of a televised tribute to rockabilly great Carl Perkins, and he was looking forward to a similar affair with Chuck Berry, who had been so influential to Clapton in his youth. However, despite the spirited music played at the concerts, much of the event's shine was diminished for Clapton when Berry made good on his reputation of being egotistical and difficult.

As Clapton remembered, "Chuck appeared and he sat down next to me on the couch and he said, 'Hi, I'm Chuck Berry, you're Eric Clapton. Nice to meet you.' Then he said, 'Hang on a second!' and shouted out, 'Bring the camera in!' So the next thing I knew, this person holding a camera and microphone walked into the situation. Then Chuck turned to me and said, 'Okay, so when was it you really got into my music?'"

Clapton found Berry's attitude perplexing. He'd seen his fair share of self-absorbed rock stars in his day, but his experiences with his elders had usually been positive. Rather than be flattered by his influence on rock history, Berry seemed hung up and embittered by people who had pinched some of his best riffs. In the end, Berry was far too self-centered for Clapton's tastes.

"I still love his music," he said, "but meeting him in some senses took the edge off it for me. I found out bit by bit that he was so concerned with money and himself, and he is such an ambitious man, that in a way kind of spoiled the feeling for the music."

Much more rewarding for Clapton was his work on the film score to the Mel Gibson movie *Lethal Weapon*. Eric had contributed his talents to a number of motion picture sound tracks over the years, dating back to his work with George Harrison on *Wonderwall Music* in 1968. More recently he had written the score for the *Edge of Darkness* television production, and *August* had included "It's in the Way That You Use It," a song he cowrote with Robbie Robertson for the movie *The Color of Money*.

At first glance, the sound track work might have appeared to be a total departure for Clapton, but it was actually a natural progression. Clapton had always been very visually oriented, so it wasn't much of a stretch for him to come up with music to accompany the images he watched on the screen. In addition, he was well accustomed to shifting musical moods and colors in his extended onstage solos; he knew how to build around an existing theme.

"You're reflecting a visual aspect and trying to enhance what's already there," Clapton remarked, mentioning that, in film work, he didn't have to concern himself with whether the music would be commercially successful. "It gives me a great deal of freedom without the pressure," he said, "and I enjoy it for that reason."

As could be expected, Clapton had his own ideas about how sound tracks should be composed, and he approached the process with the same fierce perfectionism that he brought to all aspects of his musical life. Sound tracks, he felt, should exist as fine, independent pieces of music. He loved older scores such as *The Treasure of the Sierra Madre* and *East of Eden*, and he used these as models for his own work.

Recording the *Lethal Weapon* sound track was less than ideal, as far as Clapton was concerned, in that the score's two main instruments, guitar and saxophone, weren't recorded together in the studio. Clapton laid down his guitar tracks in England, and David Sanborn did his saxophone parts in the United States. Both musicians were easily capable of working in this fashion, but it was disappointing to Clapton. Working on the project long distance prohibited some of the creative energy possible on collaborative recordings.

Nevertheless, the sound track worked out well—so much so, in fact, that Clapton would be asked to work on the scores for the movie's two sequels. Clapton couldn't have been more pleased. He'd found yet another creative outlet.

. . .

Clapton opened 1987 with a string of six concerts at the Royal Albert Hall, beginning an annual tradition that, by the early nineties, had expanded to nearly four times that many dates.

The idea behind putting together a concert series was simple enough: over the years, Clapton had felt that he might have been short-changing his own country with all his international touring, particularly in the United States. He wanted to show his appreciation for his British following. His fondness for the Royal Albert Hall dated back to his farewell concert with Cream, and he greatly preferred the venue over London's vast, and consequently less intimate, Wembley Stadium. The concerts sold out quickly, and those fortunate enough to obtain tickets wound up seeing some of Clapton's finest performances—boosted, no doubt, by the presence of Dire Straits' Mark Knopfler on second guitar.

The Clapton-Knopfler team, like Clapton's earlier collaborations with George Terry, Albert Lee, and Duane Allman, succeeded mainly because Knopfler could adapt to Clapton's style. This wasn't always easy. Clapton preferred to play rhythm when he had another accomplished guitarist onstage with him, partly because he was lazy, but mostly because he enjoyed listening to a sizzling solo as much as anyone in the audience. This, however, wasn't why people came to see an Eric Clapton show, so the second guitarist, especially one with Knopfler's reputation, had to put on a strong performance without upstaging the headliner. When asked what he looked for in a second guitarist, Clapton, without providing names, described Mark Knopfler to a tee: "I like to have someone in the band who's stable, you know, who can play and get on with people—that really is most important. I don't like to play with people who've got to prove themselves."

Clapton certainly felt no such urge. Awards honoring his achievement as a musician, such as the British Phonographic Institute achievement award given to him in February, were still timely yardsticks by which he could gauge his critical and popular appeal. His tours, such as his winter trip to Europe and spring jaunt to the United States, continued to prove that there was still greater demand than supply for tickets to his concerts. And his gold and platinum record awards kept record company executives happy. As he rolled into his middle years, Clapton had plenty of reason for self-satisfaction.

Through all of it, he remained essentially the same person he'd been in his youth, when he'd moved from Ripley to London to pursue a life in music. Professional acquaintances were quick to point out what a down-to-earth, nice guy he was. Indeed, though he was a man of expensive tastes and an occasional wild streak, he was also as acutely aware of his roots as he was of his current standing. That his heart was in the right place was rarely a matter of question; his generosity was proven by his participation in any number of large- and small-scale charity gigs. For every high-profile charity event like the Prince's Trust shows, in which he played alongside George Harrison, Ringo Starr, Elton John, and Phil Collins, there seemed to be an equal or greater number of the much more modest variety, such as Clapton's low-profile performances at the Cranleigh Golf Club and the Finchley Cricket Club. Only a handful of rock figures could come close to matching his track record.

. . .

Like most celebrities, Clapton was inundated with requests for appearances and with endorsement offers. Over the years he had allowed his name and image to be attached to selected products such as Sound City guitar strings and Music Man amplifiers, and his music was occasionally used for promotional purposes, but Clapton and his management tended to take a cautious approach in the arena of product marketing, despite the easy money that could be made from it.

One recent endorsement brought Clapton more trouble than he had bargained for. As part of its "The Night Belongs to Michelob" advertising campaign, the Michelob beer company had put together a commercial featuring Clapton performing a new version of "After Midnight." The ad was tastefully done, showing Clapton playing and singing the song. At no point was Clapton seen holding a bottle of beer or speaking on behalf of the product.

Nevertheless, he was severely criticized when the commercial hit the airwaves, the bulk of the criticism focusing on Clapton's position as a recovering alcoholic. His detractors claimed that Clapton showed extremely poor judgment in appearing in a beer commercial. Not only was he sending mixed signals to those familiar with his past, but also, to a lesser extent, he might have been guilty of lending unintended approval to underage drinking, since so many of his fans were not of legal drinking age.

Those close to Clapton realized that there was a deeper, more troubling element to the criticism: in recent years, Clapton had slipped off the wagon and was drinking again. For the most part, his drinking was light—an occasional glass of wine or beer—but given Clapton's membership in Alcoholics Anonymous, along with his tendency to become preachy with others who drank to excess, the Michelob commercial smacked of hypocrisy. (Ironically, the alcohol consumption increased and Clapton was back in Hazelden, getting further treatment for his alcoholism, when the commercial finally hit the airwaves.)

If all this weren't enough, Clapton found the ad entered into a long-standing debate among his own peers: at what point was music affected by residual commercial profit?

This was an extremely difficult issue to resolve. Rock musicians, like other creative individuals, wanted their work exposed to as many people as possible; their livelihoods, as well as their chances of recording future projects, depended on it. As the years passed, and rock 'n' roll shed much of its bad boy image and was integrated into mainstream culture, rock musicians found other ways, besides recording, performing, and publishing royalties, to earn money. The proliferation of music used in commercials, MTV ads and videos, Muzak, and other miscellaneous marketing ventures had opened up huge new avenues of potential income (and, some would say, exploitation), leaving the artist in the position of having to exchange artistic control for a sizable paycheck.

Then there was the issue of corporate sponsorship of rock tours. For many years, large corporations, particularly those gearing their product to the youth market, had been sponsoring the biggest rock tours on the circuit. Musicians rarely made artistic concessions to their sponsors, but there still lingered the nagging questions about any unintentional influence a sponsor might have on the musician's work. The debate was further fueled by such figures as Neil Young, Tom Waits, and Elvis Costello, who registered protests against corporate sponsorship of rock artists.

Clapton posed an interesting study. After all, he had left the Yardbirds because he disapproved of exchanging some of the band's purist blues principles for a commercially appealing sound, yet here he was, playing a bluesy version of "After Midnight" for a beer company, ignoring his own personal problems with alcoholism for a corporate payoff. Was he selling out?

Historically speaking, Clapton never had a problem mingling with the forces of high commerce. As a member of Cream, he'd performed the music for a Falstaff beer commercial, and in the future he would record background music for Honda automobile ads. His shows had received corporate sponsorship, including the controversial *Money and Cigarettes* tour underwritten by Camel cigarettes. By his estimation, he had done nothing to cheapen the value of his music, and he took a defiant stance in the face of his critics. He was troubled by some of the remarks made by his peers, but rather than let it eat at him, he tried to put it to good use.

"That sort of thing will make me strive more than anything a critic will say," he commented, referring specifically to negative remarks made by Elvis Costello about the Michelob commercial. "When a musician runs me down, I want to prove something to him."

As if to thumb his nose at the controversy, as well as prove that the music stood apart from the beer commercial, Clapton released the new version of "After Midnight," backed by "I Can't Stand It," as a single to promote his 1988 *Crossroads* compilation. The criticism would die down, but the music would remain.

. . .

Throughout 1987 and 1988, Clapton stayed busy in the recording studio, working with other musicians on their album projects. He recorded three brilliant new tracks with Jack Bruce for his former bandmate's forthcoming album. The songs really highlighted the different paths each had taken since their days in Cream. Yet, at the same time, they also proved how musically compatible they still were. In addition to the Bruce project, Clapton contributed to Sting's *Nothing Like the Sun* and George Harrison's *Cloud Nine* albums, both recordings giving him the opportunity to check in and work with old friends.

Oddly enough, Clapton's own projected album for 1987 had to be canceled. According to his contract with Warner Brothers, Clapton was to submit a double album of live performances. A handful of Clapton's concerts had been recorded for this purpose over the past two years, and Mike Ponczek, Clapton's engineer, had gathered an impressive fifteen-song selection from the various concerts for the album. The record's timing, however, was off. Seven of the selected songs were slated to appear in their studio versions on the forthcoming British compilation, *The Cream of Eric Clapton*, and almost all were included, in one form or another, in the huge boxed retrospective, *Crossroads*, scheduled for 1988 release. The live album was wisely put on hold.

The *Crossroads* project, released in conjunction with Clapton's silver anniversary as a performer, was nothing less than a gift to Clapton from Bill Levenson, PolyGram's director of catalog development. Levenson originally intended to release a series of double lp (or single CD) sets depicting Clapton's entire career from the Yardbirds through his solo work, but after doing his initial research, Levenson concluded that licensing problems might prohibit some of the material from being released. Rather than begin a project he might not be able to complete to his satisfaction, Levenson turned his attention to compiling an ambitious boxed set similar in format to Bob Dylan's *Biograph*. The Clapton set would be a career retrospective composed of greatest hits, previously unavailable studio and live recordings, B sides not placed on albums, and other rarities. There was a certain risk involved in pursuing such a project, since boxed sets were still relatively new in 1987 and, other than the Dylan box, there were no sales track records to go by.

The six-record (four-CD), seventy-three-track compilation remains one of the models by which all boxed sets are measured. Among the rare or previously unreleased tracks in the collection are the Yardbirds' original demos, a selection of Cream's early BBC performances, an unissued Blind Faith studio recording, cuts from the aborted second Derek and the Dominos album, and outstanding live performances from all phases of Clapton's career—all arranged in chronological order and documented in a Grammy Award–winning booklet written by Anthony DeCurtis of *Rolling Stone*. Working methodically over a year and a half, Levenson listened to every available tape of Clapton's studio and live work, and in assembling the collection, he managed to include at least one track from each Clapton album, including the Warner Brothers releases. If anyone ever questioned Clapton's contributions to rock music, the answers were in *Crossroads*.

"What comes across is just how focused and consistent a musician Clapton has been almost from the beginning," stated a reviewer for *Stereo Review*. "Eric Clapton, of all the Sixties rock guitar heroes, is the only one whose work justifies a retrospective like this."

Such sentiments were echoed by virtually everyone reviewing the anthology. *Playboy*, calling *Crossroads* "the ultimate Eric Clapton retrospective," praised the Dominos material as the most significant music in the collection, while *Rolling Stone*, in a five-star review, lauded *Crossroads* as "a rich, comprehensive portrait of a man blessed with undeniable greatness and cursed with doubts about his ability to carry that weight."

For his part, Clapton expressed mixed emotions about the compilation. He was honored that Levenson had gone to such lengths in gathering the selections on *Crossroads*, yet he admitted being overwhelmed by listening to such an accounting of his career. Each cut stirred up memories—some not entirely pleasant—of people and bands, and of time long passed. He was reminded of what a struggle his career had been and, self-critical as always, he found flaws in many of the recordings. Ultimately, however, he was pleased by the collection and even found a way to joke about what it meant to his career.

"You know what the best thing is about the whole thing?" he quipped in an interview published a short time after the release of *Crossroads*. "I haven't put out an album since *August*. So without lifting a finger, *The Cream of Clapton* did well, and this one's going to do well, so it's kind of like a great stop-gap, because it keeps me in a fairly high profile, and without me really doing much work."

. . .

Clapton, as a matter of fact, was doing plenty of work. He expanded his Royal Albert Hall appearances to nine dates, and judging from the incredible demand for tickets, it was evident that he could have booked twice as many performances.

Spring 1988 found Clapton working almost exclusively on sound track projects. In late March he recorded a guitar track for a robbery scene in *Buster*, an ill-fated movie starring Phil Collins. Six weeks later he contributed a sequence of blues tracks to a television documentary on the beginnings of World War II. These projects were relatively easy for Clapton, especially when compared to his work on the score for the Mickey Rourke film *Homeboy*. For this sound track, Clapton was reunited with Michael Kamen, the Roger Waters keyboardist who had worked with him on *Lethal Weapon*.

The work was Clapton's most challenging film work to date. Clapton had been counting on Kamen's knowledge and experience to help guide him through the project, but Kamen had other obligations to honor and departed in the early goings, leaving Eric to sort out the music on his own. The on-the-job training, though difficult at times, brought forth some innovative work, particularly on Dobro, which Clapton liked to use to create an old, country-blues feeling. However, when Mickey Rourke heard the soundtrack, he wasn't satisfied with the music written for his character, a boxer, so Clapton wound up rewriting and rerecording portions of his work, an experience that grated on him but which, he'd confess, acted as another ego test. The hard work paid off. The sound track would stand up over time as one of Clapton's better film efforts.

Clapton's demand as a studio sessions player was achieving new heights, and though his other activities left him with little time to do much in this area, he would still help out friends when they called. He played on a Davina McCall album being produced by his old California friend Rob Fraboni, and on a Gail Anne Dorsey recording being produced by his bassist Nathan East. An album by former Traffic drummer Jim Capaldi teamed Clapton up with George Harrison and Steve Winwood. Clapton was now in a position to all but mail in his contributions, and it wasn't at all uncommon to find him walking into a studio, overdubbing several guitar parts, and leaving, with little or no contact with the artist he was recording for.

Somehow, in the midst of this whirlwind of activity, Clapton cleared away the time to rehearse for and perform in a string of benefits, including the annual Prince's Trust charity concerts. With Prince Charles and Lady Diana looking on, Clapton played a brief yet white-hot set with his band and special guests Phil Collins, Elton John, and Mark Knopfler. In appreciation of Clapton's years of performing for the charity, as well as to honor his quarter century on the music scene, Prince Charles presented Clapton with a mounted model of a silver Stratocaster guitar.

For Clapton, the high point of this particular season of charity gigs was his appearance at the Free Nelson Mandela concert, held at Wembley Stadium on June 11, 1988, the imprisoned South African leader's seventieth birthday. Clapton's appearance, unannounced in flyers and advertisements for the event, was an interesting turnaround, for instead of playing with his own band, he was standing off to the side, acting as second guitarist in Mark Knopfler's Dire Straits. By now, the two guitarists had worked together enough to know each other's every move onstage, and Clapton seemed totally comfortable performing such Dire Straits hits as "Walk of Life," "Sultans of Swing," and "Money for Nothing."

The Mandela benefit, like the Live Aid concert, provided Clapton the opportunity to participate in a politically healthy project without having to headline the event or issue proclamations. Even with his growing popularity and influence, Clapton had never grown comfortable as a spokesman for political causes; he preferred to speak through his music, and hoped that his presence would be statement enough. By appearing in a huge display against apartheid, performing with the likes of Stevie Wonder, Tracy Chapman, and Sting—all known for their outspoken political opinions—Clapton was able to join in a group statement about one of the most important political issues of his time.

· · ·

Mark Knopfler was part of the Clapton entourage on its autumn trip through North America. Although he still had no new material to showcase, Clapton marked his visit to the United States and Canada with a series of high-power performances. As expected, there were plenty of powerful exchanges between Clapton and Knopfler, and each night's set list was packed with songs that encouraged extended solos. By now, old saws like "Crossroads" or "Sunshine of Your Love" seemed a lifetime removed from the mature musician Clapton had become, and Eric had to really concentrate on his solos in order to keep them from sounding too familiar to concertgoers.

"I don't *really* ever know where it's going," he said of his solo technique, a long-standing practice of improvising on the spot. "I do feel that as you get older, you have more respect for your instrument. Also, in living a different kind of life and not being into drugs or drink now, my focus has come back into the serious aspects of what I do as a guitarist and to try to improve that without going over the top."

The problem, Clapton was quick to concede, was that he had a tendency to overplay. Fans loved rapid-fire guitar riffs, but Clapton was still searching for the kind of economy that could both maintain the integrity of the song and display his mastery of his instrument.

The U.S. tour paid off in one unexpected bonus: the chance to play onstage again with Jack Bruce. Over the two decades that had passed since the disbanding of Cream, countless rumors had sprung up about the group's reforming for an album or tour, and though band members had never closed the door entirely on such a reunion, the prospects of their playing together diminished with each passing year. Clapton, for one, had little interest in backtracking; he had come too far in his career for a reprise of his early years. Nevertheless, he had remained on good terms with Jack Bruce and Ginger Baker, and had worked with both since Cream's farewell concert at the Royal Albert Hall.

Clapton set the rumor mill buzzing anew when he jammed onstage with Jack Bruce during Bruce's October 11, 1988, show at New York's Bottom Line nightclub. The two ran through "Spoonful" and "Sunshine of Your Love"—both regularly featured songs on the Bruce tour circuit—and if their playing betrayed some of the rust that had formed on the once well-oiled musical machine, none of the original enthusiasm was missing.

"I knew if I went, I'd probably play because the fans would demand it," Clapton said afterward, confessing that he'd been unnerved by the prospects of playing with Bruce in public for the first time since the breakup of Cream.

Despite the good time, there was still no serious discussion about any kind of reunion. Neither Clapton nor Bruce wanted to return to the past.

"If we got back together," Clapton reflected, comparing his time with Cream to a rocky marriage, "how far back would it go into the misery of what we experienced? Would that come back with it? It scares the living daylights out of me, because there was a lot of hostility, a lot of aggression and a lot of unpleasant personality clashes."

Although he still cared a great deal for Jack Bruce and Ginger Baker, Clapton conceded that he had changed too much over the years to be comfortable playing with them. A great deal of it had to do with his own ego. "I wouldn't select those guys to be in my band because they are lead musicians," he explained. "I'd have to get out of the way. And I don't want to get *out* of the fuckin' way. I want to be in the front now. Maybe I didn't then, but I do now."

Clapton reached closure with another important part of his past when Pattie Boyd formally filed for divorce. The action, although expected, was difficult for Clapton, a reminder of the failure of the most intense relationship of his life. Even after splitting up with Pattie, Clapton found that he had strong feelings for her. She had been the love of his life, and he accepted the blame for his marriage's failure. He deeply regretted his inability to hold down a traditional long-term relationship with a woman, yet with the divorce from Pattie, he resigned himself to it.

"We're all lonely people," he told an interviewer for *Musician*, in a conversation touching on musicians and relationships. "When it comes down to it . . . we'd all like to be normal. I can accept now that I probably never will be, but I'd still like to have that part of my life resolved and comfortable."

So it was for the journeyman bluesman. Clapton might not have reached the mythological proportions of his idol, Robert Johnson, who, according to legend, had exchanged his soul for his music, but in making music his life and identity, he had paid his own devil's price. He had sacrificed something vital, something he could never recover. He had given up his chance to lead a normal life.

• • •

In all likelihood, Clapton could have avoided recording a new studio album indefinitely, coasting on his reputation, playing an endless calendar of concert dates, and relying on crowd-pleasing songs that had propped up his career during the lean years of his past. He was now a rock institution, a surefire draw of undebatable international status. When he teamed up with other marquee names, as when he played a four-concert swing in Japan with Elton John and Mark Knopfler, he had grateful fans eating out of his hands, regardless of whether they had heard the same songs on previous occasions.

Nevertheless, Clapton had a recording contract to honor, and three years between studio albums was a long stretch, even for a man who had drastically trimmed his output over the last decade. Much of Clapton's decline in productivity could be attributed to his inability to write new songs to his liking. He had never been a prolific songwriter—certainly not in comparison to such contemporaries as Elton John, Van Morrison, or Paul McCartney—and a great many of his titles resulted from songwriting collaborations. In recent years, with the exception of his soundtrack work, he had written very little new material, on his own or in collaboration with others.

Then there was the issue of the kind of album he wanted to record. When questioned about his plans for his next project, Clapton would tell interviewers that he hoped to put together an album with a harder, back-to-basics rock 'n' roll sound. He also spoke of making an album of blues standards, a tribute to his influences. His plans, however, depended on the personnel available to work on the record. The producer, along with the studio musicians slated for the project, would have a great bearing on the direction the album would take. Phil Collins was interested in appearing on the new recording but not as its producer, which left Clapton with another issue to settle.

Despite such uncertainties, Clapton was feeling ambitious when he flew to New York in March 1989 to commence work on not one but two new projects. Beside recording his own album, he had been hired to write the soundtrack for the sequel to *Lethal Weapon*.

Fortunately, he had plenty of help. Songwriter Jerry Williams, absent on the *August* album, had a sheaf of new songs for consideration, as did George Harrison, who was presently back in the hub after the overwhelming success of his *Cloud Nine* album and his initial work with the Traveling Wilburys, and who surprised Eric by offering him a handful of new numbers to record. Clapton's core band of Nathan East, Greg Phillinganes, and drummer Steve Ferrone was boosted by Dire Straits keyboardist Alan Clark, saxophonist David Sanborn, vocalist Chaka Khan, and sessions whizzes John Tropea (guitar), Richard Tee (piano), and Jim Keltner (drums). Robert Cray, now a close friend of Clapton's, rounded off the roster. The group represented the largest roster of studio contributors since Clapton's *No Reason to Cry* album—and that adventure hadn't been planned.

Robert Cray's influence was felt immediately. When Cray arrived in the studio, Clapton was battling the flu and had nothing new to record. At producer Russ Titelman's request, the band cut a cover of Big Mama Thornton's "Hound Dog." The new version, though adequate, would never have given Elvis Presley reason to worry, but at least it was a start. Cray then suggested that they do "Before You Accuse Me," a Bo Diddley standard that had been a Clapton favorite since his youth. Clapton and Cray traded solos throughout the numerous takes of the song, Cray answering Clapton's fat, bluesy notes with stinging runs of his own.

The younger guitarist's influence was even more direct on "Old Love," a simmering blues addressing Clapton's painful, lingering feelings for Pattie. Clapton had written some basic lyrics, as well as the chord progressions for the verses, but he needed a turnaround and bridge to finish the song. He played what he had for Robert Cray, and asked if he could come up with something. By the next day, Cray had worked out the missing parts, along with additional lyrics.

A fourth song, a cover of Ray Charles's "Hard Times," added to the album's blues base. Clapton had always appreciated the full, brass-enhanced sound of Charles's blues recordings with Atlantic Records, and he'd wanted to pay homage to it for some time. However, rather than simply imitate Charles's sound, Clapton decided to try to replicate it. To achieve this, he brought in veterans David "Fathead" Newman and Hank Crawford, both former members of Charles's band, to play the saxophone lines, as well as Ray Charles's mentor, Charles Brown, to write the piano arrangement. The final version, elevated by Clapton's jazz-inspired vocal, caught listeners by surprise.

"A lot of people have said to me that their favorite track on this new album of mine is 'Hard Times,'" Clapton remarked shortly after the release of *Journeyman.* "That really shook me, because I didn't think they would like that. I thought that was almost too *ancient* in a way, in its approach, for anyone to like it. But there are people out there that want that."

With four blues songs recorded, Clapton briefly entertained the notion of cutting an album's worth of blues, but the realities of the marketplace changed his mind. It had been a long time between albums, and a more commercial venture was needed at the moment. An album with a couple hit singles would have been ideal, at least from the perspective of his record company.

For hits, Clapton had Jerry Williams. The Texas songwriter contributed five new songs to the album, including singles candidates "No Alibis," "Running on Faith," and "Pretending." In other hands, the Williams numbers might have been reasonably good yet ultimately disposable pop songs, but when augmented by Clapton's guitar solos, the tunes reached a higher status. "Running on Faith" was especially noteworthy, and Clapton cut two versions—one acoustic and one electric—of the song, deciding to go with the latter, though the Dobro arrangement would resurface when Clapton performed it on MTV's "Unplugged" program in 1992.

Journeyman as a whole was an effective album, packed with suitable songs for the concert circuit, and featuring Clapton vocals that sounded better than ever. If, over a career's time, Clapton had relinquished his role of guitar innovator, he more than made up for the concession with numerous displays of his technical proficiency. The presence of Robert Cray probably pushed Clapton into using the album as a clinic on note bending, wah-wah solos, and sustained notes, but whatever his inspiration, Clapton served up his most convincing work of the 1980s.

The album, however, constituted only the beginning of Clapton's active work period. He traditionally worked in strong bursts of creative energy, and this was no exception. His score for *Lethal Weapon 2*, highlighted by his brilliantly moody interplay with David Sanborn's saxophone, proved once again how well he could work in the film score business, and if this studio work wasn't enough, Clapton also contributed guitar solos to studio albums by Zucchero and Cyndi Lauper, followed by a session in which he and his own band recorded an arrangement of Elton John's "The Border Song" for a forthcoming Elton John–Bernie Taupin tribute anthology.

Somehow, in the midst of such frenetic activity, Clapton penciled in time to mix the tracks on *Journeyman*. The album, though pleasing to Warner Brothers officials, was still incomplete in their opinion. It definitely had commercial appeal, but it lacked the elusive monster hit single, the eighties' answer to "Layla." Presented with the challenge of coming up with such a song, Clapton went to work on what eventually became "Bad Love," a tune written to formula—and one which, ironically, would earn him his first Grammy Award.

Remembered Clapton: "I methodically thought about it and said, 'Well, I'll get a riff, I'll modulate into the verse, and there'll be a chorus where we go into a minor key with a little guitar line. Then there'll be a breakdown and I'll put "Badge" in for good measure.' "

The suggestion for the "Badge"-like bridge came from Foreigner's Mick Jones, who worked with Clapton on the song. The bridge not only beefed up the tune's musical structure but also afforded Clapton the opportunity for what turned out to be one of his best solos on the album. "Bad Love" may not have been the next "Layla," but it became the album's first single, as well as a popular concert number.

"That's something I've always shied away from doing," Clapton said on writing to formula, adding that "Bad Love," after getting a little nudge, wound up taking on a life of its own. "I've always been inclined to look outside myself for new directions. It's a big failing of mine, and something I'm trying to resolve. But this was the one occasion when I went *back* to what I knew how to do."

The statement might have been applied to Clapton's method for the whole album. His entire recording career as a solo artist had been a long search for new musical direction, and though some of his meanderings into other forms had achieved interesting results, they kept moving him away from his true identity, that of bluesman and guitarist extraordinaire.

Journeyman, released in November 1989, elicited praise from a vast majority of its reviewers. There seemed to be an attitude of relief in the air, as if critics were breathing a collective sigh of relief over Clapton's abandoning his *August* excursions into funk-and-pop in favor of the kind of music he did best.

"The journeyman may only be a hired gun, but he knows he's a damned good shot," wrote J. D. Considine for *Rolling Stone*, calling *Journeyman* "Clapton's most consistent and satisfying album since *461 Ocean Boulevard*." *People* magazine checked in with similarly favorable commentary, lauding the album as "Clapton's strongest work of the decade"; the recording, continued the reviewer, had its moments of transparent commercialism, but "it's easier to forgive his weakness for the almighty buck when he shows as much class as he so often does on this album."

. . .

The new songs, good as they were, were not a part of the Clapton concerts that commenced shortly after the recording sessions. With no time to rehearse suitable concert arrangements of the new material, Clapton and his band hit the road with their old standbys. Not that it mattered to their audiences: included in the Clapton itinerary were visits to Israel and Africa, where music fans, anything but accustomed to regular Clapton performances, were enthusiastic about anything he decided to play.

For Clapton, the trip to Africa was especially poignant. He was going back to the ancient roots of the blues. No rock star had ever performed in Mozambique, and Clapton's concert at the Machava National Stadium, held in front of 100,000 people for the benefit of the King's Trust, was a deeply moving experience. The country had been decimated by war and poverty, but the people had survived spiritually.

"It was a great honor to do something that I'd sort of touched on at Live Aid and at the Mandela concert," Clapton reflected. "To do it on the spot was what really made you choke up. You were actually playing *to* these people."

Clapton, who had been presented a tribal ceremonial shield upon arriving in the country, was especially touched when the entire audience sang along with the chorus of "Same Old Blues," which he had rearranged to carry an African sound. The drama of all the voices raised in unison, along with the spectacle of a huge banner, raised in front of the stage and reading "Mr. Clapton, thank you for bringing us some paradise," was an overwhelming experience. "The black guys in the band were just moved to tears," Clapton said. "It really choked me up."

Although he didn't tour the United States in 1989, Clapton nevertheless turned up all over the country, giving occasional interviews to plug *Journeyman* and playing as a guest performer at several high-visibility concerts. In New York, he joined the Rolling Stones during their nationally televised gig in Jersey City, playing guitar on the Stones' arrangement of Willie Dixon's "Little Red Rooster." (The song eventually appeared on the Stones' 1991 *Flashpoint* album.) He also walked onstage at an Elton John concert in Madison Square Garden, where he dished out a superb guitar solo on "Rocket Man." For Clapton, the frenetic pace was not only enjoyable; it was part of the publicity machinery needed to launch the new album and whet appetites for an exhaustive touring schedule projected for the following year.

thirteen

Tears in Heaven
1990–93

I wonder, "Why me? Why have I survived?" I have to look at that as the positive, I have survived these things and therefore I've got some kind of responsibility to remain positively creative and not dwell on the misfortune of it.

If anything, Eric Clapton appeared to be gaining a reserve of energy that belied his age. Needing neither wealth nor fame, he was in the enviable position of performing because he *chose* to, for whatever his personal reasons. Going on the road was still hard work, and infinitely more complex than it had been when he had embarked on his first large-scale tour with Cream, but he was as driven to please as ever, as compelled to put himself on the line in concert as he had been when he was doing his groundbreaking work as a young guitarist with John Mayall and the Bluesbreakers. The meaningful exchange in any concert—the musician's creative generosity for the appreciation of the masses—had settled to a comfortable level over the years, but Clapton never took it for granted.

To kick off his extensive tour in 1990, Clapton expanded the number of his annual Royal Albert Hall dates to an unprecedented eighteen nights, spread out over a three-and-a-half-week period. By now Clapton had become a fixture at the venue, which fans were jokingly referring to as Eric Hall.

"I am a very habitual person," he explained of his fondness for the annual string of concerts. "I like nothing more than to have some kind of routine in my life. And I'm also very grandiose, so I decided that this year's project had to be a really mammoth production."

And so it was. The first twelve performances featured two different Clapton bands each night—his stripped-down, four-piece unit and a thirteen-piece outfit that included a horn section, percussionist, and background singers—each unit playing half a show. The next three nights were blues nights, and the final three dates placed Clapton and his expanded group in the midst of a sixty-piece orchestra.

From an artistic standpoint, the concerts were successful to varying degrees. The four-piece unit, with Clapton front and center in the musical scheme, invited greater opportunity for improvisation and extended guitar solos. Conversely, the orchestra tended to restrict Clapton to a tighter format. The lush orchestration fleshed out songs like "Wonderful Tonight" or "Bell Bottom Blues" but bogged Clapton down in others.

The heart and soul of Clapton's 1990 Albert Hall dates were the three concerts devoted entirely to blues standards. With a backing band of Buddy Guy and Robert Cray on guitar, Johnnie Johnson on piano, Robert Cousins on bass, and Jamie Oldaker on drums, Clapton had an extremely capable unit, and the concerts moved freely from one form of blues to another, touching down on the music of Otis Rush, Willie Dixon, Big Bill Broonzy, Elmore James, Muddy Waters, Howlin' Wolf, and other blues masters. Buddy Guy, always intense and unpredictable, especially if he had been drinking, acted as the band's musical catalyst, goading Clapton and Cray—who tended to favor a more structured approach—into improvisations that had both band and audience hanging on for dear life.

Clapton appreciated the spontaneity, which gave the shows a sense of the unexpected. "With Robert Cray," he noted, "I knew we could rehearse and, once we got it, it would stay that way. And it would probably stay that way with me, too. I may take an extra solo. With Buddy, you didn't know what was going to happen. And that's what I wanted."

Not that Guy's unbridled enthusiasm was always a benefit: after the band's first performance, Clapton was fined by the hall's management for playing seventy-five minutes too long, the overrun a direct result of Guy's excessive jamming. Of course, those in attendance were not complaining.

. . .

A year and a half had passed since Clapton's last tour of the United States, and the time lapse, along with the popularity of *Journeyman*, made Clapton a very hot ticket on the American tour circuit. For the first time in nearly half a decade, Clapton had new songs in his stage repertoire, and he saw that the *Journeyman* tunes were prominently featured in his shows. A veteran of the promotion game, Clapton did all the right things to ensure that the public was aware of his new record. His appearance on "Saturday Night Live" alone exposed him to millions of potential record buyers.

The U.S. tour was divided into two lengthy parts, the first in the spring, the second later in the summer. Between the two segments, Clapton returned to England to participate in Knebworth 1990, a high-profile charity concert held on June 30 for the benefit of the Nordoff-Robbins Music Therapy Center—an institution using music as part of its treatment of physically and mentally challenged children—and a new performing arts school called the British Record Industry Trust School for Performing Arts and Technology.

Over a hundred thousand people packed Knebworth Park and tolerated intermittent rain during the all-day event, watching Robert Plant join Jimmy Page for a three-song Led Zeppelin set, and Phil Collins team up with Mike Rutherford and Tony Banks for a Genesis reunion. Paul McCartney and Pink Floyd, the day's big headliners, drew raves for their performances, McCartney adding emotional impact to his set by screening a three-song video of John Lennon performing "Help," "Strawberry Fields Forever," and "Give Peace a Chance."

Much of Clapton's set, broadcast live over BBC radio, was taped for commercial video and album release. After leading his band through several selections from *Journeyman*, Clapton brought out Mark Knopfler, his Dire Straits band, and Elton John for a superstar jam of Dire Straits and Elton

John songs, the triumphant performance ending with an encore of "Sunshine of Your Love."

Knebworth 1990 offered Clapton a respite from his torrid work schedule, giving him the chance to mingle with old friends and play for the sheer joy of it. Given what lay ahead in the months to come, it was just the break he needed.

. . .

For the second half of the tour, Clapton had two very special dates on the menu, both scheduled for Alpine Valley, a large outdoor theater located near an East Troy, Wisconsin, ski resort. The two shows, scheduled for August 25–26, were to be the ultimate blues nights, presenting full sets by Clapton, Robert Cray, and Stevie Ray Vaughan. The three guitarists were arguably the best—and without a doubt the most popular—of the younger blues musicians on the scene, and ticket holders held high hopes of seeing all three onstage at the same time, trading licks and egging one another on.

Clapton looked forward to the two performances. Although he didn't know Stevie Ray Vaughan as well as he knew Robert Cray, Clapton had grown very close to Vaughan in recent years. He and Vaughan had jammed onstage during Eric's April 15 gig in Detroit, and Clapton had walked offstage after the show convinced that Vaughan was the best blues guitarist in the business. Moreover, Clapton was well versed in Vaughan's battles with drug and alcohol addiction, and he had great admiration for the way Stevie Ray had overcome his problems and stayed clean. Clapton knew how difficult that road could be.

The concerts exceeded all expectations. Clapton, as the elder and headliner of the shows, was last to go on both nights. During the others' performances, he stood off in the wings and watched the two younger guitarists and their bands work the Alpine Valley crowds into a frenzy, which only served as a launching pad for his own inspired sets. After the first evening's show, he brought out Stevie Ray and Jimmie Vaughan,

Robert Cray, and surprise guests Bonnie Raitt and Jeff Healey for a scorching onstage jam of Robert Johnson's "Sweet Home Chicago."

The second night was even more incredible. Before beginning, Clapton posed with Robert Cray and the Vaughan brothers for a forthcoming Fender guitar ad. Then it was down to business. For this particular performance, Clapton had brought along Buddy Guy as his encore guest, but it was Stevie Ray Vaughan who stole the show, jamming with such ferocious intensity that Clapton just shook his head in disbelief. The shows had been promoted as a kind of battle of the guitarists, and no one would have disputed the billing.

"All in all, it was an evening of staggering talent," wrote *Rolling Stone* critic Mikal Gilmore, who was on hand for the August 26 show.

The musicians were as elated by the performance as their audience. Standing backstage, they congratulated each other and spoke of taking the show on the road. Clapton invited Vaughan to join him at his Albert Hall dates next year. Buddy Guy suggested that they all get together the following evening for a jam session at "Legends," his Chicago blues club.

None of it would ever occur.

After the show, the musicians and their entourage were to be flown by a fleet of helicopters to Chicago. A huge fog had rolled into the area, severely cutting visibility and making travel treacherous. Stevie Ray Vaughan, in a hurry to get back, asked if he could take the first helicopter out. Vaughan's helicopter had just taken off when it slammed into the back of a hundred-foot, fog-shrouded artificial ski slope, instantly killing Vaughan, Clapton's American agent Bobby Brooks, Eric's bodyguard Nigel Browne, assistant tour manager Colin Smythe, and pilot Jeff Brown. Clapton, who had been taken to his hotel after an uneventful flight, knew nothing of the accident or fatalities until the following morning, when Roger Forrester woke him with the news that a helicopter had not returned.

When the helicopter failed to arrive in Chicago, the FAA initiated an all-out search, focusing their efforts on the Alpine Valley area. The twisted wreckage of the helicopter had been discovered by two sheriff's deputies just before seven in the morning. All that remained was the grisly task of identifying the victims. Clapton and Jimmie Vaughan were driven by limousine to the site.

Stunned and deeply saddened, Clapton considered canceling the remainder of his tour, which would have involved calling off five shows. However, after giving the matter a lot of thought, he decided to continue.

"I had a meeting with all the bands and the managers," he recalled. "All the crew had gone on to the next show, so we got them on the phone, and we tried to come up with a unanimous decision about whether we should go home or whether we should go on. It was clearly felt that if we packed up and went home, the whole thing would just be unbearable."

Clapton reacted to the death of Stevie Ray Vaughan much the way he reacted to the loss of Jimi Hendrix: a great void had been created in the music world, and it was up to musicians like him to fill it. Vaughan and Hendrix had pushed the evolution of the blues guitar to another level, and Clapton, who had been influenced by both, owed them a personal debt. He had to see that a part of them continued to live on in his own work.

The tour's remaining shows, dedicated to Vaughan and the others, were extremely difficult to get through. For Clapton, they were nothing less than an emotional catharsis, a matter of trying to hold up professionally in the face of great personal loss. As a tribute to Vaughan, Eric improvised a blues on slide guitar as each evening's encore. It was a beautiful memorial, but to Clapton, it was still woefully inadequate. At forty-five, he had witnessed more than his fair share of untimely deaths.

• • •

The loss of Stevie Ray Vaughan darkened an otherwise radiant year for Clapton. He was honored with the Living Legend Award at the Elvis Awards, and he was named Top Rock Album Artist by the *Billboard* Music Awards. His exhaustive touring took him to Australia, the Far East, and, for the first time ever, South America.

One measure of Clapton's ambition at this time might have been found in his performances at the Royal Albert Hall, which were expanded yet again in 1991, this time to twenty-four nights. The four-band format (four-piece, nine-piece, blues, and orchestra) was identical to the previous year, with each band receiving six nights. By now the Albert Hall dates had become full-blown social events, attended by London's well-to-do, many of whom would buy tickets to as many different shows as were available, the ultimate die-hard fans attending every performance. It was joked that Clapton could have taken up residence in the Hall and made a healthy living without ever leaving London.

Clapton was determined to use this year's dates to complete his live-album obligation to Warner Brothers. He had recorded some of the previous year's Albert Hall performances, but after listening to the tapes, he had concluded that he could do better. Russ Titelman flew in to produce the concert recordings, which involved converting the stage—and the space under the stage—into a recording studio.

With the exception of the blues nights, the shows were almost identical to those of the previous year, with virtually the same personnel. Coming, as they did, on the heels of Clapton's year of constant travel, the performances were much tighter, most noticeably on the *Journeyman* material, and by the time Clapton had finished his string of dates at the Albert Hall, he had more than ample material for his live album.

The blues nights easily outshone the others. Back from 1990 were Buddy Guy and Robert Cray, who were now complemented by Jimmie Vaughan and blues legend Albert Collins. Each guitarist had a distinctive style, and Clapton had as much fun watching them play as he had working onstage himself—to the extent that some reviewers, in their accounts of the performances, complained that Clapton was too content to stand off to the side and let others play his show for him. Such disputes, however, constituted a minority opinion. As a rule, concertgoers were thrilled to be able to see that many internationally acclaimed bluesmen onstage at the same time.

The album made from the concerts, *24 Nights*, released in December, was a hodgepodge accurately reflecting the different band configurations and their sounds. Not surprisingly, the blues segment brought forth the most impassioned, wide-open playing, while the orchestra numbers sounded heavy-handed at times. Although executed flawlessly, the *Journey-*

man tunes were almost exact replicas of their studio versions, and though it only made sense that Clapton would feature the music from his most recent studio album in concert, the songs seemed unnecessarily repetitious on *24 Nights*.

Clapton's playing on the album ran the gamut. The album's liner notes boasted that there were no fixes or overdubs on the record, and that statement, as much as anything that Clapton or his critics could have said, hinted at both the positive and negative points of the album. Clapton's playing was technically superb but creatively safe, which led to an album that was pleasing but not extraordinary.

"Clapton has always been king in that paradoxical category of gentleman bluesman," observed a *Rolling Stone* critic in a favorable review. "At times, his savage and suave elements balance each other out."

To the album's detractors, this "balance" was the core of the problem: Whatever happened to the risk-taking Clapton, the guitarist who could innovate as well as interpret?

"The trouble with *24 Nights*," wrote a reviewer for *Playboy*, "is not that it's a terrible album. The problem is, it's often bland and unenergetic— and that's even more frustrating."

The artist himself seemed to recognize as much. In discussing the album, Clapton gave his work less than an unqualified endorsement. "We recorded my shows at the Albert Hall this year and the year before, and we've amalgamated it to make a live record, which is . . . well, some of it is superb, and some of it isn't superb. It's good, but . . ."

He left the sentence unfinished. *24 Nights* fulfilled a business obligation, and it certainly wasn't something to be ashamed of, but in the long run it was simply Clapton's first live album in a decade—product intended to fill the void between *Journeyman* and whatever came next.

* * *

After polishing off his most successful Albert Hall season to date, Clapton was off to New York City, where he hoped to take a good vacation after a year's hard work.

For Clapton, one of the joys of this particular trip was the opportunity to spend time with his son, Conor, who was now four and a half years old. Clapton and Lory Del Santo had remained on good terms since Conor's birth, and over the years, Clapton had seen his son as often as time and circumstances would allow. At one time, Clapton and Del Santo had discussed the notion of getting married and giving Conor a stable family environment, but both realized that it wasn't the best idea. Clapton lived the free-spirited lifestyle of a musician, spending much of his time on the road, following his career wherever it took him. It would be better for all concerned if Conor was raised in a single-parent household, with his father visiting whenever his schedule permitted it.

Clapton treasured his occasional visits with his son. Because of his own background, he appreciated the importance of a father-son relationship, even if it was less than a traditional one, and he took his role as a parent seriously. With this in mind, he hoped to back off his heavy work in 1991 and use a good portion of the year to develop a tighter relationship with Conor.

On March 19, shortly after his arrival in New York, Eric took Lory and Conor to the circus, where they had a wonderful time on a classic family outing. At the end of the evening, they agreed to meet for lunch the following afternoon, to be followed by a trip to the zoo.

Eric would never see his son again.

The next day, March 20, as he was preparing for his lunch date, Clapton received the phone call that every parent fears the most: his child had died in a horrifying accident.

"I didn't believe it," Clapton told interviewer James Henke. "I mean, I was here in this hotel when it happened, only about ten blocks down the road. And the phone rang and I picked it up and Lory was on the other end, and she was hysterical. She said that Conor was dead. And I thought, 'Well, this is ridiculous. Don't be silly.' I said, 'Are you sure?' I mean, what a silly question: 'Are you sure?' But then I just went off the edge of the world for a while. I ran down there, and I saw the paramedic equipment everywhere, and ambulances and police cars. And I thought, 'This is true.'"

The nature of the accident was almost impossible to believe. A housekeeper, cleaning the bedroom windows of Del Santo's fifty-third-floor apartment, had left one of the tilt-in windows open to dry. Conor had been playing in the apartment, and had somehow climbed out unnoticed onto the window ledge, which lacked the usual child guards. He lost his balance and fell forty-nine floors to the rooftop of an adjacent building.

Totally overwhelmed, Clapton "turned to stone," concealing his emotions while taking charge of the immediate tasks at hand. Staying busy was the only way he could cope with the tragedy. Friends called with comforting words, while thousands of fans, many of whom had recently seen him on his triumphant world tour, sent cards and letters of sympathy. Dignitaries such as the Kennedy family and Prince Charles sent their condolences. The news media covered the tragedy extensively, but the usually private Clapton didn't notice enough to care. He had withdrawn into himself.

"I wanted to get away from everybody," he explained. "The Italian side of the family . . . well, Italians are very dramatic, and it was all out in the open, this wailing and gnashing of teeth. But for me, from the way I was raised and being English, well, we go inside ourselves and keep a stiff upper lip. We pretend that we're okay, and we take care of business. But inside it's a different story."

The funeral was attended by about a hundred people, including members of the Clapton and Del Santo families, George Harrison, Phil Collins, and Pattie Boyd. Clapton was moved to tears as he sat in St. Mary Magdalene Church in Ripley, not far from where he himself was raised, and listened to Reverend Christopher Elson speak of Conor's "spirit, intelligence, and courage." After the services, Conor was laid to rest in the church's country graveyard.

Clapton remained in seclusion for months, trying to stabilize himself with regular visits to a therapist and attendance at Alcoholics Anonymous meetings, which helped keep him from backsliding into heavy drinking. He talked openly about his sense of loss and took solace in others' words of comfort. Letters continued to pour in, some from people who had lost children of their own—parents who had endured the terrible loss and could offer encouraging words. There were even letters from women volunteering to act as surrogate mothers for future Clapton children. In one case, a single mother offered to move in with her young daughter.

Over his months of reflection, Clapton forged a new philosophy that helped get him from day to day. Though it was only natural that he would question why he had experienced the tremendous tragedies of recent months, he eventually reasoned that trying to make sense of it was a futile exercise.

"When you experience death," he said, "you find there is no control over it. And whatever you think or construct as a theory as to why these things happen is, finally, nonsense. Because no one knows which of us will be gone tomorrow, or why. I learned *that* from my son. Because there is *no* explanation for his death."

Instead of searching for answers to unsolvable questions, Clapton tried to move ahead. In Conor and Stevie Ray Vaughan, he had seen how life could end suddenly and without warning, so he decided that he should consider every day a blessing. In wondering why he had survived when others had not, Clapton concluded that he had survived for a purpose.

His talent justified his life, and as long as he was around, he would use it to its fullest.

. . .

Throughout his career, Clapton's finest songs originated from emotions felt deep down in the core, and in sorting through his feelings in the aftermath of his son's death, Eric found material for an entire cycle of songs about Conor.

"I only compose songs if I'm in an emotional state, if I'm experiencing extreme happiness, extreme sadness or grief," he explained. "*Then* I compose because I have to fix myself. I compose to heal myself from damage."

The songs came freely during Clapton's months in seclusion. His therapy and AA sessions had put him in a confessional frame of mind, and the songs he wrote were disarmingly honest outpourings of his deepest feelings.

His motivation for writing the songs was profound. Besides trying to heal his emotional wounds, Clapton believed that somehow, in some spiritual way, Conor would hear his songs. In addition, he felt the need to share his grief with the countless people who had supported him during his time of sorrow.

The problem, Clapton readily admitted, was in writing songs that weren't too personal.

"Where do you draw the line?" he wondered. "I don't know. My attitude towards my son is that I owe it to him. I've lost him. What am I going to do? I have to pay my respects to that boy, in *my* way, and let the world know what I thought about him. I don't want to make it a secret."

For works written during such a brief period of time, the songs displayed great musical range and emotional depth. The first song, "Signe," was an instrumental, a surprisingly upbeat samba written while Clapton was vacationing with Roger Forrester on a chartered yacht. "The Circus Left Town" was an account of Clapton's last evening with Conor, while "My Father's Eyes" was an astonishingly frank depiction of Eric's own fatherless identity, in which Clapton confessed that the only way he could look into his father's eyes was by gazing into the eyes of his son. With each new song, Clapton found a new way to address his sense of loss.

After nearly six months in seclusion, Clapton was prepared to return to at least a minimum of public activity. He had been commissioned to write the score for *Rush*, a film dealing with the horrors of drug addiction and, to a lesser extent, the loss of a loved one, and in September he flew to Los Angeles to work on the sound track at The Village Recorder studios. The score for the Lili Zanuck–directed film found him playing Dobro and gut-string acoustic guitars, as well as his Stratocaster, the variety leading to his most wide-ranging sound track to date. A fierce electric blues featuring Buddy Guy on second guitar was balanced by smoldering, low-key blues numbers inspired, said Clapton, by the playing of Stevie Ray Vaughan.

"The album he made with his brother had some of the finest guitar sounds I've ever heard," he mentioned, referring to the posthumously released *Family Style* by Jimmie and Stevie Ray Vaughan. "It had something to do with being on an amplifier very, very low so you can *hear* the string on the fretboard, almost."

The centerpiece of the soundtrack was Clapton's stirring ballad "Tears in Heaven." The song, part of the series of numbers written shortly after Conor's death, was incomplete when Clapton was hired to write the *Rush* soundtrack, and though Clapton felt that it would fit well in the movie's story about loss, he worried that it might be too personal for release. In fact, he was so plagued by self-doubts that he offered to provide a replacement if it didn't work in the movie. "It's awfully maudlin and I still don't like the way some phrases end," he confessed to Lili Zanuck, adding that "it'll never be a hit."

Fortunately, he had changed his mind by the time Will Jennings, one of Steve Winwood's collaborators, helped him complete the song by contributing its memorable bridge. Clapton was ready to share the song with a world that had been so sympathetic in his darkest hour, and *Rush* was the proper vehicle for its debut.

"I needed the film to finish it," he noted, "because otherwise I probably would have let it go. It was also a good opportunity for me to write about the loss of my son and have somewhere to put it—to channel it—because it didn't look like I was going into the studio in the near future."

"Tears in Heaven," like "Layla" or "Wonderful Tonight," hit a universal chord, even though Clapton was writing about a deeply personal experience. Anyone who has ever lost a loved one has questioned whether there is an afterlife, and whether he or she will meet that loved one in the afterlife, and Clapton's naked feelings, sung over one of his most beautiful melodies, were genuinely moving. In just a few verses, he spoke the universal language of grief.

While staying in Los Angeles, Clapton made rough demo tapes of several of the new songs about Conor. Though he had no intention of finishing the songs in the immediate future, Clapton recognized his recording of the demo tapes for what it was—still another part of the healing process.

. . .

Another important part of that process was getting back on the road and facing live audiences again, knowing that the response to his shows would be tempered by the public's knowledge of the recent tragedies in his life. Clapton expected to be touring in 1992, but for the time being, he needed something to get his feet wet, and for this he turned to his old friend George Harrison. On numerous occasions during the previous year, as he traveled throughout the world, Clapton had been asked about Harrison, who had come out of semiretirement with his solo album and his work with the Traveling Wilburys, but who hadn't toured in fifteen years. People wanted to see Harrison onstage again.

Clapton had no trouble identifying with such wishes. He had spoken publicly of his desire to work onstage with Harrison as early as 1974, and he had talked to Harrison about the prospects of a joint concert over the years, all to no avail. Harrison's stage fright had been long established, and his last tour had been disastrous. Nevertheless, Clapton discussed the idea with Harrison, arguing that he only needed to show up with his guitar and sing. Clapton would provide the backing band and equipment, and his management would take care of all the arrangements. After agreeing and changing his mind several times, Harrison finally relented.

A thirteen-show schedule was set for Japan, a favorite touring spot of Clapton's, and a location far enough from the beaten path to allow Harrison the chance to perform without the media crush he might have experienced elsewhere. "The main thing is for George to enjoy it," Roger Forrester remarked to reporters asking about the tour, and the Clapton camp did its level best to see that this was the case.

The shows, documented in Harrison's double CD *Live in Japan*, were a delight. Sounding upbeat and confident, Harrison led Clapton and the band through such Beatles classics as "Taxman," "Something," and "Here Comes the Sun," along with selections of his solo works. The Japanese audiences responded enthusiastically when Harrison revived such chestnuts as "If I Needed Someone" and "Old Brown Shoe"—songs he had never played in concert.

Clapton reveled in his sidekick role, boosting Harrison's music with lean yet very effective solos. Each night he would take the spotlight for several of his own songs, but there was never any question that these were George Harrison shows. Predictably, the showstopper was "While My Guitar Gently Weeps," for which Clapton brought back a virtual note-for-note replay of his solo on the Beatles song. The Japanese audiences ate it up. "It is a pleasure to hear a pair of past masters bring out the best in each other," wrote a critic in a review of *Live in Japan*—a common enough sentiment expressed during the tour.

There was talk of bringing the show to Europe or the United States, but it was not to be. Clapton was booked for a tour of his own, and for Harrison, as fulfilling as the shows in Japan had been, there was no temptation to re-create the circus environment of his earlier days. The Japanese dates would have to do.

. . .

Less than a month after returning home to England, Clapton made the most important appearance of his career, on MTV's "Unplugged." Clapton had been aware of the acoustic-format program for a couple of years, and he had secretly hoped to perform on the show, but given his hectic schedule and the events in his life, he hadn't had the opportunity. Clapton was intrigued by the notion of doing an entirely acoustic concert—something he had never done as a professional—and when he was invited to do "Unplugged," he decided to use the occasion to play "Tears in Heaven," along with several other new songs written about his son, for the first time in concert.

At first Clapton was uncertain about how many players to use in the show. Instinct told him that he would probably be better off if he went out alone, or with just another guitarist or bassist, but after rehearsing with his full band, he elected to go on with six instrumentalists and two background vocalists, which gave him the opportunity to flesh out some of the songs.

He never sounded better. If anyone ever questioned his overall mastery of the guitar, he proved it time and time again throughout the program. Deprived of the effects he could have otherwise employed with his electric guitar, he put on a dazzling display of finger picking and flat picking on both six- and twelve-string acoustic guitars, as well as on Dobro. The format also accentuated the maturity of Clapton's voice, which had a different timbre in a setting in which he wasn't shouting over highly amplified instruments.

"When you're onstage with an electric band, going through a massive p.a. system, it's very artificial," Clapton explained, speaking of how he was accustomed to hearing himself only through the stage monitors. "It's such a joy to sing with a full band and be able to hear your own voice."

In recording the program, Clapton ran through most of the songs twice, giving the producers the option of selecting the best performance of each song for the program. As expected, the new songs written for Conor, particularly "Tears in Heaven," packed the greatest emotional punch, and Clapton was clearly moved by the studio audience's response. Seated in a chair in loose, comfortable surroundings, Clapton seemed quite at home when running through the blues songs, the stage suddenly transformed into a back porch, the voice singing "Malted Milk" or "Walking Blues" sounding as wise as old voices wafting across the dusty roads of the old South. The humorous false start at the beginning of "Alberta," the kazoos played in "San Francisco Bay Blues," the impromptu jamming of "Rollin' and Tumblin' "—Clapton was enjoying his own party.

The biggest surprise of the evening was Clapton's retooled version of "Layla," which he now arranged as a slow shuffle, much the way he had conceived the song prior to Duane Allman's contributing its famous guitar riff.

"I've done it the same all these years, and never considered trying to revamp it, the way a lot of artists might," said Clapton. "Bob Dylan, for instance, changes *everything* every time he plays a song. I thought this was a great opportunity to just take 'Layla' off on a different path."

Such a drastic rearrangement, given the song's stature as one of rock's greatest songs, might have been risky business, even for its author, but the

MTV audience responded to it favorably—so enthusiastically, in fact, that the new version became the single from *Unplugged*, the multiplatinum recording of the concert.

. . .

Clapton's performance on "Unplugged," reaching millions of viewers, was the perfect appetizer for his months of touring ahead. Two weeks after his television appearance, Clapton made a short, six-show run through the United Kingdom, followed by his annual Albert Hall dates, trimmed, this year, to a more manageable twelve shows.

Now in a workaholic mode, as he always was after an extended period of inactivity, Clapton pushed himself through a flurry of studio work prior to leaving for his tour of the States. He cut a single, "Runaway Train," with Elton John, and "It's Probably Me" with Sting, the latter featured in *Lethal Weapon 3*. He also worked on that movie's film score, though this latest venture paled in comparison to his music for *Rush*.

Unplugged, released in August to some of the best reviews of Clapton's career, was an unqualified success, becoming Clapton's all-time best-selling album. The record's timing, coming in the middle of a lengthy stadium tour, was fortuitous, even though Clapton was playing few of the same songs in concert. Videos of "Layla" and "Tears in Heaven," taken from the MTV special and shown frequently on television, gave *Unplugged* the kind of exposure that record company officials can only dream of, the "Tears in Heaven" effort later winning an MTV Award for best video.

Clapton's tour, which took him through the United States, then around Europe, and finally back to the States, was ambitious even by the musician's own standards. Clapton had always spoken of his great fondness for playing onstage, but in a tour of such epic proportion, where every performance seemed to be staged in a football or baseball stadium, he had reached a new plateau. This was especially apparent when he performed his highly publicized dates with Elton John at Wembley Stadium in London, Shea Stadium in New York, and Dodgers Stadium in Los Angeles. At a time when ticket prices were rising to new heights and concert attendance was subsequently dropping, the sold-out Clapton-John concerts were a scalper's delight.

Clapton was on a roll, and as the months ahead would prove, it was only the beginning.

• • •

Prior to 1993, Clapton had received a roomful of awards, but oddly enough, he had been largely (and conspicuously) overlooked by the music industry itself. As a general rule, he was a shoo-in for newspaper or magazine readers' poll awards—which, coming from fans, Clapton always appreciated—but he had taken home only one Grammy in the past, for his vocal on "Bad Love."*

The new year changed all that. For openers, Clapton, along with former bandmates Jack Bruce and Ginger Baker, were elected into the Rock 'n' Roll Hall of Fame, and then, when Grammy Award nominations were announced, Clapton found himself a candidate for nine awards. The recognition was a wonderful coda to what had been one of the most extraordinary years in his career.

The previous November, two months after his tour of the States had finally come to an end, Clapton had returned to New York to appear in a concert commemorating Bob Dylan's thirty years in the music business. The show, simulcast to countries around the world, was a feast of rock's marquee names, past and present, including Clapton, George Harrison, Tom Petty, Neil Young, and Dylan himself, with each artist performing one or two of Dylan's songs. For his segment of the show, Clapton played "Love Minus Zero—No Limit" and "Don't Think Twice (It's All Right)." His reading of "Love Minus Zero," although tight and polished, was nothing special; Clapton sounded as if he was just trying to get comfortable

---

*He also received an award for his work on George Harrison's *Concert for Bangla Desh* album, but it was a group award.

in the packed Madison Square Garden arena. "Don't Think Twice," however, was an entirely different story. Clapton tore into the song with a zeal so intense that it all but redefined the Dylan classic.

Clapton, like Dylan, had reached a point in his career where his life's work could be placed in some kind of perspective. His contributions to contemporary music were easily apparent, from his role in seeing the guitar evolve into a soloing instrument in the context of rock 'n' roll, to his catalog of recordings that had become part of the sound track of three decades' living. Only a small group of musicians and songwriters could compare to the influence he'd had on the music of his times.

Being inducted into the Rock 'n' Roll Hall of Fame for his work in Cream signified the beginning of what will certainly be continuing recognition for Clapton's achievements throughout his life. Cream had given rock a new direction, and while Clapton, in his acceptance speech in Los Angeles, claimed to have a general dislike for awards such as his Hall of Fame recognition, he was also very proud of what it stood for. Twenty-five years had passed since Cream's farewell concert, and Clapton, Bruce, and Baker were looking every bit their age, but when they picked up their instruments after the ceremony and ran through "Crossroads," "Sunshine of Your Love," and "Born Under a Bad Sign," they sounded as fresh as ever.

The Grammy Awards ceremony likewise honored Clapton's overall contributions, even if the awards were issued for the music he made on a single album. In all, Clapton received Grammys for best male vocal, best pop vocal, best rock song, song of the year, record of the year, and album of the year, making *Unplugged* one of the most awarded recordings in rock history. Clapton, who performed "Tears in Heaven" to a rousing ovation from the Grammy audience, remained humble when accepting his armload of awards. He was, he confessed, "very moved, very shaky, and very emotional."

"I want to thank a lot of people," he said, "but the one person I want to thank is my son, for the love he gave me and the song he gave me."

• • •

The recognition, coming at a time when Clapton was celebrating his thirtieth anniversary as a professional musician, was a tribute to Clapton's ability to survive on both human and creative levels. Clapton had watched his music go through many stages, some successful and others not, yet he had never failed to forge ahead. His life had been a continual challenge, and though he could stake no claim to having made all the right decisions, he had moved into middle age with a grace and dignity not often found in internationally worshipped entertainment figures. At one time he had grappled with his own celebrity, uncomfortable with his place in the spotlight and tormented by the responsibility that he felt came with it, but he had finally come to terms with it. He wasn't God, as his young fans had once claimed, but from the time he picked up a guitar and played it onstage, he wasn't simply mortal either.

"If I have to be a hero, even to myself, it's worth it because it's something to strive for," he told an interviewer in 1990. "I quite like having my mettle tested in that way. I didn't like it so long ago; I tried to avoid it, to play it down, and tried to *destroy* it. And that process nearly destroyed me, too—as a human being."

In finally accepting his position as a guitar hero to millions of people worldwide, Clapton also embraced, even if reluctantly, the idea that he had to lead by example.

"I think that the ultimate guitar hero should be a dispenser of wisdom," he said, quickly adding that, by wisdom, he meant the insight that people might gain from his example. "That should come through in the playing," he insisted. "If it doesn't come through in the playing, then it should come through in his lifestyle. I don't have a great deal of that, but that's the one thing I will say that I'm still striving after, outside of perfection as a musician: the attainment of wisdom, in any amount. And I think that's a really worthy cause."

fourteen

Pilgrim
1998-98

I've tried to play folk, C&W, jazz, and a lot of pop music, but I do blues best, and that's been given to me to do. As much as I've questioned it and railed against it and been stubborn about my path, I'm back on it. This is me, in terms of my musical identity, where I came from and what I mean. Wherever I go in the future will be as a result.

eric Clapton's triumph at the Grammy Awards ceremony capped one of the most startling, if not improbable, comebacks in rock music history. Twenty years earlier, he had been in the midst of a self-imposed retirement, hooked on heroin and uncertain as to when he would be performing in public again. A decade later, he'd made his comeback but was slipping from favor, his career lost on a meandering road that seemed to lead to nowhere significant; his name still carried currency, but more because of his history than for anything he was doing at the time.

The international exposure from Live Aid jolted Clapton's career back into motion, and from then on, Clapton, Roger Forrester, and the rest of the Clapton camp made certain that Clapton, his image, and his music were marketed with great care. There would be no backsliding, even if that meant having Clapton take a safer, middle-of-the-road approach to his act. He would be marketed as rock's ultimate survivor, the flawed but brilliant warrior who had made his way across the battlefield, scarred but victorious.

Ironically, the Grammy ceremonies and the accompanying demand for Clapton's time had a marked effect on the musician. All of a sudden, at the pinnacle of his fame, he withdrew from the public eye, declining interviews and performing only his annual Albert Hall dates and an occasional charity gig. When *Rolling Stone* decided to run a cover story on Clapton, as it had on numerous occasions in the past, the now-reclusive star turned down the magazine's interview requests, leaving the publication with a cover story offering no new material. The same was true for *Guitar Player*, which Clapton had favored over the years. For his own reasons, Eric had removed himself from the reach of the media.

The public was rife with speculation. Some observers thought Clapton simply needed time to regroup; he'd gone underground before, so there was no reason to suspect anything other than a need for privacy as the reason for his latest "disappearance." He was, after all, still performing from time to time, and he could be spotted in public often enough to reassure all concerned that he was fit and able to perform whenever the mood struck him.

Others worried that the overwhelming success of *Unplugged* had initiated a prolonged period of uncertainty, or even a creative block. Clapton had opposed the album's release other than as a limited edition, but in the wake of its gigantic critical and popular acceptance, the artist was faced with important questions: Where was his music headed, and what did the public expect from him? The main—and most obvious—question loomed very large indeed: How do you follow up an album such as *Unplugged*?

The darkest and most cynical speculation concerning Clapton's withdrawal from recording and touring focused on the way Clapton's success had played on the artist and his management. Roger Forrester had become impossible to deal with, said one observer very close to the scene. He had always been very protective of Eric's interests, but these watchdog instincts, challenged by the snowballing demands for Clapton's time, were reaching a point where old friends were being cut off and left muttering to themselves.

In all likelihood, there is truth to all of the above. Clapton always distanced himself from public scrutiny, even during those periods in which he was most receptive to being interviewed; he was wary, if not uncomfortable, talking about his music, and he loathed any discussion about his private life. Holding on to his privacy in the aftermath of his son's death and his Grammy winnings would have been impossible if he had responded to the barrage of interview requests, and the idea of honoring such requests from friends and proven journalists, while refusing all others, would have prompted angry cries about favoritism. From this standpoint, he was better off turning down everyone.

• • •

Still, Clapton couldn't stay away from the studio or off the road forever, and by early 1994, word was out that he was finally back in the studio, working on an album of blues standards. The choice of material was anything but a surprise. Clapton's 1993 and 1994 Albert Hall shows had been devoted exclusively to the blues, and Eric had been talking for years about recording an album of his favorite songs in the genre. Despite his hopes of making such a recording, he never seemed to get the project on tape.

"Things keep happening to put it on hold," he told an interviewer in 1991, mentioning that the death of his son earlier in the year had turned his creative energies to writing songs about Conor. The blues album, he intimated, might indeed be recorded, but he had no idea when it would happen.

Part of the challenge was in finding the focus of the music that he wanted to record. Clapton had been influenced by every type of blues imaginable, but it would have been impossible to include all of them on just one or two CDs. For a while, Clapton entertained the notion of sticking to a Texas blues style in the Bobby "Blue" Bland mold, complete with a heavy rhythm section and horns, or even create a kind of musical hybrid that combined classic blues styles with a rock 'n' roll kick. Clapton's work on "Hard Times" had convinced him that anything was possible, and the success of *Unplugged* had given him the confidence he needed to put more of his inner self on the line. *Unplugged*, he insisted, was a personal statement that paled in comparison to the parts of him that would stand exposed in his proposed blues album.

The project, Clapton believed, needed to catch the sense of urgency and live-wire immediacy present in the best blues numbers, and the optimum place for this to happen was onstage. However, he knew from past experience that he couldn't rely on live performances alone to complete an album on any kind of schedule; it had taken two years to put together the songs on *24 Nights*. He needed a spirited studio environment where he could do multiple takes of a song. After giving the matter some thought, Clapton arrived at a compromise: all tracks would be cut "live" in the studio, with no overdubs or fixes. This would retain an element of risk and spontaneity, but the band could record a song over and over until it delivered a track that Clapton liked.

"It's a wonderful process of working," he admitted. "We do everything live, so if one person makes a mistake, we all have to do it over again or we accept the mistake."

The sessions, conducted in London's Olympic studios, featured an entirely new band, with the exceptions of Andy Fairweather-Low, who had worked with Clapton on *Unplugged*, and keyboardist Chris Stainton, who had been with him, off and on, since the late seventies. Bassist Dave Bronze and veteran studio drummer Jim Keltner formed an excellent rhythm section, and Jerry Portnoy, who had worked with Clapton on some of his Albert Hall blues nights, contributed the best blues harp on a Clapton venture since his Bluesbreakers days.

In fact, the sessions harked back to Eric's time with John Mayall. The album was his first all-blues effort since *The Bluesbreakers with Eric Clapton*, and song for song, the new recording offered Clapton's most inspired guitar work since the Mayall record. The main difference was in Clapton's voice, which, of course, had appeared on only one song on the Mayall album, but which had sounded so vulnerable on *Unplugged*. On the new album, Clapton sang with such authority that it knocked both critics and casual listeners back a step.

"Stellar guitar-playing is expected of Clapton," wrote one reviewer, "[but] I'm not sure we expect him to sing with this kind of fervor and rough-edged power. I actually checked the liner notes on 'Blues Before Sunrise' because I thought Eric had brought in a ringer to handle the singing."

Clapton's vocals ran the gamut, from growls and snarls to a mellow, after-hours crooning, displaying an enviable range that moved effortlessly from falsetto highs to gritty lows. He might not have been able to match Buddy Guy's ferocious vocals on Guy's earlier reading of the Eddie Boyd standard "Five Long Years," or Muddy Waters on "Hoochie Coochie Man," but his vocals were finally able to stand with those of Steve Winwood or Van Morrison in the pantheon of worthy white interpreters of black music.

Not that it all came easy. Some of the songs, such as "Five Long Years" or "Sinner's Prayer" (the latter a Lowell Fulson number made popular by Ray Charles) were on the mark in just a couple of takes, while others took much longer. The band ran through "Hoochie Coochie Man" several dozen times before they met Clapton's guarded approval.

Such perfectionism had its price, at least in terms of the critical reaction to the record. People took for granted that Clapton could play the blues, and his ability on guitar was unquestionable. As a result, some critics complained that, in making *From the Cradle*, Clapton was playing safe; the new recording offered excellent covers, but it brought nothing original to the table.

"Despite Clapton's obvious feel for the form, *From the Cradle* never transcends the tradition on which it is built," noted a reviewer who labeled the album "a back-to-basics move designed to boost credibility while cashing in on a reputation forged decades ago." The album's saving grace, wrote the critic, was the way it invited listeners to consult the source material.

The criticism, if viewed from Clapton's perspective, was almost complimentary. In making the album, he was consciously returning to his roots, to days when he was initially establishing his reputation. As he was quick to point out, he had tried every form of music he could think of, but nothing pleased him as much as playing the blues. Furthermore, he had no pretense about his performing as well as his predecessors.

"I try my hardest, to save my life, to sing the blues, but I don't think I can do it half as well as an American black man from the South," he said modestly in a radio interview promoting *From the Cradle*. "I am qualified to sing the blues because of what has happened to me, but I still don't think I'll ever do it as good as a black man."

• • •

Although Clapton, throughout the nineties, would remain highly placed on lists of entertainers earning the largest annual incomes, the release of *From the Cradle*, along with the corresponding tour and television special, moved him back into the spotlight, making him once again one of the hottest commodities in the music business. Suddenly, after an extended absence, Clapton seemed to be everywhere, appearing at benefit and tribute concerts, working on movie soundtracks, and turning up in a glut of reissues of early recordings, or in new compilations. Polydor released a greatly expanded version of *Eric Clapton's Rainbow Concert*, more than doubling the rather meager initial release of the 1973 comeback concert. From a musical standpoint, the band still sounded tentative, but as a historical document, the album was important, catching Clapton gamely trying to work his way through one of the most trying periods of his life.

Conversely, *Crossroads 2*, a four-CD compilation issued in April 1996, captured Clapton as he shifted musical directions and re-established himself in the seventies. Given the fact that Clapton had already put out two live albums covering the period (*E.C. Was Here, Timepieces, Volume II: "Live in the Seventies"*), one might have expected the new compilation to be a huge redundancy of interest only to die-hards and completists; however, *Crossroads 2* held its own as a boxed set, thanks largely to the efforts of compilation producer Bill Levenson, who sifted through hundreds of hours of concert tapes from the period, choosing selections that presented Clapton at his best during an unstable time. There was indeed an overlap of material, with several entries being repeated (albeit in alternate mix form) from *E.C. Was Here*, and several songs ("Have You Ever Loved a Woman," "Ramblin' on My Mind," and "Driftin' Blues") turning up more than once in the new collection, usually as parts of medleys. Nevertheless, when judged as a whole, the recordings became a live counterpart to the earlier *Crossroads*, finding Clapton revisiting songs that he had recorded with John Mayall, Cream, Blind Faith, and Derek and the Dominos, as well as playing all the hits he'd produced as a solo artist in the seventies. There were even four previously unreleased studio numbers, though these paled in comparison to the fiery colors in the live recordings, particularly the blues numbers. Clapton's studio albums from the period had focused on a more laid-back sound, with shorter songs and less emphasis on guitar pyrotechnics; *Crossroads 2* presented his other side, showing a master bluesman still in command of his material.

Ironically, Clapton's two most notable recordings of the mid-nineties, "Change the World," written for the John Travolta movie, *Phenomenon*, and *Retail Therapy*, on which he recorded incognito for a one-off band calling itself TDF (Totally Dysfunctional Family), were greatly removed from the Clapton of two decades earlier—or even from the Clapton heard on *From the Cradle* a few years earlier. Clapton had befriended the popular producer and singer Kenneth "Babyface" Edmunds, and their soft-rock collaboration on "Change the World," in the eyes of one critic, was "a seamless blend of [Clapton's] easy-rolling folksy side and the soft-cushion soul of producer Babyface . . . the latest example of Clapton's savvy ability to tap into the musical zeitgeist without seeming crass."

Retail Therapy, in essence, was another attempt by Clapton to disappear into his music, unencumbered by his reputation or public expectation, similar in a way to his escape from John Mayall's Bluesbreakers to the Glands three decades earlier. By now, of course, Clapton was far too big an international name to simply become an anonymous member of a one-off band, so, in *Retail Therapy*, he and co-producer Simon Climie created a humorous air of mystery that kept the rumor mills grinding for months. Although the album was released on Reprise Records, longtime distributor of Clapton's Duck label, Clapton's name was not mentioned anywhere on the CD or its cover. Instead, a mysterious "x-sample" was cited as co-writer and co-producer of the album's songs. To extend the joke, the bandmembers' faces were obscured by dark helmets in the liner notes photographs.

The album itself was an interesting experiment. Most of the songs were instrumentals, with several featuring vocal samplings of Clapton and others. Some of the songs had a soft jazz or New Age feeling, with Clapton playing gorgeous arpeggios on acoustic guitar, while other entries found him grinding out electric guitar licks on numbers that owed more to Trent Reznor than to Muddy Waters. In a highly positive review, *Down Beat* praised Clapton's contribution to the unusual album. "Clapton or not," wrote the reviewer, "x-sample's guitar work is varied and tasteful, as he alternates among lovely, Mediterranean-inspired acoustic musings, spacy electric guitar treatments and rowdy blues wails."

Clapton may have enjoyed the anonymity, but from a marketing standpoint, *Retail Therapy* suffered from his refusal to attach his name openly to the product. The album went nowhere on the music charts and would ultimately stand, like Clapton's earlier contribution to Roger Waters' *The Pros and Cons of Hitch-Hiking*, as a curious footnote in the guitarist's career.

• • •

For all of his work on miscellaneous recording projects, and all the reissues and repackaging of his earlier work, Clapton was long overdue for a studio recording of new material. His last such effort had been *Journeyman* in 1989—a long time between studio albums, even for someone like Clapton, who had been content to take his time in releasing new material over the past decade and a half.

Anticipation ran high when word circulated in 1997 that Clapton was back in the studio. No one knew quite what to expect. The few new songs that he'd been playing at concerts were soft, moody ballads, and he had yet to record "My Father's Eyes" and "The Circus Left Town," two striking numbers written for his son not long after Conor's death. He had played

the songs during the *Unplugged* television sessions, but he had intentionally left the songs off the album, preferring instead to save them for a future studio recording. There was always a chance that he would record
another offering of blues standards—he had more than enough material in
his repertoire to release another outstanding recording like *From the
Cradle*—or that he might come up with something as totally unpredictable
as *Retail Therapy*—the group from the TDF sessions was with him in the
Olympic Studios, and Clapton was comfortable writing songs with Simon
Climie—but neither seemed likely. After drifting through the nineties, releasing two live albums, working on movie soundtracks, playing with a
one-off band, and contributing to other people's projects, Clapton needed
to reaffirm his identity in the studio.

The album, aptly entitled *Pilgrim*, found Clapton still at the crossroads,
still searching for love, his identity, and peace of mind in fourteen songs
that, sadly, were unified by sterile arrangements more in keeping with his
soundtrack work than his bluesman roots. "My Father's Eyes" and "The
Circus Left Town," now entitled "Circus," were on the recording, but
both seemed to lose their sense of urgency in the studio, where the edgy
Unplugged vocals were replaced by vocals that sounded entirely too measured. The contributions of such gifted session musicians as Steve Gadd,
Nathan East, Greg Phillinganes, and Paul Carrack were buried in a mix of
strings and drum programming that all too often took the heart out of
what might otherwise have been perfectly acceptable songs. With only a
few exceptions, Clapton's voice, so full of power and authority on *From the
Cradle*, seemed to be stripped of the emotional intensity necessary to sustain the songs' impact. There was no question that Clapton had put effort
and consideration into the album, but the recording, like some of his earlier recordings of the seventies and eighties, came up short.

Released in March 1998, *Pilgrim* was greeted with mixed reviews. *Rolling
Stone* praised the album in a four-star review, calling it "easily Clapton's
most ambitious, introspective piece of work since his days with the legendary, lacerating Derek and the Dominos."

"*Pilgrim,*" continued reviewer David Wild, "is the musical journal of an artist who has wandered into some dark places and come back the wiser for his troubles."

Other publications were less generous, with nearly every critic commenting on the quiet, almost funereal feeling to the album. "Unbearable loss and yearning are the central themes of *Pilgrim,*" noted *People* magazine reviewer Steve Dougherty, "and with its heartbeat bass lines, melodic, meditative guitar figures and heartbroken lyrics, it offers moments of surpassing beauty. But at 75 minutes, *Pilgrim* is one long, slow slog, interrupted by only two or three up-tempo tunes. Listening is like sitting through a film you much admire but fervently wish would hurry up and end."

Time was even more brutal. In a review entitled "A Bad Case of the Aquas," critic Christopher John Farley attacked the album from every angle, calling it "a compromised, blues-tinged pop-rock album, with drippy melodies and cautious, manicured guitar solos" that lacked the "guts" of Clapton's best work. Clapton, Farley wrote, hadn't sounded this weak in years. In Farley's opinion, the album's first single, "My Father's Eyes," lost its effectiveness by employing an arrangement "so polished and plodding it never comes close to evoking emotion in the listener—unless you consider boredom an emotion."

Ironically, for all the protests about *Pilgrim's* mellow, MOR approach, the album contained one song that placed Clapton in the center of controversy. In "Sick and Tired," one of the album's few blues numbers with some snarl to it, Clapton sang of getting a shotgun and blowing his former lover's brains out—a lyric prompting loud objections from women's rights and domestic violence groups. At a time when American rap artists were under intense scrutiny and criticism for writing explicitly violent or misogynist lyrics, it seemed inconceivable that someone of Clapton's stature would write and release such a song.

"This is 1998. Hate speech against women or people is not OK," argued Stacey Kabat, executive director of Peace at Home, a shelter for battered women in Boston, and producer of an award-winning documentary on domestic violence. Kabat, a Clapton fan who had received *Pilgrim* as a gift from her husband and son, petitioned Reprise Records with the hope of seeing Clapton re-record "Sick and Tired" with new lyrics for future pressings of the album, much the way Michael Jackson had redone "They Don't Care About Us," a number from his *History: Past, Present and Future* album that had offended Jews with what were considered to be anti-Semitic lyrics. In addition, Kabat suggested that Clapton donate some of the earnings from *Pilgrim* to antiviolence organizations.

Other groups issued similar complaints about the lyrics, but Clapton, who preferred to remain silent in the controversy, had his fair share of defenders, including some of America's most highly regarded music critics. Clapton, said *Village Voice* music editor and critic Robert Christgau, was following a longstanding tradition; many entries in *The Anthology of American Folk Music*, he pointed out, contained lyrics depicting violence toward women. Anthony DeCurtis, a former *Rolling Stone* editor and author of the award-winning liner notes to Clapton's *Crossroads* anthology, agreed that such lyrics were part of a tradition in American blues. "There's this idea that all music is an endorsement of a social viewpoint," DeCurtis said. "There isn't any sense that something might be expressing an emotion that you might even feel every once in a while . . . Maybe one of the functions of art is to give expression to emotions—even of violent anger toward people. Songs are not prescriptions for how to live."

"Sick and Tired" presented a thorny issue to critics because, on an album packed with ballads and easy-listening numbers, it offered one of the few moments of gritty, up-tempo music. *Time* magazine, which hated the album in general, had gone to the extent of singling out "Sick and Tired" (and "One Chance") as "almost worth the price of the whole album." "Sick and Tired," wrote the reviewer, "features grinding, growling guitar work by Clapton, as well as some strong, swaggering vocals."

Negative reviews and controversy aside, *Pilgrim* proved to be another winner with Clapton fans, moving up the *Billboard, Rolling Stone,* and other music charts and easily attaining triple-platinum status. "My Father's

Eyes," while not the chartbuster that "Tears in Heaven" had been a few years earlier, was nevertheless an enormous hit on the adult contemporary charts, staying high on the lists and on radio playlists for months after its release.

• • •

As always, Clapton hit the road to promote his latest album, but this time around, during his Lexus-sponsored North American tour, he found himself addressing his past in a way he would never have predicted. The autobiographical underpinnings of "My Father's Eyes" had reawakened interest in Clapton's roots, particularly in Canada, where Clapton's father had originated, and after some research and investigation, the media was able to dig up stunning new information about Clapton's previously unknown half-sister and two half-brothers, as well as information on Eric's long-lost father. The discoveries made headlines around the world.

From military records, it was determined that Edward Walter Fryer, Eric Clapton's father, had been born on March 21, 1920, in Montreal, Quebec, and by all indications, he had lived the life of a free spirit, moving constantly, marrying several times, fathering at least four children, and getting by for much of his life on a drifter's hand-to-mouth existence. He had left home at fourteen and supported himself by singing and playing piano in saloons in the Montreal area. In 1940, at age twenty, he entered the service, enlisting in the Canadian army and spending most of his tour of duty in England, where he met Patricia Clapton and fathered a son he would never know. At the end of the war, when his unit was being shipped home, Fryer was nowhere to be found. He was listed as AWOL and, on September 4, 1946, given a dishonorable discharge.

Clapton would say that he'd heard that his father was a conservative banker in Montreal, but in all likelihood, Edward Fryer never stayed still long enough to hold down a job in any "conservative" line of work. Instead, he scratched out a living through his music, playing in bars, hotels, dance clubs and even strip clubs in Canada and the United States. Years later, more than a decade after his father's death, Eric Clapton, upon hearing the truth about him, would remark that learning about Edward Fryer's lifestyle had shed some light on his own behavior.

"This desire to play and have fun and chase women," Clapton said of his father, "is all me. So it's kind of nice to know that some of this stuff got handed on."

Fryer met a classical piano teacher named Cecilia, and, in 1958, the two had a daughter, Sandra; a year later, Edward, Jr., called Ted by the family, was born. Both were musically gifted—Sandra on piano, and Ted, like his older half-brother, on guitar.

However, the similarities between Ted Fryer and Eric Clapton did not end with their choice of musical instrument. Ted aspired to make a career in music, and with this in mind, he dropped out of high school and tried to learn to play the blues like his idols, B. B. King and, ironically, a great British blues guitarist named Eric Clapton. As his older sister recalled, Ted "would sneak and pretend to go to school, but he would hide and go downstairs in the basement or go to the park with his guitar."

Ted played in a band that was talented enough to enter a Vancouver "Battle of the Bands" contest and win its first prize—the chance to cut a demo tape for a local record company—but his musical aspirations never blossomed into a successful career. Like his older half-brother, he tried and failed at marriage, and, like his older half-brother, he found that he had a taste for heroin. Unfortunately, he was unable to overcome his addiction, and by the time he reached his fortieth birthday, he was living in a flophouse and struggling to get by.

Edward Fryer walked out on his son and daughter in 1964, when Sandra was six and Ted was four. Neither would see him again. In 1965, about the time Clapton was being lionized as a guitar god in London, Fryer was playing piano in bars in Florida. He met and married Yvonne Colson, and, in 1968, they had a daughter, Eva Jane Fryer. The family moved nomadically around the United States and Canada, following Fryer's jobs and living in a number of cities, including Toronto, Ottawa, and Kingston. For a time, they operated a small dance club for teenagers.

The marriage ended in 1971. Fryer bought a sailboat, on which he lived for the rest of his life. In the summer months, he docked the boat in Port Darlington on Lake Ontario, and during the winter months he would head south, traveling along the Atlantic coastline until he reached and docked in Florida. He continued to earn his living in piano bars, and he supplemented his income by painting signs. He spent his final years with Sylvia "Goldie" Nickason, who was with him at the time of his death from leukemia in 1985.

All three of Clapton's siblings expressed great surprise when they learned, through the media, about their blood relation to the famous guitarist, but none showed any inclination to trade on Clapton's name, or to try to plug into his wealth, even though all three were living, at best, modest lives.

"I just want him to know that I am not after his fame," Eva Jane Fryer, a single mother living in a Florida trailer, told reporters. "I just want to know him. Because if he is my brother, he is part of me. And I'm part of him. I would just like to know him and maybe be a part of his life."

Sandra Fryer-Rich, an employee of American Express in North Carolina, also expressed the desire to meet Clapton, but she quickly added that if it came down to Clapton's having to choose between meeting her or her brother, she would prefer that he get together with Ted. "He can do more for Ted than he can for me," she maintained. "He could reach Ted in a way that no one else could."

When found in Vancouver, Ted Fryer admitted that he, too, would like to sit down with Clapton, but not until he had conquered his heroin addiction. If and when that time came, he hoped to show Clapton some of his own artistic endeavors. "I've got three songs that I'd like to send," he stated, "to let him know what his brother's musical capabilities are."

The unexpected revelations about his father and previously unknown siblings caught Clapton by surprise, and placed him in an awkward position. Although interested in meeting his half-brother and sisters, Clapton wanted no part in turning an otherwise joyous occasion into a media circus. He had spent more than three decades in the public eye, battling for his privacy, and he knew all too well that the tabloids would have a field day with this latest bit of news.

"I don't know quite what to do with it yet," he told reporters. "I don't want to disrupt anybody's life. I don't want to go down there and be trailed by photographers, but I do want to make the connections."

• • •

Where will Clapton go next?

There is no simple, definitive answer to the question, but it can be accurately surmised that he, and he alone, will determine his future. As a solo artist, he has stubbornly pursued whatever type of music he desired, regardless of the reaction it might receive. Like such artists as Bob Dylan, Neil Young, or Van Morrison, he always seems to be in the process of re-inventing himself, and he appears to be enjoying himself in the process, whether he is working on a soundtrack for *Lethal Weapon 4*, recording a duet with B. B. King for the bluesman's *Deuces Wild* album, making a cameo appearance in *Blues Brothers 2000*, or chipping in guitar parts for Tony Rich's album, *Birdseye*. As he has proven throughout his career, he is content to wander and explore many paths.

Whatever he decides to do in the future, all paths will lead back to the blues—to the core of Clapton's identity as a person and a musician—because Eric Clapton is, was, and always will be primarily a bluesman. For all his popularity and wealth, and whatever security they might bring him, Clapton seems to realize that, in accepting the identity of the bluesman, he must also bear the weight of its yoke.

As the title of his most recent album suggests, Clapton has learned to accept the fact that his life is one of constant searching. All he can do is forge ahead, proving with each successful album and tour what some of his blues idols have known all along: blues is *feeling*, as old as time and universal to all corners of the globe. It originates not from someone who plays and sings with the grace of a god, but from someone bold enough to act as a messenger of the heart.

fifteen

Riding with the King
(1998-2002)

When I was younger, I thought I was always in the wrong place—that there was something better right around the corner. But I'm fifty-six now, and I'm quite comfortable in my own skin. I don't want to be somewhere else.

As a commercial enterprise, Clapton's *Pilgrim* tour was another tremendous success, both in the United States and abroad. By now, Clapton was nothing less than a blues and rock institution, and fans proved that he was still a huge stadium and concert hall draw. His detractors rolled their eyes at his tour's big corporate sponsorship—Lexus in the United States, Volkswagen in Europe—but by now corporate sponsors were a regular part of large rock tours, and fans didn't seem to mind the video advertisements flashing on huge screens during intermissions. As always, critics in the United States and overseas offered wildly mixed responses to the shows, particularly the early portions of the concerts, which found Clapton accompanied by an eight-piece string section, or playing unplugged versions of his songs. Clapton, however, had been touring long enough to know how to pace his shows, and by the time his two-hour stints were winding down with first-rate renditions of his classic numbers, critics and fans alike were won over.

Three decades of touring, playing many of the same songs a hundred or more times per year, had left Clapton looking for fresh ways to present his material onstage. He wasn't a stylist like Dylan, who could change the arrangement of one of his songs from tour to tour—or even night to night—and it's unlikely that his fans would have stood for radical changes in any event. He still enjoyed the rush that he felt when he connected with his audiences, but the tours left him exhausted, reminding him that his youthful energy was long gone. He was, quite simply, growing older. Even the Albert Hall tradition had reached its end: Clapton played his last string of blues nights at the revered venue in 1996, and he showed no inclination of picking up the tradition at any time in the future.

He now looked the part of the elder statesman. He was still fit and trim, but his closely cropped hair and beard were turning grey; the trendy clothing, from the psychedelic garb of the 1960s to the Armani suits of the 1990s, had been replaced by the bluejeans, T-shirt, and work boots of the working man. He wore eyeglasses in a variety of fashions.

Somehow, though, it all seemed befitting to someone of his stature, caught between his being one of the wealthiest men in England, and being a man whose musical identity would always be connected to the hardscrabble spirit of the blues.

• • •

A quarter-century had passed since Eric Clapton kicked his heroin habit, and nearly a decade had gone by since the worst of his battles with alcohol abuse. For Clapton, addiction was a deeply personal issue that hovered often in his mind. He was keenly aware of the price he'd paid—literally, in terms of the outrageous sums of money spent on drugs and alcohol, and, more important, physically and spiritually, as substance abuse nearly destroyed him—and he'd seen what addiction had done to others. He hated the thought of being enslaved to any substance. He'd even given up a lifetime's habit of cigarette smoking.

Still, he realized that, by nature, he would always fight the impulse to overindulge. "I'll be an addict till they put me in the ground," he confessed, noting that he was speaking not only of his taste for alcohol or drugs, but of a tendency to go overboard in anything that pleased him. "It can be shopping, TV, food, sex," he pointed out. "I'll use it or think about using it. Now I don't actually participate too much in any of those things; I'm pretty much like a monk these days."

Few would have accused Clapton of living a monk's existence—he certainly wasn't as reclusive as his old friend, George Harrison, who preferred to hang around his estate and tend to his gardens—yet compared with the excessive lifestyles of other high-profile musicians, Clapton's daily routine seemed toned down. He continued to enjoy the life that his wealth provided him, but he also took time to do more than just pay lip service to his concerns about substance abuse.

Since 1996, he had been quietly working, as an unpaid volunteer, at the Priory Clinic, a treatment center not far from London. His involvement had begun innocently enough. He had dropped by to visit the clinic's director one day, and when the director told him of a young man who was refusing to attend his group therapy sessions, Clapton had stopped by the patient's room. The visit had been an eye-opener for the young addict, who couldn't believe that someone of Clapton's stature would care enough to intervene on his behalf. Clapton, in turn, was amazed that he could have such an impact on someone's life.

"I thought that I'd achieved something and felt different and good about myself," he said afterward. "All the things I'd come in to moan about were suddenly not such a big deal any more. So I said: 'Is there anyone else I could sort out?' And it snowballed from there."

From that point on, whenever he was staying in London, Clapton worked four days a week at the clinic.

This was only the beginning. Clapton envisioned starting up his own rehabilitation center, and he invested $6.5 million of his own money into the planning and construction of such a clinic. On October 15, 1998, the Crossroads Centre opened in Antigua.

Clapton loved the location. He'd kept a home on the Caribbean island for more than two decades, and, by Clapton's thinking, there was something soothing about the warm climate and nearby ocean that couldn't help but lighten the stress surrounding drug or alcohol rehabilitation. The thirty-six-bed, state-of-the-art Crossroads Centre featured living quarters, meeting halls, a swimming pool and gymnasium, all supporting a four-week, twelve-step rehabilitation program that mixed intense therapy with recreation. At a charge of $9,000 per guest, the program was substantially cheaper than what one could find elsewhere, and those unable to afford the cost could work it off after treatment. One-third of the facility's beds were reserved for the island's natives, who, Clapton explained, were largely responsible for the rehab facility's existence.

"Antigua was becoming an unhealthy place to be," he said, recalling how an upswing in crack cocaine use on the island had resulted in an increasing number of problems. "There was more begging, more violence, and I was not comfortable with it, particularly as I am still in recovery myself."

Although Clapton hired a former administrator from the Betty Ford Clinic to oversee operations at the Crossroads Centre, he remained a strong presence at the facility, offering opinions and guidance in policy decisions, and visiting the clinic and its patients whenever he was staying in Antigua. His dedication to Crossroads Centre even led to a high-profile event in June 1999, when Christie's in New York auctioned off one hundred of his old guitars, including "Brownie," the guitar he'd used during the recording of *Layla and Other Assorted Love Songs*, with the $5 million proceeds from the auction going to the rehab facility.

"I want to give it as much as I can," Clapton said of his continuing plans for involvement with the Crossroads Centre, "but I would happily do that anonymously. I want to be just a piece of furniture—I'll sneak in and just be one of the guys."

. . .

Clapton had wanted to be "one of the guys"—a journeyman, as it were—for most of his career, but one only had to look at his musical output to see that, with the exception of a rare project like TDF, he would never be just another anonymous musician.

His music had been packaged and re-packaged over the years in every imaginable way, from greatest hits compilations to newly remastered versions of his original albums, all in an effort to capitalize on his name and squeeze every possible dime out of his lengthy career. His recordings with the Yardbirds had been issued in so many permutations that Clapton himself must have wondered just how long he had been a member of the group. The same could be said about the short-lived Derek and the Dominos, who, as a working unit, had issued two-record studio and live sets; later, a three-CD boxed set of studio work and a two-CD compilation of live material were added to the star-crossed band's commercial output. The boxed set, *Those Were the Days*, gathered all of Cream's previously available studio work with the best of the trio's already released live material, along with a few previously unavailable oddities, and alternate takes. Much of all this work was the brainchild of Bill Levenson, who had done such a remarkable job on the *Crossroads* anthology, and who saw that the music was thoughtfully packaged with memorable photographs and thoughtful liner notes.

Two new projects—a compilation entitled *Blues*, and an expanded version of *Blind Faith*—surfaced in 1999. Both relied heavily upon previously available material, but each offered enough in new material to keep hungry Clapton fans content.

Blues, a two-disc set, offered one CD of studio material, and another of live performances. As compilations go, it was a winner, a strong sampling of Clapton's work as a blues artist, covering songs by Muddy Waters, Lead Belly, Elmore James, Jimmy Reed, Willie Dixon, Otis Rush, T-Bone Walker, Bo Diddley, Bobby "Blue" Bland, and, of course, Robert Johnson. Cynics asserted that this was just another rehash job, but aside from the obvious inclusion for purely commercial purposes—"Wonderful Tonight" a blues song?—and the repetition of two alternate studio takes of "Before You Accuse Me," and live and studio versions of both "Have You Ever Loved a Woman," and "Early in the Morning," the compilation was an astute assembly of blues styles. Much of the live material, in fact, had been presented in the recent *Crossroads 2* box, but for those unable or unwilling to plop down a hefty sum for the box, *Blues* would more than suffice.

"Clapton taps the musical wellspring that has sustained him for more than three decades," *Rolling Stone* applauded in a four-star review. "It may be a story you've heard parts of before, but it's compelling nonetheless—and this collection tells it with insight and flair."

That same year, Polydor issued a deluxe two-CD thirtieth anniversary edition of *Blind Faith*, containing the digitally remastered 1969 album and nine tracks absent from the original recording. Compared to *Blues*, this album was much less successful. The best of the outtakes—an electric version of "Can't Find My Way Home" and a robust reworking of Sam Myers' "Sleeping in the Ground"—had already appeared, respectively, in the Steve Winwood and Eric Clapton boxed sets, and the other studio material and jam sessions, while perhaps of some interest to die-hards or completists, had little to offer other than occasional flashes of instrumental brilliance and a glimpse into the super-group's futile struggle to find its identity as a unit.

Clapton cringed when he listened to the new recording. The work reminded him, as if he could ever forget, of the extended guitar solos he'd grown to dislike. "At the time, I thought these were magnificent things we were doing, just jamming away," he conceded. "But I was a kid. The only personality I had was within my fingers. I could play it, but I couldn't say it."

This, by now, was a familiar refrain, regularly employed by Clapton to ward off fans and critics who claimed he'd gone soft, who were always clamoring for the Eric Clapton of old. He wasn't keen on listening to his old work, he'd argue, but when he did hear an old Cream or John Mayall number, he would weigh the maturity informing his later work against the passion that fueled his youthful days.

"I hear the fire," he said of his earlier recordings, "but I'm embarrassed by the clumsiness—the ego that surrounds it. I'm more comfortable listening to something contemporary of mine that doesn't have the fire but has more self-awareness."

He was pleased, then, when he was inducted for an unprecedented third time into the Rock 'n' Roll Hall of Fame, this time for his work as a solo artist. His previous honors had been for his membership in the Yardbirds and Cream, but, for Clapton, these two groups had been short-term endeavors, known more for their influence on rock music—and, yes, for their fire—than for the number of recordings they had left behind. Clapton's work as a solo artist vastly eclipsed the work he'd done with those and other bands, and to be inducted on his own merits as a solo artist was a nod to Clapton as a singer and songwriter, as well as an instrumentalist; it was an endorsement of a large body of work.

"I don't know quite how to handle this stuff," a modest Clapton offered in his induction speech. "I'm just a messenger—I carry the message, and I hope to be able to do that as long as I live. Love and music is all you need."

• • •

Over the course of his career, Eric Clapton had played, onstage or in the recording studio, with an incredible range of blues, R&B, and soul artists. He'd learned hard lessons from the likes of Sonny Boy Williamson and Howlin' Wolf; produced an album for Buddy Guy and Junior Wells; recorded with Champion Jack Dupree, Aretha Franklin, Ray Charles, and a host of others; and jammed onstage with Muddy Waters, B.B. King, Otis Rush, and Stevie Ray Vaughan, to mention just a few. Few artists could stake such a claim. For all the critical moaning and groaning about his laid-back, adult contemporary music, Clapton remained, at heart, a bluesman, and he rarely let an interview go by without making sure that the public understood as much.

Oddly enough, for all his experiences—and the built-in demand from record buyers—he'd never recorded a full-length album of duets with a blues artist. Part of this undoubtedly had to do with scheduling and contractual issues, and part could be attributed to Clapton's own modesty. People could scribble "Clapton is God" all over subway walls, or proclaim him to be the greatest axeman in the history of the electric guitar, but in his own mind, Clapton felt that, as a blues player, he still had much to learn from the masters. He might have fantasized about recording an entire album with one of the giants, but he was far too modest to ever take the initiative on such a project.

All this changed in early 2000, when Clapton and B.B. King joined forces on *Riding with the King*, an album that would greatly boost King's career and reaffirm Clapton's credentials as a significant blues artist in his own right.

Clapton had known King, at least marginally, for a long time. They'd played together onstage at the Café A Go Go in New York City in 1967, while Clapton was still a member of Cream, and they'd run into each other, from time to time, over the next thirty years. They finally collaborated on a recording in 1997, when Clapton appeared with King on "Rock Me Baby" on King's *Deuces Wild* album. True to form, Clapton said nothing to King about wanting to work with him on an album project, and *Riding with the King* might not have happened if King had not seen Clapton on a television talk show in 1998.

"I've known Eric since the sixties, and I've always wanted to do something like this with him, but I didn't want to push it," King recalled shortly after the recording of *Riding with the King*. "About two years ago, I saw him on *Larry King Live,* and Larry asked him, 'What would you like to do?' And Eric said, 'Make a CD with B.B. King.' I almost fell out of the chair! I couldn't believe it."

The two connected and started planning an album. King asked Clapton to draw up a list of songs that he wanted to record, and Clapton returned with a selection that included some of King's own vintage material—songs that King hadn't played in decades.

"I wondered how in the world did he think of those?" King remarked. "Some of those I hadn't done since the '50s. I was very pleased and happy with his choices, but I had to relearn all of them! He knew them better than I did."

King suggested that they record some of Clapton's music, but Clapton demurred. As far as Clapton was concerned, B.B. King was gong to receive top billing all the way, and that included the selection of songs. King wasn't enthusiastic about Clapton's notion that they record a new arrangement of the Johnny Mercer and Harold Arlen classic, "Come Rain or Come Shine"—King feared he couldn't do it justice—but Clapton talked him into giving it a shot. The song eventually wound up closing out the album.

"As I get into my old age, those songs are coming up," Clapton said of some of the standards that he remembered from bygone days, when, as a boy, he'd go to the movies with his Uncle Adrian and his future Aunt Sylvia. Clapton loved the musicals from the era, and, in 2001, on his world tour, he would close out his shows with a blues version of "Over the Rainbow." "I may have to do another couple of albums to get these things out of my system," he quipped.

Clapton and King began recording in February 2000, with Clapton and Simon Climie co-producing, Alan Douglas engineering, and the two guitarists supported by a top-notch group of musicians that included old standbys Nathan East on bass and Andy Fairweather-Low on rhythm guitar, Steve Gadd on drums, and Joe Sample on keyboards. Doyle Bramhall II, a Texas native and leader of the band Smokestack, chipped in on guitar and contributed two songs. Clapton remained true to his recent practice of recording "live" in the studio. "A lot of the songs," B.B. King explained, "[were] first takes. We'd usually do two or three takes on everything to make sure. You can't ever tell: you might break something, or something gets erased."

More often than not, it was a matter of recording the unplanned but memorable moments. Alan Douglas, a veteran of the *From the Cradle* sessions, knew to expect the unexpected.

"With Eric and his band, you have to make sure you're always recording," he told an interviewer from *Guitar Player* magazine. "When you have that much talent in the room, there are a lot of musical subtleties and interactive nuances, and you have to make sure everything is captured."

Clapton agreed. "A lot of the time the best stuff is accidental," he admitted. "The guys I work with in the studio know to keep the tape running, because I play the best stuff when I don't know I'm recording and I'm just noodling."

Riding with the King contained a number of high points. On the title track, Clapton and King gave a spirited reading of the John Hiatt song, with a much heavier rhythm track than the original, and a fade that included a funny spoken-word passage from B.B. King. Clapton's revisiting of two old favorites, Big Bill Broonzy's "Key to the Highway" and Big Maceo's "Worried Life Blues," were laid back, respectful of the original material while offering beautifully subtle interplay between Clapton and King. "When My Heart Breaks Like a Hammer," one of King's older numbers, offered Clapton and King the chance to stretch out on their solos, their playing muscular and clean. The two guitarists obviously enjoyed playing together, and what the album might have been lacking in competitive fire (such as the earlier interplay between Clapton and Carlos Santana on *Crossroad II*'s "Why Does Love Got to Be So Sad?"/"Eyesight to the Blind" medley), it gained in workmanlike performances showcasing each guitarist's individual sound and talent.

The album raced up the charts when it was released in July 2000, opening at number one on the *Billboard* "Blues Albums" chart, and taking the number three position of *Billboard*'s "Top 200"; no album in B.B. King's long career had done so well. The critics, while finding the album "short on protracted fireworks," as one put it, were impressed with the album. "As celebrity blues summits go," wrote *Rolling Stone* critic David Fricke in a four-and-a-half-star review, "*Riding with the King* is refreshingly ham-free, a commercially astute meeting of like minds, hearts and voices."

Unfortunately, no tour accompanied the release of the album. Clapton appeared with King in the video of "Riding with the King," the album's single, but he stepped back from all other promotional appearances; this would be B.B. King's time in the spotlight. The recording provided a huge boost for King's career: a new solo effort, *Makin' Love Is Good for You*, released at the same time as *Riding with the King*, sold well, as did a couple of his earlier albums; a tour of Europe found the seventy-four-year-old bluesman in top demand. *Riding with the King* would hold down a top ten blues chart position well into 2002, and Clapton and King would win Grammy awards for the effort.

• • •

Throughout the 1990s, Eric Clapton grew increasingly introspective, particularly in his music. *Unplugged* and *From the Cradle* had been deeply personal forays into his musical roots, while *Pilgrim* stood as a kind of catharsis, exploring a lifetime's journey peppered with personal loss and redemptive slivers of light. Clapton had worked obsessively on *Pilgrim*, taking more than a year to work it into a state that satisfied him. Clapton's continuing efforts to stay free of alcohol and drug dependency, with their attendant counseling and group therapy sessions, placed the already sensitive musician in greater touch with his emotional landscape, which, in turn, nudged him toward a renewed exploration into his own background. He conceded that he would always have ambivalent feelings toward his mother, and with the publicity surrounding the discovery of his half-sisters and half-brother, he had little choice but to reconsider his unusual family history.

Death also had its say in directing this self-examination. It was one thing to deal with the sudden, unexpected loss of friends, bandmates, or even family members, quite another to realize, as he moved through middle age, that those close to him, or significant people in his past, would be dying of natural causes. Tragedy and loss were part of a bluesman's luggage, but they could be cumbersome. Clapton had taken a blow in 1994 when his grandmother, Rose Clapp, passed away, and then again, less then six months later, when Alice Ormsby-Gore was found dead in her home in Boscombe. Life had been difficult for Ormsby-Gore, whose battles with addiction had seen her fall from the surroundings of great wealth to a shabby apartment in a slum district. Clapton must have shuddered at the thought that he, too, could have wound up this way.

Then, in the spring of 2000, just as Clapton was completing work on *Riding with the King*, Adrian Clapton, Eric's uncle, passed away. For Eric, this represented another terrible loss, not only of a beloved family member, but of a piece of his very confused childhood.

"After a while, after attending his funeral, I found myself in a state of suspended animation, remembering my early and the precious times I had spent with him," Clapton wrote in his liner notes to *Reptile*. In the strange guise carried out by Jack and Rose Clapp, in which Clapton's mother posed as Eric's sister, Adrian Clapton had been an older brother, and Eric was greatly influenced by him. "I realize now," he stated, "that most of my tastes in music, art, clothes, cars, etc., etc., were formed in this period of my life, and were due mostly to the wonderful relationship I had with my Uncle Adrian (a.k.a. 'Son') and his wife Sylvia."

Clapton hadn't been as close to Adrian over the past decade, largely due to Eric's efforts to stay sober. Adrian liked to drink, and Eric deliberately avoided him, partly because he didn't want to fall back into his old patterns of addiction, and partly, he hinted, because he was holding the lofty position of a judgmental convert. "I became very anti-social and hardly spoke to him at all," he recalled. "For the last ten years of his life, I was not there."

Adrian, Clapton realized, had been a lovable rogue, not unlike the person he himself had been during periods of his youth, and his death gave Eric another occasion to consider the twisting path of his own life.

Inevitably, he wound up back in the recording studio, where music was always therapeutic. This time, he had no "Tears in Heaven" or "My Father's Eyes" to anchor the recording. He had written an early version of "Find Myself," which addressed his relationship with Adrian, but the song seemed stagnant. Things started to fall into place when Clapton took a short break from the studio, visited his half-sisters in Canada, and spoke to them at length about Adrian. By the time he returned to the studio, he knew that he was on the verge of another very personal album, but one noticeably different from *Pilgrim*. "*Pilgrim* was unloading a lot of sad feelings about a relationship that I'd been in for a long time," he explained. "But *Reptile* has got an even deeper meaning, in that it goes over my whole life."

One doesn't risk making a strong autobiographical statement with strangers, and for *Reptile* he stayed with old, trusted bandmates, using the same unit he'd worked with on *Pilgrim* and *Riding with the King*. Not only was Clapton comfortable working with these musicians; he also knew that they were gifted enough to take on various musical styles that, ultimately, reflected on his complex personality. There was, however, one new—and very important—wrinkle: rather than employ a couple of female background singers, as he had throughout his solo career, Clapton brought in the Impressions, Curtis Mayfield's background singers, to work on the new album. The addition proved very beneficial: the Impressions added a texture to the sound never heard on a previous Clapton album.

The songs wandered all over the musical map, from the opening title track, an instrumental samba, to the tougher-edged blues numbers, to the ballads that had long been a Clapton staple. Jazz lines could be heard in some of the songs, country blues seasonings in others. Clapton's singing, which had grown stronger and more confident over time, was as authoritative as ever, alternately strong and vulnerable, much like the singer himself. In "Come Back Baby," he proved once again that he well could be the greatest interpreter of Ray Charles's songs outside of Charles himself. His re-tooling of James Taylor's "Don't Let Me Be Lonely Tonight," though an odd choice to cover, maintained the beautiful simplicity of the original while adding Clapton's own distinct colorings. "Superman Inside," the album's single, displayed once again that Clapton could still rear back and rock. Clapton explored his familiar themes of love and loss, but to much greater effect than on the earlier *Pilgrim*.

The album's title, like the titles of earlier Clapton efforts, had its own strange background. "Reptile," Clapton explained, was a slang term of endearment, often expressed as a humorous form of put-down; a reptile was a little off-center, a bit of a rebel or outsider, but ultimately respected. In his own mind, Clapton probably felt that he fit the description, as did many of the people he knew and worked with, and, above all, as the inspiration for the new album, his Uncle Adrian.

Reptile received the predictable mixture of reviews, with some critics clamoring for a tougher-edged recording ("if only Clapton would crank up his guitar and make the rock album for which his disciples have long been starving"), while others simply dismissed it as a typical disappointment ("yet another version of the tepid corporate rock records Clapton's been making ever since 1974's *461 Ocean Boulevard*"). *Rolling Stone*, though un-

willing to label the album a classic, was typical of many of the favorable reviews, praising the album while offering a faint caveat: "Over the course of
fourteen tracks, Clapton blends virtually every style he's worked in during
the past thirty-five years. Whether it will strike your ears as something-
for-everyone generosity or a patchy jumble probably depends on how
much of a purist you are."

In a down year for music sales, *Reptile* held its own, selling respectably
but certainly nowhere near what record company executives would have
hoped. "Superman Inside" received plenty of airplay, but it, too, failed to
capture the public fancy the way "Tears in Heaven" or even "Change the
World" had pleased the public. "Reptile," the album's title track, did win a
best instrumental Grammy in early 2002, keeping Clapton's Grammy
streak alive and rewarding his faith in what had to be the strangest choice
of an album opener in his career, but over the long run, *Reptile* was destined to stand as another workmanlike effort, memorable for a handful of
songs but typical of the safe path Clapton's career had taken.

• • •

Clapton kicked off the release of *Reptile* with another ambitious world tour.
Backed by a talented four-piece band, Clapton performed a small sampling
from the new album, a handful of his blues standards like "Have You Ever
Loved a Woman" and "Hoochie Coochie Man," and the obligatory litany
of hits. Though generally well received, the shows had a comfortable,
front-porch feeling that left audiences feeling satisfied but not blown away.
One reviewer, in comparing Clapton to his old contemporary, Jeff Beck,
praised Clapton's guitar virtuosity and vocal ability, but deemed him "too
safe, too sedate" for his hungry audience. "While Jeff Beck is a big swig of
Jack Daniels," the reviewer wrote, "Eric Clapton is a cup of chamomile
tea."

Such criticism didn't seem to bother Clapton. Fans were paying much
higher ticket prices for concert seats, and he was determined to give them
their money's worth, even if fulfilling expectations meant going over such

familiar material as "Badge," "Sunshine of Your Love," "Layla," or "Have You Ever Loved a Woman."

"The tiring thing is trying to bring new songs from *Reptile* to the stage and introduce them to an audience," he admitted. "You're towing a big weight, because nobody has heard them and they're not really interested. But when you go into 'Badge,' everyone knows it."

By fall 2001, Clapton had grown road-weary. The *Reptile* tour had taken him around the globe, and while there were always those magical moments finding the guitarist connecting with his audience, those moments were greatly outnumbered by the tedium of travel, the seemingly endless number of soundchecks, the unsettling feeling of waking up every morning in a new city (or country), and the pressure to be in top form. The money could be mind boggling, but it came at a price that Clapton no longer wanted to pay. The *Reptile* tour, he announced, would be his last. "The live thing doesn't work for me anymore," he insisted, stating that he would find other ways to express himself.

It was a familiar lament in rock circles. More than thirty-five years earlier, the Beatles, at the height of their staggering popularity, had announced that they were finished touring. George Harrison in particular hated the daily grind, from the media interviews to the adulation of shrieking fans who didn't seem to know the difference between a spirited performance and a flat one; the concerts had become a circus, with music being almost beside the point. Other bands voiced the same complaints, some actually leaving the road for extended periods before the allure of the big payday brought them back.

For Clapton, the live performance had always been a vital part of self-expression; he was able to stretch out more onstage, with a greater sense of immediacy and urgency in his guitar solos, than in the studio. He'd tried the "live in the studio" approach to recording on *Riding with the King* and *From the Cradle*, and while both albums featured flashes of inspired soloing, there was something about the blues that had to be experienced and not just heard. The *Pilgrim* and *Reptile* tours, however, had underscored the great disparity between the critical and popular reaction to Clapton's latest work. Fans endorsed—or, at worst, quietly tolerated—the new work, saving their loudest ovations for such time-honored classics as "Crossroads," "Layla," and "Cocaine"; impatient critics shifted in their seats when Clapton played such personally meaningful numbers as "My Father's Eyes" and "Pilgrim." Where the hell was Slowhand? they wondered. When was he going to ditch the adult contemporary stuff, strap on his Strat, and buzz through the kind of music he was capable of playing?

"We've yearned for Clapton to slip the reins of middle-aged mediocrity and let loose the dogs of war," wrote a reviewer of Clapton's 1998 UK tour. "We've waited in vain for him to escape the prison of his own making." Offered another critic: "Even the most besotted fans must be tempted to give up. Although they're pretty sure that somewhere in the show he'll turf the string section off stage, roll up his sleeves and play some of the blues he still cites as his first love, Eric does not make it easy for them."

And these comments were in favorable reviews!

Clapton responded to his critics with typical candor. This was the kind of music that he liked and wanted to play, he'd say; he wasn't interested in resurrecting the loud, lengthy jams that characterized his early career.

Still, Clapton must have wondered whether it was worth the bother. Critics were falling all over themselves in praise of Bob Dylan's *Time Out of Mind* and *Love and Theft* albums—both magnificent efforts, yet certainly more laid back than Dylan's snarling electric albums of the mid-1960s—and reviews of Dylan's concerts bordered the reverential. Other aging rockers were similarly well treated. Clapton was still recording, and his shows were anything but nostalgic affairs.

Even as he launched into his *Reptile* tour, Clapton sounded upbeat. "The physical price of touring is very high," he told *Guitar Player* magazine, "but it's worth it when the band gets onstage and the musical chemistry happens. That's why I do it."

Despite his announcement that he was putting the touring behind him, Clapton left the door open for future live performances. There might be occasional concerts in smaller venues, he hinted, or maybe even smaller-scale tours, but as far as he was concerned, he was finished with the huge arena circuit. Only time would tell.

• • •

There might have been one other factor influencing Clapton's decision: the birth of another daughter, Julie Rose, to Clapton and his twenty-five-year-old girlfriend, Melia McEnery, while Clapton was still committed to his *Reptile* tour. Clapton had met McEnery, a graphic artist from Ohio, in Los Angeles in 1999, and the new arrival, Clapton's third child, seemed to further underscore his stated intentions of settling down, even if he showed no inclination of marrying the child's mother.

There was, however, one major, high-profile event in the immediate future—one which Clapton could never have predicted. Shortly after the September 11, 2001, terrorist attacks on the World Trade Center in New York and the Pentagon in Washington, D.C., Clapton joined an all-star lineup in a benefit concert organized by Paul McCartney. Clapton's appearance with Buddy Guy marked one of the evening's many highlights, which included another reuniting of The Who, a strong McCartney set, and a touching performance by James Taylor. Clapton and Guy traded scorching guitar solos, giving a worldwide audience a taste of what might be missed if Clapton stuck to his promise of semi-retirement from the stage.

Just a few weeks later, Clapton was saddened to learn that George Harrison had lost his long battle with cancer. Harrison had been ailing for some time, but even if his death came as no surprise to those who followed the news accounts of his struggles with throat cancer, it nonetheless served as a reminder that some of rock's great voices were growing older and, in some cases, more frail. For Baby Boomers, the Beatles had been a symbol of youth; now, half of them were gone. Clapton, of course, had much deeper reasons to mourn. His history with Harrison had been well documented; he had lost a friend and, in some regards, a spiritual compass.

On January 1, 2002, Clapton celebrated the new year in a big way. He and a group of about twenty guests gathered at St. Mary Magdalene church for the double baptism of Clapton's daughter Ruth, now sixteen, and Clapton's new daughter, Julie Rose, now six months old. For Clapton, the setting was especially poignant: his son Conor was buried in the church's cemetery, as were his grandparents. After the baptisms, Clapton shocked everyone present by exchanging wedding vows with Melia McEnery.

The wedding had taken everyone by surprise. After his divorce from Pattie Boyd, Clapton had all but sworn off the chances of his ever marrying again. But the marriage, in some respects, was simply another matter of Clapton's taking a new direction in his life. In recent years, he'd been simplifying his life. He'd sold his fine arts collection, further dedicated himself to sobriety and the calmer existence that it brought him, and announced that his days of touring were over; he'd even ended his long relationship with manager Roger Forrester. By all indications, he was tying up loose ends and moving toward a much less complicated life. Marriage was just another way of settling down.

Said Clapton's Aunt Sylvia, who witnessed the wedding ceremony: "It was like reading a wonderful book and coming to a happy ending."

• • •

Where will Clapton go next?

There is no simple, definitive answer to the question, but it can be accurately surmised that he, and he alone, will determine his future. As a solo artist, he has stubbornly pursued whatever type of music he desired, regardless of the reaction it might receive. Like such artists as Bob Dylan, Neil Young, or Van Morrison, he always seems to be in the process of reinventing himself, and he appears to be enjoying himself in the process. Whatever he decides to do, all paths will lead back to the blues—to the core of Clapton's identity as a person and a musician—because Eric Clapton is, was, and always will be primarily a bluesman. For all his popularity and wealth, and whatever security they might bring him, Clapton seems to realize that, in accepting the identity of the bluesman, he must also bear the weight of its yoke.

As the title of his album *Pilgrim* suggests, Clapton has learned to accept the fact that his life is one of constant searching. All he can do is forge ahead, proving with each successful album or tour that some of his blues idols have known all along: blues is a feeling, as old as time and universal to all corners of the globe. It originates not from someone who plays and sings with the grace of a god, but from someone bold enough to act as a messenger of the heart.

Source Notes

1: *Motherless Child*

Epigraph: J. D. Considine, "Eric Clapton Is Not God," *Musician*, November 1986.

"It's difficult . . ." Timothy White, *Rock Lives* (NY: Henry Holt, 1990), p. 315.

"very fun-loving people": Ibid., p. 314.

"We told him . . ." Ray Coleman, *Clapton!* (NY: Warner, 1987), p. 34.

"It was a very . . ." Jenny Boyd, *Musicians in Tune* (NY: Simon & Schuster, 1992), p. 22.

"As a tiny tot . . ." Ibid.

"I wanted to be different . . ." Ibid., p. 56.

"There was a funny . . ." Robert Palmer, "Eric Clapton: The Rolling Stone Interview," *Rolling Stone*, June 20, 1985.

"I couldn't really . . ." Alex Coletti, "Amazing Grace," *Guitar World*, June 1993.

"I was the one," Steve Turner, *Conversations with Eric Clapton* (London: Abacus, 1976), p. 32.

"It sounded . . ." "Off the Record" radio show, Westwood One Radio Network, December 1992.

"Guitar playing . . ." Considine, "Clapton Is Not God."

"It was almost like . . ." Peter Guralnick, "Eric Clapton at the Passion Threshold," *Musician*, February 1990.

"Both of the Robert . . ." Dan Forte, "Out from Behind the Sun," *Guitar Player*, July 1985.

"It came as something . . ." Eric Clapton, "Discovering Robert Johnson," from the liner notes of *Robert Johnson: The Complete Recordings* (Columbia 46222).

"a general nuisance": Turner, *Conversations*, p. 34.

"If you were . . ." David Mead, "Eric Clapton," *Guitarist*, June 1994.

"just a blues . . ." Turner, *Conversations*, p. 33.

"You could play . . ." Considine, "Clapton Is Not God."

"It was magic . . ." White, *Rock Lives*, p. 315.

"It was mainly . . ." Ibid., p. 316.

"I didn't know . . ." Steven Gaines, "Eric Clapton: The Inside Story of His Comeback with '461 Ocean Boulevard,'" *Circus Raves*, October 1974.

"I knew just about . . ." Palmer, "Rolling Stone Interview."

"I'd love to be . . ." "Reflections on Eric Clapton," *Guitar Player*, July 1985.

"It was a nightmare . . ." Dan Neer, "Eric Clapton Testifies," *Guitar*, June 1986.

"It was a very heavy . . ." Gaines, "Eric Clapton: Inside Story."

2: Smokestack Lightning

Epigraph: Robert Palmer, "Eric Clapton: The Rolling Stone Interview," *Rolling Stone*, June 20, 1985.

"I always used . . ." Timothy White, *Rock Lives* (NY: Henry Holt, 1990), p. 312.

"You take the rough . . ." Peter Guralnick, "Eric Clapton at the Passion Threshold," *Musician*, February 1990.

"Those Englishmen . . ." Palmer, "Rolling Stone Interview."

"When Sonny Boy . . ." Marc Roberty, *Eric Clapton: The Complete Recording Sessions* (NY: St. Martin's, 1994), p. 13.

"I knew his songs . . ." Guralnick, "Eric Clapton at Passion Threshold."

"You realize . . ." David Fricke, "Eric Clapton: Still Living on Blues Power," *Rolling Stone*, August 24, 1988.

"When you're in . . ." Dan Forte, "Dominos Fall," *Guitar Player*, August 1976.

"very instrumental . . ." Ray Coleman, *Clapton!* (NY: Warner, 1987), p. 264.

"Sam did his . . ." Steve Turner, *Conversations with Eric Clapton* (London: Abacus, 1976), p. 40.

"He could have slapped . . ." Ibid., p. 41.

"He loves the blues . . ." "Clapton Quits Yardbirds—'Too Commercial,'" *Melody Maker*, March 13, 1965.

3: Deification

Epigraph: David Mead, "Eric Clapton," *Guitarist*, June 1994.

"very lost and alone": Dan Forte, "Out from Behind the Sun," *Guitar Player*, July 1985.

"I started wondering . . ." Ibid.

"made me feel . . ." Ibid.

"My first main . . ." Richard Skelly, "John Mayall: Headmaster of the British Blues School," *Goldmine*, September 3, 1993.

"During the week . . ." Mick Fleetwood, *Fleetwood* (NY: Avon Books), pp. 21–22.

"Eric was the only . . ." "Reflections on Eric Clapton," *Guitar Player*, July 1985.

"He was totally amazing . . ." Skelly, "John Mayall: Headmaster."

"When Eric joined . . ." "Reflections on Eric Clapton."

"We did a lot . . ." Marc Roberty, *Eric Clapton: The Complete Recording Sessions* (NY: St. Martin's, 1994), p. 21.

"He didn't get you . . ." Steve Turner, *Conversations with Eric Clapton* (London: Abacus, 1976), p. 54.

"We did it straight . . ." Marc Roberty, *Eric Clapton: The New Visual Documentary* (London: Omnibus, 1990), p. 10.

"They were wino days . . ." Turner, *Conversations*, p. 53.

"There was something . . ." Roberty, *Visual Documentary*, p. 9.

"The audiences in Britain . . ." "Reflections on Eric Clapton."

"He was a very moody . . ." and "With my band . . ." Ibid.

"There were no . . ." Tom Mulhern, "Jack Bruce: Cream's Bassist on Clapton's Influence," *Guitar Player*, July 1985.

"He hit those peaks . . ." John Mayall to author.

"I had a definite . . ." James Henke, "Eric Clapton: The Rolling Stone Interview," *Rolling Stone*, October 17, 1991.

"The leap came . . ." Peter Guralnick, "Eric Clapton at the Passion Threshold," *Musician*, February 1990.

"He was a bit . . ." Roberty, *Complete Recording Sessions*, p. 27.

4: Power Trio

Epigraph: Nick Logan, "Final Goodbye from the Cream," *Hit Parader*, July 1969.

"By the time . . ." Fred Stuckey, "No More Blind Faith," *Guitar Player*, December 1970.

"It was always . . ." Dan Neer, "Eric Clapton Testifies," *Guitar*, June 1986.

"I like the way . . ." Robert Palmer, "Eric Clapton: The Rolling Stone Interview," *Rolling Stone*, June 20, 1985.

"it was the only . . ." Jim Delehant, "Jack and Ginger Make The Cream Work," *Hit Parader*, October 1968.

"I was thrown out . . ." Ibid.

"We were very poor . . ." Steve Dougherty, "Rocker Ginger Baker Now Faces 50 with a Smile," *People*, June 19, 1989.

"Jack wanted to sit . . ." Steve Roeser, "Ginger Baker: Anyone for Polo?" *Goldmine*, October 15, 1993.

"I always liked . . ." Jim Nelson, "In the Studio" radio show, Bullet Productions, March 1990.

"The trio . . ." Delehant, "Jack and Ginger Make Cream Work."

"The only jazz . . ." Tom Mulhern, "Jack Bruce: Cream's Bassist on Clapton's Influence," *Guitar Player*, July 1985.

"The minute we started . . ." Neer, "Eric Clapton Testifies."

"We're the Cream . . ." Ray Coleman, *Clapton!* (NY: Warner, 1987), p. 58.

"a sensational new . . ." Marc Roberty, *Eric Clapton: The New Visual Documentary* (London: Omnibus, 1990), p. 11.

"They will be called . . ." Ibid.

"We had maybe . . ." Neer, "Eric Clapton Testifies."

"We didn't want . . ." Steve Turner, *Conversations with Eric Clapton* (London: Abacus, 1976), p. 55.

"I had worked . . ." Chris Welch, *Cream: Strange Brew* (Surrey, England: Castle Communications, 1994), p. 116.

"It could have been . . ." Roberty, *New Visual Documentary*, p. 12.

"had a funny feeling . . ." John Hutchinson, "Eric Clapton: Farther up the Road," *Musician*, May 1982.

"He blew everybody's . . ." Turner, *Conversations*, p. 47.

"He bugs me . . ." Delehant, "Jack and Ginger Make Cream Work."

"He did everything . . ." Dan Forte, "Dominos Fall," *Guitar Player*, August 1976.

"I was still . . ." Turner, *Conversations*, p. 47.

"It . . . opened up . . ." Turner, *Conversations*, p. 56.

"I just kissed . . ." Harry Shapiro and Caesar Glebbeek, *Electric Gypsy* (NY: St. Martin's, 1992), p. 141.

"red hot": Turner, *Conversations*, p. 62.

"As a rule . . ." Ibid., p. 63.

"psychedelic hogwash": "In the Studio" radio program.

"They recorded at . . ." "Reflections on Eric Clapton," *Guitar Player*, July 1985.

"It was like . . ." Bill Graham and Robert Greenfield, *Bill Graham Presents* (NY: Doubleday, 1992), p. 215.

"the ultimate . . ." Ibid.

"Every little move . . ." and "there is less . . ." Jon Landau, "Eric Clapton," *Rolling Stone*, May 11, 1968.

"The beginning of the peak . . ." Nick Logan, "Jack Bruce: Thinking about the Future," *Hit Parader*, April 1969.

"taking a liberty" and "We leaped in . . ." Hutchinson, "Farther up the Road."

"Sometimes when we have . . ." Delehant, "Jack and Ginger Make Cream Work."

"The album got bogged . . ." Felix Pappalardi, "How Cream Made 'Wheels of Fire,'" *Hit Parader*, February 1969.

"Tom and Bill . . ." Ibid.

"Both Baker and Bruce . . ." "Blue Condition," *Newsweek*, March 19, 1968.

"The bone of contention . . ." Roeser, "Ginger Baker: Anyone for Polo?"

"I just experimented . . ." Turner, *Conversations*, p. 57.

"a master of . . ." and "Clapton's problem . . ." Jon Landau, "Cream," *Rolling Stone*, May 11, 1968.

"All during Cream . . ." Palmer, "Rolling Stone Interview."

"Once we'd got . . ." Turner, *Conversations*, p. 57.

5: Do What You Like

Epigraph: Fred Stuckey, "No More Blind Faith," *Guitar Player*, December 1970.

"I got hold . . ." Barbara Charone, "Please Take This Badge off of Me," *Crawdaddy*, November 1985.

"When I heard . . ." Dan Neer, "Eric Clapton Testifies," *Guitar*, June 1986.

"All rumors . . ." "Cream Separation Is Denied," *Rolling Stone*, July 6, 1968.

"It is simply . . ." Nick Logan, "Jack Bruce: Thinking about the Future," *Hit Parader*, April 1969.

"Cream is good . . ." Jann Wenner, "Records: Wheels of Fire," *Rolling Stone*, July 20, 1968. All citations in this passage are taken from this review.

"He wanted me . . ." Stuckey, "No More Blind Faith."

"We listened . . ." Marc Roberty, *Eric Clapton: The Complete Recording Sessions* (NY: St. Martin's, 1994), p. 39.

"I had to go . . ." John Pidgeon, "Eric Clapton: Return of the Reluctant Hero," *Creem*, April 1978.

"looked like characters . . ." Ibid.

"psychedelic loonies": Ibid.

"I was really . . ." Nick Logan, "Final Goodbye from The Cream," *Hit Parader*, July 1969.

"It was a great . . ." Ibid.

"That whole song . . ." Timothy White, *Rock Lives* (NY: Henry Holt, 1990), p. 164.

"We were writing . . ." Neer, "Eric Clapton Testifies."

"I've been on . . ." Steven Gaines, "Eric Clapton: The Inside Story of His Comeback with '461 Ocean Boulevard,'" *Circus Raves*, October 1974.

"All through Cream . . ." Dan Forte, "Out from Behind the Sun," *Guitar Player*, July 1985.

"With Cream . . ." Jeffrey Peisch, "Sittin' In with Eric Clapton: The Slowhand of God," *Record*, July 1985.

"the implication . . ." "Random Notes," *Rolling Stone*, March 1, 1969.

"I came offstage . . ." Steve Turner, *Conversations with Eric Clapton* (London: Abacus, 1976), p. 67.

"The show *was* . . ." White, *Rock Lives*, p. 251.

"No, man . . ." Robert Palmer, "The Rolling Stone Interview," *Rolling Stone*, June 20, 1985. All quotations in this passage are from this source.

"Can we pray . . ." Turner, *Conversations*, p. 94.

"I ran around . . ." Dan Neer, "Up Close with Eric Clapton," radio program, Neer Perfect Productions, 1992.

"I suppose . . ." Forte, "Out from Behind the Sun."

"The album stands . . ." White, *Rock Lives*, p. 251–52.

"I think it's . . ." David Fricke, "Eric Clapton: Still Living on Blues Power," *Rolling Stone*, August 24, 1988.

6: Why Does Love Got to Be So Sad?

Epigraph: J. D. Considine, "Clapton Is Not God," *Musician*, November 1986.

"There was a guy . . ." Robert Palmer, "Eric Clapton: The Rolling Stone Interview," *Rolling Stone*, June 20, 1985.

"It was the promoters . . ." Marc Roberty, *Eric Clapton: The New Visual Documentary* (London: Omnibus, 1990), p. 32.

"I joined Delaney's . . ." Peter Guralnick, "Eric Clapton at the Passion Threshold," *Musician*, February 1990.

"There is some . . ." "Random Notes," *Rolling Stone*, November 29, 1969.

"I just grabbed . . ." Timothy White, *Rock Lives* (NY: Henry Holt, 1990), p. 164.

"He was prepared . . ." David Fricke, "Eric Clapton: Still Living on Blues Power," *Rolling Stone*, August 24, 1988.

"He's such an enthusiastic . . ." Steve Turner, *Conversations with Eric Clapton* (London: Abacus, 1976), p. 70.

"I left the tapes . . ." Marc Roberty, *Eric Clapton: The Complete Recording Sessions* (NY: St. Martin's, 1994), p. 55.

"The other reason . . ." Dan Forte, "Dominos Fall," *Guitar Player*, August 1976.

"Hubert ended up . . ." Roberty, *Complete Recording Sessions*, p. 58.

"His attitude . . ." Guralnick, "Eric Clapton at Passion Threshold."

"The hardest confrontation . . ." John Hutchinson, "Farther up the Road," *Musician*, May 1982.

"It introduced . . ." Guralnick, "Eric Clapton at Passion Threshold."

"He took me down . . ." Alan Paul, "Of Wolf and Man," *Guitar Legends '94*.

"Take it, man . . ." Ibid.

"The basic concept . . ." Gene Santoro, "The Layla Sessions," liner notes for *The Layla Sessions: Twentieth Anniversary Edition* (Polidor, 847083-2).

"I went to Esher . . ." Ray Coleman, *Clapton!* (NY: Warner, 1987), p. 181.

7: Crossroads

Epigraph: Steve Turner, *Conversations with Eric Clapton* (London: Abacus, 1976), p. 86.

"I'm *dying* . . ." "Reflections on Eric Clapton," *Guitar Player*, July 1985.

"I just remember . . ." Turner, *Conversations*, p. 73.

"They had a barricade . . ." Gene Santoro, "The Layla Sessions," liner notes from *The Layla Sessions: Twentieth Anniversary Edition* (Polidor, 847083-2).

"It scared Duane . . ." "Reflections on Eric Clapton."

"When you get . . ." Dan Neer, "Eric Clapton Testifies," *Guitar*, June 1986.

"Get out . . ." "Reflections on Eric Clapton."

"He wrote the riff . . ." John Hutchinson, "Farther up the Road," *Musician*, May 1982.

"When I finished . . ." "Reflections on Eric Clapton."

"I'm as proud . . ." Ibid.

"We were dabbling . . ." Turner, *Conversations*, p. 83.

"He was in a box . . ." Harry Shapiro and Caesar Glebbeek, *Electric Gypsy* (NY: St. Martin's, 1992), p. 61.

"When Jimi died . . ." Robert Palmer, "Eric Clapton: The Rolling Stone Interview," *Rolling Stone*, June 20, 1985.

"Well, maybe not . . ." Turner, *Conversations*, p. 98. All quotations in this passage from this source.

"I was completely . . ." Donald E. Wilcock with Buddy Guy, *Damn Right I've Got the Blues* (San Francisco: Woodford, 1993), p. 93.

"I don't know . . ." David Fricke, "Eric Clapton: Still Living on Blues Power," *Rolling Stone*, August 24, 1988.

"Well, the Dixie . . ." James Henke, "Eric Clapton: The Rolling Stone Interview," *Rolling Stone*, October 17, 1991.

"There was no . . ." Fricke, "Still Living on Blues Power."

"I remember . . ." Palmer, "Rolling Stone Interview."

"When I first . . ." Ibid.

"All I learned . . ." *Musician*, February 1992.

"It wasn't me . . ." Turner, *Conversations*, p. 87.

"That whole show . . ." Timothy White, *Rock Lives* (NY: Henry Holt, 1990), p. 190.

"The John and Yoko . . ." "Random Notes," *Rolling Stone*, November 25, 1971.

"a kind of . . ." John Lennon and Yoko Ono to Eric Clapton, reprinted in Ray Coleman, *Clapton!* (NY: Warner, 1987), pp. 93–94.

"I was very . . ." "Eric Clapton Packs Rainbow in Triumphant Comeback Gig," *Rolling Stone*, March 1, 1973.

8: *Return of Slowhand*

Epigraph: Steve Turner, *Conversations with Eric Clapton* (London: Abacus, 1976), p. 95.

"It finally came . . ." Ibid., p. 88.

"I wasn't actually . . ." Barbara Charone, "Please Take This Badge Off of Me," *Crawdaddy*, November 1985.

"In this life . . ." Geoffrey Giuliano, *Dark Horse* (NY: Plume Books, 1991), p. 146.

"Robert Stigwood . . ." "Clapton Cutting LP in Miami," *Circus*, August 1974.

"At press time . . ." Ibid.

"I just wanted . . ." Frank Rose, "Eric Clapton: Happy at Last, with Patti and Reggae in Jamaica," *Circus*, June 1975.

"That's why . . ." "Reflections on Eric Clapton," *Guitar Player*, July 1985.

"I didn't think . . ." Robert Palmer, "Eric Clapton: The Rolling Stone Interview," *Rolling Stone*, June 20, 1985.

"He was just . . ." Timothy White, *Rock Lives* (NY: Henry Holt, 1990), p. 310.

"Eric Clapton is . . ." "Eric Clapton in US: Something's Happening Here," *Rolling Stone*, May 23, 1974.

"Without a doubt . . ." Janis Schacht, "Record Reviews," *Circus*, November 1974.

"Between laid-back . . ." Ken Emerson, "The Sound of Slow-Hand Clapton," *Rolling Stone*, August 29, 1974.

"probably the truest . . ." *Circus Raves*, October 1974.

"His singing . . ." Alan Rosoff, "Clapton Lays Back," *Crawdaddy*, October 1974.

"Clapton's voice . . ." Arthur Levy, "Clapton at the Crossroads: Why *Does* Love Got to Be So Sad?" *Zoo World*, September 26, 1974.

"silliness": Chris Charlesworth, "Electric, Clapton!" *Melody Maker*, July 6, 1974.

"That tour . . ." Rose, "Eric Clapton: Happy at Last."

"I'm friends . . ." "Random Notes," *Rolling Stone*, December 5, 1974.

"I wanted . . ." Charone, "Please Take This Badge."

"no growth . . ." Bud Scoppa, "There's One in Every Crowd," *Rolling Stone*, May 22, 1975.

9: *Further on up the Road*

Epigraph: David Mead, "Eric Clapton," *Guitarist*, June 1994.

"Eric's sitting . . ." Frank Rose, "Eric Clapton: The Comeback That Just Won't Quit," *Circus*, October 1975.

"It was too quick . . ." Steve Turner, *Conversations with Eric Clapton* (London: Abacus, 1976), p. 17.

"We did a show . . ." "Reflections on Eric Clapton," *Guitar Player*, June 1985.

"Erratic performances . . ." Barbara Charone, "Please Take This Badge Off of Me," *Crawdaddy*, November 1985.

"George Terry . . ." Steve Lake, "Southern Fried Clapton," *Melody Maker*, June 26, 1975.

"He doesn't *owe* . . ." Charone, "Please Take This Badge."

"a triumph . . ." Wayne Robins, "Records: *E.C. Was Here*," *Creem*, November 1975.

"Clapton sings . . ." Jean-Charles Costa, "Clapton's Back: Fluid Phrasings, Basic Blues," *Rolling Stone*, October 9, 1975.

"What's happened . . ." "Random Notes," *Rolling Stone*, September 11, 1975.

"There were a lot . . ." Charone, "Please Take This Badge."

"used it as a clubhouse . . ." Levon Helm with Stephen Davis, *This Wheel's on Fire: Levon Helm and the Story of the Band* (NY: William Morrow, 1993), p. 245.

"One of the reviews . . ." John Pidgeon, "Eric Clapton: Return of the Reluctant Hero," *Creem*, April 1978.

"He came down . . ." Ibid.

"There's little here . . ." Kevin Doyle, "Eric Clapton: No Reason to Cry," *Creem*, January 1977.

"This riskless . . ." Dave Marsh, "Clapton Takes a Slide," *Rolling Stone*, November 18, 1976.

"What started it . . ." Pidgeon, "Return of Reluctant Hero."

"one foreigner . . ." "Letters," *Sounds*, September 1976.

"It still lives . . ." Pidgeon, "Return of Reluctant Hero."

"I also question . . ." J. D. Considine, "Clapton Is Not God," *Musician*, November 1986.

"Every now and then . . ." Marc Roberty, *Eric Clapton in His Own Words* (London: Omnibus, 1993), p. 40.

"He was just . . ." Bill Graham and Robert Greenfield, *Bill Graham Presents* (NY: Doubleday, 1992), p. 391.

"That show . . ." Ray Coleman, *Clapton!* (NY: Warner, 1987), p. 244.

"really lightweight": Marc Roberty, *Eric Clapton: The Complete Recording Sessions* (NY: St. Martin's, 1994), p. 103.

"The only people . . ." Michael Davis, "Records: Eric Clapton—Slowhand," *Creem*, February 1978.

"a few good . . ." John Swanson, "Slowhand—Eric Clapton," *Rolling Stone*, December 29, 1977.

"It is the only . . ." Marc Roberty, *Eric Clapton: The New Visual Documentary* (London: Omnibus, 1990), p. 63.

"It was all . . ." Ibid.

10: The Shape You're In

Epigraph: Robert Palmer, "Eric Clapton: The Rolling Stone Interview," *Rolling Stone*, June 20, 1985.

"in order . . ." Steve Turner, *Conversations with Eric Clapton* (London: Abacus, 1976), p. 27.

"Ten thousand quid . . ." Ray Coleman, *Clapton!* (NY: Warner, 1987), p. 199.

"I love . . ." Peter Guralnick, "Eric Clapton at the Passion Threshold," *Musician*, February 1990.

"I think . . ." J. D. Considine, "Clapton Is Not God," *Musician*, November 1986.

"I hold myself . . ." Marc Roberty, *Eric Clapton in His Own Words* (London: Omnibus, 1993), p. 43.

"Anywhere else . . ." Marc Roberty, *Eric Clapton: The New Visual Documentary* (London: Omnibus, 1990), p. 73.

"How could I play . . ." Coleman, *Clapton!*, p. 2.

"As an artist . . ." John Piccarella, "Eric Clapton with a Bullet," *Rolling Stone*, June 23, 1981.

"My mind . . ." Considine, "Clapton Is Not God."

"It was the first . . ." Ibid.

"That was . . ." Timothy White, *Rock Lives* (NY: Henry Holt, 1990), p. 305.

"Whenever I get . . ." John Hutchinson, "Farther up the Road," *Musician*, May 1982.

"The thrill . . ." Palmer, "The Rolling Stone Interview."

"If one focuses . . ." Tom Wheeler, "Money and Cigarettes," *Guitar Player*, July 1985.

11: Behind the Sun

Epigraph: Marc Roberty, *Eric Clapton in His Own Words* (London: Omnibus, 1993), p. 50.

"the music of . . ." Marc Roberty, *Eric Clapton: The New Visual Documentary* (London: Omnibus, 1990), p. 80.

"When I saw . . ." Kurt Loder and Michael Goldberg, "Rock of Ages: Ronnie Lane & Co.," *Rolling Stone*, January 19, 1984.

"After the Albert . . ." Ibid.

"I heard the way . . ." Jeffrey Peisch, "Sittin' In with Eric Clapton: The Slowhand of God," *Record*, July 1985.

"Eric's last couple . . ." Marc Roberty, *Eric Clapton: The Complete Recording Sessions* (NY: St. Martin's, 1994), p. 122.

"It really was . . ." Peisch, "Sittin' In with Eric Clapton."

"It really did . . ." Ibid.

"It was fun . . ." Dan Forte, "Out from Behind the Sun," *Guitar Player*, July 1985.

"It was very . . ." Ibid.

"We found out . . ." Peisch, "Sittin' In with Eric Clapton."

"Here was rock's . . ." Jonathan Gregg, "On Stage: E.C. Returns to Form," *Record*, July 1985.

"It was more . . ." "Paternity suits him fine, but Eric Clapton's baby makes four and his marriage ends," *People*, December 1, 1986.

"my mortality . . ." Roberty, *In His Own Words*, p. 50.

"They were . . ." Dan Neer, "Up Close with Eric Clapton," radio program.

"the holy madman": Timothy White, *Rock Lives* (NY: Henry Holt, 1990), p. 308.

"People will say . . ." David Fricke, "Eric Clapton: The Rolling Stone Interview," *Rolling Stone*, August 25, 1988.

"I sat . . ." Roberty, *In His Own Words*, p. 71.

12: Journeyman

Epigraph: Marc Roberty, *Eric Clapton in His Own Words* (London: Omnibus, 1993), p. 91.

"This new lp . . ." Lydia Carole De Fretos, "A Strong Comeback from One of Rock's Forefathers," *East Coast Rocker*, December 10, 1986.

"Clapton's best . . ." Ibid.

"Chuck appeared . . ." Roberty, *In His Own Words*, p. 75.

"I still love . . ." Ibid.

"You're reflecting . . ." Dan Forte, "Just Another Crossroads," *Guitar Player*, July 1988.

"I like to have . . ." Dan Forte, "Dominos Fall," *Guitar Player*, August 1976.

"That sort of thing . . ." Dan Forte, "Tribute to Slowhand," *Guitar Player*, September 1989.

"What comes across . . ." Steven Simels, "A Portrait of Eric Clapton," *Stereo Review*, July 1988.

"the ultimate . . ." Vic Garbarini, "Crossroads," *Playboy*, June 1988.

"a rich . . ." David Fricke, "The Best of God," *Rolling Stone*, April 21, 1988.

"You know what . . ." Forte, "Just Another Crossroads."

"I don't *really* . . ." Joe Jackson, "Heartbreaks and Blessings," *Musician*, February 1992.

"I knew . . ." "Cream Reunion: A Heaping 'Spoonful,'" *Rolling Stone*, December 1, 1988.

"If we got . . ." James Henke, "Eric Clapton: The Rolling Stone Interview," *Rolling Stone*, October 17, 1991.

"I wouldn't select . . ." Forte, "Tribute to Slowhand."

"We're all lonely . . ." Peter Guralnick, "Eric Clapton at the Passion Threshold," *Musician*, February 1990.

"A lot of people . . ." Ibid.

"I methodically thought . . ." Forte, "Tribute to Slowhand."

"That's something . . ." Timothy White, *Rock Lives* (NY: Henry Holt, 1990), p. 300.

"The journeyman . . ." J. D. Considine, "Journeyman," *Rolling Stone,* November 30, 1989.

"Clapton's strongest . . ." Andrew Abrahams, "Picks & Pans: Journeyman," *People,* January 8, 1990.

"It was a great . . ." Forte, "Tribute to Slowhand."

"The black guys . . ." Ibid.

13: Tears in Heaven

Epigraph: James Henke, "Eric Clapton: The Rolling Stone Interview," *Rolling Stone,* October 17, 1991.

"I am a very . . ." Robert Sandall, "The House of God," *Rolling Stone,* March 22, 1990.

"With Robert Cray . . ." Donald E. Wilcock with Buddy Guy, *Damn Right I've Got the Blues* (San Francisco: Woodford, 1993), p. 119.

"All in all . . ." Mikal Gilmore, "Blues Summit: The Fateful Weekend," *Rolling Stone,* October 4, 1990.

"I had a meeting . . ." Henke, "Rolling Stone Interview."

"Clapton has always . . ." Josef Woodard, "24 Nights," *Rolling Stone,* October 31, 1991.

"The trouble with . . ." Vic Garbarini, "Music," *Playboy,* February 1992.

"We recorded . . ." Henke, "Rolling Stone Interview."

"I didn't believe . . ." Ibid.

"turned to stone": Steve Dougherty, "Eric Clapton," *People,* March 1, 1993.

"I wanted to get . . ." Henke, "Rolling Stone Interview."

"spirit, intelligence, and courage": "In an English Country Churchyard, Eric Clapton and Friends Mourn the Death of His Son, Conor, 4," *People,* April 19, 1991.

"When you experience . . ." Joe Jackson, "Heartbreaks and Blessings," *Musician,* February 1992.

"I only compose . . ." Ibid.

"Where do you . . ." Ibid.

"The album . . ." Ibid.

"It's awfully . . ." Charles Leerhsen, "His Saddest Song," *Newsweek,* March 23, 1992.

"I needed . . ." Alex Coletti, "Amazing Grace," *Guitar World,* June 1993.

"The main thing . . ." Michael Goldberg, "Harrison, Clapton Plan Tour of Japan," *Rolling Stone,* September 5, 1991.

"It is a pleasure . . ." Parke Puterbaugh, "Wrap Up," *Rolling Stone,* August 6, 1992.

"When you're onstage . . ." Coletti, "Amazing Grace."

"I've done it . . ." Ibid.

"very moved . . ." Edna Gundersen, "Grammy 'Heaven' for Eric Clapton," *USA Today*, February 25, 1993.

"If I have . . ." Dan Forte, "Tribute to Slowhand," *Guitar Player*, September 1989.

"I think . . ." J. D. Considine, "Eric Clapton Is Not God," *Musician*, November 1986.

14: Pilgrim

Epigraph: Mike Baker, "Eric Clapton: My Long Overdue Testament to the Blues," *Guitar Player*, November 1994.

"Things keep happening . . ." Peter Guralnick, "Eric Clapton at the Passion Threshold," *Musician*, February 1990.

"It's a wonderful . . ." Baker, "My Long Overdue Testament."

"Stellar guitar playing . . ." Dave Tianen, "Clapton Circles Back to Blues," *Milwaukee Sentinel*, September 18, 1994.

"Despite Clapton's obvious feel . . ." Greg Kot, "From Safe to Sorry," *Chicago Tribune*, September 16, 1994.

"a ringing tribute . . ." David Hiltbrand, "Eric Clapton's Nothing But the Blues," *People*, May 15, 1995.

"a seamless blend . . ." David Browne, "Phenomenon," *Entertainment Weekly*, July 26, 1996.

"Clapton or not . . ." Jon Andrews, "Retail Therapy," *Down Beat*, July 1997.

"easily Clapton's most . . ." David Wild, "A Deeper Shade of Blue," *Rolling Stone*, March 19, 1998.

"Unbearable loss . . ." Steve Dougherty, "Pilgrim," *People*, March 14, 1998.

"a compromised, blues-tinged . . ." "guts," and "so polished . . ." Christopher John Farley, "A Bad Case of the Aquas," *Time*, March 30, 1998.

"This is 1998 . . ." Daniel Rubin, "Eric Clapton Song with Violent Lyrics Sparks Outcry from Some Quarters," *Philadelphia Inquirer*, April 15, 1998. All other citations in the passage are from this source.

"almost worth . . ." Farley, "Bad Case of Aquas."

"This desire to play . . ." n.a., "Clapton Relieved with News of Dad," *Vancouver Province*, March 30, 1998.

"would sneak and pretend . . ." Michael Woloschuk, "'Please Help Our Brother, Eric,'" *Vancouver Province*, April 1, 1998.

"I just want . . ." Michael Woloschuk, "Family Learns of Link to Clapton," *Calgary Herald*, March 26, 1998.

"He can do more . . ." Woloschuk, " 'Please Save Our Brother.' "

"I've got three . . ." Belinda Luscombe, "He Is Heavy, He's My Half Brother," *Time*, April 20,1998.

"I don't know . . ." n.a., "Clapton Relieved."

15: Riding with the King

"I'll be an addict . . ." Harvey Solomon, "A More Mellow Clapton Comes to Crossroads," *Boston Globe*, October 28, 1998.

"I thought that I'd achieved . . ." Jan Moir, "Clapton Comes Clean," *Chicago Sun-Times*, December 29, 1998.

"Antigua was becoming . . ." Ibid.

"Clapton taps . . ." Anthony DeCurtis, "Clapton in Blue," *Rolling Stone*, August 19, 1999.

"At the time . . ." David Fricke, "Clapton at the End of the Highway," *Rolling Stone*, June 21, 2001.

"I hear the fire . . ." Richard Johnson, "Eric Clapton's Golden Age," *Rolling Stone*, April 12, 2001.

"I'm just a messenger . . ." Anthony Bozza, "Clapton, Raitt, Taylor Lead Hall of Fame Class of 2000," *Rolling Stone*, April 13, 2000.

"About two years ago . . ." Anthony DeCurtis, "Q&A: B.B. King," *Rolling Stone*, September 14, 2000.

"I wondered . . ." Melinda Newman, "Bluesmen Eric Clapton, B.B. King Join Forces on Duck/Reprise Album," *Billboard*, June 3, 2000.

"As I get into my old age . . ." Fricke, "Clapton at the End of the Highway."

"A lot of the songs . . ." Newman, "Bluesmen Eric Clapton, B.B. King."

"With Eric and his band . . ." Darrin Fox, "Alan Douglas on Recording *Reptile*, *Guitar Player*, June 2001.

"A lot of the time . . ." Darrin Fox, "Right Here Right Now," *Guitar Player*, June 2001.

"short on protracted . . ." David Fricke, "A Pair of Kings," *Rolling Stone*, July 6, 2000.

"As celebrity summits go . . ." Ibid.

"I realize now . . ." Eric Clapton, Liner Notes to *Reptile*.

"Pilgrim was an unloading . . ." Richard Johnson, "Eric Clapton's Golden Age."

"if only Clapton . . ." Michael Paoletta, "Albums: Pop," *Billboard*, March 24, 2001.

"yet another version . . ." Will Hermes, "E.C. Listening," *Entertainment Weekly*, March 16, 2001.

"Over the course . . ." Anthony DeCurtis, "Eric Clapton's Many Moods," *Rolling Stone*, March 19, 2001.

"too safe, too sedate . . ." Kerry Gold, "Clapton Too Safe, Too Sedate for Rock 'n' Roll Fans," *Vancouver Sun*, Sugust 7, 2001.

"The tiring thing . . ." Fox, "Right Here Right Now."

"The live thing . . ." Emily Fasten, "Journeyman No More: Eric Clapton," *Guitar Player*, October 2001.

"We've yearned . . ." Paul Cole, "Cropped Hair and Loafers! But Eric is Still Sheer Class," (Birmingham) *Evening Mail*, October 16, 1998.

"Even the most besotted . . ." n.a., "Clapton Gives Us the Blues," (London) *Guardian*, October 17, 1998.

"The physical price . . ." Fox, "Right Here Right Now."

"It was like . . ." n.a., "Double Feature," *People*, January 21, 2002.

Selected Discography
1964–2002

Over the years, the songs of Eric Clapton have been packaged and re-packaged so many times that it is virtually impossible—and unnecessary—to present a complete listing. The following represents Clapton's singles and albums officially issued in the United States and Great Britain, as well as a large selection of official compilations and bootlegs. Clapton's work as a guest or sessions artist is also listed, with the titles of the tracks on which he appeared.

Yardbirds

SINGLES

Great Britain:

"I Wish You Would"/"A Certain Girl" (1964).
"Good Morning Little Schoolgirl"/"I Ain't Got You" (1964).
"For Your Love"/"Got to Hurry" (1965).

United States:

"I Wish You Would"/"A Certain Girl" (1964).
"For Your Love"/"Heart Full of Soul" (1966). (EC does *not* play on "Heart Full of Soul.")

ALBUMS

Great Britain:

Five Live Yardbirds (1964). "Too Much Monkey Business"/"I Got Love If You Want It"/"Smokestack Lightning"/"Good Morning Little Schoolgirl"/"Respectable"/"Five Long Years"/"Pretty Girl"/ "Louise"/"I'm a Man"/"Here 'Tis."

Sonny Boy Williamson and the Yardbirds (1965). "Bye Bye Bird"/"Mister Downchild"/"23 Hours Too Long"/"Out on the Water Coast"/"Baby Don't Worry"/"Pontiac Blues"/"Take It Easy Baby"/"I Don't Care No More"/"Do the Weston" (entitled "Western Arizona" on subsequent releases).

United States:

For Your Love (1965). EC plays on six of the album's ten cuts: "For Your Love"/"I Ain't Got You"/"Got to Hurry"/"I Wish You Would"/ "A Certain Girl"/"Good Morning Little Schoolgirl.

Having a Rave Up with the Yardbirds (1966). EC plays on three cuts, taken from *Five Live Yardbirds*: "Smokestack Lightning"/ "Respectable"/"Here 'Tis."

Yardbirds' Greatest Hits (1967). EC plays on two cuts: "For Your Love"/ "Smokestack Lightning."

ANTHOLOGIES

The Yardbirds, Volume 1: Smokestack Lightning (1991). EC plays on the following cuts: "For Your Love"/"I'm Not Talking"/"Putty (in Your Hands)"/"I Ain't Got You"/"Got to Hurry"/"I Ain't Done Wrong"/"I Wish You Would"/"A Certain Girl"/"Sweet Music"/ "Good Morning Little Schoolgirl"/"Good Morning Little Schoolgirl"

(live)/"I'm Talking about You"/"Got to Hurry" (alternative take)/
"Smokestack Lightning" (live)/"Respectable" (live)/"I'm a Man" (live)/
"Here 'Tis" (live)/"Boom Boom"/"Honey in Your Hips"/"I Wish You
Would" (live).

The Yardbirds, Volume 2: Blues, Backtracks and Shapes of Things (1991).
EC plays on the following cuts: "Smokestack Lightning"/"Let It
Rock"/"Honey in Your Hips"/"I Wish You Would"/"You Can't Judge
a Book by the Cover"/"I'm Talking about You"/"Bye Bye Bird"
(live, with Sonny Boy Williamson)/"Mr. Downchild" (live, with SBW)/
"The River Rhine" (live, with SBW)/"Twenty-three Hours Too
Long" (live, with SBW)/"A Lost Care" (live, with SBW)/"Pontiac
Blues" (live, with SBW)/"Take It Easy Baby" (live, with SBW)/
"Out on Water Coast" (live, with SBW)/"I Don't Care No More"
(live, with SBW)/"Western Arizona" (live, with SBW)/"Boom
Boom"/"Good Morning Little Schoolgirl"/"Good Morning Little
Schoolgirl" (backing track)/"Too Much Monkey Business" (live)/
"Got Love If You Want It" (live)/"Five Long Years" (live)/"Pretty
Girl" (live)/"Louise" (live).

John Mayall/John Mayall and the Bluesbreakers

SINGLES

"I'm Your Witchdoctor"/"Telephone Blues" (1965).
"Lonely Years"/"Bernard Jenkins" (1966).

ALBUMS

John Mayall's Bluesbreakers with Eric Clapton (1966). "All Your Love"/
"Hideaway"/"Little Girl"/"Another Man"/"Double Crossing
Time"/"What'd I Say"/"Key to Love"/"Parchman Farm"/"Have You
Heard"/"Ramblin' on My Mind"/"Steppin' Out"/"It Ain't Right."

Looking Back (1969). A Mayall compilation. EC plays on one cut: "They Call It Stormy Monday."

Back to the Roots (1971). EC plays on six cuts: "Prisons on the Road"/ "Accidental Suicide"/"Home Again"/"Looking at Tomorrow"/ "Force of Nature"/"Goodbye December."

Primal Solos (1983). A live album, on which EC plays on five cuts: "Maudie"/"It Hurts to Be in Love"/"Have You Ever Loved a Woman?"/ "Bye Bye Bird"/"I'm Your Hoochie Coochie Man."

Miscellaneous

What's Shakin? (1966). Three EC tracks with the Powerhouse (EC, Jack Bruce, Steve Winwood, Paul Jones, and Pete York): "I Want to Know"/"Crossroads"/"Steppin' Out."

Blues Anytime Vol. 1 (1968). EC plays on five cuts: "Snake Drive"/ "Tribute to Elmore"/"West Coast Idea" (recorded with Jimmy Page, Mick Jagger, Bill Wyman, Ian Stewart, and Chris Winters), and "I'm Your Witchdoctor"/"Telephone Blues" (his single with John Mayall and the Bluesbreakers).

Blues Anytime Vol. 2 (1968). EC plays on four cuts: "Draggin' My Tail"/ "Freight Loader"/"Choker" (from the same Jimmy Page–produced sessions noted above), and "On Top of the World" (recorded with John Mayall and the Bluesbreakers).

Blues Anytime Vol. 3 (1968). EC plays on one cut, from the Jimmy Page–produced sessions: "Miles Road."

White Boy Blues (1987). A compilation of early British blues tracks, featuring EC performances with John Mayall and the Bluesbreakers and EC's studio sessions with Jimmy Page. EC plays on the following cuts: "Snake Drive"/"West Coast Idea"/"Choker"/"I'm Your Witchdoctor"/

"Tribute to Elmore"/"Freight Loader"/"Miles Road"/"Telephone Blues"/"Draggin' My Tail."

Cream

SINGLES

"Wrapping Paper"/"Cat's Squirrel" (1966).

"I Feel Free"/"NSU" (1966).

"Strange Brew"/"Tales of Brave Ulysses" (1967).

"Anyone for Tennis?"/"Pressed Rat and Warthog" (1968).

"Sunshine of Your Love"/"SWLABR" (1968).

"White Room"/"Those Were the Days" (1969).

"Badge"/"What a Bringdown" (1969).

"Crossroads"/"Passing the Time" (1969, U.S. only).

ALBUMS

Fresh Cream (British version) (1966). "NSU"/"Sleepy Time Time"/ "Dreaming"/"Sweet Wine"/"Spoonful"/"Cat's Squirrel"/"Four Until Late"/"Rollin' and Tumblin' "/"I'm So Glad"/"Toad."

Fresh Cream (American version) (1966). "I Feel Free"/"NSU"/"Sleepy Time Time"/"Dreaming"/"Sweet Wine"/"Cat's Squirrel"/"Four Until Late"/"Rollin' and Tumblin' "/"I'm So Glad"/"Toad." (CD bonus tracks include "The Coffee Song" and "Wrapping Paper.")

Disraeli Gears (1967). "Strange Brew"/"Sunshine of Your Love"/ "World of Pain"/"Dance the Night Away"/"Blue Condition"/

"Tales of Brave Ulysses"/"SWLABR"/"We're Going Wrong"/
"Outside Woman Blues"/"Take It Back"/"Mother's Lament."

Wheels of Fire (1968). "White Room"/"Sitting on Top of the World"/
"Passing the Time"/"As You Said"/"Pressed Rat and Warthog"/
"Politician"/"Those Were the Days"/"Born under a Bad Sign"/
"Deserted Cities of the Heart"/"Crossroads"/"Spoonful"/
"Traintime"/"Toad."

Goodbye (1969). "I'm So Glad"/"Politician""Sitting on Top of the
World"/"Badge"/"Doing That Scrapyard Thing"/"What a Bringdown."
(CD includes "Anyone for Tennis?" as bonus track.)

Best of Cream (1969). "Sunshine of Your Love"/"Badge"/
"Crossroads"/"White Room"/"SWLABR"/"Born under a Bad
Sign"/"Spoonful"/"Tales of Brave Ulysses"/"Strange Brew"/"I Feel
Free."

Live Cream (1970). "NSU"/"Sleepy Time Time"/"Hey Lawdy
Mama"/"Sweet Wine"/"Rollin' and Tumblin.'"

Live Cream Vol. II (1972). "Deserted Cities of the Heart"/"White
Room"/"Politician"/"Tales of Brave Ulysses"/"Sunshine of Your
Love"/"Steppin' Out."

Strange Brew: The Very Best of Cream (1983). "Badge"/"Sunshine of
Your Love"/"Crossroads"/"White Room"/"Born under a Bad Sign"/
"SWLABR"/"Strange Brew"/"Anyone for Tennis?"/"I Feel Free"/
"Politician"/"Tales of Brave Ulysses"/"Spoonful."

Those Were the Days (1997). "Wrapping Paper" (in the studio) "I Feel
Free" (in the studio)/"NSU" (in the studio)/"Sleepy Time Time"
(in the studio)/"Dreaming" (in the studio)/"Sweet Wine" (in the
studio)/"Spoonful" (in the studio)/"Cat's Squirrel" (in the studio)/
"Four Until Late" (in the studio)/"Rollin' and Tumblin' " (in the
studio)/ "I'm So Glad" (in the studio)/ "Toad" (in the studio)/

"Lawdy Mama" (version 1) (take)/"Strange Brew" (in the studio)/
"Sunshine of Your Love" (in the studio)/"World of Pain" (in the studio)/
"Dance the Night Away" (in the studio)/"Blue Condition" (in the
studio)/"Tales of Brave Ulysses" (in the studio)/"SWLABR" (in the
studio)/ "We're Going Wrong" (in the studio)/"Outside Woman Blues"
(in the studio)/"Take It Back" (in the studio)/"Mother's Lament" (in the
studio) "White Room" (in the studio)/"Sitting on Top of the World" (in
the studio)/"Passing the Time" (alternate version) (take)/"As You Said"
(in the studio)/"Pressed Rat and Warthog" (in the studio)/"Politician" (in
the studio)/"Those Were the Days" (in the studio)/"Born Under a Bad
Sign" (in the studio)/"Deserted Cities of the Heart" (in the
studio)/"Anyone for Tennis?" (in the studio)/"Badge" (in the
studio)/"Doing That Scrapyard Thing" (in the studio)/"What a
Bringdown" (in the studio)/"The Coffee Song" (in the studio)/"Lawdy
Mama" (version 2) (take)/"You Make Me Feel" (in the studio) (demo
version)/"We're Going Wrong" (in the studio) (demo version)/"Hey
Now Princess" (in the studio) (demo version)/"SWLABR" (in the
studio) (demo version)/"Weird of Hermiston" (in the studio) (demo
version)/"Clearout" (in the studio) (demo version)/"Falstaff Beer
Commercial" (in the studio) N.S.U. (live) "Sleepy Time Time"
(live)/"Rollin' and Tumblin' " (live)/"Crossroads" (live)/"Spoonful"
(live)/"Tales of Brave Ulysses" (live)/"Sunshine of Your Love"
(live)/"Sweet Wine" (live) "White Room" (live)"Politician" (live)/"I'm So
Glad" (live)/"Sitting on Top of the World" (live)/"Steppin' Out"
(live)/"Train Time" (live)/"Toad" (live)/"Deserted Cities of the Heart"
(live)/"Sunshine of Your Love" (live)

Blind Faith

Blind Faith (1969). "Had to Cry Today"/"Can't Find My Way Home"/
"Well All Right"/"Presence of the Lord"/"Sea of Joy"/"Do What
You Like."

Delaney and Bonnie

SINGLE

"Comin' Home"/"Groupie (Superstar)" (1969).

ALBUM

On Tour with Eric Clapton (1970). "Things Get Better"/"Poor Elijah—Tribute to Johnson (Medley)"/"Only You Know and I Know"/"I Don't Want to Discuss It"/"That's What My Man Is For"/"Where There's a Will, There's a Way"/"Coming Home"/"Little Richard Medley."

Derek and the Dominos

SINGLES

"Tell the Truth"/"Roll It Over" (1970). This single was withdrawn almost as soon as it was released.

"Layla"/"Bell Bottom Blues" (1970). Reissued in 1972.

"Why Does Love Got to Be So Sad?" (live)/"Presence of the Lord" (live) (1973).

ALBUMS

Layla and Other Assorted Love Songs (1970). "I Looked Away"/"Bell Bottom Blues"/"Keep on Growing"/"Nobody Knows You When You're Down and Out"/"I Am Yours"/"Anyday"/"Key to the Highway"/"Tell the Truth"/"Why Does Love Got to Be So Sad?"/"Have You Ever Loved a Woman?"/"Little Wing"/"It's Too Late"/"Layla"/"Thorn Tree in the Garden."

Live in Concert (1973). "Why Does Love Got to Be So Sad?"/"Got to Get Better in a Little While"/"Let It Rain"/"Presence of the Lord"/"Tell the Truth"/"Bottle of Red Wine"/"Roll It Over"/"Blues Power"/"Have You Ever Loved a Woman?"

The Layla Sessions—Twentieth Anniversary Edition (1990). "I Looked Away"/"Bell Bottom Blues"/"Keep on Growing"/"Nobody Knows You When You're Down and Out"/"I Am Yours"/"Anyday"/"Key to the Highway"/"Tell the Truth"/"Why Does Love Got to Be So Sad?"/"Have You Ever Loved a Woman?"/"Little Wing"/"It's Too Late"/"Layla"/"Thorn Tree in the Garden"/"Jam I"/"Jam II"/"Jam III"/"Jam IV"/"Jam V"/"Have You Ever Loved a Woman?" (alternate master #1)/"Have You Ever Loved a Woman?" (alternate master #2)/"Tell the Truth" (jam #1)/"Tell the Truth" (jam #2)/"Mean Old World" (rehearsal)/"Mean Old World" (band version, master take)/"Mean Old World" (duet version, master take)/"(When Things Go Wrong) It Hurts Me Too" (jam)/"Tender Love" (incomplete master)/"It's Too Late" (alternate master).

Live at the Fillmore (1994). "Got to Get Better in a Little While"/"Why Does Love Got to Be So Sad?"/"Key to the Highway"/"Blues Power"/"Have You Ever Loved a Woman?"/"Bottle of Red Wine"/"Tell the Truth"/"Nobody Knows You When You're Down and Out"/"Roll It Over"/"Presence of the Lord"/"Little Wing"/"Let It Rain"/"Crossroads."

EC as Solo Artist

SINGLES

"After Midnight"/"Easy Now" (1970).
"I Shot the Sheriff"/"Give Me Strength" (1974).
"Willie and the Hand Jive"/"Mainline Florida" (1974).

"Swing Low Sweet Chariot"/"Pretty Blue Eyes" (1975).

"Knockin' on Heaven's Door"/"Someone Like You" (1975).

"Hello Old Friend"/"All Our Past Times" (1976).

"Carnival"/"Hungry" (1977).

"Lay Down Sally"/"Cocaine" (1977).

"Wonderful Tonight"/"Peaches and Diesel" (1978).

"Promises"/"Watch Out for Lucy" (1978).

"If I Don't Be There by Morning"/"Tulsa Time" (1979).

"I Can't Stand It"/"Black Rose" (1981).

"Another Ticket"/"Rita Mae" (1981).

"Layla"/"Wonderful Tonight" (live) (1982).

"I Shot the Sheriff"/"Cocaine" (1982). (12-inch includes live version of "Knockin' on Heaven's Door.")

"I've Got a Rock and Roll Heart"/"Man in Love" (1983). (12-inch includes "Everybody Oughta Make a Change.")

"The Shape You're In"/"Crosscut Saw" (1983). (12-inch includes "Pretty Girl.")

"Slow Down Linda"/"Crazy Country Hop" (1983).

"Wonderful Tonight"/"Cocaine" (1984).

"You Don't Know Like I Know"/"Knock on Wood" (Australia only) (1984).

"Edge of Darkness"/"Shoot Out" (UK only) (12-inch includes "Obituary," "Escape from Northmoor," "Oxford Circus," and "Northmoor.") (1985).

"Forever Man"/"Too Bad" (1985). (12-inch includes "Something's Happening.")

"She's Waiting"/"Jailbait" (1985).

"Behind the Mask"/"Grand Illusion" (1987). (12-inch includes "Wanna Make Love to You.")

"It's in the Way That You Use It"/"Bad Influence" (1987). (12-inch includes "Same Old Blues" and "Pretty Girl.")

"Tearing Us Apart"/"Hold On" (1987). (12-inch includes live version of "Run.")

"Wonderful Tonight"/"Layla" (1987). (12-inch includes "I Shot the Sheriff" and live version of "Wonderful Tonight.")

"Holy Mother"/"Tangled in Love" (1987). (12-inch includes "Forever Man" and "Behind the Mask.")

"After Midnight" (commercial version)/"I Can't Stand It" (1988). (12-inch includes "Whatcha Gonna Do"; CD single includes "Whatcha Gonna Do" and live version of "Sunshine of Your Love.")

"Bad Love"/"Before You Accuse Me" (1989). (12-inch and CD single include live versions of "Badge" and "Let It Rain.")

"No Alibis"/"Running on Faith" (1990). (12-inch and CD single include live version of "Behind the Mask.")

"Pretending"/"Hard Times" (1990). (12-inch includes "Knock on Wood"; CD single includes "Behind the Sun.")

"Wonderful Tonight" (live)/"Edge of Darkness" (live) (1991). (CD single includes live versions of "Layla Intro" and "Cocaine"; limited edition CD single includes live versions of "I Shot the Sheriff " and "No Alibis.")

"Tears in Heaven"/"White Room" (live) (1992). (12-inch and CD single include "Tracks and Lines" and live version of "Bad Love.")

"Layla" (live)/"Tears in Heaven" (live) (1992). (CD single includes excerpts from MTV interview.)

"Motherless Child"/"Driftin'" (1994). (CD single includes live version of "County Jail" and "32-20.")

ALBUMS

Eric Clapton (1970). "Slunky"/"Bad Boy"/"Lonesome and a Long Way from Home"/"After Midnight"/"Easy Now"/"Blues Power"/"Bottle of Red Wine"/"Lovin' You Lovin' Me"/"Told You for the Last Time"/"Don't Know Why"/"Let It Rain."

Eric Clapton's Rainbow Concert (1973). "Badge"/"Roll It Over"/"Presence of the Lord"/"Pearly Queen"/"After Midnight"/"Little Wing."

461 Ocean Boulevard (1974). "Motherless Children"/"Better Make It Through Today"/"Willie and the Hand Jive"/"Get Ready"/"I Shot the Sheriff"/"I Can't Hold Out"/"Please Be with Me"/"Let It Grow"/"Steady Rollin' Man"/"Mainline Florida"/"Give Me Strength."

There's One in Every Crowd (1975). "We've Been Told (Jesus Coming Soon)"/"Swing Low Sweet Chariot"/"Little Rachel"/"Don't Blame Me"/"The Sky Is Crying"/"Singin' the Blues"/"Better Make It Through Today"/"Pretty Blue Eyes"/"High"/"Opposites."

E.C. Was Here (1975). "Have You Ever Loved a Woman?"/"Presence of the Lord"/"Drifting Blues"/"Can't Find My Way Home"/"Rambling on My Mind"/"Further on up the Road."

No Reason to Cry (1976). "Beautiful Thing"/"Carnival"/"Sign Language"/"County Jail Blues"/"All Our Past Times"/"Hello Old Friend"/"Double Trouble"/"Innocent Times"/"Hungry"/"Black Summer Rain"/"Last Night."

Slowhand (1977). "Cocaine"/"Wonderful Tonight"/"Lay Down Sally"/"Next Time You See Her"/"We're All the Way"/"The Core"/"May You Never"/"Mean Old Frisco"/"Peaches and Diesel."

Backless (1978). "Walk Out in the Rain"/"Watch Out for Lucy"/"I'll Make Love to You Anytime"/"Roll It"/"Tell Me That You Love Me"/"If I Don't

Be There by Morning"/"Early in the Morning"/"Promises"/"Golden Ring"/"Tulsa Time."

Just One Night (1980). "Tulsa Time"/"Early in the Morning"/"Lay Down Sally"/"Wonderful Tonight"/"If I Don't Be There by Morning"/ "Worried Life Blues"/"All Our Pastimes"/"After Midnight"/"Double Trouble"/"Setting Me Up"/"Blues Power"/"Rambling on My Mind"/"Cocaine"/"Further on up the Road."

Another Ticket (1981). "Something Special"/"Black Rose"/"Blow Wind Blow"/"Another Ticket"/"I Can't Stand It"/"Hold Me Lord"/"Floating Bridge"/"Catch Me If You Can"/"Rita Mae."

Money and Cigarettes (1983). "Everybody Oughta Make a Change"/"The Shape You're In"/"Ain't Going Down"/"(I've Got a) Rock 'n' Roll Heart"/"Man Overboard"/"Pretty Girl"/"Man in Love"/"Crosscut Saw"/"Slow Down Linda"/"Crazy Country Hop."

Behind the Sun (1985). "She's Waiting"/"See What Love Can Do"/"Same Old Blues"/"Knock on Wood"/"Something's Happening"/"Forever Man"/"It All Depends"/"Tangled in Love"/"Never Make You Cry"/"Just Like a Prisoner"/"Behind the Sun."

August (1986). "It's in the Way That You Use It"/"Run"/"Tearing Us Apart"/"Bad Influence"/"Walk Away"/"Hung up on Your Love"/"Take a Chance"/"Hold On"/"Miss You"/"Holy Mother"/"Behind the Mask"/"Grand Illusion."

Journeyman (1989). "Pretending"/"Anything for Your Love"/"Bad Love"/"Running on Faith"/"Hard Times"/"Hound Dog"/"No Alibis"/"Run So Far"/"Old Love"/"Breaking Point"/"Lead Me On"/"Before You Accuse Me."

24 Nights (1991). "Badge"/"Running on Faith"/"White Room"/"Sunshine of Your Love"/"Watch Yourself"/"Have You Ever Loved a

Woman?"/"Worried Life Blues"/"Hoodoo Man"/"Pretending"/"Bad Love"/"Old Love"/"Wonderful Tonight"/"Bell Bottom Blues"/"Hard Times"/"Edge of Darkness."

Unplugged (1992). "Signe"/"Before You Accuse Me"/"Hey Hey"/"Tears in Heaven"/"Lonely Stranger"/"Nobody Knows You When You're Down and Out"/"Layla"/"Running on Faith"/"Walkin' Blues"/"Alberta"/"San Francisco Bay Blues"/"Malted Milk"/"Old Love"/"Rollin' and Tumblin.' "

From the Cradle (1994). "Blues Before Sunrise"/"Third Degree"/"Reconsider Baby"/"Hoochie Coochie Man"/"Five Long Years"/"I'm Tore Down"/"How Long Blues"/"Goin' Away Baby"/"Blues Leave Me Alone"/"Sinner's Prayer"/"Motherless Child"/"It Hurts Me Too"/"Someday after a While"/"Standin' Round Crying"/"Driftin' " "Groaning the Blues."

Pilgrim (1998). "My Father's Eyes"/"River of Tears"/"Pilgrim"/"Broken Hearted"/"One Chance"/"Circus"/"Going Down Slow"/"Fall Like Rain"/"Born in Time"/"Sick & Tired"/"Needs His Woman"/"She's Gone"/"You Were There"/"Inside of Me."

Riding with the King (with B.B. King) (2000). "Riding with the King"/"Ten Long Years"/"Key to the Highway"/"Marry You"/"Three O'Clock Blues"/"Help the Poor"/"I Wanna Be"/"Worried Life Blues"/"Days of Old"/"When My Heart Beats Like a Hammer"/"Hold on! I'm Comin' "/"Come Rain or Come Shine."

Reptile (2001). "Reptile"/"Got You on My Mind"/"Travelin' Light"/"Believe in Life"/"Come Back Baby"/"Broken Down Find Myself"/"I Ain't Gonna Stand for It"/"I Want a Little Girl"/"Second Nature"/"Don't Let Me Be Lonely Tonight"/"Modern Girl"/"Superman Inside"/"Son & Sylvia."

One More Car, One More Road: Live on Tour 2001 (2002). Live album with accompanying concert DVD.

ANTHOLOGIES AND COMPILATIONS

History of Eric Clapton (1972). "I Ain't Got You"/"Hideaway"/"Tales of Brave Ulysses"/"I Want to Know"/"Sunshine of Your Love"/ "Crossroads"/"Sea of Joy"/"Only You Know and I Know"/"I Don't Want to Discuss It"/"Teasin'"/"Blues Power"/"Spoonful"/"Badge"/"Tell the Truth"/"Tell the Truth" (jam)/"Layla."

Timepieces—Best of Eric Clapton (1982). "I Shot the Sheriff"/"After Midnight"/"Knockin' on Heaven's Door"/"Wonderful Tonight"/"Layla"/"Cocaine"/"Lay Down Sally"/"Willie and the Hand Jive"/"Promises"/"Swing Low Sweet Chariot"/"Let It Grow."

Timepieces Volume 2—"Live" in the Seventies (1983). "Tulsa Time"/"Knockin' on Heaven's Door"/"If I Don't Be There by Morning"/"Rambling on My Mind"/"Presence of the Lord"/"Can't Find My Way Home"/"Smile"/"Blues Power."

Backtrackin' (1984). "I Shot the Sheriff"/"Knockin' on Heaven's Door"/"Lay Down Sally"/"Promises"/"Swing Low Sweet Chariot"/"Wonderful Tonight"/"Sunshine of Your Love"/"Tales of Brave Ulysses"/"Badge"/"Little Wing"/"Layla"/"Cocaine"/"Strange Brew"/ "Spoonful"/"Let It Rain"/"Have You Ever Loved a Woman?"/"Presence of the Lord"/"Crossroads"/"Roll It Over"/"Can't Find My Way Home"/"Blues Power"/"Further on up the Road."

The Cream of Eric Clapton (1987). "Layla"/"Badge"/"I Feel Free"/ "Sunshine of Your Love"/"Crossroads"/"Strange Brew"/"White Room"/"Bell Bottom Blues"/"Cocaine"/"I Shot the Sheriff"/"After Midnight"/"Swing Low Sweet Chariot"/"Lay Down Sally"/"Knockin' on Heaven's Door"/"Wonderful Tonight"/"Let It Grow"/"Promises"/"I Can't Stand It."

Crossroads (1988). "Boom Boom"/"Honey in Your Hips"/"Baby What's Wrong"/"I Wish You Would"/"A Certain Girl"/"Good Morning Little

Schoolgirl"/"I Ain't Got You"/"For Your Love"/"Got to Hurry"/"Lonely Years"/"Bernard Jenkins"/"Hideaway"/"All Your Love"/"Ramblin' on My Mind"/"Have You Ever Loved a Woman?"/"Wrapping Paper"/"I Feel Free"/"Spoonful"/"Hey Lawdy Mama"/"Strange Brew"/"Sunshine of Your Love"/"Tales of Brave Ulysses"/"Steppin' Out"/"Anyone for Tennis?"/"White Room"/"Crossroads"/"Badge"/"Presence of the Lord"/"Can't Find My Way Home"/"Sleeping in the Ground"/"Comin' Home"/"Blues Power"/"After Midnight"/"Let It Rain"/"Tell the Truth"/"Roll It Over"/"Layla"/"Mean Old World"/"Key to the Highway"/"Crossroads"/"Got to Get Better in a Little While"/ "Evil"/"One More Chance"/"Mean Old Frisco"/"Snake Lake Blues"/"Let It Grow"/"Ain't That Lovin' You"/"Motherless Children"/ "I Shot the Sheriff"/"Better Make It Through Today"/"The Sky Is Crying"/ "I Found a Love"/"(When Things Go Wrong) It Hurts Me Too"/"Whatcha Gonna Do"/"Someone Like You"/"Hello Old Friend"/"Sign Language"/"Further on up the Road"/"Lay Down Sally"/"Wonderful Tonight"/"Cocaine"/"Promises"/"If I Don't Be There by Morning"/"Double Trouble"/"I Can't Stand It"/"The Shape You're In"/"Heaven Is One Step Away"/"She's Waiting"/"Too Bad"/"Miss You"/"Wanna Make Love to You"/"After Midnight."

Early Clapton (1988). "Got to Hurry"/"I Ain't Got You"/"Good Morning Little Schoolgirl"/"Let It Rock"/"A Certain Girl"/"Take It Easy Baby"/ "Too Much Monkey Business"/"Draggin' My Tail"/"Tribute to Elmore"/ "Snake Drive"/"West Coast Idea"/"Choker"/"Freight Loader"/"Miles Road"/"Maudie"/"Lonely Years"/"I'm Your Witchdoctor"/"Telephone Blues"/"On Top of the World."

Stages (1993). "Steppin' Out"/"Ramblin' on My Mind"/"Hideaway"/ "Have You Heard"/"Outside Woman Blues"/"Crossroads"/"They Call It Stormy Monday"/"Well All Right"/"Bell Bottom Blues"/"Blues Power"/ "Drifting Blues"/"Mean Old Frisco."

Crossroads 2 Live in the Seventies (1996). "Walkin' Down the Road"/"Have

You Ever Loved a Woman"/"Willie and the Hand Jive"/"Get Ready"/
"Can't Find My Way Home"/"Driftin' Blues"/"Ramblin' on My Mind"/
"Presence of the Lord"/"Ramblin' on My Mind"/"Have You Ever Loved
a Woman"/"Little Wing"/"The Sky Is Crying"/"Have You Ever Loved a
Woman"/"Rambling on My Mind"/"Layla"/"Further on up the Road"/
"I Shot the Sheriff"/"Badge"/"Driftin' Blues"/"Eyesight to the Blind"/
"Why Does Love Got to Be So Sad?"/"Tell the Truth"/"Knockin' on
Heaven's Door"—Clapton, Eric/"Stormy Monday"—Clapton, Eric/"Lay
Down Sally"/"The Core"/"We're all the Way"/"Cocaine"/"Goin'
Down"/"Slow"/"Ramblin' on My Mind"/"Mean Old Frisco"—Clapton,
Eric/"Loving You Is Sweeter Than Ever"/"Worried Life Blues"/"Tulsa
Time"/"Early in the Morning"/"Wonderful Tonight"/"Double Trouble"/
"Crossroads"/"To Make Somebody Happy"/"Cryin' "/"Water on the
Ground"/"Kind Hearted Woman."

The Blues (1999). "Before You Accuse Me" (Take a Look at Yourself)/
"Mean Old World"/"Ain't That Loving You"/"The Sky Is Crying"/
"Cryin' "/"Have You Ever Loved a Woman"/"Alberta"/"Early in the
Morning"/"Give Me Strength"/"Down at the Bottom" (Meet Me) /
"County Jail Blues"/"Floating Bridge"/"Blow Wind Blow"/"To Make
Somebody Happy"/"Before You Accuse Me" (Take a Look at Yourself)
(version 2)/"Stormy Monday" (live)/"Worried Life Blues" (live)/"Early in
the Morning" (live)/"Have You Ever Loved a Woman" (live)/"Wonderful
Tonight" (live)/"Kind Hearted Woman" (live)/"Double Trouble"
(live)/"Driftin' Blues" (live)/"Crossroads" (live)/"Further on up the
Road" (live).

SOUND TRACKS

Edge of Darkness (1985). "Edge of Darkness"/"Shoot
Out"/"Obituary"/"Escape from Northmoor"/"Oxford Circus"/
"Northmoor."

Lethal Weapon (1987). "Armanda"/"Meet Martin Riggs"/"Roger"/"Coke

Deal"/"Mr. Joshua"/"They've Got My Daughter"/"The Desert"/
"Nightclub"/"The Weapon."

Homeboy (1988). "Travelling East"/"Johnny"/"Bridge"/"Dixie"/"Ruby's
Loft"/"Country Bikin' "/"Bike Ride"/"Ruby"/"Party"/"Training"/"Final
Fight"/"Chase"/"Dixie 2"/"Homeboy."

Lethal Weapon 2 (1988). "Knockin' on Heaven's Door"/"Riggs"/"The
Embassy"/"Riggs and Roger"/"Leo"/"Goodnight Rika"/"The Stilt
House"/"The Shipyard"/"Knockin' on Heaven's Door."

Rush (1992). "Tracks and Lines"/"Realization"/"Kristen and
Jim"/"Preludin' Fugue"/"Cold Turkey"/"Will Gaines"/"Don't Know
Which Way to Go"/"Help Me Up"/"Tears in Heaven."

Lethal Weapon 3 (1992). "It's Probably Me"/"Runaway Train"/"Grab"/
"Riggs and Rog"/"Roger's Boat"/"Armour Piercing Bullets"/"God Judges
Us by Our Scars"/"Lorna—A Quiet Evening by the Fire."

Eric Clapton as Sessions Musician

(Includes guest appearances on soundtracks,
concerts, anthologies, etc.)

Duane Allman. *An Anthology* (1972). "Mean Old World," "Layla." Both
songs recorded while Allman worked as a member of Derek and the
Dominos.

Ashton Gardner and Dyke. *The Worst of Ashton Gardner and Dyke* (1971).
"I'm Your Spiritual Breadman."

John Astley. *Everyone Loves the Pilot* (1987). "Jane's Getting Serious."

The Band. *The Last Waltz* (1978). "Further on up the Road," "I Shall Be
Released."

The Beatles. *The Beatles* (White Album) (1968). "While My Guitar
Gently Weeps."

Marc Benno. *Lost in Austin* (1979). "Hotfoot Blues," "Chasin' Rainbows," "Me and a Friend of Mine," "New Romance," "Last Train," "Lost in Austin," "Splish Splash," "Monterey Pen," "The Drifter," "Hey There Señorita."

Chuck Berry. *Hail! Hail! Rock 'n' Roll* (1987). "Wee Wee Hours," "Rock 'n' Roll Music."

Stephen Bishop. *Bowling in Paris* (1989). "Hall Light," "Save It for a Rainy Day."

———. *Red Cab to Manhattan* (1982). "Little Moon," "Sex Kittens Go to College."

Leona Boyd. *Persona* (1986). "Labyrinth."

Paul Brady. *Back to the Centre* (1986). "Deep in Your Heart."

Gary Brooker. "Leave the Candle," "Chasing the Chop" (single, 1981).

———. "Home Lovin' " (Side A of single, 1982).

———. *Lead Me to the Water* (1982). "Lead Me to the Water."

———. *Echoes in the Night* (1985). "Echoes in the Night."

Jack Bruce. *SomethinElse* (1993). "Waiting on a Word," "Willpower," "Ships in the Night."

———. *Willpower* (1989). "Willpower," "Ships in the Night."

Buckwheat Zydeco. *Taking It Home* (1988). "Why Does Love Got to Be So Sad?"

The Bunburys. *Bunbury Tails* (1992). "Fight (the Good Fight)."

———. "Fight (the Good Fight)" (Side A of single, 1988).

Jim Capaldi. *Some Come Running* (1988). "You Are the One," "Oh Lord Why Lord."

Ray Charles. *My World* (1993). "None of Us Are Free."

Joe Cocker. *Stingray* (1976). "Worrier."

Phil Collins. *Face Value* (1981). "If Leaving Me Is Easy."

————. *But Seriously* (1989). "I Wish It Would Rain."

The Crickets. *Rockin' 50s Rock 'n' Roll* (1971). "Rockin' 50s Rock 'n' Roll," "That'll Be the Day."

Brendan Crocker. *Brendan Crocker and the Five O'Clock Shadows* (1989). "This Kind of Life."

King Curtis. "Teasin'" (Side A of single, 1970).

Roger Daltry. *One of the Boys* (1977). EC is listed on the credits for this album, but no specific information on individual cuts is known.

Rick Danko. *Rick Danko* (1978). "New Mexico."

Jesse Ed Davis. *Jesse Davis* (1971). "Reno Street Incident," "Tulsa County," "Washita Love Child," "Every Night Is Saturday Night," "You Bella Donna You," "Rock and Roll Gypsies," "Golden Sun Goddess," "Crazy Love."

James Luther Dickenson. *Dixie Fried* (1972). "The Judgement."

Dr. John. *Hollywood Be Thy Name* (1975). "Reggae Doctor."

————. *The Sun, Moon and Herbs* (1971). "Black John the Conqueror," "Where Ya At Mule?" "Craney Crow," "Pots on Fiyo (File Gumbo)," "Who I Got to Fall On (If the Pot Get Heavy)?" "Zu Zu Mamou," "Familiar Reality (reprise)."

Gail Anne Dorsey. *The Corporate World* (1988). "Wasted Country."

Danny Douma. *Night Eyes* (1979). "I Hate You."

Lamont Dozier. *Inside Seduction* (1991). "That Ain't Me."

Champion Jack Dupree. *From New Orleans to Chicago* (1966). "Third Degree," "Shim-Sham-Shimmy."

Bob Dylan. *Desire* (1975). "Romance in Durango."

———. *Hearts of Fire* (1987). "The Usual," "Had a Dream about You," "Five and Dimmer."

———. *The 30th Anniversary Concert Celebration* (1993). "Don't Think Twice (It's All Right)," "My Back Pages," "Knockin' on Heaven's Door."

Aretha Franklin. *Lady Soul* (1968). "Good to Me as I Am to You."

Kinky Friedman. *Lasso from El Paso* (1976). "Kinky," "Ol' Ben Lucas."

Bob Geldof. *Deep in the Heart of Nowhere* (1986). "Love Like a Rocket," "August Was a Heavy Month," "The Beat of the Night," "Good Boys in the Wrong."

———. "Love Like a Rocket" (single, 1986).

Buddy Guy. *Damn Right I've Got the Blues* (1991). "Early in the Morning."

Buddy Guy and Junior Wells. *Play the Blues* (1971). "A Man of Many Words," "My Baby She Left Me (She Left Me a Mule to Ride)," "Come on in This House," "Have Mercy Baby," "T-Bone Shuffle," "A Poor Man's Plea," "Messin' with the Kid," "I Don't Know," "Bad Bad Whiskey."

George Harrison. *All Things Must Pass* (1970). "Wah-Wah," "Isn't It a Pity? (version #1)," "What Is Life," "Run of the Mill," "Beware of Darkness," "Awaiting on You All," "Out of the Blue," "Plug Me In," "I Remember Jeep," "Thanks for the Pepperoni."

———. *Cloud Nine* (1987). "Cloud Nine," "That's What It Takes," "Devil's Radio," "Wreck of the Hesperus."

———. *The Concert for Bangla Desh* (1972). "Wah-Wah," "My Sweet Lord," "Awaiting on You All," "That's the Way God Planned It,"

"It Don't Come Easy," "Beware of Darkness," "While My Guitar Gently Weeps," "Jumping Jack Flash," "Youngblood," "Something," "Bangla Desh."

———. *George Harrison* (1979). "Love Comes to Everyone."

———. *Live in Japan* (1992). "I Want to Tell You," "Old Brown Shoe," "Taxman," "Give Me Love," "If I Needed Someone," "Something," "What Is Life," "Dark Horse," "Piggies," "Got My Mind Set on You," "Cloud Nine," "Here Comes the Sun," "My Sweet Lord," "All Those Years Ago," "Cheer Down," "Devil's Radio," "Isn't It a Pity," "While My Guitar Gently Weeps," "Roll Over Beethoven."

———. *Wonderwall Music* (1968). "Ski-ing."

Corey Hart. *First Offence* (1984). "Jenney Fey."

Howlin' Wolf. *The London Howlin' Wolf Sessions* (1971). "Rockin' Daddy," "I Ain't Superstitious," "Sitting on Top of the World," "Worried about My Baby," "What a Woman," "Poor Boy," "Built for Comfort," "Who's Been Talking?" "The Red Rooster," "Do the Do," "Highway 49," "Wang-Dang-Doodle."

———. *London Revisited* (1974). "Going Down Slow," "The Killing Floor," "I Want to Have a Word with You."

Elton John. *The One* (1992). "Runaway Train."

Johnnie Johnson. *Johnnie B. Bad* (1991). "Creek Mud," "Blues #572."

Michael Kamen. *Concerto for Saxophone and Orchestra* (1990). "Sandra."

Thomas Jefferson Kaye. *Not Alone* (1993).

Jonathan Kelly. *Don't You Believe It* (1970). "Don't You Believe It" (Side A of single, 1970).

Bobby Keys. *Bobby Keys* (1972). "Steal from a King," "Bootleg," "Command Performance," "Crispy Duck."

Carole King. *City Streets* (1988). "City Streets," "Ain't That the Way."

Freddie King. *Burglar* (1974). "Sugar Sweet."

———. *1934–1976* (1977). "Sugar Sweet," "TV Mama," "Gambling Woman Blues," "Further on up the Road."

Alexis Korner. *The Party Album* (1980). "Hey Pretty Mama," "Hi-Heel Sneakers," "Stormy Monday Blues."

Corky Laing. *Makin' It on the Street* (1977). "On My Way."

Ronnie Lane. *See Me* (1980). "Lad's Got Money," "Barcelona," "Way up Yonder."

Ronnie Lane and Pete Townshend. *Rough Mix* (1977). "Rough Mix," "Annie," "April Fool," "Till the Rivers Run Dry."

Cyndi Lauper. *A Night to Remember* (1989). "Insecurious."

Jackie Lomax. "New Day" (Side A of single, 1969).

———. *Is This What You Want?* (1969). "Sour Milk Sea," "The Eagle Laughs at You," "You've Got Me Thinking." CD bonus track: "New Day."

———. "Sour Milk Sea," "The Eagle Laughs at You" (single, 1969).

Arthur Louis. *Knockin' on Heaven's Door* (1988). "Knockin' on Heaven's Door," "Plum," "The Dealer," "Still It Feels Good," "Come On and Love Me," "Train 444," "Go Out and Make It Happen." (Reissue of *Arthur Louis' First Album*, 1975, previously available only in Japan.)

———. "Knockin' on Heaven's Door," "Plum" (single, 1975).

———. "Knockin' on Heaven's Door," "The Dealer" (single, 1978).

———. "Still It Feels Good," "Come On and Love Me" (single, 1981).

John Martyn. *Glorious Fool* (1981). "Couldn't Love You More."

Christine McVie. *Christine McVie* (1984). "The Challenge."

Shawn Phillips. *Contribution* (1970). "Man Hole Covered Wagon."

Billy Preston. *Encouraging Words* (1970). "Right Now," "Encouraging Words."

———. *That's the Way God Planned It* (1969). "That's the Way God Planned It, parts 1 & 2," "Do What You Want to Do."

———. "That's the Way God Planned It," "Do What You Want to Do" (single, 1969).

Lionel Richie. *Dancing on the Ceiling* (1986). "Tonight Will Be Alright."

Rolling Stones. *Flashpoint* (1990). "Little Red Rooster."

Leon Russell. *Leon Russell* (1970). "Prince of Peace."

———. *Leon Russell and the Shelter People* (1971). "Alcatraz," "Beware of Darkness."

Richie Sambora. *Stranger in This Town* (1991). "Mr. Bluesman."

David Sanborn. *Upfront* (1992). "Full House."

Otis Spann. *The Blues of Otis Spann* (1964). "Pretty Girls Everywhere."

———. "Stirs Me Up" (Side B of single, 1964).

Vivian Stanshall. "Labio-Dental Fricative," "Paper Round" (single, 1970).

Ringo Starr. *Old Wave* (1983). "Everybody's in a Hurry but Me."

———. *Rotogravure* (1976). "This Be Called a Song."

Stephen Stills. *Stephen Stills* (1970). "Go Back Home."

———. *Stephen Stills 2* (1971). "Fishes and Scorpions."

Sting. *Nothing Like the Sun* (1987). "They Dance Alone."

Doris Troy. "Ain't That Cute" (Side A of single, 1970).

———. *Doris Troy* (1970). "Ain't That Cute," "Give Me Back My Dynamite," "I've Got to Be Strong," "You Give Me Joy Joy," "Don't Call Me No More," "Get Back."

———. "Get Back" (Side B of single, 1970).

Tina Turner. *Live in Europe* (1988). "Tearing Us Apart."

———. "What You See Is What You Get" (12-inch single, 1987).

Various Artists. *Buster* (motion picture soundtrack, 1988). "The Robbery."

———. *The Color of Money* (motion picture soundtrack, 1988). "The Gift (It's in the Way That You Use It)."

———. *Knebworth* (1990). "Think I Love You Too Much," "Money for Nothing," "Sad Songs," "Saturday Night's Alright for Fighting," "Sunshine of Your Love."

———. *Music from Free Creek* (1973). "Road Song," "Getting Back to Molly," "No One Knows."

———. *Nobody's Child* (1990). "That Kind of Woman."

———. *Prince's Trust 10th Birthday Party* (1986). "Better Be Good to Me," "Tearing Us Apart," "Call of the Wild," "Money for Nothing," "Everytime You Go Away," "Reach Out," "No One Is to Blame," "Sailing," "I'm Still Standing," "Long Tall Sally," "Get Back."

———. *Prince's Trust Concert 1987* (1987). "Running in the Family," "If I Was," "Wonderful Tonight," "Behind the Mask," "Stand by Me," "You've Lost That Loving Feeling," "Through the Barricades," "Saturday Night's Alright for Fighting," "While My Guitar Gently Weeps," "It's the Same Old Song," "I Can't Help Myself," "Reach Out, I'll Be There," "With a Little Help from My Friends."

———. *Secret Policeman's Other Ball: The Music* (1982). "Crossroads," " 'Cause We Ended as Lovers," "Further on up the Road."

———. *Stone Free* (1993). "Stone Free."

———. *Tommy* (motion picture soundtrack, 1978). "Eyesight to the Blind," "Sally Simpson."

———. A Tribute to Curtis Mayfield (1994). "You Must Believe Me."

———. *Two Rooms* (1991). "The Border Song."

———. *Wayne's World* (motion picture soundtrack, 1992). "Loving Your Lovin'."

———. *White Mansions* (1978). "White Trash," "Kentucky Racehorse."

Martha Velez. *Fiends and Angels* (1969). "It Takes a Lot to Laugh, It Takes a Train to Cry," "I'm Gonna Leave You," "Feel So Bad," "In My Girlish Days."

Roger Waters. *The Pros and Cons of Hitch-Hiking* (1984). "4.30am (Apparently They Were Travelling Abroad)," "4.33am (Running Shoes)," "4.37am (Arabs with Knives and West German Skies)," "4.39am (For the First Time Today—part 2)," "4.41am (Sexual Revolution)," "4.47am (The Remains of Our Love)," "4.50am (Go Fishing)," "4.56am (For the First Time Today—part 1)," "4.58am (Dunroamin Duncarin Dunlivin)," "5.01am (The Pros and Cons of Hitch-Hiking)," "5.06am (Every Stranger's Eyes)," "5.11am (The Moment of Clarity)."

Bobby Whitlock. *Bobby Whitlock* (1971). "Where There's a Will There's a Way," "A Day Without Jesus," "Back in My Life Again," "The Scenery Has Slowly Changed."

———. Raw Velvet (1972). "The Dreams of a Hobo," "Hello LA, Bye Bye Birmingham."

Zucchero. *Zucchero* (1989). "Wonderful World."

BOOTLEGS

Cream

The BBC Files 1965–1968 (Pyramic PY CD 021). "I Feel Free"/"N.S.U."/ "Four Until Late"/"Strange Brew"/"Tales of Brave Ulysses"/"Outside Woman Blues"/"Born under a Bad Sign"/"Steppin' Out"/"Politician"/ "Sweet Wine"/"Wrapping Paper"/"Hey Lawdy Mama"/"Train-time."

BBC '66. "Cat's Squirrel"/"Train-time"/"Hey Lawdy Mama"/"I'm So Glad"/"Steppin' Out"/"Big Mama Blues"/"Sleepy Time Time"/ "Crossroads."

Cream: Secret History. "Cat's Squirrel"/"Beauty Queen"/"Rollin' and Tumblin' "/"Coffee Song"/"Toad"/"Sweet Wine #1"/"Sweet Wine #2"/ "I Feel Free #1"/"I Feel Free #2"/"I Feel Free #3"/"I Feel Free #4"/ "Wrapping Paper #1"/"Wrapping Paper #2"/"You Make Me Feel #1"/ "You Make Me Feel #2"/"Sleepy Time Time"/"Sweet Wine"/"I'm So Glad"/"Wrapping Paper"/"Four Until Late"/"Cat's Squirrel"/"White Room"/"Sing Along"/"Anyone for Tennis?"/"Pressed Rat and Warthog"/ "Falstaff Beer #1"/"Falstaff Beer #2"/"Piano and Acoustic Guitar Jam"/"N.S.U."/"Cat's Squirrel"/"Train-time"/"Lawdy Mama"/"I'm So Glad"/"Four until Late"/"I Feel Free"/"N.S.U."/"Strange Brew"/"Tales of Brave Ulysses"/"We're Going Wrong."

Creamer (Oh Boy 1-9107). "White Room"/"Crossroads"/"Sunshine of Your Love"/"Train-time"/"Toad"/"Spoonful"/"I'm So Glad."

Concerthouse: Winterland (Koine K880803). "N.S.U."/"Steppin' Out"/ "Train-time"/"Toad"/"I'm So Glad"/"Sleepy Time Time"/"Tales of Brave Ulysses"/"Crossroads"/"We're Going Wrong."

Creme de la Creme (Bird Brain BBR 010). "Sweet Wine"/"Wrapping Paper"/"Hey Lawdy Mama"/"Train-time"/"I Feel Free"/"N.S.U."/"Four until Late"/"Strange Brew"/"Tales of Brave Ulysses"/"Outside Woman Blues"/"Born under a Bad Sign"/"Politician"/"I'm So Glad."

Eric Clapton's Cream Live (CDDV 2039). "Strange Brew"/"I Feel Free"/"Born under a Bad Sign"/"Hey Lawdy Mama"/"Politician"/ "Crossroads"/"Sleepy Time Time"/"I'm So Glad"/"N.S.U."/"Outside Woman Blues"/"Tales of Brave Ulysses."

Hello Again on Tour. "Steppin' Out"/"Sweet Wine"/"Lost Love"/ "N.S.U."/ "Big Mama Blues"/"Sleepy Time Time"/"Crossroads."

Live Cream, Volume 3 (BTM ARTZ). "White Room"/"Politician"/ "Crossroads"/"Sunshine of Your Love"/"Spoonful"/"Deserted Cities of the Heart"/"Passing the Time"/"Drum Solo"/"I'm So Glad."

Royal Albert Hall 1968 (WRMB 366). "Cat's Squirrel"/"Hey Lawdy Mama"/"Spoonful"/"Crossroads"/"N.S.U."/"White Room"/"Sunshine of Your Love."

'67–'68 (CMB 47-106). "Steppin' Out"/"Sweet Wine"/"Lost Love"/ "N.S.U."/"Big Black Woman Blues"/"Sleepy Time Time"/"Crossroads"/"White Room"/"Politician"/"Crossroads"/"Sitting on Top of the World"/"I'm So Glad"/"Sunshine of Your Love."

Stepping Stones, Part 1 (Silver Rarities SIRA-CD 23). "White Room"/ "Politician"/"I'm So Glad"/"Sittin' on Top of the World"/ "Crossroads"/ "Sunshine of Your Love"/"Well All Right"/"Sleeping in the Ground"/ "Sea of Joy."

Stepping Out (The Swingin' Pig TSP CD 014). "N.S.U."/"Steppin' Out"/"Train-time"/"Toad"/"I'm So Glad"/"Outside Woman Blues"/ "Born under a Bad Sign"/"Strange Brew"/"Tales of Brave Ulysses"/"Four Until Late.

Three Wheels of Fire (The Genuine Pig TGP CD126). "White Room"/ "Politician"/"Sunshine of Your Love"/"Toad"/"Spoonful"/"I'm So Glad"/ "Introduction"/"Sweet Wine"/"Wrapping Paper"/"Hey Lawdy Mama"/ "Train-time"/"Introduction"/"I Feel Free"/"N.S.U."/"Four Until Late."

Blind Faith

Gothenburg 1969 (Moby Dick Records MDCD 003). "Sleeping in the Ground"/"Sea of Joy"/"Under My Thumb"/"Presence of the Lord"/"Had to Cry Today"/"Do What You Like."

Stepping Stones, Part 2 (Silver Rarities SIRA-CD 24). "Under My Thumb"/"Can't Find My Way Home"/"Do What You Like"/"Presence of the Lord"/"Means to an End"/"Had to Cry Today."

U.S. Tour (TARKL 1902). "Crossroads"/"Presence of the Lord"/"Means to an End"/"Well All Right"/"Can't Find My Way Home"/"Had to Cry Today."

Eric Clapton

Alberta, Layla, and All My Love (Speedball Company SCB 026). "Before You Accuse Me"/"Lonely Stranger"/"Running on Faith"/"Nobody Knows You When You're Down and Out"/"Layla"/"Tears in Heaven"/ "Circus Left Town"/"Alberta"/"Hold On."

Alone with My Guitar (OHM Digital Recordings OHM 1 CD). "Before You Accuse Me"/"Lonely Stranger"/"Running on Faith"/"Nobody Knows You When You're Down and Out"/"Layla"/"Tears in Heaven"/ "Circus Left Town"/"Alberta"/"Hold On."

American Tour '78 (The Swingin' Pig TSP CD 063). "Knockin' on Heaven's Door"/"Lay Down Sally"/"Next Time You See Her"/"Cocaine"/"Badge"/"Sign Language."

Another Page (Red Phantom RPCD 2073/2074). "Anything for Your Love"/"Pretending"/"I Shot the Sheriff"/"Running on Faith"/"My Father's Eyes"/"She's Waiting"/"Circus Left Town"/"Tears in Heaven"/"Signe"/"Before You Accuse Me"/"Old Love"/

"Badge"/"Wonderful Tonight"/"Tearing Us Apart"/"Layla"/
"Crossroads"/"Sunshine of Your Love."

A Blues Evening (Golden Stars JVCD 1144). "All Your Love"/"Have You
Ever Loved a Woman?"/"Ramblin' on My Mind"/"Jam"/"Pretending"/
"Running on Faith"/"White Room"/"Bad Love"/"Wonderful Tonight"/
"Layla."

The Blue Sheriff (Golden Stars TKCD 1042). "Tulsa Time"/"I Shot the
Sheriff"/"Lay Down Sally"/"Worried Life Blues"/"Let It Rain"/"Double
Trouble"/"Sweet Eliza"/"Wonderful Tonight"/"Blues Power"/"Have You
Ever Loved a Woman?"/"Cocaine"/"Layla."

Blues Night (Star Records STAR 2). "Watch Yourself"/"Hoodoo
Man"/"The Stumble"/"Standin' Around Cryin' "/"All Your Love"/"Have
You Ever Loved a Woman?"/"Who's Lovin' You Tonight"/"Key to the
Highway"/"Wee Wee Baby"/"Long Time Comin' "/"Piano Shuffle"/
"Leavin' Town"/"I Can See Your Lights On" (But I Can't See Nobody
Home)"/"Black Cat Bone"/"I'm So Glad"/"Low Down and Dirty"/
"Stranger Blues"/"Hoochie Coochie Man"/"Little by Little"/"My Time
after a While"/"Sweet Home Chicago."

Bluespower (Chapter One CO 25137). "Have You Ever Loved a
Woman?"/"Blues Power"/"Key to the Highway"/"Bright Lights Big
City"/"I Can't Hold Out"/"Willie and the Hand Jive"/"Get Ready"/
"Little Wing"/"Layla"/"Little Queenie."

Bright Lights in Blues City (Big Music BIG 033). "Smile"/"Let It
Grow"/"Can't Find My Way Home"/"Willie and the Hand Jive"/"Let It
Rain"/"Key to the Highway"/"Blues Power"/"Have You Ever Loved a
Woman?"/"Layla"/"Presence of the Lord"/"Steady Rollin' Man"/
"Crossroads."

Caught in the Act (Rockdreams ROCKS 92026/27). "White Room"/
"I Shot the Sheriff"/"Wonderful Tonight"/"Layla"/"Sunshine of Your

Love"/"Hung up on Your Love"/"Tearing Us Apart"/"Badge"/"Let It Rain"/"Crossroads"/"Cocaine"/"Same Old Blues."

Claptonmania (Archivio ARC CD 004). "Hello Old Friend"/"Sign Language"/"Alberta"/"Tell the Truth"/"Can't Find My Way Home"/"Double Trouble"/"I Shot the Sheriff"/"Knockin' on Heaven's Door"/"Further on up the Road"/"Badge."

Class Blues (Buccaneer Records BUC 004). "I Shot the Sheriff"/"White Room"/"No Alibis"/"Tearing Us Apart"/"Wonderful Tonight"/"Cocaine."

Crossroads '87 (Taifun Records 0073 203). "Crossroads"/"White Room"/ "I Shot the Sheriff "/"Hung Up on Your Love"/"Wonderful Tonight"/ "Miss You"/"Same Old Blues"/"Tearing Us Apart"/"Holy Mother"/ "Badge"/"Let It Rain"/"Cocaine"/"Layla"/"Sunshine of Your Love"/ "Money for Nothing."

Dire Circumstances (Turtle Records TR-210). "Hello Old Friend"/"Sign Language"/"Badge"/"Wonderful Tonight"/"Tell the Truth"/"Layla"/ "I Shot the Sheriff"/"Tearing Us Apart"/"Can't Find My Way Home"/ "Badge."

An Eclectic Collection 1974 (ZAP 7851). "Easy Now"/"Let It Grow"/"I Shot the Sheriff"/"Layla"/"Smile"/"Little Wing"/"Willie and the Hand Jive"/"Get Ready."

An Eclectic Collection 1974, Part 2 (ZAP 7852). "Badge"/"Can't Find My Way Home"/"Driftin' Blues"/"Let It Rain"/"Presence of the Lord"/"Crossroads"/"Steady Rollin' Man"/"Little Queenie."

The End of Summer Night (Dynamite Studio DS 92NO43/44). "Layla"/ "Bell Bottom Blues"/"Key to the Highway"/"Mainline Florida"/"Can't Find My Way Home"/"Further on up the Road"/"Knockin' on Heaven's Door"/"Blues Power"/"Teach Me to Be Your Man"/"Stormy Monday"/"Badge"/"Carnival"/"Little Wing/""Eyesight to the Blind."

Eric Clapton and His Band 1981 (UD 6551/2). "Tulsa Time"/"Early in the Morning"/"Lay Down Sally"/"Wonderful Tonight"/"If I Don't Be There by Morning"/"Someday Babe"/"Country Boy"/"Double Trouble"/"All Our Past Times"/"Blues Power"/"Knockin' on Heaven's Door"/"Settin' Me Up"/"Ramblin' on My Mind"/"Have You Ever Loved a Woman?"/"After Midnight"/"Cocaine"/"Layla"/"Further on up the Road."

Forever Man (RSR/Inter-National RSR 232). "Tulsa Time"/"Tangled in Love"/"Behind the Sun"/"Wonderful Tonight"/"I Shot the Sheriff"/ "Same Old Blues"/"Blues Power"/"She's Waiting"/"Badge"/"Let It Rain"/"Layla"/"Forever Man"/"Further on up the Road."

Forever Man (See For Miles Records Ltd.). "Motherless Children"/ "Tangled in Love"/"Blues Power"/"Lay Down Sally"/"Wonderful Tonight"/"Badge"/"Let It Rain"/"She's Waiting"/"Layla"/"Forever Man"/"White Room"/"Wanna Make Love to You"/"Run"/"Miss You"/"Tearing Us Apart"/"In the Air Tonight"/"Cocaine"/"Further on up the Road."

Frankfurt (Pharting Pharoah Records 13162). "Motherless Children"/ "Tangled in Love"/"Blues Power"/"Lay Down Sally"/"Badge"/"Let It Rain"/"She's Waiting"/"Same Old Blues"/"Wonderful Tonight"/"Layla"/"Forever Man."

Gentleman's Appearance (American Concert Series ACS 205). "Knockin' on Heaven's Door"/"Lay Down Sally"/"Next Time You See Her"/ "Cocaine"/"Badge"/"Sign Language"/"Layla."

Georgia Peach (FLAT 8223). "Hello Old Friend"/"Badge"/"Knockin' on Heaven's Door"/"One Night with You"/"Whole Lotta Shakin' "/"Can't Find My Way Home"/"Blues Power."

German Tour '83 (Deadend Prod. EC). "I Shot the Sheriff"/"Someday Baby"/"Let It Rain"/"Key to the Highway"/"The Shape You're In"/

"That's All Right"/"Have You Ever Loved a Woman?"/"Ramblin' on My Mind"/"Layla."

The Guitar World (Flashback 07900123). "Hello Old Friend"/"Sign Language"/"Badge"/"Knockin' on Heaven's Door"/"One Night with You"/"Whole Lotta Shakin' "/"Can't Find My Way Home."

Hand Jive (ZAP 7884). "Willie and the Hand Jive"/"Get Ready"/ "Untitled"/"Layla"/"Little Queenie"/"Badge"/"Layla Reprise."

In Concert 1977 (Super Golden Radio Shows 018). "Hello Old Friend"/ "Sign Language"/"Alberta"/"Tell the Truth"/"Can't Find My Way Home"/"Double Trouble"/"I Shot the Sheriff"/"Knockin' on Heaven's Door"/"Further on up the Road"/"Badge."

Jamming with Eric Clapton and Santana (501). "Layla"/"I Shot the Sheriff"/ "Can't Find My Way Home"/"Jam Session: Wish You Could See My Eyes"/"Soul Sacrifice"/"Indications"/"Blues Power."

Keep on Knockin' (Red Calendar RC 2118). "Stormy Monday"/"Knockin' on Heaven's Door"/"Badge"/"Can't Find My Way Home"/"Carnival"/ "Key to the Highway"/"Blues Power"/"Little Wing"/"Tell the Truth."

Layla (On Stage 12001). "Tulsa Time"/"Ramblin' on My Mind"/"Knockin' on Heaven's Door"/"Cocaine"/"Lay Down Sally"/ "Badge"/"Sign Language"/"Layla"/"Next Time You See Her."

Layla's Birthday (Sugarcane Records SC 52010). "Hello Old Friend"/ "Sign Language"/"Layla"/"Key to the Highway"/"Tell the Truth"/"All Our Past Times"/"Blues Power"/"One Night"/"I Shot the Sheriff."

The Legendary L.A. Forum Show (Oh Boy 2-9052). "Layla"/"Further on up the Road"/"Knockin' on Heaven's Door"/"It's Only Love"/"Can't Find My Way Home"/"Tell the Truth"/"Stormy Monday"/"Why Does Love Got to Be So Sad"/"Teach Me to Be Your Woman"/"Badge"/"Jam Session."

Little Wing (Living Legend Records LLRCD 095). "Have You Ever Loved a Woman?"/"Blues Power"/"Key to the Highway"/"Bright Lights Big City"/"I Can't Hold Out"/"Willie and the Hand Jive"/"Get Ready"/"Little Wing"/"Layla"/"Little Queenie."

Live in London (Caution Music). "I Shot the Sheriff"/"Little Wing"/"Let It Grow"/"Get Ready"/"Badge"/"All I Have to Do Is Dream."

Live in Rome (CN-01). "White Room"/"I Shot the Sheriff"/"Wanna Make Love to You"/"Wonderful Tonight"/"Miss You"/"Same Old Blues"/"Badge."

Living on Blues Power, Vol. 1 (Extremely Rare EXR 015/016). "Motherless Children #1"/"Motherless Children #2"/"High Up on a Mountain Top #1"/"High Up on a Mountain Top #2"/"High Up on a Mountain Top #3"/"Why Does Love Got to Be So Sad"/"Bell Bottom Blues #1"/"Keep On Growing #1"/"Knockin' on Heaven's Door #1"/"Knockin' on Heaven's Door #2"/"Knockin' on Heaven's Door #3"/"Eyesight to the Blind #1"/"Easy Now"/"Twist and Shout"/"After Midnight"/"Eyesight to the Blind #2"/"Knockin' on Heaven's Door #4"/"It's Too Late"/"Well Allright"/"Keep on Growing #2"/"Bell Bottom Blues #2"/"High up on a Mountain Top #4"/"Motherless Children #4"/"Layla"/"Mainline Florida"/"Knockin' on Heaven's Door #5"/"Knockin' on Heaven's Door #6."

Living Stories (The Genuine Pig Records TGP-CD-140). "Tulsa Time"/"Tangled in Love"/"Behind the Sun"/"Wonderful Tonight"/"She's Waiting"/"Badge"/"Let It Rain"/"I Shot the Sheriff"/"Same Old Blues"/"Layla"/"Forever Man"/"Further on up the Road."

London at Night, Vol. 1 (Bad Man Records BD 1). "Pretending"/"Running on Faith"/"I Shot the Sheriff"/"White Room"/"Bad Love"/"Lay Down Sally"/"Before You Accuse Me"/"Old Love."

London at Night, Vol. 2 (Bad Man Records BD 2). "No Alibis"/"Tearing

Us Apart"/"Wonderful Tonight"/"Cocaine"/"Crossroads"/"Sunshine of Your Love."

Milk Cow Blues (Unbelievable Music UM 008/9). "Badge"/"Milk Cow Blues"/"Have You Ever Loved a Woman?"/"Steady Rollin' Man"/"Let It Rain"/"Nobody Knows You When You're Down and Out"/"I Shot the Sheriff"/"Layla"/"All I Have to Do Is Dream"/"Little Wing"/"Smile"/ "Easy Now"/"Let It Grow"/"Badge"/"Willie and the Hand Jive"/"Get Ready"/"Blues Power."

Mountain Dew (Buccaneer Records BUC-019). "Tulsa Time"/"Tangled in Love"/"Behind the Sun"/"Wonderful Tonight"/"I Shot the Sheriff"/ "Same Old Blues"/"Blues Power"/"She's Waiting"/"Badge"/"Let It Rain"/"Layla"/"Forever Man"/"Further on up the Road."

A Night at the Crossroads (Triangle Records PYCD 077). "Tell the Truth"/"Mainline Florida"/"Mean Old World"/"Blues Power"/"Steady Rollin' Man"/"Crossroads"/"I Shot the Sheriff"/"Let It Rain"/"Willie and the Hand Jive"/"Get Ready"/"Can't Find My Way Home."

A Night in Copenhagen (Lost Rose LR CD 09). "Sign Language"/"Further on up the Road"/"Knockin' on Heaven's Door"/"Stormy Monday"/"Tell the Truth"/"Key to the Highway"/"Nobody Knows You When You're Down and Out"/"Layla."

One Night in Dallas (Seagull Records SEA 042). "Hello Old Friend"/ "Sign Language"/"Knockin' on Heaven's Door"/"One Night"/"Can't Find My Way Home"/"Blues Power"/"Layla."

On Tour. "The Core"/"Double Trouble"/"Knockin' on Heaven's Door"/ "Blues Power"/"Have You Ever Loved a Woman?"/"All the Way"/"Sign Language"/"Tell the Truth"/"Stormy Monday"/"Layla."

Play with Fire (Blues Power 3003-1945-002). "Intro"/"Pretending"/"No Alibis"/"Running on Faith"/"I Shot the Sheriff"/"White Room"/"Can't Find My Way Home"/"Bad Love"/"Before You Accuse Me"/"Old

Love"/"Badge"/"Wonderful Tonight"/"Cocaine"/"Layla"/"Crossroads"/
"Sunshine of Your Love."

Reziprocal Affection (Oh Boy 1-9103). "Tulsa Time"/"I Shot the Sheriff"/
"Wonderful Tonight"/"She's Waiting"/"Lay Down Sally"/"Badge"/"Let
It Rain"/"Poor Little Man"/"Layla."

R&R Heart (Scorpio Records SC-LP-503). "I Shot the
Sheriff"/"Worried Life Blues"/"Key to the Highway"/"After
Midnight"/"The Shape You're In"/"Wonderful
Tonight"/"Cocaine"/"Further on up the Road."

Royal Treatment (Oedipus Records 01990). "Pretending"/"Running on
Faith"/"I Shot the Sheriff"/"White Room"/"Bad Love"/"Lay Down
Sally"/"Before You Accuse Me"/"Old Love"/"No Alibis"/"Tearing Us
Apart"/"Cocaine"/"Wonderful Tonight"/"Crossroads"/"Sunshine of Your
Love."

Same Old Blues. "Everybody Ought to Change Sometime"/"Motherless
Children"/"I Shot the Sheriff"/"Same Old Blues"/"Blues Power"/
"Tangled in Love"/"Steppin' Out"/"Tulsa Time"/"Lay Down Sally"/
"Something's Happening"/"Badge"/"Behind the Sun"/"Wonderful
Tonight"/"Let It Rain"/"Who's Loving You Tonight"/"Have You Ever
Loved a Woman?"/"Rambling on My Mind"/"Cocaine"/"Layla"/"Knock
on Wood"/"Further on up the Road."

Same Old Blues. "Crossroads"/"White Room"/"Cocaine"/"She's Waiting"/
"Same Old Blues"/"Holy Mother."

The Sentimentalist (Sunset Records Eric ER 841125/3). "Tulsa Time"/
"Motherless Children"/"I Shot the Sheriff"/"Same Old Blues"/"Tangled
in Love"/"White Room"/"Hungry"/"Wonderful Tonight"/"She's
Waiting"/"Lay Down Sally"/"Badge"/"Let It Rain"/"Double Trouble"/
"Cocaine"/"You Don't Know Like I Know"/"Matchbox Blues"/"Blue
Suede Shoes"/"Goodnight Irene"/"Mean Woman Blues."

'74 (Berkeley Records). "Can't Find My Way Home"/"Willie and the Hand Jive"/"Layla"/"Presence of the Lord"/"Blues Power"/"Badge."

The Shape You're In (XL 1549/50/51). "Tulsa Time"/"I Shot the Sheriff"/ "Lay Down Sally"/"Someday Baby"/"Let It Rain"/"Double Trouble"/ "Sweet Eliza"/"Key to the Highway"/"After Midnight"/"The Shape You're In"/"Wonderful Tonight"/"Blues Power"/"Ramblin' on My Mind"/"Have You Ever Loved a Woman?"/"Cocaine"/"Layla"/"Further on up the Road"/"Driftin' Blues"/"Motherless Children"/"A Whiter Shade of Pale"/"Setting Me Up"/"Another Ticket"/"Badge."

Slowhand Blues (ECD1/3793 ECD2/3793). "How Long"/"Alabama Women"/"Terraplane Blues"/"Four Until Late"/"Kidman Blues"/ "County Jail Blues"/"32–20"/"Chicago Breakdown"/"Hey Hey"/"Walkin' Blues"/"Long Distance Call"/"Blow Wind Blow"/"Key to the Highway"/ "Tell Me Mama"/"Juke"/"Blues Leave Me Alone"/"Goin' Away Baby"/ "Coming Home"/"Meet Me in the Bottom"/"Forty Four"/"It's My Life"/"Love Her with a Feeling"/"Tore Down"/"Born under a Bad Sign"/"Let Me Love You Baby"/"Groaning the Blues"/"Hear Me Calling"/"Ain't Nobody's Business"/"Sweet Home Chicago."

Slowhand Live in Boston (ZAP 7880). "Smile"/"Have You Ever Loved a Woman?"/"Blues Power"/"Can't Find My Way Home"/"Presence of the Lord"/"Bright Lights Big City."

Slowhand Serenade (Sleepy Dragon Records DRA 5506). "Crossroads"/ "White Room"/"I Shot the Sheriff"/"Falling for Your Love"/"Wonderful Tonight"/"Tearing Us Apart"/"Holy Mother"/"Badge"/"Let It Rain"/"Cocaine"/"Layla"/"Who Do You Love"/"Sunshine of Your Love."

Smile (ZAP 7881). "Smile"/"Let It Grow"/"Willie and the Hand Jive"/ "Layla"/"Boogie"/"Little Queenie."

Snowhead (EC 1978). "Knockin' on Heaven's Door"/"Lay Down Sally"/ "Next Time You See Her"/"Cocaine"/"Badge"/"Sign Language"/"Layla."

Stormy Monday Blues (Great Dane Records GDR CD 9109). "Layla"/ "Further on up the Road"/"Knockin' on Heaven's Door"/"Can't Find My Way Home"/"Tell the Truth"/"Why Does Love Got to Be So Sad"/ "Teach Me to Be Your Woman"/"Badge"/"Jam Session."

Unplugged (Pluto Records PLR CD 9220). "Before You Accuse Me"/ "Lonely Stranger"/"Running on Faith"/"Nobody Knows You When You're Down and Out"/"Layla"/"Tears in Heaven"/"Circus Left Town"/"Alberta"/"Rollin' and Tumblin'"/"Old Love."

The Unsurpassed Eric Clapton (Yellow Dog YD 022). "Slunky"/"Bad Boy"/ "Lonesome and a Long Way from Home"/"After Midnight"/"Blues Power"/"Bottle of Red Wine"/"Lovin' You Lovin' Me"/"Told You for the Last Time"/"Don't Know Why"/"Let It Rain"/"Easy Now"/"Lonesome and a Long Way from Home #2"/"Don't Know Why #2."

Virginia (Beech Marten 028). "Motherless Children"/"Tangled in Love"/ "Blues Power"/"Tulsa Time"/"I Shot the Sheriff"/"Wonderful Tonight"/ "She's Waiting"/"Lay Down Sally"/"Badge"/"Let It Rain"/"Forever Man"/"Layla."

A Wednesday Night at the Tokyo Dome (Great Live Records GLR 9237/38). "Crossroads"/"White Room"/"I Shot the Sheriff"/"Money for Nothing"/ "I Don't Wanna Do Like That"/"Wonderful Tonight"/"Cocaine"/"Layla"/ "Solid Rock"/"Saturday Night"/"Sunshine of Your Love."

Wonderful Tonight (Raindrop POD ECB83). "Tulsa Time"/"I Shot the Sheriff"/"Lay Down Sally"/"Worried Life Blues"/"Let It Rain"/"Double Trouble"/"Sweet Eliza"/"After Midnight"/"The Shape You're In"/ "Wonderful Tonight"/"Blues Power"/"Have You Ever Loved a Woman?"/"Trouble"/"Cocaine"/"Layla"/"Further on up the Road."

Appendix:
Eric Clapton's Bands

1963—The Roosters (March–September). EC (guitar), Ben Palmer (piano), Tom McGuinness (guitar/bass), Robin Mason (drums), Terry Brennan (vocals).

Casey Jones and the Engineers (September). EC (guitar), Tom McGuinness (guitar), Brian Casser (vocals), Ray Stock (drums), Dave McCumisky (bass).

The Yardbirds (October–December). EC (guitar), Keith Relf (vocals/harmonica), Paul Samwell-Smith (bass), Jim McCarty (drums), Chris Dreja (guitar).

1964—The Yardbirds. Albums: *Sonny Boy Williamson and the Yardbirds*; Five Live Yardbirds.

1965—The Yardbirds (January–March).

John Mayall and the Bluesbreakers (April–August, October–December). EC (guitar), John Mayall (keyboards/ guitar/harmonica/vocals), John McVie (bass), Hughie Flint (drums). (Jack Bruce sat in with the band, playing alongside EC, in October.)

The Glands (August–October). EC (guitar), Ben Palmer (piano), Jake Milton (drums), Bob Ray (bass), Bernie Greenwood (sax), John Baily (vocals).

1966—John Mayall and the Bluesbreakers (January–June). Album: *John Mayall's Bluesbreakers with Eric Clapton.*

Eric Clapton and the Powerhouse (April). EC (guitar), Jack Bruce (bass), Stevie Winwood (organ/vocals), Paul Jones (harmonica), Pete York (drums), Ben Palmer (piano). Album: *What's Shakin'* (three tracks).

Cream (June–December). EC (guitar/vocals), Jack Bruce (bass/harmonica/vocals), Ginger Baker (drums). Album: *Fresh Cream.*

1967—Cream. Album: *Disraeli Gears.*

1968—Cream. Albums: *Wheels of Fire*; *Goodbye.*

1969—Blind Faith. EC (guitar/vocals), Stevie Winwood (keyboards/guitar/vocals), Rick Grech (bass/violin), Ginger Baker (drums). Album: *Blind Faith.*

Plastic Ono Band (September 13). EC (guitar), John Lennon (guitar/vocals), Yoko Ono (vocals), Klaus Voorman (bass), Alan White (drums). Album: *Live Peace in Toronto.*

Delaney and Bonnie and Friends (November–December). EC (guitar), Delaney Bramlett (guitar/vocals), Bonnie Bramlett (vocals), Carl Radle (bass), Bobby Whitlock (keyboards/vocals), Jim Gordon (drums), Jim Price (trumpet), Bobby Keys (sax), Rita Coolidge (vocals), Dave Mason (guitar).

1970—Delaney and Bonnie and Friends (January–March). Albums: *Delaney and Bonnie on Tour with Eric Clapton*; *Eric Clapton.*

Derek and the Dominos (May–December). EC (guitar/vocals), Bobby Whitlock (keyboards/vocals), Carl Radle (bass), Jim Gordon (drums). Duane Allman played guitar on the band's studio recording, and Dave Mason played with the group on its first single and its first gig only. Albums: *Layla and Other Assorted Love Songs*; *Derek and the Dominos—Live in Concert*.

1971—Derek and the Dominos (January–April).

George Harrison's Concert for Bangla Desh (August 1). EC (guitar), George Harrison (guitar/vocals), Leon Russell (piano/vocals), Ringo Starr (drums/vocals), Klaus Voorman (bass), Billy Preston (organ/vocals), Jim Keltner (drums), Carl Radle (bass), Jesse Ed Davis (guitar), Don Preston (guitar), Pete Ham (guitar/vocals). Album: *Concert for Bangla Desh*.

1972—Did not perform.

1973—Eric Clapton's Rainbow Concert Band (January 13). EC (guitar/vocals), Pete Townshend (guitar), Ronnie Wood (guitar), Stevie Winwood (keyboards/vocals), Rick Grech (bass), Jim Capaldi (drums), Jimmy Karstein (drums), Rebop (percussion). Album: *Eric Clapton's Rainbow Concert*.

1974—Eric Clapton and His Band (A) (April–December). EC (guitar/vocals), Carl Radle (bass), George Terry (guitar/vocals), Dick Sims (keyboards), Jamie Oldaker (drums) Yvonne Elliman (vocals), Marcy Levy (vocals), Sergio Pastora Rodriguez (percussion). Album: *461 Ocean Boulevard*. [Also appearing on the album: Albhy Galuten (keyboards), Jim Fox (drums), Al Jackson (drums).]

1975—Eric Clapton and His Band (A). Albums: *There's One in Every Crowd*; *E.C. Was Here*.

1976—Eric Clapton and His Band (A). Album: *No Reason to Cry*. [Also appearing on the album: Robbie Robertson (guitar), Ronnie Wood (guitar), Bob Dylan (guitar/vocals), Billy Preston (keyboards/vocals), Georgie Fame (keyboards), Rick Danko (bass/vocals), Garth Hudson (organ), Richard Manuel (piano/vocals), Levon Helm (drums/vocals).]

1977—Eric Clapton and His Band (A). Album: *Slowhand*. [Also appearing on the album: Mel Collins (sax).] Yvonne Elliman and Sergio Pastora Rodriguez left the group in June.

1978—Eric Clapton and His Band (A). Album: *Backless*. [Also appearing on the album: Benny Gallagher (vocals), Graham Lyle (vocals).] George Terry and Marcy Levy left the band in August.

1979—Eric Clapton and His Band (B) (January–September). EC (guitar/vocals), Albert Lee (guitar), Carl Radle (bass), Dick Sims (keyboards), Jamie Oldaker (drums).

Eric Clapton and His Band (C) (October–December). EC (guitar/vocals), Albert Lee (guitar/vocals), Chris Stainton (keyboards), Dave Markee (bass), Henry Spinetti (drums). Album: *Just One Night*.

1980—Eric Clapton and His Band (D). EC (guitar/vocals), Gary Brooker (keyboards/vocals), Albert Lee (guitar/vocals), Chris Stainton (keyboards), Dave Markee (bass), Henry Spinetti (drums).

1981—Eric Clapton and His Band (D). Album: *Another Ticket*.

1982—Eric Clapton and His Band (D) (January–August).

Eric Clapton and His Band (E) (August–December). EC (guitar/vocals), Albert Lee (guitar/vocals), Donald "Duck" Dunn (bass), Chris Stainton (keyboards), Roger Hawkins (drums). Album: *Money and Cigarettes*. [Also appearing on the album: Ry Cooder (guitar).]

1983—Eric Clapton and His Band (E) (January–February).

Eric Clapton and His Band (F) (February–August). EC (guitar/vocals), Albert Lee (guitar/vocals), Donald "Duck" Dunn (bass), Chris Stainton (keyboards), Jamie Oldaker (drums).

ARMS Benefit Tour Band (September–December). EC (guitar/vocals), Ronnie Lane (vocals), Joe Cocker (vocals), Paul Rogers (vocals), Jeff Beck (guitar), Jimmy Page (guitar), Charlie Watts (drums), Simon Phillips (drums), Kenney Jones (drums), Andy Fairweather-Low (guitar/vocals), Bill Wyman (bass), Chris Stainton (keyboards), Tony Hymas (keyboards), Fernando Saunders (bass/vocals), Ray Cooper (drums/percussion), James Hooker (keyboards). Steve Winwood played keyboards and mandolin, and sang, in the UK concerts.

1984—Roger Waters "Pros and Cons" Touring Band (May–July). EC (guitar), Roger Waters (bass/vocals), Chris Stainton (keyboards), Tim Renwick (guitar), Andy Newmark (drums), Michael Kamen (keyboards), Mel Collins (sax), Katie Kissoon (vocals), Doreen Chanter (vocals).

Eric Clapton and His Band (G) (March–December). EC (guitar/vocals), Donald "Duck" Dunn (bass), Jamie Oldaker (drums), Chris Stainton (keyboards), Peter Robinson (keyboards), Shaun Murphy (vocals), Marcy Levy (vocals). Album: *Behind the Sun*. [Also appearing on the album: Phil Collins (drums/percussion/vocals), Jeff Porcaro (drums), John Robinson (drums), Nathan East (bass), Steve Lukather (guitar), Lindsay Buckingham (guitar), Michael Omartian (keyboards), Greg Phillinganes (keyboards), Nathan Howard (keyboards), Lenny Castro (congas), Jerry Williams (vocals), Ted Templeman (percussion).]

1985—Eric Clapton and His Band (H). EC (guitar/vocals), Tim Renwick (guitar), Donald "Duck" Dunn (bass), Jamie Oldaker (drums), Chris Stainton (keyboards), Shaun Murphy (vocals), Laura Creamer (vocals). Marcy Levy left the band in July.

1986—Eric Clapton and His Band (I) (January–August). EC (guitar/vo-
cals), Phil Collins (drums/vocals), Nathan East (bass/vocals), Greg
Phillinganes (keyboards/vocals). Album: *August*. [Also appearing
on the album: Tessa Niles (vocals), Katie Kissoon (vocals), Tina
Turner (vocals), Michael Brecker (sax), Randy Brecker (trumpet),
Jon Faddis (trumpet), Dave Bargerone (trombone).]

Eric Clapton and His Band (J) September–December). EC (gui-
tar/vocals), Steve Ferrone (drums), Nathan East (bass/vocals),
Greg Phillinganes (keyboards/vocals).

1987—Eric Clapton and His Band (J).

1988—Eric Clapton and His Band (J).

Eric Clapton/Elton John Japanese Tour Band (November). EC
(guitar/vocals), Elton John (piano/vocals), Mark Knopfler
(guitar/vocals), Nathan East (bass/vocals), Greg Phillinganes (key-
boards/vocals), Steve Ferrone (drums), Ray Cooper (percussion).

1989—Eric Clapton and His Band (I) (January–February). (Royal Albert
Hall Four-Piece Band)

Eric Clapton and His Band (K) (January–February). EC
(guitar/vocals), Mark Knopfler (guitar/vocals), Nathan East
(bass/vocals), Alan Clark (keyboards), Steve Ferrone (drums), Ray
Cooper (percussion), Tessa Niles (vocals), Katie Kissoon (vocals).
(Royal Albert Hall Big Band)

Eric Clapton and His Band (L). EC (guitar/vocals), Phil Palmer
(guitar), Nathan East (bass/vocals), Alan Clark (keyboards), Steve
Ferrone (drums), Ray Cooper (percussion), Tessa Niles (vocals),
Katie Kissoon (vocals). Album: *Journeyman*. [Also appearing on
the album: Phil Collins (drums/vocals), George Harrison
(guitar/vocals), Robert Cray (guitar/vocals), Jim Keltner (drums),
Darryl Jones (bass), Cecil Womack (guitar/vocals), Linda Womack

(vocals), Jerry Williams (guitar/vocals), Jeff Bova (keyboards), Chaka Khan (vocals), Richard Tee (piano), Robbie Kondor (keyboards), Carol Steele (congas), John Tropea (guitar), David Sanborn (sax), Vaneese Thomas (vocals), Taawatha Agee (vocals), Pinaa Palladino (bass).]

1990—Eric Clapton and His Band (J) (February). (Royal Albert Hall Four-Piece Band)

Eric Clapton and His Band (M) (February). EC (guitar/vocals), Robert Cray (guitar/vocals), Buddy Guy (guitar/vocals), Johnnie Johnson (piano), Robert Cousins (bass), Jamie Oldaker (drums). (Royal Albert Hall Blues Band)

Eric Clapton and His Band (L) (February–March). (Royal Albert Hall Big Band)

Eric Clapton and His Band (N). EC (guitar/vocals), Phil Palmer (guitar), Nathan East (bass/vocals), Greg Phillinganes (keyboards/vocals), Steve Ferrone (drums), Ray Cooper (percussion), Tessa Niles (vocals), Katie Kissoon (vocals).

1991—Eric Clapton and His Band (J) (February). (Royal Albert Hall Four-Piece Band)

Eric Clapton and His Band (O) (February). EC (guitar/vocals), Johnnie Johnson (piano), Jimmie Vaughan (guitar/vocals), Buddy Guy (guitar/vocals), Chuck Leavell (keyboards), Jamie Oldaker (drums), Albert Collins (guitar/vocals), Robert Cray (guitar/vocals), Greg Phillinganes (keyboards/vocals), Joey Spampinato (bass), Jerry Portnoy (harmonica). (Royal Albert Hall Blues Band)

Eric Clapton and His Band (P) (February–March). EC (guitar/vocals), Phil Palmer (guitar), Nathan East (bass/vocals), Steve Ferrone (drums), Greg Phillinganes (keyboard/vocals), Chuck

Leavell (keyboards), Ray Cooper (percussion), Tessa Niles (vocals), Katie Kissoon (vocals). (Royal Albert Hall Big Band)

George Harrison Japanese Tour Band (December). EC (guitar/vocals), George Harrison (guitar/vocals), Andy Fairweather-Low (guitar), Nathan East (bass/vocals), Chuck Leavell (keyboards), Greg Phillinganes (keyboards/vocals), Steve Ferrone (drums), Ray Cooper (percussion), Tessa Niles (vocals), Katie Kissoon (vocals). Album: *Live in Japan*.

1992—Eric Clapton and His Band (Q) (January). EC (guitar/vocals), Nathan East (bass/vocals), Andy Fairweather-Low (guitar/vocals), Chuck Leavell (keyboards), Steve Ferrone (drums), Ray Cooper (percussion), Tessa Niles (vocals), Katie Kissoon (vocals). Album: *Unplugged*.

Eric Clapton and His Band (R) (April–September). EC (guitar/vocals), Nathan East (bass/vocals), Andy Fairweather-Low (guitar/vocals), Chuck Leavell (keyboards), Steve Ferrone (drums), Ray Cooper (percussion), Gina Foster (vocals), Katie Kissoon (vocals).

1993—Eric Clapton and His Band (S) (February–March). EC (guitar/vocals), Andy Fairweather-Low (guitar), Jimmie Vaughan (guitar/vocals), Donald "Duck" Dunn (bass), Richie Hayward (drums), Jerry Portnoy (harmonica), Chris Stainton (keyboards), Tim Sanders (sax), Simon Clarke (sax), Roddy Lorimer. (Royal Albert Hall Blues Band)

1994—Eric Clapton and His Band (T). EC (guitar/vocals), Dave Bronze (bass), Jim Keltner (drums), Andy Fairweather-Low (guitar), Jerry Portnoy (harmonica), Chris Stainton (keyboards), Roddy Lorimer (trumpet), Simon Clarke (sax), Tim Sanders (sax). Album: *From the Cradle*.

Eric Clapton and His Band (U) (September–December). EC (guitar/vocals), Dave Bronze (bass), Andy Newmark (drums), Andy Fairweather-Low (guitar/vocals), Jerry Portnoy (harmonica), Chris Stainton (keyboards), Roddy Lorimer (trumpet), Simon Clarke (sax), Tim Sanders (sax).

Index

407

ICE AND SNOW NEAR THE GANGES' SOURCE

FOG DESCENDS ON BIRCH-COVERED MOUNTAIN IN KHUMBU, NEPAL

NALTA, A GLACIAL LAKE IN THE KARAKORAMS

THE HIMALAYAS

THE WORLD'S WILD PLACES/TIME-LIFE BOOKS/AMSTERDAM

BY NIGEL NICOLSON
AND THE EDITORS OF TIME-LIFE BOOKS

THE WORLD'S WILD PLACES

Editorial Staff for *The Himalayas*:
EDITOR: John Man
Deputy Editor: Christopher Farman
Picture Editor: Pamela Marke
Design Consultant: Louis Klein
Staff Writers:
Michael Brown, Mally Cox, Kate Dorment,
Dan Freeman, Heather Sherlock,
Timberlake Wertenbaker
Art Director: Graham Davis
Assistant Art Director: Roy Williams
Design Assistant: Joyce Mason
Picture Researchers:
Karin Pearce, Susan Stratton
Editorial Researcher: Vanessa Kramer
Editorial Co-ordinator: Jackie Matthews

Consultants
Botany: Christopher Grey-Wilson, Phyllis Edwards
Invertebrates: Michael Tweedie
Geology: Dr. Peter Stubbs
Geomorphology: John Tyson
Ornithology: I. J. Ferguson-Lees
Zoology: Dr. P. J. K. Burton

The captions and text of the picture essays are written
by the staff of Time-Life Books.

Valuable assistance was given in the preparation of
this volume by the following Time-Life correspondents:
Elizabeth Hawley, Kathmandu, and Jim Shepherd,
New Delhi.

Published by Time-Life International (Nederland) B.V.
5 Ottho Heldringstraat, Amsterdam 18

The Author: Nigel Nicolson first visited Nepal for two weeks in 1965, and has subsequently spent almost four months in the Himalayas in order to write this book. An accomplished author of many books on architecture, history, and politics, his most recent ones include *Portrait of a Marriage*, and *Alex*, a widely acclaimed biography of Earl Alexander of Tunis.

The Consultant: Lord Hunt of Llanvair Waterdine is a distinguished mountaineer who led the successful assault on Mount Everest in 1953. Other expeditions have taken him to Russia, Greenland, Greece and Poland. He is a strong supporter of international mountaineering projects. Among the books he has written are: *The Ascent of Everest* and *The Red Snows*.

The Cover: Beyond a shadow-darkened ridge in north-west Jammu-Kashmir, Nanga Parbat soars 26,660 feet into the clouds. Thirty men died climbing this peak before it was conquered by a German and Austrian team in 1953.

Contents

The World's Highest Mountain Chain

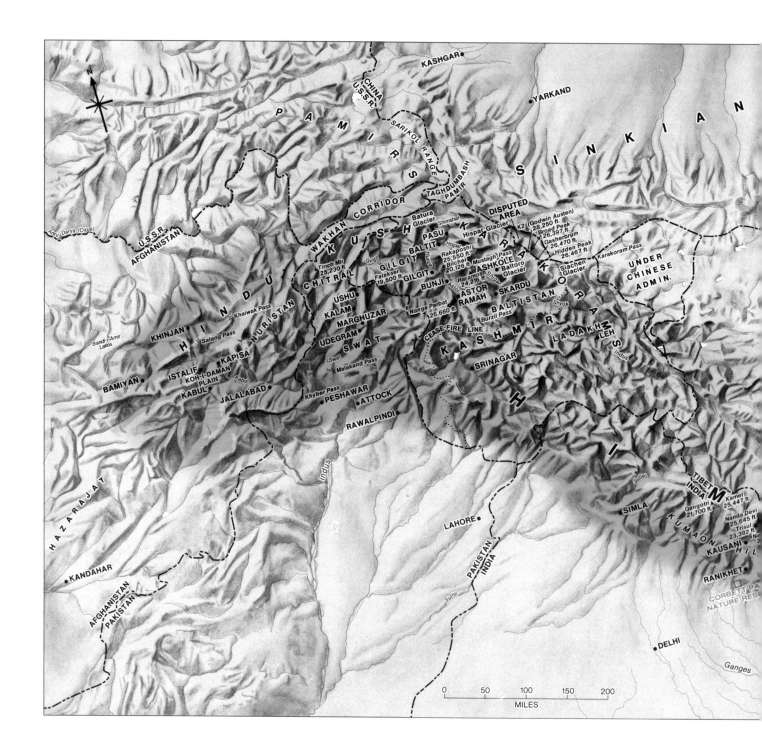

The extensive mountain chain, the Himalayas, indicated by the green rectangle on the outline map (right), stretches across the thick neck of the Indian sub-continent for about 1,700 miles, from Afghanistan in the west to Assam in the south-east. Roughly 100 to 150 miles wide, its awesome bulk straddles eight countries, dividing India from Tibet. Distinguished by enormous variety of climate, vegetation and wild life, the Himalayas consist of three major ranges. Typically Himalayan are the Everest and Karakoram ranges with their lush tropical valleys and their titan peaks perpetually covered by snow. The Hindu Kush range in the far west lies beyond the reach of the monsoons, and its slopes are therefore bleaker. On the relief map (below) dark green stands for vegetation up to the tree-line at 12,000 feet; light green represents the alpine zone at 15,000 feet. The nature reserves and national parks are in red. Passes are marked) (. Peaks are indicated by a triangle. Rivers and lakes are in blue.

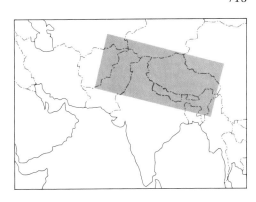

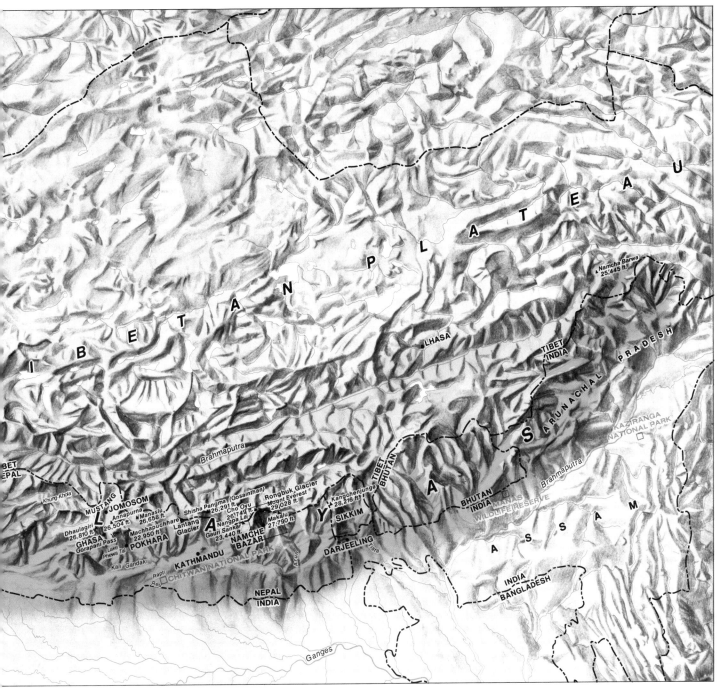

"Himalaya" means

1/ "Abode of Snow"

A hundred divine epochs would not suffice to describe
all the marvels of the Himalayas.   SANSKRIT PROVERB

Some years ago I flew from Delhi to Moscow. The clouds rolled in heavily over Delhi's airport, and with the resigned despondency of all long-distance travellers I foresaw a dull, tiring flight. But gloom and clouds can both be penetrated. The clouds persisted until Moscow, but within a few minutes from take-off we rose above them. I glanced out of the window. There, piercing the clouds, was a sight that made me grip my neighbour's arm. "Look!" I cried, "the Himalayas!" He was not impressed: I had spilled his coffee.

I had never seen them before, and there they were, or at least the middle section of them, from Kashmir to Nepal, stretched across the wide angle of my vision at a mean distance of 200 miles. My first impression was of their whiteness; the second of their regularity; the third of their unexpected smallness. The range rose suddenly as a toothed ridge above the plain of the clouds, taut as the blade of a band-saw, glitter-white in the sun, its narrowness accentuated by its length. It seemed to me a small protuberance for so great an earth. But five vertical miles were dwarfed by the 500 horizontal miles I could see from the aeroplane.

Something of their immensity became clearer as we flew close to the Karakorams, the north-west section of the Himalayas in northern Kashmir. The range now appeared like a coastline, the clouds a grey sea washing its feet and penetrating its fjords. The ground was heavily broken, and black began to appear against the white, the black of huge rock-faces too steep to hold the snow. I was able to distinguish individual peaks: K2, the second highest in the world; Nanga Parbat, which killed 30 men before it was climbed. Their beauty was cruel, terrifyingly silent. They assumed defiant attitudes, basically pyramidal in deference to the only law that they were forced to acknowledge, the law of gravity, but their crowns were formed by geological accident—sharp as thorns, or domed and sullen. They seemed to possess every characteristic of living people.

Nine years later I returned to the Himalayas for this book with photographer Terry Spencer. Now we confronted them without the advantage of a height greater than their own. At dusk I looked out from the Indian village that was our base, towards the huge mountain-island of Nanda Devi and Nanda Kot 30 miles away, an island because both peaks are separated from their neighbours by vast ravines on each side. Nanda Devi, 25,645 feet high, is considered by many the pearl of the Himalayas, so symmetrical, so simple that a child could draw it, the double peaks linked by a straight edge as fine as a chisel's, the blade formed by a 10,000-foot ice-wall, grooved but immaculate.

Our village was called Kausani, which crowns a high ridge where Mahatma Gandhi once spent three months writing one of his best-known books, *Anashakti Yog*. The man in charge of his bungalow, now a shrine, said that we could stay there the night if we wished, but there were certain rules. We asked what they were. "First you must take off your shoes." We took off our shoes. "You must not eat meat while you are in this place." I wondered, but did not dare ask, whether eggs counted as meat, for hard-boiled eggs were all we had brought with us. "Next," he said, "we have a service in memory of the Mahatma every evening at six sharp." There is no person in the recent history of the East whose memory I revere more greatly, but we both knew instinctively that neither in body nor in spirit were we worthy to occupy Gandhi's bungalow even for a single night. We managed to find rooms in a government rest-house a little way along the ridge. It was very uncomfortable, but we had a magnificent view of Nanda Devi.

Below us the ground fell away in terraces to a deep valley and then mounted again to another ridge, and beyond it to another, and then another, respectively the gallery, dress-circle and stalls facing a vast proscenium. We saw before us a frontier written against the sky, an ultimate lift of the earth's surface, a frontier between much more than India and Tibet, for it divides climates, cultures, religions and centuries. It is the most authentic wilderness in the world. Men can inhabit swamps and deserts and even polar wastes, but few living things can exist for long in the frozen fastness that we saw so clearly from so safe a distance. Ruled out of bounds by their permanent covering of snow, the upper few thousand feet were spectacular seen through binoculars. Himalaya means "Abode of Snow". There lay its roof-top. The ridges rode upwards supported by precipices to such needle-points that if it were architecture one could not believe that stone thus suspended could retain its stability.

Occasionally a small cloud hitched itself to a peak and flew for an hour like a tattered pennant, but most of the range remained untarnished-white until shortly before sundown. The light then dropped like sound receding. The valleys, last to receive it, first to lose it, returned to the lap of darkness, but for long afterwards the snow-mountains were swept by colour. Nothing changes in mountains but visibility and the intensity of light, Promethean light upon Promethean rock, one elemental force reacting upon another.

The clouds, streakily horizontal or rising in flares, now gathered huger than the mountains but made them seem higher, just as a man swaddled in bedclothes seems taller than when upright. As the sun sank, the clouds retained its light till at last they were little balls of filmy gauze, such as you see accompanied by cherubim in the background of Italian paintings. Then rose the full moon, the great compensator, and late that night I left my bed to discover whether it could restore the mountains to me. It did, vestigially. If I had not known that they were there, I would have doubted what I saw: sheets of distant whiteness, rhomboid-shaped, like yachts in mist, pale, irregular and spectral.

A third scene comes to my mind, no longer from outside the Himalayas but from within them. We were camped on the western slopes of Annapurna. It had been a hard day's walking, and fearing to risk the precipitous path in darkness, Terry and I decided to call a halt. We pitched our tents in a small field on the valley floor, and sat over the camp-fire between them. Suddenly I spotted a brilliant point of light almost directly overhead.

"It's a planet," I said.

"No planet is as bright as that," said Terry.

"Then it's Skylab."

"No, it's not moving."

"I know," I said, with sudden inspiration. "It's the Kohoutek comet," of which the imminent approach had just been announced.

"Far too soon for that," Terry replied.

Then what? We consulted our head porter, a Sherpa. He laughed. "It's a shepherd's bonfire." It did not seem possible. The thing was in the sky. But he was right, as we saw clearly when daylight returned. Darkness had not only obliterated detail; it had erased from our short-lived memories the gradient of the mountainside. From its five linked peaks, Annapurna does not flow or tumble to man-level. It shoots down. We had been looking at a spot barely 2,000 feet over our heads. The mountain rose a further 20,000 feet above it.

In all our travels I never experienced a more dramatic reminder of the scale of the Himalayas. It is well known that they contain the greatest mountains on earth, but few people realize how much greater they are than any others. In all of North America the highest peak is 20,320 feet (Mount McKinley, Alaska); in the Andes, Aconcagua (22,834); in Africa, Kilimanjaro (19,340); in Europe, Mont Blanc (15,781); in Australasia, Mount Cook (12,349). But in the Himalayas, Karakorams and Hindu Kush, all connected geologically and ecologically, there are three peaks —Everest, K2 and Kangchenjunga—over 28,000 feet, and 13 others over 26,000. Their names are as majestic as their appearance: Lhotse, Makalu, Dhaulagiri, Cho Oyu, Nanga Parbat, Manaslu, Annapurna I and II, Hidden Peak, Broad Peak, Gasherbrum II, Shisha Pangma (also named Gosainthan), Gasherbrum IV. So many others exceed in height the tallest mountains elsewhere in the world that while they have now all been mapped, comparatively few have been named.

The Himalayas, Karakorams and Hindu Kush cover by their joint length of some 1,700 miles parts of eight countries: India, Bhutan, Sikkim, Nepal, Pakistan, China (including Tibet) and Afghanistan. The Pamirs are also geologically part of the group, but spring away from it northwards, and are outside the scope of this book.

The Himalayas do not make a neat pattern on a relief map. They present no clean arc like the Alps, no line as firmly ruled as the Andes. The range runs north-east through Afghanistan, east and south through Kashmir, south-east through India, east through Nepal, Sikkim and Bhutan, and north-east again to the Brahmaputra. The foothills on the "Indian" side would qualify on most maps as considerable mountain ranges by themselves, while the high plateau of Tibet and its continuation into southern China maintain a general level of 15,000 feet, splashing the map with wide areas of a disconcerting dark brown and speckling it with the white of permanent snow. One would be tempted to ask: Where *are* the Himalayas?

On the ground it is different. Nobody standing on a hilltop in the Kumaons or on the airfield of Pokhara in central Nepal would have any doubt where the Himalayas are. At Pokhara the valley floor lies at 2,900 feet. In front, with scarcely an intervening foothill, rises Machhapuchhare, nearly 23,000 feet high, and beyond it, the colossal curve of the Annapurnas, five summits in a row. In no place on earth is there so great a vertical rise in so short a horizontal distance.

The Himalayas demand superlatives. They *are* superlative: the highest mountain, the highest pass, the deepest gorge, the highest-living animals—the mountains confront us with phenomena that exist nowhere else on earth. Other mountain ranges can be digested by the landscape: they are penetrable, harnessed by roads and railways. But no railways cross the Himalayas, and few roads. They are mountains so stupendous that they can be overflown, but not tunnelled; climbed, but never tamed; mapped, but seldom visited. They are, and look like, what Kenneth Mason, formerly a Superintendent of the Survey of India, has called "the greatest physical feature of the earth." Why do they reach so high? Why, to twist the famous phrase, *why* are they there?

In Kathmandu I met a young French geologist. I do not like geology because I do not understand its language, but I very much liked this geologist, because he was able to explain to me by two simple gestures how the Himalayas were formed.

First he held his hands palms down, fingers pointing inward, some six inches apart, and slowly moved one hand into the other. His fingers bent under pressure; some folded downwards to lie alongside each other, but most yielded upwards into peaks.

"My hands," he said, "are two continents. When they meet, and if pressure is maintained, two things can happen. They can fold under each other; or they can be forced into the air. The Himalayas are my upper fingers, the buckled edges of two continents that clashed."

"But if they were forced up as you say, why are they so pointed? After all, rocks aren't like your fingers. They lose their shape under pressure. One would have expected a tumbled mass, not those elegant pyramids and spires."

Then he gave me his second demonstration. He held up one hand, vertically, and separated his fingers. The gaps between them represented the valleys and glaciers—the fissures—and he explained that rocks can be easily cut by water, ice, wind, landslide and avalanche into sharp shapes. He pointed to his middle finger: "Machhapuchhare!" he said with a smile, and strode off.

A shaggy male yak pauses briefly from his grazing on grass and lichen in one of the few photographs ever taken of the wild yak in its natural environment. Hunted almost to extinction, most of the wild yak have retreated to the remotest heights of the 15,000-foot Tibetan plateau. During spring the yak's under-fur—which in winter insulates it from temperatures of −40° F.— moults, giving it this dishevelled look.

I had never wondered before why mountains exist. To me they had simply been part of the natural scene. But mountains are not that permanent. Enormous pressures built them, pressures exerted by the movement of primeval continents, in a continuing process known to geologists as Continental Drift. Continents, or pieces of the continents as we know them, and all the oceans, are carried on rafts or "plates" some 40 miles thick, and these plates float on the viscous rock beneath the earth's crust. They move with inexorable slowness, from half an inch to four inches in a year, away from or towards each other. When they move away, new ocean floors form in their wake; when they collide, they raise mountains because their coastal and submarine rocks, after a bit of undershuffling, have no place to go but upwards.

This process, of course, is very gradual and began between 40 and 60 million years ago, when the plate bearing what was then the separate continent of India collided with that of the huge northern continent of Asia. But quite recently there came a climax. Between half a million and two million years ago the Himalayas shot up another 10,000 feet, at a rate unknown in any other geological event. They are, therefore, the youngest as well as the highest mountains in the world, and they are high because they are young. There has been no time for erosion to wear them down.

As you walk in the Himalayas, and if you have been taught to look for it, you can find evidence of these cataclysmic events. The first is the presence of fossilized sea-animals high up on the slopes. One day in central Nepal a boy brought me a round piece of dark-blue shale that he cracked open on a rock. Inside was the perfectly preserved fossil of an ammonite, a sea creature that flourished for hundreds of millions of years and then become extinct. These ammonites have been found in the Himalayas as high as 18,000 feet. The uppermost levels are limestone, a rock formed by the gradual deposit on the seabed of the shells of marine creatures. There can be only one explanation: as the continents collided and reared upwards at their edges, part of the original seabed between them was carried up with the deeper rocks.

Another and even more startling effect of Continental Drift is the direction taken by Himalayan rivers. One might have supposed that the greatest mountain range on earth would also form its most impressive watershed. The rain and melting snow must surely flow down the northern slopes into Tibet and down the southern slopes into the Indian plain. Instead they form rivers that cut through the relatively new and soft structure of the mountains on their way to the lowlands and the sea. In this respect, too, they are unique among the mountains of the

Under clumps of bankside grass, a swift glacial stream flows through a sharply-angled channel in rock 20,000 feet up on Annapurna South. The stripes are the tilted strata of alternating sediments— such as limestone and shale—that have been exposed by the water's persistent erosive action over thousands of years.

world. Thus, the great water-divide is not the crest-line of the mountains, but the edge of the Tibetan plateau, 100 miles to the north of it and, on average, 10,000 feet lower down.

The result is seen in the huge trans-Himalayan gorges, the deepest in the world. Two of the main rivers, the Indus and the Brahmaputra, which rise a few miles from each other in Tibet, wend nearly 1,000 miles west and east before they turn abruptly southwards to cut through the Himalayas to the Indian Ocean. But a smaller river like the Arun, which flows between the Everest massif and Kangchenjunga, rises 80 miles north of Everest and breaks directly through the chain in a gorge over 18,000 feet deep. (Its headwaters are less than two miles from the course of the Brahmaputra. The Arun, with its violently erosive strength and steep gradient, must sooner or later claw its way through this narrow watershed and "capture" the Brahmaputra, thus reducing one of the greatest rivers of the world to a miserable trickle.)

The geologists explain this curious phenomenon by supposing that the rivers must already have been there before the Himalayas rose to their present height. The Arun, and many others like it, found their natural way to the ocean southwards from the highest mountains then existing. When, in their final convulsion, the Himalayas topped the Tibetan mountains, the rivers were strong enough to hold their course through the rising barrier, cutting their gorges in the soft sedimentary rocks and the tougher granites.

The process is still not complete. The rocks are being forced upwards by the continuing pressure beneath them. It is difficult to gauge the rate of rise because measurements do not extend back for more than a century, but there is no doubt that the highest Himalayas are growing higher under the pressure of the still-merging continents. The annual growth has been calculated at between three and four inches. But this does not allow for erosion, and the net growth is estimated at a few inches a century. However, this is definite enough for a geologist to have warned mountaineers facetiously in 1952 that they must climb Everest before it became too high to climb. The British expedition did so in the following year.

Appalling disasters accompany the movement of the rocks. The huge natural forces of uplift and gravity and cleavage by ice and water can render futile man's attempts to control them. The Himalayas are a region of constant earthquake, landslip and flood. In 1841 a mass of rock from the west side of Nanga Parbat was precipitated into the Indus, holding back the waters to form a lake 40 miles long, and when a few months later the dam burst, the flood was catastrophic, drowning an entire Sikh army camped at Attock 100 miles lower down. The Nepal earthquake of 1934 killed more than 10,000 people.

Everywhere in the Himalayas one can see evidence of changes on a lesser scale. Turning the corner of a mountain path, I came upon a scene of devastation caused by a landslip only three weeks before. A fraction of a mountain spur, giving way suddenly in the middle of the night, had obliterated in a few seconds a fraction of human endeavour. It had sheared a path clean through a village centre. Twelve sleeping people were killed instantly. The timbers of their houses were strewn like matchsticks, and boulders as big as cottages lay heavily where cottages had stood. Five hundred feet above, the cliff showed a clean scar; five hundred feet below, the torrent of rocks lay expended on the valley floor. Such disasters will occur over and over again, unpredictably, when a last drop of surface-water tips the precarious balance. "Abode of Snow"! How homely a name for something so implacably cruel!

Yet these inhospitable carcasses of shifting rock are also sources of sustenance, and are feared and worshipped by their inhabitants. Annapurna means "Giver of Life" and the Tibetan name for the Everest group is Chomolungma, "Goddess Mother of the Earth." Their snows feed the valleys, water the animals and crops, nourish the primula and the pine. On their lower slopes the monsoon adds its heavy load to this massive process of irrigation.

The monsoon is not itself a rain, but a wind that carries rain. It originates in the Indian Ocean and, flowing water-laden across India, rides up the slopes of the mountains, expanding and cooling as it ascends. Eventually, the vapour condenses and rain pours down in torrents between April and mid-October, according to the longitude. "Upon what a gigantic scale does nature here operate!" wrote the British naturalist, Joseph Dalton Hooker, in 1848. "Vapours raised from an ocean whose nearest route is more than 400 miles distant are safely transported without the loss of one drop of water to support the rank luxuriance of this far distant region. This and other offices fulfilled, the waste waters are returned by the rivers to the ocean, and again exhaled, exported, recollected and returned!"

Today we express our admiration of nature less extravagantly, and also more precisely, because Hooker was wrong in attributing to the monsoon such miraculous powers of containment: on its way to the Himalayas it leaks considerably. On arrival it releases its water on the southern and middle slopes of the mountains. Above 20,000 feet little remains to fall, which is one reason why Everest's summit is usually seen as a pyramid of black rock; and none of it on the Tibetan plateau beyond. The Himalayas are a climatic barrier: southwards, they absorb the monsoon like a hydraulic buffer; northwards, they shield the plains from the cruel climate of Tibet, its searing summer winds and bitter winter gales. As it moves westward, the monsoon's load decreases. At Darjeeling, on the border of Sikkim, the rainfall is 123 inches in the year; at Simla, north of Delhi, it is 63 inches; at Leh, in Kashmir, only three.

At the end of the rains, the climate of the monsoon Himalayas is delightful. In three months of travel I experienced only one short spatter of rain, and walked shirt-sleeved as high as 13,000 feet in sunshine that was unbroken for days on end, and in air so pure that a mountain peak 20 miles away appeared but five. In the mountains the temperature varies greatly from place to place and from hour to hour, so thin is the air and so intense the radiation. In the daytime you can suffer from sunstroke; at night from acute frost-bite. When the temperature drops sharply at dusk, there is always (for the casual walker) the refuge of the plains, where true winter never comes. One is reluctant to seek it. The height lost must be painfully regained next day; and what is a horizon closed by nearby trees compared to the view at dawn from the upper hills, of sunlit mountains rising above gulfs of encircling mist?

The monsoon is partly responsible for the variety of Himalayan vegetation, but more important is the rapid change of altitude. Just as the southern slopes of the mountains are quite different from the northern, the first freshened by the monsoon and vigorous, the others bleak and sterile, so in ascending from the *terai*, or jungle, in the lower valleys to the tree-line and then the snow-line, one passes through botanical layers that could only be discovered in the flat lands of Europe and America by a south-north journey of 3,000 miles. If in the plains the temperature is 80°F., it will be −40°F. at the summit of Everest. Almost the whole range of the world's climate, and hence its flora and fauna, are concentrated within four or five vertical miles, from tropical jungle to frozen slopes.

The part of the *terai* that I visited was not particularly dense. The sal tree, which is its main constituent, is a fine, straight-limbed evergreen that discourages the undergrowth, and the jungle is more like a thick Western forest than the nightmare litter of decaying branches, weeds, vines and brambles, that I had imagined. The ground is clear, patinated by starry flowers. Much of the *terai* is open country, but only in the sense

One of the most eminent of 19th-Century scientists and a close confidant of Darwin, Sir Joseph Dalton Hooker (above) travelled through India to study the distribution and evolution of plant species. In 1848-50, he explored Sikkim where he discovered some 22 new species of rhododendron, a common Himalayan flowering shrub. Among these was the Rhododendron dalhousiae (shown right in Hooker's own drawing), named after Lady Dalhousie, wife of the then Governor-General of India.

of being treeless, for the view across it is even more restricted than in the jungle proper—by grasses and bamboo that by the autumn have grown as much as 25 feet high.

From the *terai* we worked our way up to Ranikhet in the Kumaon Hills, a vertical distance of some 8,000 feet, and by degrees, with deep interpenetration, the vegetation changed. The lower forest is alive with insect and animal life, rank with growth; the upper is distinguished by its silence. The sal gives place to pine, the pine to oak, the oak to juniper and rhododendron, and above that comes birch, which marks the tree-line. At intervals we found solitary specimens of maple, Indian horse-chestnut (*Aesculus india*), the silk-cotton tree, and the imported eucalyptus. The most interesting sight was a marvellous example of the banyan tree, trailing aerial roots until they anchored in the earth and grew as satellite trunks, turning a tree into a marquee.

Freaks like the banyan do not form forests. Of those trees that do, by far the loveliest are not the oaks, which in Asia have lost the graceful boles and crowns of their European and North American cousins, but the conifers. Here there are not only pines, but also spruce, larch, fir and juniper. They are old in geological time. They have stood in the snow and cold and darkness, yet are evergreen, reminders that all winters come to an end, that life endures. The king of them all in the Kumaons is the chir pine. They stride along a sky-silhouetted ridge, or in glades that sweep down slopes so steep that the roots of one are level with its neighbour's spire. The forest floor is thick with their fallen needles. These prevent intrusive growth, so that the view between their well-spaced trunks is unimpeded, and they wend to the valley bottoms like colonnades. Sometimes the chir will vary its slim triangular shape to grow tufts at intervals up the trunk, terminating in a spidery puff-ball at the top, a growth as unattractive as the tufts of hair on a clipped poodle and an indication that branches have been lopped off. It can, however, stand its endless symmetrical repetition, adorning rather than clothing the brown hills, and filling the air with the sweet scent of resin.

Where the trees have light and soil enough beneath them, or on the naked hillsides and above the line where the trees end, flowers grow in such profusion and variety that for many people the Himalayan region means primarily the greatest horticultural treasure-house on earth. I was not there at the season of their greatest blossoming, for like their dreaded companions, the leeches, they flourish best during the monsoon. But there is no need to visit the Himalayas in spring or summer to know their flowers: we can find them in our own gardens, thanks to the work of botanists like Joseph Dalton Hooker, Brian Hodgson, Bishop Heber, Frank Kingdon Ward and Frank Ludlow.

In the Himalayas, most of these flowers extend wild in sheets where the Western city-dweller would boast of a small patch. But some, like the Himalayan blue poppy, which the gardener would propagate to fill a bed, are often extremely elusive in their natural state. One of the joys of Himalayan travel is to find flowers in their greatest variety and numbers above 12,000 feet, between tree and snow, the scale of the flowers diminishing in inverse proportion to the enlargement of the landscape, and their colours deepening in the intensified ultra-violet rays of the sun. The primulas, purple-pink, blue, white and yellow, push up in early spring at the base of great cliffs or in sunny places under the shelter of giant boulders. Others emerge through the snow before it is melted, their buds and leaves wrapped in a scaly protective covering. In July, the meadows between 13,000 and 15,000 feet are bright with potentillas in their millions, anemones, *Corydalis*, several species of aconite and edelweiss, saxifrages, irises, asters, blue, lilac and white gentians (which carpet the ground), and the cotoneaster.

But the pride of the Himalayan flowers, particularly in the east, are the rhododendrons. Among the first shrubs to blossom, from February to April, before the monsoon has time to ravish them, they range from the tiny dwarf carpeter to the tall tree rhododendron, the national flower of Nepal. Flourishing as complete forests at heights between 5,000 and 10,000 feet, the blooms are a multitude of colours from scarlet to pure white. As a shrub, the rhododendron is easily transplantable, and has spread throughout the world. But how different are the clumps in the wilderness sections of large Edwardian gardens from the Himalayan species from which they emerged! In Nepal the tree rhododendrons grow as high as 60 feet, their dark brown limbs twisting like vegetable Laocoons, and staining red whole mountain-sides with their vivid and glorious abundance.

The flowers and the mountains—together they suggest the opposite ends of the scale on which nature works. At one extreme operate the vast, apocalyptic forces that created the mountains; at the other, the intricate subtleties that produced a perfect flower; the first beyond man's capacity to control; the second beyond his present capacity to comprehend. But both equally deserving of his awe.

The Shaping Ice

Since the onset of the first Ice Age nearly two million years ago, ice has been incessantly reshaping the Himalayas. On the mountain summits, where the snow clings precariously, thin sheets of ice have chiselled the peaks to ever finer points (right). Then, from as high as 24,000 feet, where enough ice and snow have accumulated, glaciers have gouged out the rock. Inching down the valleys to some 4,000 feet below the snowline, they have broadened the profiles from a narrow "V", carved by prehistoric rivers, to a smooth-based "U".

Though apparently inert, glaciers actually move at a steady pace, partly by slipping and sliding and partly by a form of plastic motion deep beneath their surface. As snow accumulates, its star-shaped crystals are compressed into rounded granules of ice. As successive layers build up to a depth of several thousands of feet, the pressure of their weight causes the lower levels slowly to flow. This "plastic" core of the glacier drags with it the brittle surface layers. The layers do not move uniformly, however, because their edges are slowed by friction with the valley walls. Wracked by different rates of flow, the edges of the glacier-ribbon continually split into crevasses and reform when the stresses diminish.

As the glacier travels, it bites into the rock over which it travels. At its head, it scoops out an armchair-shaped *cirque*. On Mt. Everest —as on many high peaks—a ring of *cirques* progressively sharpens the mountain's outline.

As the glacier moves down the valley, grinding debris from the floor and walls, it may be joined by tributaries. Because the trunk glacier usually gouges its valley at a faster rate and digs deeper, the tributaries are left "hanging", linked to the main glacier by steep ice-falls.

Glaciers transport most of the rock debris deep within, but some debris accumulates on the surface, in fringing bands called lateral moraines. When glaciers converge, these moraines meet in the centre of the trunk glacier, colouring it like a striped monster.

Most Himalayan glaciers are two to three miles long but the longest, the Siachen, gouges a 45-mile-long valley through the eastern Karakorams. Where they end, their meltwaters expose jumbles of debris in terminal moraines, where mosses and grasses may eventually take root.

Towering more than 23,000 feet near the western face of Everest, Mt. Pumori has been sculpted by ice into a near-perfect pyramid. High on the peak, melting snow has percolated behind the rock faces. In freezing as ice and expanding, it has acted like a giant chisel, exerting pressures of up to nearly one ton per square inch to split off the outer rock. At the base, where enough snow has accumulated, glaciers have gouged out cirques.

High on the Nepal-Tibet frontier, a maze of crevasses scars the surface of glacial ice in Everest's Western Cwm (Welsh: "valley"). This valley-sized cirque, carved westwards from Everest by the Khumbu Glacier, was named by the British explorer, George Mallory, apparently as an expression of his affection for the Welsh highlands. Here, as the glacier curves towards Mt. Pumori (background), it is wracked by stresses that crack open its left-hand edge.

At the head of the 2,000-foot ice-fall that joins the Western Cwm with the Khumbu Glacier, seasonal layers of winter and monsoonal snow are cleft by fissures up to 50 feet deep. Once fractured, the firmly packed snow may be weakened by weathering, causing it to collapse into a mass of icy debris.

In the Hindu Kush, the cumbrous mass of an unnamed glacier grinds an ever-widening passage through the Warm Pass. Heaving over an uneven floor, its surface has been rent by a crevasse whose near-side lip has subsided to a depth of 50 feet. Past glacial action has hollowed the flanks of the distant peaks.

Jumbled morainic debris marks the slow retreat of the Lantang Glacier in northern Nepal. The glacier once filled the valley, fanning out to a point just beyond the foreground of this photograph. The melting ice exposed a ridged terminal moraine, part of which is visible (right). As the glacier's load of ice diminished with a progressively warmer climate, the snout retreated, exposing less debris each warm season.

The rounded outlines of the Khung Khola Valley in northern Nepal bear witness to the shaping power of a vanished glacier. Skirting the jagged ridge (centre background), the glacier planed smooth the contours of the valley, depositing debris in hollows in the walls and floor. A dry stream bed now meanders towards lower ground and sedges and grasses emerge from soil-filled gaps between the rocks.

2/ In the Giant's Shadow

*Far higher in the sky than imagination dared to suggest, a
prodigious white fang—an excrescence from the jaw of the
world—the summit of Everest appeared.*

GEORGE LEIGH MALLORY QUOTED BY CAPTAIN JOHN NOEL/ *THROUGH TIBET TO EVEREST*

According to legend, an official of the Indian Trigonometrical Survey
burst into the office of his superior in New Delhi one day in 1852 and
exclaimed: "Sir, I have discovered the highest mountain in the world."
In fact, the discovery was less dramatic. It was the final product of labor-
ious cross-checking of figures from the field-survey. At the time, and
for almost a century afterwards, Nepal was closed to Europeans, and the
height of its major peaks could be calculated only from the Indian hills,
nearly 100 miles away, by dragging up heavy surveying equipment on
poles slung between two men. Their measurements were remarkably accurate. Everest was said to be 29,002 feet high. The latest recalculation,
in 1953-5, gives its height as 29,028 feet (plus or minus 0.8 feet, a nice
qualification, for it is the depth of a single fall of snow).

Everest, before 1852, was unknown to Westerners because it was inaccessible, and all but its peak was hidden from the Indian plains by its
giant neighbours Lhotse and Nuptse. In 1848 Joseph Dalton Hooker,
looking westwards from a spur of Kangchenjunga, had had a glimpse of
it: "There was no continuous snowy chain; the Himalayas seemed suddenly to decline into black and rugged peaks, till in the far north-west it
rose again in a white mountain mass of stupendous elevation at 80 miles
distance, called by my Nepal people, 'Tsungau'."

The name Tsungau does not reappear in history. The newly-discovered
peak was known for several years by its code-number XV in the survey-

book, and it was not until 1865 that Sir Andrew Waugh, Director of the Indian Survey, suggested that it should be called after his great predecessor, Sir George Everest, Surveyor-General of India from 1830 to 1843. Everest is the only mountain in the entire range that bears the name of an individual. When it was proposed that K2 in the Karakorams should be named after Colonel H. H. Godwin Austen who surveyed its glaciers, the suggestion displeased both the Indian Survey and the Royal Geographical Society, and was not officially adopted. There have been second thoughts even about Everest. Shortly after its christening, the Tibetan name Chomolungma was discovered, and it has been proposed as more suitable for a mountain that had been venerated under that name for centuries before Sir George Everest's was known. Some scholars, however, say that Chomolungma refers to the whole group of peaks in that area, not to Everest alone. For that reason, and also for its subsequent fame, Everest is likely to remain unchanged as the name of the highest elevation upon the earth.

A view of Everest is today easy to come by. The approach to it from the lowlands of Nepal is normally made by aeroplane. Terry Spencer and I accomplished in an hour the approach journey that took the Everest expeditions 17 days; in the season of our visit over 6,000 people made the four-day trek northwards from the airstrip at Lukla to the base-camp at the foot of the Khumbu ice-fall below Everest. There is even a Japanese-run hotel on a spur just north of Namche Bazar, the main Sherpa village of the Khumbu region. From it, we could retrace through field-glasses every agonizing footstep taken by Edmund Hillary and Tenzing Norgay up the last 2,000 feet of Everest to its summit.

But Everest is not humbled by its present-day conveniences, any more than it was diminished by surrendering to the British expedition in 1953 the blue riband of inaccessibility. It still exacts its penalties: from the mountaineer, death; from the mere trekker, mountain-sickness and a hard slog up steep paths and glacial moraines. Everest is terrifyingly eternal, and we are mortal. More than 20 men have reached its summit, but at what price in human life and suffering! The ascent becomes no easier, except psychologically, because it has been done before. There is a remoteness about this peak that must be measured by a scale more subtle than mere altitude. It stands aloof, stern rather than beautiful, graceless even, and, if one can attribute to a mass of rock the antithesis of the feeling it arouses, contemptuous. Nobody has ever loved Everest as they might love Nanda Devi, the giant of the Indian Himalayas. "It is a place," one early mountaineer remarked, "to have been to; not to go to."

Peaks of the Everest chain, swathed in snow, present the world's most spectacular horizon as they jut massively above the humble Nepalese foothills. The distant triangular peak on the left is Mount Everest (29,028 feet), the highest mountain on earth. Running in front of it is the Nuptse ridge (25,850 feet) and to its right is Lhotse (27,890 feet). The high peak at right is Makalu (27,790), first scaled in 1955.

We flew up for a closer look at the mountain in a light aeroplane piloted by an adventurous Swiss who was determined to display to best advantage not only his skill but the mountains to which he was accredited. Flying east from Kathmandu over the rumpled foothills, we saw the few roads around the Nepalese capital drop away, then the houses, then the terraced fields. As we turned north up the valley of the Dudh Kosi River, the classic approach to Everest, we found it surprisingly regular, both in gradient and direction, a straight cleft rising steadily between brown hills. I watched the altimeter climb, 15,000, 16,000, 18,000 feet. The pilot handed me his oxygen mask, and I took a few gulps, though I didn't feel I needed them yet. Suddenly we found ourselves above the snow-line, and the pilot pointed ahead:

"Everest!"

At first I was not sure which it was. We were in an amphitheatre of peaks, one poised with astonishing precariousness (it turned out to be Ama Dablam), others level with our wings. But as the direction of flight was north and Everest lies northernmost at the head of the valley, it could only be the black pyramid I saw rising clear above the rock-wall that closed the upper end. It was. I was disappointed that so little of it was visible, and what there was did not conform to my notion of supremacy. It looked almost shy. The pilot pointed out other landmarks: Namche Bazar; Thyangboche Monastery, neat on its saddle-spur. These names, so familiar from newspaper accounts of the great expeditions, achieved sudden substance in such small huddles.

Terry Spencer, sitting behind me, was busy taking photographs from the cabin door which he had opened above a 10,000-foot drop, insisting that nothing, not even a sheet of clear plastic, should come between his lens and the astounding view. We flew to the top of the valley—a mosquito among wedding-cakes—and circled in a huge parabola (to use up our overload of petrol, the pilot explained, but we suspected him of being a man who took pleasure in giving pleasure), allowing us a closer look at Lhotse's ice-wall. I watched him anxiously as he floated the aircraft away from it with a falcon's ease. Then we returned down the valley towards Namche's landing-strip. It was a joke of an air-strip, the highest in the world, a finger held out waist-high by a mountain on which we took our chance to perch.

When you step suddenly on to ground 12,000 feet above sea-level, you expect to feel different. We had been warned of the effects of altitude, and heard that the Japanese hotel had oxygen on tap for those who needed it. I took my first few steps as if I was walking on a newly-frozen

Like a vast watchtower, Mount Everest stands on the borders of Tibet and Nepal. Clustered around it are many of the Himalayas' greatest peaks; all those rising above 20,000 feet are marked on the map of the Everest region (right). Between the mountains flow long glaciers and rivers (shown blue), cutting their way down thousands of feet, southwards towards the Indian plains.

N

TIBET
NEPAL

Nangpa La
18,753 ft.

Cho Oyu
26,749 ft.

Gyachung Kang
25,991 ft.

Rongbuk Glacier

East Rongbuk Glacier

Lungsampa Glacier

Sumna Glacier

Ngojumba Glacier

Nup La
19,636 ft.

West Rongbuk Glacier

Khartaphu
23,720 ft.

Karma Changri
20,560 ft.

Lingtren Nup
20,866 ft.

Pumori
Glacier

Lingtren
21,972 ft.

Changtse
24,770 ft.

Kartse
21,350 ft.

LUNAK

Chumbu
22,483 ft.

Pumori
23,442 ft.

Khumbutse
21,785 ft.

Lho La
19,705 ft.

Ice
fall

Western Cwm Glacier

Mount Everest
29,028 ft.

Kangshung Glacier

Khumbu Glacier

Lobujya West
20,161 ft.

Lobujya East
20,075 ft.

Lobujya
Glacier

Nuptse
25,850 ft.

South Col
26,200 ft.

Lhotse
27,890 ft.

"Peak 38"
24,898 ft.

Pethangtse
22,014 ft.

TIBET
NEPAL

LOBUJYA

Nuptse Glacier

Lhotse Shar
27,503 ft.

Kyajo Ri
20,295 ft.

"Island Peak"
20,305 ft.

Cho Polu
22,093 ft.

Chago
22,590 ft.

Makalu II
25,130 ft.

Cholatse
21,129 ft.

Lhotse Glacier

Bhote Kosi

Taweche
20,889 ft.

PHERICHE

DINGBOCHE

CHUKHUNG

Ama
Dablam
Glacier

Baruntse
23,688 ft.

Barun Glacier

Makalu
27,790 ft.

Langmoche Khola

Imja Khola

PANGBOCHE

Ama Dablam
22,493 ft.

Hongu Glacier

Dudh Kosi

THYANGBOCHE

Thami Khola

"Peak 4"
22,047 ft.

NAMCHE BAZAR

Hongu South Peak
20,013 ft.

"Pyramid Peak"
22,430 ft.

Teng Kangpoche
21,325 ft.

Kwangde
20,299 ft.

Thamserku
21,680 ft.

Kangtega
21,932 ft.

Hongu Khola

Dudh Kosi

Kyangshar Khola

"Peak 41"
21,830 ft.

Chamlang
24,012 ft.

"Peak 43"
22,208 ft.

Karyolung
21,920 ft.

Mera
21,120 ft.

LUKLA

0   2   4   6   8   10
MILES

pond. It was quite unnecessary. I felt exhilarated or light-headed more than breathless, and suffered nothing more than a slight headache.

Later that day we took a more prolonged look at our exalted surroundings. The Dudh Kosi Valley was an amazing sight. Mist swam into it from each end, changing its shape and colour every half-minute. Downwards, towards the plain, the hills descended in flying buttresses, matching each other on both sides of the river, while northwards they broke into the peaks of the great snow-mountains. Ama Dablam, as I had noticed from the air, was dominant because it stands alone, its head nodding seemingly in defiance of the law of gravity. To the north was the *bombe glacée* of Taweche, and alongside us a graceful mountain of which I had never previously heard, Kangtega (21,932 feet), rising in lacey *arêtes* to a summit fluted by ice-furrows. A cloud broke its outline at mid-point. Mountains like this need clouds to assert their height, and a cloud's movement to emphasize their stability. I have seen the Himalayas, cloud-free at dawn, lose all their colour and majesty, looking like Swiss replicas of themselves. They need clouds for the same reason that emperors need robes and trappings.

Ahead was Everest. Now I could focus field-glasses on its crest. In the wonderfully clear air every detail of its structure was visible, black rocks lightly streaked with snow, rising in ribs to form a tent-like summit. From this vantage point there was no sign of its culminating snow-dome, on to which Hillary had cut the final steps "with a few whacks of the ice-axe." But there was the south summit, notching the skyline a little lower down; and there the 40-foot step of rock that so nearly defeated him in the last hour of his ascent. The base of the summit-triangle was cut off just above the South Col by Nuptse's battlemented crest, scarcely deserving to be named a mountain in its own right, I thought resentfully; but at its far end rose Lhotse, proud and positive. The sun was setting. Heavy clouds drifted across the crimson cloth of Nuptse's wall. The colours were those of a Turner painting: first, strawberry streaked with cream, changing into a dying fire as rapidly as Terry could capture it, and finally into amber. As the snow-slopes lost the sun, only the peaks blazed out, like candles, to be extinguished one by one. Everest's was the last to go, as if to proclaim in this unmistakable manner that it was, in fact, supreme.

It might be imagined that so great a barrier as Everest and its satellites is impenetrable except by the most intrepid mountaineers. But the Everest group, like all others in the Himalayas, is bordered by passes on each side, and men have crossed them immemorially for trade and cultural exchange. The Sherpas came south by these routes in the Middle Ages, and within very recent times double their number of Tibetan refugees. In the reverse direction, the Nepalese have climbed the passes to barter their goods and skills in Tibetan markets. The frontier has been closed to foreigners since 1950, when the Chinese occupied Tibet, but trade, now mostly in smuggled goods, still goes on.

The Sherpas form a tiny tribe of a few thousand people, unknown and cut off by the mountains until some few years ago, and now world-symbols for good-natured endurance. Trade and mountain-porterage have given them a higher standard of living than their neighbours to the south, and their religion is a source of joy evident in their courtesy and creased smiles. "Compassion with all animate creatures," wrote C. F. Haimendorf, the eminent anthropologist, who knows them best, "is in their eyes the essence of human virtue;" and creatures include man. These are the people, Mongol by origin, Nepalese by adoption, who have chosen to inhabit one of the most intractable corners of the globe.

Namche Bazar itself is at the junction of the Dudh Kosi with a lateral valley that leads to the frontier pass of Nangpa La, over 18,000 feet above sea-level. The outside world has already left its mark on Namche since the first European entered it in 1950. There is now a school, a police-post, several open-fronted shops selling beer and canned peaches to the trekkers, and touching hand-painted notices advertising "restaurants" and "hotels" that turn out to be little more than invitations to share a family's meal and the mat-covered bedstead in their only room. In essence, however, the character of the village is unchanged. It has its air-strip high above, but no road; and a squat temple, with a stream of clear water flowing past it, as it always had. The village street opens into a small piazza where yak-wool is spun and woven into carpets. Prayer-flags flutter over every house, and the inscription that they carry, *Om mane padme hum* ("Hail to the jewel in the lotus") is endlessly repeated in paint or carving on prominent rocks. There is a mood of propitiation in these hills. In the small chapel, the wall-paintings depicted the Himalayas euphemistically as the size of the Apennines in Italian primitives.

Next day we began walking towards Everest, with a Sherpa to carry our camera equipment. We walked the Thyangboche path, 2,000 feet down to the bed of the Dudh Kosi, to get the feel of the mountains and to acclimatize. The path is steep, but it was easy walking on the way down, rubber soles cupping the strewn stones, and the path led through delightful country, across sloping meadows and through groves of

Icicles hang in a heavy curtain across the Khumbu Glacier, west of Everest. The curtain—like the rest of the glacier surface that is littered here with morainic debris of pebbles and boulders—is in a constant state of change and motion. Within days, or perhaps even hours, the melting of the ice and the irregular movement of the glacier will have obliterated the curtain and the crevasse below it.

twisted juniper and birch dripping with pale green lichen. The Dudh Kosi was white with constant turmoil and its granite boulders shone with specks of mica. (Hence its name, Dudh Kosi which means "Milk River.") When suspended in great cliffs, the rock is almost indistinguishable from blocks of ice.

So this stream was the collected outpouring of the Everest massif! It seemed unexpectedly small; but then I remembered that snow does not fall thickly at great heights, and most of what does fall is eternally retained there if it is not blown away or burnt off by evaporation before it melts. A bridge crosses the river at this point, and as we sat beside it, a team of yaks picked its way across—heavy, hairy oxen, that combine the rôles of porters and domestic cattle, supplying the mountain people with milk and the soft wool of their bellies for the weaving of blankets and many items of clothing.

From the river the path zig-zags up to the Thyangboche spur, on which an aging Buddhist monk was moved in the 1920s to build a monastery facing the most dramatic backdrop in the world, and beyond it Tibet, the source of his inspiration. An earthquake destroyed the buildings in 1934 and the abbot died from the shock a few weeks later, aged 85. But it was soon rebuilt by his successor, who now presides over a community of some 40 lamas. The small compound is almost the last inhabited locality on the Everest route. The main channel of the Dudh Kosi breaks northwest to collect the water of Cho Oyu, and a relatively minor torrent called the Imja Khola leads up the moraine of the Khumbu Glacier. The route, though now well-trodden, is appropriately barren. It is easy walking, since the glacial debris provides a firm footing and the upward slope is gradual. But the way is long and the nights sharp with frost, and the rising altitude cuts every gulp of air in half.

The base-camp lies at nearly 18,000 feet, at the foot of the Khumbu ice-fall. There is no feature on the approach to a mountain more familiar than this. The majority of us who enjoy our mountaineering vicariously, by reading about it, tend to skip lower ordeals and are only interested in the summit. With Everest it is different. Its features are as familiar to us as our own favourite park. The ice-fall, the Western Cwm, the southwest face. the Lhotse wall, the South Col, the south summit, are milestones on a journey that we have taken in the imagination many times: those of an older generation will add the Rongbuk Glacier and the North Col from memories of pre-war expeditions. But the greatest of all is the ice-fall, because it is infinitely spectacular and dangerous. It looks like the ruins of a great city encased in ice and slowly subsiding down a

chute 2,000 feet high. It is composed of vast blocks of ice-masonry—
towers and walls and pinnacles—all of which must eventually topple as
the steady pressure of the glacier above it forces the whole cracking mass
forwards and downwards. It is the ladder by which all expeditions
mount to the platform from which the summit must be scaled; but it is a
ladder with rotten rungs. It is never the same from one hour to the next;
never stable; never silent. A sudden rattle, and down comes an ice-
tower: a deep sigh, and a crevasse opens. The ice-fall separates men
from boys, mountaineers from tourists.

Beyond and above it lies the great snow-bath of the Western Cwm,
formed by Nuptse on one side, by Everest's own south-west face on the
other, and by Lhotse at the far end. It is a long, slow drag across it to the
base of the encircling walls, and then Everest makes its third, or fourth,
beginning, for it is a mountain that must be divided not into chapters,
but into volumes. Snow and ice give place to bare rock. Skills that would
be regarded as commonplace in Snowdonia or the Appalachians must
now be exercised in the teeth of a 100 m.p.h. gale, a temperature drop to
−40°F, and an altitude that makes a man catch each breath with pain.
The actual danger is not so great, once the ice-fall has been surmounted.
It is the attrition of weeks of bitter cold and wind that eventually wears
down the strongest men.

Everest has a character quite different from that of any other mountain. It would be disappointing if it were like its neighbour Cho Oyu, only
2,000 feet lower and according to Chris Bonington, who led the British
Everest expedition in 1972, "little more than a very high-altitude fell
walk"; or Nuptse, which never makes up its mind to be a mountain at all.
Everest is formidably masculine and certain, a giant who knows his
rights. But there is a special grace, too, in the long sweeps of ice and rock
that mitigates its extreme aloofness. I gazed at it with admiration, regret-
ting that because its peak marks a sealed frontier, I would never be able
to see its far side, by all accounts even more stupendous.

NATURE WALK /Through Kali Gandaki Gorge

PHOTOGRAPHS BY TERENCE SPENCER

The valley of the Kali Gandaki in central Nepal is said to be the deepest gorge in the world. It separates two of the world's largest mountain massifs—Dhaulagiri and Annapurna—each of which has a main peak of over 26,000 feet. The distance between them is 22 miles, and the bed of the river at its central point lies 18,500 feet below.

But the word gorge needs some qualification: it suggests a narrow slit cut by a river between vertical rock walls. The Kali Gandaki certainly has its dramatic passages, but much of its upper course, carved by glaciers in the remote past, is a mile wide, and its banks, though sometimes extremely precipitous, are more often gently inclined. No road runs along it, but there is a path that can be followed from village to village by men and pack-animals, and it has been known for centuries to pilgrims, traders and migrant families as one of the easiest breaches of the Himalayan chain.

The Kali Gandaki claims another distinction. Its upper part is a "dry" valley. The monsoon exhausts itself against the southern slopes, and although rain or at least humid mist can creep along the mountain walls, it does not penetrate the valley floor. A dessicating wind blowing from the south dries it still further, and the increasing altitude completes the process. The valley becomes a semi-desert, spotted with spiny shrub, only 20 miles beyond the point where its vegetation is riotously tropical. In the space of a day's march one can descend from the sharp dry sunshine and wind-blown Tibetan flora around the village of Jomosom to the steamy humidity and sub-tropical monsoon flora of the gorges below the village of Ghasa. The abruptness of the change is astonishing.

Terry Spencer and I took four days to cover the length of the gorge. He with cameras, I with notebook, walked those 20 miles in the month of November, when the monsoon finally ended and sparkling sun irradiated unsullied snow.

As we flew from Kathmandu we swung north up the valley that we were to descend on foot and could pick out the thin silver chain of the Kali Gandaki River snaking between the two vast mountains. We landed at Jomosom on sand and gravel, at an altitude of 9,000 feet, 20 miles from the nearest point in Tibet, and were met by the seven porters whom we had engaged to carry our tents and stores during the coming trek.

As we took our first steps away from the airstrip, we noticed at once that the mountain slopes were treeless until some 2,500 feet above the valley floor, and there a few birches drifted hesitantly across them, encouraged by the last flicker of the forked monsoon rainfall.

GANDAKI AT ITS WIDEST

Looking north towards the Mustang district, we saw that even these few wanderers gave up the struggle, and the ground was quite barren.

Terry and I did not stay with the porters, for they remained on the path while we hurried from one dramatic scene to another, making notes and taking photographs. The valley floor swelled in humps like dunes, but there were patches of

TOWERING WALLS DWARF A TRAIL ALONG THE KALI GANDAKI GORGE

SEMI-DESERT LAND

they do not approach each other too closely. If they do, a twist of the wings and a sharp turn to left or right avoids a collision and harmony is once more restored.

We crossed the river, a tumbling torrent grey with cold, and made our way up the east slopes to a small lake that I had spotted from the aeroplane. Tiny balls of cloud hung in the sky, as if they had been fired there by anti-aircraft guns. Every sound was audible from a mile away, the chinking of shod boots against a stone, the bells of a distant donkey team, and somewhere a woman was singing in the quavering fashion of the East. Growing out of the bank of a small tributary of the Gandaki was a birch with tawny leaves—the first splash of colour we had seen—and its branches leaned in a graceful curve towards the open river bed. They had yielded to the persistent wind that we were soon to experience.

Below the Snow Kingdom

An hour later we reached the lake, a silver salver dropped flat between the mountains and crumpled at its edges. The hillside above it was streaked with bright streams carrying the melting snow from the surrounding peaks. The summit of Dhaulagiri I was always visible. Through binoculars I could walk it in imagination so clear was the air. A mattress of snow 50 feet thick lay on a ridge above its glacier, poised to collapse in a soft smothering avalanche. These gigantic forces have a gentle way (gentle, it seemed, from that distance) of restoring

vegetation that stained the sterile sweeps of sand: scattered pincushions of caragana, another creeping plant barely recognizable as a thwarted honeysuckle, and bushy junipers that lower down the valley I was to see growing to 50 feet. This was semi-desert. Wind-borne particles had carved the valley walls into fluted cliffs down which sheep and yaks picked their way to the water in the river-bed. The Tibetan plateau is said to be the only region of the earth's surface where desert and arctic conditions coexist; and you will not find the next forest to the north for another 2,000 miles, in the wasteland of Siberia.

High in the sky cranes, storks and eagles glide over Jomosom on thermals. The birds are at ease as long as

TAWNY-LEAVED BIRCH

SUMMIT OF DHAULAGIRI

soil onto the rocks and whipping it into delicately spiralled patterns. Pools of water at my feet were imprisoned by a scattering of loose stones and edged by crackling ice.

Then a yard away on the ground I saw an ammonite. This, I knew, was evidence that the mountains were raised up from parts of what had once been the sea-bed between India and northern Asia like a primordial Atlantis in reverse. However, our first day was closing in on us. In failing light and increasing cold, our porters erected our tents and fed us a warming meal of mutton, carrots and cauliflower, and tea laced with rum. We felt very content as, wrapped in all our spare clothing to keep out the cold, we crawled into our sleeping bags.

their equilibrium: a puff of snow and a million tons find a new level; and then the process begins again.

But the peace of the scene was illusory. A plume of snow flying from the summit indicated freezing gales up there, and we were told that a British expedition had been six weeks aloft, struggling to climb the last 2,000 feet of Dhaulagiri IV. Two men, we later heard, an Englishman and a Sherpa, were killed, and the others withdrew defeated, like nine expeditions before them. The fourth peak of Dhaulagiri—that companion of our easy walk, that enemy of their brutal climb—remains unconquered.

The wind began to rise predictably at noon, a strong funnelling of cool air from the south, blowing sandy

FOSSIL AMMONITE

We were tired and the night passed quickly. When we woke at 6 a.m., after 11 hours' darkness, the sun was breaking over the eastern crests. The crisp freshness of the new day was inspiring—off came the anorak, off the sweater and we could stride the moraines in exultation before breakfast.

By 7 a.m. we were on our way. I

SAND BLOWN ON TO ROCK

was scarcely aware of losing height as we walked, until I glanced down at the tumbling river; and walking was very easy along the flats of the widening valley or on a narrow path cut from the cliff walls. Down a side valley a glacier of mud had carried whole tree-trunks from the upper levels. Here, too, was more evidence of the uplifted sea-bed that became the Himalayas. A great boulder striped with orange was calcium carbonate—the consolidated remains of sea animals.

A black juniper came down to the valley floor at the village of Tukche, and in a sheltered corner stood a bush with orange berries: *Hippophae*, the buckthorn. Here the country began to change perceptibly. Along the ridges from the south strode the advance guard of an army of conifers: the east Himalayan fir,

CALCIUM CARBONATE ROCK

Abies spectabilis, and its more common neighbour, the Bhutan pine, *Pinus wallichiana*, a magnificent tree of gleaming colour and beautiful texture.

The path climbed again along the cliff-face towards Larjung, where we were to make our second camp, and we looked down on a string of donkeys crossing the valley floor—microscopic reminders of the scale of the breach we were following. At Larjung we found a pleasant field near the river, where we ate before wrapping ourselves up against the cold of night. We could hear dogs barking loudly in the village.

Life in High Forests

In the morning, we rose refreshed, exhilarated by the prospect of the day's march. This was to be the day when we crossed into the splendours of tropical Kali Gandaki. We set off in perfect walking weather, the sun shining above us. Although the gorge was still wide and the river was still comparatively small within it, there was now an urgency about its passage and it seemed to share our enthusiasm to reach greener pastures ahead. Even the vegetation closed in on it so that it appeared to run more directly towards its goal. Thick forests of pine clung to the valley slopes and also to the river-bed itself. The river soon narrowed to its first gorge, where the yellow spike of *Gynura cusimbua*, grew in profusion among the pines. Ice-age glaciers had not penetrated this far, and the passage of the Kali Gandaki farther south was left to its own

GYNURA CUSIMBUA

SUB-TROPICAL KALI GANDAKI GORGE

GRIFFON VULTURE

SILHOUETTED RAVENS

erosive powers. The drop in altitude —we had now come down to 4,800 feet—the growing influence of the monsoon and melting snows were collectively responsible for the lusher vegetation that now began to surround us. With the encroaching flowers and the evergreen came birds, insects and small reptiles and amphibians. None of them was numerous for they were hidden. In the surrounding forest, I was later told, we must have passed a hundred species of birds, but they were silent and reluctant to rise above tree-height. But we did see Himalayan griffon vultures and ravens. The former is a powerful scavenger and it sailed over the valley, its keen eyes scanning the ground for a decaying carcass. The ravens, among the largest members of the crow family, performed remarkable aerial contortions around high precipices. But of the lovely flycatchers and the laughing thrushes of the Himalayas there was no sign.

Before the village of Ghasa we had lunch overlooking a splendid water-fall. It was 50 feet high, a huge, black slab of smooth rock down which a narrow trickle of water made its way. We could easily imagine the volume of water that must come cascading over this ridge during the full force of the monsoon rains. In the afternoon we made little pro-gress, fearing for our lives as we walked the steep and stony paths with an almost precipitous drop on one side. We stopped at Kobre and shared a field with some cattle. It was a depressing camp-site, but the welcome night warmth enabled us to sleep loosely clad, cradled on pine needles.

In the morning sunlight flooded the valley and we set off through our first rhododendron forest. Its trees grew to 40 feet and their twisted brown branches were hung with lichen—an isolated jungle among the stateliness of the pines.

SHEER WATERFALL

One of the porters brought us a miraculous creature. The birds and mammals may have been hidden, but he had found a huge praying mantis. The extraordinary monster-insect sat frozen on a rock, hoping by its immobility to avoid detection. It must be among the most delicately formed of all creatures, I thought, with its long spidery legs and twig-thin fuselage. Strangest of all is its head. It is lifted from legend, from nightmares, peering with fixed eyes, tremulous with antennae, aggres-sive in aspect and intent, but so vulnerable that its dragon-like fea-tures seemed absurd.

Torrential Waters

We walked on past Ghasa. The stands of chir and pines were touched by the sun, pale green, dark green. A white *Delias* butterfly sailed past us and settled mo-mentarily on a little flowerhead. It closed its wings and revealed a shock of bright red and yellow on

RHODODENDRON GROVE

PRAYING MANTIS

DELIAS BUTTERFLY

their underside—enough to frighten any predator, I thought—before it launched itself into the air again.

Now the water of the main river was whipped into a sudden frenzy and poured with demonic force through two narrow channels each side of a boulder. Lower down the scene was repeated with augmented violence. Here the Gandaki strained in a final effort to carve its way between the constraining bulks of Annapurna and Dhaulagiri. From a mile wide the river was compressed into a tea-pot's spout, its banks forming a true gorge for a few yards at a time. Sometimes we had to climb high over its shoulders to make any progress at all.

Sub-tropical Nepal rose to meet us. Flowers and trees grew in cups of soil right down to the river's edge. We stopped to look back and saw with surprise that the great mountains were behind us. We had walked clean through the Himalayas from north to south.

GANDAKI SURGING THROUGH NARROW GORGE

3/ Predator and Prey

Why should animals and insects and birds choose to come and dwell in such barren wastes? Possibly they may be attracted by the sanctuary they find here. Yet what an intense and uncertain struggle mere existence means at those heights!

CAPTAIN JOHN NOEL/ *THROUGH TIBET TO EVEREST*

The Himalayas from plain to snow give shelter to such a variety of wild animals that if an Ark were to be stocked from no other source, it would preserve an élite of the animal kingdom. The richest level is the lowest, the jungle or *terai*, where are found most of the animals of children's story-books or Uccello's paintings, among them the tiger, leopard, monkey, elephant, crocodile and rhinoceros. The last three do not wander far from the lowest foothills, but the others climb from the jungle in their insatiable quest for food, and come into contact and conflict with the creatures of the middle zone: the bear, the jackal, the red panda—and man. These give place to the animals of the rich grassland above the trees, the yaks and wild asses, the sheep and goats which carry an armoury of strangely contorted horns. Throughout the three zones are spread the deer, prey for the carnivores, and they, too, vary in species according to the altitude, as do the creeping creatures and the birds.

At both extremes, the severity of the struggle for existence is at its maximum; but while in the rain forest it is the struggle between one animal and another that counts, in the high mountains it is the struggle with altitude and the elements. In one case there is usually an over-abundance of food; in the other, extreme scarcity. Most animals stop where the plants stop, at about 19,000 feet. But climbers on Everest have seen the tracks of mountain sheep at 20,000 feet, of hares and foxes at 21,000, of wolves at 21,500. The birds and tiny crawling things survive highest. They alone, or some of them, would have no need to enter the Ark. Jumping spiders were found at 22,000 feet by the 1924 Everest expedition. Neither freaks nor wanderers, they have since been shown to be part of a small but hardy community in permanent residence. Here, in the lofty wastes, the predatory instinct that governs life on the forested slopes reasserts itself. To survive, the spiders feed on spring-tails, insects one-fifth of an inch long, which derive their name from a trigger-like mechanism under their bodies capable of throwing them a few inches into the air. These feed, in their turn, on the detritus of the lower slopes, blown upwards by the wind: pollen, dead flies, rotting leaf fragments and the young of various insects and spiders that disperse by rising on a "parachute" of thread, and drift with the wind.

At such heights the cold is always intense. But this presents no problem for the permanent community above the snow-line. During the day the spider's dark-brown body soaks in the sun's heat and the springtail obtains warmth from the stones. Both creatures withstand drops in temperature by going into a state resembling hibernation. It is possible that in these frozen regions there exist other colonies of spiders and insects, so far unstudied because their habitat is lethal to all but the fittest of men. It may even be that insurgent life, with all the pressure of millions of years of reproduction and evolution behind it, has managed to scale the highest peaks on earth.

The realm of Himalayan fauna may be seen diagrammatically as a layered pyramid. As the seasons change, animals ascend or descend the pyramid to escape the worst of the heat or the cold, some using larger lungs to make the most of rarefied air, others equipped with sweat glands to compensate for the oven-heat of the tropical plains. Darwin would have found here within a few thousand feet concentrated proof of his theory that it is the fittest that survive.

It is, however, only in menageries, like those at Delhi or Kabul, or stuffed, glittering with glass eyes, in the lounges of hotels or airports, that one is likely to see more than a tiny proportion of these animals. All but the birds and monkeys are very shy, and many species are now extremely rare. They range over vast and thickly sheltered territories; they fear each other, with reason; they move with stealth, and their coats are camouflaged; many of them are nocturnal in their habits; others hibernate. Only in specially favoured areas like the state-protected reserves can they be seen in any numbers, or at a great distance in open country and above the trees.

By far the most ubiquitous and visible animal in the Himalayas is man, and he is slowly destroying the other spieces. The main reason is that man is in direct competition with other animals for space. To win more land for agriculture, the hill-farmers fell or burn back virgin forests, as in the Nepalese *terai*. Deprived of normal food supplies, the animals begin raiding crops and domestic livestock. In turn they are killed by farmers with livelihoods to protect. (There is no blame here: all over the Himalayan region and in every part of the civilized world the cry is raised, Protect the animals. Yet it is often overlooked that man is also an animal, and if he is in competition with other animals, his livelihood, too, deserves at least an equal degree of protection.)

Hunting and poaching also take their toll of the wild life. Tourists pay £3,000 to shoot a Marco Polo sheep, with its horns that curve into a complete circle and then sweep outwards, and only a little less for the near-extinct markhor, a goat with corkscrew horns that are often more than four feet long. The pelt of a snow-leopard can fetch £100 and the musk pod of the musk-deer—used in the manufacture of high-grade perfume—at least £1,000. Many inhabitants of the Himalayas have religious taboos against killing far more effective than any government directive, but many more have no qualms about hunting meat for the pot or snaring the valuable musk-deer. Traplines extend for miles along the slopes of the Mailung Khola River, in Central Nepal, and whole villages make their living from poaching and hunting.

Nevertheless, there are regions of the world where men and animals in their sparse numbers can co-exist. Terry Spencer and I went to one Indian reserve, a 500-square-mile tract of jungle and open grassland in the lowest of the Himalayan foothills. The experience was both thrilling and shaming. We wished to see in their natural state some of the animals that penetrate the higher hills. The game warden promised to arrange for us to photograph a tiger. Late that night he tethered a buffalo some two miles from the bungalow where we stayed, and while we ate and slept, the terrible kill took place, fortunately out of earshot. The warden confirmed in the morning that "the bait had been taken"—a nice euphemism, I thought—and the tiger was in the area. So off we went on an elephant to view the scene of the night's carnage.

From our elevated platform we could observe a world in which Adam and Eve would have felt at home. Brilliantly coloured parakeets scattered at our approach, vultures (the nastiest-looking creatures I have ever seen apart from bats) watched obscenely from the branches of dead sal trees, and several types of deer bounded from under our feet. When we came to

Frozen by the flash, two musk-deer are photographed on their nocturnal search for plant food. These rare inhabitants of the Himalayan forests are extremely shy—and with good reason. Both males and females have a gland under the tail that secretes pungent musk, a substance that is extremely valuable as a perfume base, and for which the deer are hunted and killed. Another unusual feature of the animal, evident in this photograph, is the long tusk-like canine teeth, which it uses in territorial combat and for defence.

the site of the kill, we were told to climb a wooden tower. A man with a rifle, I noticed, took up position behind us, just in case.

The beat began. Our elephant lumbered off to join five others, and, urged on by the cries of the *mahouts*, they moved away a quarter of a mile, to drive into our clearing the tiger that was supposed to be lying up in the jungle fast asleep, sated by its enormous meal. We were to remain completely quiet. Terry focused his camera on the clearing. We could see the high grass and bushes violently agitated as the elephants moved forwards. Birds began to scream across the clearing. Then came an absurd anti-climax. The elephants emerged into the open, their trunks hanging foolishly; but no tiger. The jungle was then beaten from the opposite direction, again with no result. The tiger had loped off else-where; the trick had been played on it once too often.

As we swayed slowly back to camp, we felt less disappointment than shame. I was actually glad not to have seen the tiger. In compensation there was evidence around us of the less ferocious life of the jungle. The chital, the loveliest of all deer, were moving in small herds, a blaze of white dots on their chestnut flanks; their duller cousins, the hog deer, roamed nearby. Rhesus monkeys swung from tree to tree in play; and then, suddenly, one of the noblest beasts of the forest, a sambur, rose at a few yards' distance to stare at us—frozen by fear more than curiosity, big as a pony, its graceful antlers spread against a background of green.

We sensed fear all around us, as if every living thing was holding its breath. The jungle, at least in daytime, is a silent place. There was fear in the movements of the chital, a tentative dance of hooves preceding a sudden prance and gallop; fear in the darting eyes of the monkeys; fear in the desertion of the sambur by its mate. I wondered why they chose to inhabit a place where danger lurked so continuously, where there were 50 tigers out of the 2,000 left in the entire Indian sub-continent.

Yet, on reflection, there is a balance in this savage process that is admirable, an assurance that rich and complex ecologies can be preserved. Evolution has provided each herbivore with defences: teeth, claws, horns, thick skins, acute hearing or eyesight or sense of smell, fleetness of foot, stealth, vocal cords to give warning, camouflage for concealment, nocturnal habits, the protection of the herd. But none of these attributes is a guarantee of survival. Male antlers and horns, efficient enough weapons or deterrents against rivals of the same species, are useless against serious attack by carnivores; and the chital's bright dappled coat, excellent camouflage in broken ground, draws attention to the creature when it strays into the forest fringes. Predators, adapted to exploit any opportunity, help ensure a healthy herbivorous population, limited in number so that no strain is imposed by overgrazing on the resources of their habitat.

I asked the warden about these things. He was a likeable Indian with a great love of animals, but he described with evident admiration how a tiger kills. It can pursue its quarry for about 200 yards, and if not out-distanced, bowls it over, breaking its neck on the run. With its jaws it severs the jugular vein. Then it looks for signs of a rival that could steal its prey. If all is clear, it places one paw on its victim's shoulder, the other on the ground, and gnaws at the neck. Having tasted the meal, the tiger eviscerates the kill with a single stroke of its claws, and drags the carcass away to thicker cover, where it begins the serious eating, start-ing always with the hindquarters. The warden had witnessed this procedure many times, and it had never varied. It did not horrify him; it was "mathematical balance." If there were no deer, he argued, the vegeta-tion would grow rank: if there were no tigers, the deer would multiply so rapidly that they would destroy it all.

Man must, of course, occasionally act as executioner. When I reached the Gorapani Pass, in Nepal, I heard that only two days earlier a tiger had killed a water-buffalo in the village. When I descended the Kali Gandaki Gorge a schoolmaster told me that every summer tigers raid the neighbourhood for cattle, and the children are locked up. But control may be exercised without cruelty. In his classic, *Man Eaters of Kumaon*, Jim Corbett describes how he shot half a dozen of the most notorious killers in the very district we were visiting. One tiger had killed 434 people before it fell to Corbett's rifle. Yet he loved the tigers and leopards that he was employed to kill. He once shot a man-eater when it was asleep, and felt the need to write a whole paragraph of apology. For the tiger is not the natural enemy of man, as man is of the tiger. "It is only when tigers have been incapacitated through wounds or old age," Corbett writes, "that, in order to live, they are compelled to take to a diet of human flesh"—presumably because men are less agile in escaping than deer. Corbett spent 32 years in the pursuit of carnivores, "and though I have seen sights which would cause a stone to weep, I have not seen a case where the tiger has been deliberately cruel, or killed more than was necessary to satisfy its hunger or its cubs."

Of the leopards he wrote: "Those who have never seen a leopard under favourable conditions in his natural surroundings can have no conception of the grace of movement and beauty of colouring of this most graceful and beautiful of all animals.... To class such an animal as

Its plumed ears alert, a lynx pads warily through the Upper Indus Valley in search of deer, which it kills with a single bite to the neck.

vermin, as is done in some parts of India, is a crime which only those could perpetrate whose knowledge is limited to the miserable, underfed and mangy specimens seen in captivity." It is the most convincing argument for preservation that I have read anywhere. Supreme in the development of tooth and claw, in grace, strength and agility, in sight, sense, hearing and the craft of hunting, and with an intelligence surpassed only by that of man and the higher apes, the great cats of the jungle are masterpieces of creation, and should not in any circumstances that I can imagine be eliminated from it.

Tigers and leopards are rarities, and I saw none. Nor did I see in the wild any of the smaller cats that have found a home in the Himalayas. They include the leopard cat, only two feet long, a miniature panther that preys on small birds and mammals, sleeps in tree hollows, and is seen, though rarely, from plain level up to 9,000 feet; the jungle cat, about the same size as a domestic cat, which prefers drier and more open ground, and is found quite commonly near the villages of Kashmir; the lynx, a little larger, and possessing the proverbial eyesight and hearing of its European and Canadian cousins, which frequents the Upper Indus Valley as high as 11,000 feet; and, oddest of all, the fishing cat, an inhabitant of heavy jungle, which can scoop up fish from the water with its paw and has been known to attack sheep and even children.

I did, however, see troops of monkeys at the most unexpected places—by the roadside, on bridge parapets, and in a thicket between two Nepalese villages that was so small that it was more like a playground than serious cover. They are the tamest of untamed animals, and have been known in India to throng the platforms of railway stations awaiting passenger trains from which to pilfer discarded sandwiches. Two species of monkey predominate in the lower Himalayas up to 8,000 feet; the rhesus and the langur. Of the two, the rhesus is the uglier, with its frowning face and red behind. The langurs are supremely graceful and have endearing little faces and very long tails. Each is endowed with amazing agility in trees and on the ground, using spindly branches to catapult itself up to 30 feet, seldom misjudging the distance or the capacity of a branch to bear its flung weight. At other times they are still, or relatively still, for no monkey out of the scores I watched remained quite motionless for a second. They were catching at leaves, nibbling at shoots, darting glances from side to side, or picking at their fur, not, as is generally supposed, for vermin, for monkeys are remarkably free from them, but for minute burrs or pieces of loose skin. (At other times mutual

A red panda, or cat-bear, browses through the mountain forest in search of leaves and fruit. In fact a member of the racoon family with only superficial similarities to cat and bear, the red panda leads a mostly arboreal existence at altitudes between 7,000 and 12,000 feet. It sleeps in trees for most of the day, feeding at ground level in the early morning and evening. Its toy-like appearance is deceptive. The panda has razor-sharp claws and a vicious bite.

social grooming takes place.) Their wide range of facial expression and vocal calls and their companionableness towards each other and to man make them the Pucks of the forest. But they also are prey. A leopard can seize a monkey from a tree by a quick lunge and scramble, and if a python traps one in its coils, the monkey has no chance. Unlike the baboon, it has never learnt to use a stick or stone as a weapon of defence.

From foothills to mountain peaks live the bears, three different species of them, each to its own altitude. The sloth bear inhabits the foothills, the black bear prefers the lower forested slopes, and the immense brown bear dwells on the open peaks above the tree-line. Although none of them is entirely carnivorous, feeding mainly on grass, roots and insects, all are potentially dangerous to man and are feared by the natives more than any other animal, except possibly the wild dogs. If disturbed they can break into a lumbering gallop and rear up in a terrifying manner. They kill, not by hugging, but by striking, and their great claws can inflict terrible wounds. The sloth bear, which can grow up to six feet and weigh 250 pounds, is particularly dangerous because of its poor vision and hearing. Approached from downwind, it will not be aware of an interloper until he is almost on top of it. Then, in a panic, the sloth bear will charge, knocking its enemy flat and mauling him before rushing off.

The black bear, however, which may grow to five feet and weigh up to 500 pounds, shows little fear of man and sometimes descends to raid crops. Some members of the species also acquire a taste for flesh and the black bear has been cited as one of the main predators on the Kashmir stag. Its most unusual talent is curling up in a ball and rolling downhill. On the open slopes above the tree-line, the brown bear, which can grow to over nine feet and weigh as much as 650 pounds, avoids contact with man and is rarely seen.

Both black and brown bears hibernate during the winter, in caves or nooks of trees. All their bodily functions—digestion, heartbeat, respiration—are so greatly reduced that they emerge after four or five months almost as fat as at the start. They hibernate not in order to avoid the cold, because they can, and do, move to lower and more sheltered ground, but for lack of food. The brown bear in springtime wakes from its long sleep to follow the receding snow-line to its permanent level, where throughout the summer it lives isolated and unloved, turning over stones for voles, digging marmots from their burrows and occasionally raiding the high grazings for sheep and goats. But awake or sleeping the bear invests the forest with terror.

A more innocuous if less impressive inhabitant of Nepal, Sikkim and the mountains eastward is the cat-bear or red panda. About the same size and shape as a fox, it is bright chestnut in colour, with a long bushy tail ringed by bars of white, and seems to have little in common with either the bear or the giant panda, whose home is the bamboo forests of south-west China. Although both pandas do have several similarities, including "sixth fingers"—pads on the front paws that help them to hold bamboo stems when feeding—and are usually classed as members of the racoon family, some zoologists doubt if they are related, asserting that the Chinese but not the Himalayan variety belongs to the bear family. Whatever its origins, it is easy to understand why the red panda makes such a popular pet. A lovely, silky little creature that pads around in a friendly way, it is as much at home in a drawing-room as in a forest.

Another creature that has become popular in the West—though few would want it in their drawing-room—is the *Yeti* or "Abominable Snowman." Robert Fleming jr., the foremost zoologist in Nepal, told me that he discounted many of the stories told about the *Yeti* as "hobgoblin legends" invented to frighten children. A Sherpa hunter of his acquaintance, with 40 years' experience of the mountains, had never seen one. "Still," Fleming concluded, "there *is* something unexplained." The porter whom we engaged was more cynical. "Only old men have seen a *Yeti*," he declared emphatically. I formed a sudden picture of garrulous dotards boasting by the fireside of an encounter invented in their youth, and retold so often that they had come to believe in it themselves.

Nevertheless, according to the anthropologist, C. F. Haimendorf: "Most Sherpas have seen Yeti at some time or other, and wall-paintings in monasteries and temples depict two types of them—one resembling a bear and one resembling a large monkey. It is generally known that there are two such types, and in hard winters they come into the valleys and prey on the Sherpas' potato stores, or even on cattle." Shortly after my departure from the Himalayas it was reported from Kathmandu that a female yak-herder in the Everest region had been knocked unconscious by a *Yeti*, which then killed five of her animals by twisting their horns.

There are said to be two main types of *Yeti*—a small variety that feeds on humans and a large variety that prefers yaks. J. A. McNeely, an American zoologist, who was still in Nepal looking for *Yeti* at the time of my visit, has published a detailed description of the smaller variety by combining all the eye-witness accounts available. "It is a stocky ape-like creature about 5 to $5\frac{1}{2}$ feet tall, covered with short coarse hair, reddish brown or greyish brown in colour, and longer on the shoulders.

The large head has a high-pointed crown and a marked sagittal crest. Small ears lie close to the head and the face is hairless and rather flat. The teeth are quite large, though not fangs, and the mouth is wide. The arms are long, reaching to the knees. The Yeti normally walks on two legs, with a shuffling gait; he may drop to all fours when in a hurry or climbing over rocks. The feet are large, with two large prehensile toes and three smaller toes. There is no tail."

Professor R. N. Wojkowitz, an Austrian ethnologist who spent three years living among the peoples of Sikkim and Tibet, has also used eye-witness accounts to construct an equally vivid description of the larger variety of Yeti. It is said to be between seven and seven and a half feet tall when erect on its hind legs, with long arms and a powerful body covered with dark brown hair. It has an oval head running to a point at the top and an ape-like face. Both face and head are only sparsely covered with hair. "He fears the light of a fire," says Wojkowitz, "and in spite of his great strength is regarded by the less superstitious inhabitants of the Himalayas as a harmless creature that would attack a man only if wounded. From what native hunters say, the term 'snowman' is a mis-nomer, since firstly it is not human and secondly it does not live in the zone of snow. Its habitat is rather the impenetrable thickets of the high-est tracts of Himalayan forests. During the day it sleeps in its lair, which it does not leave until nightfall. Then its approach may be recognized by the cracking of branches and its peculiar whistling call.... Why does the creature undertake what must certainly be extremely wearisome expedi-tions into the inhospitable regions of snow? The natives have what sounds a very credible explanation: they say the Snowman likes a saline moss which it finds on the rocks of the moraine fields. While searching for this moss it leaves its characteristic tracks on the snowfields. When it has satisfied its hunger for salt it returns to the forest."

It is easy, of course, to dismiss such observations as superstitious fantasy or wishful thinking. But there is other evidence that is more difficult to explain. The tracks of unidentified beasts have been seen and photographed several times by mountaineers from East and West. Perhaps the most impressive evidence of this kind was provided by Eric Shipton, one of the pioneers of Himalayan exploration, on the Menlung Glacier during a reconnaissance of Everest in 1951. Dr. Michael Ward, another British climber who accompanied Shipton, has described the incident. "Our height was probably between 18,000 and 19,000 feet, and we were approaching the lower part of the Menlung Glacier. Some of the tracks that we saw were well formed, and others were rather indistinct.

This 12-inch-long footprint, reproduced here life size, is the strongest evidence of the legendary Yeti or "Abominable Snowman." It was photographed on the Menlung Glacier by Eric Shipton, leader of the 1951 Everest Reconnaissance Expedition. The footprints, which matched those of no known animal, appeared to have been made by a creature weighing more than 200 pounds. According to one popular theory, the "Snowmen" may constitute a relict community of Gigantopithecus, a prehistoric anthropoid known only from a few fossilized bones and teeth.

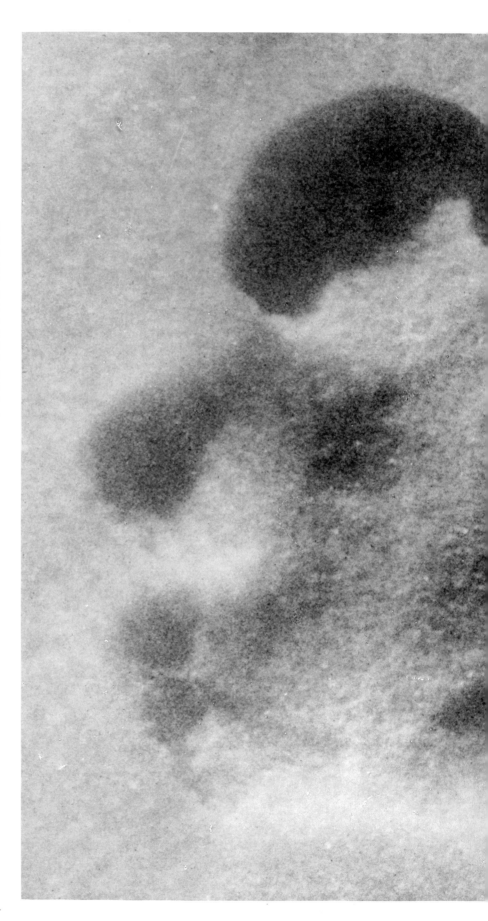

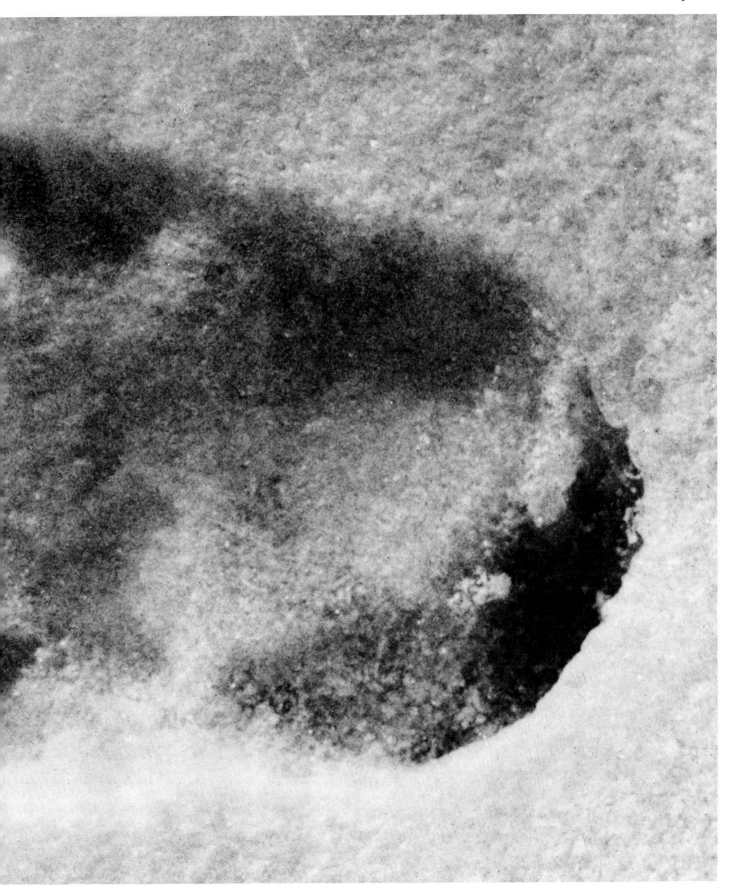

From their number it looked as though there had been more than one animal making them. They kept more or less to the middle of the glacier, and we followed the tracks for about a quarter of a mile before turning off on to a lateral moraine which led us down to some upper grassland."

From their depth the tracks had obviously been made by creatures weighing at least 200 pounds apiece. The prints were 12 to 14 inches long and about six inches wide. "The imprint that we photographed," Ward recalled, "had the impression of five definite toes. The most medial toe being the largest, as in a human foot. The small toe left very little imprint at all. The rest of the foot was very similar to that of a human being, except that, of course, it was broader. One feature was that where the animal had crossed a small crevasse one could see where the toes had dug in to gain purchase on landing, and also it appeared as though there might be the imprints of nails."

One fascinating conjecture is that *Yeti* may be related to *Gigantopithecus*, a huge anthropoid known from the fossils of mandibles and teeth, which flourished in southern China and India about half a million years ago, when the Himalayas were still being formed and the new genus *Homo* was evolving. Driven upwards by fire-using and weapon-wielding man, *Gigantopithecus* could have taken refuge in the rising mountains and may still find sanctuary there.

But if such a creature exists, it does not appear to have survived in the western Himalayas and Karakorams, for the locals to whom I mentioned it had never heard of it. Also absent from this region are several species commonly found from Nepal to Burma. The panda, sambur, crestless porcupine and hog-badger are to be found neither in Kashmir nor farther west, and those curious goat-antelope, the grey goral and maned serow, with their short, backward-sloping horns, do not range west of Kashmir. Instead, one finds others more adapted to life in the barren mountains: the Kashmir stag (looking uncannily like its Landseer equivalent), the ibex—a goat with scimitar horns—the Marco Polo sheep and the markhor. Northwards, in the Tibetan plateau, live the wild ass, the bharal or blue sheep, the snow-leopard and the yak.

The snow-leopard, also a native of the higher Himalayas, is slightly smaller than the common leopard, with a longer tail. Its coat is soft grey to pure white, starred with pale rosettes. It rarely comes below 6,000 feet in winter, and in summer has been found in areas as high as 18,000, where it preys on the wild sheep and goats. I was always meeting people who had met other people who had seen one in the wild. Only once, in northern Pakistan, did I find an actual eye-witness. He said that the leopard was "very stupid," not reacting to danger like other wild animals. "I shot it as it stood motionless, gazing at me."

The yak is the highest-dwelling mammal in the world. Rarely, in its wild state, will it come below 14,000 feet. The domestic yak is employed in the Himalayas as low as 10,000, but when one was brought to the plains of Afghanistan, it died of liver-disease within a few months. Its favoured habitat is the bleak Tibetan plateau, where it lives off wiry tufts of grass. It is the largest native animal in Tibet—a bull can weigh 1,200 pounds and stand six feet at the shoulder—and untamed is exceedingly fierce: even its tongue is so harsh that it can rasp flesh off bones. But nothing could be gentler than the domestic yaks that the Sherpas employ, moving in single file over high snowbound passes, uncanny in their power to detect hidden rocks or clefts. They are excellent riding animals. In Hunza I sat astride a yak, and found it difficult to distinguish between ascent and descent so short are its legs, so sure its gait, and so deep and soft the natural saddle of its back.

With its thick, matted coat and large lungs the yak is supremely well adapted to survive the intense cold and thin air of maximum heights. With other mammals, too, the rule is almost invariable: the higher their habitat, the larger their lungs. Birds, however, seem unaffected by the rarefied air, and expend no greater effort on sailing level with the highest peaks than low in the valleys. One Everest expedition watched lammergeyers sailing at 25,000 feet, and another was effortlessly followed by choughs—members of the crow family—to 27,000. They have no obvious reason to fly so high: there is no food for them there. Why do they do it? I put the question to Robert Fleming. He explained that high flying puts no strain upon them. They are helped by up-draughts of warm air, and can descend with equal ease whenever they wish, covering great distances very quickly. They seem to find little difficulty in breathing: a man cannot talk and breathe simultaneously at 18,000 feet, but birds twitter happily at even higher altitudes.

"So they fly high for fun?"

"Yes, for play and pleasure."

It was nice to find in the wilderness of the Himalayas a living thing that actually enjoyed it.

Denizens of the "Moist Lands"

For the eastern two-thirds of its length, the base of the Himalayas is fringed by a narrow fertile strip, 10-20 miles wide, known as the *terai*, the "moist land." Although much of it is now heavily farmed, many areas are still unchanged from the original tracts of treacherous marsh and jungle and they still provide sanctuary for a unique cross-section of Asia's wildlife.

The *terai* owes its fertile extravagance to two factors besides its rich soil: heat and water. Lying far inland at an altitude of less than 600 feet, it receives few cooling breezes, and summer temperatures exceed 100°F. Abundant water is supplied by seepage from the monsoon rains that soak the mountains at the height of summer.

After running down the foothills, the rain-water disappears into the loose gravel and rubble at their base to filter downwards at depths accessible to the roots of the trees that form the *terai*'s northern protective screen. After a gradual drop of around a thousand feet, the water seeps through to the surface when the ground levels off. Consequently, the untamed areas of the *terai* are almost impenetrable complexes of muddy, wandering streams, thick,

low bush, and dim, tall forest. Nepal's Chitwan National Park, where these pictures were taken, is one such area.

Chitwan is a wildlife haven. Here roams a tenth of the world's tiger population: more than 200 of these great cats pad along the game trails in the evening and wait silently amid dense reed beds for deer and wild pig. Chitwan also provides lush pastures for 200 of the world's estimated 800 Indian rhinos, foraging through twelve-foot cuckoo grass like antique ironclad ships ploughing through heavy seas.

The *terai*'s two species of monkey exploit it in different ways. The stocky rhesus swings through its tree canopy, seeking fruit and grubs, while the long-limbed langur combs the ground for the best of root, seed and shoot. Both types are raucous and can be detected even at night by occasional bursts of screeching—perhaps a warning at the sight of a passing leopard. In the creeks and rivers lurk crocodiles, some of them fish-eaters, others lying in ambush for land-dwelling animals like the dappled deer that wander along the water's margin, almost invisible against the leaves and filtering sunlight.

In a northward view over the river Reu in Chitwan National Park, the principal animal habitats of the damp region known as the terai emerge from morning mist. Tall rushes, sedges and grass in the foreground flank the muddy waters of the Reu. The dense, marshy thickets across the river lie half-hidden by mist. Behind them thick sal-tree jungle hedges the terai. The Siwalik foothills rise into the background haze.

A group of chital deer (above) pauses on
the alert at the forest edge. Content to
graze pasture or browse among the trees,
they are at home in both marsh and
jungle. Although their spotted
camouflage is least effective against the
background of rivers, they take to the
water if pursued, and can swim well.

A langur mother and young (right),
away from their tree sanctuary and
hence doubly alert, interrupt suckling
to identify a disturbance. Although
more vulnerable when they descend,
langurs spend most of their day on the
ground, tempted down by succulent
young growth on the forest floor.

Alert for a trace of game, a tiger pauses in its patrol of terai animal trails—a daily journey that will cover several miles of jungle, marsh and riverside. Since its nose is not keen enough for tracking, the tiger stalks by sound, and its eyes pick out quarry from thick cover only on the final approach at quite short range.

Nearly submerged in its favourite bathing pool, an Indian rhinoceros escapes the heat and the myriad flies of midday. Jungle mynah birds perch on the island of its massive back, attracted by both the rhino's parasites and by insects stirred up during the great animal's wallowings.

At cooler times of the day, the rhino grazes, shoulder-deep in tall cuckoo-grass (right). Mynah birds—well known as brilliant mimics—continue in permanent attendance, feeding on the grass- and ground-dwelling insects that are scattered by the trampling progress of their six-foot high, two-ton benefactor.

A gharial (or gavial) crocodile cleaves the water with its thin, club-like snout as it maintains position against the current. The snout, armed with even, needle-like teeth, is an adaptation to the gharial's diet of fish: it offers little resistance to the water when the crocodile strikes with an abrupt sideways slash of the head. Though fearsome to behold—the gharial can grow to 20 feet long—this reptile is of little danger to humans; if approached, it simply sinks into the water.

4/ To the Edge of the World

At one moment we would find ourselves climbing rugged rock-faces, at another we would be forced to make our way between steep walls of detritus knowing full well that we might at any moment be struck by falling stones.

ARDITO DESIO/ *ASCENT OF K2*

The Karakorams are one of the highest mountain barriers in the world, where a mile can be swallowed up by a single curve of river or mountain-flank. Extending for some 300 miles from the Afghan border to the Shyok River, they divide Pakistan from China and run parallel to the Punjab Himalayas, separated from them only by the Indus Valley. Created by immense forces over astronomic periods of time, the environment is so vast, so exuberant, so menacing, that it is beyond human capacity to comprehend or constrain. Here rock and water are in perpetual but unequal competition, for rock must always yield eventually to water, shouldering it aside in one place only to admit its passage in another.

Looking south to Nanga Parbat, I saw how that huge mass delays and diverts but cannot prevent the incision of the Indus on its impetuous course to the Arabian Sea. I was standing at the confluence of the Indus with one of the major tributaries of its upper valley, the Gilgit. Each river arrives at this point apparently equal in width and vigour. But when they merge there can be no question which is master, for the Indus accepts the Gilgit in a flurry of bubbles and broken eddies that are smoothed away a quarter of a mile downstream, and then flows onwards as if nothing special had happened. That the two rivers have reached this same point at the same level is a fact of geography that one takes for granted, since it is bound to occur somewhere. But their headstreams lie 1,000 miles apart, and in hustling to their junction each drops 13,000 feet and forces its way through the mighty Karakorams.

It is possible to drive from the base of Rakaposhi in the Karakorams to the base of Nanga Parbat in the Himalayas in half a day, and as you cross the Indus by a quivering bridge of planks suspended from high wires, it seems less a frontier than a jugular vein. The Indus, like the Brahmaputra, rises in Tibet from the slopes of the superbly symmetrical Mount Kailas, sacred to Buddhist and Hindu alike.

The two rivers to which Kailas gives birth are the greatest in the Himalayas, greater than either the Irrawaddy or the Ganges, which also spring from the mountains. The Brahmaputra and the Indus are the same length—1,800 miles—and both flow parallel to the Himalayan range before breaking through it at opposite ends. The Brahmaputra receives a lot of rainfall; the Indus flows for the first part of its length in the Karakoram-Himalaya trough, which is seldom visited by rain, but is fed by melt-water, and then receives tributaries in such abundance that it carries at its mouth twice the volume of the Nile.

Such rivers make geography intelligible. They have a sense of purpose and destination; mountains have none. They are alive; mountains are inert, like the Bilcher, which presides over the Indus-Gilgit confluence. The green-blue water was the only movement in the scene before me, and added the only colour to mountain-brown and summit-white. The land is semi-desert, the water slipping past in chasms too deep to rise and irrigate the shoulder levels, where the cauldron heat of summer completes the desiccation begun by sheep and goats. The steppes are tufted by camel-thorn and sage-brush, but are otherwise barren, and the course of minor tributaries is indicated in winter only by fernlike patterns in the dust. So empty is the upper valley of the Indus that the dirt road and bridge by which I travelled were the only human marks upon it, strikingly economical in their effort compared to the wastage of mountain and river in theirs. And yet I was amazed, seeing it for the first time, that the mighty Indus, which gave its name to a whole sub-continent and to a civilization that lasted a thousand years, could make so little impact upon its surroundings.

Nanga Parbat is the western sentinel not only of the Indus Valley but of the entire Himalayan range. Its name means "naked mountain," because its steely cliffs can hold no permanent snow; and to German climbers it is known as Murder Mountain from its reputation as a man-killer. From the north it cannot be described as beautiful, for beauty in a mountain demands a certain symmetry, while Nanga is ill-proportioned, rising to 26,660 feet by a series of barren shoulders, each shrugging higher than the last and culminating in the summit of curving snow.

From other directions it seems more graceful and certainly less tame, particularly to those climbing it. I understood something of their hardships when I flew from Rawalpindi to Gilgit at 18,000 feet past its western flanks. This must be the most dramatic of all scheduled flights, but so dependent upon weather that the pilot turned back in mid-air on our first three attempts. As I was sitting next to him, I felt more grateful than frustrated. Clouds rose ahead of us larger than the mountains. We could not fly over them because the ceiling of the little Fokker aeroplane is only 20,000 feet; and we could not fly through them because Nanga might lurk like a tiger inside. Our fourth attempt succeeded, and we climbed from the plain to cross ridges that soon gathered into quills slanting steeply to minor peaks, with streams running between them like spilled ink. Against their sides stood banks of pine, no longer green from this height, but tiny black exclamation marks.

For the mountaineers this is merely the approach march, lasting weeks. Then their real difficulties begin. I looked down, then across, then upwards, at Nanga Parbat as it rose above us, and chose the routes by which I imagined myself overcoming ice-walls and crevasses, just as a huntsman can follow a scent cross-country from the windows of a train. The summit was domed and smooth and seemed easy to me. Then I remembered Hermann Buhl of Innsbruck, who in 1953 climbed the last 4,400 feet alone, leaving his companion in the highest camp at 2.30 a.m. and took till 7 that evening to reach the top, too late to descend. He spent the night under a crescent moon a few hundred feet below the summit, without oxygen, food or tent and somehow survived. When his friends went up next day to retrieve his corpse, they met him stumbling down.

Having finally landed at Gilgit, I wanted to see Nanga Parbat from closer to, and so I followed the track that climbs eventually up the eastern side of the mountain near the village of Astor. This track will take only the toughest of vehicles and it is impossible to drive from Gilgit to Astor—a distance of 70 miles—in less than five or six hours. The slowness of the journey is an indication of its hazards. For the first 40 miles, until well beyond the Indus bridge and the solitary village of Bunji, the road was rough but fairly level. It was only when our Jeep swayed over the bridge at the foot of the Astor Gorge that I began to wonder whether I should have come at all.

Here a Jeep must behave like a goat. The track is scarcely wider than the Jeep itself, and is cut from the cliff-face in a ledge that sometimes runs at river-level, but more often four or five hundred feet above it. It is slippery with ice or dust (how odd to see the two in juxtaposition), and there is no parapet of any kind on the river side to guard against the precipitous drop. As the track winds steeply upwards to hug the mountainside and gain height, there are frequent hairpin bends that the driver must approach at speed to gain the necessary impetus to round them, and these are the most alarming moments of the 30-mile ascent. He hurtles into apparently empty space, and at the last second wrenches the wheels around the corner, hoping that they will grip the ice and that there will not be a herd of goats on the other side. Then there are bends so tight that they can be turned only by reversing to the very edge of the abyss. And if you should meet a descending vehicle, which on my journey happened only once, the impasse must be overcome by retreating backwards to a strip of slightly wider path where one vehicle can squeeze past the other hub to hub, the outer wheels scraping the rock wall or manoeuvring to within an inch of oblivion. I did not want to ask how many fatal accidents there had been and, tactfully, I was not told. Still, we made it safely: up, and then down again.

Actually Nanga Parbat became less visible the nearer I approached it; and was completely out of sight once I was on its slopes. We were obliged to drive up another 2,000 feet to Ramah before the mountain began to reveal itself again, and at 13,000 I was still less than halfway up.

Ramah is a delectable place. It is not a village, but a single hut, built by British officers in the 1930s for rest and recreation. I was the first foreigner to come there in winter for five years, said the caretaker of the rest-hut. The last was another Englishman. "He had a lady with him," the caretaker added disapprovingly. The hut lies at one end of a valley that has been carved into the rock by a minor glacier. In summer it is a meadow grazed by yaks and spangled with flowers; in January it is snow-filled from end to end. Streams feed into it, flowing fast under translucent hoods of ice or past waterfalls frozen solid into glacial pillars. It is ringed by trees, mostly *Pinus wallichiana* and the edible pine, *Pinus gerardiana*, which stand ruddy in the sunlight against the snow. At the far end, two miles from the hut, is a lake in which are reflected snowpeaks 20,000 feet high. I first mistook the highest of them for Nanga Parbat itself, but the summit still lies hidden many miles beyond, and you can see it only by climbing another thousand feet up a steep spur (which the lady refused to do, said the caretaker with a sniff). On these slopes are found ibex and musk-deer, he told me. And he had often come across prints of snow-leopards.

I felt myself embraced by the Himalayas in a way I never felt at Everest or in the Gandaki Valley, for my feet were treading untrodden snow, and here at last was the stillness found only in high mountains far from human habitation. As the steel tip of my walking-stick punctured the surface ice, I imagined it an alpenstock and felt the upward tug to which all mountaineers succumb. I began to understand how they can risk their lives for the purity of it all, the purity of old rock and new snow, of the crystalline air, the cleanliness of the very danger to which they are exposed, for there could be nothing mean about death in such a place: terrible, perhaps, but never squalid.

On the return journey I stopped at Astor. It is called by its inhabitants "the city", in the sense, I suppose, of the ancient Greek concept of a city, for although it is nothing but a huddle of mean houses, it has a tradition of bellicose independence, and is now the main frontier village between Pakistan and Indian Kashmir. It is little known except to its inhabitants, who imagine it to be world-renowned as a trade route and battleground. They live a life of excruciating hardship, although it would be a simple matter to tap the great Indus River in the valley at their feet and flood and fertilize the barren plains. The streams flowing off the mountains could also be trapped and split into life-giving rivulets. My companions expressed agreement. "Come," they said. "Come to Hunza, and we will show you where it has been done."

The Hunza River splits the Karakorams from north to south, rising on the Chinese border and flowing into the Gilgit River, which, in turn, flows into the Indus. Enclosed by mountains rising to 25,000 feet, its floor cultivated like a garden, the Hunza Valley deserves Eric Shipton's encomium as "the ultimate manifestation of mountain grandeur." Poplars, thin and pale as wands in their winter nakedness, ride dead-still up the slopes or curve in groves along the river-banks. Between them are terraced orchards of apricots, apples and almonds, some interwoven with vines, and irrigated by rivulets of the clearest water falling in tresses from the nearer hills. At one point a gorge gapes at its summit to disclose the white triangle of a glacier and near by rises the tremendous granite needle known as Princess Bubula's Peak; opposite, growing misty with distance, is the glen that forms the bed of the Hispar Glacier; and at the southernmost end of the valley towers Rakaposhi, a queen of a mountain, with pink clouds streaming at sunset from a summit ridge that thrusts into the sky like a blade of steel.

One can drive the entire length of the Hunza Valley by Jeep, and for me the excitement of the journey was not so much the fabled central

A snow-leopard lazes outside its lair; sadly, the species is becoming scarce because its superb coat is highly prized by fur hunters.

section where the Hunza people live, but the gorge itself and the almost uninhabited country at its northern end. The dirt road we followed is cut much more boldly in the face of the cliff than the track to Astor. It follows grander curves, affording dizzy views downwards of the torrent swirling past rock-precipices, and upwards to sudden glimpses of mountains that appear to belong to another world. The Hunza River has literally torn the Karakorams apart. But as the process was so gradual, it has left, instead of the jagged edges found in the Astor Gorge, smooth canyon walls striped at intervals by horizontal strata of a different colour. So deep is the gorge that it receives little light direct from the sun, but the honey-coloured cliffs fill the basin with a warm glow, and we never felt claustrophobically enclosed. Turning a final bend, we saw in front of us the entrance porch to the canyon, a 10,000-foot wall of rock, pierced by the river, and crenellated by a row of sharp peaks very close together and almost equal in height. As they caught the setting sun, each one became a Gothic flambeau.

This was the route, I suddenly remembered, by which Peter Fleming in 1935 had descended to India after his six-month, 3,500-mile journey overland from Peking. On my return to England I re-read his *News from Tartary* and was amused to find with what relief he had greeted this grim scene as the first outpost of civilization. To him it had powerfully suggested Scotland. To me it was the end of the known world. In his day there was nothing but a mule-track cut in the cliff, but today the road, barely passable from Gilgit, becomes unbelievably good about eight miles beyond Baltit, the capital of Hunza. The dirt road and swaying suspension bridges give place to a three-lane highway with stone bridges, curves and gradients as smooth as a glacier's, and a surface incomparably better. It was built by the Chinese as a peace-offering to Pakistan, and parts of it are labelled with appropriate titles: Friendship Bridge; Chou En-Lai Pass. The road is still bordered by immense mountains, high enough—and thus important enough—to be named and measured. Several of them are over 25,000 feet high. From their northern slopes descend glaciers 20 or 30 miles long, two of them extending to within a quarter of a mile of the road. It is very cold—the valley lies in the middle of a natural refrigerator—and in the evening the wind from the south howls through the canyon towards Pasu.

Just beyond Pasu we were halted by a barrier across the road. It was not the Chinese frontier, which lies several miles ahead, but a Pakistani checkpoint where we were informed with courtesy and many jokes that we could go no farther. It was disappointing, but the soldiers

Throwing up clouds of sand and dust, a wave of broken rock rolls down the scree slopes of a barren valley in Hunza province.

allowed us to walk across the bed of the Hunza—mainly dry at this time of the year—to inspect its confluence with the Shimshal and sent a guide to show us the way across the half mile of stone and ice.

Lord, this is a dreadful place. I began to understand why our ancestors pictured Hell as cold. On a summer's day, perhaps, the deep valley could acquire grandeur and even charm. But this was mid-January and night was falling. The wind increased in force and bitterness, veering from point to point in violent gusts, and all around us the cliffs turned menacing and sullen-yellow. The two great glaciers ended in dirty snouts faintly visible in the gloom, and other ice-falls were clamped to chutes of fallen rock. Mist canopied the valley. There were no birds, no trees, no plants, no animals and no people except the soldiers in their unenviable outpost. Ahead of us, as we picked a path between ice-coated boulders, we could hear the increasing roar of the Hunza River, and when we reached it, we saw the Shimshal, which rises 100 miles away to the east, forcing its way through the opposite cliff. This was no confluence; it was an ejaculation. The anger of the Hunza was simply doubled. It poured away into the mounting darkness, marking its passage by irritable white flares. As we turned back across the stones, the sky surrendered the last of the day's light, and all that remained to guide us were vast shapes blacker than the blackness that surrounded them.

Northwards from Pasu the valley opens out into a wide basin to collect the water of a large area, and we had a glimpse of it before walking to the Hunza. It seemed suddenly familiar, then I realized that I was remembering photographs of the moon. There was the same dusty plain split by bare mountains and ravines, the same motionless boulders strewn across it, the same flat light. For the most part it is empty wilderness, and at its centre, within 50 miles of where we stood, three frontiers converge, those of the Soviet Union, China and Afghanistan, while a fourth, Pakistan's, lies near by. The neighbouring places of their junctions are clearly marked on the map; on the ground they are minor peaks, and have been visited only by the most intrepid travellers. The mountains are fleshless bones that will look little different half a million years hence. No boundary fences are possible or required, and though their assumed courses have been formalized by treaty and toasted by foreign ministers in glasses of champagne, the frontiers merge in a desolate no-man's-land where all the winds of Asia meet to howl a common dirge.

Apart from a few favoured valleys like Hunza, the Karakorams are inhospitable to man, and the poverty of the people and the great distances between settlements are proof of it. Linked to the rest of Pakistan only in the last 25 years by an unreliable air service and a single Jeep track, the region has tended to look northwards towards China for its material and spiritual sustenance, rather than south to India. The carved woodwork of the Mir (Rajah) of Hunza's ancient palace at Baltit, purely Chinese in character, is one example of this. Attitudes are changing, however, as communications improve and more visitors come to Hunza.

But while Gilgit and Hunza are already feeling the effect, the eastern end of the Karakoram range, where the greatest mountains rise, is scarcely more penetrable than in 1887, when Francis Younghusband became the first European to attempt a crossing at its most perilous point. His story is worth retelling as an example of earlier explorations of this wilderness. Younghusband was a captain in the King's Dragoon Guards. Stationed in China, he determined to walk from Peking to India across the Gobi Desert and the Karakorams, a journey of 3,000 miles never previously attempted.

The first stage went well: with eight camels, a guide, a servant and a Mongol assistant, he plodded 1,000 miles through the interminable desert, mostly at night, before he came to the first house he had seen since starting. From there it was another 40 days' march to Kashgar in Chinese Turkestan, and thence south to Yarkand, where he had his first view of the mountains. He had the choice between the easier Karakoram Pass, leading to Leh, in Ladakh, or the much higher and virtually unexplored Mustagh Pass into Kashmir. He chose the latter. His guide, Wali, who had crossed this pass 30 years before—from the opposite direction—was the last man known to have done so. There were seven other men with them, and 13 ponies to carry their supplies.

But Wali, it transpired, had forgotten the way. As they entered the mountain belt, they were in pathless country untenanted by man; and on reaching the top of a 15,000-foot pass, the first, they saw ahead of them tiers of peaks—25,000, 26,000 and, in one case, 28,000 feet high. "It was a scene," wrote Younghusband, "which, as I viewed it, and realized that this seemingly impregnable array must be pierced and overcome, seemed to put the iron into my soul." They descended a steep valley, then climbed again to another pass, "where I chanced to look upwards rather suddenly, and a sight met my eyes which fairly staggered me. We had just turned a corner which brought into view a peak of appalling height, which could be no other than K2. Viewed from this direction, it seemed to rise in an almost perfect cone, but to an inconceivable height. We were quite close under it, and here on the northern side, where it is literally clothed in glacier, there must have been 14,000 to 16,000 feet of solid ice."

They advanced to the foot of the pass and found their way along a glacier composed of blocks of ice 200 feet tall. Incredibly, they led the ponies through it, hauling and pushing, slipping and falling, for 15 miles, taking advantage of whatever moraine they could find at the edges. From that point the ponies could go no farther, and leaving them with a couple of men to lead them by the alternative route, Younghusband and the six others started to climb the final pass. For equipment they had only one bedroll, a sheepskin coat for each man, some native biscuits, a large kettle, a packet of tea, an ordinary pick-axe and a bottle of brandy that Younghusband had brought all the way from Peking, promising himself not to open it until he reached India.

The ascent of the Mustagh Pass was breathless but not too hard, and they reached the top (19,030 feet) at midday. On the far side they looked down an ice-slope as steep as a house roof terminating in a precipice several thousand feet high. "To get down," wrote Younghusband, "seemed to me an impossibility. I had had no experience of Alpine climbing, and had no ice-axe or other mountain appliances. I had not even any proper boots. All I had for footgear were some native boots of soft leather without nails and without heels ... which gave me no sort of grip on an icy surface ... I kept quite silent as I looked over the pass, and waited to hear what the men had to say about it. They meanwhile were looking at me, and imagining that an Englishman never went back from an enterprise he had once started, took it as a matter of course that as I gave no order to go back, I meant to go on."

So they started down the ice-slope, Wali cutting steps with the pick-axe, the others following him holding a rope of which one end was tied round Wali's waist. But they did not have the sense to loop it round their own. Younghusband tied handkerchiefs round his boots to give them extra grip, and they advanced to the edge of the precipice. At that point one man turned back unable to face it. But Younghusband and the five others began their descent, taking advantage of slight holds that the rugged surface of the rock presented: "Even then we seldom got a hold for a whole hand or a whole foot. All we generally found was a little ledge, upon which we could grip with the tips of the fingers or side of the foot ... For six hours we descended the precipice, partly rock and partly ice slope, and when I reached the bottom and looked back, it seemed impossible that any man could have come down such a place."

As the sun set, they reached the head of the Baltoro Glacier and made camp. The only casualty of the descent was the bottle of brandy, smashed in a fall. It took the party two more days to traverse the glacier, and a further two to reach Ashkole, the first inhabited spot in India—"a repulsively dirty place" where the inhabitants were most inhospitable, dismayed to find that their village was approachable from the north. Younghusband and his party continued to Skardu in Baltistan and then walked on to Srinagar. There the political agent, the first fellow-countryman he had seen for seven months, greeted Younghusband with the words, "Don't you think you should have a wash?"

Mountains and remote villages do not change much in 90 years, and Ashkole still lies three days' journey from Skardu, for the Jeep-track extends only part of the way up the Shigar Valley which leads to it, and the path is rough and steep. Shigar is not unlike Hunza. Fertile with almond trees and even grapes and tobacco, it is fed by several glaciers of which the Baltoro is one of the longest in the world outside the Polar regions. In Ashkole itself you will still find the huddle of squalid houses that represented to Younghusband the fingertips of civilization reaching out to guide him home.

This region of Baltistan contains a larger number of clustered peaks over 24,000 feet than any other area, even in the Himalayas. Sixty of them are over 22,000. The highest, K2 (28,250), is exceeded only by Everest, and the three Gasherbrums are all over 26,000. They are infinitely remote. The base of K2 lies 100 miles from the nearest point approachable on wheels, and an expedition can take three weeks to reach it before the serious climbing begins. I saw only the approaches, but enough to realize the hardship of the full journey and the dangers of the climb. The Karakorams rather than the Pamirs, to which the title is usually applied, are the Roof of the World.

The Mountain Fliers

The Himalayan slopes are home to a cosmopolitan population of birds, most of them immigrants that have colonized this apparently hostile world. They represent species from as far as Europe and Africa and as close as the neighbouring uplands of the Orient. And their life-styles reflect a vast range of habitats— from the frozen, wind-torn snow-fields of the world's highest peaks to the hot and forested foothills.

The highest realm belongs to the birds of prey and carrion. The perils of life near the snow-line ensure a constant supply of car-cases: predators leave the remains of their kills and any mountain sheep or goat that weakens soon succumbs to cold. This food supply attracts huge griffon vultures. Their ominous shadows are as familiar on the Himalayan snows as are those of their counterparts on the African plains, and they spiral on wind currents up to 25,000 feet. Their more ornate cousins, the lammer-geyers, now almost extinct in their European homeland, also skim the high contours, and alpine choughs —members of the crow family—have been seen as high as 27,000 feet.

On and below the snow-line at 9-15,000 feet, where melting snow provides water for the alpine pastures and attendant insects, lies an area rich in food for the smaller birds. This is the summer home of many species; redstarts and ac-centors, sparrow-sized insect-hunters, flit from boulder to boulder or dash, mouse-like, in pursuit of their minute prey. Pheasants, par-tridges and pigeons from the heights of China feed on shoots and bulbs; their colours blend with the patch-work of grass, boulders and snow, helping them avoid the attention of eagles and hawks.

Many of the snow-line birds are seasonal commuters. Nesting at summer-time in the safety of the snows, they fly down to the forests of the foothills, as low as 5,000 feet in winter. There they must adopt an entirely different style of life. Al-though food and shelter are readily available, competition is fierce, for the lower jungles and forests teem with birds: green parakeets scream from the treetops, flocks of strutting mynahs flit restlessly from clearing to clearing, and undulating files of thrush-like brown babblers flop heavily from bush to bush, seeking seeds. It is a world rich in food, and vastly different from the austere and lonely heights.

As pre-monsoon clouds swirl around the snow-line, griffon vultures wheel effortlessly. With wings that can span 10 feet, griffons are masters of gliding, so the savage updraughts caused by drastic temperature changes and towering rockfaces enable them to cover great distances in quest of food.

This rare picture of a lammergeyer on
the ground—it is resting on the stony
fringes of an alpine pasture—reveals
the rich tawny colour of the bird's
breast, which is so difficult to see when
the bird is flying against a bright sky.
Also visible is the moustache of black
feathers that gives the lammergeyer
its other name of bearded vulture.

In flight, the lammergeyer specializes
in fast, contour-hugging glides. It can
reach 80 m.p.h. in its sweeping
searches for skeletons picked clean by
its cousins, the griffon vultures. When
successful, it seizes a large bone in
its talons, flies high over rocks,
drops its burden to shatter it and then
lands to make a meal of the marrow.

Blood pheasants forage for pine shoots, mosses, ferns and lichen in the world's highest pheasant habitat: the melting snow at 9-15,000 feet. In contrast to the eye-catching plumage of the males (centre)—their stripes account for the "blood" of their name—the females (far right) are a dowdy brown. Their dull colour provides camouflage when they incubate their eggs in grass-lined gaps between boulders.

An insect-hunter of the upper slopes, the alpine accentor (left) scours crevices for flies and beetles. Winter drives it down to the forest, where it must compete for food, but the accentor, with a muscular throat that can break up hard seeds, is adapted to the change.

Snow pigeons (right) glide the last few hundred feet to feeding grounds in the cliffs and forests at around 9,000 feet. They make this downhill journey once a day, flying back up before dusk, no matter what the weather, to roost in valleys above the snow-line, where they gather to be secure from predators.

Alert to every movement in the tangled undergrowth, a spiny babbler sits on its nest in the low scrubland of Nepal. Among the shyest of hill-side birds and a weak flier, it keeps to the low bushes in its search for insects. Although occasionally tempted from cover to feed in near by grasslands, the spiny babbler seldom ventures into regions that are above 6,000 feet.

5/ The Great Divide

*The general impression of the great range is of a wild,
desolate, little-known country, a country of great peaks and
deep valleys, of precipitous gorges and rushing grey-green
rivers; a barren beautiful country of intense sunlight, clear
sparkling air and wonderful colouring.*

W. K. FRASER-TYTLER/ *AFGHANISTAN*

Before I left London I rang up the Afghan Embassy.

"Please, I want a visa for Afghanistan."

"Why exactly?"

"Because I am writing a book about the Himalayas."

"We have no Himalayas in Afghanistan."

The voice at the other end sounded like a high-class florist from whom I had ordered two dozen saucepans.

"Yes, you have: the Hindu Kush."

"The Hindu Kush are not part of the Himalayas."

"They are as much part of them as a bridal train is part of a wedding-dress."

This was too elaborate an argument to sustain over the telephone with a complete stranger, and the voice repeated, more emphatically, its earlier denial, and rang off.

Later, when I went to the Embassy in person, they were just as sceptical, but put it more kindly.

"The Hindu Kush are hardly the Himalayas themselves. Are you quite sure that you wish to include them?"

I was quite sure. Geographically they are extensions of the Himalayas, I said, and if we left them out we would make ourselves look ridiculous.

I got my visa with no trouble at all, indeed with great courtesy, and

being committed, went to see the Hindu Kush. There is no difficulty in
seeing them: you have only to look out of a hotel window in Kabul, the
Afghan capital. They smash across the horizon like great towers. To
visit them, in mid-winter, when I was there, is a different matter. The
range is 600 miles long, rising to 25,000 feet, and is crossed by three
roads that lead northwards from Kabul to the Russian frontier. Only
one, however, remains motorable throughout the year. Elsewhere, the
range is impenetrable, except on foot and with great endurance. Even
the hardy nomads who live deep within the hills are driven to seek
shelter in the valleys. Having chosen to arrive in February, I crawled up
the lower slopes of the range, hammered at its portals, flew over it, and
once crossed it by car. I fought the Hindu Kush, but did not fight it very
hard, and cannot claim to know it. I simply came to realize that there
was more to know than any human being could compass in a lifetime.

The name Hindu Kush means "Hindu killer", and it first appears in a
book of travels by the Arabian, Ibn Batuta, in 1334, in which he
explains: "Many of the slaves, male and female, brought from India, die
on the passage of this mountain owing to the severe cold and quantity of
snow." The Greeks called it Parapamisus, derived from the Persian
uparisena—"the peaks over which the eagle cannot fly". It is a sprawling
range, with a well-defined crest-line, but serrated by deep gorges and
throwing off subsidiary ridges north and south—"a barren beautiful
country of intense sunlight," wrote W. K. Fraser-Tytler, the former
British Minister in Afghanistan, in his classic book, *Afghanistan*,
"clear sparkling air and wonderful colouring as the shadows lengthen
and the peaks and rocks above turn gold and pink and mauve in the
light of the setting sun".

The range curves across Afghanistan like a giant backbone, dividing
the country into two unequal parts. About a third lies north of this
watershed. There the peaks gradually give way to high plateaux and the
plains beside the low Amu Darya (as the Oxus River is now known).
Southwards from the main massif, rocky tendrils stretch in all directions, split by a series of ice-fed rivers, until they peter out in the desert
flats of Iran and the plains of Kandahar. In the east the Hindu Kush
narrows to the Wakhan Corridor, a spur of Afghanistan that was deliberately created in the late 19th Century to separate Russia from
northern India at a time when international tensions were too great to
risk a common frontier.

It is a region that few travellers have visited, and those who have find
themselves overwhelmed by the violence of the terrain. "It is a country of

extremes," wrote Fraser-Tytler, "of high barren plateaux and wide open stretches of sun-baked desert, of narrow fertile valleys, and rocky mountain spurs. Its climate varies from the bitter cold of the Kabul winter when the temperature frequently drops below zero Fahrenheit, to the great heat of the Oxus Valley where in summer a temperature of 110°F. is normal. It is a treeless wind-swept country, where in winter an icy blast blows off the high ridges, and in summer whirling 'devils' of sand and dust sweep across the open plains."

Unlike the Himalayan range itself, the Hindu Kush gets little benefit from the seasonal monsoon rains that turn the valleys of Nepal and Sikkim into lush green gardens. The average rainfall for the whole of Afghanistan is only seven inches a year, and the Hindu Kush is almost entirely bare of plants and trees except where the valleys are watered by the streams from high glaciers and winter snows. "That which most forcibly strikes a traveller in these regions," wrote Captain John Wood of his journey through the Hindu Kush in 1837-38, "is the total absence of wood—the nakedness of the country. There are no timber-yielding trees indigenous to the Hindu Kush . . . except the Arch, a dwarfish fir, which never equals in size its congeners of the Himalayan forest. It serves, however, for the building purposes of the natives, and is too valuable to be used as fuel. The poplar is seen by the sides of most rivulets, but never in great numbers, and always in localities which indicate that man has placed it there. The same may be said of fruit-bearing trees, except the almond and pistachio-nut, which are evidently natives of the lower portions of the Hindu Kush."

It is probable that there are even fewer trees in the area now than when Captain Wood was there. Droughts have increased the aridity and in 1969-70 and 1970-71 there was no winter snow at all. The immediate effect of this latest drought, however, was too much water. Without fresh falls of snow to reinforce it, the ancient snow-crust high up on the Hindu Kush began to melt, causing floods and landslip. On the southern slopes the snow-line crept upwards by as much as 1,000 feet. As well as natural disasters, the drought also brought a minor civil war. As the snow melted, new veins of semi-precious lapis lazuli were exposed and rival claims to mining rights ended in bloody fighting.

Despite this region's general aridity, however, wildlife, though scarce, is varied. There are wolves, bears, foxes, wildcats, hares, wild sheep, ibexes, porcupines, striped hyenas and the occasional leopard. Tigers have also been reported in the mountains, but evidence is scarce. Bears are present in the wooded areas of east Afghanistan and

Receiving virtually no rainfall from the monsoon, the starkly rugged heights of the Hindu Kush can only support scant vegetation.

hyenas are to be found in the south, close to the Pakistan border. The only monkeys are the rhesus, which inhabit the woods alongside the Bagshal River. Trout teem almost undisturbed in the mountain rivers, and the Amu Darya contains giant sturgeon. But the wildlife that is most visible in the mountains is the birds. The high skies are rarely clear of birds of prey, wheeling and soaring on powerful upcurrents of air. There are buzzards, eagles, occasional black kites, hawks and vultures, including lammergeyers, with their distinctive feathered necks and long wings. In the valleys snipe step cautiously through marshland and kingfishers dart over the water in a flash of bright blue.

Some of the smaller birds fall victim to the tribesmen's passion for falconry, which is evident in many of the mountain villages where men and boys can be seen with trained birds on their wrists. Hawking was probably introduced into Afghanistan by the Mongols who, in turn, are thought to have learned the sport in China where it was known as early as 2,000 B.C. Fortunately for other bird life in the Hindu Kush, a trained falcon is extremely expensive and the bird is not easy to trap. The hunter crouches in a hole in the ground and is covered with a large flat stone that has an opening in it large enough for him to put a hand through. A small bird is then tethered to the top of the stone. When the falcon drops from the sky to grab the bait, the hunter thrusts his gloved hand through the hole and grabs the predator by its talons.

I first glimpsed the eastern Hindu Kush from two valleys that ride northwards from the plain of Peshawar in Pakistan—the valleys of Swat and Chitral. I visited them both before journeying on to Kabul. The Swat is a paradise that deserves to be better known, a happy country of unique beauty and historic richness. No European had entered it for 2,000 years before British soldiers penetrated the Malakand Pass in 1895. But it was and is thickly populated, and the ruins of a hundred Buddhist monuments of an earlier age still stand as blunted cones in the corners of fields. In A.D. 519 a Chinese traveller, Sung Yun, reported that the sound of temple bells filled the whole country. Since the 16th Century it has been the home of the Yusafzai tribe, who combine a fierce disposition with remarkable skill in the arts of agriculture.

The road through Swat from Malakand is not a Jeep-track, but well-engineered tarmacadam lined with poplars. I drove up a side-valley that ended at Marghuzar below high wooded mountains, and all the way the terraced fields were green with the shoots of a very early spring. Deodar cedars dropped their ruddy needles on pale grey boulders. Aloft there were bold ridges sprouting trees and streams tumbling between euca-

Banking heavily with splayed wings, a griffon vulture strays accidentally across the flight-path of a lammergeyer that is preparing to land.

lyptus. The water is put to excellent use: first, it runs through cottages to provide a permanent tap and sink; flowing onwards, it works a water-mill; then it irrigates the upper fields; and finally—not a drop wasted—it falls in cascades to perform the same service lower down.

Quite close to Marghuzar is Udegram, the town that has been identi-fied with Ora, captured by Alexander the Great at his first assault. The present ruins are of a later fortress on the same site, and I climbed them, led by a shepherd boy. We toiled up a slope of sliding shale ridged at intervals by the foundations of houses, until, at 2,000 feet above the valley, we reached the drum-towers and ceremonial staircase of the citadel. Looking across the Swat River to the mountains on the far side, it was easy to imagine the terror inspired by the sight of Alexander's cavalry, his 30,000 infantry, his 30 elephants, flooding through the passes to the valley floor. Northwards on the horizon was the Hindu Kush, the bare hills of the middle-ground lifting suddenly into snow peaks, Falakser prominent among them at 19,500 feet. The higher and farther I gazed above the valley mist, the sharper became the outlines. The distant ice was streaked with dark shadow.

Next day I drove with a guide towards the northern wall. At first the road led along level ground on one side of the three-mile-wide valley. Then we entered the hills, and fields gave place to forest, plainsmen to highlanders. With the mountain named Mankial now presiding over the gorge, we entered the first snow. On each side of the Swat Gorge oak merged with deodar, and pine marched with gleaming needles to the frost of the river bed. Soon snow obliterated all detail of the ground, except where the trees rose thick and high and held it like a canopy over the bare rock. Eventually we reached Kalam, at 7,000 feet, where two rivers meet to form the Swat, and the driver protested that he could go no farther because the good road ends there and the Jeep-track was far too dangerous. So we walked.

We walked for three hours up the path towards Ushu and the border with Gilgit. All the way we were enclosed by the deodar forest, the cedar that can shoot up 45 feet in 20 years. Here in the northern extremity of Pakistan the tree is particularly magnificent, rising 100 feet before the first branches, marvellously symmetrical and regal. It was a Wenceslas scene: the snowtrack winding between pillar-like boles, the roar of the torrent, the high peaks beyond. In spring the ground is starred with pale-blue violets, but I was glad to see it in its winter dress. The thin mountain air awakes all one's senses: smells are sharper, sounds echo, eyesight is keener. The trodden snow is springy and aching limbs seem suddenly to be suffused with new energy at these exciting altitudes.

Chitral, the neighbouring valley, is much more difficult of access than Swat. The rough road is open for only three months in the year, and the best approach is by air from Peshawar. The journey is worth its minor perils. The state is about the size of Wales, hemmed in by mountains more than 20,000 feet high. In deep valleys nature is kind and they are filled with fruit trees, but beyond, wrote Sir George Robertson of his journey in 1890, "are vast silent mountains cloaked in eternal snow, wild glacier-born torrents, cruel precipices, and pastureless hillsides where the ibex and the markhor find a precarious subsistence. It takes time for the mind to recover from the depression which the stillness and melancholy of the landscape at first compel. All colour is purged away by the sun-glare, and no birds sing."

It is very different at the other exit from the Peshawar plain, the Khyber Pass. Here the mountains descend to manageable size (the highest point of the road is only 3,500 feet), so manageable, indeed, that men have taken over the defences from nature. The very name Khyber has a cutlass ring about it. Not only has it been throughout history a main route of invasion between India and Central Asia, but it is the home of the Afridi tribe, estimated to be 200,000 strong, and possibly the most ferocious, independent and warlike race ever known. The pass is not like Malakand, a knife-edge approached by a tortuous ascent, but a tumbled mass of hills extending 50 miles from side to side, not so much a gorge as a series of ambush positions.

I drove across it from Peshawar to Kabul in an easy day. I had ordered a car. I was given a small bus. "But I don't want a bus," I protested. "I am your only passenger." The driver, an Afridi, looked at me through a slit of the garment that swaddled him from head to foot. "I have friends," he said; and I did not dare challenge the look in his eyes. So we set off, and at intervals stopped to pick up the friends, who mounted alongside me, saying nothing, gripping rifles.

At the mouth of the pass the villages and individual farms are contained within high mud walls, like minor forts, windowless but loopholed for small-arms. We began to twist into the first hills by an excellent road, the railway winding above and below it, the old caravan route braided between them. A team of donkeys trotted past below us, bearing huge rubber tyres, slung like panniers one to each side. A fort or fortlet crowned each hill, and on the few faces of sheer rock were carved the crests of British regiments. It was all very reassuring. Then my driver began signalling to other friends on the road in what appeared to be a finger-code—two fingers, three, one bent double—and I imagined how sinister such signs could seem in less peaceful times. I barely noticed when we reached the summit, for the whole Khyber is less a crossing than a weaving between huge mounds. The frontier was like a Mafia headquarters, but the soldiers on each side were friendly. I entered Afghanistan with the sense of having survived an unpleasant experience, though nothing unpleasant had occurred. It is a haunted place: the tension of past history is still felt.

During the long drive onwards to Kabul the Hindu Kush kept me company on the horizon. I bought oranges and bananas in Jalalabad and shared them with my silent companions, and we drove on and on through wide plains covered with herds of goats, and then through the three long gorges of the Kabul River, very narrow and turbulent. Walled villages were flung at intervals against the lower hills, the houses catching the light or throwing strong shadows, as in a cubist painting.

From Kabul the Hindu Kush is seen in all its splendid eminence, enlarged in winter by the spreading of the snow to cover the foothills and part of the plain. The crest-line is more regular than that of the Himalayas, forming a rampart some 15,000 feet high. I was determined to cross it. I headed across the plain of Koh-i-Daman, leaving on the right the site of Kapisa where Alexander probably wintered his troops before attempting the ascent, and on the left the village of Istalif, which was loved by Babur, the first Mogul emperor of India. Camels stalked beside the road. There were big mulberries everywhere and well-tended vines, and many of the houses had drying-floors for the grapes, lined with holes like a columbarium for the warm air to blow through.

The road leads to the Salang Pass and leaps from the plain like a thrown coil. From this point it is Russian-built, and as it mounts higher its engineering grows more extravagant, carried on vast embankments and protected from the snow by concrete galleries, until, at 11,000 feet, it pierces the crest by a tunnel one and half miles long, gloomy, cold, faintly lit by fluctuating electricity, like a mine. On the far side the road twists down again, littered with the wreckage of lorries. Failing brakes spell disaster on this descent. An hour before I reached the spot, a lorry had run amok and hurtled across the loop of a hairpin bend. Ploughing across a field of boulders, the chassis was stopped abruptly by one of them, leaving the cab and its load of grain to shoot onwards another 100 yards and disintegrate. All three occupants were killed.

I had intended to stay a few days on the summit of the Salang in a

Spiny tussocks of mauve Acantholimons stand firm while the hot, dry wind of the Hindu Kush buffets the silky threads of Stipa grass.

shanty village euphemistically renamed a skiing centre, but there were no skiers, and conditions were impossibly grim. It shares its electric current with the tunnel, and as the tunnel takes priority, the illumination of the huts is reduced to glow-worm insignificance in the evening, and to total darkness at 8 pm. I would have been miserable to no purpose throughout the long cold nights, and in daylight I would have had the choice between walks on the road, breathing diesel fumes, or stumbling across slopes obscured by snowfields so blinding that already I was forced to cover my eyes and peer through slatted fingers. I would have learned nothing; enjoyed nothing but the recollection of my misery. So I descended the north side of the pass to the valley at Khinjan, and there I spent five happy days exploring as much of the Hindu Kush as was accessible by long walks.

The Hindu Kush is a Great Divide, and its crest, as jagged as a cock's, as arrogant as Guelph architecture, was penetrable only in summer before the Russians built the all-seasons road. The passes are true passes, not clefts, and the history of Afghanistan is dominated by attempts to cross them. Alexander in 328 B.C. and Timur (Tamerlane) in A.D. 1398, used the Khaiwak Pass (11,640 feet); Babur in 1504 crossed by the Qipchak Pass (13,900), and Genghis Khan in 1220 took the lower route by Bamiyan. Alexander led 32,000 men over the Khaiwak in May, when snow still masked the northern tracks, and they suffered terribly, not so much from cold as hunger, for the ascent took a week, the descent ten days, and there was no edible vegetation on the route, no beasts except their own horses to kill, and they ate the flesh raw for lack of fuel to cook it on. When Timur took his Mongols across he could see no way down the far side except by ordering them to slide on their behinds. Timur himself had a wicker basket made, in which he was lowered by ropes to their full extent. Then a platform was cut in the snow, and the process repeated five times until he reached more level ground. The pack-animals were tied to wooden sledges and swung by ropes across the ravines. More men were lost in that crossing than in the whole of the subsequent campaign.

I saw something of this, in even crueller weather, from the foot of the passes, and suffered in imagination the agony of their climb. Snowfields one can cross with relative security, probing with a stick ahead; if necessary, glaciers can be traversed, as they were by Timur, on hands and knees; bare rock affords hand- and toe-holds. But smooth snow, covering a cascade of boulders, obliterating goat-paths, filling crevasses, creates the worst of all conditions, particularly when there are

Two pikas emerge from their hole under the rocks to forage for the grasses and scrub plants on which they feed. Small rodents that are particularly well adapted to survive extreme cold, they have been found living at 17,500 feet in the Himalayas—higher than any other mammal. Well insulated by their dense grey-brown fur, they also have furred soles enabling them to move over smooth rock. Instead of hibernating they live on grass that they have collected and stored near their burrows during the summer months.

no trees to mark the depth of snow and provide roots and trailing branches to climb by. At night there was no shelter from the smothering blizzard; no hot food; a man once frost-bitten was left to die; and those who survived had to endure all this for two weeks or more, and probably fight a battle when they reached the plain.

I fought no battle, except against the elements. Day after day I strode the paths radiating from Khinjan, away from the village and the road, and up the mountainside to the point where man-made tracks gave place to goat-paths, strewn with lumps of schist that sounded musically when kicked. These led me to the first thin slivers of encrusted ice. It is always a splendid moment. To feel ice beneath your boots and the sun reflected on your face by mirror-surfaces, to walk onwards with caution but also with mounting exhilaration, is to know what the earliest travellers knew, for these things do not change. I was soon lost in hanging valleys, lost but for one sure guide—that downward slopes at this medium height must always lead back to safety. But there can be accidents up here: a twisted ankle, if nothing worse, can immobilize a man, and the proximity of help a few thousand feet below is little consolation if his voice will carry no farther than a few hundred.

Once I thought I had come near to disaster. There was a conveniently placed thorn-bush above me on a low cliff, but it came away as I grasped it, and I fell backwards upon a bed of rocks. The fall was no more than a few feet, and the rocks were fortunately rounded, but I was hurt enough to convince myself momentarily that I had suffered some crippling injury. Of course, I hadn't. Because the human body is supple and cushioned, a superficial abrasion does no damage to its structure. But as I lay there, all the pleasure of the climb drained from me. The mountain had become hostile, the snow-couch on to which I eased myself seemed suddenly a mortuary slab. So small a space does a man occupy in this vastness that he is reduced in spirit by the contrast when he is in trouble, just as he is enlarged by it when he strides the moraines freely and alone.

That day I limped down humbled. But there were other days when I rose at dawn and walked till dusk, and the world seemed to hold no greater joy than this, and no more splendid mountains than the Hindu Kush. Their summits were unattainable by me, but in miniature I could scale them by imagining each ridge and hummock to be the highest point. It is a slow business. Each footfall must be calculated ahead, every fresh advance measured against the difficulty of retreat. At various

This lake is set like a sheet of lapis lazuli deep into the rough, arid terrain of the Hazarajat range of the Hindu Kush in Afghanistan. It is one of five lakes fed by waters of the Band-i-Amir River. Lying at an altitude of 10,000 feet in a series of terrace-like levels, they are separated and surrounded by vertical cliffs. Even during the summer months their vivid blue waters are ice-cold.

points I crossed in ignorance thin bridges of snow, soft and all-smothering, a deceptive disguise for what lay beneath. There was no need for maps, for the very shape of the mountains is a sufficient guide for a day's slow journey, and no map will warn the climber of hazards that can only be measured by the eye and tested by the foot or stick.

In these high mountains winter seems the natural, the permanent, season. The descent of the snow-line by a few thousand feet merely makes it more accessible from the valleys, the summits more remote. The conditions aloft are duplicated by conditions lower down. One can share the experience of mountaineers without being one. What in summer is a cleft of rock becomes in winter a crevasse; a scree-slope turns into a temporary glacier. All life is extinguished where animals grazed three months before, and where they will graze again when spring returns. The levels merge. A snow-filled gully leads to a greave of ice that from its convex thickness seems perennial. A rocky outcrop is sheathed in white armour not unlike the mica of its summer state. The wilderness is extended downwards until it meets the foothills, and expectant nature rests and waits.

Conditions in other parts of the Hindu Kush are even sterner. The Anglo-Russian boundary commission of 1895 described the eastern end of the Wakhan Corridor in terms unusually vivid for an official report: "A rugged and inaccessible spur of the Sarikol range carries the boundary into regions of perpetual ice and snow to its junction with the main range. Here, amidst a solitary wilderness 20,000 feet above sea level, absolutely inaccessible to man and within the ken of no living creatures except the Pamir eagles, the three great Empires [of Britain, Russia and China] actually meet."

To the south-west of the Wakhan Corridor lies Nuristan. Walled in on all sides by mountains, it is impassable in the winter months. It is so isolated that until recent times the inhabitants were able to maintain their ancient pagan religion in a country peopled elsewhere entirely by Muslims. Until 1895, when the area was invaded, the central government in Kabul had no control of these deep upland valleys. The old name of Kafiristan, "country of unbelievers," was then changed to Nuristan, "country of light," to mark the forcible conversion of these wild people to the state religion.

They are quite unlike other races to be found in Afghanistan. The legend that they are descended from the stragglers of Alexander's army, which skirted the country on its way to Samarkand, sounds too fantastic to believe. But Eric Newby, the British explorer and travel writer, saw many people who had a distinctly southern European appearance. "They were all extraordinary," he wrote, "because they were all different, no two alike. They were tall and short, light-skinned and dark-skinned . . . There were men like gypsies with a lock of hair brought forward in ringlets on either side of the forehead. There were men with great bushy beards and moustaches that made them look like Arctic explorers. There were others like early Mormons with a fuzz of beard round their faces but without moustaches. . . . Those who were hatless had cropped hair and the younger ones, especially those with rudimentary beards, looked as strange and dated as the existentialists of St. Germain des Prés; while those whose beards were still in embryo were as contemporary as the clients of a *Café Espresso*."

From Kabul I flew to Teheran. Rising from the snow-scraped airport, I looked down upon the foothills of the Hindu Kush, white and rumpled like bedclothes. The few villages were besieged by winter; not a man-made track approached them. Above rose minor peaks untrodden since the creation. I could see clearly etched in the snow the pattern of watercourses, the gullies leading to streams, the streams to rivers, the rivers sometimes to the sea, but more often to the deserts or swamps round Kandahar, where they evaporate in temperatures as high as 115° F. It was difficult to identify places, for height, form and colour tended to merge into one, but I thought I saw the Bamiyan Valley, a slot between parallel ridges, where the Hindu Kush slowly dies away.

Above, a dark-blue sky shaded downwards to pale blue, and pale blue to misty white, soon indistinguishable from the snow with which it merged on the horizon. I followed the racing landscape through binoculars, as if equipped with magic boots. A huge plain rushed to meet us, wrinkled like leather. The pilot told us we were crossing the border of Iran. Snow again, streaked as if by monster ski-tracks, and then 1,000 miles of nothing. The Hindu Kush, and with it the whole backbone of Central Asia, had finally surrendered to the plain.

The War of the Flowers

"Plants, in a state of nature, are always warring with one another, contending for the monopoly of the soil," wrote Sir Joseph Dalton Hooker, one of the first botanists to make an extensive study of Himalayan flora in the 19th Century. "Every modification of climate, every disturbance of the soil . . . favours some species at the expense of others." Perhaps the best place to observe the effects of this struggle is the Himalayas, where the extreme height and mass of the mountains, their position between the plains of India and the highlands of Central Asia and the fact that much of the area lies in the track of the monsoon rains, provide a wide variety of growing conditions.

Although the Himalayas contain numerous habitats, they can be broken down for the sake of convenience into four broad and contrasting regions: the rain forest of the east, drenched by the monsoon and ranging up to an altitude of 6,000 feet; the wet alpine zone above the tree-line beginning at about 10,000 and rising to 18,000 feet or more; a transitional semi-wet region in the central portion of the mountains, where the precipitation from the monsoon diminishes mark-edly; and an arid region in the high Hindu Kush, far to the west.

In each of these regions, the plants are magnificently adapted to the exacting demands of their particular environment—some, as the pictures on the following pages demonstrate, in ingenious ways. Where living room is at a premium, as in the overgrown jungle of the lower slopes, they must compete with one another for available space and light. But the higher up the mountains or the farther west they live, the more they must engage in another, even harsher battle. Pitted against the raking winds, often covered by snow for long winter periods and oppressed by temperatures that may reach tropical intensity by summer day and plunge below zero at night, most hug the ground and may insulate themselves in a protective cocoon of fluff. Many —like the blue poppy at right—have evolved brilliant colours to lure the few available insects. A few are even qualified by evolutionary combat to survive on the wind-blasted upper slopes. One tiny plant, *Stellaria decumbens*, grows as far up as 20,130 feet, which makes it one of the highest living plants in the world, a true veteran of the war.

Considered one of the most beautiful of Himalayan plants, a species of blue poppy, Meconopsis horridula, glittering here with rain, adorns meadows and screes from 13,000 to 17,000 feet. Its forbidding Latin name is derived from the plant's armoury of straw-coloured spines which, protruding from its leafy rosettes, stems and sepals, discourage browsing animals.

LEONTOPODIUM STRACHEYI—HIMALAYAN EDELWEISS

Weathering the Heights

In the alpine zone of the eastern Himalayas, flowering plants have two fundamental problems to contend with—the cold and the heavy precipitation of the monsoon.

The saussurea (right) wraps itself in a gauze of fibres that not only serve as insulation, but may prevent it from being bowed down or even undermined by torrential rain. The edelweiss (top left)—taller by several inches in the Himalayas than its cousin in the Alps—has fuzzy petals that are, in fact, protective leaves surrounding the real flowers. These are no more than tiny clusters at the centre. The leaves may also provide firm footing for pollinating insects.

The gentian's vase-shaped flowers (bottom left) dwarf the mother plant from which they spring in an effort to attract insects, but they close up tightly with the first drops of rain, a reaction that prevents them from filling up and drowning. They reopen within minutes of the sun reappearing.

GENTIANA DEPRESSA—HIMALAYAN TRUMPET GENTIAN

IMPATIENS GLANDULIFERA—HIMALAYAN BALSAM

The Space Searchers

Below the alpine zone in the eastern Himalayas lies the steamy jungle. Here on the damp slopes, different species exploit every possible niche in an intensely competitive search for space and energy-producing light.

Some are rampant climbers, with twining shoots or tendrils that clasp the trunks of evergreen oaks, sal and other trees as they reach towards the sun. *Raphidophora glauca*, whose flower is seen right, extends long aerial roots (in addition to the main root at its base) that sink into the moss of trunks soaring to 100 feet or more. Its lofty perch ensures efficient propagation: birds eat its fruits and excrete the seeds on to the ground.

The Himalayan balsam, *Impatiens glandulifera* (left) occupies an entirely different habitat. It nestles in shady gullies, tolerant of both wet and shade. When its fruit is ripe, the pod explodes, shooting seeds as much as eight feet across the forest floor to help propagation.

RAPHIDOPHORA GLAUCA FLOWER

DELPHINIUM BRUNONIANUM

Plants in the Middle

In western Nepal and the eastern Hindu Kush, where the monsoon dissipates itself, the Himalayas are a meeting place for the most adaptable species of the wetter and drier regions to the east and west.

Here large tufts of *Aster flaccidus* (right) colour the rocky mountain slopes, and the common gentian of the region is the earth-hugging *Gentiana falcata* (bottom left). *Delphinium brunonianum* (left) proliferates between 12,000 and 18,000 feet but, thwarted finally by the altitude, produces dwarf-size plants in the hard conditions at higher levels.

GENTIANA FALCATA

Western Way of Life

In the arid Hindu Kush, in the Himalayan far west, plants can withstand long periods of drought. Many have leaves that are little more than spines, thus diminishing water loss and discouraging browsing by goats and yaks. Some produce airborne seeds that allow them to propagate themselves over a wide area: those of *Acantholimon lycopodioides* (below) are wafted away in paper-thin "shuttlecocks".

Cardamine loxostemonoides (right) also releases tiny seeds to the winds, but it has an additional means of propagation: its tiny bulbs subdivide into bulblets that roll beneath the scree to suitable environments in which to sprout.

ACANTHOLIMON LYCOPODIOIDES

CARDAMINE LOXOSTEMONOIDES

6/ Man Against the Wilderness

Both man and mountain have emerged from the same original Earth and therefore have something in common between them.

SIR FRANCIS YOUNGHUSBAND/ *THE EPIC OF MOUNT EVEREST*

I sometimes tell myself an imaginary story. Long before the Europeans came to the Himalayas, a young man of the mountains looked up at the great peak that overhung his village, and without telling anyone he set out one early dawn to climb it. For days he struggled up ice and rock, hauling himself from ledge to ledge, sleeping wrapped in his cloak on perilous shelves and gnawing the frozen lump of yak's meat that he carried. On the twentieth day he reached the summit. He had climbed the highest point on earth, though he did not know it. When he came down, nobody credited that he had done what he claimed, so he gave up talking about it. But there was one person who did believe him: his son, who passed on the story to his own son, and he to his, and so on for many generations, until the Englishmen came to the village. They heard the story, and laughed. But when they, too, reached the peak of Everest, they wondered: was it possible that someone had stood there before them?

I tell myself the story only to refute it. It could not have happened. No man could reach or live at that altitude without equipment; and no Sherpa would have wished to attempt it, for the people who are forced to live permanently among the mountains look upon them with very different attitudes from those of Westerners.

In the recent past mountaineers tended to attribute to their porters romantic notions of adventure and appreciation of scenic grandeur that were unknown to the people who wrest their living from these desolate regions. The fact is that if some of them have made a profession of portering for the foreigner, this is only because it is lucrative. Most still see the peaks as holy places, the slopes as the birthplace of catastrophes, the climate as a burden, the forests as potential farmland. When one lives with the mountains instead of merely visiting them, one accepts different values. And so it is that through the eyes of the local inhabitants I learned to see the Himalayas in a new light.

To many of the mountain people, the idea of climbing these peaks seems nearly as sacrilegious as for a devout Catholic to scale St. Peter's. Every prominent peak in the Himalayas is said to be the resort of gods or demons and is credited with supernatural powers of defence. The sacred mountain of Kangchenjunga, which means "the five jewels of eternal snow," is the place where the Tibetan god of wealth kept his treasure, and the British expedition of 1955 turned back five feet from the summit in order not to offend their Sherpas. Of Ama Dablam, Machhapuchhare, Nanda Devi and Nanga Parbat, equivalent legends are repeated at length.

The local inhabitants of the Himalayas look upon their mountains not so much with admiration as with fear or, at least, fatalism. I was walking with one of them on the slopes of Nanga Parbat through a scene of dazzling beauty, and he turned to me without any preface to remark: "The first night of marriage is the last night of love." Hoping to avoid a melancholy autobiography, I began to rhapsodize about the mountains around us. It was no good. "We who live in nature," he replied, for he had a habit of speaking in proverbs, "have no eyes with which to see it."

It is true and inevitable. The world is a cruel place, and life a constant struggle, in the plains as in the mountains. But in the mountains it is crueller, because there all the forces of nature are ranged against men's puny efforts. They fight back, but the mountain is stronger. My companion grew bitter, recalling the friends he had lost, the labour of years destroyed overnight.

"Why do you come here?" he asked. "Do you not have kinder places in your own country?" He pointed downwards at his village. "See there, that black mark. That was our bazaar, until two weeks ago. It was burnt to the ground, not because some woman was careless with her lamp, but it was struck by lightning. And look there," swinging round to an amphitheatre of once neatly terraced slopes, now a chaos of tumbled stones. "That happened last winter, when a stream suddenly altered its course. How do you expect us to love this place?"

"Why not leave it for the plains?"

"And where in the plains? They are either desert, or already crowded with people to the point of suffocation. Let us change places: I will go to England; you can live here.'"

The catastrophes that he pointed out to me had not rated a mention even in Pakistani newspapers. They were known only to the villagers. But others on a larger scale have become history. In 1840 an ice-causeway formed on the Shyok River, creating a temporary lake 12 miles long and 400 feet deep. When it collapsed six months later, the wave was 30 feet high and did not exhaust itself until it had thundered 200 miles below. There was the winter when the Yengutsa Glacier inexplicably advanced three miles in eight days, as unstoppable as volcanic lava, to overwhelm three Hunza villages. Lower down the same valley I saw evidence of what had happened only two summers before. The river, swollen suddenly by an immense avalanche 50 miles upstream, had shorn away the cliff on which a village stood, carrying with it half the houses. The other half still stood on the verge, ruined and abandoned except for the two or three farthest from the edge which the owners had re-occupied at their peril, to be within reach of the surviving fields. Everywhere you see signs of even greater disasters, now long past but at the time creating unimaginable terror: landslides that have obliterated entire plains; rivers that have changed their courses by as much as 30 miles; earthquakes and floods that have left their mark in broken strata or streaks of a deeper colour on canyon walls. I have only to raise my eyes from where I write this, in the Hindu Kush of Afghanistan, to see on the opposite hillside a boulder as large as an omnibus, poised on a cliff-edge. It may have rested there a million years, but who can tell when it will come crashing down on the village beneath?

Thus those who live close to this wilderness view it apprehensively. It is not only impending catastrophe that menaces them, but the predictable fluctuation of climate against which they have never been able to equip themselves. There is no more pathetic sight than a Kashmiri or a Pathan shivering in the winter's cold, unless it be the same man working himself to exhaustion in the summer's heat. They have no change of clothing. The same cotton gown does duty for all seasons, and the only difference is that in winter they will take a loose fold and swathe it round their heads. A woman, too, has but one garment: she wears it every day, works in it, sleeps in it, and as likely as not it will form her shroud. It is a light sari, retaining its elegance even in extreme shabbiness, but utterly impracticable for tending flocks or cutting wood, and in cold weather lamentably inadequate.

In their dwellings one sees another aspect of the Himalayas. Built of the stone or mud or bamboo that surrounds them, many types of hut or cottage speckle the hillsides. They look pretty, but are pitiful defences against rain and cold. Leaky and draughty, lacking glass even when they have windows, damp and vermin ridden, they are traps for every infectious and pulmonary disease. In winter whole families crouch round their fire, looking up wraithlike at the passerby, sustained perhaps by a single meal a day. And what have they to look forward to? A summer of torrid heat alternating with unrelenting rain, hailstones so big that in Nepal they can incapacitate a man for weeks, and wind in gusts up to 100 miles an hour against which he can barely stand. With the humid heat come mildew and insects, recurrent spoliators of his few possessions. It is worse than a nomad's life, for the nomad can at least escape the mud and refuse of his own making.

Because of such hardships the people have been formed by the land— a hardy race inured to their wearisome life. In this world there are no roads, and man himself must often act as pack-animal. The British explorer and ornithologist Guy Mountfort quotes Hsun Tsang, a Chinese traveller who passed through these regions in A.D. 631: "Perilous were the roads and dark the gorges . . . Here were ledges hanging in mid-air; there flying bridges across abysses; elsewhere paths cut with a chisel, or footings to climb by." It is little different today. I have in my mind three pictures. One is of girls carrying on their backs large sheets of plywood that caught the wind like sails. At least this amenity of civilization might help to provide a more durable shelter. But meanwhile the journey of these girls was a purgatory, lasting many days. The second sight is of a young man with a sick friend mounted on his back, taking him—but where? There was no doctor within 50 miles. The third is of a girl, having stumbled from a footbridge with her heavy pack, struggling in the torrent below, from which she was rescued with great difficulty. Such sights are common in Nepal. Few people can afford animals to carry themselves or their burdens. We saw no mules, and the only donkeys were slung with stores for the army in the far north, a jolly cavalcade that we christened the 4th Annapurna Hussars. Even in the Kumaon Himalayas of India, where roads are plentiful, women carry on their heads loads of fodder as tall as themselves, swinging along with unselfconscious grace. The cart is unknown in the remoter regions, even where level ground pleads for its use. Within a few miles of Kathmandu, a wheelbarrow, like the

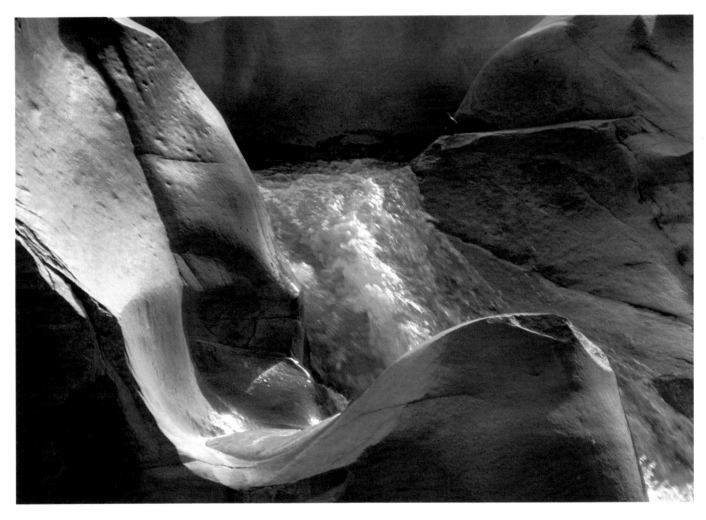

More than 10,000 feet above sea level, one of the headstreams of the river Ganges tumbles down its course, through rocks carved and polished by ice (above) and water (right). To the Hindu faith, this part of the river is especially sacred. Here, near its source, below Gangotri Peak, in the Indian Himalayas, the fast-flowing waters of the mountain stream look very different from the huge, sluggish river that finally empties its muddy waters into the Bay of Bengal, 1,500 miles away.

plough, is never seen; and this among the descendants of a people who were some of the greatest artificers and traders of the East.

Born to a life of porterage, they take it for granted, carrying burdens that would buckle the knees of most other men. I tried to lift one of the packs that our Sherpas carried to 10,000 feet. It weighed a mere 80 pounds, and nearly swung me off my feet, but to them it was no hardship or indignity. Indeed, they are quite capable of carrying loads equalling their own weight—from 150 to 180 pounds. They have developed a padding stride, unvaried for hours on end, over clusters of small loose stones, bare mountainside or steps constructed up the steeper gradients for 1,000 feet or more, like the approaches to Heaven seen in a dream. At intervals the Nepalese have built resting places, a bench to sit upon and behind it a stone table to rest the pack, and often in the centre of the table they plant a cherry or walnut tree, to give shade. You find them in places known from experience to be points of maximum exhaustion, at the top of long ascents where the ground becomes reasonably level. But for great stretches between them the path is relentless. Sometimes in traversing the length of a canyon the route is cut out of the sheer rock-face—half a tunnel, the outer side open to a precipice, and the inner hollowed to allow the passage of a crouching man. Or if the rock is too hard even for this, the path is a plank held against the canyon wall by forked trunks resting on the river-bed below.

The track is a highway, the village street its market-place. We passed beggars, merry youths, the halt and blind, a store-keeper carrying stock for a month on his back, a whole family leaving the higher ground to winter in the valley, a lama, an official of consequence in fine clothes and attended by his servant. The effect is curiously mediaeval. Because the pace is of a walk and all traffic is canalized along a single route, there is every excuse to stop and gossip: the path is a channel of communication in more than one sense. You pass and you re-pass, right and left. One has to watch the track continuously, for each stone is a dangerous new shape set at a new angle. The rhythm of ascent is different from the rhythm of descent, and there are those who say—though I am not one of them—that it is easier to go up than down. But exhaustion lies mostly in the mind: when the sun begins to shine between the boles of trees instead of through their crowns, you know you are reaching the top of the pass, and energy can flow back as rapidly as lethargy seeps in.

Then the bridges. The simplest of them are pines felled across a stream, which you must cross with a panther's tread. Others are crazily cantilevered—a design so traditional that I saw it repeated from Nepal

A Nepalese villager, accustomed since childhood to bearing heavy loads, brings a large bundle of wood up from the village. Around many high-lying villages, the trees have long since been used for firewood; those who are too poor to possess a pony or yak must collect wood themselves and carry it up the mountain to their homes.

to Afghanistan; tree-trunks anchored in stone bastions on opposite banks, reaching towards each other at a slight angle till they form a gap narrow enough to be spanned by planks. But the most exciting and enjoyable are the bridges suspended from ropes of wire or twisted vines, swaying over a river a hundred feet below. They move in rhythm to every footfall—jellified cat-walks, and in places where the planks have fallen or rotted, you walk upon the wires themselves. It is not quite so dangerous as it looks, because the wires are firmly anchored and form hand-rails on each side. They are at their most alarming where they have been widened in the Karakorams to take Jeeps. I crossed one near Gilgit which we approached on level ground, but the far side ended at a sheer cliff-face, with a tunnel that twisted ingeniously up through the rock to gain the flat shelf above. Another bridge hung over the Astor Gorge swinging freely between its bastions.

The leeches that infest the track during the summer deserve to be pilloried in a separate paragraph of their own. They arrive with the monsoon and hang as obscenely as slugs from every bush and clump of grass, reaching out to attach themselves to passing men and animals. They penetrate to the flesh through openings as tiny as lace-holes or between the threads of woollen socks to pierce a blood-vessel with their tripartite suckers, emitting a chemical fluid that prevents the coagulation of the blood. Dozens can feed off a single limb, and so painless is their suction that a man can sleep through it, waking to find his bed-clothes soaked in blood. The wound will continue to bleed long after the leech has sucked its fill and fallen off its victim. Men are slightly better off than sheep or cows which cannot reach parts of their bodies, but it is better not to pull off a leech; this may lacerate the flesh, and the wound can turn septic. The best way to shake off a leech is with a liberal sprinkling of salt or a burning cigarette-end.

The people are a part of the mountains. Just as the mountains are majestic and unyielding, the people lead heroic lives of ceaseless toil and danger. In the most distant regions they have no outside aid. They are self-supporting, self-reliant—and nearly as unchanging as the mountains themselves. There may be a primitive open-air school for the children, but their parents behave the same, look the same and lead the same lives as their remote ancestors. The ladder by which I climbed to the flat roof of a house was hewn from a tree trunk, in much the same way as a river-canoe. Despite their sophistication in other ways, the Sherpas continue to till their fields with the *kodali*, a short-handled mattock or hoe, which has scarcely changed its form since the stone-age. Their medical facilities, too, are archaic. Average life expectation in Nepal is only 30 years. Goitres are commonplace and the inhabitants have never become immune to the tropical diseases, dysentery, cholera, typhoid, smallpox, jaundice and malaria. Many a devout peasant-woman will never see a doctor all her life, for shame of allowing a stranger to touch her body. In Nepal a woman came to us with her index finger half severed by an axe. Terry Spencer, who has a little more medical knowledge than I have, muttered to me that he should take the axe and complete the amputation, for the finger would probably turn gangrenous, but we disinfected and bound it, and she went away grateful for even this degree of skill in a place nine days' walk from the nearest doctor.

Fortified by inoculation against every known virus, clothed in anoraks and fur-lined boots, equipped with field-glasses, cameras and a travelling *batterie de cuisine*, we were passengers through a rocky prison in which those around us were serving lifelong sentences. We wondered whether we were wrong to pity them. If they had a road, who could afford a motor-vehicle to travel it, or the luxury goods it would bring from the plains? Would tourists enrich their culture, or would they destroy it? We wished for these people the impossible: the benefits of modern technology without its penalties.

A leech clings to a leaf with its powerful posterior sucker and cranes forward towards a possible host. The leech, related to the earthworm, operates like a predatory blood bank. After dropping on to a passing man or animal, it punctures the skin with its jaws and siphons off a sufficient quantity of blood to sustain it for months.

All our values were turned upside down: despite the suffering, there was cheerfulness on every side. It seemed to be proof of an astonishing resilience. And many of the villages have their simple amenities—and even a few beauties like the poinsettia, which the Nepalese plant with such abandon round their houses. An old man sitting cross-legged on a rock splitting bamboo and shaping it into baskets; a group of naked young children playing in a river; a woman slowly turning a prayer wheel—these people would not understand our compassion, nor like it if they could. All around were terraces of young maize or irrigated rice, representing the successful effort of generations; and humble beasts shared their lives and homes quasi-biblically. If the old look older and the young more vulnerable than they do in the West, none of them miss what they do not know about. Their simplicity and religion give them a peace of mind that we might envy.

I sat in a tiny mill-house in the Karakorams, frying eggs on an open fire, and talking to the group of villagers that soon collected. The background noises were the awkward churning of the mill-stone, the rush of water that drove it, the spitting of the eggs. The headman of the village had been a sergeant in a British-Indian regiment and looked the part, but as I questioned him I felt like one of the inquisitors of a 19th-Century Highland commission:

"How high does the river rise in summer?"

"About 20 feet above what you see now."

"Does it flood the fields?"

"Sometimes; and then our crops are destroyed."

"How much rain do you have?"

"Almost none: the river is fed by melting snow."

"How do you water your crops?"

"We lead the stream-water into the fields."

"What crops do you grow?"

"Maize, buck-wheat, potatoes, rice, and some fruit, like apricots."

"What animals do you keep?"

"Goats, sheep, cows, chickens."

"Are there any wild animals or game-birds in the mountains?"

"Yes; ibex, markhor, chukkor—and once I saw a snow-leopard."

"Do you have any tools, like saws?"

"Only axes. What need have we of saws? The pine . . . ", and he glanced almost with affection at the simple roof of lashed logs, ". . . has a perfect shape for building houses. We have no need to cut it up."

"What do you obtain from outside the village?"

"We need nothing. But I have this flask that my father bought in China." (It was the largest, gaudiest tin I have ever seen.)

"How do you make clothes?"

"From sheep's wool mixed with goat-hair. We spin and weave it."

"Is the population of the village increasing?"

"It has doubled in the last 20 years."

"Do you ever go into the mountains?"

"Only to collect wood."

In his last two answers lie the most serious threats to his village, to hundreds more like it—and to the Himalayan ecology: over-population of the habitable areas and the slow destruction of the forests in the quest for cultivable land. In the 19th Century the process was called "the conquest of the forest", as if the forest were the enemy of man. It took some time to recognize it as man's greatest friend. After all, there were many peasants, and an unlimited jungle. It seemed sensible for one to clear the other. In 1848 the great naturalist and traveller Joseph Dalton Hooker watched with delight the forests of the Sikkim Himalayas going up in smoke: "At this season (April) the firing of the jungle is a frequent practice, and the effect by night is exceedingly fine: a forest so dry and full of bamboo, extending over such steep hills, afforded grand blazing spectacles. The voices of birds and insects being hushed, nothing is audible but the harsh roar of the rivers, and occasionally, rising far above it, that of the forest fires."

It is as if a man, watching a neighbour's house burn down, were to remark: "The spare bedroom is *nicely* alight now." But Hooker compounded his ignorance of what he was witnessing by adding without censure that the native of the region "never inhabits one spot for more than three successive years. He squats in any place which he can render profitable for that period, and then moves to another."

It was easier to move on after three years and burn another piece of forest because the ash does not remain a natural fertilizer for much longer. Therefore in one man's working life he might clear an area equivalent to 16 separate farms.

The effect can be seen almost anywhere in the Himalayas. The plains and lower hills are almost bare of vegetation of any kind, and the goats are busy eating what is left. It is not simply that the trees that were once there cannot grow again; the soil itself is washed away. When the rains come, both rain and earth are lost. In a forest the canopy of leaves absorbs the shock of the monsoon, so that the water reaches the ground with comparative gentleness. The trees act like sponges for the rain, retaining its moisture in the tissues of the wood and soil by a close network of roots and deep mattresses of humus, where it is protected from evaporation. The insects find a haven there, making it porous and absorbent, and every winter adds a new quota of fallen leaves and dead branches. It is a natural cycle. Now, with the trees gone, the insects die, and the water quickly runs off, carving new erosion channels and creating bare rock above and floods and landslides below. Great ravines are rapidly gouged out and large areas of plain overwhelmed by sandy outwash. The consequence is a man-made wilderness in the very places where men count most upon fertility.

Of course, there are compensations. Snow and glaciers release their waters as gradually as forests: and for generations the farmers have practised the greatest of all their skills, the terracing and irrigation of the lower slopes, which makes the most of what land and water remain. There is no more pleasing or frequent sight in the Himalayas than that of ice-cold water running swiftly in channels 40 feet above the lower plains, to drop through controlled apertures on to fields patterned like a jig-saw by their retaining walls. These considerable feats of engineering were accomplished by hand, aided by the most primitive tools. In Hunza, until quite recently, they used wooden paddles for spades, and ibex horns for picks.

In the Himalayas of northern Assam erosion is less of a problem, for the population is thin and the rain-forests immense. Few people have dared to go there, since the natives are reputed to be resentful of intruders, and thus geographers are still not quite certain how the Himalayas tail off in the east beyond Namcha Barwa. O. K. Spate, the great geographer of the Indian sub-continent, calls it one of the last unsolved topographical problems in the world.

One of the few explorers who went there was the anthropologist, C. F. Haimendorf. He took his wife with him, in order, he explained, to soften by her mere presence the indignation of the natives, a function that she accomplished with engaging charm and courage. In 1955 he published a delightful book called *Himalayan Barbary*, which did something to rehabilitate the reputation of the tribes. "The spontaneous hospitality with which we were received in the remotest villages," he wrote, "always filled me with warmth and renewed my belief in the fundamental friendliness of man." That is, so long as man is not provoked. When he is, this sort of thing can happen: "If he were to find that his wife had been unfaithful, a Dafla man would be so upset that he would be unable either to eat or sleep. He would not hesitate to kill her lover, tear him limb from limb, and show her the dismembered parts: then, roasting the flesh, he would stuff it into her mouth."

Haimendorf never reached the highest mountains that divide Assam from China, although he saw them from a distance. Once again his belief in human nature survived all his tribulations. "Far from being the treacherous savages of popular belief, the Miris of these hills struck me as cheerful companions, and the most warm-hearted of friends." On that optimistic note we can leave man in one of the two most extreme wildernesses that the Himalayas contains. The other is far fiercer: the part that lies more than 20,000 feet above the level of the sea.

Journey Through Five Realms

PHOTOGRAPHS BY CAPTAIN JOHN NOEL

The famous British expedition that attempted to conquer Everest in 1924 failed when two climbers, George Mallory and Andrew Irvine, died in an attempt on the summit. Among the survivors was photographer Captain John Noel (right). A keen amateur naturalist and a walker rather than a skilled mountaineer, Noel had been a member of a pioneering expedition to Everest two years before.

According to a contemporary account, Noel wanted "to catch and express the spirit of the mountains, the awe they inspire, their terrible character, their might and their glory, and withal their irresistible attraction". This he set out to do with a telescopic camera especially designed to work in temperatures as low as −25°F.: the mechanism to advance the film ran on ball-bearings instead of oil, which would have frozen. Noel made careful colour notes of his photographic subjects and used them later as a guide to transform his delicate black and white glass slides into hand-tinted images.

Noel's pictures provide a unique photographic record not only of the progress of the expedition, but also —as the pictures on the following pages show—of the effects of changing altitude on Himalayan vegetation. These scenes have an additional historic interest: the Nepalese government at the time forbade an approach to Everest through their territory to the south of the mountain, and so the expedition marched through Sikkim to attack Everest from Tibet—a route that has been closed to Westerners since China invaded this territory in 1950.

The expedition, which set off in March, took 35 days to reach the Base Camp, 12,000 feet below the summit. The climbers passed through five main zones of vegetation. The first hard trek through tropical jungle took them upwards to more temperate forested areas. Then they emerged to cross clear alpine pastures speckled with spring flowers, continued upwards to the almost barren Tibetan plateau, and finally reached the wasteland of ice and snow around Everest.

One of the first natural wonderlands the party traversed was the valley of the river Tista in Sikkim (far right), only 750 feet above sea level. The photograph, looking down to the river 6,000 feet below, shows the densely forested slopes that covered their route northwards.

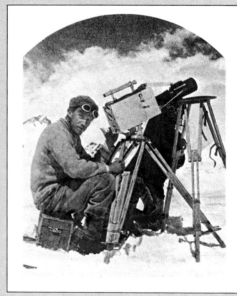

CAPTAIN NOEL AND CAMERA

THE WINDING TISTA VALLEY

CAMP IN THE FOOTHILLS

From Thick Jungle to Alpine Meadow

For the first few days, the expedition sweated through the tangled jungle of the Tista valley, where a constant 90°F. heat evaporates the drenching rains—250 inches a year—into steaming mists. Exotic butterflies and tropical birds fluttered among 20-foot high giant ferns, bamboo trees and palms entwined with creepers, vines and many varieties of orchids. The camp scene near the Tista River (left), taken by a native porter, shows Noel himself standing beside his tent, a tripod camera set for action.

At about 7,000 feet above sea level the thick jungle gradually opened out to a more temperate zone (right) where spruce, pine and other conifers grew beside oaks and magnolia trees. These upland forests were splashed with blue irises and crimson, yellow and pink rhododendrons. But as Noel and his companions reached 10,000 feet, the birch and pine trees gave way to cool green alpine pastures, carpeted with dark purple and yellow primulas, blue gentian, saxifrage and edelweiss.

UPLAND FORESTS AND MEADOWS

LAKE ON THE TIBETAN PLATEAU

Across Tibet's Stark and Lofty Plateau

As the expedition left the green alpine belt behind and below, the vegetation became scantier and the scenery increasingly desolate. This was the beginning of another world, a lofty, arid wilderness: the Tibetan Plateau. The plateau lies at an average height of 15,000 feet, extends 1,500 miles east to west and is 1,000 miles wide from north to south.

The landscape is forbidding; snow-dusted hills rise to several thousand feet above the surface of the near-barren plateau. Rainfall is minimal, but in spring rivers of melted snow and ice flow down from the mountains, supplying water to hundreds of lakes that reflect the brilliant azure sky.

Surprisingly, domestic yak herds and wild animals thrive on the area's sparse scrub. Colonel Norton (the expedition leader) observed of one occasion: "The plain appears utterly devoid of vegetation, yet herds of kyang (wild asses) and Tibetan gazelle surrounded us . . . all looking as sleek and round as if their chosen habitat were the finest pasture in Asia."

But to the climbers, the climate was as hostile as the land. Freezing nights, followed by days of bitter, piercing wind, sapped the strength of the party. "It used to be a saying among us," wrote Noel later, "that Everest's 'long arm' [the local name for the wind that batters the mountain] started to hit us before we ever reached her."

MELT WATER FROM THE RONGBUK GLACIER

At the Portals of an Ice Kingdom

A month after their departure from Darjeeling, the expedition set up Base Camp near the 50-foot thick snout of the Rongbuk Glacier, at an altitude of 16,400 feet (left; Noel's photographic tent is visible at the right of the picture.)

In this realm of rock and ice dominated by the Everest massif, the wind, water and ice eat into boulder surfaces until they resemble coral. Vegetation, though restricted to meagre patches of lichen, is still enough to support a few birds, spiders and insects, many of which are especially adapted to the harsh conditions of the environment.

Higher up, at 18,000 feet on the glacier proper, the expedition encountered a fairytale world of ice pinnacles rearing up 100 feet. In Noel's photograph (right) a solitary Sherpa, on the ledge bottom to the left, is dwarfed by Rongbuk's colossal glacial spires sculptured and notched by evaporation and wind.

Towards the Great Untrodden Summit

The heights at which the climbers established the final camps on the route up Everest presented them with sublime views; but such heights also imposed treacherous and debilitating conditions. The weather, of a severity unknown in the previous 30 years, forced the climbers to turn back from several attempts on the summit. The thin air made every tiny effort a trial of willpower and physical strength.

To their surprise, they found that they were not the only living creatures to defy such altitude. Major R. Hingston, the expedition's naturalist, found tiny attid spiders in rock crevices at 22,000 feet; and choughs flew around the climbers to their highest bivouac at 27,000 feet, becoming tame and welcome companions in the wilderness.

Captain Noel, who climbed up to 23,000 feet to photograph the final assault from as close as possible, wrote of Everest: "It made a prodigious sight as I looked—a forbidding pyramid of grey and white with rugged sides. In the marvellously thin and clear air it stood bleak and menacing."

From snowfields above the Rongbuk Glacier he photographed the north-east ridge of Everest (right), dramatically lit by the evening sun. A few days later, the mountain claimed the lives of Mallory and Irvine, last seen within 600 feet of the summit, and the 1924 expedition conceded a tragic defeat.

7/ Into the Zone of Death

As he looks at the mountains the climber's heart swells with joy and pain. It is so beautiful and yet so inaccessible. Oh! to set foot on those virgin slopes—even though death waits poised above! EDMUND HILLARY/ *HIMALAYAS*

The peaks of the Himalayas are a different universe from the one we inhabit. One can fly over the high wilderness of snow and ice or focus on it with binoculars from the safety of the slopes thousands of feet below. But it remains remote from both the traveller and the native. Only one group of people have penetrated it—the mountaineers and their porters—and it is through their eyes that this strange universe stands revealed.

Those who challenge this wilderness are confronted by difficulties and dangers appalling in their frequency and magnitude. In the Alps, unless a climber chooses deliberately the most difficult approach, an ascent is usually predictable and well-tried. But in the Himalayas, every hazard of the lower ranges is magnified. The glaciers may be convenient routes to the summit, but they are also traps that can close with terrifying violence, breaking away in ice-blocks weighing hundreds of tons. An ice-wall a thousand feet wide and a hundred high, apparently clamped to the rock's surface, topples slowly forward in cataclysmic ruin. An avalanche of snow, fallen overnight and loosened again by the morning sun, strikes at a man with the force of a torrent and carries him helpless over a precipice. If he tries to avoid these dangers by ascending the ridges, a whole new category of risks awaits him. The knife-edge is so sharp, its sides so steep, that a single moment of inattention can plunge him to his death. An ice-cornice suddenly collapses under his added weight. A slab of rock sloping like a roof-tile, one of a thousand others safely traversed, is found, too late, to be unsupported.

The weather is equally unpredictable. Sometimes the sun can be so violent, piercing the thin air with X-ray intensity doubled by reflection from the snow, that a man can suffer as acutely from sunburn as in an equatorial desert; that same night he may endure agonies of polar cold. The range of temperature at these altitudes is extraordinary: it has been measured as high as 219° F. in direct sunlight, and as low as —40° F. at night. The wind can suddenly rise to hurricane force, filling the air with snow to create an airborne avalanche against which a climber cannot stand. His tent, if he has one, can be as difficult to erect as to furl a mainsail in a gale, or it may be whipped from his sleeping body. Such gales can last for weeks, making all movement, upwards or downwards, impossible. At the start of their successful attempt on K2 in 1954 the Italians were scarcely able to move from their tents for 40 days. In 1934 Willy Merkl, the German climber, was isolated by a blizzard on Nanga Parbat and endured nine torturing days of cold and starvation until he died in a snowdrift, where his body was found four years later.

Then there is the debilitating effect of altitude. Acclimatization helps, but nobody can predict its effect. A young man, perhaps the strongest in a team, like Mario Puchoz on K2, can die suddenly of pneumonia. Another will be attacked by phlebitis. Age seems to have little to do with it. Mountaineers are not Olympic athletes. The age fittest for the mountains seems to lie between 25 and 40, since experience has shown that younger men do not have the physical or mental stamina.

Altitude can totally alter a man's character. The will is weakened; friendship is threatened. "Your friend in civilization," Frank Smythe, the conqueror of Kamet, has written, "may become your enemy on a mountain; his very snore assumes a new and repellent note; his tricks at the mess-table, the sound of his mastication, the scarcely concealed triumph with which he appropriates the choicest tit-bits, the absurd manner in which he walks, even the cut of his clothes and the colour of the patch on the seat of his trousers, may induce an irritation and loathing almost beyond endurance."

The ascent of Annapurna I by Maurice Herzog and his party of Frenchmen in 1950 provides what is perhaps the most dramatic example of the Himalayas' effect on man; it also produced one of mountaineering's finest books, *Annapurna*. Herzog's own account of the expedition's achievements and ordeals. No mountain over 26,000 feet had ever been climbed before. Nepal was opened to Westerners only that year.

The country was quite unknown, the approaches to Annapurna unexplored, and the local porters unorganized and untrained. Judging by the experience of climbers in British India during the previous half-century, it seemed impossible that so formidable a peak could be reconnoitred and climbed at the first attempt. But this is what the Frenchmen achieved, and their story still arouses wonder and vicarious suffering.

They had originally intended to climb Dhaulagiri (26,810 feet), but were beaten by its crevasses and a 15,000-foot wall, twice as high as the north face of the Eiger, and switched their effort across the Kali Gandaki Valley to Annapurna I, 26,504 feet high. The early stages of the ascent were very difficult, but Herzog himself (unusual for an expedition's leader) and one companion, Louis Lachenal, were in good condition when they found themselves at the highest camp poised for the summit attempt. In Herzog's words, "We took it in turns to make the track, and often stopped without any word having passed between us. Each of us lived in a closed and private world of his own . . . We remembered the days of marching in sweltering heat, the hard pitches we had overcome, the tremendous efforts we had all made to lay siege to the mountain, the daily heroism of all my friends in establishing the camps. Now we were nearing our goal. In an hour or two perhaps victory would be ours. Must we give up? No, that would be impossible. My whole being revolted against the idea. Today we were consecrating an ideal, and no sacrifice was too great. An astonishing happiness welled up in me." It was not to last for long.

They reached the summit at 3 p.m. on June 3, 1950, photographed each other, and pulled from the bottom of their rucksack a French pennant, stained with sweat and stale food. Then their troubles began. As they started down, one of Herzog's gloves blew away. He realized what this meant—"the start of a race with death". Lachenal stumbled ahead, sensing that his feet were freezing. At the highest camp they found two of their friends, Lionel Terray and Gaston Rébuffat, to whom they told the news of their success, but when Terray clasped Herzog's hand in congratulation, he found it as hard and cold as stone, white and violet with frostbite. Lachenal had lost ice-axe, cap, gloves and one crampon in a fall, his feet and both hands were frozen solid, and he was in a state of semi-delirium. All that night the fresher men worked on their two friends, massaging their numbed limbs. In the morning a gale-force blizzard was blowing. The four of them set out again with only two ice-axes between them, and the mist and snow were so thick that they could scarcely see from one end of the rope to the other.

Snow whirls above Lhotse whipped by winds that, funneling through a valley below the mountain, are forced up by the immense wall of rock.

Sinking up to their waists in new snow, they searched vainly for the camp below, where they knew help awaited them. Failing to find it, they spent the night in a vertical tunnel of ice, huddling together to share the warmth of their bodies, talking in signs more than words. "There was still a breath of life in me," wrote Herzog, "but it dwindled steadily as the hours went by. Was this cavern not the most beautiful grave I could hope for?" In the early morning an avalanche spread into it, half burying them. Terray and Rébuffat struggled out, only to find that the previous day's exertions had left them snow-blind. So they were now four men, two crippled, two blind, all lost. Herzog whispered to Terray, "Lionel, I am dying." They shouted for help: their voices carried only ten feet in the gale. Somehow they struggled on, the maimed now leading the blind. With inexpressible relief they discovered that the camp was only 200 yards from the hole where they had spent the night, and two Frenchmen and four Sherpas were there to help them. The farther journey was slow torture, but the will to live had returned. They descended ice-walls by rope, but frost-bite made their efforts so clumsy that the skin was torn from their hands and hung in strips. They reached Camp II, still at 20,000 feet, and there was the expedition's doctor, who injected their arteries with azetylcholin to stimulate the agonizing recirculation of the blood.

That was not the end of their ordeal. Camp II was turned into a casualty clearing station, but it was no hospital. The men must be taken down at once to save their lives. Herzog and Lachenal were gently lowered from ledge to ledge until they reached the valley, and from that point they were carried on stretchers for three weeks in the pouring rain of the monsoon to the Indian frontier. The doctor snipped off their fingers and toes one by one to prevent the spread of gangrene to their whole bodies. All Lachenal's toes were amputated: Herzog lost all his toes and all his fingers.

Why then do they do it? Many of the world's greatest climbers find it difficult to explain. At Kathmandu I met one of the American mountaineers who reached the summit of Everest in 1963. He was a short man, built like a jockey, who bore on his young face the marks of great exertion: the skin around his eyes was lined like a sailor's. He and three companions had survived a night at 28,000 feet without tent or sleeping-bags, but fortunately there had been no wind. I asked him whether it was true that a sort of euphoria numbs the senses when one is in this lofty wilderness. "Well," he replied, "only in so far as you feel quite isolated from your companions. You are in a world of your own. If

A monstrous avalanche—released by warm weather, rain or sudden vibration —hurtles down the 25,850-foot Nuptse ridge, near Mount Everest (left). In its fearsome descent it dislodges thousands of tons of piled snow and flings them billowing down the valley.

you have to talk, you do so by signals or grunts. You cannot speak and breathe simultaneously at that height. I felt at one moment that I wouldn't live through it. Then suddenly, at about 4 a.m., came the realization that I would survive. That was the best moment: you might say that it was the only happy moment. When I got to the top, I had thought only of the enormous difficulty of getting down. It was like being in combat. Only a day or two later, when the lower camps had nursed us down, did I experience any sense of achievement and triumph. I looked back at Everest and thought, 'Was I really there? Well, I need never go there again.'" And then he added, as so many other climbers do: "I can't think why it is that I go on doing it."

It cannot be because they enjoy the mountain scenery. Danger and exhaustion and sickness of mind and body dull the appreciation of natural beauty, and rarely can a climber lift his eyes from the place where his next footstep will fall. If they loved mountains for their splendour, they would walk the foothills parallel to the crest, as I did. Mountaineers are only interested in height and the Himalayas offer the greatest heights of all. Achievement is measured in hundreds and thousands of feet, vertically, and for them the mountain has no other dimension. Sometimes, however, a climber of unusual sensibility, like Christian Bonington, will pause to contemplate with wonder the devastation around him. For devastation it is. There is no construction here, except very temporarily; only destruction, and it can take ugly as well as terrifying forms. A glacier that has lost its snow is "a mournful place of grit-covered ice, decaying towers and dark, yawning holes," as Bonington wrote of the glacier that sweeps up to the south face of Annapurna. "In bright sunlight it is like an abandoned scrapyard." Only the mist and the moon can soften hard outlines, obliterate the hideous detail of decay and flood gloomy sockets with translucency.

It is the view from the mountains, not the view the struggling climber has of his own painful route, that fills with occasional rapture a mind however tired. The neighbouring summits seem beautiful: the summit immediately above rarely does. But it is the view downwards that exalts the spirit—the ice giving place to rock, the rock to scrub, the scrub to trees, the distant trees to cultivation and the unseen life of the valleys and the plains. It is the view, as in an historical diorama, of the emergence of man.

A wilderness presumes a non-wilderness, and when both are visible simultaneously, the effect of both is magnified. You can see them in juxtaposition, comfortably from below; but how much more eloquent is the contrast from above! There are no seasons here. You are isolated in a prehistoric world, a frozen world, where even a bee's sting would be a welcome reminder of things known. But there are no bees. Nature is shorn of its gentle impertinences and of all its delicacy except for the changing colours. You are confronted by the rawest elements of which the globe is made. It is a miserable world, yet sublime.

All this comes to the mountaineer, however, only in retrospect. During the climb, far from being an object of admiration, the mountain is an enemy. "The five of us sat that night in an atmosphere of hatred for the mountains," said Ian Rowe of the unsuccessful attempt on Dhaulagiri in 1973. "All we now wanted was to get off." Mountaineers conceive their adventures in para-military terms. The very language of mountaineering reveals it: expedition, assault, conquest, defeat. Their camps, like army corps, are identified with Roman numerals from I to VIII or IX. Just as a soldier can respect his enemy, so the mountaineer is humbled by his failure. "We slugged into Kathmandu," wrote Dennis Gray after his unsuccessful attempt on the 23,400-foot Gauri Sankar, "weary, dejected, unwashed, ragged, fed up with ourselves and with each other. The mountain gleamed high in the sky on the horizon, a reminder that time would heal the wounds."

What is it that drives a man to risk his very life on the summits? Undoubtedly, there is an element of glory-seeking, personal or patriotic, as there is in war. Karl Herrligkoffer assembled his party at the base of Nanga Parbat to pledge themselves to victory in "an Olympic oath" for the honour of Germany. When the Italians reached the summit of K2, Ardito Desio, their leader, issued an order of the day: "Lift up your hearts, dear comrades. By your efforts you have won great glory for your native land." The British, the Americans, the French, the Japanese and the Russians have been equally aware that national prestige is involved in their efforts.

But the greatest attraction, of course, is the danger, which this environment presents as no other can. The mountains offer the opportunity to test nerve, skill and endurance to the limit. The mountaineers are driven by that streak in men, as Robin Lane Fox wrote of Alexander the Great, that drives them to dare what other men have not thought possible. Take away the hazards, says John Hunt, leader of the successful British expedition to Everest in 1953, and you will rob mountaineering of its pleasure. Long before anyone thought of climbing the Himalayas, Byron, who might almost have had mountaineers in mind, put it thus:

Perils he sought not, but ne'er shrank to meet;
The scene was savage, but the scene was new;
This made the ceaseless toil of travel sweet.
Beat back keen winter's blast, and welcomed summer's heat.
And Francis Younghusband: "What is the secret of it? Quite certainly it
is the power of the mountains to force the best out of men. Man likes to
be his best. But often nothing short of a Himalayan peak can extract it
from him, can compel him to be fittest in body, alertist in mind and
firmest in soul." Wilfred Noyce has written: "By climbing mountains, by
extending himself beyond the bounds of everyday experience, a man can
set up a new relationship with something bigger than himself."

Because mountaineering is a matter of the spirit and the emotions,
the reactions of the mountaineers differ. To some, the scaling of a peak
is the infinite magnification of a child's pleasure in treading a lawn of
virgin snow. "The contest," said Edmund Hillary, who reached the
summit of Everest in the 1953 assault, "brings fear and joy—and a
deep respect, whatever the result of the struggle". The greys of ordinary
life become blacks and whites. To some, the barren wastes are places
where a man can be alone with himself and his God. To succeed is almost
a sacrilege, like shooting a tiger. Bill Tilman wrote of his conquest of
Nanda Devi in 1936: "The feeling which predominated over all was one
of remorse at the fall of a giant."

Sometimes normal emotions are suspended. When Dougal Haston and
Don Whillans reached the top of Annapurna by the south face, in 1970,
"there was only a kind of numbness". Smythe wrote of his ascent to the
Mana peak: "It was as though I had been led blindfold up the mountain,
and the bandage had been removed on the summit. But of all my memories, one stands pre-eminent: the silence. The silence of dead places
where not even a plant grows or a bird dwells . . . I seemed on the very
boundary of things knowable and unknowable."

Others have found themselves over the boundary, into hallucina-
tion, and Smythe himself, climbing alone on Everest in 1933, was convinced that he was roped to another man. So clear was the impression
that he divided his piece of cake into two. Later he saw, in a mirage, two
kites hanging motionless before him in the air. On Nanga Parbat
Hermann Buhl turned to talk to a friend who he knew, with another
part of his mind, was not there. Herbert Tichy, who also experienced
this condition, said there was nothing terrifying about it. It arises
because the mind is not anchored by the bonds of reason, as it is lower
down, and seems to roam freely to the very verge of insanity. Extreme

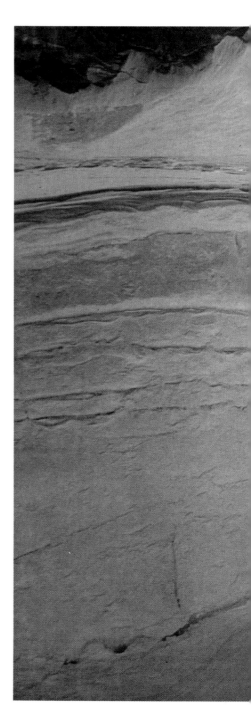

An English mountaineering team skirting the gaping jaws of a massive crevasse on the south face of Annapurna in 1970.

cold and lack of oxygen, added to great exhaustion, engenders a sense of complete indifference, and conjures up phantom companions.

Such is the scale of the mountains that it is difficult to imagine the success of an unsupported climber. Solo attempts on Himalayan peaks have always ended in failure. Friends, in the flesh, become a spur to success, an insurance against danger. An expedition is a team. The planning of it, from its conception in a Welsh pub or a Zürich inn—what Lord Hunt calls "the mental preparation"—the long approach march, the establishment of lower camps, the shared hazards and exhilaration, create a spirit of joint endeavour that pushes men to the limits of endurance. The process is one of slow pyramidical building, the reduction of tons of stores at the base camp to the last bottle of oxygen that will make the difference (as to Hillary in 1953) between success and failure at the top.

The total effort may be in the order of one-tenth climbing and nine-tenths porterage, forcing the flow of supplies to run uphill, and this can only be achieved by collaboration. Rivalry and envy, so far as this is humanly possible, are suppressed. The success of one is the triumph of all. Routes and camps can be planned but not settled in advance. The variety of circumstances being infinite, success depends upon such small things as the angle of a rock-face, the breadth of a cornice, the position of a hand- or toe-hold, an illness, the loss of a crampon, a change in weather—in fact, the element of chance that man cannot foretell.

It all began in the Alps in the 18th Century. Techniques of mountain-climbing were evolved; a literature was created. When the major Alpine peaks had been climbed, men looked farther afield, and higher, and the Himalayas became their natural target, for there their sights could be raised to the limit. The surveyors led the way, because the British needed more information about India's northern frontiers, and many accomplished extraordinary journeys. In 1855 Adolphe and Robert Schlagintweit, two brothers employed by the Magnetic Survey, approached Kamet from the Tibetan side and reached 22,300 feet.

The first northern circuit of Everest, from Darjeeling to Kathmandu, was made in 1871. In 1895 came the first attempt to climb a major peak as an exploit for its own sake, when A. F. Mummery, an experienced British Alpinist, was killed on Nanga Parbat. The first monster peak to fall was Trisul (23,382 feet), to Tom Longstaff in 1907. Everest was first attempted in 1922, and in 1924 came the gallant deaths of George Leigh Mallory and Andrew Irvine, which created a legend still familiar 50 years later to every schoolboy. In 1931 Kamet fell to Frank Smythe. In 1936

Bill Tilman and N. E. Odell climbed Nanda Devi. But none of the supreme mountains—the 13 that top 26,000 feet—was climbed until after the Second World War. Now all of them have been, some several times.

What, it may be wondered, is there left to do? Plenty. There are several famous peaks like Macchapuchhare (22,950 feet) that have not been climbed to the top, and others of equivalent height have hardly been explored. There are more difficult routes to attempt up mountains already climbed, like Annapurna's south face, which was conquered by Chris Bonington's expedition of 1970, and the south-west face of Everest, which he attempted in 1972. There is the challenge to smaller parties to repeat the achievements of previous expeditions that were backed by great resources of money and manpower.

No doubt, too, the technological aids to climbing will continue to evolve. The Victorians would use no gear that "modified the face of the mountain", allowing only the cutting of ice-steps, since ice (they argued illogically) was not part of the mountain. They climbed in knicker-bockers and motoring gloves. When special clothing, crampons and pitons were introduced, the old-stagers condemned those who used the new climbing aids for "throwing unwarrantable resources at magnificent peaks". Oxygen was worse, and early expeditions climbed without it. Then a more realistic attitude became acceptable. On Hunt's 1953 expedition to Everest, they carried extensible aluminium ladders, rope ladders, pulleys, a light mortar to bring down avalanches, radios, special high-altitude clothing and newly-designed tents. On K2 in 1954 the Italians used a ropeway to slide stores up the steepest slopes by a hand-operated windlass. Then came the use of aircraft to cut out the exhausting rigours of the long approach march.

But no artificial aids can prevent the ultimate confrontation between men and the merciless defences of nature. Nothing can mitigate the awfulness of crumpled, ice-coated rocks, the violence of an avalanche or blizzard, the terror of a slip at great heights. This book has been about a wilderness. If wilderness is what men seek as a refuge from their civilizations and as a test of their courage, here in the Himalayas above 25,000 feet, in what Herbert Tichy called his "zone of death", they will find it untamed, in perpetuity.

Celestial Heights

Mountain peaks are never really conquered. Man may stand on them boastfully—for a moment after a struggle to the top—but his victory is short-lived. To the people of the Himalayas this is as it should be, since to them the peaks constitute a wilderness apart, the rightful dwelling place not of men, but of the gods. The rolling clouds and shades of light captured in the pictures on these pages may vary, but the massiveness of these regal monoliths conveys a sense of the Eternal.

To the Hindus the Himalayas are central to their cosmology. The peaks are the petals of the Golden Lotus that the god Vishnu created as a first step in the formation of the universe. On one of these peaks, Mt. Kailas, sits Shiva in a state of perpetual meditation, generating the spiritual force that sustains the cosmos. And when Vishnu caused the Ganges to flow from Heaven, he made it reach the Earth on the highest peaks where Shiva caught it up in his eyebrow.

To the Tibetans the Himalayan peaks are the sacred ground for a multitude of gods and devils. On one peak dwells the red goddess who owns a nine-headed tortoise, on another, the brown goddess who rides a turquoise-maned horse, and on a third 361 demons, all brothers.

The names of many peaks reflect this mystical tradition. The highest of them all, Everest, is called Chomolungma by the Tibetans, meaning Goddess Mother of the Earth. Annapurna translates as Giver of Life. The mountain richest in Tibetan mythology is Kangchenjunga: Five Treasures of the Eternal Snows. Tibetans believe that the god of wealth lives there, storing on its five peaks the five treasures: gold, silver, copper, corn and sacred books.

In 1955, Kangchenjunga's divinity threatened a British climbing expedition. The governments of Sikkim, India and Nepal refused to allow the climb because their peoples feared that the enterprise might provoke the anger of the god and bring serious harm to the land. Eventually a compromise was reached. The climbers halted within a stone's throw of the summit: the Sherpas buried offerings to their god; and the group went back down the mountain without defiling the holy peak. Such deference was once articulated by a Hindu pilgrim, who said, "In the midst of such peaks, one can draw near to what is truly placeless, the really divine."

KANGTEGA IN A CORONET OF CLOUDS

THAMSERKU AT SUNRISE

KANGCHENJUNGA LOOMING IN A DISTANT HAZE

MACHHAPUCHHARE, "THE FISH'S TAIL," A SYMBOL OF VISHNU

NUPTSE, THE WESTERN OUTPOST OF EVEREST

ANNAPURNA, "GIVER OF LIFE"

EVEREST AT SUNSET

Bibliography

Bauer, Paul, *The Siege of Nanga Parbat.* Rupert Hart-Davis, 1956.

Bonington, Chris, *Annapurna South Face.* Cassell, 1971.

Bonington, Chris, *Everest, South West Face.* Hodder and Stoughton, 1973.

Calder, Nigel, *Restless Earth.* BBC Publications, 1972.

Corbett, Jim, *Man-eaters of Kumaon.* Oxford University Press, 1944.

Cornwall, Ian, *Ice Ages: Their Nature and Effects.* John Baker Ltd., 1970.

Desio, Ardito, *Ascent of K2.* Elek Books, 1955.

Dyhrenfurth, G. O., *To the Third Pole.* Werner Laurie, 1955.

Dyson, James L., *The World of Ice.* Cresset Press, 1963.

Eiselin, Max, *The Ascent of Dhaulagiri.* Oxford University Press, 1961.

Etherton, P. T., *Across the Roof of the World.* Constable and Co., 1911.

Fraser-Tytler, W. K., *Afghanistan.* Oxford University Press, 1950.

Fukada, Kyuya, *The Great Himalayas.* Abrams, 1973.

Gee, E. P., *The Wild Life of India.* Collins, 4th edition, 1969.

Gray, Dennis, *Rope Boy.* Gollancz, 1970.

Hagen, Toni, *Mount Everest.* Oxford University Press, 1963. (includes contributions by G. O. Dyhrenfurth, C. F. Haimendorf and E. Schneider).

Hagen, Toni, *Nepal.* Kunnerley and Frey, Berne, 1961.

Haimendorf, C. F., *Himalayan Barbary.* John Murray, 1955.

Herrligkoffer, Karl M., *Nanga Parbat.* Elek Books, 1954.

Herzog, Maurice, *Annapurna.* Jonathan Cape, 1952.

Heuvelmans, Bernard, *On the Track of Unknown Animals.* Paladin, 1970.

Hillary, Edmund, *High Adventure.* Hodder and Stoughton, 1955.

Hindley, Geoffrey, *The Roof of the World.* Aldus Books, 1971.

Hooker, J. D., *Himalayan Journals* (2) (2 vols.). John Murray, 1854.

Hooker, J. D. and Thomson, T., *Introductory Essay to Flora Indica.* W. Pamplin, 1855.

Hooker, J. D. and W. J. Hooker, ed., *Rhododendrons of Sikkim-Himalaya.* Reeve, 1849.

Hunt, John, *The Ascent of Everest.* Hodder and Stoughton, 1953.

Huxley, Leonard, *Life and Letters of J. D. Hooker.* John Murray, 1918.

Izzard, Ralph, *The Abominable Snowman Adventure.* Hodder and Stoughton, 1955.

Jackson, John A., *More than Mountains.* George G. Harrap and Co., 1955.

Lane Fox, Robin, *Alexander the Great.* Allan Lane, 1973.

Leifer Walter, *Himalaya: Mountains of Destiny.* Galley Press Ltd., 1962.

Long, Tony, *Mountain Animals.* Macdonald, 1971.

Maraini, Fosco, *Where Four Worlds Meet.* Hamish Hamilton Ltd., 1964.

Mason, Kenneth, *Abode of Snow.* Rupert Hart-Davis, 1955.

Mountford, Guy, *The Vanishing Jungle.* Collins, 1969.

Murray, W. H., *The Story of Everest 1921-1952.* J. M. Dent and Sons Ltd., 1953.

Nebesky-Wojkowitz, René von, *Where the Gods are Mountains.* Weidenfeld and Nicolson, 1956.

Newby, Eric, *A Short Walk in the Hindu Kush.* Hodder and Stoughton, 1958.

Noel, Captain J. B. L., *Through Tibet to Everest.* Edward Arnold and Co., 1927.

Norton, Lt-Col. E. F., *The Fight for Everest 1924.* Edward Arnold and Co., 1925.

Noyce, Wilfred, *Climbing the Fish's Tail.* William Heinemann, 1958.

Prater, S. H., *The Book of Indian Animals.* Bombay Natural Historical Society, 3rd edition, 1971.

Salim, Ali, *Indian Hill Birds.* Oxford University Press, 1949.

Sayed Khan Qamer, A., *The Lure of the Karakorams.* Rawalpindi, 1973.

Shirakawa, Yoshikazu, *Himalayas.* Tokyo, 1971. (Includes contributions by Edmund Hillary, Arnold Toynbee.)

Smythe, F. S., *Kamet Conquered.* Gollancz, 1932.

Smythe, F. S., *The Valley of Flowers.* Hodder and Stoughton, 1938.

Spate, O. H. K., *India and Pakistan.* Methuen, 1954.

Stainton, J. D. A., *Forests of Nepal.* John Murray, 1972.

Swinson, Arthur, *North West Frontier.* Hutchinson, 1967.

Tichy, Herbert, *Himalaya.* Hale, 1971.

Tilman, H. W., *The Ascent of Nanda Devi.* Cambridge University Press, 1937.

Tilman, H. W., *Nepal Himalaya.* Cambridge University Press, 1952.

Whistler, Hugh, *Popular Handbook of Indian Birds.* Gurney and Jackson, 1928.

Wood, Captain John, *Journey to the Source of the Oxus.* John Murray, 1872.

Younghusband, Sir Francis, *The Epic of Mount Everest.* Edward Arnold and Co., 1926.

Younghusband, Sir Francis, *Everest: The Challenge.* Thomas Nelson and Sons Ltd., 1936.

Younghusband, Captain Frank E., *The Heart of a Continent,* John Murray, 1896.

Acknowledgements

The author and editors of this book wish to thank the following: Jack Amos, London; Mike Cheyney, Kathmandu; Dr. C. Embleton, London; Robert E. Fleming, Kathmandu; Sally Foy, London; Dr. Colin Harrison, Tring; Imtiaz Hussein, Rawalpindi; Tony Long, Rye; Susan Pinkus, London; The Library of Royal Botanical Gardens, Kew; Captain John Noel, New Romney; The Library of Royal Geographical Society, London; G. C. Tripathi, Ranikhet.

Picture Credits

Sources for pictures in this book are shown below. Credits for pictures from top to bottom are separated by dashes.

Cover–Jim Burke, Time-Life Picture Agency, 1965, Time Incorporated. Front end papers 1, 2–Dorothy Mierow. Front end paper 3, page 1–Raghubir Singh. 2, 3–Goetz D. Plage from Bruce Coleman Ltd., London. 4, 5–F. Jackson from Robert Harding Associates, London. 6, 7–Su Gooders from Ardea Photographics, London. 8, 9–B. N. Kelly. 10, 11–S. V. Kimber. 12, 13–G. Bell. 18, 19–Maps by Hunting Surveys Ltd., London. 25–Mark Boulton. 27–N. A. Callow from Natural History Photographic Agency, Westerham, Kent. 30, 31–Eileen Tweedy, courtesy of The Director, Royal Botanic Gardens, Kew. 35–G. Bell. 36, 37–John Cleare. 38–B. N. Kelly. 39–Christopher Grey-Wilson. 40, 41–Mark Boulton. 42, 43–Christopher Grey-Wilson from Robert Harding Associates. 46, 47–B. N. Kelly. 49–Hunting Surveys Ltd. 52, 53–G. S. Bishop C.B., O.B.E. 56 to 63–Terence Spencer. 66–Gustav R. Zimek from Tierbilder Okapia, Frankfurt. 69–Wilfried D. Schurig from Tierbilder Okapia. 70–Richard Waller from Ardea Photographics. 74, 75–Eric Shipton F.R.G.S., courtesy of the Royal Geographical Society, London. 79–John Gooders from Ardea Photographics. 80–M. D. England from Ardea Photographics. 81–M. Krishnan from Ardea Photograph-

ics. 82, 83–Goetz D. Plage from Survival Anglia Ltd., London. 84, 85–Mark Boulton. 86, 87–John Gooders from Ardea Photographics. 93–George Schaller from Bruce Coleman Inc., New York. 95–Harrison Forman, New York. 101–George Silk, Time-Life Picture Agency, 1972, Time Incorporated. 102–G. J. Broekhuyson from Ardea Photographics. 103 to 105–Goetz D. Plage from Bruce Coleman Ltd. 106–Robert L. Fleming from Ardea Photographics. 107–Goetz D. Plage from Bruce Coleman Ltd. 108, 109–Robert L. Fleming from Ardea Photographics. 113–Harrison Forman. 115–Goetz D. Plage from Bruce Coleman Ltd. 119–Nancy Tapper. 120–Christopher Grey-Wilson. 122, 123–F. Jackson from Robert Harding Associates. 127–Christopher Grey-Wilson from Robert Harding Associates. 128–Goetz D. Plage from Bruce Coleman Ltd. 129 to 135–Christopher Grey-Wilson from Robert Harding Associates. 140–Raghubir Singh. 141–Jim Burke, Time-Life Picture Agency, 1965, Time Incorporated. 142–Terence Spencer. 144–Christopher Grey-Wilson from Robert Harding Associates. 148 to 157–Captain John Noel. 161–B. N. Kelly. 163–G. S. Bishop C.B., O.B.E. 167–Christian Bonington. 171–B. N. Kelly. 172, 173–Goetz D. Plage from Survival Anglia Ltd. 174–Keith Hyatt from Natural Science Photos, London. 175–Terence Spencer. 176–B. N. Kelly. 177–N. A. Callow from Natural History Photographic Agency. 178, 179–G. S. Bishop C.B., O.B.E.

Index

Colour reproduction by
Printing Developments International Ltd.,
Leeds, England—a Time Inc. subsidiary.
Filmsetting by C. E. Dawkins (Typesetters) Ltd., London, SE1 1UN.
Smeets Lithographers, Weert. Printed in Holland.
Bound by Proost en Brandt N.V., Amsterdam.